ALSO BY SHELDON M. NOVICK

Henry James: The Young Master

Honorable Justice: The Life of Oliver Wendell Holmes

The Collected Works of Justice Holmes
(edited by Sheldon M. Novick)

HENRY JAMES

HENRY JAMES

The Mature Master

SHELDON M. NOVICK

RANDOM HOUSE NEW YORK

Published in the United States by Random House, an imprint of
The Random House Publishing Group, a division of
Random House, Inc., New York.

RANDOM HOUSE and colophon are registered trademarks of
Random House, Inc.

Frontispiece image: charcoal drawing by John Singer Sargent,
1912 (The Royal Collection, Windsor Castle; digital image
copyright © 2005 by Queen Elizabeth II).

ISBN 978-0-679-45023-8

Printed in the United States of America on acid-free paper

www.atrandom.com

2 4 6 8 9 7 5 3 1

FIRST EDITION

Book design by Simon M. Sullivan

For Carolyn

PREFACE AND ACKNOWLEDGMENTS

Although this is the second and concluding volume of a biography of Henry James, it is meant also to be read as a self-contained account of a man who was both great and good, and of a civilization he feared was dying.

After the first volume of my biography of James was published, recounting his childhood and youth, my work was interrupted for several years, but the delay has been salutary in some ways. In the intervening time, scholars have unearthed and made accessible a great mass of new material concerning the years of James's maturity, when he wrote the books for which he is now mainly remembered, that was not available to earlier biographers and from which I have greatly benefited.

James's published work and his copious notebooks contain a singular record of the manner in which a writer of fiction converts the raw materials of experience into works of art. James's letters—most of which have never been published—provide a parallel report of his private life, the rich experiences that were his raw materials, his loves and his domestic concerns, his successes and failures in a lifelong effort to harmonize passion and duty, life and art in Europe and America, in a time that calls across the gulf of the twentieth century to ours. He recorded the gradual development of his practice of fiction, his invention of dramatic imagery that conveys with startling realism passionate, fully rounded human beings held together by strong forces. In his life and in his art he sought an ideal of civilization: a humanist garden. His constant theme was the limits, material and moral, on freedom. We have the raw materials with which he worked, or some of them, and an account of the manner in which they were transmuted into art.

Taken together these materials allow one to tell a reasonably well rounded story. While there are a half-dozen previous biographies, and an enormous critical literature, I have taken a fresh look at the primary materials, including the hundreds of James's letters that have only recently been made available. Many of James's letters, such as those in the late

Adeline Tintner's extensive collection, now in the Berg Collection of the New York Public Library, were not available to previous biographers; many other of the roughly 10,500 surviving letters that James wrote, scattered in various locations and often close to illegible, although nominally open to scholars, have now been transcribed or published, making them practically accessible. I have also benefited greatly from recent scholarly studies that have not yet been reflected in work for a general audience, as well from older works that have fallen into obscurity. I have been reassured by such studies as Michael Egan's *Henry James: The Ibsen Years* that literary and biographical views may converge, and give a rounded image.

The Henry James the reader will meet in these pages may seem unfamiliar, both in detail and in general outline, however. This is a matter in part of new materials and in part of selection. In an epilogue to this volume I describe the manner in which an image of James formed and achieved the force of an ideal in the years that followed his death. The received view of James was of a passive, fearful man, a detached observer of the life around him, in which he did not participate. He was vaguely thought to have had ample independent means and so to have been able to write self-indulgent works that never found a wide audience. His brief career as a playwright has been repeatedly described as an utter failure, one in which he at last was driven from the stage by the scorn of the audience. This canonical image is likely to remain with us, despite the evidence that it is incorrect in detail and misleading overall.

The following account is based on primary materials, James's own writings and those of his contemporaries, and is an attempt to portray James in his years of maturity and success freshly and in some ways for the first time. Far from passive or detached, he was an active and engaged man, passionate and energetic, for whom relationships were the ground of life and the subject of his art.

Henry James's surviving letters have been catalogued, and much of the information they contain summarized in the online calendar assembled by Steven H. Jobe, who was kind enough to share his work in progress with me. Susan E. Gunter and Steven H. Jobe have published valuable editions of James's letters to women and young men and shared typescripts of unpublished letters. Philip Horne has recovered and published many of James's letters to writers, editors, and agents. Peter A. Walker and Greg W. Zacharias have undertaken to assemble and publish all of James's letters, and they too have shared their work in progress. I am indebted for advice and support to Roger Asselineau, especially for his illuminating suggestions concerning James's plays; to my old friend Samuel R. Delany, who shared his helpful thoughts about James's ghost stories; and to Fred Kaplan, who shared research notes with me when I began this project. Early in my work, the late Leon Edel courteously answered my questions about James, and the materials he assembled and published during his lifetime, frequently cited in the pages that follow, were an invaluable aid. Adele de Cruz has helped me in numerous ways to understand the world of art and artists in which James flourished.

It is a particular pleasure to acknowledge my numerous debts to Susan E. Gunter, who read and commented on successive drafts. Professor Gunter's biography of Alice Howe James, shortly to be published, was particularly helpful. John R. Bradley read a draft of the first chapter of this book, and his encouragement and advice have been helpful in many ways. As editor of two collections of essays on James, he gave me an opportunity to explore some of the ideas developed more fully here; as did the editors of *The Henry James Review* and *DoubleTake* magazine.

Equally helpful has been the work of modern scholars studying the late Victorian and Edwardian era, the last half of the "long" nineteenth century, in which James lived and worked. The twentieth century was anxious to forget its parents and to make a new world for itself, but the twenty-first seems eager to remember that lost world, before the era of revolutions, genocides, and world wars. Several authors have done much to recover the rich details of a working writer's life in James's London; Michael Anesko's reconstruction of James's dealings with publishers was particularly valuable to me and is frequently cited in what follows. Also valuable have been recent biographies of women who were among James's closest friends: Mary Ward, Edith Wharton, Violet Paget, Elizabeth Robins, and Gertrude Bell, as well as recent doctoral dissertations— I am particularly obliged to Tamie Watters for her unpublished dissertation on Rhoda Broughton and her transcripts of Broughton's letters, which saved me much labor. The Victorian bachelor has also emerged from the shadows in excellent recent biographies of Edmund Gosse, J. A. Symonds, and Oscar Wilde, and shorter studies of Morton Fullerton, Howard Sturgis, and others. Also helpful to me in recovering James's intellectual world were Theoharis C. Theoharis's study of the passing of the classical tradition, *Ibsen's Drama: Right Action and Tragic Joy*; and Sarah Gibbons's *Kant's Theory of Imagination*.

Personal and particular thanks are owed to many more individuals than I can be confident of naming. Priscilla Glucksman ably assisted my research at an early stage, and Scott Russell assisted with transcriptions and translations of Paul Zhukowsky's letters. Laura Gillen and Joanne Legg helped in many ways. My thanks again also to Ralph Curtis, for his hospitality at the Palazzo Barbaro; Ione and John Martin, for their hospitality while tenants of Lamb House; Dr. Ione, for her thoughts on James's depression; Dr. Sari Galanes, for her thoughts on Alice James's numerous ailments; the late Miss C. F. Kingdon, for sharing Mary Weld's unpublished diary; the late Henry James Vaux and Alice James Vaux, for their hospitality and assistance; the late Alexander Robertson James and his daughter Bay, for courteous answers to my questions and for permission to quote extensively from the James family archives in my earlier volume. The works of James and his contemporaries have emerged from copyright, but acknowledgment is happily made for permission to quote from James family materials in the possession of Harvard University.

The students in my courses and seminars at Vermont Law School on the construction of national identity, and the students in my occasional courses on Henry James at the Institute for Lifelong Education at Dartmouth, have done much to enrich my understanding and to revive my enthusiasm for this work over the course of many years, interrupted as it has been.

My thanks go also to the curators, librarians, and staff of the libraries and museums listed at the head of the endnotes to this volume, precious walled gardens in which the memory of James's world is preserved, for their unfailing diligence and courtesy and for their permission to quote from their collections. The Dartmouth College libraries have been particularly generous and helpful, as have the librarians and reading room staff of the Houghton Library at Harvard, who have helped me through various projects over the course of the last twenty years. My thanks also to Florence Roth, Conservateur de la Bibliothéque de la Société des Auteurs et Compositeurs Dramatiques, for information about adaptions of Henry James's work for stage and screen; to Carren Kaston, for her friendly advice about portraits of Henry James; to Elena Di Majo, director of the Museo Hendrik Christian Andersen, and Prof. Massimo Colesanti, president of Fondazione Primoli, for numerous courtesies.

I have profound debts to Robert D. Loomis, my editor, and Elizabeth Kaplan, who made the marriage, that I am happy to acknowledge.

My thanks above all to people close to me who have tolerated Henry James's intrusion into their lives and who have supported me over the years; first among whom is my wife, Carolyn Clinton, to whom this book is dedicated, who has given me, along with her patience and affection, the benefits of her intelligence and moral clarity. I am happy also to acknowledge the affectionate advice and support of my son, Michael, and my daughter, Melia.

Contents

BOOK III
Artist of Experience, 1896–1904

BOOK IV
A Mild Glory, 1905–1916

EPILOGUE

Henry James at Home, 1904

A late afternoon in spring, and the weather is still cool. James is in his upstairs study, a small, green-paneled room. A sea-coal fire flickers silently in the corner grate. Sitting at his desk, his back to the fire, James is correcting the typescript of the morning's dictation; he is at work on his new novel, *The Golden Bowl*. To his right, a narrow window between glass-fronted bookcases looks over a walled garden and the gabled roofs of Rye.

Winters here within sight of the Channel are dark and windy but mild, and frosts are rare. Violets and snowdrops bloomed in the garden in February; now, in March, crocuses, hyacinths, and jonquils are blossoming within the embrace of the sun-warmed redbrick garden walls. The little English market town of Rye is huddled all around but out of sight. James is in an eagle's nest, spiritually and materially, a high redoubt of privacy and civilization. At sixty years of age, at the peak of his powers and artistic success, he is an international figure, and the society of Europe and America are spread before him, making in his eyes a single, intricate figure, a vast garden of right order. He is a citizen of this great world, a cosmopolite, but after years of struggle he is at home on his hilltop, a home that he has made for himself in which, bachelor that he is, he has founded a family.

Lamb House is more than James's home, it is the seat of his family in Europe. He who was born into a provincial, middle-class American family has made of himself an international figure and the master of a feudal inheritance. His brother William and William's wife, Alice, have made Lamb House their home on and off for two years, while William has struggled to recoup his health and to prepare a series of lectures, *The Varieties of Religious Experience*. James's nieces and nephews are accustomed to making long visits, and he has taken a particular interest in his oldest nephew and namesake, Harry, who is known in London and in Rye as Henry James, Jr.

When the weather turns warm, a thin but steady stream of callers and seekers after autographs comes unannounced to his door, sometimes bearing letters of introduction. When James is at work, the parlor maid, Alice Skinner, turns them away. Friends come down from London on weekend visits. Howard Sturgis has just been by; James had been reading the proofs of his novel *Belchamber.* Joseph Conrad, H. G. Wells, Ford Madox Ford, and others stop in the evenings to read their work for the master's criticism. Young Forrest Reid has just sent a copy of his ambitious first novel and received an encouraging letter in reply. Mary Ward, whose books sell more widely than James's, is a friend and distant neighbor, as is Rudyard Kipling; Edith Wharton, early in her career as a writer, has just made the first of many visits. James's good friend John Hay, the American secretary of state, has written a long letter, enclosing with it a few words of praise for James's work from Senator Edward O. Wolcott, a fellow Progressive. Hay is eager to enlist James in private diplomacy, especially in efforts to bring the United States and Great Britain into a globe-girdling partnership.

A few younger men visit singly on those weekends when there are no other guests. The most eagerly sought and happily welcomed of these visitors at present is an expatriate American sculptor, Hendrik Andersen, who lives in Rome. When their separate lives and careers keep them apart, James writes frank love letters to him.

His books in recent years have not been so successful financially and have not achieved the mass audience or the influence on events for which he once hoped. His ventures into the mass media, the newspapers, and the stage have not been commercially successful; the illustrated magazines, once a staple of his work, have turned to a mass audience, leaving him behind. The editors who are the gatekeepers of the new mass marketplace do not care for James's work; the newspaper reviewers do not understand his purposes. Commercial failures, stinging reviews, and the still worse silences that greeted some of his most ambitious works were deeply painful, and he complains about his lack of success; but in truth he has been reconciled for the past decade to these limitations and on the whole is content, within the boundaries of his sufficient means, with the esteem of writers and his faithful circle of readers. "Dear Mrs. Atherton," he has just written to an American novelist, one of many who admire him,

> It would give me great pleasure that you should dedicate a book to me. . . . May my name contribute to bring your work better fortune than it usually contributes to bring mine. I am greatly obliged at any

rate to your so friendly appreciation of my good influence. . . . Such assurances give one a lift, send back echoes of one's voice.

He has achieved much, "a kind of mild glory," as he will say of himself. He stands on a height that he shares with few others in the world of letters and strives to content himself within the limits of his straitened means. He thinks, however, that it is unnecessary and perhaps even wrong to be moderate in *artistic* aspiration. The only thing that can justify art, as he wrote years before and continues to feel, is "the effort to carry it as far as one can." His work is ever more ambitious. The novel he is completing, *The Golden Bowl*, is the latest culmination of his work. "I can work only in my own way," he writes to his agent, explaining the lengthening delays in completing this novel. He minutely revises the typescripts that Miss Weld produces and then revises again. He is, he says, producing the best book that he has ever done, a judgment that later ages will confirm. Free to compose his novel as a whole, instead of hastily in monthly installments for a magazine, and with the leisure to rewrite, he revises "with such perfection that every inch is done over and over."

Book I

A Bachelor in the
Capital of the World,
1881–1890

1

LONDON IN WINTER

Henry James's first major novel, *The Portrait of a Lady*, was published in the fall of 1881 and was an immediate success. He was at the time a middle-aged bachelor living in furnished lodgings at 3 Bolton Street, in the heart of London, two doors in from Piccadilly. Bolton Street was an enclave of transients, of furnished lodgings in what had once been modest town houses between shops and galleries to the east and the great houses and gentlemen's clubs to the west. The broad, mile-long neighboring avenue of Piccadilly was noisy with carriages, cabs, vans; there was a cab rank at his corner, and in the evenings prostitutes were numerous as one walked up toward the crowded hub of Piccadilly Circus.

His rooms were on the "parlor floor" of the house, up a set of stairs from the street, and comprised a dim, high-ceilinged front sitting room, whose tall corniced windows looked out upon the blank side wall of the great house opposite, and a dark back bedroom: a place to work and a place to sleep. His landlady was on the ground floor; her daughter opened the outside door to visitors. A kitchen maid brought tea and toast in the mornings, a chop and a boiled potato for his lunch, from the subterranean kitchen. For a small fee, a stout red-faced woman carried off his dirty linen once each week and returned it heavily starched and pressed. In the evenings he dined out, walking the winter streets for exercise and to save cab fare.

The city's essential characteristic was its immensity: on such a scale, violence became grandeur. James's image for London was masculine, the city was a giant, or an ogre that fed on human flesh. On winter afternoons, a filthy yellowish brown fog hung over the city; gas lamps were lighted, but their weak gleam barely penetrated the fog. A dim red glow on the horizon might have been the light of the setting sun or the flames of gasworks, it was impossible to tell. Indoors in the warmly lit Reform Club fog lay on the lower steps of the broad marble staircase, and only in the library upstairs did firelight and lamplight fully dispel the gloom. As he wrote to his brother Robertson in America:

> You know that I am very much settled in London & have pretty well adopted the place as my permanent residence. It agrees with me in every particular & I feel thoroughly at home here. It is a wonderful, brutal great Babylon of a place, & if one doesn't like it very much, one must hate it: but fortunately I like it. I have every reason to do so, having had a good deal of success here, & put my fame & fortune on a sufficiently promising footing.

His father, the elder Henry James, had restlessly uprooted his family, had fled the confining village atmosphere of pre–Civil War Manhattan, with wife, five children, nursemaid, and tutors trailing after him. The family had lived for a time in Paris, until their funds ran out, and then in a succession of seaside resorts, and finally landed in what had seemed to Henry the desert of Cambridge, Massachusetts. He had fled, in his turn, to Paris and now at last to London, the world city.

In London every race and nation, every form of worship, were represented. As Baedeker famously said, there were more Scots in London than in Aberdeen, more Jews than in Palestine, more Catholics than in Rome. Cosmopolitan to the last degree, London was the capital of the world and the present home of its ruling class, who over centuries had created a highly distinct and elaborated civilization, a cosmopolitan community that for James approached the "ideal of a convenient society," one in which he had a place:

> a society in which intimacy is possible, in which the associated meet often and sound and select and measure and inspire each other, and relations and combinations have time to form themselves.

The most important part of London life, the center to which he was drawn, was James's circle of men active in the arts, whose position or means allowed them to serve as mentors and patrons to younger men. He had found his way into it slowly. His principal guides were Lord Houghton, Lord Rosebery, and Charles Hamilton Aïdé, the last a man who still kept his youthful appearance although he was at this time about fifty years old. Aïdé would come to typify the bachelors of this world. He was slender and below average height: "A dapper little gentleman with dark hyacinthine locks . . . most exquisite of exquisites," as a mutual friend knowingly said. Aïdé was French as well as English and had the graceful manner and conscious carriage of a Parisian. "An aesthetic bachelor of a certain age," James called him, expecting to be understood, "excellent and amiable."

In later years, when Aïdé visited America and presumed on their long friendship to call on James's family and friends, James awkwardly distanced himself and disavowed their intimacy; but in his early years in London, Aïdé was a valued and close friend. Like Houghton and Rosebery, Aïdé entertained regularly, and his musical evenings were well attended by actors and patrons of the theater; at his little dinners James also met the most promising of painters and poets. Aïdé introduced James to overlapping, vaguely defined circles that a later generation—not entirely accurately or fairly—would call aristocratic and homosexual and that the middle-class press satirized as "aesthetic": the sculptor and patron Lord Ronald Gower and his protégé Morton Fullerton, the painter Sir Frederick Leighton and his pupil the sculptor Hamo Thornycroft; the poet and critic J. A. Symonds, who would publish a celebrated defense of homosexuality; Thornycroft's intimate friend Edmund Gosse; and a shifting circle of other young painters, actors, and writers. These men, many of whom had shared public school and university experiences, would be among James's closest friends. His beloved Hendrik Andersen would later join the circle, first as Gower's protégé and then as James's.

Aïdé wrote light verse and had made an early success with a novel, *Rita*, the fictional autobiography of a young woman. His sentimental love songs, sonnets, and ballads, sometimes set to his own music, were addressed to a genderless "you" and were popular in Great Britain and America. He was, like James, a habitué of the theater, and for his friend the actor George Alexander, for whom James too would eventually write a play, he would adapt a French farce. Again like James, he was always carefully dressed; perhaps too carefully. A friend said of James, "He was always well dressed," not meaning precisely a compliment:

> he gave the impression—with his rather conspicuous spats and extra shiny boots—of having just come from an ultra-smart wedding.

At Aïdé's frequent small dinners for artists and writers, in his flat in Hanover Square, or at weekends at his house in Lyndhurst (and later in Ascot), James met many of the leading painters and illustrators of the day, especially George du Maurier, Alfred Parsons, and his young protégé the American Edwin Abbey, who would be among his most intimate friends. James would draw Aïdé's portrait, dressed in rags, as "Hyacinth Robinson," the hero of *The Princess Casamassima*, James's novel of the dark side of London.

In many ways, Aïdé embodied the distinctive attractions of London. Elizabeth Robins had called him "hyacinthine," and James would call his fictional avatar "Hyacinth," after the beautiful youth loved and slain by Apollo, using a name that was a slang reference to a man attractive to other men. Aïdé was charming but by no means effeminate; he was aristocratic in a particular sense, he was cosmopolitan—which was to say not precisely English, as James was not precisely or only American. There were as yet no salons like Aïdé's in New York or Boston; in Paris, salons were conducted by women, and their dynamics were driven by heterosexual attractions. In Rome and in London, however, James found gatherings of men like himself, cultivated and intelligent, artists and their mentors who were attracted to other men as well as to women, some who were absolute bachelors and some who were married and fathers: cosmopolitan men who were at home in the languages and capitals of Europe. They and the women of their class and generation were the keepers of transmitted culture. When James returned to the United States later in life, he would record his dismay that American men had abandoned their obligations to civilized life and left art and religion solely in the keeping of women.

James had not shared the public school and university life of the gentleman, but he had assiduously made himself familiar with the best of European culture, with German philosophy and Italian Renaissance painting, with French literature and criticism, and what he considered the distinctively English contribution to civilization, their social arrangements. He looked benignly upon the institutions of European aristocracy and its Church, which over the centuries had found a place for everyone and everything. He was, in short, a cosmopolite with aristocratic tastes in an age when European institutions still bore the marks of their feudal origins. His belongings were in truth provincial, American, and middle class, and he shared his family's republican principles; but he was most at his ease among other men of aristocratic manner and tastes.

Certain advantages accrued to his cosmopolitan habits. He had that most attaching of aristocratic qualities, a sense of being at ease in his own skin and at home in the world, wherever he found himself. It was necessary for his social relations that he be at ease, as he evidently was, with the closeted sexual relations among many of the men that he knew. Such relations were thought to be peculiarities of the cosmopolitan, aristocratic world, of the men and women who traveled regularly among the capitals of the West. James followed their migrations, as well as his limited means would allow, to Paris and Rome, where love affairs might be conducted more openly. He had no private means, however, and supported himself by his pen, which put some strain on his ability to participate fully in their lives. He lacked the town house and country estate that were the poles of social life in London; but gentlemen's clubs, a precious invention, allowed him to entertain male friends and so made up for those deficiencies to a degree.

London winters, in short, were masculine and cosmopolitan, and it was in winter that James enjoyed the city most thoroughly. Days were short and dark, and the pleasures of London lay indoors at night, in enclaves of lamplight, in the gentlemen's clubs and houses of the West End, surrounded as they were by dampness and darkness, muddy streets, poisonous brown fogs, long rows of little black houses that somehow were necessary to the overall effect. As James remarked early in his stay:

> We are far from liking London well enough till we like its defects: the dense darkness of much of its winter, the soot on the chimney-pots and everywhere else, the early lamplight, the brown blur of the houses, the splashing of hansoms in Oxford Street or the Strand on December afternoons.
>
> Christmas week, when the country houses are crowded at the expense of the capital: Then it is that I am most haunted with the London of Dickens. . . . Then the big fires blaze in the lone twilight of the clubs. . . . It is not a small matter, either, to a man of letters, that this is the best time for writing, and that during the lamplit days the white page he tries to blacken becomes, on his table, in the circle of the lamp, with the screen of the climate folding him in, more vivid and absorbent.

The darkness of the scene was necessary to bring out the highlights, morally as well as materially; the "immense misery" of London was like the fog itself, in which there were warm enclaves of light:

> The uglinesses, the "rookeries," the brutalities, the night-aspect of many of the streets, the gin-shops and the hour when they are cleared out before closing—there are many elements of this kind. . . . I think it is

partly because we are irremediably conscious of that dark gulf that the
most general appeal of the great city remains exactly what it is, the
largest chapter of human accidents. . . the impression of suffering is a
part of the general vibration; it is one of the things that mingle with all
the others to make the sound that is supremely dear to the consistent
London-lover—the rumble of the tremendous human mill. This is the
note which, in all its modulations, haunts and fascinates and inspires
him. And whether or no he may succeed in keeping the misery out of
the picture, he will freely confess that the latter is not spoiled for him
by some of its duskiest shades.

This was dangerously close to taking a merely aesthetic view of moral
questions. A prolonged agricultural depression had driven millions of
men to the cities, seeking work. Of London's four and a half million inhabitants, fully one third were recent immigrants. There was little work
and almost no housing for them. Families shared a single room in decay-
ing tenements; thousands were homeless. Their plight was not yet
thought to be among the responsibilities of government, and a whole
new realm of charitable enterprises was being organized, largely by
women of the Ten Thousand, to ameliorate urban ills. Arnold Toynbee
had delivered his lectures "On the Industrial Revolution," speaking especially of the plight of the displaced farm workers who had migrated in
large numbers to London, in 1880–1881; a lurid series of illustrated articles in *Pictorial World*, "How the Poor Live," created a stir and was followed by similar articles in other newspapers. The *Daily News* and *The
Daily Telegraph* began to carry regular columns calling for reform in the
provision of housing. An anonymous pamphlet, *The Bitter Cry of Outcast
London*, gave a sensational picture of incest and prostitution in the
crowded, miserable lodgings of the immigrants. Prostitutes, children
among them, loitering on Piccadilly were a nightly reminder of the horrors.

But the aesthetic principle of London was chiaroscuro: the masculine
darkness of winter provided a contrasting background for the brilliance
of the London Season, what James called the "Protestant carnival"—the
busy summertime of dinners, balls, and late parties from the Monday following Easter until Parliament rose in mid-August and "everyone" scattered to country houses in cooler climates. The Season was the reign of
beautiful women; a time when the poor stood in the streets in the
evening to watch gorgeously dressed ladies stepping from their carriages

in Mayfair and Belgravia. The coal-smoke fogs dispersed, the pale northern sun shone, and sheep were pastured in the parks. In the summer days,
workingmen would sit on the grass in Hyde Park to watch the carriages
carrying gorgeously dressed ladies. For a penny one could sit on a bench
and watch the riders on the bridle path called Rotten Row.

James had on principle from his earliest arrival in London sought admission to this more brightly lit circle. He maintained that it was immature and unmanly, a weak yielding to temptation, to remain within
single-sex communities. Manhood and art required a full experience of
life. George W. Smalley, the *New-York Tribune*'s correspondent in London, helped James make his way in middle-class, heterosexual London.
Smalley and his wife, Phoebe, had given James a family fireside in their
house in Hyde Park Square. Smalley was tall, strong, blond, and Saxon,
ten years older than James; Phoebe was delicate and dark. They had four
small children when James came to London, all still at home, and their
house was a busy meeting place for visiting Americans and their English
friends. Smalley counted himself one of the unofficial ambassadors of the
United States, one who had worked to keep the peace between the two
English-speaking nations during the American Civil War. He had been a
fierce Abolitionist, a correspondent for the antislavery *Tribune;* Phoebe
was the adopted daughter of Wendell Phillips, the renowned antislavery
agitator, and as a girl had labored in the Abolitionist cause. Twelve years
after the war, the Smalleys were now comfortably established in the
transatlantic community of victors. They had grown more conservative
with age, however, and viewed with suspicion and condescension the radical agitation for women's rights and Irish independence.

James had Christmas dinner with the Smalleys his first winter alone in
London, and at that charming meal they renewed their invitation for the
following year, establishing a tradition that would be maintained year
after year for twenty years. James was godfather to their youngest child
and a witness at their eldest daughter's wedding.

Another mentor in London was Fanny Kemble, an heiress of the great
Kemble theatrical family, who had married an American and into whose
transatlantic family James had also entered, befriending Kemble's daughters and grandchildren. Through her he had a ticket of admission to London society, and it was through her that he had been taken up by her
friend Monckton Milnes, Lord Houghton, and became a regular guest at
the country-house gatherings of Lord Rosebery and his Rothschild wife.
Through Kemble he met the hostesses who reigned in the Season and

became a regular dinner guest and Sunday visitor in the great houses of the West End.

James found the festive Season of spring and early summer paradoxically oppressive. His masculine, social London of cozy enclaves was overwhelmed by crowds, he was deluged with invitations from hostesses whom he did not feel free to ignore, and he was distracted by the press of people. He was no longer able to make unannounced calls, and conversation was banished, replaced by flirtatious badinage and gossip, nor was he able to join very much in the spirit of flirtation and celebration. Rather, he felt his hard-won identity and individuality overwhelmed; he compared the Season in London to a room so crowded that it was impossible for one to move. Then, too, he was troubled by the image of the ragged poor watching the ladies of the Ten Thousand going in to dinner; it reminded him of *A Tale of Two Cities*, of the excesses of the old regime. Chiaroscuro was not an adequate moral basis for a civilization.

> The condition of [the English upper class] seems to me to be in many ways very much the same rotten & *collapsible* one as that of the French aristocracy before the revolution—minus cleverness & conversation; or perhaps it's more like the heavy, congested & depraved Roman world upon which the barbarians came down.

He was nevertheless popular with the hostesses whose entertainments made him uneasy. Though he did not hunt or shoot and lacked violence or sexual threat, he was a personable bachelor, fashionably American, who posed no danger to unmarried daughters. He received a great many invitations and knew a great many people—too many, as he often ruefully remarked—and dined out often. But so far as status went, he found that his accomplishments as a writer counted for little. In America, he went in to dinner with the hostess or the most beautiful woman on his arm, but in London he came in at the tail end of the party and was seated with no one in particular. Personal attainments counted for little in London: "However exalted, however rich, however renowned you may be, there are too many people at least as much so for your own idiosyncrasies to count," he observed; and then added with an edge of envy:

> I think it is only by being beautiful that you may really prevail very much; for the loveliness of women it has long been noticeable that

London will go most out of her way. It is when she hunts that particular lion that she becomes most dangerous.

In his stories and novels, he frequently imagined himself in the place of a beautiful young woman who was a season's hit, who was in danger of thinking that London would continue to be kind and even generous to her.

Sunday afternoons in winter, between the rituals of Christmas holidays in the country and Easter holidays abroad, were set aside for visits to women friends. Since his unhappy years in Cambridge, Massachusetts, he had made it a principle to call regularly on a circle of female friends, a ritual and a duty that allowed him to join in the wider life around him and to become better acquainted with his readers and their concerns. James reveled in gossip, studied his hostesses, and stored up their anecdotes. Fanny Kemble was his most treasured resource, with her anecdotes stretching back into the early Victorian age, but he slowly enlarged his circle. Mary (Mrs. Humphry) Ward, for instance, a young matron who was to be the most successful novelist of her generation, whose books would be historic events, sent him polite but insistent invitations. She would later recall a visit he paid to her one summer at the beginning of their long friendship:

> It was a very hot day; the western sun was beating on the drawing-room windows, though the room within was comparatively dark and cool. The children were languid with the heat, and the youngest, Janet, then five, stole into the drawing-room and stood looking at Mr. James. He put out a half-conscious hand to her; she came nearer, while we talked on. Presently she climbed on his knee. I suppose I made a maternal protest. He took no notice, and folded his arm round her. We talked on; and presently the abnormal stillness of Janet recalled her to me and made me look closely through the dark of the room. She was fast asleep, her pale little face on the young man's shoulder, her long hair streaming over his arm.

Mary Ward had a lovely white-and-pink complexion, dark brows, and unruly hair, a nose out of proportion to her face, and a small, habitually pursed mouth. She was too thin for beauty by the standards of the day, and as she grew older, her expression became more severe. But she was very bright and passionately eager to learn, and, although barred by her sex from admission to the public school and university with which her family was so closely identified—her grandfather was the famous Thomas Arnold of Rugby, her father and husband had both taught at Oxford, and the still more famous Oxonian Matthew Arnold was her uncle—she nevertheless immersed herself in Oxford, found a succession of mentors and educated herself under their direction. She was in some ways, therefore, very much like Henry James and might have served to represent the majority of readers of his books.

Ward made a point of meeting James because she hoped to emulate him. She had embarked on a career in letters and greatly admired his new novel, *The Portrait of a Lady*, which was appearing in serial form. James seemed to her the head of a new school of fiction, a morally sound realism: "this American art has the promise of the morning in it," she confided to her journal.

His calls upon women were in part research; the audience for fiction was largely female, and his tales for illustrated magazines were about young women and their loves. Kemble had provided him with several plots and had even appeared in a couple of his stories; Ward too would give him a plot and introduce him to a young actress who would be model for one of his heroines. He felt now, however, that he must move away from tales that turned on marriage. *The Portrait of a Lady*, his most ambitious novel to date, was the story of a young American woman betrayed into making a bad marriage with an artistic, cosmopolitan man whom she loved but whose inner and most private affairs she had failed to understand. The novel was masterly, but the subject was not on the grand scale, and his work was not yet taken seriously in the men's world. When his American friend William Dean Howells published an essay comparing him to Dickens and Thackeray, there were cries of outrage in London. His brother William spoke for convention when he remarked that James's stories were concerned only with the relations of women to men and that he needed a larger canvas.

Here in the London winter it was spread before him: the great shadowed landscape of injustice, the black little houses in the sooty streets, the pall of fog; the threat of violence, of a final cataclysm.

Nothing *lives* in England today but politics. They are all-devouring, & their mental uproar crowds everything out. This is more & more the

case; we are evidently on the edge of an enormous political cycle. . . .
The air is full of events, of changes, of movement (some people wd. say
of revolution, but I don't think that).

James, in short, through strenuous effort had found both a place
among the bachelors and men of arts who were his closest friends, and
a social position that gave him entree to the great houses of London
in the Season, a vantage point for observation of the society he had
set himself to portray, a pinnacle from which he could begin to paint
the political landscape and the great tide of change and destruction
that was rising. There was a price to be paid for his position. His
speech and quiet manner, those of a European gentleman, were not
precisely English or American, any more than he was a husband or a father. He was a cosmopolite, uprooted from his origins. His wide and
deeply set gray eyes were remarkable—they were emphasized in every
portrait—and when he was tête-à-tête with an intimate they were
expressive, his manner open and affectionate. But, when he was in
company, he often withdrew behind his beard and his British dress
and watched his companions from behind heavy lids. He lived in
London as if on a stage, conscious of observing and being observed.
Edmund Gosse, meeting him in London at this time, described James
as hidden behind the mask of his reserve, his repose, and his full
beard.

James's quiet manner, self-possession, and repose paradoxically drew
others to him. But his aristocratic composure and tastes would also bring
him into conflict with the middle-class audience upon whom he depended, and with the gatekeepers of middle-class morality, hostile as
they were to the privileged, cosmopolitan circles in which he found his
footing. He felt these conflicts in his own person and in his work: the
struggle of the young against the old, the conflict of democratic freedom
against ancient civilization, the ancient war between justice and beauty.
James's conflicts were resolved for him only in the realm of intimacy, behind closed doors, where he found freedom within the liberal constraints
of an old order. His only indisputable love letters were written to men.
His romantic affections were drawn to young men who were beautiful
and who were gentlemen—who seemed to him to represent not only an
object of desire but an ideal. For James's sensibility we have only the
clumsy word "closeted." Privacy and secrecy were essential for these relations: privacy was not only a condition but a necessary part of a fully
realized life.

His ambition was grandiose: he meant to secure a position at the top of the world, to be a public figure of the first order, yet maintain an enclave of privacy within which he and his most intimate friends could maintain their relations—a garden of civilized delights like those at the center of his tales. All this was to be done virtuously, without falsehood and without treating another person merely as an appliance of his own pleasure. James lived by his labors, but dreamed of wealth, freedom, and privacy.

2

THE PAST INTRUDES

Yet a life is not a linear progression. Before plunging into a novel of London politics James went to America, to refresh his sense of himself and to begin his works of social commentary on home ground. *The Portrait of a Lady* had run in London and Boston magazines for a year, in monthly serial installments, before book editions were published in the fall of 1881 in time for Christmas sales. The magazine installments had prompted much gratifying comment, and the book editions' success seemed assured. He had the intense pleasure of seeing the three-volume British edition prominently displayed in London booksellers' windows, but he felt the need to refresh himself after years of struggle.

Newspaper reviews of his new novel were mixed, and the reviewers were evidently puzzled. *The Portrait of a Lady* set its heroine, a newly wealthy American girl, in a corrupt and cosmopolitan Europe. Among other things, it was a retelling of the story of the Garden of Eden, of freedom gained through knowledge of evil. The men who wrote for newspapers declined to recognize the essentially Christian moral principles when stripped of their orthodox dress. American reviewers were particularly severe on what they took to be an irreligious book, one that failed to punish adultery or to condemn an illegitimate birth, and that seemed to partake of the corrupt European society it described. Even the liberal *Spectator* of London, which had praised the opening chapters when they first appeared in *Macmillan's Magazine*, did not care for the completed book. *The Spectator* headed its review "The Cloven Foot of Mr. James's Agnosticism," and the conservative *Saturday Review* was even more disapproving.

The "lady" of the title, Isabel Archer, was portrayed with intimate understanding. James entered warmly into her passionate friendships, her rebellions, her loves, her mistaken marriage. Readers shared her dawning realization of betrayal, of evil. The portrait of Isabel would ensure the popularity of the book over the generations. But the book was lacking in conventional sentiment. "There is no heart in it," *The Independent* pronounced, and even the faithful, Bostonian *Atlantic* seemed to agree. Many reviewers found the heroine too intellectual, perhaps too manly, an artificial creation. In Great Britain, furthermore, James's portrayal of his American heroine as superior to her English sisters, in both moral character and personal attractions, was not well received.

Part of the trouble was that James was a foreigner, a guest in London, and his criticisms of the English were resented by his hosts. It was not only that he turned a cold, somewhat intellectual eye on his characters, all but the few young men who were described as objects of desire. Thackeray and Trollope had hardly been flattering in their portraits of England, and each had portrayed attractive American heroines who were superior in some respects to their English cousins. But English authors measured their countrymen by their own standards and attributed English failings to universal human nature. James was more distanced, more analytical than his predecessors and employed a more modern, comparative method. He showed what he thought were the characteristic flaws of the English by placing them beside an idealized American, Isabel Archer, with whom all the English men were made to fall in love. This method of comparison, for all its analytical advantages, was guaranteed to outrage and offend, especially when employed by a foreign guest; which James perhaps was not sorry to do.

He was hurt but not greatly troubled by the poor reviews or greatly moved by newspaper praise. In an earlier volume, he had infuriated American reviewers by his criticisms of his native country; a degree of scandal was a part of his popular success. "I care for the newspapers only enough to loathe them," James wrote to Henry Adams, and this was not merely bravado. Newspaper reviewers had limited influence, other than to publicize the book edition, for his novel had already made itself known through the magazine serials that had been appearing for the past year; readers liked James's story, and sales of the book edition were brisk, despite the lukewarm reviews. Three thousand copies of the one-volume American edition (at two dollars a copy) and a thousand sets of the far more expensive, three-volume British edition (at one and a half guineas, about eight dollars then, roughly one hundred twenty dollars today) had sold by Christmas. In the end, about seven thousand of the American edition and two thousand sets (including a second, cheaper edition) in Great Britain would be printed and sold; James was one of the more popular novelists of the day.

Readers have continued to keep the book alive for almost a century and a half, although the style—not much out of place in a Victorian monthly magazine—now seems mannered and ornate, its stiffness leavened only by James's gentle humor. James is amused to see men pouring out tea for themselves, for instance:

> The implements of the little feast had been disposed upon the lawn of an old English country house. . . . The persons concerned in it were taking their pleasure quietly, and they were not of the sex which is supposed to furnish the regular votaries of the ceremony I have mentioned.

James goes to great lengths to find elegant substitutes for ordinary nouns, but the language is not beautiful and there is little imagery. His efforts to render the badinage of young people and the rapid, clever talk of the dinner table are embarrassingly clumsy. These defects of style will be corrected to some degree twenty-five years later, in the "definitive" New York Edition, and it will be the revised text that remains popular, in numerous editions. But even in this original text, many will consider it James's finest work, and all will agree with his own assessment that it is the masterpiece of his early period, the culmination of his long apprenticeship, marking his admission to the small guild of major authors. In retrospect, it stands securely among the best novels then being written in English. George Eliot was dead, and Thomas Hardy had finished his major work; Herman Melville's novels of the previous generation had been forgotten for the time. Of those who were still writing, George Meredith's highly elaborate style and mythic allusions, although much admired, would soon drop into obscurity; Anthony Trollope was popular but was something of a guilty pleasure. *The Portrait of a Lady* almost alone from this time would remain in print for the century to come.

It was a step above James's earlier novels as well. This is saying much, for *Roderick Hudson, The Bostonians, Washington Square,* the modest *The Europeans,* and his short story "Daisy Miller" were classics of their kind. They are still popular in their original form, simply and plainly written; but it is a measure of the richness and beauty of *The Portrait of a Lady* that, unlike these earlier efforts, it would benefit from the revisions James made for the New York Edition late in his career; the imagery that he added would only deepen the portrayal of a young woman's thoughts and feelings.

Isabel Archer has the graceful intelligence and moral spontaneity that James admires. She is not conventionally beautiful by Victorian standards—she does not have the buxom figure, the low forehead, the dimpled smile of the illustrated romance novel—she is a modern young woman, tall and boyishly slim, long-necked, and athletically graceful. She has luxuriant, unfashionably red hair, clear gray eyes, and a wide, expressive mouth. Exquisitely young, she stands erect with the consciousness of her power, but her innocence is touching and vulnerable; one fears for her.

Isabel Archer is a type, a heroine of mythic stature. Her surname suggests the virgin huntress of classical mythology. There are echoes of Christian imagery as well. She is Eve in the Garden, and the Virgin; James will make repeated references to *Paradise Lost;* she will be marked by tragedy and become the mature goddess. And yet she is the ideal of the American woman of the future as well: she embodies hope and an idea.

All of these references are managed quietly and unobtrusively, and Isabel accordingly is not an abstraction; she is peculiarly and vividly individual. She has a characteristic manner and James's precise memories. She comes to cosmopolitan Europe alone, very much as James did, and falls in love with her mentor and guide, Gilbert Osmond. We see events from her perspective, enter into her intimate thoughts, feel for ourselves her friendship with the entrancing villain Mme. Merle. The heart of the novel is Isabel's dawning realization that Merle has betrayed her and that her friend has sold her into marriage with Osmond for the sake of her money.

None of this would matter to us, perhaps, if we had not fallen in love with Isabel, and entered wholly into her youthful passionate consciousness. We struggle along with her to make sense of clues; share her awakening knowledge in a long night's vigil, as she recalls the sight, glimpsed through a doorway, of Mme. Merle standing as Gilbert Osmond sprawls languidly before her in a chair. There is something magical, in the portrayal of her thoughts and feelings, that carries us along with them as if we were observing the performance of a great actor. James's portrayal from within of a woman's coming of age has a realism and tact that will not easily be equaled. As a later critic would observe:

James's sympathy for his female characters would be unusual in any country and era; but coming as they do from the same culture that gave us Melville's sailors, Twain's picaresque heroes, and Howells's business-men, James's women are nothing short of thrilling.

Tired, his writer's sack emptied, James prepared for his return to America. The dilemma for him, in dealing with his native land, was that it *was* the place of his birth and the matrix in which he had grown, his first source of shared identity, but he had found it impossible to live there. Even in New York, his native city, when he tried to settle himself there to please his family, he had failed to find the social atmosphere, the conveniences, the circle of fellow men artists, that he felt he needed for his work and for the realization of a complete life as a man; nor had he found in America the suitable social role, the comfortable identity—the costume, as it were—that he wore as a bachelor in London. But he was reluctant to surrender any part of his personal identity, and he could not cease to be an American in the eyes of the British, even if he would. As a man of letters he was expected to know and write about his native land as well as his adopted London. He accordingly planned not merely a visit to his family but a tour of the American South and West that would allow him to write as an American about America.

He sailed in October from Liverpool to Quebec and went first to Cambridge, Massachusetts, where his parents had settled in a quiet, white-clapboard, tree-shaded house on Quincy Street, opposite Harvard College.

After his six years' absence, James found the town little changed. From Harvard Square, rattling wooden horsecars, straw spread on their floors against spitting, carried workingmen into Cambridgeport in the mornings and college boys to Boston in the evenings. Cambridge was still a half-rural suburb. The people lived indoors, and there was little public life; yet Cambridge lacked any real enclaves of privacy. Houses looked into each other's windows, the college was spread along the streets, unprotected by gates or fences. It was still the village he had fled, democratically refusing differentiation or selection, equally lacking in privacy and society.

His younger brothers, Wilky and Bob, who had settled in the Midwest after their service in the Union Army, were visiting when he arrived. His older brother, William, and his younger sister, Alice, had remained in Cambridge, however, and at Christmas in 1881 the family assembled for the first time in many years, to welcome Henry on his return.

• • •

Let us imagine—as a means of summarizing what is known of them at this time—that the family is being photographed in their quiet parlor.

The elder Henry James, the father, is an old man; his untrimmed beard is white and spreads over his chest. With his cap and his beard, he is like an ancient scholar of the Talmud; he remains seated. He has grown feeble and somewhat querulous. His wife, Mary Robertson James, sits beside him, her brightness now dimmed by age, close to death. Her vigorous sister, Catherine, the children's Aunt Kate, we may imagine standing beside her chair and looking straight into the camera lens, unsmiling, although there is a certain fierce humor in her manner. The four sons undoubtedly stand, beside and behind their parents. They are middle-aged, disparate in appearance. William, at forty the eldest, is thin, clean-shaven, rather intense; old photographs do not capture the fierce blue of his eyes. Henry is stout, composed. Garth Wilkinson—Wilky—is something more than stout, mild, blond, his expression characteristically open. Robertson—Bob—the youngest son, is thin, dark, bearded, troubled.

We imagine Alice, the youngest, seated beside her father and surrounded by her brothers. With her round face and gray eyes, she looks a good deal like her father and her brother Henry, except that while Henry is at ease, accustomed to being observed, she is uncomfortable and consequently looks a little angry and uncertain.

When they were children, Henry and Wilky were together a great deal. Alice and Bob, as the youngest, were in the nursery together; William as the eldest was for the most part alone or with his father.

They had all scattered at the time of the Civil War and the years following. William and Henry did not enlist, kept out of the fighting by poor health and their father's early opposition to the war. When it became a crusade against slavery, however, Wilky and Bob—barely old enough to serve—had been encouraged to volunteer as officers in black regiments. Wilky was wounded in the Battle of Fort Wagner, where his colonel and so many of their men were killed, and never entirely recovered his health. Bob, too, was wounded and was invalided home. After the war, the youngest brothers were sent to Florida, to manage a cotton plantation that was part of a utopian plan for reconstruction of the South; but this project, like the father's earlier socialist schemes, was a failure, and both boys went west with the railroads.

Henry, for his part, after the war went to Europe to try his hand as a journalist and man of letters; William took up the study of medicine. Alice remained at home, caring for the father and serving as his secretary, and being cared for in turn during episodes of deep depression. The children had little contact in the intervening years, but now they were together again.

Despite his injuries and illnesses, Wilky had remained cheerful and optimistic, fundamentally healthy-minded and good-natured. This set him apart, for the other children were all troubled to some degree with a family ailment, a disturbance of the nervous system that was sometimes known as melancholia and in a later age would be called depression. The father had suffered periods of depression and hypochondria, and the youngest son, Bob, had the affliction to a marked degree. Periods of depression would alternate with periods of euphoria, exacerbated (after his years in the army) by drink, which made the subsequent drops even deeper. Alice too was afflicted by periods of deep depression, anxiety, and hysterical paralysis. William and Henry suffered in a milder degree, and the ailment was less disabling in them than in Alice or Bob, but only Wilky had escaped it entirely.

The problem evidently lay in the James line. Mother and Aunt Kate were stoutly healthy, well able to care for their family of invalids. Alice received the most up-to-date treatment for hysteria, a course of pelvic massage and vigorous exercise with dumbbells, administered in his home by a New York physician, Charles Taylor. The success of the treatment induced Henry to try a version of it himself. He hired a young man to administer the massages and like Alice was for a time relieved of his symptoms. William, through his medical studies, was led to experiment with electrical stimulation of the back and bowels and was encouraged regularly to visit the "water cures" of Europe, to ease his various ailments and the hypochondria of depression. But these scientific cures were rarely helpful, and William in the years of their shared youth was the invalid of the family.

As in many families, shared illnesses and shared secrets were woven into the fabric of their intimate relations. The children were drawn together by their illnesses, and the letters that passed among the adults were always filled with talk of depression, constipation, and bad backs, and in late years heart disease, often described in their father's vocabulary, a blend of scientific and biblical language. The siblings were conscious that their shared ailments were hereditary, and formed a bond of blood as well as sentiment. When Robertson became engaged to Catherine van Buren, a first cousin on his father's side, parents and siblings were united in distress; William wrote for them all, warning of the hazards of consanguinity in a family such as theirs. But they took a certain pleasure in the shared ills of the body and the shared experiences of treatment.

These ties of blood and affection drew them all to the mother, who struck a joyous tone: the bodies in her care were to be healthy, happy, free of anxiety: "My bosom seems as if it must burst with its burden of love and tenderness," she wrote to her dutiful son Henry, early in his travels in Europe, urging him to "drink in health of body and mind in following out your own safe and innocent attractions." She was always clear and firm in her regard for a healthy and virtuous satisfaction of appetites, particularly the sexual, and at times sounded the Protestant divine Henry Ward Beecher's note, "Man was made for enjoyment." The father too gave the message a spiritual grounding, not unlike his friend Beecher's. The elder James had written often about Christian socialism, about an ideal society ordered in accord with the natural passions, and had generously supported the utopian, communist experiment at Brook Farm. For his Romantic generation, rebels against orthodoxy, the central principle of Christianity was the embodiment of love. He had attacked the civil institution of marriage, when it acted as an arbitrary denial of healthy instinct, and was an early champion of divorce. When young Bob, still in the army and not yet married, wrote about a sexual liaison that seemed to him a sin, his father replied

> [God] has no anger, *and can have no anger with you for anything you have done* . . . all that he cares for is that you should do nothing hurtful to your spiritual life, which you do by doing things injurious to other people—& in no other way. The gratification of the sexual appetite in you cannot be in anywise contrary to his will, which is one with your highest inward manhood, save insofar as it is gratified in a way to involve some other person's personal degradation or your own.

Again and again, the father returned to the point, so that it would not be overlooked

> Understand then that God would cease to be before he could blame you for anything . . . especially for doing what your own natural instincts enjoin upon you, so long as they can be obliged without degrading yourself or others.

Henry James was raised in this atmosphere of the idea embodied, an atmosphere in which pleasures of the flesh were sanctified by virtue. In Henry James's tales, his heroines seek a treasure (only rarely found): the joy of innocent passion realized, a healthy, happy union of body and spirit. Evil arises only when others are degraded by passion; when a woman becomes a victim, used by other men and women solely as a means of pleasure or gain rather than as an end in herself.

The five James siblings have little in common now, except shared memories of childhood. Wilky and Bob are in business in Milwaukee; William and Alice remain in Cambridge and have entered the academic world. After years of teaching biology to undergraduates, William at forty has at last been admitted to the philosophy department of Harvard College and is an assistant professor there. Alice has joined with friends in operating a correspondence school for women, and serves also as her father's secretary and companion. All except Henry have formed new families, new alliances. William, Wilky, and Bob have married and are fathers; Alice has a life partner, Katherine Loring. But Henry lives alone, in London, and answers questions about his plans a little irritably. He is "a bachelor," he says, too good a bachelor to spoil by marriage. Of the intimate friendships that he has formed, he says nothing.

From his parents' house in Cambridge, after the winter holidays were past, James went by rail to New York, stopping there briefly for visits with relatives and friends, and then on to Washington.

In the capital he stayed with old friends, Marian Adams—always known as "Clover"—and her husband, Henry Adams, who had settled in Washington, where Adams was at work on a history of the republic.

It was an interesting time to be there. The ruling Republican Party had repeatedly shown itself to be corrupt in the most primitive fashion; former senator James G. Blaine, now secretary of state and chief of patronage for the faction called the "Half-Breeds" (for their failure to support President Ulysses S. Grant for a third term), was widely believed to have taken bribes. President James Garfield, head of the faction, had been assassinated just weeks earlier by a madman who called himself a member of the rival "Stalwarts"; he had murdered the president, he frankly explained, so that Vice President Chester A. Arthur, a Stalwart, could take control of the patronage. The assassin, Charles Guiteau, was confidently awaiting rescue from jail by what he imagined to be a grateful president.

Although the new president did not pardon Guiteau, he did dismiss Half-Breeds from office and, nothing abashed, appointed Stalwart ambassadors, postmasters, and collectors of customs in their places. Office seekers accordingly filled the city, figuratively stepping over the corpses of their predecessors; those who had been in power were suddenly at loose ends; the world of Washington was upside down. James prepared for his visit with some apprehension. He had come equipped with letters of introduction, including one to the outgoing secretary of state, James G. Blaine, about whose corruption he had been reading and hearing. Blaine was cordial, and invited him to a dinner party to meet the newly ascended president, a distant relation of James's through Albany cousins. In a story James wrote the following year, "Pandora," he described the sensation of meeting the president in such surroundings, the great man appearing—despite the recent assassination—without attendants and chatting informally with the guests. In letters, James called him "a good fellow—even attractive."With an air of surprise, James remarked that the president "is a gentleman." Other guests at the dinner party included Andrew Carnegie, General William Tecumseh Sherman, the governor of California, and the British ambassador. Newspapers concluded their list of the distinguished guests with "that eminent novelist and anglicized American, Henry James, Jr."

He saw the sights of Washington, paid calls on houses where he had letters of introduction, and spent most of his evenings with Clover and Henry Adams at their house on Lafayette Square. There he met a select sampling of the diplomatic community and of the permanent residents of Washington, among whom was Jérôme Bonaparte, the grandson of Napoleon's youngest brother. James was already slightly acquainted with Mme. Bonaparte, the former Miss Edgar, whom he had met during his year in Paris. A restoration of the Bonapartes would make her, perhaps, a princess.

"I have learned no state secrets, nor obtained the inside view of anything," he wrote Robertson in Cambridge, denying, with a little edge of sarcasm, Bob's speculations. "Neither have I acquired any valuable acquaintances." But here he paused and struck out "acquaintances," for he was meeting a great many people, and substituted "familiarities." No, he would not seek to be appointed secretary to a consul or ambassador. A friend, James Russell Lowell, was the newly appointed ambassador to

Great Britain, and Lowell might have spoken for him. But James had never wanted a job, even a sinecure at an embassy.

Bob in his reply reported that their mother was suffering from bronchitis but there was no reason for alarm; the doctor assured them that she was in no danger. "I should only be in the way," Henry wrote back. "I earnestly hope moreover that she has seen the worst & I depend upon your writing to me again immediately to let me know how she prospers."

On January 22, 1882, James established an acquaintance, if not a familiarity, with Oscar Wilde. An elderly family friend, retired judge Edward G. Loring, held a reception to which James was invited, to introduce Wilde, who was on a lecture tour arranged by the impresario Richard D'Oyly Carte.

As a public spectacle, Wilde's tour was running a close second to the trial of Garfield's assassin. Wilde's lectures were a publicity stunt for Gilbert and Sullivan's comic opera *Patience*, which D'Oyly Carte had just opened in New York, a satire on the aesthetic movement. Wilde made the tour in costume, as it were, and was willing to go along with the joke, with a degree of self-mockery, because he needed money. He wore his hair long and straight, parted in the center and carefully waved. He wore a bizarre outfit of velvet and lace when he lectured, and even when paying calls he wore a black silk cutaway coat, a colorful foulard around a low, wide collar, a yellow silk waistcoat, tight knee breeches, and silk stockings. He wore low-cut patent-leather pumps with broad buckles, better to display his plump, shapely legs, and the overall effect of a big man dressed in this manner—Wilde was a stout six foot three—was startling. At a time when a man could not appear in mixed company in shirtsleeves, his was a deliberately provocative outfit, somewhat in the spirit of his friends Sarah Bernhardt and Lillie Langtry, who cheerfully traded on their sexual notoriety.

In his lectures, Wilde forthrightly embraced the aestheticism with which he was charged and attempted to explain the critical theory of the day: art for art's sake, the mindful appreciation of beauty. His appearance and manner pointed constantly to the sexual, which was certainly part of the message. His costume, consciously theatrical as it was, was a part of the double-sided lesson:

We have lost all nobility of dress, and in doing so have almost annihilated the modern sculptor. . . . To see the frock-coat of the drawing room done in bronze or the double waistcoat perpetuated in marble adds a new horror to death.

Wilde was violently attacked by the newspapers, which obligingly provided the desired publicity for his lectures and for the road tour of *Patience*. At the time of his meeting with James, *The Washington Post* caricatured Wilde on its front page (with characteristic racism) as "the Wild Man of Borneo," and he was reviled even by a fellow lecturer on the D'Oyly Carte circuit—a military man who in this way took his share of the publicity. Women flocked to Wilde's lectures, and men in the audience tried to shout him down. He was subjected to a steady stream of shouted insults—which he returned with the panache of long practice—as he made his way southward from New York to Washington.

He and James were aware of each other and had many mutual friends but had not met before. Wilde told a Washington newspaper reporter, in a compliment to America, that *The Portrait of a Lady* was better than anything then being written by English authors. James read this and was flattered. After meeting Wilde at the Lorings' party, James asked Clover if he might bring Wilde to tea one afternoon at the Adamses'. She declined to have Wilde in the house, however, and James accordingly called on him at his hotel instead. The call was mildly courageous, considering Wilde's notoriety, and was to some degree an expression of solidarity with a fellow artist who was under violent attack.

They could not have presented a more striking contrast. Wilde was twenty-seven years old, a young man with a sly smile and a knowing air, constantly on stage, doing his best to be outrageous, mocking his own publicity stunt. James was thirty-eight, balding, completely self-contained behind his quiet, watchful gray eyes, sitting a little stiffly because of his bad back, in his frock coat and double waistcoat.

James politely expressed surprise that they had not met before, in London, and confessed that he missed the city. The younger man drawled, with feigned astonishment, "Reelly, you care for places?" This touched on a question that was indeed of the greatest importance to James, but in a manner that precluded serious reply. There is no further record of what was said, but afterward, James said that Wilde was a "cad."

A few days after this meeting, a telegram summoned James to Cambridge. His mother had died suddenly, of heart failure.

• • •

The family gathered in Cambridge again, around the now vacant center of their shared lives. There was no public ceremony. A Unitarian minister, Dr. James Freeman Clarke, read a simple burial service at the house for the members of the family; the children asked him not to say anything about Mary James personally, although he knew her well, but only to read some passages from scripture that she cherished. Mrs. James had abandoned the Presbyterian Church, if not her Calvinist beliefs, when she married, and she and the children had all accepted the father's independence, his hostility to churches and dogma. The Unitarian Church provided them with the modest minimum of ceremony needed for such occasions.

Mary James's four sons carried their mother's coffin to the Cambridge city cemetery and placed it in a temporary vault until it would be possible to bury it in the spring. "We four boys took her coffin to the grave and kissed her quiet face for the last time," the youngest brother, Bob, wrote to his wife.

We have all been educated by Father to feel that death was the only reality & that life was simply an experimental thing & for this reason it may be that we have taken Mother's going as such an orderly transition. . . . [W]e feel that we are more near to her now than ever before, simply because she is already at the goal for which we all cheerfully bend our steps. I do not think that either Father, Alice or myself have shed a tear. But the boys coming later were very much shocked, Harry especially who had a passionate childlike devotion to her.

3

HEAD OF HIS FAMILY

For some time before her mother died, Alice had been doing well, bolstered by her intimate friendship with Katherine Loring. With funds provided by her father, Alice had purchased a parcel of land in Manchester, on the seashore north of Boston, and had begun building a summer house there, which she and Katherine had planned to share. They had spoken of traveling to Europe together.

When her mother died, these plans were thrown into confusion. Her father plunged into a deep depression after his wife's death, and it was evident that William and his wife would not be able to care for him. As often happened, care of the father fell to the daughter, Alice.

Perhaps in part because the old man plainly could not live long, Alice was able to rise to the occasion with considerable energy and good spirits, somewhat to the surprise of her family. When Henry returned from Washington, he found Alice and Aunt Kate managing the old man and the household very ably between them. In the summer, Alice planned to take her father to the new house she and Katherine were building.

Bob was with them on Quincy Street when their mother died, but his wife and children had not accompanied him from Milwaukee, where they had all settled. Thin, intense, muscular, and sunburned, with his full beard and unruly dark hair, wide pale blue eyes under the heavy James brows, Robertson was fierce, almost wild. Attractive and intelligent, his manner could be imperious. He was a brilliant talker, a master of conversation in a household of talkers. He had settled in Milwaukee and had married Mary Holton, a lovely, reserved, affectionate, and dutiful daughter of a leading Milwaukee family. It was not in Bob's nature to settle quietly into family and business life, however. Unable to keep a job in an office, he had resigned from his position at the Chicago, Milwaukee & St. Paul Railway Company, and in the hope that hard physical work would improve his health, he and Mary had purchased a farm near Milwaukee. But the isolation, darkness, and inactivity in the hard winters made matters worse. His manner to Mary became abusive, and she sometimes fled with her children to her father's house. Early in 1881, Bob came back alone to his family in Cambridge and remained on Quincy Street to be cared for. Now, with his mother dead and his father an invalid, Bob left Cambridge; the others assumed that he had returned to Milwaukee.

Wilky, too, departed. Having followed Robertson into the railroad, he too had married into a substantial Milwaukee family, the Carys. The taciturn Mr. Cary would sit to James for his portrait as Whitney Dosson in *The Reverberator*. As Wilky described him in a letter, the old man was now retired: "He is a good, simple, very straightforward man with as little imagination as can be. He is rather cold & undemonstrative & has no occupation save of sitting on his piazza & reading the papers & looking at the thermometer & opening & closing the window-blinds."

Wilky had grown very stout, his wounded left leg still troubled him greatly, and he walked with a cane but with undiminished energy. With borrowed funds, he had invested in a new enterprise that supplied hardware to the burgeoning railroads. When this investment prospered, Wilky began to acquire real estate and business properties. Borrowing heavily against his new properties, he became a principal in a project to build iron bridges for the rapidly growing railroad lines. But the speculative bubble of railroad expansion burst in the panic of 1873, and the country sank into recession, very inopportunely, while his first bridge was still under construction. When Robertson's telegram arrived, telling him of their mother's death, his health was in further decline, and he was again working in an office, for a salary. He had come east with money lent to him by Henry.

The second reunion of the James siblings, accordingly, was both sad and brief. Wilky and Bob departed; William returned to his family in Boston; and Henry alone remained in Cambridge with Alice and their father.

A few days after his brothers' departure, Henry received an unhappy letter from Bob. He had not returned to Milwaukee as they all had thought. Bob had gone into Boston with his luggage but instead of boarding a train for Milwaukee had on impulse shipped as crew on a sloop bound for the Azores. He planned to remain there for an extended period of time, hoping to recover his health by hard work in a warm climate. He asked if he might draw on Henry periodically for expenses.

Abandoned by his brothers, Henry dutifully kept Alice company in Cambridge, managing the distribution of their mother's estate and assisting in their father's care. He gave up his own plans for travel. The house on Quincy Street was quickly sold. Henry helped Alice and their father move into a smaller house in Boston, on Louisburg Square, near William and his family. He then rented rooms of his own nearby and settled down in Boston to keep his sister and their father company for the winter. Alice, indeed, was managing well; but there was a considerable strain, as the old man was very ill. He suffered two small strokes, after which his speech was slurred and increasingly whimsical; he began to say that he had already died. He lost his taste for food and refused to eat.

"Harry James is spending the winter only a few doors from us," his old companion William Dean Howells wrote to a mutual friend.

> He had a plan of traveling all about the country this winter and then of returning to England in April; but this has been broken up by the sudden death of his mother, and I doubt if he will stay continuously abroad again while his father lives.

The winter passed quietly. Louisburg Square, near the flattened crest of Beacon Hill, was paved with cobbles and held a little oval of green in its center, a garden surrounded by an iron fence. The square, now approaching its sixtieth birthday, had an air of comparative age in the booming, postwar Boston of those years. Its trees were fully grown, and its houses sat in their shade behind little lawns, unostentatious three- and four-story redbrick houses, shoulder to shoulder, with plain, Greek Revival bow fronts.

On the far slope of Beacon Hill was little Ashburton Street, where the James family had lived for a brief time during the Civil War years, a time that had remained vivid in Henry's memory as his "prime," his first awakening to the common experiences of mankind: of sexuality, of money, of encounters with death. Now approaching his fortieth birthday, with half a lifetime intervening, he was back on Beacon Hill. His older brother, William, with whom he had shared a bedroom in Ashburton Place, was nearby, and the friends of that time were still in Boston. William Dean Howells was in Louisburg Square; Oliver Wendell Holmes and his bride, Fanny Dixwell, were in a modest apartment on Beacon Hill.

The self-absorbed Holmes was surprisingly sympathetic and under-standing. Wendell Holmes, Henry, and William had shared a moment in their young manhood when all three were friends and neighbors and as-pired to be men of letters. They were to be philosophers and poets and in memorable summer afternoons made a charmed circle that revolved about their slender, pale cousin Mary Temple, who seemed to Henry the embodiment of youth and innocent passion, who shared their aspirations but was trapped in the cage of gender and meager surroundings. Wendell and William were in love with her, and Henry, who loved her, saw the men through her gray eyes, so much like his own.

Holmes was the first to go to London, the capital to which they all looked, Holmes who had been determined to pursue the path of letters. But Holmes had since become a lawyer (kicked into the profession by his father, he said) and had just been appointed to the Harvard Law School faculty, after years of private practice. In his spare hours Holmes had written a book in which he attempted a newly scientific, empirical study of law, and it was on the strength of this book that he had become a teacher (and still hoped to be a judge), approaching somewhat obliquely the intellectual questions that had interested his circle in their youth.

William had drifted. After studying art, for which he showed great ap-titude, he, too, had been kicked into a profession and a career. Henry alone had taken the path of independence that led to the great cos-mopolitan world of art and letters. Facing Holmes again across a dinner table, he seemed to see the personification of another choice, of a life he had not lived.

Another old and intimate friend was in Boston that winter: the slight, dark-eyed Elizabeth Boott. She and her father, Francis, had returned to Boston from a long sojourn in Italy and were living on Beacon Hill. Lizzie Boott, three years younger than James, had been his closest woman friend; they had ridden romantically together in the Campagna outside Rome. They were two self-possessed, serious young artists—Lizzie was a painter of great ability—they had shared many experiences and become intimate friends in the years when they were learning their crafts in Eu-rope. Many years later she would be the model for Maggie Verver, the heroine of James's greatest novel, *The Golden Bowl*.

Other old friends were in Boston. At the end of a well-remembered walk down the sharp westward slope of Mount Vernon Street, James's early mentor Annie Fields still maintained her salon, in a house on Charles Street stuffed with antiquities and memorabilia. Her husband was dead; within days of his death, the writer Sarah Orne Jewett had moved into Annie's house, and the two women thenceforth had been inseparable. Henry called upon them and revived their old friendship. They and their house would provide the armature, as it were, for the central figures of his next novel, *The Bostonians.*

Another Beacon Hill hostess, Isabella Stewart Gardner, was also keeping a salon in the European fashion and was "at home" every weekday at five. She was an old friend, and James, now a frequent visitor, often found Holmes there; he met also many of the young writers and artists of Boston, among them handsome Marion Crawford, a young musician with whom Mrs. Gardner was conducting a fully European flirtation.

James wrote in the mornings and walked over the bridge to Cambridge to have tea with his father and sister three or four afternoons every week—their principal meal was still the old-fashioned "tea" of his childhood—taking a horsecar back to Boston in the evening. His pain at his mother's death receded into melancholy, and he remembered those months in Boston afterward as "a simple, serious, wholesome, time. Mother's death appeared to have left behind it a soft, beneficent hush."

Newspapers noted James's presence in Boston for the winter, and his friend Howells wrote an admiring appreciation of his recent fiction, accompanied by an engraved portrait, for *The Century* magazine. The illustration showed a rather sweet young man in profile, with a receding hairline emphasizing a strongly modeled head and large, liquid eyes, a full beard, and a mouth that seemed about to speak.

His long stay in Boston revived his sense that London was the only place in which he could live and work, and he was impatient to return. In April, his father's health improved, surprisingly; Alice, with Katherine's help and support, seemed well and able to manage. James accordingly gave up his rented rooms and booked a stateroom for the journey to England, planning, however, to remain in London only until his presence would again be required in Boston.

He went by rail to New York City, paid calls, and boarded his ship at the foot of Manhattan. Wendell and Fanny Holmes had a stateroom on the same ship, as Fanny was treating her husband to a visit to London for the Season, which he adored (and she detested), in the summer before his first year as a teacher at the Harvard Law School. On the two-week voyage, Holmes and James renewed their old friendship. Henry gave Wendell introductions to men in London and Oxford who were likely to share his interests, and invited Fanny and Wendell to call on him in London, which they promised to do.

James did not accompany them to Liverpool, however, but disembarked when the ship docked in Queenstown (now Cobh), in Ireland. In need of cash after the depredations of the American journey and pursuing his plan to begin writing works of social commentary, James undertook a journalistic expedition, for *The Nation*, to see the renewed rebellion in Ireland against British rule; but after spending three or four days in Dublin, he gave it up. As he wrote to *The Nation* editor E. L. Godkin:

> I soon perceived that to get even a glimpse of the Irish revolution I shld. have to take several days & wander about the country—a course for which I am not prepared.

In London, returning after long absence to his flat on Bolton Street, he opened the door to find his brother Bob reclining on the sofa. The voyage to the Azores had been a disaster, and Bob was in a state of collapse.

> My dear Mary. . . . I am able to give you some news of poor Bob, who is at present with me. . . . You will already have heard of his having come to England. . . [and] will know what a dismal failure his attempt to go to the Azores in a small schooner was, & how little comfort or well-being he found at Fayal. . . . I am keeping him here with me, & he seems glad to remain for the present.

Despite the burden of Bob's presence, James returned to work. He was not yet ready to undertake a big novel of social commentary that would be a task of years, however. Instead he set to work on short pieces for monthly magazines, whose editors he had carefully cultivated, that would refresh his income. He thought also of writing for the stage, which might be even more remunerative. While in America he had drafted a play based on his popular and widely pirated story "Daisy Miller"; now, as he busied himself with short stories and travel articles for *The Century* in New York and *The Atlantic Monthly* in Boston, he kept himself open to opportunities for "dramatic work."

Among his first essays for *The Century* was a particularly self-revealing one. He began with a long personal reminiscence. Perhaps the effect was strengthened by his return to America and by Bob's presence in his rooms in London that summer, but as he wrote he was plunged into memories of his childhood, the year or two that had preceded his twelfth birthday, before his father had broken up their New York home and hauled the family through years of wandering. They had lived on Fourteenth Street in Manhattan, and he had played solitary games in Union Square and walked down Sixth Avenue to school. With pennies given him for treats he had purchased little four-page booklets of ruled paper, in each of which the fourth page was left blank, as if to invite an illustration. Alone in his room on Fourteenth Street, in the quiet at the back of the house, he would fill in the first three pages with a little story and then on the fourth page would draw a climactic scene, a tableau of performers on a stage.

Illustrated texts—the illustrated Dickens, whose drawings he had studied in his grandmother's house; the illustrated children's books that arrived from London at Christmastime; the deluxe edition of the works of Sir Walter Scott; and above all the illustrated *Punch*, which arrived weekly—fed his childish ambition.

Now in London himself, preparing to write his monthly contribution to *The Century*, on the subject of George du Maurier's drawings, he leafed through back numbers of *Punch* and was transplanted back to those early years when he had lived in imagination in full-page drawings of handsome people riding in Rotten Row, of cabmen and costermongers, of page boys in buttons, of bathing machines at the seaside, of gentlemen riding to hounds, of pretty girls in striped petticoats and coiffures shaped like mushrooms, wondrous exotic scenes unknown in America.

The drawings in *Punch* were little dramas, like the scenes he himself had tried to portray, gripping his pencil tightly, in those distant days. He felt a kinship with the illustrator's art that drew him to George du Maurier, who had elevated the charming cartoons to the plane of high art. A constant cast of characters, a sort of repertory theater, appeared regularly in du Maurier's drawings, sometimes in the foreground and sometimes in the crowd: caricatures of du Maurier's friends and imaginary characters who stood for classes and nations: tall, manly English gentlemen, impossibly beautiful and graceful English ladies; a short, plump Frenchman with bulging calves; the German-Jewish beer baron Sir Gorgius Midas, oozing vulgarity from every pore; the aesthetes Postlethwaite and Maudl, who greatly resembled James McNeill Whistler and Oscar Wilde; and James's favorite, the beautiful Mrs. Ponsonby de Tomkyns:

> This lady is a real creation . . . she is the modern social spirit. She is prepared for everything; she is ready to take advantage of everything . . . .

She is the little London lady who is determined to be a greater one . . . .
She tires poor Ponsonby completely out . . . He is not, like his wife, a
person of imagination. She leaves him far behind.

In his letters, James would sometimes refer to clever Mrs. Ponsonby
and her stolid, dim husband as if they were actual persons. She would appear many years later, in *The Golden Bowl*, satirically renamed Fanny Assingham and still accompanied by her bemused husband.

Preparing to write his essay, James went out to Hampstead to visit du
Maurier. They were acquainted, having met years before at one of Hamilton Aïdé's dinners, and du Maurier had drawn the illustrations for
monthly installments of James's *Washington Square* when it appeared in
Cornhill Magazine. James disliked having his fiction illustrated with portraits of the characters, but the two men had developed a mutual understanding, and now when James walked out to Hampstead to interview du
Maurier, they became friends.

The artist was short and frail, and wore a mustache and goatee. His
wife, Emma, and their five children, then all still at home, and their ancient giant of a St. Bernard dog, Chang, were all familiar figures from du
Maurier's evocative drawings, and James fell in happily with the family as
if they were old friends. Du Maurier showed him the house, his workroom, his drawings; told James of his near blindness—he had lost the sight
of one eye when still a young man, and his remaining eye was failing—
which obliged him now to make his drawings very large; they would be
photographically reduced for the magazine. He was a raconteur and rattled along steadily while they walked on Hampstead Heath. There was an
attractive tinge of melancholy behind his cheerful tales. He was half
French and half English, had been educated in both countries, but had
settled in London, as James had, and the French language and a shared
fondness for Paris strengthened the bond between them. In the evening,
du Maurier sat at the piano and the girls sang. He took a deep pleasure in
the music, in the expression of feeling by his beautiful daughters.

After some weeks of rest and recuperation under Henry's care, Bob left
London for a health resort in Malvern, the James family's ancient refuge.
By September, Henry was able to persuade him to return to Milwaukee.
Although not yet able to join his own family, by the fall Bob was back at
his farm, while Mary and their children remained with her father in
town.

The news from Boston was good for a time; Father and Alice seemed to get a fresh start, and Aunt Kate returned to New York. The old man wrote lucid, affectionate letters to his sons and daughters-in-law. For July and August, Alice brought him to the house in Manchester, although it was not entirely completed, to escape the miserable heat of Boston. Katherine Loring joined them there.

With Bob on his way home and his father seemingly in better health, James undertook a rapid tour of the south of France, to give himself a vacation and collect material for more travel writing. (The monthly essays that resulted would be collected in a slim volume, *A Little Tour in France*, another of his potboilers destined to become a classic.)

But solitude was short-lived, and his family quickly reasserted themselves. On his return to London, his brother William arrived, planning to stay for an indefinite visit.

This was one of William's frequent escapes from the demands of family. Duty had kept him at home during his wife's latest pregnancy, but when their second son had safely been delivered, William had fled to Europe. His Alice was absorbed by her two children, and William felt both burdened and neglected at home. There was work for him to do in Europe, but his restlessness may also have been an expression of the family ailment, which seemed to affect him most strongly when his wife was less available. To save money, she with her two babies returned to her mother's house in Cambridge, and let their own house when William went abroad.

William had gone first to Germany, to treat his various ailments at water cures, and to visit centers of scientific research. The water cures (and his escape from cares at home) were beneficent, and it was in good spirits as winter fell that he came to London. Henry was glad to see him, despite the renewed distractions from his work, and did his best to help William find his way into academic circles. Henry arranged for him to meet Frederic W. H. Myers, who was founding a society for psychic research and with whom William would form a lifelong association. Henry arranged also for a guest membership at the Athenaeum Club and gave William various letters of introduction.

Letters from his sister, Alice, in Boston reporting on their father's condition ceased, worrisomely, and were replaced as winter came on by letters from Katherine Loring. Alice had succumbed to the prolonged strain and on return from the seaside was bedridden, unable to write. Loring's letters on her behalf were warm, frank, and straightforward:

Alice sends much love . . . & would write if she were able . . . but until today, she has not been well enough even to tell me what to write. Today she is about again, and saw your father . . . . His brain has rapidly given out these past three days, & he now talks more than before about the spiritual life in a foolish way, still objecting to food; more now, because of the bad taste, whereas before it was because it would keep him alive . . . he is interested in the people who come with messages, flowers, etc. His pulse is strong & regular . . . the Doctor can not at all judge how long life will last.

Aunt Kate returned to Boston and took up residence at Mount Vernon Street for the duration, which was to be brief. The old man did not want his sons to be summoned, but Alice asked to have Harry sent for, and Aunt Kate accordingly wired to him in London that it was time to return. When Henry replied that William and he would book passage, Aunt Kate wired again, saying that he should come alone; the old man insisted that frail William was not to come. This seemed callous, but they had all been taught that death was not a tragedy and William was always treated as an invalid, himself in need of care. For assistance with the practical affairs that followed a death, Alice and Aunt Kate would rely on Henry. William sourly agreed, and, hastily breaking appointments, Henry set off alone on the bitter midwinter passage across the North Atlantic. He was too late to say farewell to the old man. A note from Alice was waiting for him when his boat docked: "Darling father's weary longings were all happily ended on Monday at 3 p.m. . . . He had no suffering but we were devoutly thankful when the rest came to him, he longed so to go."

The old man was buried beside his wife. The simple ceremony—the burial service was again read by a Unitarian minister—had already been concluded by the time Henry arrived in Boston, exhausted and ill from his voyage. Bob had arrived in time for the funeral but would stay for only a day or two. Wilky had been too ill to come at all.

The diminished family was together in the rented house in Boston only briefly. The day after Henry's arrival, Katherine Loring bundled Alice off to the Loring family home for a few days, and Bob boarded the train for Milwaukee. Aunt Kate and Henry remained alone together in the little brick house on Mount Vernon Street, now emptied of the father's powerful presence. Christmas approached, and in Louisburg Square in the long evenings candles shone in the windows.

• • •

In the new year, Alice returned from her visit to the Lorings, "wonderfully better," as Henry said. He made no effort to find bachelor quarters for himself but remained with Alice in the house where their father had died. Aunt Kate remained for Alice's sake, and the three settled down in Louisburg Square for the winter. William was still in London, but a packet arrived with his letter of farewell to their father. Henry took this letter to Cambridge cemetery and, standing beside their father's grave, read William's words aloud to the still air. Then, in the quiet upstairs bedroom of the Mount Vernon Street house, he wrote a full account of their father's death and sent it off to William, urging him to remain in London for the winter and offering the use of his own flat. He called on William's Alice and dutifully offered his company and his assistance to the young mother while William was away. She was ill at ease and wrote to her husband that

> Harry makes one miserable in a fine, inexplicable fashion. He is trying all the time to do his whole duty to me, but I know it is adverse fortune which thrusts me upon him, and I try to temper myself to him and be as slight a shock as possible.

Henry had loved his father and had answered the call of duty to come to his deathbed, but he was greatly occupied almost from the moment of the father's death by practical concerns, and, perhaps partly for this reason, neither the accounts of others nor the record he kept in his own journal suggests that he felt the same profound grief and loss that had followed his mother's death.

For William, however, the father's death was the more difficult to bear. He remained in London, feeling slighted and perhaps somewhat guilty for having avoided the death scene, envious of the attentions Harry was receiving, and it may have been by way of making amends and restoring his self-respect that for a good part of the next two years he would occupy himself in editing and preparing for publication a volume of his father's work, including the large part of a book that the old man had left incomplete at the end, which for many years would be William's own principal accomplishment as a scholar. When this memorial volume was completed and shown to her, his sister, Alice, burst into tears: "How beautiful it is that William should have done it!

isn't it, isn't it beautiful? And how good William is, how good, how good!"

In a long preface, William entered sympathetically into his father's philosophy and gave a decent and respectful summary of ideas against which he had struggled during the father's life. In doing so, he made himself in a sense his father's heir, and twenty years later, with the writing of *The Varieties of Religious Experience,* he would still be trying to redeem his promise to join his own very different labors to his father's.

Henry's reaction was very different: affectionate as he was, and saddened by the loss of his father, the old man and he had remained at arm's length. Of William's memorial edition of the father's "literary remains," Henry said only:

> It comes over me as I read them (more than ever before,) how intensely original & personal his whole system was, & how indispensable it is that those who go in for religion should take some heed of it. I can't enter into it (much) myself—I can't be so theological, nor grant his extraordinary premises, nor [throw] myself into conceptions of heavens & hells, nor be sure that the keynote of nature is humanity &c. But I can enjoy greatly the spirit, the feeling & the manner of the whole thing . . . & feel really that poor Father, struggling so alone all his life, & so destitute of every worldly or literary ambition, was yet a great writer. At any rate your task is beautifully & honorably done.

With regard to practical affairs, however, it was Henry rather than William who assumed the principal responsibilities. Henry wrote to Wilky and then to Bob, who was now back in Milwaukee with his wife and children, about their father's will:

> My dear Bob.
>
> Father appointed me executor of his will, & I have had to open it & take the necessary steps in consequence. One of these is to send you a copy of it, which I have asked Aunt Kate to make. I enclose it herewith. You will see that Father has placed a limit upon your share of the estate; but what will strike you more than that is the fact that he has omitted Wilky altogether. I won't make any remarks upon either of these facts now, because I have just written a long letter to Wilky, & because I mean very soon to come out to Milwaukee, to see both of you

& talk with you about the whole matter. Wait till then, dear Bob, & we shall all understand each other.

The will had been written that summer, while Henry was traveling in France, and he did not know its contents until after the old man's death. The elder Henry James had never expressed interest in making a will, but Aunt Kate, as the end drew near, insisted that one be drawn and evidently had helped in its composition. Aunt Kate, who had herself invested in the doomed Florida plantation and then in Wilky's bridge-building venture, likely was responsible for the meager provision made for Bob and for the failure to make any bequest to Wilky. The two Milwaukee daughters-in-law had means of their own; to the hard-minded Aunt Kate it was evident that Wilky would not long outlive his father and that Wilky's heirs would need no help from the James estate. Wilky had debts to them all dating from the failed business ventures, and from a purely practical perspective there was no need for him to share in the inheritance. Alice, on the other hand, would depend on her inheritance from her father.

Letters flew among them. Wilky reacted with understandable bitterness and promised to bring legal proceedings to break the will; he suspected that it was Aunt Kate who had suggested he be disinherited, but his father had signed the will, and that seemed a "death stab." Alice expressed great uneasiness about both the deduction from Robertson's share and the failure to make any provision at all for Wilky; she who was the intended beneficiary of these maneuvers suggested that they ignore the provisions of the will and divide the estate equally among them.

The estate, the remains of their paternal grandfather's investments in real estate, had been greatly eroded by inflation and much had been spent or given away, invested and lost in utopian schemes. But a mortgaged property in Florida (the defunct plantation) and four houses in downtown Syracuse remained. The Syracuse properties produced some income, and their value would likely rise, as they were beside the planned site of new Syracuse city offices. With the proceeds of the sale of the family house in Cambridge, the estate was valued at almost $100,000 (roughly $1.5 million today).

William, writing at length from Henry's flat in London, proposed a complex scheme for selling one of the Syracuse houses and, with the proceeds, creating a fund to make payments on the Florida mortgage. Wilky's share of the remaining income would be reduced to take account of his debt to the estate. Dividing the income from the unsold properties among the five siblings according to the proper proportions, he calculated, Wilky would receive $23.46 per month and each of the others would receive $31.25 per month from the remaining Syracuse rents.

William wrote also to Alice, saying that he planned to return to Boston immediately. He was having difficulty making his way socially in London, which he did not enjoy, and in any case wished to be back at home.

Henry disregarded William's proposed scheme and made plans for the simple, equal division of the estate that Alice had suggested. He wrote and telegraphed to William, urging him to remain in London for the winter; Henry would send more letters of introduction, as many as he would like. There was really nowhere for William to live in Boston at the moment, as William's own house was rented and there was no room for him in his mother-in-law's small house. William would have to rent rooms for himself in bleak, wintry Cambridge; in short, it was senseless for him to make the midwinter passage across the Atlantic, and such an abrupt return might give the appearance that his journey to centers of learning in Europe had been a failure.

This continuing exclusion from family affairs was difficult for William, who as the eldest son might have expected to be his father's executor. He did not really dispute the judgment that, so far as practical matters were concerned, his place should be taken by Henry. But it certainly felt a slight that their father had named Henry sole executor of his estate and that the choice had been approved, apparently by common consent, by the other children. Even now, William was not wanted at home. With some reluctance and evident resentment, he acquiesced in the suggestion that he remain abroad, smarting under Henry's implied authority, and evidently stung by the suggestion that his trip was turning out badly. In subsequent letters, William made a great point of his ties and obligations as a married man, the father of two children, accomplishments that Henry lacked. Henry did send him more letters of introduction to London friends, however; William remained in London and eventually made a success of his visit.

In mid-January, in subzero weather, Henry went to Milwaukee to talk at leisure with Bob and Wilky. He went by rail, stopping briefly in Chicago, and then continued westward a hundred miles into heartland he had never before visited and that in winter seemed a particularly barren wilderness. "These parts make New England seem like Italy, and Chicago renders Boston—as seen from there—adorable," he wrote grumpily to Fanny Kemble in London. "The worst of the West is that it is a great country, with an extraordinary material civilization, and doesn't care one straw what one thinks of it." For the first time he met his broth-

ers' wives and children, with whom he would henceforth maintain a lifelong correspondence. He stayed with Wilky and his wife, Caroline, in the
charming suburban house that her father had helped them buy. Wilky
was sadly changed, his health broken and his spirits depressed, although
"his old gentleness and softness" remained. He had lost a great deal of
weight and strength; he suffered from heart disease, pains in his joints,
and a gradual collapse of his kidneys that the doctors had now diagnosed
as Bright's disease; it was plain he could not live long. Robertson, for his
part, was struggling with demons and trying to separate permanently
from his wife. He asked that the Syracuse properties be sold so that he
could receive his share in cash and discharge his obligations to her and
the children once and for all. Henry managed to put both brothers at
ease, and Wilky wrote gratefully afterward that

> Your visit here, the fact of your coming here this long distance to see
> us, has prepared me for almost any exhibition of kinship from you.
> Your extreme kindness and kinship to me while you were here, your
> loving, tender, moderate and wise counsels to me had peremptorily dis-
> armed me of all the fancied abuses and isolations under which my ex-
> istence labored.

On the return trip, Henry stopped in Syracuse, visited the family
properties, and talked over the situation there with their agent, Munroe,
who strongly urged keeping the four parcels together and holding them
for at least four years, which to Henry seemed good advice. After their in-
spection of the properties, Munroe drove him along James Street, named
for the paternal grandfather, which Henry found touching: it seemed to
him the Fifth Avenue of Syracuse and one of the "handsomest" of American streets. Henry was pleased to find himself at ease in the world of
practical affairs and even to discover in himself a certain talent for managing them.

Wilky and Bob had gratefully agreed to Henry's proposal to divide the
inheritance simply and equally among the five children and to make no
accounting of disputed transactions between them and their late father,
and with some reluctance Bob agreed not to insist on the sale of the Syracuse property but simply to transfer his interest to Mary, who would
henceforth receive and administer his share of the income. Henry would
leave Wilky to make whatever amends he thought appropriate concerning the debts he had incurred to the estate. The Florida venture had been
undertaken at their father's insistence and very much to the sons' cost;

nothing perhaps was owed on that score; and as to the failed bridge venture, perhaps it was best simply forgotten. William continued to protest,
however, against an equal division of the property and asked that at least
the $5,000 owed from the failed bridge venture should be returned to
the estate from Wilky's share. Henry hastily replied:

> What you say about deducting $5000 has something to be said for it,
> but my *strong* feeling is now, & it is in a high degree Bob's & Alice's, that
> as things are at present this had better not be insisted upon . . . in def-
> erence to Wilk's broken down condition. He strikes me so much (& so
> pitiably) [as] not having long to live, that it doesn't seem well, in these
> last *months* (perhaps) to attempt to give him a lesson.

Without waiting for William's acquiescence, Henry asked the family
attorney, Joseph Warner, who had drawn the original will, to draw up
what amounted to a new one—an agreement among the five siblings for
a redivision of the estate in equal shares. The Quincy Street house had
been sold, and the proceeds, which amounted to roughly a fifth of the
total estate, were invested in railroad bonds. Alice would receive that
portion of the estate and with it an immediate assured income. The Syracuse and Florida properties were to be put in trust for the four brothers,
who had less need for cash. There was a complex provision made at
William's insistence to ensure that Wilky's share in the trust would pass
to his children, and not to his wife's prosperous family, after his death;
Henry agreed to pay certain debts of honor from Wilky's share of the estate, presumably by borrowing against Wilky's share of the principal and
paying off the loans from his share of the income.

Concerned that Alice's income would still not be sufficient, Henry
turned over to her, for her lifetime, his own quarter share of the Syracuse
rents. So long as Alice lived, Henry would receive nothing from the estate, but she would have the means to live as she wished; like a character
in one of his stories, he conferred upon Alice the freedom that an independent income afforded.

"You are rapidly becoming the 'rich bachelor uncle' of fiction & the
drama," William wrote rather coolly to Henry. He was leaving London,
which he continued to dislike, for Paris and Florence. Would Henry
please send him an advance against his share of the Syracuse rents, to
cover the expenses of the trip? William continued to object to the complete reformation of their father's will, but in the end he signed the
agreement that Henry sent him.

And so matters were resolved. Alice seemed well, and on Henry's fortieth birthday, April 15, 1883, brother and sister celebrated quietly together in Louisburg Square. "I have proposed to my sister to return with me to England, and set up a common ménage with me in London," he reported to Mrs. Kemble,

> but she has shrewdly declined that proposal: for we are really both much too fond of our individual independence, and she has a dread of exchanging the comfortable *knowns* of Boston for the vast unknowns of London. But after I return myself she will come to Europe from time to time, and that will allow me to feel settled and permanent there.

It was time to take stock and get back to work. He opened a fresh notebook, purchased in London. We can imagine him in the sitting room in Louisburg Square, writing in his journal. He addressed himself, or perhaps the journal itself, as "my friend"; in later years, he would address it as *"mon bon,"* his spirit or genius. He assessed his state at this turning of the road:

> If I can only *concentrate* myself: this is the great lesson of life. . . . When I am really at work, I'm happy, I feel strong, I see many opportunities ahead. It is the only thing that makes life endurable. I must make some great efforts during the next few years, however, if I wish not to have been on the whole a failure. I shall be a failure unless I do something *great*!

In that Boston spring and summer he wrote three short stories for quick magazine publication, later to be collected in book form; he negotiated with Macmillan, at long range, for a collected edition of his short stories to be published in London; wrote a prospectus for a novel, for his Boston publishers; wrote a half-dozen reviews of books and plays and another half-dozen articles about people and places; he began work as well on the travel sketches for *The Atlantic* that would be published the following year as *A Little Tour in France*, the fruit of his last summer's journey. He wrote each article or story in a fresh, blue-lined copybook, from a supply brought from London. In a word, he began again to *produce* in phenomenal, copious quantity. He wrote rapidly and carefully, generally writing only a single draft, beginning with a title and writing straight through to signature and date at the end. He read over each piece when it was done, making minor corrections, and sent it off. He now signed himself simply "Henry James," omitting the "Jr." he had affixed to his name while his father was alive.

He held stubbornly to his plan to write about America. His tour of the South and West was impossible to carry out, as he must return to work and to London, but he had managed a glimpse of Washington, where the phenomenon of political democracy was on display, and had thoroughly refreshed his sense of Boston and New York; he would make these do. In the short stories and essays he wrote before his return to London, so many sketches for a portrait, he approached from different angles the central fact of the American nationality, of the young national character, that had emerged from the Civil War. America posed for him among her elderly European relations, her clear gray eyes gazing candidly at her audience, conscious that the future would be hers.

The sketches were made in preparation for the novel that he had proposed to his Boston publishers, the planned fruit of his American journeys. The novel was to be a satire of democracy, and he cheerfully told Clover Adams that "I expect the success in this country that *Democracy* has had in England."

His heroine was to be a young woman just emerging from adolescence, with a magnificent voice and a charismatic presence, a gifted performer on the public stage, wielding the power of her talent and beauty. As James first conceived her, she was to be "Verena Tarrant," a Bostonian, the daughter of Abolitionists, radical reformers who plan a career for her as a public speaker, a stage performer. "They cherish her, as a kind of apostle and redeemer," James notes. Her parents seek to parade Verena on the stage; a clumsy, vulgar newspaperman seeks to exploit her. A wealthy Old World dowager tries to buy her for her son. These are the hazards of the marketplace, the dangers of freedom and democracy.

Another young woman, from a different social circle, befriends her: Olive Chancellor, from a rich, conservative, exclusive family, who lives alone. She is a spinster whose affections are directed exclusively toward other women; she has devoted herself to the women's movement, and she too wishes to exploit Verena.

> She . . . has thrown herself into these questions [of women's rights] with intense ardor & has conceived a passionate admiration for our young girl, over whom, by the force of a completely different character,

she has acquired a great influence. She has money of her own, but no talent for appearing in public & she has a dream that her friend & she together . . . may, working side by side, really revolutionize the condition of women.

The two form an intense, intimate friendship. Young Verena moves into her mentor's town house in Boston; they make what has come to be called a "Boston marriage." Their relationship is to be the center of the novel. "The subject is strong and good, with a large interest," James tells himself.

The greatest sacrifice his mother had made for her family, James confided to his journal, was to remain in Cambridge with her invalid husband and daughter. "She passed her nights & her days in that dry, flat, hot, stale & odious Cambridge, & had never a thought while she did so but for father & Alice." Mary Robertson James was a New Yorker from birth and had grown up in Washington Square, in the Calvinist Dutch, Scottish, and Huguenot New York of an older time. Her mother's family, the Robertsons, Scottish merchants, were founders of Presbyterian churches; they were of a generation that sent their children to school in Switzerland to learn French. Cosmopolites in a vanishing transatlantic world, their Calvinist orthodoxy mixed oddly with Continental culture and American spontaneity. She was at home in Manhattan and Geneva, but rural Cambridge, Massachusetts, was a land of exile for her, or so it appeared to her son. Cambridge, in James's eyes, was a sort of desert, lacking in an absolute degree what much of America lacked, the civilization that he found in London and to some degree in New York. After their father's death, Henry had urged William to remain in London; he must not forgo an opportunity to experience Europe. Not until he had that experience to the full should he return to the "barren scene" of Cambridge in the midst of its "harsh and rasping winter":

this morning I went out to poor nudified & staring Cambridge & thought that *that* & your life there is what you are in such a hurry to get back to! At furthest you will take up that life soon enough—*interpose* therefore as much as you can before that day—continue to interpose the Europe that you are already in possession of. Do this even at the cost of sacrifices.

This was the core of his reports of American national character. He made a note in his journal for future use:

In a story, someone says—"Oh yes, the United States—a country without a sovereign, without a court, without a nobility, without an army, without a church or a clergy, without a diplomatic service, without a picturesque peasantry, without palaces or castles, or country seats, or ruins, without a literature, without novels, without an Oxford or a Cambridge, without cathedrals or ivied churches, without latticed cottages or village ale-houses, without political society, without sport, without fox-hunting or country gentlemen, without an Epsom or an Ascot, an Eton or a Rugby . . . !"

This passage caused an uproar when it was later published (with slight changes) in the United States. James was aware that the feudal institutions on his list were the product of long-continued injustices and had been consciously rejected by his democratic countrymen; that indeed his country existed in large degree in opposition to them. In *The Point of View*, a collection of fictional letters from visitors to America, James gave a more sympathetic view of the democratic experiment. Acknowledging America's great advances in justice and freedom and that the absence of hierarchical authority, of ancient institutions, of differentiation and distinction, was part and parcel of the democratic experiment, their absence was felt all the same. James once said of his friend Fanny Kemble that she had democratic convictions but aristocratic tastes; one could say the same of him. When writing a long appreciation of Ivan Turgenev, and evidently thinking also of himself, he said that the Russian author was

out of harmony with his native land—having what one may call a poet's quarrel with it. He loves the old, and he is unable to see where the new is drifting. American readers will peculiarly appreciate this state of mind: if they had a native novelist of a large pattern, it would probably be in a degree his own.

Some of his American contemporaries spoke in similar terms, and many followed him to Europe. His friends Clover and Henry Adams expressed similar views, even more pungently. Wendell Holmes, in public addresses and private conversation, warned of the dreary world cut into half-acre lots that America was constructing; Holmes escaped to London whenever he could. George Santayana described the plight of poets in Boston and Cambridge in the 1880s:

> visibly killed by the lack of air to breathe. People individually were kind and appreciative to them, as they were to me, but the system was deadly, and they hadn't any alternative [European] tradition to fall back upon (as I had).

And here is Ernest Renan, writing in his *Recollections*, which James has just respectfully reviewed:

> The world is moving in the direction of what I may call a kind of Americanism, which shocks our refined ideas. . . . A society in which personal distinction is of little account . . . in which exalted functions do not ennoble, in which politics are left to men devoid of standing or ability, in which the recompenses of life are accorded by preference to intrigue, to vulgarity, to charlatans who cultivate the art of puffing.

This was the national culture that Henry Adams had described in *Democracy*, and Renan's was not far from James's own judgment, although James with more divided loyalties and divided mind saw the moral progress in democracy. He had difficulty expressing what was being lost, the vanishing world in which his own ambitions were fixed. His list of aristocratic institutions, while quotable, did not convey much. It was not feudal institutions, as such, nor aristocracy nor an established church that James missed. In James's stories, where the values of an old civilization make up so much of the background, they are left largely to be imagined; the distinctions and contrasts that made both society and privacy adorable were difficult to convey.

Part of what James meant by "civilization" was simply Matthew Arnold's "best that has been thought and said." James's "best" was to be found in Europe: Italian painting, German philosophy, English social arrangements, the French stage. James's catalogue of the best that had been thought and said was a very different list from the one he made of American absences, however. Even in his late novel *The Spoils of Poynton*, where the artifacts of civilization are the subject of the tale, they are left largely to be imagined. Plainly, he was trying to get at the background, or prior condition, for accomplishing great works—the environment for which he himself felt the need—rather than the works themselves.

Partly he faced the difficulty of describing an atmosphere in which he lived and that he could not easily see from the outside. For the quality that was missing in America, the precondition of all art, James did not have a simple word or expression. At times he fell back on the word "privacy" and at others "individuality" or Renan's "distinction," but none of these words quite captured the quality that he seemed to have in mind and that he missed in America. Partly too he was hindered by the lack of adequate language, the impossibility of being frank about embodied life. It was easier to describe absence than presence, an absence symbolized by the open doors, the too-frequent windows, the lack of barriers and enclosures. The missing quality was something that took time to develop, that could be acquired only over centuries, and that appeared only where leisure and privacy were provided.

Louisburg Square and Gramercy Park had some of the quality James sought, not because of the elegance of the buildings (which was not great) nor the exclusiveness of the enclave. What he seemed to admire was long-continued cultivation of a particular place and character. He admired England for its walled gardens, tiny imitations of John Milton's Paradise: the height of civilization had seemed to him, when he first visited it, the fellows' garden in Oriel College. In Rye, he would cultivate such a garden of his own. Within walls, within a frame, as it were, one could make a work of art. Performing for an educated and critical audience, one could live as if life itself were an art. Within four walls, given time and leisure, one could construct and maintain a repository of civilization. But what would happen to the country houses, to the churches, to the drawing rooms, if they had no locks, no guards?

An enclosure, of course, was not enough; it must be filled with life. Density of life, the accumulation of civilized life that James found in London and Paris, was in itself a great value, but it was also the soil in which alone a modern imagination could be cultivated. The growth of an imagination required constant exposure to beauty, to experiments, to variety, to extremes. The harmony of disparate elements, the composition of contrasting elements within a frame—that was the definition of civilized life, itself the highest art.

James accordingly assessed lives as if they were elements in a painting or a moral landscape, planted and pruned in harmony with the design of a park. Each life was, or should be, a noble specimen of its kind. To be beautiful, a life, like a story, should embody some moral principle, in harmony with the order of its surroundings. When he spoke of his mother, one could see this passionate desire for order at work. Shortly after his mother died, he made a copious entry in his journal:

She was our life, she was the house, she was the keystone of the arch. She held us all together, & without her we are scattered reeds. She was patience, she was wisdom, she was exquisite maternity. Her sweetness, her mildness, her great natural beneficence were unspeakable, & it is infinitely touching to me to write about her here as one that *was.*

Mother was not an abstract ideal, she *embodied* one. He had been raised in the atmosphere of idealist philosophy and Protestant thought; the Word as Flesh. His mother was the *house,* he wrote, and nothing could be warmer or more tangible and rooted. Her excellence was her ability to make and support *their* family, *their* little community, and she was so much herself the fabric of their relations that Henry could hardly accept she was gone.

Her death has given me a passionate belief in certain transcendent things—the immanence of [a] being as nobly created as hers—the immortality of such a virtue as that—the reunion of spirits in better conditions than these. She is no more of an angel today than she had always been; but I can't believe that by the accident of her death all her unspeakable tenderness is lost to the beings she so dearly loved. She is with us, she is of us—the eternal stillness is but a form of her love. One can hear her voice in it—one can feel, forever, the inextinguishable vibration of her devotion.

New York City, where James spent his childhood, was partly exempt from his criticisms of America, and although his detour among *ses miens* had now lasted a full two years, he arranged to spend a few days more in New York before returning to London. Despite the pressure of arranging his father's affairs and mediating among his warring siblings, of writing for magazines to replenish his supply of cash and making proposals for books to be published later, he spent a week visiting his mother's family in Gramercy Park and attending to business affairs. Manhattan had its share of American deficiencies, but he had a fond regard for the city, which he described in a novel as "the American capital":

I never return to this wonderful city without being entertained & impressed afresh. New York is full of types & figures & curious social idiosyncrasies. . . . It is altogether an extraordinary growing, swarming, flittering, pushing, chattering, good-natured, cosmopolitan place, &

perhaps in some ways the best imitation of Paris that can be found (yet with a great originality of its own).

Perhaps, in time, New York City would have its turn as capital of the world, but for the moment his subject matter and his life were in London, and he was impatient to return.

He had a few remaining duties yet to perform. Wilky had gone to Florida for the winter, in an attempt to salvage his health, and was working his way north to spend the summer in salubrious New England. Henry came down by rail from New York as far as Washington to meet him and brought him back to Boston. It was the last visit he would have with his younger brother, the one to whom he had been closest when they were all children. By August, James was back in New York, writing a few farewell notes to friends before boarding a steamer for his return voyage.

4

THE CONTINUAL RENEWAL
OF DAILY LIFE

In November 1883, shortly after James returned to London, a telegram
arrived with the news of Wilky's death. The report was not a surprise,
but it was a great loss and another shock to James. He had little chance
to mourn, however, as a new flurry of letters and telegrams arose from
the effort to settle Wilky's tangled affairs, still entwined with their father's. In Henry's absence, William had succeeded to the duties of admin-
istrator of the trust holding the Syracuse properties, but William's wife
and Henry together still carried out the larger part of the transactions
that were required after Wilky's death. Alice wrote to Bob in Milwaukee
about arrangements that were needed, apparently to pay the remainder
of Wilky's debts: mortgaged properties in Florida and Washington were
to be sold; William K. Loring could provide information about the Washington property. There were sums due to Wilky from his last post in a
government office; sums still to be paid out on his behalf to a former em-
ployee. Henry, as executor of his father's estate, saw to it that these matters were attended to and Wilky's share of the income from the Syracuse
properties was made over to his children so that, as agreed, the money
would go in due course to the children themselves or their heirs, and not
to the well-to-do widow or her family. Henry sent a legal description of
the Syracuse properties to Bob's wife, Mary, so that Bob's share of the estate could be put in a second trust, administered for his and Mary's interest, and for their children after they were gone. Slowly, Wilky's debts
were paid and the various interests in and claims to the Syracuse properties came to rest.

Wilky's widow was distraught, and after the quarrels over the father's and his estates, Henry alone of the family managed to retain his ties with her. She wrote to Henry that she wished she and the children could lie beside Wilky and die; Henry answered as best he could.

James picked up the threads of his complex, dutiful social life, the vantage point from which to write the books of social commentary he now planned. He was at home in a Liberal circle whose center was the Reform Club, of which he was a member, and was a good friend of Lord Rosebery, who had just entered William Gladstone's cabinet and would succeed Gladstone as leader of the party. James's lodgings on Bolton Street were near Rosebery's town house and the Savile Club, to which Rosebery had given comfortable new quarters on Piccadilly. He was a frequent guest of the energetic Louisa Wolseley, whose dinners in her little house on Hill Street, Mayfair—only a few paces from Bolton Street—were an essential element of her husband's career. When, the previous summer, the prime minister had chosen her husband, Garnet Wolseley, to head an armed force to put down the nationalist movement in Egypt, James had shared Louisa Wolseley's anxieties and had joined her in celebrating her husband's eventual victory at Tel-al-Kabir. James had no qualms at this time over British imperialism in Africa, where Wolseley was said to be defending civilization. He listened quietly to Louisa's tales of intrigue in the court of Queen Victoria and enjoyed her successes on her husband's behalf, as she maneuvered between the mutually mistrustful queen and prime minister.

James was not intimate with political men, but his glimpses of life high and low were sufficient for his purpose: portraying Anglo-American civilization, as Honoré de Balzac had portrayed the France of his day. James worked very hard to maintain his observation post near the pinnacle of transatlantic society, and the effort required a strenuous way of life: concentrated mornings of work at his desk, dining out almost every night, walking home through the darkened streets, often sitting up past midnight writing letters; back at work in the morning. "I know too many people—I have gone in too much for society," he told his journal, but immediately reassured himself that he was "seeing the world."

James Russell Lowell was the newly appointed ambassador to the Court of St. James's. Lowell was an old friend from Parisian days, and while James had chosen not to ask for an embassy appointment, he dropped in at the U.S. Embassy regularly, calls that he would memorialize in his uncompleted novel *The Sense of the Past*. He tried to be helpful to Lowell and would come at teatime, on days when the queen was holding her "drawing room" receptions, to be introduced to the new arrivals from America who had been presented there and whose entry into London he could sometimes assist. At the embassy teas, he sometimes met French consul Jules Jusserand, with whom he also formed a friendship. James took pleasure, in his capacity of private ambassador, in introducing both Lowell and Jusserand to George du Maurier.

When he was not within visiting distance of his friends, as was often the case, he wrote. James corresponded regularly with Hamilton Aïdé, Fanny Kemble, and other friends during his stay in America; he sent a card to congratulate Mrs. Thomas Huxley on her daughter's marriage; in reply, she wrote to his London address, inviting him to a dinner; he answered from his hotel in Paris. Ivan Turgenev was dying painfully of cancer at nearby Bougival; James wrote to mutual friends for news and visited Turgenev when he could. His beloved friend Paul Zhukowsky had gone to Moscow to join the court of the new czar, Alexander III; James tried to maintain over lengthening distances the lifelong friendship he had pledged. Once back in London, he wrote to the editor of *Lippincott's Magazine* in Philadelphia, recommending travel pieces written by his old friend in Boston Julia Ward Howe. He was so busy and overwhelmed with commitments that Matthew Arnold confided to their mutual friend William Dean Howells that despite repeated efforts he had "never yet succeeded in decoying Henry James" to his "small hovel in Surrey."

Maintaining this high level of connectedness while continuing to produce a steady stream of articles and book chapters required unremitting, unresting effort, of which he frequently complained.

There were times, especially at the end of winter, when depression overtook him and the labor of simply opening his mail seemed too much. To keep up his spirits he exercised, drank a good deal of tea, coffee, and cocoa, and regularly took guarana, a popular stimulant that helped him to maintain his energy level and fight off depression.

On January 30, 1884, James called on Mary and Humphry Ward, at teatime, to meet the young American actress Mary Anderson, and afterward went with them to the Lyceum Theatre (at Miss Anderson's invitation), to see her perform the female lead in *Comedy and Tragedy*, written for her by W. S. Gilbert. Anderson, a remarkably lovely young woman,

had grown up in Louisville, Kentucky, where the local accent preserved
the British English of an earlier day; her soft southern speech, unlike the
harshly nasal Yankee accents, fell kindly on English ears. She was a plump
young woman with beautiful skin, an ample bosom, and big features—
widely set eyes, a full mouth, and pouting lips—and had been a tremendous hit since her debut at the Lyceum the previous September. She was
a great beauty by the standards of the day and a romantic figure—her father, an Englishman, had served as an officer in the Confederate Army
and had died in the war—but not a skillful actress. James and Mary Ward
discussed the lack of artfulness in Anderson's performance, and by summer their conversations about it had borne fruit: Ward sketched for
James the outlines of a story she thought of writing, and he recorded the
idea in his journal, already beginning to make it his own, the germ of *The
Tragic Muse.*

Tributes to his success had begun to appear in print. *The Century* in July
1883 had listed him as one of the half-dozen leading American writers,
with his friends Constance Fenimore Woolson and William Dean Howells; he was the leader of a new school of realists. *Revue des Deux Mondes*
carried a forty-page essay by "Mme Bentzon," an intelligent appreciation
of his work; his articles, reviews, and stories were now solicited by magazine editors in London, New York, and Boston.

Arrangements with publishers had grown complex. Having signed
over the income from his inheritance to his sister, he depended on his
earnings as a writer, and this was a difficult position for a writer with serious intentions. In Great Britain, where he had staked his claim, the markets were narrow and pay was small; book and magazine publishing for
the middle class was considered a genteel profession, rather than a remunerative trade. Macmillan and Company, James's principal publisher in
those years, was characteristic. Founded in 1843 by the brothers Daniel
and Alexander Macmillan, it had remained a family affair. James's editor,
Frederick Macmillan, was a son of the senior founding brother, Daniel;
fellow editors included his cousins Maurice and George Macmillan. They
were perhaps the premier literary house, publishers of Alfred, Lord Tennyson, Matthew Arnold, and Thomas Hardy. There was little money to
be made by publishing literary books, even by these great names, however, and Macmillan like other genteel houses had settled on a strategy of
bringing out literary novels in a handsome format at a high price. Its novels were usually published in two or three volumes, set by hand and

printed on good paper, with wide margins; purchasers often had them re-covered in leather or vellum for their libraries (providing custom for a large bookbinding trade in London). Books were expensive, sales limited, and profits meager. Like academic publishers today, literary publishers in Britain in the Victorian era printed only a few hundred sets of a new novel, and sold them for one or one and a half guineas—perhaps seventy-five to a hundred dollars today.

The Portrait of a Lady, for instance, as we have seen, was published in a three-volume edition for one and a half guineas, and only five hundred sets were printed. (When this edition sold out, however, a cheaper single-volume edition was issued, of which a thousand copies were sold.) To reach a wider audience, publishers relied principally on the lending li-brary chains, Mudie's and W. H. Smith, which might purchase several hundred sets to lend from local shops.

Lending-library customers were most often women, and the some-what priggish and fearful proprietors of the libraries considered it their duty to protect their female audience from dangerous materials. (A gen-tleman, if he read novels at all, would find the latest volumes at his club.) The educated wife and mother of a family was James's reader; but the lending library adjusted itself not to her but to her daughters:

> We have the [suburban] villa well in our mind. The father who goes to the city in the morning, the grown-up girls waiting to be married, the big drawing-room where they play waltz music and talk of dancing parties. But waltzes will not entirely suffice, nor even tennis; the girls must read. Mother cannot keep a censor (it is as much as she can do to keep a cook, housemaid and page-boy). . . . Out of such circumstances the circulating library was hatched.

A middle-class family could subscribe to Mudie's or W. H. Smith's cir-culating library for two guineas per year and borrow the popular three-decker novels one volume at a time. Sales to the general public of a serious novel would be only in the hundreds; but the circulating libraries might buy hundreds or thousands of copies more, and it was on the cir-culating libraries that the book publishers depended.

The result, of which James and other authors often complained, was a relentless prudishness in literary fiction. There were sensational novels, to be sure; published in thirty-page monthly pamphlets or serialized weekly in newspapers, these often dreadful books were sold directly to the pub-lic, did not depend on the lending libraries, and were often far racier than the literary fiction of the day; but James's novels were not mass-market affairs.

Literary agents were few; authors usually negotiated their own agreements, and contracts were one-sided. The ordinary British book contract was a printed form, under which author and publisher agreed to "share profits," if any. It was not unusual for authors to bear part of the initial expense of typesetting and printing, and there rarely were any profits to be shared. Editors were avuncular and considered it their task to bring good books into print, rather than to make money for authors. As James said of the Macmillans, despite their friendliness, "the delicious ring of the sovereign is conspicuous in our intercourse by its absence." Editors sometimes made small advances against royalties, but for an author without independent means, who wrote for money, the situation was difficult.

Illustrated magazines made a difference. Weekly, monthly, and quarterly magazines poured from the new high-speed presses, a vast stream of paper that had to be covered with print for the entertainment of the women of the burgeoning middle class, newly educated and freed by servants from household drudgery and child care. An author could write reviews, essays, profiles, and short stories suitable for illustration, to keep the pot boiling. James's income in those early years was derived mainly from such articles and serialized novels in upscale, illustrated magazines in the United States, *The Century, The Atlantic Monthly,* Harper and Brothers' weekly and monthly magazines, *The Nation, The Galaxy,* and *Scribner's Magazine;* and in Great Britain, *Macmillan's Magazine, The Cornhill Magazine, The English Illustrated Magazine, The Fortnightly Review, Longman's Magazine,* and *The Pall Mall Gazette.* These were glossy, expensive magazines with finely engraved illustrations and paid their authors well. Most valuable of all, an illustrated magazine might purchase the right to publish a novel in monthly installments, before book publication, and thus provide a substantial stream of cash over the course of a year or more as the serial installments appeared.

The drawbacks of serialization were considerable, however. Magazines imposed artificial constraints of space and time, as well as male editors' sometimes arbitrary judgments of what was appropriate for and would appeal to their youngest female readers. Potentially the most serious danger was that James, like other authors in his position, began to rely on the monthly payments from magazines for his day-to-day expenses, and a serialized novel became a long race against deadlines. The opening chapters of a novel, hurried into print, would appear before he had written the closing chapters. The pressure to meet deadlines was intense, and he had little chance to revise. Chapters were sent off to the typist in first draft and were forwarded to the printer with only slight corrections.

Bending to the necessities of the market, James had disciplined himself to write clean, well-composed first drafts. He always seemed to be composing his thoughts into finished sentences; his letters and even his conversation were produced as if ready for publication. He conceived his books as organic wholes; his method was to explore outward from a central situation, what he called the donnée, the given premise, feeling his way into the natural form of a book. But a novel, no matter how carefully prepared beforehand, is to some degree made in the writing. Nearly all of James's early stories and novels began copiously, expanding to fill the seemingly vast canvas before him; but by its end each had become severely truncated, hastily sliding to the planned conclusion. In *The Portrait of a Lady*, a great deal of needed development had to be omitted for lack of space; in *The Bostonians*, the tone would alter markedly as the tale proceeded. But he had neither time nor patience to revise a novel as a whole; like James's short stories and occasional pieces, each was written from front to back, once for all.

The connection with Macmillan was particularly valuable for him, for it was a publisher of a monthly literary magazine as well as books; he could make a bargain for a book on the basis of a comparatively brief proposal that would provide a substantial flow of cash sufficient for him to undertake large projects. He became a regular visitor at Frederick Macmillan's modest house in Saint John's Wood, a suburb of London, and befriended the whole family: Frederick's young American wife and his uncle Alexander Macmillan, who was now the senior partner in the firm. "The Macmillans are everything that's friendly—caressing," James gleefully reported to his brother William, "old [Alexander] Macmillan physically *hugs* me."

Even with such arrangements in place, the income from British sales was modest; James earned only perhaps £400 for a novel published in magazine serial and book form by Macmillan, roughly $30,000 today, for a year of work. But he could often double his income by arranging for simultaneous American publication. American book publishers relied more often on large printings of inexpensive, single-volume editions; but because of their low price and consequently small royalties, the returns to authors were rarely much better than in Britain. Serial publication of novels in monthly magazines and even in newspapers was also quite popular in America, however, and so with American magazine and book editions there was a substantial second stream of cash for each of James's novels.

He had early established warm personal relations with James and Annie Fields, the Boston publishers of both *The Atlantic Monthly* and Ticknor & Fields books, and with William Dean Howells, editor of *The Atlantic*. Through them, as with Macmillan's in London, James often was able to make a single advance arrangement for both magazine and book editions of a novel, that would provide a flow of cash while it was being written. *The Portrait of a Lady* was serialized simultaneously in *The Atlantic* in Boston and *Macmillan's Magazine* in London, for instance, and then published simultaneously in three volumes in Great Britain and one volume in the United States (James perforce reading and correcting two sets of proofs at each stage). But James Fields was dead, and his widow no longer played an active role in the publishing business. Howells had moved to New York City, and the new editor of *The Atlantic*, Thomas Bailey Aldrich, was markedly less receptive to James's proposals than Howells had been. There was a priggish side to Aldrich's taste, and unlike Howells he was hostile to the new realist movement. When James proposed a higher rate of payment for his next novel, to reflect the success of *The Portrait of a Lady*, Aldrich separated himself from the project entirely.

This was a serious setback, especially because of the quirks of copyright law in each country. The U.S. Congress, jealously protective of American industry, had refused to grant copyright protection to works published abroad. Any work that was published first in Great Britain was in danger of being pirated by an American publisher. James's first great popular success, "Daisy Miller," for instance, having appeared first in a British magazine, was copied and sold in the United States in a pirated edition before he was able to arrange an authorized publication there, so that he earned little from his first American success. In order to secure rights in both the American and British markets, one was obliged to make arrangements beforehand to publish simultaneously in both countries, securing copyright protection in each. Each form of a work had to be separately registered; at this time it was necessary to secure copyright separately for each magazine installment, then for the book, and then again for any dramatization.

Friendly relations with the *The Atlantic Monthly* and Macmillan had somewhat simplified these complexities for James; he could make advance arrangements for simultaneous magazine and book publication of a work with his two reliable publishers, who would secure copyrights in both countries for him at each step. Now the loss of his easy understanding with *The Atlantic* and Ticknor & Fields threatened to jeopardize the whole complex structure of magazine and book publication on which his livelihood depended. At this opportune moment, James R. Osgood returned to the scene. Osgood was a Boston book publisher who had brought out some of James's first work; when James now proposed what was to be a short novel in perhaps six installments, *The Bostonians*, Osgood offered the substantial sum of $4,000 for all rights, for a term of five years. Osgood himself would then arrange for simultaneous magazine serialization, followed by book publication on both sides of the Atlantic.

Osgood was courting a new generation of young novelists, including Bret Harte, William Dean Howells, and James himself. Several would be tempted by Osgood's generous offers and join his list of authors. Osgood, unfortunately, was a better editor than businessman, and those generous advances would in time lead to trouble, but for the moment he was the answer to a prayer.

With the help of Fred Macmillan in London and James Osgood in the United States, accordingly, the arrangements for James's next novel, *The Bostonians*, were completed. Serial installments were to appear in *The Century* magazine in the United States and *Macmillan's* in Great Britain; James had the promise of ample cash for a year's work, which (supplemented by the occasional stories and essays he continued to sell) would carry him through *The Bostonians* and well along toward his next book, already planned, his ambitious study of social justice and revolutionary politics in London, *The Princess Casamassima*.

But there were distractions, and work on *The Bostonians* was slow and painful. "Infinitely oppressed & depressed by the sense of being behindhand with the novel," he confided to his journal on August 6; he had not yet really begun writing *The Bostonians*, although he had engaged with Osgood for it a full year before.

Once he sat down to it in earnest, the difficulty of imagining distant America was considerable. He had made few notes, other than his published sketches, done no research specifically for the novel during his visit; the subject of the women's movement—prompted by a story by Alphonse Daudet—had occurred to him only shortly before his departure, and he had little direct knowledge of the world of American business and politics. For plot and characters he relied not on Boston but on an anecdote Fanny Kemble had told him about Lady Byron, who had counseled—and envied—a young woman lecturer in London. For the setting of his drama, James was obliged to draw upon his few early memories of Boston. Perhaps in part because his materials were thin, James was not averse to giving the story an air of realism by using mildly scandalous references. He placed the two women of the story in Annie Fields's very recognizable house on the water side of Charles Street, with its familiar view of the Back Bay, the house Fields now shared with her life partner, Sarah Orne Jewett. Katherine Loring sat for the portrait of the mannish Dr. Prance. The principal male character, Basil Ransome, in the proposal a Boston lawyer and Civil War veteran, was initially modeled on Wendell Holmes and was given Holmes's youthful ambitions and ideas, although when the work began in earnest, the character was rewritten as a southerner in order to make the tale more broadly national.

James began expansively, as usual, and the novel grew longer and more detailed than he had planned. The opening chapters were filled with a cast of minor characters and portrayals of public meetings, punctuated by the author's arch commentary. His lack of sympathy with the political movement he was describing, his lack of sympathy with democratic politics in general, was readily apparent.

In February, he made his annual pilgrimage to Paris. Instead of tea and cold toast in the morning, there were coffee and a buttery hot brioche, followed by a stroll to the bathhouse on the Seine. The thin winter light was more pleasant than the coal fog of London; in cafés and salons the talk was of art and literature; he received mercifully few dinner invitations. Paris was sensation: odors, tastes, sounds, sights, friendships, a revel of innocent pleasures. He had maintained a separate set of intimate friendships in Paris dating from his sojourn there ten years earlier, about whom he rarely spoke when he was in England or America.

Ivan Turgenev, who had been at the center of life in Paris for James, had died, however, and his absence was greatly felt. Gustave Flaubert, too, was dead, but James traveled out to Auteuil for a morning with Edmond de Goncourt, called on Émile Zola at his house in Paris, spent an evening with the celebrated novelist Alphonse Daudet. As he reported to his friend Grace Norton:

> Daudet is a dear little man, extraordinarily beautiful, but very sad, and looking to me exhausted with all the brilliant ingenuities he has dug out of his heart. He and two or three others here interest me much;

they have gone so far in the art of expression. But they are the children of a decadence, I think . . . strangely corrupt and prodigiously ignorant.

To Howells he wrote:

There is nothing more interesting to me now than the effort and experiment of this little group, with its truly infernal intelligence of art, form, manner—its intense artistic life. . . . The floods of tepid soap and water which under the name of novels are being vomited forth in England, seem to me, by contrast, to do little honour to our race.

He formed what would be a lifelong friendship with Daudet and wrote in praise of his newest novel, *Sapho,* that it was wonderfully true to life; that it was not fiction but history.

Another writer whose acquaintance James made on this visit, Paul Bourget, was a charming young man, although his work was not of the magnitude of Daudet's or Zola's. James arranged to see him again that summer.

When in later years he wrote about Paris, however, he rarely mentioned the French writers he had known, rarely wrote about the French at all, except obliquely, as seen through the eyes of Americans. Painters interested him more, especially the young Americans in Paris, struggling like himself to acquire both classical learning and the newest techniques. Painters' studios, especially those of portrait painters, were masculine salons where artists and writers called upon one another, chatted with a sitter or a model, gossiped among themselves, flirted, formed intimate friendships.

Not long after this visit to Paris, James wrote a novel, *The Reverberator,* set in that city. The hero was a Europeanized American, fond of painters and paintings: Gaston Probert, who mused on his acute appreciation of beauty:

the society of artists, the talk of studios, the attentive study of beautiful works, the sight of a thousand forms of curious research and experiment, had produced in his mind a new sense, the exercise of which was a conscious enjoyment, and the supreme gratification of which on several occasions, had given him as many ineffaceable memories.

This was James himself; his own art was in a certain sense visual; he liked to picture relationships and situations in visual terms; he was a

painter of tableaux more than a teller of stories. He cultivated his remarkably faithful visual memory as a principal resource; he was evidently
able to call up remembered faces as images projected against the closed
eyelids of memory. An education among artists and the greatest works of
the past, and the habit of careful analysis, combined to create what he
called a new sense, a sensitive photographic plate "that nature (with culture added) enabled him to carry in his brain."

On this visit to Paris, James met John Singer Sargent, an American
painter then working in Paris. Sargent was a cosmopolite, raised in Florence and educated in Europe. Flushed with recent success, Sargent had
abandoned his fifth-floor flat in the squalor of Montparnasse, hired a
cook and a manservant, and taken a little house with a studio in the Seventeenth Arrondissement, on the wide new Boulevard Berthier. (In *The
Reverberator*, James would place his characters in a studio very much like
Sargent's, on the nearby Avenue de Villiers.) James visited his studio and
admired (albeit hesitantly) a portrait on which Sargent had been laboring for the past year: a full-length, near-life-size portrait of Virginie
Gautreau. She, too, was a Europeanized American making an early success in Paris; the portrait was a kind of collaboration between painter and
model, the product of months of studies and experiments, suffused with
controlled erotic power; the boyish head, in profile, was oddly reminiscent of Albert de Belleroche, Sargent's young friend and frequent model.
She would be known to generations of the painting's admirers as
"Madame X." Sargent had posed Mme. Gautreau dramatically against a
plain background, her head to one side, her profile sharply etched as if on
a medallion: a portrait of beauty as a form of power and a professional
beauty as a new social type, a conqueror; *une femme du monde*, as James
observed to Lizzie Boott, "half-stripped and covered with paint—blue,
green, white, black."

Sargent planned a visit to London that winter, and James asked to be
allowed to make introductions for him. He urged Sargent, as he had formerly urged Paul Zhukowsky, to establish a studio in London and paint
portraits there at the center of the world. Sargent agreed to have introductions made; but he did not yet consider leaving Paris.

Back in London, James returned to his writing table and his routine. The
talk in London was only of politics, of labor unrest and parliamentary reform, the extension of the franchise to working men. The contrast was
painful, especially as James had slipped into a mild late-winter depression:

I find life *possible* in London (on condition of swearing at it). . . . I have settled down again into . . . the matutinal tea & toast, the British coal scuttle, the dark back-bedroom, the dim front sitting room, the *Times*, the hansom cab, the London dinner. . . . This place *is* hideously political & there don't seem to me to be three people in it who care for questions of art, or form, or taste. I am lonely & speechless.

When Sargent arrived, however, James spent a week with him, and his spirits revived. James proposed him for a guest membership in the Savile Club and wrote to Edmund Gosse, proudly asking him to second "my young man." He hosted a dinner for Sargent at the Reform Club, to which he invited Sir Frederick Leighton, Sir Edward Burne-Jones, and other luminaries of the Royal Academy whose acquaintance he had made through Aïdé; he brought Sargent to Burne-Jones's studio and generally made what efforts he could to ease Sargent's entry into London, introducing him to Aïdé, Alfred Parsons, Ned Abbey, and others of the bachelor circle. For the moment, Sargent was still focused on Paris; his portrait of Mme. Gautreau was to be shown at that year's Salon and Sargent had great hopes for it; but he submitted with a good grace to James's patronage.

James was not a churchgoer, but (characteristically) the only clergyman he knew at all well was Edward White Benson, the archbishop of Canterbury. Benson could recite long passages, seemingly whole pages, of James's early novel *Roderick Hudson;* the characters of James's novels, Benson's sons later recalled, were familiar topics of dinner-table conversation and seemed almost friends of the family. His wife, Mary Benson, at forty still young and handsome, stout and strong-featured, was devoted to her husband and dutifully played her role as hostess of Lambeth Palace, the archbishop's London residence, a sprawling collection of ancient structures on the south bank of the Thames. Their son Fred later recalled that she "loved entertaining on a great scale, and being entertained: to meet and be in the midst of those who carried on the government of Church and State was a rich pleasure to her." She and Henry James became friends, and he shared her "rich pleasure" in observing the rulers of the empire: "The sights and shows, the debates and ceremonials, the state functions and ecclesiastical occasions, bishops and princes and prime ministers." As with other women friends, he entered into her interests and concerns; her five children, as they grew, became his friends as well. The eldest boy, Arthur, was twenty-two years old when they met and was completing his studies at King's College, Cambridge. He would be among the most intimate of James's friends.

Arthur Benson and Henry James met outside the family circle for the first time at a luncheon party at Kings College given by Fred Myers. After the lunch, Benson invited James and another guest, Laura Tenant, to see the new chapel of Kings College. They had tea in Benson's rooms; it was a memorable day for the young man, and, as Benson later recalled, he and James never lost touch again during their joint lives. Arthur Benson was a slender, reserved, manly, and serious young man, supernaturally bright, with a good deal of unconscious charm; setting aside his usual graceful reserve he would sometimes, throwing his head back, burst into hearty, openmouthed laughter.

In the summer of 1884, James and Robert Louis Stevenson began to correspond. They had been acquainted for some years, although neither at first had much impressed the other. They had most likely encountered each other at the Savile and at the occasional dinners of the Rabelais Club, of which they both were members. James had attended the opening of a play, *Deacon Brodie*, that Stevenson had written in collaboration with W. E. Henley, a mutual friend. James liked Stevenson's work, but they had never gotten beyond a nodding acquaintance. The premise for their friendship now was an essay James wrote in the summer of 1884.

A popular author, Walter Besant, had given a talk afterward published as a pamphlet pleading the case for the novel to be taken seriously as one of the fine arts. Poetry and painting were universally understood to be serious forms of artistic expression, but the novel was merely popular entertainment. Besant blamed the novelists, particularly women writing for other women in the illustrated magazines. He thought novels would be taken more seriously if novelists were better craftsmen, more manly, hewing as poetry did to certain classical conventions.

Besant prescribed what he thought was needed to make the novel respectable, a poetics of fiction. If the novel was to emulate traditional masculine arts, authors should keep to their place, describing familiar scenes in familiar terms. Besant did not think highly of women's novels, but if the ladies were to write, a woman was not to attempt to describe army garrison life; a middle-class author was not to attempt to "introduce his characters into society." The novel was to have a "conscious moral purpose" and, above all, "to tell a story"—which was to say that it should restrict itself to familiar sorts of narratives.

Shortly after Besant's pamphlet was published, an anonymous reviewer in *The Pall Mall Gazette* used it as a stick with which to beat James, whom he held up as the representative of the new, ladylike "psychological" school, a writer of doubtful moral purpose, an outsider making free with the society of his betters.

This gave James a chance to unburden himself. The priggishness of editors and reviewers thus spread before him, James unsheathed his knives and flayed Besant and his anonymous ally slowly and gracefully, in a long essay for *Longman's Magazine*. (The public enjoyed such quarrels; Besant's essay and James's reply were widely read and quickly republished for American readers in a pirated pamphlet.)

James said he would not like to disagree with Besant's plea that novels should reflect the author's experience, have a high moral purpose, and tell a story. It would be difficult to disagree but equally difficult to assent. What did any of these prescriptions mean? The novel was a portrayal of reality, as much as a painting or a history; but how was one to set down truths? There were no rules for realistic fiction; to write truthfully, one needed only and above all to have imagination, the organ of perception that in Paris was being scientifically refined until it amounted to a new sense.

> The young lady living in a village has only to be a damsel upon whom nothing is lost to make it quite unfair (as it seems to me) to declare to her that she shall have nothing to say about the military. Greater miracles have been seen than that, imagination assisting, she should speak the truth about some of these gentlemen.

Obliquely citing as his authority George Eliot, a lady who had not shrunk from portraying men's affairs and political movements of which she had little direct experience, James insisted that imagination was the organ through which the fiction writer perceived and learned to portray reality and that the power of imagination justified his claim to truth:

> The power to guess the unseen from the seen, to trace the implication of things, to judge the whole piece by the pattern, the condition of feeling life in general so completely that you are well on your way to knowing any particular corner of it—this cluster of gifts may almost be

said to constitute experience, and they occur in country and in town, and in the most differing stages of education. . . . Therefore, if I should certainly say to a novice, "Write from experience and experience only," I should feel that this was rather a tantalizing admonition if I were not careful immediately to add, "Try to be one of the people on whom nothing is lost!"

We must pause if only for a moment here upon this remarkable, coolly passionate essay, "The Art of Fiction," which quickly became popular with writers and extended its influence well into the next century.

The essay's popularity stemmed in part from James's cheerful, energetic attack on the prudish and philistine arbiters of British taste, the lending libraries and illustrated magazines, and the "moral timidity" of the English novelists who were making a "bouquet for Mrs. Grundy." In the essay he made a second plea, however, one that was equally important to him and that was slower in being answered, a plea for the importance of theory:

> The successful application of any art is a delightful spectacle, but the theory too is interesting. . . . I suspect there has never been a genuine success that has not had a latent core of conviction.

James had the temerity to hold up French writers as an example from whom, despite their failings, the British could learn. He touched for only a moment on the dreaded word "theory," but it stood like a flag planted at the head of his essay.

What, then, is the theory that James expounds? He lays out its premises in order.

He begins by agreeing with the French naturalists that the writing of fiction is an empirical investigation, a search for truthful representation. Censorship, the self-censorship of the publishers and libraries, was its enemy. Art, like science, lives upon discussion, "upon curiosity, upon variety of attempt," and the search for truthful representation progresses only through free experiment. "The only reason for the existence of a novel is that it does attempt to represent life," and the novelist therefore is no less "occupied in looking for truth" by exploring memories of the past than are historians like Gibbon and Macaulay. Walter Besant's formalism would stifle this effort and reduce the novel to repetition of conventional platitudes.

James had in mind his own circle of friends in London and Paris, and he returned repeatedly to comparisons with painting: he said that the novelist and the painter, especially the portrait painter, were engaged in the same enterprise. But the novel, unlike a painting, is extended in time. Even Nathaniel Hawthorne's and Stevenson's fanciful tales, expressly defended by James, are "history"—not metaphorically but in the same literal sense that Gibbon's *Decline and Fall* is a history of the Roman Empire.

> To represent and illustrate the past, the actions of men, is the task of either writer [the novelist or the historian], and the only difference I can see is, in proportion as he succeeds, to the honor of the novelist, consisting as it does in his having more difficulty in collecting his evidence.

James addresses this mysterious assertion obliquely. Not all fiction succeeds in being history; presumably Besant's formulaic novels do not. "Humanity," James says, "is immense, and reality has myriad forms; the most one can affirm is that some of the flowers of fiction have the odor of it, and others have not."

If the conventional, sentimental English novel does not have the smell of human life, the French mechanistic, materialist view is not necessarily better. James rejects Émile Zola's "pessimism," his view that history can be reduced to natural science, that heredity and environment, measured with calipers, completely determine the behavior of his characters. Reality, James tells us, is richer than that.

We are plunged suddenly into idealist philosophy. Novel writing is a serious affair, and part of the dignity of the novelist is that he has much in common with the philosopher. What we know of reality is only what we experience, what we make of sense impressions, and this is what James means when he says that because "humanity is immense," therefore "reality has myriad forms." James is the son and brother of philosophers, raised in an atmosphere of German and French philosophy, of American Transcendentalism and Unitarian belief, and in a series of vivid images he gives his understanding of how the world is known. Each person sees it from a particular window, through the frame made by his own history, language, and culture. The atoms of experience are captured and given meaning by the mind of the observer, the embodied consciousness:

> Experience is never limited, and it is never complete; it is an immense sensibility, a kind of huge spider-web of the finest silken threads sus-

pended in the chambers of consciousness, and catching every air-borne particle in its tissue.

The patterned web, the figures into which it is spun, give shape and beauty to experience. James has absorbed Immanuel Kant's transcendental idealism from the atmosphere of his youth. Myths and fables reflect the inner structure of experience. The tales on which fiction is constructed therefore may be richly expressive of universal truths. Narrative fiction can give coherence and meaning to remembered experience.

An imagination may be strong or weak, or indeed absent. When it is powerful, however, "when it happens to be that of a man of genius—it takes to itself the faintest hints of life, it converts the very pulses of the air into revelations."

Every author, in short, looks out of her own window at the world, and her vision and practice are shaped by her knowledge and limitations. The only general principle James lays down is that the author ought to cultivate experience in all its forms and live in each moment imaginatively; but every author has her own perspective and point of view, the frame she holds up to the world; the fabric on which her experience is embroidered. The completed novel, like life itself, will not be a deductive system, a set of propositions. It will be an organic whole, "a living thing, all one and continuous"; a passionate expression of her coherent vision of embodied life. James finally advised the young writer:

> If one must indulge in conclusions, let them have the taste of a wide knowledge. Remember that your first duty is to be as complete as possible—to make as perfect a work. Be generous and delicate and pursue the prize.

This essay was only the first part of what James meant eventually to write: "my pages, in *Longman's*, were simply a plea for liberty: they were only half of what I had to say." He evidently had in mind to write also about the practice of fiction, and the place of narrative, the art of storytelling in it. The story, after all, was the author's stock-in-trade, and held whatever measure of truth he had.

The plot was a distinct element of the work and carried its moral content: at their best, stories had the truths of universal myths and fables. But such stories must be presented as mysteries. James had early settled on a method that was like his description of Turgenev's: the reader was to be drawn into the novel by curiosity; a story was to have the fascination of an unopened telegram. The reader seeking to understand what was happening to the characters of a tale would be obliged to exercise her imagination, and it was her imagination that would give life and meaning to the scattered hints that language conveyed.

Robert Louis Stevenson read James's "The Art of Fiction" when it appeared in *Longman's Magazine*, and although he found himself praised there in passing, he was prompted to write a rebuttal of his own. James compared novels to paintings, emphasized their scenic and portrait quality; there had not been space or time for his discussion of storytelling. Stevenson regretted the omission of that element, for he believed that the art of fiction was preeminently the art of storytelling. The tale itself indeed must be true, but the action of a tale told clearly and simply might carry a novel along, without the strenuous imaginative efforts of which James was so fond.

Stevenson made some other gentle criticisms. In James's stories, crucial action too often took place offstage or behind closed doors. The essentials of storytelling were simplicity of character and simplicity of action. James's elaborate, imaginative depictions were often inconsistent with good storytelling, and his counsels of perfection might be discouraging to the young writer.

Stevenson's courteous rebuttal appeared in *Longman's* in due course, under the title "A Humble Remonstrance," and James—who entirely agreed with Stevenson about the importance of narrative but was perhaps unpersuaded of the need for simplicity—wrote him a short and friendly letter:

My dear Robert Louis Stevenson, I read only last night your paper . . . and the result of that charming half-hour is a friendly desire to send you three words. Not words of discussion, dissent, retort or remonstrance, but of hearty sympathy, charged with the assurance of my enjoyment of everything you write . . . we agree, I think, more than we disagree, and though there are points as to which a more irrepressible spirit than mine would like to try a fall, that is not what I want to say— but on the contrary, to thank you for so much that is suggestive and felicitous in your remarks—justly felt and brilliantly said.

Stevenson, for his part, replied with equally friendly warmth and invited James to visit him in Bournemouth, where he had settled that summer in the hope that its climate and quiet would be good for his tuberculosis:

As you know, I belong to that besotted class of man, the invalid: this puts me to a stand in the way of visits. But it is possible that some day you may feel that a day near the sea and among pinewoods would be a pleasant change from town. If so, please let us know; and my wife and I will be delighted to put you up, and give you what we can to eat and drink (I have a fair bottle of claret).

But it would be some time before James was able to take up this invitation.

In the summer of 1884, James cultivated instead his budding friendship with Paul Bourget, whom he had met in Paris and who now visited him in London in turn. Ten years younger than James, Bourget was handsome and slender, with large dark eyes and a soft mustache. He was well turned out, slightly affected, gentlemanly. Bourget was a character out of Balzac: a young man from the provinces who had come to Paris and had just begun to make his mark as a critic and man of letters, who supported himself by his pen and advanced his career through intimate friendships with both men and women. Bourget had just begun to write novels that showed the influence of James's work and ideas, and he was eager to cultivate James. When he came to London, they walked together in Hyde Park and Kensington Gardens and dined together repeatedly. They agreed to meet more privately in Dover, where James planned to take lodgings for the month of August and where the two solidified their lifelong friendship. If James ever broke his habitual reticence to speak of the weeks they spent together in the seaport, the record has been lost.

5

BOURNEMOUTH AND BROADWAY

Alice, living alone in Boston, had promised to visit her brother often in Europe. But while she shared many of James's reservations about America in general and Boston in particular, she did not want to emigrate. She had a place in Boston society and had a good deal of company, keeping in her house in Louisburg Square what she called her "salon." Her small dinner parties were popular and well known. With the adequate means that Henry had arranged for her, she was able to hire servants and to palliate her regular episodes of anxiety and depression with visits to New York, exercise, galvanic treatments, and massage. Her neighbor Dr. Holmes inveighed in those years against colleagues who spoke of "cures"; in the limited state of medical knowledge the best one could hope for was palliation of symptoms and to avoid doing harm; so it was with Alice, who regularly submitted to the treatments recommended by William or Aunt Kate and would succumb for a time to the blandishments of charming and clever physicians. She would return resignedly after a few days or weeks to her routine of exercise and massage.

In the summer of 1884, however, Katherine Loring accompanied her own ailing sister Louisa to Europe, and by the fall Alice began to find the solitude of lengthening nights intolerable. She decided to join the Loring sisters for a winter in the comparatively mild climate of Bournemouth on the south coast of England, followed by a summer in Switzerland. Katherine obligingly returned from Europe to accompany Alice on her voyage. Alice and Katherine sailed together from New York early in November. Alice cabled that she was coming, and Henry hired a lady's maid, receiving advice from a cousin, Mrs. Stanley Clarke, on how to do this, and made plans to meet Alice on her arrival, bringing the maid with him.

To Henry's considerable distress, however, when her ship docked at

Liverpool, Alice was carried ashore by two porters. She had fallen ill shortly before the voyage and had greatly worsened en route. She had been overcome by a combination of seasickness and a puzzling, chronic exhaustion accompanied by severe pains in her head, back, and legs. She was unable to walk and too ill to go on to Bournemouth with her friends. James accordingly took rooms for himself, Alice, and her new maid at his old, familiar Adelphi Hotel in Liverpool. A doctor was consulted, and James found a nurse to care for Alice.

They remained in Liverpool for two weeks, until Alice seemed sufficiently recovered to travel, but instead of continuing on to Bournemouth as she had planned, Alice accompanied Henry to London, where he found lodgings for her and her little entourage of nurse and servant on Clarges Street, near his own rooms on Bolton Street.

There followed a series of consultations with the great masters of the medical profession in London. Alice submitted patiently, if not entirely gracefully, to long waits in reception rooms, followed by interviews and manipulations of her person. She did not find the physicians congenial, and the examinations were humiliating:

> It requires the strength of a horse to survive the fatigue of waiting hour after hour for the great man & then the fierce struggle to recover one's self-respect. . . . I think the difficulty is my inability to assume the receptive attitude, the cardinal virtue in woman, the absence of which has always made me so uncharming to & uncharmed by the male sex.

The diagnosis of her new illness was "gout," although Alice, skeptical of physicians, found it strange that the disease had come on so abruptly and resulted in such general weakness and debilitation. She suffered a good deal of pain and weakness in her legs, which deprived her of the outdoor exercise that she had relied upon to stave off anxiety and depression in the past. It was difficult to be immobilized: "To have a tornado going on within one, whilst one is chained to a sofa, is no joke, I can assure you," she confided to Aunt Kate. Whatever the true nature of the illness, there was no effective treatment for it, and Alice slowly came to accept that this new affliction was not simply another attack of her old anxiety but a new and protracted affair, and she began to speak of years, rather than months, for it to run its course.

Henry visited twice each day and helped Alice to find a nurse and servant for a long stay. He introduced her to Mary Ward, who called regularly; to Alice Stopford Green, the historian and recent widow of J. R.

Green, who was at work on a new edition of her late husband's *Short History of the English People*, a book that Alice had much admired; to Fanny Kemble and her daughter Frances Leigh. Katherine Loring came up regularly from Bournemouth, when she could be spared from the care of her own sister, Louisa, and Alice's old friend Sara Sedgwick, who had married the late Charles Darwin's eldest son, William, came up from Southampton or stopped on her way through London to Cambridge, to visit the invalid. James Russell Lowell and his wife, Frances, extended their hospitality; Frances called and invited Alice to share their Christmas dinner. James slowly reconstructed Alice's daily life, and Alice wrote to their brother William:

> His kindness & devotion are not to be described by mortal pen, he shows no outward sign of impatience at having an Old Man of the Sea indefinitely launched upon him, I am afraid that he will find me attached to his coat-tails for the rest of my mortal career.

She slowly recovered, to a degree, and for a time, to escape the London winter fog, Alice, with a maid and a nurse-companion, took lodgings in Bournemouth, near the Lorings, and Henry came down to visit her there. Katherine was evidently torn between friendship and family. When the time came for her sister to go to Switzerland and it was plain that Alice could neither go with them nor remain alone in Bournemouth, Katherine promised she would return after a month to Alice, as a permanent arrangement. James would remain with Alice until Katherine's return.

James wrote tactfully to Aunt Kate, who had never approved of Alice's intimacy with Katherine and who still hoped that Alice would marry, reporting the women's renewed and permanent partnership:

> We must accept it with gratitude. One may think that [Katherine's] being with [Alice] is not in the long run the best thing for A.; but the latter is *too ill* to make the long run the main thing to think about. There *may* be no "long run" at all; & if there is, a *long* period with K. will work better than a *short* one, especially if it is free from the baleful element of Louisa's conflicting claims & K.'s divided duty . . . a devotion so perfect & generous as K.L.'s is a gift of providence.

James accordingly went to Bournemouth that summer, while London was having its Season, to be on hand during Katherine's absence. May and June were pleasant months to be in Bournemouth; the weather was mild, there were miles of cliffs overlooking sandy beaches on which to walk and think, and in those days there were few summer visitors.

The Bostonians had dragged on far longer than he had planned, into twelve monthly numbers; but it was done at last, and he was able to get to work on his long-planned novel of revolutionary politics in London, *The Princess Casamassima*. In lodgings in Bournemouth, James wrote in the mornings, lunched with Alice, took long walks on the cliffs in the afternoons, visited Alice again at teatime. His evenings were free, and the turn of events had brought him within visiting distance of Robert Louis Stevenson. On his first summer evening in Bournemouth, therefore, James walked out to the house Stevenson and his family had rented—a modest two-story, yellow-brick house with a blue slate roof, covered with ivy. It stood in a suburban half acre of heather and lawn, on the bank of a little ravine filled with laurel then prettily in bloom. James knocked at what turned out to be the rear door and waited in the kitchen while a maid, evidently taking him for a tradesman, took in his card. But there was no awkwardness about the visit that followed. James returned the next evening, and the next. He spent nearly every evening for eight weeks with the Stevensons.

Stevenson was very ill, emaciated and wracked with coughs. It seemed to James that Stevenson was dying; but illness had not affected his ebullient spirits, his boyish charm, his intelligence, or his energy. Stevenson was thirty-four years old in that summer of 1885. Tall and exquisitely thin even before his disease, Stevenson was emaciated and pale. He paced about his small parlor, head bent a little under the low ceiling, smoking, coughing, and gesticulating. Fanny, his wife, sat silent for the most part as the two men conversed; she was evidently older than Louis, but she shared Stevenson's youthful and passionate temper and the air of improvisation with which they lived, like students in temporary lodgings.

Their circumstances gradually unfolded for James. Stevenson and the red-bearded Henley, madly enthusiastic, were collaborating on a series of projects intended to make them rich. Their jointly written play, *Deacon Brodie*, had not succeeded, but more plays were in the offing. In still another collaboration, with Fanny, Stevenson had written a detective-story novel, *The Dynamiters*, for whose commercial (if not artistic) success he had high hopes. *A Child's Garden of Verses* had just been published, his novel *Prince Otto*—which dealt with social justice and revolution—was running in serial form, and he was at work on yet another new book: *Kidnapped*.

The Stevensons were in Bournemouth partly on the theory that the mild climate would benefit Stevenson's lungs, partly because Fanny's son, Lloyd, was at school there, partly because it was cheap. Fanny, stout and plain, her hair descending in unbecoming ringlets over her forehead, was an American, and to Stevenson's British friends and family, who formed a large and demanding circle around him, her speech and manners seemed coarse. Fanny struggled against their jealousy and resentment, struggled to maintain her household on the very limited income that Stevenson's writing provided. Alone among Stevenson's friends and family, James accepted Fanny's place in her husband's life and was seemingly free from jealousies and resentments. As Fanny wrote happily to her in-laws, "He is a gentle, amiable, soothing, sleepy sort, fat and dimpled. We find ourselves excessively fond of him."

Each evening, on his arrival, James settled into an ancient blue armchair, thenceforth to be known as "Henry James's chair," and was served a drink or a glass of wine. Sometimes he had a cigarette to keep Louis company. So quickly did they become intimate that on May 19, the Stevensons' wedding anniversary, James dined with them, their only guest. Fanny served American dishes in his honor, and James took second helpings of everything. Later, fondly recalling these evenings in a letter to James, she remembered that "You sat enthroned in your own blue chair, and we grouped ourselves about you."

James and Stevenson talked about their theories of fiction and about their works in progress. They most likely also talked about politics and dynamiters, about whom both were writing. Stevenson admired James's portraits of women, a weak point in his own work, and Louis composed a sonnet in honor of these visits, imagining that James came accompanied by his vivid creations,

> But he, attended by these shining names,
> Comes (best of all) himself—our welcome James.

Letters and telegrams followed James from London, bringing sad news. Frances Lowell, who had been so welcoming to him and to Alice, had died, and Lowell was being recalled from his post. The new Democratic president, Grover Cleveland, wished to appoint his own man. To James, Lowell's forced return to barren Cambridge seemed as great a misfortune as Frances's death. He wrote to Grace Norton that such a retirement was "a cruel, a barbaric, fortune." From Bournemouth, he sent a tender farewell to his old friend:

> I give you my blessing and every good wish for a happy voyage. I wish I could receive you over there—and assist at your arrival and impressions—little as I want you to go back. Don't forget that you have produced a relation between England and the U.S. which is really a gain to civilization and that you must come back to look after your work. . . . The only way you can be a good American is to return to our dear old stupid, satisfactory London, and to yours ever affectionately and faithfully,
>
> Henry James

The first installments of *The Bostonians* were already appearing in *The Century*, where Osgood had placed it. Under his agreement with the author, when the last installment was submitted, Osgood was to pay James $4,000 for the American serial and book rights, and James was looking forward to receiving the money. The last chapter was with his typist in London and had only to be read over and sent in. The family Syracuse properties needed renovation, and the owners were being asked to provide a capital of $1,000 each. James had assigned his share of the income to Alice but as part owner was still liable for the assessment, which he planned to pay from the Osgood advance.

He now also expected his expenses to increase. For some time, he had been looking for more comfortable quarters. In Bolton Street he was at the center of things, but he was both lonely and distracted by society. He confessed to a neighbor that he had a vision of a "semi-detached villa" in suburban Saint John's Wood, near the Frederick Macmillans, "with man and wife to wait on him scrub & cook—& a dog as a companion & a spare room for a friend & nice little dinners of six twice a week."

The villa did not materialize, but he found a sunny flat in South Kensington, in walking distance (or cheap hackney fare) from Mayfair and central London, yet away from the noise and crowds of Piccadilly and with room for the desired visitors and entertainments. De Vere Mansions was built to meet a new demand for self-contained apartments, with cooking facilities and rooms for servants, and was admirably designed for a bachelor. James would have a spare room for guests and a suitably neat little dining room in which six could be seated.

With the prospect of a handsome lump-sum payment from Osgood

for *The Bostonians,* advances for *The Princess Casamassima,* and payments for his steady production of short stories, he could now think of
taking these larger, brighter rooms; of keeping servants, taking his meals
at home, entertaining. He had no reason to suppose that his income
would decline. He had engaged for the flat, which would not be available
for several months, and had happily planned to spend the summer in
Bournemouth while awaiting his new quarters.

It was accordingly with considerable alarm that one summer morning
in Bournemouth he opened *The Times* and found the following notice
among the telegrams from America: "Messrs. James R. Osgood and Co.,
publishers, of Boston, have suspended payment." Osgood's business had
failed, and he had sought the protection of the bankruptcy laws.

Until that moment, James had received no payment for *The Bostonians* or for two collections of short stories that Osgood had published for
him in America. Altogether he was owed about $5,000. This was a year's
wages, and he could not easily afford the loss, just when he had committed himself to a substantially more expensive mode of existence. He
feared that Osgood had already collected payment for the serial installments of *The Bostonians* from *The Century,* money that surely had been
swallowed up in the bankruptcy. Numberless questions abruptly posed
themselves. Could he ask *The Century* to pay him directly for the serialization of *The Bostonians,* on the chance it had not yet paid Osgood?
What about the promised advance on the book edition? He was obliged
by his agreement to deliver the last chapter to Osgood and was not entitled to any payment until then; but surely, if he sent the last copy to Osgood in Boston, he would not be paid, and rights to the book would be
enmeshed in the bankruptcy.

James wrote immediately to Frederick Macmillan, posing all of these
questions and asking his advice, and Macmillan answered the next day,
reassuringly. He advised against sending the last chapter to Osgood; the
money for serial rights was probably lost, but Osgood was in no position
to pay for or to publish the book edition.

> "The Bostonians" being again your property you will have no difficulty
> in getting it published by someone else. We, for instance, should be very
> glad to publish it, paying you whatever royalty you have been in the
> habit of receiving from Osgood.

The next day Macmillan wrote again, having consulted his solicitor;
the matter was not quite so simple as it had seemed to him. James had

agreed to deliver the completed novel before being paid; it might be necessary to make some gesture toward performing his side of the bargain, obliging Osgood to confess failure to perform his. Osgood had acquired the rights to publish *The Bostonians* in Great Britain as well as America, and there would be a good deal of maneuvering yet before the situation was untangled. James was obliged to retain the family lawyer in Boston, Joseph Warner, and telegrams flew. The trustees of Osgood's estate claimed to be willing to perform their side of the bargain, to pay for and publish *The Bostonians*, if James insisted upon that; but James most emphatically did not insist, sensibly preferring to recover the rights to the novel than to become one of Osgood's creditors. Macmillan offered to pay him £500 ($2,500) for rights to the book edition, against a royalty of 15 percent, roughly what Osgood had offered for the book edition alone; but the payments for the American serial rights had been given to and spent by Osgood, and Macmillan could not make up that loss. Eventually, an agreement was negotiated with Osgood's trustees and submitted to James, but there were further complexities: Warner agreed on James's behalf to pay for the typesetting work that had been done on the early chapters of the book, but this was unwise—James thought Macmillan would do a better job of design and declined to approve that purchase—and it was not until August that the distressing negotiations were completed and a new agreement entered into with Macmillan, who would be James's publisher in both Great Britain and America. The payments from *The Century* were lost, as were the promised advances against royalties for his short stories; but Macmillan's £500 were safely deposited in his account; Macmillan would publish the novel in two handsome editions, in three volumes in Great Britain and a one-volume edition in America.

It was not difficult for Macmillan so promptly to offer to publish *The Bostonians*, for the early chapters had been very well received in Great Britain. The notices were flattering, and as Alice wrote cheerfully to Aunt Kate, Lord Derby had congratulated James enthusiastically and the archbishop of Canterbury had invited him (once again) to dine in company as a lion of the season.

Reactions in the United States were not so warm as in Great Britain, however, and a flurry of controversy added to the confusions and anxiety of that summer. By a piece of exceptionally bad luck, James's opening chapters were running beside the closing chapters of William Dean Howells's masterpiece, *The Rise of Silas Lapham*. Howells's novel was also set in Boston. It was a realistic portrait of that new social type, the wealthy merchant, intruding clumsily upon the semifeudal certainties of Beacon

Hill. The story was simple and engaging, the portraits clear and persuasive; there was nothing to disturb or displease in it, yet it was something quite new—a portrait of an ordinary, somewhat vulgar family, unremarkable in themselves but moved by great historical forces.

The contrast to James's satire of Boston life could not have been sharper. James's leisurely opening chapters were uneventful, and the editor of *The Century*, R. W. Gilder, wrote complaining of the leisurely pace of the narrative:

> Leaving aside any question of literary merit, I am afraid Mr. Howells has beaten you in the matter of readers. The movement of "The Bostonians" is so slow that people seem to be dropping off from it. To me it is extremely enjoyable, but I can see reasons for impatience on the part of your readers.

The slow start of the novel created another sort of problem: it began with a procession of minor characters, some of whom resembled well-known figures, and it appeared to be a satire on Boston personalities. Instead of an account of the changed position of women in a democracy and the fundamental alteration of the nation's character that this portended, the tale seemed to be an unkind satire of Bostonian liberalism. This was causing a stir in the United States; newspapers pointed out that some of the unflattering portraits of Bostonians were drawn from life and gleefully exaggerated the private complaints.

James complimented Howells on his novel but complained sadly about the newspaper outcry over his own: "I am sickened by the idiotic, impudent outcry against my tale . . . attacked on the grounds of 'personality' and 'invasion of privacy'!"

A character who appeared early in the tale, "Miss Birdseye," was said to be a portrait of Elizabeth Peabody, a veteran leader of reform movements, then just eighty-one years old and still vigorously active. The fictional Miss Birdseye did not greatly resemble her; but Miss Peabody was an elderly female Abolitionist, the last survivor of the great generation, whose image was in every mind's eye, and such a character as "Miss Birdseye" could not fail to suggest her. James compounded the trouble by bedecking his fictional Miss Birdseye with Elizabeth Peabody's eyeglasses famously askew, and the damage was done. Brother William wrote from Cambridge reporting the gossip, calling it a "bad business," and hinting that Miss Peabody was deeply offended.

More serious for his book was James's slighting portrayal of feminists.

In James's tale, the women's movement was represented by Olive Chancellor, a neurotically dutiful and unhappy young woman, who appeared in the early chapters as a spinster inclined toward other women, one whose smile "was like moonlight on a prison wall."

The fictional Olive Chancellor and her beautiful young ward, Verena Tarrant, were made to live together in Annie Fields's famous and very recognizable house on Charles Street, and readers were bound to think that some reference was being made to Fields and her young partner, Sarah Orne Jewett. It was the suggestion of lesbianism that stirred furious complaints. The Boston *Evening Traveler* reported that the first installments of the novel appeared

> amid such a tumult of indignation, remonstrance, disgust and exasperation as, perhaps, never before disturbed the serene atmosphere of this city. . . . Its localities were pointed out even to the exact number and ownership of the Charles Street house where Mr. James located his heroine . . . Miss Olive Chancellor, a wealthy young woman [and] "a signal old maid."

The staid Springfield *Republican* complained that "The novelist has taken great liberties with Boston people and . . . [has] helped himself to the house of a well-known literary couple." There was great indignation over the title of the book itself, which was taken to be a sly reference to the "Boston marriages" supposed to be common among women of the city. James's disclaimers availed little and, as his portrayal of the movement for political rights for women was condescending at best, did little to mollify his readers. By portraying leaders of the women's movement as ineffectual and frivolous spinsters, moved by their anger toward men, he offended many of the educated women who were his principal audience.

The later installments of the tale were better in every respect. They were far more lively than the first, the action picked up, and the characterizations deepened. Miss Birdseye was put to rest with honor; Olive Chancellor emerged as a tragic heroine; Basil Ransome became James's most successful portrayal of a man's heterosexual passion and the rivalry for Verena Tarrant correspondingly compelling. In the end it was perhaps the best novel James had yet written, as he then thought it; but as social commentary it was a failure, and American sales of the book edition were disappointing. Although Macmillan had saved him from financial disaster, James was in danger of losing his audience.

. . .

Late in the summer of 1895 he made his first visit to the village of Broadway, a hundred miles northwest of London. It lay among fields; its single
street wound gently away into the green Cotswold Hills. Stone cottages,
grayish brown with lichen and half covered in ivy under steeply pitched,
thatched, and mossy roofs, lined the street. A bachelor friend, the American writer Laurence Hutton, had happened upon the place one recent
summer, and now a half-dozen artists and writers, mutual friends, had
adopted it as a summer resort. James went down that summer to join
them. They were a circle of bachelors, for the most part American and
British writers and illustrators for the monthly magazines: Alfred Parsons,
Edwin Abbey, George Boughton, and Charles Reinhart. That summer for
the first time they were joined by John Singer Sargent, who had come
over to paint in the English countryside. Broadway would be his port of
entry into English life.

The village inn was the Lygon Arms, a former manor house that for
centuries had been an inn. The vanished Lygon family's coat of arms
hung on a swinging signboard on the village green. Opposite the inn was
another grand old relic of the Tudor era, Farnham House, rented the summer before by the American painter Frank Millet and his family. Beside
the house, in a walled garden, stood a half-ruined medieval structure,
known locally as "the Abbott's Grange." It was a sort of ecclesiastical
farmhouse of brown stone, picturesque to the last degree. Its modest hall
was lighted by tall windows and made an excellent studio.

James, Abbey, and some of the bachelors stayed at the Lygon Arms,
and others stayed with Millet at Farnham House opposite. The illustrators shared with Millet the studio space in the Abbott's Grange or
sketched Tudor houses and cottage gardens in the village. The Lygon
Arms would be immortalized in Abbey's illustrations, drawn that summer, for *She Stoops to Conquer.* Sargent, adopting the French manner of
painting outdoors, was at work on a huge canvas in Millet's garden, *Car-
nation, Lily, Lily, Rose.*

Alfred Parsons, then forty-five, and Ned Abbey, who was twenty-three,
lived together in London. Parsons was an Englishman who had spent
some years in the United States. Parsons's genius was to capture the spirit
of a place, the particularities of landscape and garden. He was a gardener
and a painter of flower gardens; it was Parsons who would illustrate
James's essays on the Broadway circle and the book into which he would
put them, and who years later would design James's own garden at Lamb

House. Handsome Ned Abbey would serve as the model for Nick Dormer in *The Tragic Muse*.

James felt a kinship with these men that he rarely seemed to find among writers, and he wrote afterward of "the delightful, irresponsible, visual, sensual, pictorial, capricious impressions of a painter in a strange land, the person surely whom at particular moments one would give most to be."

They drew portraits of each other in words and pictures: Sargent drew James full face and then discarded the drawing and drew him in profile. George Boughton had just returned from a sketching expedition in Holland with Ned Abbey, and James wrote a frankly envious and admiring review of the book that they published jointly that summer: "If there be anything happier than the impressions of a painter, it is the impressions of two, and the combination is set forth with uncommon spirit and humor in this frank record of the innocent lust of the eyes."

James, too, worked in the mornings, taking the ruined living quarters of the Abbott's Grange for his own studio. By four, work was abandoned and the young people played tennis or went rowing on the Avon. James usually went for a walk in the late afternoon with one or two of the older men, Parsons or Boughton, or Edmund Gosse, who joined the party late in the summer. On one afternoon, James joined a rowing expedition in a barge down the Avon. Abbey played the banjo while the others sang, and James sat in the bow "like a beneficent deity," Gosse recalled. The painters' models joined them at dinner, and after dinner there were music and dancing in the studio. James joined in a cakewalk, and Sargent began singing his way through *The Ring of the Nibelungen*, recitatives and all. One night there was a birthday celebration, and James wore a garland of flowers. "We all treated him with some involuntary respect," Edmund Gosse wrote years later, "although he asked for none."

At the end of July, Sargent went to Bournemouth to paint a portrait of Stevenson, and James went with him. Alice had not been doing well; the damp climate did not agree with her, and a course of galvanic treatments for her legs, prescribed by a local physician, had been painful and unsuccessful—"nearly fatal," she said. It seemed best to bring Alice back up to London, where James remained with her for a few days. He arranged temporary quarters for her in a cottage in Hampstead, helped her get settled, and, back in his own rooms on Bolton Street, sifted through his own accumulated mail.

The letters and telegrams that awaited him carried more bad news. William's Alice and their third son, the baby Herman, had fallen ill with whooping cough; and while Alice had slowly recovered, Herman had not. The baby's cough had deepened into pneumonia, and after weeks of high fever and convulsions, the poor child had died. William's characteristic letter was waiting on James's little table:

> He was a broad generous patient little nature; and as I now look back it seems to me as if I had hardly known him or seen him at all—I left him so to his mother, thinking he would *keep*. We buried him three or four hours ago under the little pine tree at the corner of the ancestral lot, with a space between him and father's side, and our little family circle now seems remarkably contracted and bare.

Henry responded immediately, with a long letter:

> You have my full sympathy, & above all Alice has it—in the loss of a little tender innocent clinging belonging like that. Poor little mortal, with his small toddling promenade here below, one wonders whence he came & whither he is gone.

When Katherine Loring had returned from Switzerland and James to London, she and Alice spent the late summer and fall together in the little cottage at the top of Hampstead Heath. Alice would remember the cottage fondly: four small rooms downstairs and servants' rooms above, into which she and Katherine squeezed their household. Katherine purchased a bath chair and walked beside Alice while an attendant pushed her about on the heath in the benevolent afternoons.

As winter came on, James found for Alice and Katherine a flat in Bolton Row (now Curzon Street) at the head of his own Bolton Street, on the edge of Mayfair. The little detached house had light and air and was more convenient in winter than rural Hampstead, but was still so close that James could conveniently call twice a day. He found a new nurse-companion, a Mrs. Ward, to stay with Alice in the winter. Mrs. Ward was a lady in reduced circumstances, "and consequently cheap," Alice chortled, her health and spirits much improved. A modest circle of female friends called at teatime, although there was no tea, and sat in Alice's overheated rooms to talk.

Under Katherine's care, Alice's health continued to improve through the winter, and she confessed that she had begun to like London very much, in the way that Henry did: "I adore the darkness & the roar of the city," she wrote to Aunt Kate. Her sleep was no longer disturbed, and depression had given way to elevated moods. She was not going to return to America and wrote to William and his Alice to use her household furnishings, which were in storage, as their own. She and Katherine began to think of moving in the summer to Leamington, a fashionable watering place not far from London, thought to be beneficial for gout sufferers, where rents were cheaper. Fanny Kemble's daughter Frances Leigh would help them get settled there. Alice's landlady remarked that she no longer seemed an invalid; "You seem very comfortable, you are always 'appy within yourself, Miss."

Alice's friendship with Katherine was a blessing to Henry as well: it relieved both his worry and his responsibility. Once they were settled in Leamington for the summer, he fled from London and all social engagements and took lodgings in Dover for a month, to recover his privacy and to work on his big political novel.

6

THE PRINCESS CASAMASSIMA

In an elevated, joyous mood in the summer sea light, James began to describe the dark underworld of London, or, more precisely, the dim sense of dangers there.

He had decided to write about anarchist terror. The invention of dynamite had unleashed a democracy of violence. A new era of human history was opening, in which the material world would cease to be a barrier, mountains would open paths for railroads, rocky coasts would yield new harbors, and a terrible new freedom would be born. Anyone could purchase a stick of dynamite. Careless of their own lives, assassins were setting off dynamite bombs in public places, destroying monuments, murdering political leaders. These acts of "propaganda by the deed," instantly communicated to a mass audience by telegraph and newspaper, were meant to stir the manhood of the oppressed and to provoke an overreaction by government, further fomenting rebellion. Nationalist movements took up the new tactic, perfected by anarchists. Egyptians and Sudanese challenged British authority, compelling Gladstone reluctantly to send troops to assert British rule. The Irish rebellion turned violent; Lord Frederick Cavendish, home secretary for Ireland, and his chief assistant, Thomas Burke, were murdered in May 1882, in Phoenix Park, Dublin, sending a tremor through London and provoking repressions. Later that year, the first Irish dynamite bombs exploded in London itself, at the Local Government Board and at the offices of *The Times*. Vague threats were made against the queen and the prince of Wales. No one could doubt, *The Times* solemnly pronounced, that there were now men in London who hesitate at nothing . . . men to whom human life and the works of human hands, and the fabric of society itself, are as nothing in comparison with the satisfaction of their own wild demands.

The following year, two of London's new underground railway stations were dynamited. In 1884, the attacks increased in number, with explosions at Victoria Station, Scotland Yard, St. James's Square, Nelson's column, London Bridge, the House of Commons, and the Tower of London. The attackers were said to be Irish "moonlighters," but the press connected these various nationalist and anarchist movements into a single threat, imagining a vast conspiracy, centrally directed.

"The country is gloomy, anxious, and London reflects its gloom," James wrote to a friend in Boston, "Westminster Hall and the Tower were half blown up two days ago."

The popular image of a vast, international terrorist organization was carefully nurtured by an exiled Russian, Mikhail Bakunin, and his young ally Sergei Gennadiyevich Nechayev, who eagerly proclaimed themselves its leaders and who published an infamous catechism for revolutionaries:

The revolutionary despises and hates present-day social morality in all its forms . . . he regards everything as moral which helps the triumph of the revolution. . . . All soft and enervating feelings of friendship, relationship, love, gratitude, even honor, must be stifled in him by a cold passion for the revolutionary cause. . . . Day and night he must have one thought, one aim—merciless destruction.

Czar Alexander II was murdered by a self-proclaimed anarchist, a young man who carried a dynamite bomb, having made of himself a weapon.

The assassination of the czar was deeply shocking to the English, for Alexander had just been in London on a state visit to celebrate the wedding of his daughter to Queen Victoria's son. London newspapers claimed that the international conspiracy threatened all monarchs, including Victoria herself. The conspiracy supposedly reached its tentacles into every capital. Governments in Germany, Italy, Switzerland, and Denmark were said by the newspapers to have uncovered anarchist plots aimed at their overthrow.

When a young man named Friedrich Reinsdorf botched an attempt to dynamite a gathering of German royalty, he was arrested and tried, to great publicity. The London *Times* carried daily reports of the trial, in which this pathetic person, betrayed by his confederates, was described as a master criminal: "Tall, thin, and haggard, with keen and deep-set eyes," *The Times* described him, imagining him to be the leader of a movement. In James's novel, the master anarchist pulling the strings of his web of terror would be a German anarchist.

The evil conditions of the working class in London, and the corrupt state of the Ten Thousand, gave force to the vague fears of revolution. There was an army of unemployed men who had fled the countryside for hopes of work in London, and various figures were offering themselves as leaders. One H. M. Hyndman had just published a pamphlet, *England for All*, making the case for a socialist revolution, and was seeking to organize workers into a socialist association, and while there was no connection at all between trade-union socialism and the nationalist movements abroad, his efforts contributed to the general unease.

Tens of thousands of women and boys without other work were prostitutes in London; James had encountered them every evening in Piccadilly, many of them terribly young. Prostitution had been tolerated in more peaceful and prosperous times and as a practical matter had been licensed under the Contagious Diseases Act. The laissez-faire view had been that people ought to be allowed to follow any trade that they chose, and the age of consent was only thirteen. New organizations of women, however, led by the firebrand Josephine Butler, now joined the debate and argued that prostitution was hardly voluntary, that it was a form of slavery, another sign of the disorder of the time.

The case against prostitution was strongly made in a series of articles in *The Pall Mall Gazette* in the summer of 1885, by W. T. Stead, who attacked the "white slave trade." These efforts led to adoption of the Criminal Law Amendment Act of 1885, which raised the age of consent to fifteen and forbade brothels and procuring. The bill as first proposed would have protected only women and girls, but a radical MP, Henry Labouchère, introduced an amendment that extended the reach of the bill to male prostitutes and raised the age of consent for boys as well as girls. This provision was carelessly drafted. Intended to protect boys from assault, abuse, and from the evils of prostitution (and also perhaps partly to embarrass the hypocrisy of Liberal crusaders against female prostitution), the Labouchère Amendment applied by its terms to all sexual contacts between men, even in private, and so for the first time made homosexual conduct (short of the common-law offense of buggery) a crime in Britain. Although the amendment provoked little discussion in Parliament, it caused a good deal of anger and anxiety among James's friends. Edmund Gosse and J. A. Symonds exchanged letters filled with angry denunciations of Butler, Labouchère, Stead, and *The Pall Mall Gazette*.

To James these were all symptoms of a general malaise. The empire was under pressure: the Irish were in rebellion; a conflict with Russia in Afghanistan threatened an outbreak of war on the threshold of India; renewed rebellions in Egypt and Sudan seemed to threaten the Suez Canal; and there was growing resentment at home over the taxes needed to maintain control over the vast empire. The governing class seemed mired in corruption, unable to deal with the linked problems of poverty and prostitution. Economic depression was spreading from the countryside to the cities; an industrial depression was deepening, with a great exacerbation of unemployment. There were no reliable employment statistics, and the government denied the reports of decline. Yet the unemployed gathered in the slums. James, in a letter to America, remarked:

> I can imagine no spectacle more touching, more thrilling & even dramatic, than to see this great, precarious, artificial empire . . . struggling with forces which perhaps, in the long run, will prove too many for it.

In these circumstances one could easily imagine vast conspiracies gathering in the darkness. Most figures of importance in James's world of letters were addressing the questions of injustice and violent rebellion. Robert Louis Stevenson was writing of dynamiters and revolutionists; Turgenev's last work, *Virgin Soil*, was a bleak portrayal of the Russian aristocracy, on the one hand, and "nihilist" violence, on the other. Émile Zola's bestselling novel *L'Assommoir* painted the oppression of working people in Paris; he was at work on *Germinal*, a story of socialist revolt in the coalfields. Victorien Sardou's new hit play, *Fedora*, which James had seen in Paris, revolved around supposed nihilist assassins in Russia. In the United States, William Dean Howells was turning to socialist themes; John Hay, James's friend and mentor, published *The Bread-Winners*, a bestselling novel in which he held up to scorn the revolutionary violence of the labor movement. In England, Anthony Trollope, in the last year of his life, had written *The Landleaguers*, about the unrest in Ireland, and this novel had just been published posthumously. The novelists George Gissing and Walter Besant were having considerable success with sentimental novels centered on aristocratic ladies doing charitable work in the crowded slums. Oscar Wilde's *Vera*, which James had likely seen at its premiere in New York, told the story of a Russian nihilist plot to assassinate a czar; alarm over the actual assassination had led the lord chamberlain to bar any production in London. Mary Ward was at work on a new novel, *Robert Elsmere*, describing the conditions of the poor and the movement for reform.

After Turgenev's death, James reread *Virgin Soil*, and it evidently gave him ideas for a central character and some of the settings of the story on which he was at work. As in Turgenev's novel, the protagonist of *The Princess Casamassima* was the illegitimate son of an English aristocrat and a French prostitute. In James's hands, the protagonist became "Hyacinth" and began to resemble the Anglo-French, hyacinthine Hamilton Aïdé.

Hyacinth is recruited for a terrorist mission by his radical friends. For portraits of the anarchist characters, James drew on his own past acquaintance: curious to say, he had known a number of revolutionists. His father had been a socialist, a follower of Charles Fourier, and during one of the family's sojourns in Paris, James had attended a Fourierist school and had met veterans of the socialist revolution of 1848. Through Turgenev, James had met a number of exiled Russian revolutionists, the "Decembrists" who had attempted the overthrow of the monarchy. James's intimate friend Paul Zhukowsky had introduced James to Russian anarchist friends of their own generation, including an exiled Russian aristocrat traveling under the nom de guerre "Onégin," who had been the model for the "nihilist" in *Virgin Soil*.

With these sources and memories in mind, secluded at Dover, James pursued his most ambitious novel. It slowly took shape. The central situation, the donnée, was simple and clear: a triangle. The beautiful princess (a character carried forward from an early novel, *Roderick Hudson*) and a male revolutionary—Paul Muniment, the working-class leader of a nascent labor party and a future prime minister—were rivals for the loyalty and affection of the sweet protagonist, Hyacinth Robinson.

Young Hyacinth is vividly drawn; one believes that both men and women should be fond of him. He is gentle and uncertain, poised between worlds, he has no definite nationality; even his gender is vague. He is raised in working-class surroundings, recruited into the vast terrorist conspiracy, and assigned a task by his invisible masters. On a given signal, he is to murder an aristocrat. (James's terrorist conspiracy is wholly fanciful; it lacks even the quasi-military organization into "cells" that Turgenev carefully describes; it is merely a vague presence that reaches out a hand of violence.)

But the princess takes up Hyacinth, educates him, introduces him to civilization. She attempts to rescue him from his suicidal mission. The young man must choose between the princess and the labor leader, to whom he is merely cannon fodder, choose between civilization and barbarism. He makes the manly choice and chooses civilization, but, knowing that he is doomed by his confederates if he fails in his mission, he kills himself rather than commit the murder to which he has been assigned.

James worked slowly and carefully to flesh out the skeleton of his plot, and, notwithstanding the pressures of time, money, and recurrent illness, he was happy, even exalted.

He did field research. Margate, up the coast from Dover, he was told, was the resort of London "cads," and he came back from a visit there with widened eyes, as he told Louisa Wolseley. In Margate, he found the model for the shabby-genteel Captain Sholto, the princess's factotum, who went where she could not go herself and who brought back for her interesting young men like Hyacinth. Captain Sholto was an aesthete, with suggestions of sexual licentiousness, and was given Oscar Wilde's distinctive manner of wearing his hair. In the shops and pubs of Dover, James collected fragments of conversation, bits of colloquialism: "That takes the gilt off, you know"; "He cuts it very fine"; " 'Ere today, somewhere else tomorrow: that's 'is motto." Before leaving London he had arranged to tour the hideous, fever-riddled Millbank Prison on the insalubrious bank of the Thames, visiting the stone cells and the infirmary in which he would place Hyacinth's doomed mother. James was a naturalist, botanizing, as it were; the names of his characters evoked their genus and species, and their natural setting: Bowerbank, Vetch, Rosy, Amanda Pynsent, Lady Aurora.

He places them in the dark streets of Soho, crowded with vendors' stalls and street fairs, illumined by flares at night. Hyacinth's delicate features and slender hands bespeak his noble paternity; his childhood friend Millicent Henning is a robust and handsome English girl, but her large feet and thick fingers, her lack of moral sensitivity, mark her common origin. "Eustace Poupin" is the very type of Frenchman, lost in theories of socialist utopia; "Schinkel" could not be more typically German; "Vetch" is a garden-variety English radical. James puts them in their places and arranges for them to meet and to revolve about one another, while slowly, Hyacinth's dilemma emerges.

The poverty James describes is not the desperate privation of the unemployed immigrant but the common poverty of the working class: narrow circumstances, a cage of ceaseless labor from which it was difficult to escape. James did not describe and only alluded to the crowding and desperation of the slums, the prostitution, incest, and child abuse that enlivened highly colored reports in the newspapers and that he knew only by report. The master anarchist Hoffendahl was described only at second hand, and the vast invisible conspiracy of "nihilists" supposed to be planning the destruction of European aristocracy remained submerged and out of sight; the reader was to see only the hand it reached up to seize Hyacinth.

He sent the first chapters off as they were written, and the serial began appearing in September 1885, in *The Atlantic*, while *The Bostonians* was still running in *The Century*. He had been preparing his big political novel for the past two years, and although the chapters were printed as quickly as they were written, the story moved forward steadily and consistently, unmarred by changes of tone and pace. The characters deepened and developed; Hyacinth Robinson became the little hero of the tale; gradually the princess and her rival for Hyacinth's loyalty, Paul Muniment, moved to the background. James was very fond of the delicate Hyacinth, trapped in poverty, burdened by helpless love of the beautiful. As James worked, he endowed the frail Hyacinth with some of his own memories, and this French-English youth, so unlike James in other ways, recalled to him his own early years, early experiences.

He ran up to London for a day in August, for one of the few occasions that would take him from his work: an opportunity to help cement the American and British alliance. Ulysses S. Grant, the leader of Union forces in the Civil War and twice president of the United States, had died on July 23, and there was to be a memorial service in Westminster Abbey. James was invited to join those representing his country, and he was happy to attend. The service was a fine one, despite a somewhat vulgar and political sermon. The number of the British "illustrious" was creditable and included the eighty-five-year-old Lord Houghton, Fanny Kemble's friend and contemporary, who had been so kind to James on his first arrival in London and who, like Kemble, had given James a window on a vanished age. A few days after the service, on August 11, the old man died. James recalled:

I gave poor old Lord Houghton my arm to come out, & that was the last I saw of him. I liked him (in spite of some of his little objectionableness), & he was always only kind to me. A great deal of the past disappears with him.

After a month in Dover, he crossed the channel and went to Paris, where two old friends were dying. William H. Huntington, the *New York Tribune*'s political correspondent, had helped him find his way in the city and showed him some of its less conventional facets. Huntington was a bachelor, now gravely ill and alone. He had been in pain for some time, and James hoped for his sake that a release was near. Ill and dying also was Blanche de Triqueti, a distinguished and graceful Frenchwoman who had married a New Englander, Lee Childe. It was Madame Childe who had given James his glimpses of royalist, Old World aristocracy during his first sojourn in Paris. He had admired her as, elegant in black velvet, she had received guests in her Parisian salon and at the Château de Varennes, the Triqueti family estate. James dutifully returned to Paris and took his old third-floor apartment on rue Cambon for a month, to sit at the bedsides of his friends.

He followed his familiar Parisian routine: coffee and brioche on rising in the chilly flat, heated only by the feeble wood fire that Paris provided; followed by a walk, perhaps a visit to a bathing establishment in the Seine, then to work at his writing desk. He kept at work through his noon meal and on alternate afternoons went to sit by Huntington's or Madame Childe's bedside. The discipline was difficult, but there was no choice: as he wrote to Fanny Stevenson, in the Franglais diction that descended on him when he was for the most part speaking French,

Ah, to whom do you say it—that the devil of the serial at one's back mortifies the man & murders the artist?—If some one would make me *des rentes* [an income] I would write [only] 20 lines a day.

His visit drew toward its sad and inevitable conclusion, with the death of both his friends. But the interesting and sympathetic Paul Bourget was expected to return to Paris from the country in October, and James decided to extend his visit to await his arrival.

On the first of November, he was back in his flat at 3 Bolton Street. In contrast with Paris, the winter darkness, foul fogs, and bad food depressed him. To cheer himself he made a note of London's bright points: coal fires, fresh butter and eggs. He made a quick trip to Bournemouth to visit the Stevensons and was distressed to find Louis even thinner and more fragile than on their last meeting: "He was bright and charming," James reported to their mutual friend Sidney Colvin, "but struck me as of a humbler vitality then when I saw him last—a very frail and delicate thread of strength."

There was sad news from America; his friend Clover Adams, too, was dead, a suicide. Henry Adams was distraught.

Now that James was in London again, Katherine Loring went off to visit her sister in the more salubrious climate of the south of France, leaving Alice in his care for the winter. James visited Alice daily and attended to her needs. He brought people to see her, and when Alice complained of drafts, he bought a screen to keep them off.

Elizabeth Boott had decided at last to marry her old friend and teacher Frank Duveneck, from whom she had separated years before. After a brief wedding journey, they planned to settle in Florence, where Duveneck had established his studio. James wrote congratulating her "with all the warmth & confidence of old friendship." Elizabeth's father, Francis, had made the match possible by supporting Duveneck's studio, allowing him to support a wife. She in turn insisted that her father live with them when they were married. The widower and his forty-year-old daughter were determined to preserve their relationship, into which Duveneck had intruded. When in time Lizzie bore a child, a little boy, father and daughter drew even closer; almost twenty years later James would record the happiness of their moment in *The Golden Bowl*.

The winter was bitterly cold, the worst in memory, and snow was heaped in great frozen mounds in the streets. The sufferings of the new immigrants from the countryside were exacerbated, and on Monday, February 8, 1886, while James was still in Bournemouth, a mass demonstration against unemployment was held in Trafalgar Square. The large crowd spilled out of the square along Pall Mall toward Hyde Park, and then rioting began. What was now a mob began to spread, some of the rioters streaming across Green Park and into Piccadilly, where they halted carriages and overturned them, robbed their occupants, smashed windows, and pillaged shops.

James, having narrowly missed the excitement, was leaving Piccadilly entirely. His flat was ready for him in a new brown-and-yellow-brick building on a short, broad street, De Vere Gardens, that ran south from Kensington Gardens. The flat was at the south end of the block and on the top floor, which meant that it had ample light and a view across rooftops. James now had a dining room, a guest room, and two parlors, large and small, one of which he thought might be fitted out as a library and the other as a workroom. There were big, modern bow windows with expanses of glass, and the flat was "flooded with light like a photographer's studio."

Snow went on falling well into March, and when spring should have been well advanced there were still skaters on the frozen ponds in Kensington Gardens. In the new flat the small parlor was a sunny blue and yellow, however, and James installed his writing desk there; he jocularly called it his "boudoir." On March 6, he moved his household westward up the great artery of Piccadilly and Kensington Road.

When the weather permitted, James would walk beside the stream of traffic to the Reform Club on Pall Mall or to shops in Piccadilly or the Strand. He needed furniture, dishes, silverware, and all the apparatus of a household. Alice arranged to have sent to him from America the two-hundred-year-old, blue-on-white Robertson china and Grandmother Walsh's portrait from the Washington Square house that had come to Alice on their mother's death and had been in storage. Louisa Wolseley entered with enthusiasm into his furnishing and decorating and offered to help him to find a manservant from among retired noncommissioned officers. After some reflection, however, he kept to his old idea of hiring a man and wife and found through an agency a childless couple, the Smiths: she to cook and clean, he to serve as butler and valet.

In the afternoons, after work, he shopped for furniture in company with Lady Wolseley. They found an antique French writing desk that he wanted and that somehow evoked for him images of marital dramas, money problems, divorce court. He came upon a bookcase that he liked in Pratt's, an antique shop, and after some delay for reflection asked Louisa to see if it was still unsold and to inquire the true ultimate price. Together they looked at a mirror that he liked and bought.

As he wrote happily to William on his new notepaper:

The place is excellent in every respect, improves on acquaintance every hour. . . . I commune with the unobstructed sky & have an immense birdseye view of housetops & streets. . . . I shall do far better work here than I have ever done before.

He was a householder with servants dependent upon him now. More than ever, he needed to produce. To ensure his ability to work despite the shifting limitations imposed by his bad back, James equipped his study with an upright desk at which he could write standing, a daybed with a swivel desk, so that he could write reclining, and a kneehole desk at the window, where he could sit.

One of the great virtues as well as burdens of the new flat, with its servant quarters and cooking facilities, was that it allowed him to entertain overnight visitors easily and in privacy. He could also return luncheon and dinner invitations from ladies, who could not be invited to his club. Louisa Wolseley, and Mrs. Benson with her son Arthur, were among his first luncheon visitors; Arthur would later be among the overnight guests and a recipient of James's erotically charged love letters. James, somewhat flurried, as Benson later recalled, saw them down to the street door, absentmindedly, in his smoking jacket and then, realizing his state of undress, retreated "to the shelter of the porch, where he stood, waving mute and intricate benedictions."

James Russell Lowell was in town, on his first visit since the end of his posting as ambassador; James had him to lunch and invited to meet him, among other guests, the young writer Violet Paget, who published under the pen name Vernon Lee.

The Season descended upon him with its obligations and distractions, multiplied by his new duty to entertain as well as be entertained, but he kept to his desk in the mornings and avoided visits to country houses entirely or made day trips rather than weekends.

Invitations and correspondence multiplied even beyond what was customary, however. A prominent American, Dr. Oliver Wendell Holmes, father of his intimate friend Wendell, was visiting England. The seventy-six-year-old Dr. Holmes arrived in London on May 12, accompanied by his plain, middle-aged daughter, Amelia, and was immediately the lion of the Season. James received a steady series of invitations to greet Dr. Holmes. Lowell played host to a quiet, welcoming dinner; Lord Rosebery had a dinner, followed by a reception that was mobbed by two thousand, and Gosse gave a dinner to introduce Dr. Holmes to Robert Browning. So celebrated was the Autocrat of the Breakfast Table that James found himself answering requests to intercede for autographs. "Dear Miss Townley," he wrote dutifully, "I have none in my possession of Dr. Holmes's, but can easily obtain one & will do so within a few days."

Despite his need to keep ahead of the monthly publication schedule of *The Princess Casamassima*, James attended these dinners and receptions and answered these requests, treating them as a duty, one owed both to an old friend and to the great project of cementing ties between his two nations, of which the Grant memorial service, the introductions he made for visiting Americans, the letters of introduction he provided for departing Londoners, the little dinners of six were all part.

The pressure of duty eased somewhat when Katherine Loring returned from her winter visit to the Continent and relieved James of his duties to Alice. The two women gave up their winter lodgings in London and removed themselves to the air and waters of Leamington, where James called upon them at longer intervals.

Freed from daily attendance on his sister, for several days in July he visited the bachelor illustrators at Broadway, staying with Ned Abbey and Frank Millet. There he was able to work in the mornings, undisturbed by the distractions of the Season, while the painters went off sketching. In the afternoons he often went for drives in an open carriage with Ned. "We drove about seventy miles altogether," Abbey recalled, "and went through the most primitive part of England I ever saw. We only saw a railway once in all this distance."

In August, back in London just as the Season was dissipating, two new visitors arrived. Guy de Maupassant came from Paris with a note from Paul Bourget asking James to show him around, and de Maupassant— who spoke no English and was not enjoying himself—introduced James to a friend who was also in England at the time, Count Joseph Primoli.

Primoli was a man who interested James greatly. Maupassant introduced him as "a Bonaparte," and the count somewhat resembled the illustrious Napoleon. He was an amiable man, eight years younger than James, and despite his youth gave James a window on an old regime and a slowly vanishing world. He was stout, a little below average height, bearded, and balding. He had the aquiline Bonaparte profile, the eagle's beak, in somewhat softened form. A contemporary described him thus:

Compte Joseph Primoli . . . had numerous friends in every world and every milieu, and the diminutive *Gégé*, by which people readily referred to him, showed that he lent himself with a good grace to the most diverse familiarities. In fact, this Napoleonide, the son of a Roman patrician and a Bonaparte princess, was devoid of all arrogance and free of many prejudices, but his smiling condescension and gracious affability were none the less evident to anyone who failed to take account of the imperceptible distance that he expected people to keep from him.

Primoli at thirty-five was still a bachelor. He and a younger brother were caring for their aged mother in their little Roman palace. He was, like James, a cosmopolite, a Roman in Paris and a Parisian in Rome, as much at home in London as in either. He was an intimate friend of the Empress Eugénie, visited her regularly at Chislehurst in Kent, her home in exile, and made regular annual visits to Paris, where his cousin and intimate friend the Princess Mathilde—the empress's bitter rival—held court. He had a remarkable fund of anecdotes about the Bonapartes and the courtiers of the Second Empire, the great literary figures of the last generation—Renan, Taine, Flaubert, the Goncourts, Dumas fils—and ribald stories about his own generation.

Primoli and James quickly established a cordial relationship; Maupassant invited Primoli to another gathering in London, where he held out as an inducement that they would meet Henry James again there. After these meetings, James invited Maupassant and Primoli to dine at the Prospect of Whitby, an ancient, famously picturesque, somewhat seedy tavern on the riverside in Wapping. He brought George du Maurier and Edmund Gosse with him to meet the visitors, and the dinner was so much a success that both James and Primoli remembered it years afterward.

Primoli carried about him the atmosphere of the Old World, and more than anyone else whom James had known intimately, he bore with him as part of his identity "the doings, the crimes, the follies" of a ruling family. In future years he would be the model for the Roman prince in *The Golden Bowl*.

Despite these adventures, James clove to his writing desk and *The Princess*, gradually ceasing even to make entries in his journal, giving up even tea and petits fours at Louisa Wolseley's house on Hill Street. Summer slipped into fall, darkness and smoke covered London, but James remained at his desk, correcting proofs.

The Bostonians was published in hard covers while *The Princess Casamassima* was still running in monthly installments, and James thought sales were "goodish," although plainly *The Bostonians* would not be the hit for which he had hoped. He sent copies to friends and worked away at the closing chapters of *The Princess*, which ran for fourteen numbers of *The Atlantic Monthly*. Macmillan brought out the book edition of *The Princess* promptly in December 1886, treading on the heels of *The Bostonians*, hurrying the new novel out in time for Christmas sale as soon as the serial was complete. In London, as usual, his novel was published in a handsome three volumes with dark, blue-green cloth covers, priced at one and a half guineas, and in America in a single volume with cardboard covers for $1.75.

The American reviews of *The Princess* were the best that he had yet received. His friends, led by William Dean Howells, called it his best work, his "greatest" novel, "incomparably the greatest novel of the year in our language," a novel without fault. And while other reviewers were less hyperbolic, American newspapers and magazines uniformly praised this portrayal of terror in working-class London.

The English reviewers were more moderate in their assessment. Aside from their customary complaints about James's intellectualism and subtlety, the London papers generally missed the point of the story. Anarchist terror had subsided and had been for the moment forgotten, overshadowed as it had been for the past year or two by the rise of socialist labor unions, the Trafalgar Square riot, the very visible and practical political agitation for Irish home rule. Zola's novel *Germinal*, published while James was at work, an immense success, told a story of socialist-led strikes in coalfields during an economic depression. George Gissing's *Demos* (subtitled *A Story of English Socialism*) had just appeared. The newspapers therefore generally ignored James's effort to portray fears of a shadowy, anarchist underworld; for the most part, they wrote of *The Princess Casamassima* as if it were a study of the labor movement, albeit a peculiar one. *Punch*'s review, for instance, was headed "Socialism in Three Volumes":

> Hyacinth Robinson and Paul Muniment are very far indeed from being average British workmen, and they and their story, it must be feared, would pretty considerably puzzle any handicraft member of the Social Democratic Federation who took up *The Princess Casamassima*.

The Scottish Review went out of its way to praise James for showing "what an utter sham socialism, so called, is." His vast portrait of European society, his scientific comparison of national types, was understood and noted without much interest: "Mr. James's specimens . . . are very select, and, as the Darwinite would say, 'highly specialised.' " *The Times* was bored, as it so often was: "the reader is kept waiting while the characters converse with one another with amused curiosity, as if they were so many psychological specimens."

Despite these irritable complaints, the British reviews were generally favorable, and even the newspaper reviewers who had been at best luke-warm in the past recognized and approved James's ambitious efforts, in *The Bostonians* and *The Princess Casamassima*, to master new, more manly themes: to don, as one American reviewer put it, the toga virilis. James's new effort "was like the resolve of an artist already proficient in *genre* painting to risk his fame in the grand style." In London, *The Saturday Review* (which had disliked *The Portrait of a Lady*) recognized *The Princess* for a study of anarchist terror and announced that

> Mr. Henry James has broken what is for him new ground, and taken a fresh departure. Hitherto he has been the poet of the Fine Shades, the artist in emotions. . . . Surprising as it seems, it is none the less a posi-tive fact that he has made a real story. . . . To say that his achievement is complete would be to say what is not. There is a great amount of su-perfluous analysis, much of the dialog is far too subtle. . . . But, consid-ered as a first attempt, the book is wonderfully good. . . . Mr. James has made an immense advance upon himself, in ambition and material alike.

James's style had shed its awkward mannerisms and the arch, satiric quality of *The Bostonians*. He had written seriously and simply, as if he were writing history rather than fiction.

7

INTERVAL IN ITALY

Florence in December: a cool gray light. The weather is dark and wet, and James is depressed; he wonders whether he has made a mistake—perhaps Italy has lost its charm for him. He lingers in the green-and-gray gardens of the Pitti Palace. The gravel walks have not been swept, the formal shrubbery has not been clipped; the gardens are nearly deserted and have an abandoned air.

James is at rest, the immense work of his two political novels behind him, the relentless pressure of serial publication now in remission. Newspapers and letters confirm that despite some complaints from reviewers he has accomplished his purpose. William has written to apologize for his earlier bad temper about *The Bostonians* and to praise James's new efforts; Stevenson writes with enthusiasm about the closing chapters of *The Princess Casamassima*. The reviews confirm James in his belief that these novels have lifted him into the rank of serious authors.

Alice's health has been steadily improving, and Katherine Loring will be back in London after the first of the year. And so, early in December, James has fled to Florence from the darkness of winter in London.

He has brought with him an inscribed set of *The Bostonians* as a gift for Constance Fenimore Woolson, who was among the expatriates in Florence. She had been glad to rent her furnished apartment in the Villa Brichieri to him for a month; she had taken it on a two-year lease but was not yet ready to move and lingered in Villa Castellani on the village square. When they first met in Florence, almost seven years before, she was a stout, somewhat deaf, forty-year-old spinster on her first journey to Europe, struggling to make herself known and to support herself as a writer. Now she was older and more deaf, so that conversation was becoming difficult, but she was recognized as one of the leading writers of the realist school, and they met on more equal terms, as old friends. Her novel *Anne* had been a popular and critical success, running serially in an American magazine and selling well as a book; she was now financially secure and able to be generous to James; he in turn was able to introduce her to the society of Florence, as he had not done on their earlier meetings.

He wrote to Francis Boott, Lizzie, and Frank Duveneck, who were in Florence, and asked them to call on Miss Woolson, which they did. At James's prompting, Boott befriended Woolson, and James began half-seriously joking about the budding friendship between the widower and the spinster, the inevitability of their marrying.

Woolson had been lonely and was grateful for James's company and his interest. She praised his new novels, and during his stay in Florence she wrote a story of her own, "At the Chateau of Corinne," that was a delicate compliment to him and his much-abused *Bostonians*. In Woolson's story, a strong-minded woman, Katherine Winthrop—her name and character redolent of Boston—falls in love with a domineering man, John Ford, and gives up her independence to him. The brief tale recapitulates James's themes in *The Bostonians*, and, to make the compliment more pointed, Ford is made to resemble James himself: he has dark brown hair, gray eyes, and a full beard; his elegant profile is more revealing of his character than the aspect of his full, round face.

James would quickly return the compliment, in a long review for *Harper's New Monthly* of her work, capped by her new novel, *East Angels*: "Flooded as we have been in these latter days with copious discussion as to the admission of women to various offices," he began,

> it is no longer a question of their admission into the world of literature: they are there in force; they have been admitted, with all the honors, on a perfectly equal footing. In America, at least, one feels tempted to exclaim that they are in themselves the world of literature. . . . The work of Miss Constance Fenimore Woolson is an excellent example.

James reviewed her work, however, not from the perspective of her sex but simply as a contribution to the new realism. Her latest novel, *East Angels*, he says is her best. It tells most successfully her favorite tale, of a person who loves in secret and ministers in silence to those she loves; a story that can exist only in the private realm. Her mastery of character makes her novel a great success, "a picture of the actual, of the characteristic—a study of human types and passions, of the evolution of personal relations."

• • •

The other asset of his leisure was the Paget household in Via Garibaldi, where there was a salon of foreigners from four to seven every afternoon, to which James introduced the Boott-Duvenecks and Miss Woolson, making a little circle of his friends. The great attraction of the Paget household in Florence was Violet Paget, the remarkable young woman who had begun writing at an early age under the name Vernon Lee and had published her first book, *The Adventures of a Coin*, in French at the age of fourteen. Now still only thirty years old, fluent in French, Italian, German, and English, she had several volumes of critical studies and a novel to her credit. She presided over afternoon gatherings, her invalid brother, Eugene, comfortably ensconced on a sofa at her side.

Violet was slight, pale, and lantern-jawed. She wore disfiguring spectacles and cut her blond hair carelessly short. Anatole France described her as she appeared at this time: "pleasant and plain, with short hair and slim, flat figure, almost graceful in her tailor-made coat and skirt of masculine cut."

Paget's first novel, *Miss Brown*, was dedicated to James. He had delayed very long in thanking her for the first copy from the press when it was sent to him. The book was an "interesting failure," he thought; Paget did not have the same talent for fiction that she showed in her historical and critical essays; her novel showed "an awful want of taste & tact."

The difficulty James had with the book was its portrayal of the bachelor character, Walter Hamlin, by whom the eponymous Miss Brown was raised like a hothouse peach. He and his friends were portrayed as aesthetes and brutally satirized. "You are really too savage with your painters & poets & diletanti," James told her. The recognizable portraits of Oscar Wilde, Frederick Leighton, and other well-known painters and poets, some of whom were among James's bachelor friends, were indeed savage. The men were portrayed as profligate and effeminate, posing as homosexual but lacking courage to commit the sins at which they hinted in their poetry. The heroine of the tale was made to resemble Jane Morris, the favorite model of the pre-Raphaelites, and her husband, William Morris, appeared by name. Paget had been their houseguest but seemed to have no intimation of the offense she would give. James chided her, and Paget replied promptly in a friendly letter, agreeing that her caricatures of aesthetes were too harsh but confessing that a certain "rabidness" of opinion was integral to her nature. Over the years, there would be other outbreaks of Paget's "rabidness" of opinion, which would be followed by apologies and renewed expressions of friendship.

Conversation at the Paget salon was light and gossipy. Eugene Lee-Hamilton, Violet's bedridden brother, liked to tell stories from their shared childhood with the Sargents, and he repeated one of Sargent's tales, about a curious ship captain named Silsbee, that James would turn into one of his most celebrated tales, "The Aspern Papers."

James noted the anecdote in his journal, and shortly afterward he turned it into a short story, lightly disguising the characters. He moved the setting from Florence to Venice and turned Captain Silsbee into a villain, an American magazine editor. But Captain Silsbee was still alive and was still the intimate friend of the Pagets. Years later, in a preface for the story, he wrote somewhat defensively that he had not been indiscreet, presumably because the characters and settings were so completely altered as not to be recognizable. But it was *The Bostonians* all over again; the story was patently Silsbee's.

Violet Paget had sinned in this way herself, but she complained that James was a little too observant, a little too much the student of his friends's affairs. She said in private letters that he was cold and disingenuous and exploited his friends' confidences. Paget got her revenge in suitable fashion: in a short story of her own, "Lady Tal," she drew a wickedly satirical portrait of "Jervase Marion," a caricature of James:

> All those years of work, of success, of experience (or was it not rather of study?) of others, bringing with them a certain heaviness, baldness, and scepticism. . . . Jervase Marion knew it all so well, so well.

At its core, "Lady Tal" is a smart, good-natured story about writers who use one another. The story ends well: the eponymous heroine, a writer like Paget, proposes a collaboration with Jervase Marion that may or may not be a marriage. But, there are outbreaks of Paget's rabidness, of malicious humor: Marion is portrayed not merely as reserved but as incapable of feeling; there is some slapstick humor at his expense; he is shown being bullied and embarrassed by his titled lady friends; a tomboy cousin of the heroine calls him "Mary Anne." James never read the story, but when he later heard of its existence, Paget would again apologize, and he would strive once again to ignore her outbreak.

. . .

Toward the end of the year, the bad weather broke and the sun came out. James settled comfortably among the expatriates, in his element; rested and entertained, his spirits improved. On the first of the year, Miss Woolson was obliged to reclaim her apartment in the Villa Brichieri, her lease at the larger and more expensive Villa Castellani having at last run out, and James moved down the hill into Florence, to the Hotel du Sud, on the rocky embankment of the Lung'Arno, where it was cold but where sunlight flooded his rooms in the mornings. He planned to go on to Rome for a brief visit and then to return to London. James felt he should return home soon to be with Alice. And then there was the double expense of maintaining his new flat and his new servants, the Smiths, while he lived in Italy.

But his plans changed abruptly. Paul Bourget wrote to say that he would be in Venice for the spring and invited James to join him there. An exchange of letters and telegrams sufficed to alter James's plans: Alice and Katherine Loring would take his flat, instead of lodgings, for the winter and would bear the expense of maintaining the household. Alice assured him that his presence in London was not required.

While the reviews of *The Princess Casamassima* had been among the best he had received, sales of the book edition were disappointing. Female readers, already disenchanted by *The Bostonians*, evidently did not share male reviewers' enthusiasm for James's new themes of honor and class conflict in *The Princess Casamassima*. To capitalize on his new celebrity, Macmillan began to reissue earlier James novels in cheap editions with colorful jackets, for sale in railroad stations, and these sold reasonably well, broadening the audience for James's work, but did little by way of earning royalties for the author. Unless he went back to his writing desk in earnest, his income would soon decline drastically.

And so, after a long period of concentration on two big novels to the exclusion of nearly all other work, and after only a brief rest in Bellosguardo, James again began at a rapid pace to write stories, articles, and reviews for American and British illustrated magazines, and to plan new novels. His uphill climb had resumed, and he addressed himself to recovering his audience and his income. He returned to older themes, interior settings and personal relations, for which he mined anecdotes told by his friends, and stories in the newspapers, for plots.

On earlier visits to Italy, he had fallen in love with Venice, the thousand-year-old republic, but it was seven years since, as a young man poised at the brink of great popular success, he had taken lodgings on the Riva degli Schiavoni to finish *The Portrait of a Lady*. Then he had wandered deserted footpaths along the canals, rested in the half-deserted, grass-grown squares, each with its church and its fountain, and looked for the fluttering white slips in the windows of houses that advertised rooms for rent. He had imagined himself keeping a pied-à-terre, or rather a "foot in the water," in this magical city of reflections, of mirrors, water, and glass.

Now he was a middle-aged veteran of disappointments and bitterly won successes, a social lion in danger of being submerged by his celebrity. He was afraid that Venice had lost its charm for his familiarized eye; but it had not. There was no longer, perhaps, a distinctly Venetian society; at least he had not yet gained admission to one. The long decline of the republic had emptied the old palaces of their owners; the figures strolling in the *campi* and lingering at the fountains now were tourists, red guidebooks in hand, peering into the dark doorways of little churches. In James's images of this time, Venice is a great country house deserted by its owners; one that provides a setting for a new cast of characters. A Mr. Peabody Russell has purchased two Contarini palaces and proposes to knock them together, into something truly grand; James's old friends Katherine Bronson and the Daniel Curtises have each purchased a palace on the Grand Canal; Robert Browning is shopping for another. Venice seems to absorb the newcomers; the history of the city is embedded in its stones, and the spirit of the place is genially accommodating.

James was a guest in one of the old houses, Casa Alvisi, crowded between great palaces on the bank of the Grand Canal opposite the domed church of Santa Maria della Salute. It was a modest house, recently purchased by Katherine Bronson. Mrs. Bronson had been James's neighbor in Newport when they were both children. Now she was a widow, living in Venice with her daughter, occupying herself by keeping one of the precious salons in which a bachelor or a widow could find congenial company. The generous Mrs. Bronson provided James not only with comfortable lodging but with a gondola and a gondolier and encouraged him to be her guest for the remainder of the winter and spring; but two weeks after his arrival, he fell ill.

The illness began with a severe headache, much to his distress, as he had been free of headaches for some time; then a fever set in, and jaundice. The illness was evidently infectious hepatitis, transmitted by polluted water or food; James's generation called it simply "jaundice." He was bedridden for two weeks, and his Italian gondolier became his able nurse and servant. Suspecting, reasonably, that the source of the illness was the insalubrious environment of the Casa Alvisi, he fled back to Florence, to the airy hilltop of Bellosguardo, where Constance Woolson kindly made a separate apartment for him on the ground floor of the Villa Brichieri. There he gradually recovered.

Bourget arrived in Venice shortly after James departed, expecting to find him there, and lingered, waiting to learn what had become of him. They corresponded, and at last in May with his health restored, James returned to Venice to join him.

Prudently, he did not return to Mrs. Bronson's apartment in Venice but accepted another invitation, from Ariana and Daniel Curtis, who offered him an apartment in their newly acquired Palazzo Barbaro, a little farther up the Grand Canal from Casa Alvisi and just short of the Accademia Bridge. They owned the upper and more desirable stories of a fifteenth-century Gothic palace, with entrances from land and water, to which an addition amounting to a second palace had been joined at the end of the seventeenth century. One mounted worn stone steps in an inner courtyard framed by the two conjoined palaces to the Curtis apartments and its great *piano nobile* overlooking the canal and the Salute Church opposite. Tall windows opened from the Curtises' formal parlor—a sumptuous, stuccoed and frescoed former ballroom—onto little cushioned balconies, just large enough for two, where one could linger and watch the endless variety of traffic on the canal. Within, rugs were scattered on the marble floor; the plaster reliefs and medallions and the painted ceiling of the grand salon were stained with tobacco smoke. James was given a bed on the top floor, in a back room known as the "green room" for the faded, tattered pale green damask wall coverings. It was an old family dining room, with a Tiepolo ceiling, whose windows looked into the courtyard.

He worked in the mornings at a glass-fronted writing desk in the library at the front of the house. This was a long room of lacquered glass-fronted bookcases, built onto the roof of the palace in the eighteenth century; it was filled with sunlight and looked out over the Grand Canal to the south and over the red tile roofs and gardens of Venice to the north. Pigeons nested in the high window embrasures. James recalled long afterward the pleasures of that visit:

> As you live in it day after day its beauty and its interest sink more deeply into your spirit; it has its moods and its hours and its mystic voices and its shifting expressions. If in the absence of its masters you have happened to have it to yourself for twenty-four hours you will never forget the charm of its haunted stillness, late in the summer afternoon for instance, when the call of playing children comes in behind from the campo, nor the way the old ghosts seem to pass on tip-toe on the marble floors.

Daniel and Ariana Curtis were good hosts and left James alone to work in the mornings in the library. He joined them on afternoon outings to the Lido, or to the garden that Ariana kept on the island of Torcello. He had the use of a gondola again and enjoyed as always the strange sensation of being carried over the water, of entering the dimly lit water gate of a palace with a sense of mystery even when only going to tea. But James spent most of his evenings with the young, the handsome, the "sympathetic Bourget."

James filled his notebook with raw material: gossip picked up in conversation or related to him in letters. Bourget gave him an anecdote that he turned into "A London Life." A letter from Fanny Kemble provided the germ of "Georgina's Reasons." His sister, Alice, wrote to him with an anecdote about their cousin-in-law, Sir John Rose, a widower who planned to marry again, over his daughter's objections: "it is simply forty years of her mother's life wiped out." This would become a story, "The Marriages."

Plot followed plot: "The idea of a worldly mother & a worldly daughter . . . [who] excels and surpasses her, & the mother, who has some principle of goodness left in her composition, is appalled at her own work." This would become the story "Louisa Pallant." An incident struck him: an American woman, Marcy McClellan (the daughter of General George B. McClellan), had written a letter to *The New York World*, a tabloid, describing in intimate detail the Venetian society whose hospitality she had been enjoying, and causing something of a scandal in Venice. Miss McClellan's gaffe seemed to him characteristic of the age:

One sketches one's age but imperfectly if one doesn't touch on that particular matter: the invasion, the impudence & shamelessness, of the newspaper & the interviewer, the devouring *publicity* of life, the extinction of all sense between public & private . . . the sinking of *manners*, in so many ways, which the democratization of the world brings with it.

This would become a short novel, *The Reverberator*, with the setting moved to Paris to conceal its origin. It would take some time to elaborate these nuggets of plot into full-blown stories; but he had no major work in progress and so gave his full attention to each tale as it came to hand. Howells had advised him that American magazines would buy an almost unlimited quantity of his "international" tales.

"Never say you know the last word about any human heart!" So memorably begins "Louisa Pallant," the first of the stories that James fashioned from these improbable materials, scraps of gossip, in that pleasant winter and spring in Italy. The story was written simply, in the first person, by an unreliable observer—the clueless male American who had been a stock character since James's earliest tales. The device was admirably chosen to draw the reader into his puzzled speculation about the worldly mother and daughter. His eye is that of the detached bachelor; the women are once again described scientifically; we see no soft bosoms or bare, seductive shoulders; indeed, if any of James's female characters have breasts they are never mentioned. The young Miss Pallant's cultivated charm is acutely observed and indelibly rendered, as if seen by a older woman's eye:

> More than any girl I ever saw she was the result of a process of calculation; a process patiently educative . . . her music, her singing, her German, her French, her English, her step, her tone, her glance, her manner, and everything in her person and movement, from the shade and twist of her hair to the way you saw her finger-nails were pink when she raised her hand.

The setting of the story at a European watering place and the opening scenes deliberately evoke James's early success, "Daisy Miller." The story is a little mystery that the reader is invited to unravel; the Pallant women have a secret, and as in "Daisy Miller," at the end an exasperated woman must explain the situation in so many words to the clueless male.

The whole little story is a performance by the author, who speaks easily in the voice of each character. His next tale, "The Aspern Papers," the curious anecdote concerning Captain Silsbee, might have been written by another man entirely. Silsbee had sought to acquire the poet Percy Bysshe Shelley's papers from a female friend. In James's tale, the dead poet is renamed "Aspern" and the story is told by a worldly American, who takes advantage of comparatively innocent women who have the papers in their keeping. He speaks simply and in James's own voice, although he is a villain. The bachelor American befriends the custodian of the papers, but when she makes marriage the price he turns away from her in distaste.

The story was a cruel joke, and it concerned people who were still living; but the story was a great success. The atmosphere of Venice is beautifully evoked, much of the action occurs in an improbable garden, and the narrator's evil deception is at home in the atmosphere of mingled innocence and corruption. Of the tales written in this sunny moment, in Italy, with Bourget—and it partakes somewhat of Bourget's wicked air—it was the only one that would live. It would indeed become an esoteric classic and would supply the libretto for an opera.

8

EMINENT VICTORIANS

London, after Italy, was again jarring. To Daniel Curtis:

> I can't tell you what an emotion hovers over every memory of those
> delicious weeks I spent under your roof so lately & yet so remotely, as
> it seems. They were surely not the same stuff as the rest of life; they
> were as cloth of gold to *this* fog-coloured tweed.

James found his servants the Smiths pleasantly welcoming but as shy
and wooden as when he had first employed them, in sad contrast to the
congenial gondolier of the Palazzo Barbaro. Mrs. Smith presented herself
each morning for instructions as to the meals of the day, making no suggestions of her own but quietly awaiting her instructions. She seemed
somewhat intimidated by James; perhaps her experience of middle-aged
American bachelor novelists was limited.

Alice and Katherine had returned to Leamington Spa, where they had
taken rooms in a lodging house. Immediately on his return, James ran up
to see them, briefly. They had the parlor floor of the house, and their sitting room was the big formal parlor, with tall windows and a capacious
fireplace. The bedroom at the rear faced south and was correspondingly
sunny. Alice spent her mornings there, and on mild afternoons, accompanied by Katherine, she went out, wheeled in a bath chair by a servant,
with Katherine walking beside her.

His next hurried visit was to Bournemouth to see Stevenson, who had
had a bad winter. Despite his own illness, Stevenson had been obliged to
travel to Edinburgh to see his father before he died. The old man had
been ill for some time, but his death was a shock. There was some confusion about the will, which was ambiguously drafted, but eventually it be-

came clear that Louis would receive a substantial bequest. His uncle Graham Balfour, a physician, advised Louis not to return to England, where the climate was killing him, and suggested mountain air, perhaps a sanatorium in Colorado. With the aid of his father's bequest, Colorado would be possible. James accordingly found the Stevensons in a flurry of packing, arranging steamer accommodations, and trying to sublet their house.

On August 20, the Stevensons came to London and stayed overnight at the South Place Hotel in Finsbury Square, in the City of London, preparing to board their steamer for America. It was a Sunday, and the somewhat shabby commercial hotel was all but deserted. Louis was dressed with uncharacteristic formality in newly purchased mourning, and his manner was subdued.

James was flustered. He had been to the Albert Dock hoping to place a case of champagne on board ship, but neither captain nor steward was available, and he was unable to go on board himself. Eventually, he managed to convey the champagne via Sidney Colvin's brother, who had made all arrangements for the Stevensons' departure. James was in some distress, not knowing where they were—they had changed their hotel at the last minute—and fearing that he would not see them, but at last he found the correct hotel and called in the last moment before their departure, when there was a gathering of their mutual friends—Edmund Gosse, William Archer, W. E. Henley, Sidney Colvin—and accordingly little chance for a real farewell. For James it was a difficult parting: he feared that Stevenson was dying and they would not meet again. On Monday morning, the Stevensons' big, shabby steamer *Ludgate Hill* departed, sailing first to Le Havre to pick up a load of freight—horses and (bizarrely) monkeys. Stevenson went ashore at Le Havre and sent a brief note of thanks and farewell:

> It is a fine James, & a very fine Henry James, and a remarkably fine wine; and as for the boat, it is a dam bad boat, and we are all very rough mariners. We wish you were with us. . . . All salute you: all drink to you daily.

Louis wrote again when he arrived in New York. He had decided to spend the first winter in the Adirondack Mountains in New York instead of immediately going west, and James replied, "May you find what you need—white, sunny winter hours, not too stove-heated nor too pork-fed, with a crisp dry air and a frequent leisure. . . . May the American air rest lightly on you, my dear friend." As the months passed, Louis seemed to grow more distant. Little by little, his letters grew more impersonal. James called out to him:

> My dear Louis, You are too far away—you are too absent—too invisible, inaudible, inconceivable. Life is too short a business and friendship too delicate a matter for such tricks—for cutting great gory masses out of 'em by the year at a time. Therefore come back. Hang it all—sink it all and come back. . . . This is a selfish personal cry: I wish you back; for literature is lonely and Bournemouth is barren without you. Your place in my affection has not been usurped by another—for there is not the least little scrap of another to usurp it. If there were I would perversely try to care for him. But there isn't—I repeat, and I literally care for nothing but your return.

Despite these courtly protestations, James began at this time to pay regular Sunday calls on Edmund Gosse, who had assiduously cultivated his acquaintance ever since publication of *The Portrait of a Lady*. Like James, he had little formal education but despite this handicap was making his way as a man of letters. He had published some volumes of poetry and criticism and had managed to befriend Matthew Arnold, Lord Tennyson, and Robert Browning. On the strength of their recommendations he had been appointed a university lecturer at Cambridge, where his principal duty was to give a course of open lectures on English poetry. His first set of talks, collected into a slim volume in October 1886, was the subject of a devastating review by a sometime friend, Churton Collins.

Gosse was an engaging lecturer but did not have the training or temperament of a scholar. He composed his lectures hastily, without revision, relying on his memory and not troubling very much to verify his recollections. In the review Collins, not content with pointing out Gosse's numerous errors, solemnly denounced the favoritism and logrolling that had propelled the unscholarly Gosse into a university lectureship.

Gosse was depressed for a time by the malice of this attack from a friend and thought of resigning his lectureship, perhaps in part because the review was on the mark. Gosse, as James remarked privately, was in a false position. But James was a steadfast friend and, having had his own

experience of malicious reviews, recommended that Gosse take no notice, predicting correctly that Cambridge University, feeling itself attacked, would stand by him.

Gosse was grateful for James's loyalty and kindness, but did not take
James's advice. He wrote a long reply to Collins's review, which
prompted a storm of rebuttals and rerebuttals in *The Pall Mall Gazette*
and *The Times*. The storm had gradually subsided during James's absence,
and now on his return he found that Gosse, spirits revived, was beginning
a new course of lectures. The episode would not be entirely forgotten,
and Gosse's appointment would not be renewed; but he and James had
become fast friends.

Gladstone's Liberal government had collapsed after proposing home rule
for Ireland. The time for reform measures seemed to have passed; terror-
ism was again ascendant, and the marquess of Salisbury's new Tory government adopted a policy of repression. James's young bachelor friend
Arthur Balfour, Salisbury's nephew, was chief secretary for Ireland and
would be responsible for its success. As if to bring him up to date on political changes, Balfour invited James to join him for a country-house
weekend, and they went together to Percy and Madeline Wyndham's
house, "Clouds," in Wiltshire one Saturday in September.

Clouds was a new house, built for weekend parties, conveniently near
to London but secluded on its two thousand acres of forest and garden, a
gorgeous extension of Madeline Wyndham's ambitious political entertainments, "a palace of week-ending for politicians." Mrs. Wyndham was
beautiful and clever and would sit for her portrait as "Julia Dallow" in
James's *The Tragic Muse*. Her children and the children of friends, the
Tennants, were the nucleus of the celebrated Souls whose portraits James
would sketch in *The Awkward Age*. Margot Tennant, the future wife of a
prime minister, became James's lifelong friend. Her future husband, Herbert Asquith, was another member of the circle, who as prime minister a
lifetime later would help James become a British subject.

In the party that weekend was Wilfrid Scawen Blunt, Percy Wyndham's cousin and Madeline Wyndham's admirer. Blunt was an Irish nationalist and advocate of home rule. To goad him, Balfour indulged in
some sarcasm concerning the Irish members of Parliament. "I am sorry
for Dillon," Balfour said, speaking of the Irish nationalist member John
Dillon, "as if he gets into prison it is likely to kill him. He will have hard
labour."

Balfour was at leisure, and this was evidently said negligently and to annoy. But he was chief secretary for Ireland, with the authority to commence prosecutions, and Blunt chose to take the remark as a threat. The conversation became public some weeks later, when Blunt himself was jailed. On his return to Ireland, he had addressed a public meeting held in defiance of a government order. He was arrested and charged, and in due course sentenced to two months' imprisonment in Galway Gaol. This was not the sort of sentence with which Balfour had seemed to threaten him, but from jail Blunt angrily told newspaper reporters his version of the conversation at Clouds. Blunt named the others present at Clouds as evidence of his account, and James thought for a time that he, too, would be drawn into the public dispute and asked to testify at a parliamentary inquiry.

Balfour was a friend, but James's sympathies were with the humorless and disagreeable Blunt. As he remarked to William, "Balfour I should think indeed a prodigy of amiable heartlessness."

Although James and Louisa Wolseley were old friends, her husband had been serving abroad for much of the time they had known each other in London, and it was in that summer of 1887 that James conversed with Lord Wolseley for the first time at any length. James was spending a weekend at Oakdene, the Wolseleys' new country house in Surrey. The Wolseleys were much alike: little, blond, blue-eyed, energetic, with handsome athletic figures, beautiful peaches-and-cream complexions, and commanding manners. They had a little, blond, blue-eyed daughter, Frances, and were now entertaining energetically, partly on her behalf and partly in the interests of Wolseley's career.

Garnet Wolseley was recognized as a man of the future. Born into the landed gentry, the rural Tory middle class, he had advanced rapidly through an officer corps dominated by hereditary peers. He had become a public figure: the image and embodiment of the new professional soldier, the imperialist. He was a reformer, and "reform" in military matters was controversial. Reform meant professionalization of a still aristocratic order. After the disasters of the Crimean War, some reform measures had been enacted, but had only been partly put into effect, and the army remained a semifeudal institution. Wolseley had become the spokesman for reform in an era of high explosives and machine guns, forecasting a future in which Great Britain would no longer be able to retire behind its navy but would need a large, conscripted army. He put his questions into the newspapers, and into the political arena, and reform was so widely discussed that Gilbert and Sullivan in their comic opera *The Pirates of Penzance* made gentle fun of the old-fashioned "model major general," who had attended university and had a classical education but knew nothing of modern weapons or tactics.

The publicity Wolseley created, to circumvent the reluctance of his superiors, would have ruined the career of a traditional officer: Wolseley's activities were frowned upon by the commander in chief, the queen's cousin the duke of Cambridge, and by the queen herself; but battlefield successes had given him unique authority. He had won victories in China, Burma, and Canada and had served as governor-general of Cyprus, but his greatest popular triumphs were in Africa. He had brushed aside the armies of the Asante Empire in what is now Ghana, breaking up its slave trade, exacting tribute, and wresting from it the wealthy Gold Coast; imposed a British constitution on the Boer colony in Transvaal, where gold had been discovered; vanquished a nascent Egyptian nationalist movement at Tel-al-Kabir; and imposed British rule over Egypt. On the strength of his victories, Prime Minister Benjamin Disraeli was able to force his elevation to the peerage, to serve as the spokesman for reform in the House of Lords. Louisa had been at his side through all the maneuvering that each step forward had required. A son of the middle class, with no resources beyond his government salary, Garnet had become Lord Wolseley.

His luck had run out in 1885. The vast Sudan, annexed to British Egypt, was in rebellion. The leader of the rebellion was Mohammed Ahmed, called "the Mahdi" for the savior of Islam who was to appear at the end of the world. His forces had encircled and destroyed an Egyptian army, and he had established an Islamist regime and imposed Koranic law in Sudan. His army was now besieging Khartoum, the last stronghold of British rule. A friend and former subordinate of Wolseley, General Charles Gordon, had allowed himself to become entrapped in Khartoum, evidently hoping to force a British expedition to rescue him and wrest control of the Sudan back from the Mahdi.

Gladstone had wished to abandon Sudan. Wolseley and others through a campaign of publicity had forced him, after long delay, to authorize a relief expedition, however. Wolseley, as field commander in Egypt, sent a small force to break the siege of Khartoum, but it arrived forty-eight hours too late. Gordon and his force had all been killed before the relief expedition arrived. Gladstone was blamed for temporizing and delay and was called "the murderer of Gordon" by the press. Wolseley had just returned from this disaster when he and James formed their friendship. Having been one of the earliest advocates of prompt action, Wolseley had escaped blame for the disaster; he had been promoted to adjutant general of the army, and with characteristic energy had taken up his duties in London, resuming his campaign for reform.

James did not disapprove of the career the Wolseleys were making, nor of the conquests in which they played a part. He accepted the argument that Britain was a civilizing force, liberating native peoples from corrupt regimes in south Asia and from ancient slave-trading empires in Africa. Britain was defending India against threats from the brutal czarist regime in Russia and from the Ottoman Turkish Empire, which Gladstone considered literally satanic. In his first years in London, James had written a series of political essays for the American weekly *The Nation*, in which he reported approvingly on Britain's Afghan and Zulu wars. He spoke of British losses as "massacres" and of the Zulu as "bloodthirsty savages," in the accepted journalese of the day, and was gently disapproving of his Liberal friends' reluctance to pay the taxes needed to support the wars of empire.

In coming years, he would help forge links between British imperialists and their American counterparts, Progressive Republicans like John Hay and Wendell Holmes, and at the end of his life he would devote himself to helping bring America into the European war. One was obliged to choose, and James sided with what he considered the future of civilization, with the English-speaking peoples and the young soldiers who embodied their ideals.

Autumn drew toward its close, and he returned to De Vere Gardens and his writing desk, sharply curtailing visits to the country, dining out, Sunday calls. The winter was to be devoted to writing for magazines; the demands of the cash box were becoming insistent. To lighten his solitude, James had long spoken of his wish to have a dog, however, and now that he had a household and servants, he acted on his wish. On his visit to Oakdene in September, he and Louisa Wolseley evidently spoke of this, for she agreed to help him find a dog suitable for life in a flat. There was a litter of black-and-tan terriers at Oakdene, and she suggested James come down in about six weeks. In November, accordingly, he went down to Surrey again, to fetch one of the litter. So it was that he acquired his first and beloved dog, a terrier bitch that would live out its life with him and would be buried at the foot of his garden in Lamb House. He named her Tosca after the beautiful, tragic heroine of Sardou's lurid play that had just opened in Paris with Sarah Bernhardt in the title role—a somewhat extravagant name for a puppy.

Alice's care fell to him once more. Katherine Loring had been obliged to return to America, as her sister and her father both were now ailing, and she would be away for many months, perhaps years. Despite Katherine's departure, Alice "for many small reasons" decided to stay on alone in her lodgings in Leamington through the winter, and so Henry traveled to Leamington every few days. In her letters, Alice enumerated the small reasons: her lodgings were better than any she had found in London; her circle of friends in London was too stimulating, too exciting, and she felt the need for quiet and rest. In Katherine's absence her "attacks" of anxiety had become more frequent and severe. A new physician held out the possibility of restoring the strength of her atrophied leg muscles through electrical stimulation—galvanic treatments—and despite her unhappy experience with galvanic treatments in Bournemouth she was willing to undertake another trial. But she would first have to show improvement in the matter of the attacks. For that rest was needed, and it was easier to be quiet in Leamington than in London. Underlying these small reasons there seemed to be a larger one that had drained her spirit and left her reluctant to move: "Since Kath. has again been wrenched away from me & has now definitively passed from within my horizon for yrs. I am stranded here until my bones fall asunder." Despite the hopes held out by her new doctor, she began to speak more often of the prospect of dying.

She treasured Henry's visits, which cheered her, and she even ventured to praise him to William: "At the risk of stirring Wm.'s evil passions I will state that Harry's virtues transcend as ever the natural." Henry brought gossip from London and told her his news; they talked politics, which interested Alice greatly. She was particularly engaged by the struggle for Irish home rule, and when Gladstone's effort failed she became fiercely hostile to his opponents, the Unionists:

> Nearly all my friends [in Leamington] are imbecile Unionist abortions. Their hideous, patronizing, doctrinaire, all-for-Ireland's-good, little measured out globules of remedies make my blood boil.

James shared her views on home rule for Ireland, but he was not so fierce about its opponents and thought Alice might be more moderate in her views if she went out in the world more; but as he told William, these spouts of rage were at least lively. For his own part, he began again that winter to think of making a trip to Ireland, to collect material for a short book about the Irish rebellion.

He had been exhausted by the long labor and intense concentration required to write three-decker novels in monthly serials, and the poor returns on *The Princess Casamassima* and *The Bostonians* had persuaded him to abandon the big novel, at least for a while. But while weary, he was not discouraged. On the contrary, his spirits were higher than ever. He was saturated with impressions of the great world, felt indeed that he had enough material for ten years' work. As he wrote to Grace Norton:

> I look forward to some quiet months of work. I am trying, not without success, to drop out of society—as hard as some people try to get in. I want to be dropped & cut & consummately ignored. This only demands a little patience, & I hope eventually to elbow my way to the bottom.

He had learned what there was to learn by "going out," and he looked forward now to leisure and work. He wrote to William as he had to Grace Norton, filled with self-confidence and a kind of euphoria:

> [N]ow that autumn is closing in & one's fireside begins to glow I only long to settle down to work & gilded halls are simply a nuisance. They have been beco[m]ing so for a long time past. . . . I have very large accumulations (of "observations of the world" &c) & I now simply want elbow-room for the exercise, as it were, of my art. I hope during the next ten years to do some things of a certain importance; if I don't, it won't be that I haven't tried hard or that I am wanting in an extreme ambition.

James began again to write reviews, profiles, short stories, and travel pieces for the illustrated magazines, as he had when he first began to make his way as a man of letters. He wrote theater reviews, and was able to justify a pretty regular attendance at the theaters of London and Paris, which he adored, as being in the line of duty. He wrote an admiring review of Constant Coquelin's performances, masterpieces of meticulous observation and rendering. Coquelin had been one of the great stars of the Comédie-Française, but came to London that winter with his own company. James went to see him so often that his frequent companion

Rhoda Broughton begged off on account of the expense ("It is really too beastly dear. Two stalls cost 27/6!"). In the Comédie-Française, Coquelin had been limited to comic parts, but now with his own company he cast himself in tragic roles in which James thought him magnificent. In *Gabrielle*, for instance,

> Coquelin was remarkable . . . as an injured but magnanimous husband. He wept so beautifully when he found his wife loved another, yet even with his ugly face distorted by a blubber he was not ridiculous.

Coquelin was "enchanted" with James's review of his work, and the two men met and talked. Coquelin said it was "the first time he had been understood," and James for his part was struck by the brilliance of Coquelin's conversation, the beauty of his manner, the completeness of his art.

By November 1887, James had written and sent to magazines in London, Boston, and New York nine short stories and essays, but not a single one had yet appeared, and as he sat down to write still more he was seized with agonies of impatience. The delay in publishing an appreciation of Robert Louis Stevenson was particularly infuriating. His cash flow problems were growing serious; he had a household now to maintain, and no income except from his writing, but magazines generally did not pay until publication. Inquiring of Gilder at *The Century*, James found that his essay on Stevenson was being held for an illustration. At *The Atlantic, Harper's New Monthly*, and *Macmillan's*, the editors were all personal friends and continued to welcome his submissions and ask for more; but they maddeningly did not publish—and hence did not pay—him. They claimed to be holding his articles for just the right moment. He complained to Howells, to Stevenson, to everyone he knew. At the end of the year, he invited his new young friend Edmund Gosse for a dinner tête-à-tête, and evidently complained to him, too.

Unlike the others, Gosse had a suggestion: James should engage a literary agent. This was a novel arrangement, but a few popular authors were working with A. P. Watt and Son. Walter Besant, for instance, was represented by the firm. Gosse would be glad to say a word to Besant, if James wished. James seized eagerly on the suggestion and early in the new year agreed to retain Watt. His mind was greatly relieved, and soon, indeed, his stories and essays again began to appear in print, which perhaps they would have done in any case, accompanied by the illustrations that it had taken so long to obtain.

At that dinner, James and Gosse also discussed Oscar Wilde, who had been proposed for membership in the Savile Club. This was of course a controversial proposal. James and Gosse were both members of the Savile and they joined in sponsoring Wilde's application for membership, but it was defeated.

James was determined to keep to his desk. He usually dined at home, at the early hour of seven, to avoid late evenings. He took fencing lessons, the Victorian gentleman's calisthenics; William also sent him a set of chest weights with which to exercise. He largely kept to his resolution to avoid society, but as Christmas drew near, keeping up an annual tradition, he paid a brief visit to Lord and Lady Rosebery at their Georgian house in Epsom, which James called the most beautiful house in England.

In March, 1888, utterly without warning, came news from Paris that Lizzie Boott, the intimate friend of his youth and of his first ventures to Europe, was dead. She had begun to paint again, with her son out of infancy, and the family was in Paris when she contracted pneumonia and within weeks died.

It was altogether a difficult winter indeed, with Lizzie's death, Stevenson's departure, Alice's renewed dependence and deepening depression. Paul Bourget announced that he was engaged to be married, and James, dutifully freeing himself of jealousy or resentment, wrote words of congratulation to Bourget and his fiancée, Minnie David. In James's stories, from some of his earliest to *The Bostonians*, he had often told the familiar tale of same-sex friendships giving way to the heterosexual, of men betraying each other for the sake of a woman, of women for a man. He was aware that Edmund Gosse's beloved friend the sculptor Hamo Thornycroft, a member of the Aïdé circle, had married. He wrote to Stevenson in a spasm of loneliness:

> I miss you too sensibly. . . . I won't question you—'twere vain—but I wish I knew more about you. I want to *see* you—where you live and *how*—and the complexion of your days. But I don't know even the name of your habitat.

· · ·

He had not seen Mary Ward for some months. She had been occupied with writing and revising her second novel, *Robert Elsmere*. In February, the novel had appeared in bookshops, in three fat volumes, and a set arrived in a bulky parcel at De Vere Gardens. After reading most of the first two volumes, James forwarded the set to Alice and sent a hasty note of congratulations to Mrs. Ward, calling her novel "a distinguished & remarkable production" and promising fuller comments later; then he returned to his own work. *Robert Elsmere* had not been serialized, no reviews appeared at the time of publication, Mary Ward still being an unknown quantity, and so far as early indications went her second novel might have vanished without a trace, as the first had done. James began to compose in his mind a thoughtful criticism. He did not at first send this letter. *Robert Elsmere* reflected immense labor, but it was not an artful work, and he was unsure how to say what he thought. As James observed a little later to Edmund Gosse:

> [Mrs. Ward] is incorrig[i]bly wise & good, & has a moral nature as Patti has a voice . . . but, somehow I don't, especially when talking art & letters, *communicate* with her worth a damn. All the same, she's a dear.

When at last he did write to her more fully, prodded by a dinner invitation from Humphry Ward, his criticisms were mild and interspersed with warm praise. By then, however, *Robert Elsmere* was a runaway bestseller and had become not merely a book but a "momentous public event."

Despite the absence of early notices, the book was immediately popular with lending-library patrons, and libraries hastened to purchase additional copies. The first small printings were quickly exhausted, and the publisher went back to press repeatedly. Mary Ward's friends and family pushed the novel shamelessly, and reviews began to appear. Walter Pater wrote a glowing review for *The Manchester Guardian*, and in April *The Times* ran an anonymous review. Other leading journals quickly followed suit, and in May—most remarkably—William Ewart Gladstone, the Grand Old Man of the Liberal Party, past and future prime minister, wrote a 10,000-word review-essay in the *Nineteenth Century Magazine*. Gladstone was an Oxonian and former member of Parliament for Oxford; he knew Ward, and the people and settings of her book, very well. Ward had addressed questions concerning the established church that were of great importance to him. His review was argumentative, but it marked the book as the topic of the day. Printings of the three-decker grew larger but still were quickly exhausted; pirated editions appeared in the United States, no arrangements having been made for an authorized edition there. Gradually it became apparent that *Robert Elsmere* would be the most popular novel of the season, on both sides of the Atlantic. In Britain, roughly 40,000 copies of the book were sold in the first year after publication, and at least 100,000 copies were pirated and sold in the American market.

The enormous popular and commercial success of *Robert Elsmere* was difficult for James to accept without resentment. At first, he attributed Mary Ward's success to the puffing her book received from her family and the influence of her Oxford circle. He unburdened himself to Gosse, to whom he complained of the "clique" that put Ward forward. The remarkable success of *Robert Elsmere* could not really be attributed solely to the workings of an Oxford clique, however, and James quickly apologized to Gosse for his "plaintive accents"—"I feel as if I had whined & am ashamed of it." *Robert Elsmere* was an immediate and enduring hit with precisely the audience that James was losing, the middle-class women who patronized lending libraries.

9

A Private Season

Early in 1888, Tom Aldrich—pleased that James had returned to earlier, more popular themes—had asked him for a new novel to be serialized in *The Atlantic Monthly.* James answered that he had in mind for his next novel the story of an actress, *The Tragic Muse.* It would make only a short novel, running for perhaps six months; he had thought of publishing it without prior serialization. Aldrich wanted something more substantial, however, a novel that would run for a full year. James demurred at first, not wishing to undertake another big novel, but Aldrich offered fifteen dollars per printed page, and James replied, "I succumb to your arguments." He promised to deliver the first of twelve monthly installments by October, to appear the following January.

To make a novel long enough to run for a full year, he told Aldrich, he would combine *The Tragic Muse* with another story that he had in mind, the tale of a painter tempted by politics and marriage to abandon his art. The two stories had a certain symmetry and combined would make the long novel that Aldrich wanted. After delays and with some reluctance, James sat down to the sustained intensity of effort of writing a big novel for serial publication, with these two stories in mind but as yet no clear idea of how they would fit together.

Nor did the new novel promise any immediate flow of cash. Payment would be made only upon publication, which meant that he faced months of strenuous effort before any reward could be expected. He wrote, a little desperately, to Fred Macmillan, pleading for help: Would Macmillan agree to publish two volumes of short stories that had already appeared in magazines and make some payment in advance against royalties? "I must tell you that an essential part of the idea, for me, is to have some money." For the sake, again, of cash he agreed to prepare a transla-

tion of Alphonse Daudet's latest novel, as yet unpublished, the last in his
Tartarin series, for Harper's; it would appear in English in America before
the book had been published in France. He agreed to write four reviews
for American magazines. These were all meant only to keep his pot boiling; his principal task was *The Tragic Muse.*

On Christmas Day he went out to Leamington to have dinner with his
sister. He found Alice quite ill, very much worse than he had last seen
her. He remained in Leamington for a week, although he had not
planned beforehand to make such a long visit, but Alice was suffering
from a heart ailment, in addition to her other distresses, and a sad episode
had brought on an attack. A young couple, the woman far advanced in
pregnancy, had taken an upstairs room in Alice's lodging house, and on
Christmas Eve the woman went into labor. "It was very curious," Alice
wrote afterward, "to lie here, and to hear the Xmas rejoicings through the
gossamer walls on one side, and the groans of the woman in labor in the
room above." She at first thought of removing herself to a hotel, but collapsed with an attack of angina before she could carry out this plan; her
nurse administered digitalis for her heart, and gave her a sedative, potas-
sium bromide, to calm her. Alice listened until late at night to the cries of
the woman in labor, and to the husband tramping up and down the stairs,
keeping up his courage with brandy and soda. "How my heart burned
within me at the cruelty of men!" she confided to Aunt Kate.

The baby lived only an hour. "The little waxen image held a feeble
spark of life which flickered out at the end of an hour, beneficent Death
rescuing it from a mother who was 'glad' when she heard it would not
live, & who had not prepared a rag to wrap it in."

Henry remained in Leamington until Alice had recovered from the
excitement of this episode. While she was still recovering, there came the
news that Aunt Kate was seriously ill. Symptoms of the dementia of old
age had been gathering about her for some time, and now she had fallen
and evidently had broken her hip. She was bedridden, and her situation
apparently was grave.

Shortly after his return from Leamington, James dined with Mary and
Humphry Ward, who had invited him to meet a young man, Wolcott
Balestier, newly arrived in London. Balestier was very much an Ameri-
can, as James had described the type: tall, lean, with a well-shaped head,

strongly marked features, and a long jaw. He was the subtype "cultured American," as James would describe him: handsome, pale, stooping, painfully thin. Clean-shaven, he had the characteristic open expression of the American. He had grown up in Rochester, New York—"the West," as that term had been understood in James's youth. He was just twenty-seven years old, and had been in London only a matter of weeks. A wealthy grandfather, a French planter from Martinique, had died the year before at his country estate in Vermont, and Balestier had taken his modest share of the inheritance to London, inspired by an all but Napoleonic ambition. He was an author and a poet, but first of all a man of business, and he had a prescient vision of a global publishing empire.

Great Britain had entered into the Berne Convention and with thirteen European nations agreed to extend the same copyright protection to authors of member countries that it provided to its own subjects. The United States had not joined, but the pirating of Mary Ward's immensely successful novel, which in America had been given away as a premium with soap purchases, had outraged the British and prompted them to insist on protection for their authors. Legislation was pending in Congress that would recognize most foreign copyrights. Anticipating a new international copyright regime, Balestier had come to London hoping to exploit it. He had a commission from a New York publisher, J. W. Lovell, to contract with English authors for American publication, but this commission was only a beginning. Within a few months of his arrival, he was agent or publisher in Europe and America for some of the leading authors in London: Mary Ward, Henry James, Edmund Gosse, and Rudyard Kipling among them.

His idea was simply to obtain world rights to the best fiction in English, to arrange publication in America and Great Britain and separate editions on the Continent. He had approached Mary Ward shortly after his arrival in London, knowing how badly she had suffered from the pirating of her work in America; he had charmed her, and she had invited James to dinner to meet him. James was enchanted. Balestier seemed to him to be dedicated to his authors, almost as a spouse would be; he had an "acute and sympathetic interest in the fruits of literary labor" that amounted to genius.

Balestier established himself in an office just inside the arch of the Dean's Yard of Westminster Abbey, a leisurely walk from James's flat in South Kensington. He was the eldest of four children, and as their father was dead he was despite his youth the head of his family. As soon as he was settled in London, his mother came over to join him, bringing his two sisters: Caroline, who was clever and energetic, and Josephine, who was the beauty. The youngest son, Beatty, a charming scapegrace, briefly joined them as well. Calling at Wolcott's office, one was likely to find Caroline there, as she quickly took command of its management; and young Rudyard Kipling, recently arrived from India, who had taken lodgings nearby.

The office became a salon for young writers, and James in his characteristic fashion befriended the whole circle. Although James already had a literary agent, Balestier involved himself, in friendly fashion, in James's business affairs, and his friendship and his interest would make a great difference in James's life.

Earlier that winter, James had received a proposal to which he had not responded. Edward Compton, the actor-manager of a provincial theater troupe, had written to James suggesting that he turn his early novel *The American* into a play. *The American* had been reissued in a two-shilling paper-cover edition, and this presumably had prompted Compton's suggestion; but James did not at first respond. Balestier now encouraged him to accept the proposal, and then on James's behalf negotiated with Compton an advance of £250.

When James had essayed living in Paris, he had thought of making a career as a man of letters in the Parisian style and of writing plays. He had long ago written a stage version of his popular early story "Daisy Miller," but that project had foundered, and he had not found the experience encouraging. When he settled in London he had given up these ideas, as he confided to his journal:

> I had practically given up my old, valued, long cherished dream of doing something for the stage, for fame's sake, & art's, & fortune's: overcome by the vulgarity, the brutality, the baseness of the condition of the English-speaking theatre today.

Now, however, it was simply a question of income. Under the stimulus of need and of a new friendship, the old dream revived,

> but on a new & a very much humbler basis, & especially under the lash of necessity. Of art or fame *il est maintenant fort peu question* [it is now scarcely a question]: I simply *must* try, & try seriously, to produce half-a-dozen—a dozen, five dozen—plays for the sake of my pocket, my ma-

terial future. . . . To accept the circumstances, in their extreme humility,
& do the best I can *in* them: this is the moral of my present situation.

Two hundred and fifty pounds, in advance, was promising. If he could
produce plays for touring companies at the same rate that he wrote stories, or chapters of novels, the damages to his income would be repaired
and there was always a chance of a hit, a play that would succeed in the
West End and have a long run, a success that would allow him at last to
save for his old age, and to cease living from hand to mouth.

The great theatrical spectacle of the Parnell Commission had begun in
the fall. The new Tory administration had undertaken to link Irish political leaders to bombings and murders. A commission was empaneled to
investigate the involvement of the Irish members of Parliament in violent
crimes, and when the hearings of the commission opened in the new Law
Courts chamber, they focused on Charles Stewart Parnell, the gaunt and
charismatic leader of the Irish parliamentary party, who in the eyes of the
government and the press embodied Irish nationalism.

The case against Parnell now unfolded in the new year. The case rested
upon intelligence gathered by private agents and published in *The Times:*
letters apparently bearing Parnell's signature encouraged beforehand the
Phoenix Park murders and praised them after the fact. The self-styled secret agent who had brought forward the damning evidence was one
Richard Pigott, a former Irish nationalist and comrade of Parnell. He produced the incriminating letters and testified at the hearing to Parnell's
complicity in the crimes. The government's charges seemed to be
proven: the apparently moderate, reformist movement for home rule was
only a screen for terrorist violence and a step to creating an independent
state, hostile to England, on its own doorstep.

The government's case dramatically collapsed midway in the hearings,
however, when Pigott was cross-examined. The letters seemingly signed
by Parnell were oddly phrased and filled with inaccuracies. On the witness stand, Pigott was asked to spell "hesitancy" and misspelled the word
just as it had been misspelled in the letters. The following day he failed to
appear in court; he fled and was later found, an apparent suicide, in a
hotel in Madrid.

For James, the whole affair was riveting—politics as high theater—and
in letter after letter he confessed his addiction to the commission hearings, which he attended faithfully. To Louis Stevenson he reported:

two or three of the most interesting days I ever passed were lately in
the crowded, throbbing, thrilling, little court of the Special Commission, over the astounding drama of the forged *Times* letters.

He gave regular reports to his sister, Alice, who was even more en-
grossed in the progress of the hearings. To his sister-in-law, William's
Alice, he wrote:

I . . . think, just now, like everyone else here, almost only of the high
Irish imbroglio & the wonderful abyss into which the tiresome *Times*
has fallen, with its abominable Pigott & its abominable malignity. Seen
so near as this (& I have spent two quite thrilling days in the courtroom) it is all a very palpitating drama, the successive scenes of which
give—or have given—zest to each day's rising.

To Charles Eliot Norton in Cambridge he wrote saying that he had attended

the thrilling, throbbing Parnell trial, during the infinitely interesting
episode of the letters, which if one had been once & tasted blood, one
was quite hungry to go again & wanted to give up everything & live
there.

He confessed that it was only the difficulty of securing tickets to the
crowded little courtroom that kept him from devoting himself entirely to
the hearings. Balfour, he thought, was their principal architect.

In the midst of the Parnell excitement, he learned that Aunt Kate had
died. After a month of bedridden illness, on March 6, 1889, she had died
of pneumonia.

Aunt Kate was his last close tie to his mother's family, the Scottish
Robertsons and Scots-Irish Walshes, the extended family among whom
he had spent his New York childhood. Her death prompted much sor-
rowful reflection. But there was also the usual stress over the terms of a
will to distract him. For a short time it appeared that James might have a
substantial sum coming to him: Aunt Kate left a large estate, and he had
been her favorite. But, after a bequest to William of $10,000—her view
evidently having been that William was not able to support his family
without assistance—and one to Wilky's widow, Cary, a gesture of recon-

ciliation, the remainder of the estate went to Walsh cousins. There was nothing at all for Robertson, the youngest child, whose drinking and mistreatment of his wife had so distressed Aunt Kate. Henry was given a choice of some heirlooms. Alice also received some heirlooms, including her mother's family silver, and a treasured shawl; but Aunt Kate, hardminded as ever, gave Alice only a life interest, presumably to ensure that these precious things would return to the family after Alice's death, rather than go to Katherine Loring, of whom Aunt Kate had never approved.

"A life interest in a shawl!" Alice exclaimed, half in bitterness and half amused. She and William exchanged some barbed letters: she was already angry with him for taking her stored furniture to his country house in New Hampshire and was now sharply sarcastic about the very large bequest to the "favored nephew." But the $10,000 was very welcome to William, who made no apologies and did not offer to share the bequest. It would allow him to build a house in Cambridge, to accommodate his growing family. He now planned a trip to Europe, to nurse himself at watering places and meet with scientists while his wife remained at home with their children, supervising the building and furnishing of their new house.

Henry James and George du Maurier had grown closer since du Maurier had begun to spend winters in London. His oldest daughter, Beatrix, had married—James had attended the wedding, had declared the couple the handsomest of the year, and stood godfather to their first child. The oldest son, Guy du Maurier, had gone to Sandhurst; at the time of Beatrix's wedding he received his commission in the Royal Fusiliers, and after the ceremony left to join his regiment in India. The second son, Gerald, was in school; only Sylvia and May remained at home with their parents. The house in Hampstead had begun to seem rather large and empty, especially in winter when guests were reluctant to make the journey from London. The du Mauriers decided to let their Hampstead house for the winter months and take another in Bayswater, from December through March. This brought them close at hand for James, in the winter months when he most enjoyed London, and his Sunday visits to du Maurier became more frequent and were supplemented by weekday dinners as well. They walked in the afternoons and early evenings, and du Maurier told stories of his childhood, and of his aristocratic French ancestors, as he believed them to be. His conversation, James remembered afterward, was a sort of running novel, densely peopled like a big London party. Du Maurier's health was failing—he was nine years older than James—and they walked slowly in Bayswater Road. Du Maurier was a fount of fantastic tales, as well as of reminiscences and speculations; he would spin out long stories, like his tale of two enchanted lovers who took the shape of seabirds. The boy was obliged to return to human form and wandered the earth seeking his beloved. "Plots!" du Maurier would say, "I am full of plots," and offered them to James to use as he wished.

> Last evening before dinner I took a walk with G. du Maurier, in the mild March twilight (there was a blessed sense of spring in the air), through the empty streets near Porchester Terrace, & he told me over an idea of his which he thought very good—& I do too . . . it struck me as curious, picturesque & distinctly usable: though the want of musical knowledge would hinder *me* somewhat in handling it. . . . It is the history of the servant girl with a wonderful rich voice but no musical genius who is mesmerized & made to sing by a little foreign Jew who has mesmeric power.

"But you ought to write that story," James said. Encouraged by his friend, du Maurier did indeed begin to write, sitting down to it that very evening, although what he wrote at first was not this tale.

Wendell Holmes wrote to say that he would be coming to London shortly. As his court did not sit during the summer, Holmes was at leisure, and Fanny sent him off to pay a visit to London while she remained at home to care for the ailing Dr. Holmes.

Wendell was hesitant about venturing into London alone and unacquainted during the Season and invited Owen Wister—Fanny Kemble's American grandson—to accompany him: Wister was a young man who knew his way about in London society. When Wister begged off, Holmes wrote to Henry James. He wrote a friendly, even affectionate, letter; James replied promptly and warmly and prepared to make Holmes welcome, to reintroduce him to London.

By an odd coincidence, Holmes sailed from New York in June on the same ship, the *Cephalonia*, that carried William to Europe. Wendell and William renewed their old friendship, and evidently spoke of William's work in psychology, for when his book appeared the following year, Holmes wrote to him at length, as if continuing a conversation.

William did not go straight to London but left the *Cephalonia* at its first landfall in Queenstown and spent a week traveling to the north of Ireland, where his father's family had originated, then to Glasgow and across Scotland to Edinburgh, and finally south to London, arriving three weeks later than Henry had expected him.

Holmes came directly to London, however, and while awaiting William's arrival Henry did his best to make his old friend feel at home in London. They reverted to a pattern from their youth, James quietly facilitating Holmes's friendships with women. Tall, slim, and handsome, still youthful at forty-six, and an engaging conversationalist, Holmes was an eligible dinner guest. James introduced him to a pretty young widow, Lucy Clifford, who was earning her way as a writer; to the young matrons of the Souls, and to the widowed Alice Stopford Green. James also introduced him, on request, to a lovely young woman Holmes encountered at a picture gallery and who proved to be a distant connection of James's: Clare St. Leger, Lady Castletown, whose husband was a sportsman and was not often in London.

Romantic friendships between Holmes and the women to whom James introduced him on that visit would prosper. Margot Tennant wrote confiding letters, and Holmes opened a lifelong correspondence with Lucy Clifford. After Holmes's return to Boston in the fall, James told him that "Mrs. Clifford happened to confide to me yesterday how madly she loves you," with an echo of the jocular, manly tone, slightly off-key, of his earliest letters to Holmes. The acquaintance with Lady Castletown would become a prolonged flirtation, and perhaps something more.

When William at last turned up, he came to stay with Henry at his flat. On July 10, the brothers went out to Leamington for the day to visit Alice; it would be the first meeting of the three since their father's death.

Alice's summer had been a happy one. She had settled into her lodgings at Leamington and had begun keeping a journal. Best of all, Katherine Loring, freed for a time from duties to her ailing father and sister, was coming to spend three months with her. And so Alice was in particularly good spirits on July 18, when Henry came to lunch after an absence of a few days. When they had finished their meal and were talking easily, James said, "I must tell you something." Alice, thinking he had a queer look, said, "You're not going to be married!"

"No, but William is here."

Apprehensive of Alice's reaction, and her heart ailment, Henry had tried to ease the shock of the news. William waited outside for the signal to enter, while Henry explained his presence. If Alice was too upset, the meeting could be postponed. But Alice only asked for a bromide to calm her nerves, and Henry signaled to William from the little wrought-iron balcony. After a short interval, William joined them in the high-ceilinged sitting room.

Alice reclined on a chaise longue beside a floor-to-ceiling window, and Henry stood beside her. It was a difficult moment for William, finding the two younger siblings side by side, each with their father's round face and gray eyes. Henry had managed the meeting carefully, however, and it went well. He had assured William beforehand that Alice no longer resented Aunt Kate's bequest and was well disposed toward him despite their quarrels. William, when he entered, came forward and embraced her.

William remained with Henry for ten days, and they established a new friendship as adults. William was now a full professor of philosophy, but his circumstances were modest and he had not yet published any substantial scientific work. In the new edition of Appleton's *Cyclopedia of American Biography*, issued that year, a full column was given to his father and another to his brother Henry, but William himself was given only a single paragraph sandwiched between them, in which he was identified as the editor of a posthumous volume of his father's work. Henry was a world figure, while William was still struggling to write a book about the new empirical psychology. Perhaps in compensation, William took a condescending tone toward his younger brother and wrote home to his wife rather sourly that despite Henry's success,

> I am sorry to say that he is saving not a cent of money, so that my vision of him, paralyzed, in our spare room, is stronger than ever. He seems quite helpless in that regard.

Henry was tactful and did not challenge this picture of himself. He and William got on well during their brief visit, and it seemed to mark a change in their relations, a new openness and friendliness.

10

❧✦❧

AN END TO NOVEL WRITING

Macmillan's advance for the short-story volumes was meager, and while Tom Aldrich had agreed to publish the book edition of *The Tragic Muse* in the United States, he would not pay an advance over and above the fees for serialization. Well and good; perhaps he would instead pay James for the serial installments on receipt, instead of on publication? This proposal was accepted, and James received a fat check from Boston in payment for the initial chapters that had already been submitted.

Fred Macmillan, too, was reluctant to pay much in advance for *The Tragic Muse*. Already committed to two volumes of James's stories, he offered only £70 as an advance against sales of the novel. Emboldened by the friendly interest Wolcott Balestier and Balestier's partner William Heinemann had taken in his work, James expressed regret and suggested that he and Macmillan part company.

> Unless I can put the matter on a more remunerative footing all round I shall give up my English "market"—heaven save the market! & confine myself to my American. But I must experiment a bit first—& to experiment is of course to say farewell to you. Farewell then, my dear Macmillan, with deep regret.

Macmillan was not prepared to see James proposing his novel to other publishers, however, especially as Macmillan had already begun setting type from the magazine pages, and so at last he offered an advance of £250 for British rights. James left it to his literary agent in Great Britain, A. P. Watt, to work through the final agreement.

James received roughly $6,000 for *The Tragic Muse*, while the early chapters of the book were still being written, but he was spending his income as it came, as William had sourly observed. He had a household staff and a position to maintain, Alice more than ever needed the security of the income from his share of the father's estate, and so he must continue to produce at a prodigious pace. In 1890, with the advances on *The Tragic Muse* pocketed and no further royalties from the book edition to be expected, he would be obliged to begin all over again in some fashion, perhaps in the theater.

The two stories of which *The Tragic Muse* was to be made were clear enough. The first, the original story of "The Tragic Muse," was based on the debut of the actress Mary Anderson that he had witnessed with Mary Ward and recorded in his notebook four years earlier. Anderson had married and retired from the stage but James's fictional actress was to take wing as an artist. His heroine would be "Miriam Rooth," a very young woman whose beauty and poverty, like Mary Anderson's, would lead her to a career on the stage. But unlike Mary Anderson, the fictional tragic muse was to have both talent and ambition. James had his heroine begin by reciting for a retired actress of the Comédie-Française, "Madame Carré," a character modeled on Adelaide Ristori, demanding the training that Anderson never received. Young Miriam in Paris stands in the famous greenroom of the Théâtre-Français before a famous life-size portrait of Rachel Félix. The painted image gazes sadly out of her dark eyes at the newest incarnation of the muse. The fictional Miriam, we perceive, is the very personification of the actor's art. However clumsy she appears at the outset, Miriam is to be an English Rachel who will learn French technique and theory and adapt them to the London stage. She will, like Rachel, revive the national classics and spur a new generation of authors to write great plays for her. She is pure will, pure ambition.

Her admirer is Peter Sherringham, a Europeanized Englishman, an aristocrat. He is a young man with a bright future in the diplomatic service, who has been posted to Paris, where he indulges a young man's interest in the theater. Sherringham falls in love with Miriam and eventually realizes that—with his help—she can have a great success, one that will transform the London stage. But he wishes to advance himself in the diplomatic service, and while he might take up an actress from the Comédie-Française without hurting his career, Miriam is an embarrassment. She is virtuous, and Sherringham is in the ludicrous position of loving and supporting a woman who is not his mistress. He tries to resolve his dilemma by proposing marriage, on condition that Miriam give up the stage. (He, of course, cannot be married to an actress.) She firmly refuses him, takes wing, and soars away to become the English Rachel without him.

Miriam is the center of this tale, and James circles around her from the outside, rarely intruding into her thoughts or feelings, seeing her only through the eyes of the other characters, as an actress is seen on the stage. She is a mystery to the reader, who is set to puzzling over her, and it is this interest that drives the story along. We see her assiduously studying the diction, poses, and mannerisms of the classic theater; we see her slow mastery of herself and of the traditional arts of the actor. The story unfolds scene by scene, like a French play, largely through dialogue. The reader gradually learns that Miriam is an authentic artist and indeed a genius, driven by a powerful ambition. "I will, I will, I will," she cries in James's own voice. "I will succeed, I will be great." As the story unfolds, we are able to see her coming of age, her maturing intelligence, her experiences of loving and being loved, her eventual self-mastery; she is another of James's magnificent young women.

The second story that is to make up *The Tragic Muse* is equally clear. A handsome blond young Englishman, Nick Dormer (who greatly resembles Ned Abbey), is the second son of an old family. He is expected to have a political career, like his late father's; he has been "brought up in the temple" of politics where his father was high priest. But he is dreamy and artistic, and dabbles in paint, and hesitates.

There are two rivals for his loyalty and affection, male and female. The male rival is a chum of Nick's from university days—Gabriel Nash—an extreme aesthete who is made to speak like Oscar Wilde and to express Wilde's opinions. The Wildean Nash is a cosmopolite and an original, in his own person a modernist work of art. While he is to be the villain of the piece—he is, as Nick's little sister Biddy excitedly observes, "the highest expression of irresponsibility that she had ever seen"—he is affectionately drawn, and Nick's fondness for him is palpable. James conveys a deep sympathy for this worldly man.

As the story begins, Nick Dormer and Gabriel Nash meet in Paris after several years of separation, and they have a brief conversation, very much like James's own first meeting with Wilde. Nash tries to persuade Nick to give up his political career and join Nash in a life of aesthetic revels. He is seductive, and opens Nick Dormer's eyes to beauty.

The rival for Nick's affection and loyalty is Julia Dallow. Clever, beautiful, and wealthy, she is modeled on Madeline Wyndham. A widow, she keeps a political salon, and has political ambitions. She loves Dormer and wishes to marry him; she dreams of helping him become prime minister. But she cannot understand or share his interest in painting and does not want to be a painter's wife.

Awakened to beauty by Gabriel Nash, Nick Dormer throws over Julia Dallow and her wealth and the political career she promises him. But instead of drifting from sensation to sensation with Nash, Dormer in all seriousness sets out to become a painter of portraits, a working artist, and throws over Nash as well, abandoning his adolescent infatuation.

Between the painter's story and the actor's there is no apparent link. They are merely complementary: one artist must give up private domesticity in order to pursue her art; the other must give up public life and retreat into his private realm to pursue his art.

James found a link to unite the stories in Miriam herself. The actress would be the center of both tales, linking them. She would fall in love with Nick Dormer, and he would paint her portrait as the newest incarnation of the tragic muse. But he would see her only as a work of art and would not return her love, ensuring the tragic conclusion that was required.

The relations among the characters then became clear. Gabriel Nash would enter both tales as the serpent in the garden: meaning only mischief, but putting the machinery of both stories into motion.

Slowly the architecture of the novel raised itself in James's mind's eye: a structure of symmetries and reflections. Each character was a performer, with his or her proper role to play. Julia Dallow's political ambitions, Nick's painting, Sherringham's diplomacy, and Miriam's acting: each was an art, each art was ultimately a performance. " 'To be what one *may* be, really and efficaciously . . . to feel it and understand it, to accept it, adopt it, embrace it—that's conduct, that's life.' "

Gabriel Nash is the negative principle: he is mere sensuous, wild adolescence; he creates nothing, is self-indulgent, self-regarding, blind to duty. As Biddy says, he is irresponsible, and uses other people solely for his own amusement. Repeatedly during the tale he is said to be a devil or devilish; his name vaguely evokes a fallen angel; Nick at last calls him Mephistopheles. His part of the tale ends when Nick paints his portrait, reducing him from grandiose theory to frail practice. Nick's painting of Miriam brings her to life; his painting of Nash puts an end to him:

From being outside of the universe he was suddenly brought into it, and from the position of a free commentator and critic, a sort of amateurish editor, of the whole affair, reduced to that of humble ingredient and contributor.

Once his picture is painted, Nash disappears "without a trace," like a person in a fairy tale. The painting then begins to fade, little by little, "for all the world as in some delicate Hawthorne tale." Nash will not return until the last traces of paint have disappeared, when he can resume his career as a free and irresponsible critic.

Oscar Wilde certainly read the book and sardonically embraced the portrait of himself, just as he had laughingly toured America as one of George du Maurier's caricatures. Within the year, he wrote *The Picture of Dorian Gray*, in which he defiantly reversed James's image: the irresponsible hero of Wilde's tale continued to carry on in Mephistophelian fashion and remained uncannily young, while his dutiful, embodied portrait aged and faded away.

The Tragic Muse was praised by many, especially in America. William Dean Howells and J. R. Lowell were even more complimentary than usual. Horace Scudder, who had just taken over the editorship of *The Atlantic Monthly* from Tom Aldrich, wrote an admiring, unsigned review of the completed book. Scudder thought readers who had enjoyed the serial would be able to see the structure of the novel as a whole in the book edition and their attention would be held "by what may be called the spiritual plot of the tale." Scudder sent James a copy of the magazine in which this appeared, and James replied with feeling:

> I have been able to read the pages of charming sympathy you have . . . dedicated to *The Tragic Muse*. They have really brought tears to my eyes—giving me a luxurious sense of being understood, perceived, felt. Your words are delightful & I thank you for them with all my heart.

William wrote with unaccustomed enthusiasm. He had refrained from reading the serial installments, and came to the book as a whole with a fresh eye:

> At last you've done it and no mistake. The Tragic Muse caps the climax. It is a most original, wonderful, delightful and admirable produc-

tion. . . . The whole thing hangs together most intimately and well; and it is truly a spectacle for rejoicing to see that by the sort of practice a man gives himself he attains the plenitude and richness which you have at last got. . . . The whole thing is an exquisite mirage which remains afloat in the air of one's mind.

Fifteen years later, writing his preface, James would insist on the merits of the novel, its perfect architecture, its symmetry and its beauty. Indeed, in his initial plan for the selective, definitive, edition of his fiction, he placed it at the climax of his first long period. But he will concede the novel's defects. Its principal failing is that Nick Dormer is not seen intimately, either as a man or as an artist, and his sacrifices and passion must be imagined; we see him only at his easel, with his back turned to the reader. Nick's passion for his art, the circle of men in which it flourishes, are to be supplied by the reader. Instead of emerging as the second center of the novel, his art performed in intimate privacy among friends, Nick disappears into his secluded realm.

American reviewers liked the book edition, when it appeared, and treated it seriously. James had managed the feat of returning to his earlier plots and themes, without losing the depth of social commentary introduced in his big novels. The whole structure of Anglo-American society was portrayed, lightly, and a theory of art and a philosophy of life lay in the background.

But British reviews for the most part were rudely negative. James had portrayed middle-class Englishmen as philistines, and repeatedly suggested that the English were racially insensitive to art. English reviewers obligingly displayed the philistinism with which James charged them. Several found the portrait of Biddy, the quintessentially English girl suited only for marriage, the best thing in the book but complained that there was too much French thought and language for an English novel.

More serious than the bad reviews in Great Britain was the falling off of James's audience on both sides of the Atlantic. His readers evidently were not engaged by the characters or their stories. James's tale was of the essential tragedy, that love is always unequal. Miriam must sacrifice her love for Nick and make a marriage of reason with a fellow actor; Biddy must marry Peter, who loves Miriam; Julia must give up Nick, whose own passions are too deeply hidden to be seen.

Nor were most of James's educated readers, then or later, pleased with his characterizations of men's and women's roles, of national character, and race. Realistic as statements of social fact, James presented them as essential truths. Little Biddy's ambition to be a sculptor was portrayed as ludicrous, her true medium of expression marriage; Julia Dallow's political ambition could be achieved only through a man; Peter Sherringham accepted as a necessary truth that he could not marry an actress. The aesthetic bachelor Nash's role was purely negative. The English were incapable of creating their own drama and must have the assistance of the cosmopolite Jew Miriam; she alone had the genius to become English or Jewish, masculine or feminine, as her will and ambition directed.

James's portrayals of women, of men whom today we would refer to as homosexual, and of racial character, were in some ways troubling at the time and have become even more disturbing today. In other stories, although his heroines were wonderful, he also drew portraits of conventionally foolish women like Biddy and, as in the case of Fanny Assignham, made their foolishness essentially female. In *The Tragic Muse* he gave what now seems an all-but-explicit and negative portrayal of an openly gay man. This latter has been particularly puzzling, because James's own loves were, so far as is known, exclusively male.

Critics have extensively explored James's seeming ambivalence toward Oscar Wilde in particular and homosexuality in general. James's Nash is a villain, and his villainy seems inextricably linked to his aestheticism and sexuality. Here and elsewhere, James seems to accept the conventional view that homosexual love is essentially immature and irresponsible. There is certainly a problem here.

But complexity of attitude is not ambivalence. James filled his stories with conventional types and employed here the conventional image of the homosexual; but it was no more a self-portrait than the lanky American men of his novels were self-portraits. While he somewhat lugubriously embraced the role of cosmopolitan bachelor, he was, and dutifully considered himself, a responsible man among men.

James's acceptance of conventional roles and stereotypes of race and gender, his belief in their essential truth, is distasteful. But there is not a great deal of difference, in the end, between his view of roles as realities that must be accepted, and the very modern view that while real, they are socially constructed. In one interesting scene, he has Miriam—who has inherited her father's Hebrew race—and her English mother reverse roles. The mother becomes for a moment conventionally Jewish and avaricious, while Miriam becomes an English gentlewoman. The artist of genius in any medium—of course we are to understand that this includes James—is free within limits to fashion herself.

One should not neglect James's message, that while the reality of social roles must be accepted, any role may be played with genius. Miriam is able to transcend usual roles, to have masculine talents and ambitions, to wear the costumes of France and England, and to make a rational marriage with a man who is content to play the role of wife. Nick eschews conventional marriage, but does not lapse into aestheticism; he begins to make of himself a creative artist. Nash is a villain, not because he is homosexual but because—although he is a man of genius—he refuses to make anything of himself other than a passive observer and manipulator: that vile being, a critic.

The serial was received in silence, and the book edition did not sell well. Macmillan ordered only a single printing of five hundred, Houghton, Mifflin printed only one thousand, and neither edition sold out; with advances long ago spent, James's income from his novels had fallen to nothing.

This commercial collapse was a serious matter, for artistically speaking the novel was the best he had yet written and seemed to meet all the criteria of popularity. It was narrated in simple, direct, and beautiful language; the characters were well drawn, the dialogue through which the action often proceeded was realistic, and the story was well told. The tragic conclusion emerged, as it were, ineluctably from the situation.

A large part of the problem, certainly, was James's implicit message that in a world of revolutions and the collapse of empires, most people— geniuses like Miriam and himself only excepted, and even they were free only within narrow limits—most people were obliged to accept their places in an ordered hierarchy of gender and race; that there were arts suitable for men, and others for women; that political democracy and class struggles were only so many performances. The convention-bound characters, despite their exquisitely detailed realism, were lifeless; they were on display like static works of art. James seemed able to be frank and exuberant only when playing the parts of the young heroine Miriam, and the villain Nash.

Whatever the trouble was, James had done his best, and had written what he knew to be a great novel. He was unwilling to devote another spell of years to such an effort, with so little reward, and accordingly decided to close at least for a time the first long chapter in his career as a man of letters. He was rightly confident of his mastery of his art, but the serialized novels that had supported him were evidently not going to continue to be profitable. While still at work on the closing chapters of *The Tragic Muse*, with the poor reception for the opening chapters already known, he wrote to Stevenson that it would be his last big novel, at least for "a longish period," and that he would instead devote himself to short works for the illustrated monthlies, and perhaps for the stage, that promised better returns for his labors:

> I want to leave a multitude of pictures of my time, projecting my small circular frame upon as many different spots as possible and going in for number as well as quality, so that the number may constitute a total having a certain value as observation and testimony.

When *The Tragic Muse* was at last done, and the two book editions seen through the press, he sent a copy to William, saying "*The Tragic Muse* is to be my last long novel."

While he was at his desk in De Vere Gardens, struggling to complete *The Tragic Muse*, the streets of the East End were filling with crowds, and the radical press gave them a voice. The success of a match girls' strike the summer before had spurred a peaceful revolution. Gas workers, who labored at ovens where high-sulfur coal was baked to make coal gas, working long hours in life-threatening conditions, demanded to bargain with their employers as a group. They struck and won shorter hours and the right to bargain on their own behalf. In August 1889, thousands of longshoremen, "dockers," following their example, went on strike, halting the flow of goods into the port of London. Huge street demonstrations were held, Cardinal Henry Manning spoke publicly on behalf of the striking workers, the Salvation Army provided assistance to them; public collections were taken up to support the strikers, and by the end of September the dockers had won a penny rise in the hourly wage and, most important of all, although not yet expressed formally, recognition of their right to join together and bargain as a group. The common-law doctrine that a labor union was a criminal conspiracy and a strike a crime was fading from memory. As Alice put it in her passionate way:

> Since the immortal Docker's Strike the face of *Labour* has been transformed, such a shaking up & "awakening" of humanity was never be-

fore seen, all brought about by the most peaceful & absolutely legitimate means & organization . . . 200 trades in London had gained 10%
increase of wages in consequence, the masters caving in to keep the
men from going on strike, Lord Rosebery & Sir Chas. Russell taking the
chair at 3. a. m. at great meetings of the tram & omnibus-men.

Just as the dockers' strike was concluding, a radical weekly, *The North
London Press*, picked up a story about the closing of a brothel on Cleveland Street. Police were conducting a futile campaign against the brothels of London, under the criminal law amendment of 1885, and two boys
had been charged with prostituting themselves. Ernest Parke, the editor
of the weekly, learned from police that the Cleveland Street brothel had
genteel customers and that aristocrats had been allowed to flee, while the
working-class boys they had corrupted were imprisoned. He announced
in his pages in September that there had been a cover-up, in which the
government was complicit. The trial of the "Telegraph Boys" made sensational copy. In November, Parke claimed that the earl of Euston and Lord
Somerset were among the gentlemen who had been allowed to flee. The
radical MP Henry Labouchère, whose 1885 bill had made the prosecution possible and who had his own tabloid newspaper, *Truth*, from which
to trumpet his views, took up the cry of conspiracy. He insisted that a
cover-up had been concocted by the Tory prime minister, Lord Salisbury,
to protect a member of the royal family. The names of Liberal leaders, including James's friend Rosebery, were thrown into the speculations as
well. There was a great uproar in the press, and Labouchère demanded an
investigation. The popular press had a new tone, moreover, a note of class
outrage. Great and powerful men were corrupting working-class boys, introducing them to the vices of the aristocracy, exploiting their poverty.

James was well aware of the Cleveland Street scandal and took note of
the political turn it had taken. He found it convenient to go to Paris for
several weeks at the time of the boys' trial, supposedly to consult with
Alphonse Daudet about his translation of Daudet's novel. A number of
other London men, including some of his friends who had expressed concern about the Labouchère Amendment, also found it convenient to be
abroad just then.

William Dean Howells again brought out a big novel, *A Hazard of New
Fortunes*, that ran in monthly installments simultaneously with James's.
Howells's novel too was about artists, writers, and illustrators, but the

background of Howells's tale was the gathering conflict of labor and capital. One saw a new industrial order rising, the injustices that it was creating, and the rebellion by labor. Battles were fought, a character was shot and killed. The author pointed out his moral, nothing was left to the reader's imagination. Howells's novel was not constructed or composed like a painting or a play, the story alone carried one forward to a happy ending.

James was unselfishly pleased for Howells's success and only a little jealous:

> I have just been reading with wonder & admiration Howells' last big novel, which I think so prodigiously good & able, & so beyond what he at one time seemed in danger of reducing himself to. . . . It seems to me to have an extraordinary life & truth, observation & feeling, & to contain, in old Dryfoos [the rapacious capitalist], a marvelous portrait. What one doesn't like in it doesn't in the least matter—it lives independently of all that. [Howells's] abundance & facility are my constant wonder & envy—or rather not perhaps envy inasmuch as he has purchased them by throwing the whole question of form, style & composition over board into the deep sea—from which, on my side, I am perpetually trying to fish them up.

He was reading also the advance sheets of Stevenson's new novel, *The Master of Ballantrae*, which he adored and thought would have a success. It was a short, ripping tale of men fighting for the lost Tory cause; there were pirates and an East Indian fakir and naked savages. There was no hint of serious purpose, the novel had only the ragged structure of a dream. It was written in Stevenson's matchless prose, and the mysterious charm of the dying author shone through his characters like the flame of a lamp. Reading it was "the intensest throb of my literary life . . . a pure hard crystal, my boy," James told Stevenson, "a work of ineffable and exquisite art." He was immensely cheered by the prospect that the Stevensons would be coming back to England soon. The family had lingered in Honolulu and put off their return, but Fanny had written to say they planned to make the trip home in September.

"Lead him on blushing, lead him back blooming, by the hand, dear Mrs. Louis," James replied, "and we will talk over everything, as we used to lang syne at Skerryvore."

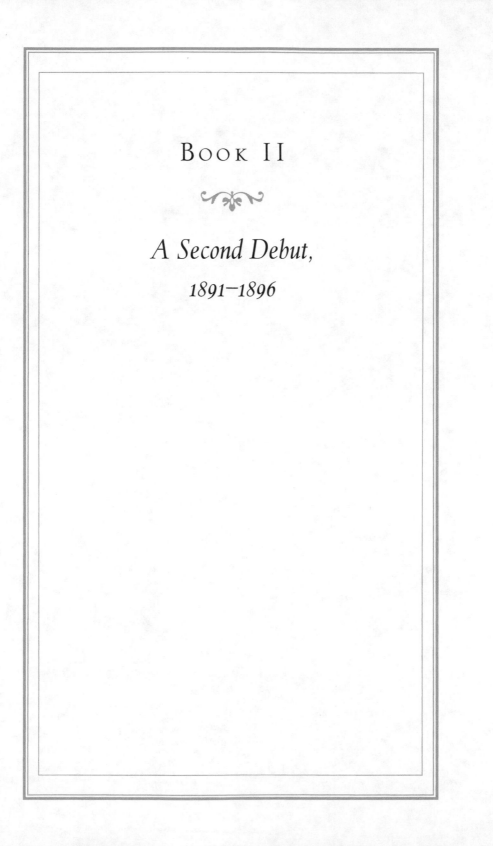

Book II

A Second Debut,

1891–1896

11

❧❀❧

COLLABORATION

When Henry James was thirteen years old and his family was at its most prosperous, they had lived for a summer in Paris, on the Champs-Élysées, in a great house between a walled courtyard and walled garden. Nearby were relatives and friends, including an Anglo-Irish family, Sir Joseph Olliffe and his wife and daughter. Olliffe had settled in Paris and was at that time physician to the British Embassy.

Henry sometimes joined his younger siblings on walks with their Parisian governess, Mlle. Danse, along the Champs-Élysées, where the governess pointed out ladies of fashion in their open carriages. It was the age of the Second Empire, and James always remembered the appearances of the young Empress Eugénie riding in her carriage from the Tuileries Palace to the Bois de Boulogne, and of the infant prince imperial in his quite separate appearances with his wet nurse, in an open carriage surrounded by troops of the mounted Imperial Guard, resplendent and erect in their light blue and silver uniforms, pistols raised and cocked; memories that would return to him at the end of his life.

Florence Olliffe, the daughter of their neighbor, was of an age with James's sister, Alice, and shared their experiences of that summer. More than twenty years later, Florence had married a young widower, Hugh Bell, and settled in London. James and she became friends, and her house on Sloane Street became one of the regular stops on his round of winter visits.

Florence Bell had a talent for languages, as James had; it had helped her to supervise the education of her talented stepdaughter, Gertrude Bell, who would be famous in her own right as an Arabist and architect of a new order in the Middle East. Florence was fluent in German and Italian as well as her native English and French, and was in the process of learning Gaelic; later, she would teach herself Norwegian and assist in making the first English translation of Henrik Ibsen's *The Master Builder*. She knew the French theater well, Coquelin was a mutual friend, and it was often in her company (and as her guest) that James saw new plays in the West End. He was a garrulous companion, and in her box felt free to comment audibly on performances.

Early in 1890, James began to write his own play, the adaptation of *The American* for which Edward Compton had asked. The novel was not ideally suited to dramatization, but this first effort would give him needed experience. He hoped to write a number of light plays for acting companies, beginning with the Comptons'.

The bar of commercial success did not seem to be set very high: hits of recent seasons had included Frances Hodgson Burnett's sentimental *Little Lord Fauntleroy*, based on her novel, and Arthur Pinero's saccharine Cinderella tale, *Sweet Lavender*. Pinero's popular farces, written for Marion Terry's company at the Royal Court Theatre, were making him a wealthy man. James thought he could do as well. The theater, after all, was booming. Until recently, the London stage had been controlled by a few holders of royal patents, who were permitted to perform only those plays licensed by the master of the royal household, the lord chamberlain. But theaters and acting companies were now multiplying rapidly, newly released from the system of monopolies and free to serve the swelling middle class who came in on suburban trains for an evening's entertainment. Any successful actor whose name was known to the public could organize his or her own company. An actor-manager would raise money, lease a theater (the most successful were building new theaters), and obtain a license from the lord chamberlain's office for it. The actor-manager would then buy a play, assemble a cast, and obtain a second license to perform the play. This second licensing step was often a matter of negotiation, in which the royal censors insisted on changes in a script before it could be performed.

The playwright was only a modest participant in this process. Many of the plays performed in London were hack translations from the French, prepared for a flat fee and freely altered by actors and censors, or old warhorses from the repertory bowdlerized to meet current sensibilities. While old monopolies were breaking up, a handful of leading actors held licenses to the principal venues of the West End—Henry Irving and Ellen Terry, John Hare, Herbert Beerbohm Tree, George Alexander, and a few others—and relied heavily on Shakespeare, Goldsmith, and other classic authors. *The Merchant of Venice* was a particular favorite, revived dozens of times in the late Victorian Age. Acting styles were old-fashioned, suited to the repertory. Actors spoke their lines in declamatory fashion and performed in a stylized manner, striking dramatic poses and holding them for minutes at a time while delivering their speeches—the "hand-to-forehead" style that would be recorded in early silent films.

Censorship by the royal household had recently been reaffirmed by statute, and Queen Victoria's lord chamberlain strictly maintained the old standards. The general tone of the West End theater therefore was that of polite conversation when young persons were present: sex, religion, and politics were not to be openly discussed. Living persons could not be portrayed (preventing political commentary or satire), clergymen of the Church of England could not be portrayed in an unfavorable light. Quotations or stories from the Bible, and references to the Deity, were forbidden (a relic of the Puritan wars against Catholicism and idolatry). Many of the standard plays of the French stage were banned because of their content. Classics by Corneille and Racine, and most modern French plays, could be performed in Britain only after violent emendation. It was for this stilted and stultified stage that Henry James was to write.

Edward Compton, who had asked James for a play, stood sturdily within Victorian tradition. He was a scion of the great Kemble-Siddons acting clan, genteel and preeminent royal patent holders for fifty years; but Compton was hoping to do something modern. At thirty-four, handsome and blond, he was the actor-manager of the Compton Comedy Company, which had been touring for several years. He was engaged to marry his leading lady, Virginia Bateman, herself the daughter of an old theatrical family. James found them cultured, polite, and respectful, and eager to put his work on the stage. It was pleasant to be among such handsome, intelligent young people, carrying forward traditions of the theater into the modern age. He allied himself with their plans and entered with enthusiasm into the project of turning his novel *The American* into a play. Written within the constraints of the illustrated magazines and lending libraries, James's work was eminently suitable for the censored stage.

"I must extract the simplest, strongest, baldest, most rudimentary, at once most humorous & most touching [play]" from his novel, James told himself; making no bones about art. "Oh, how it must not be too good & how very bad it must be!" The Comptons would perform the play first in provincial theaters, but they were thinking of leasing a theater in London, and if James's play succeeded on tour they might bring it to the West End.

. . .

In *The American*, as in the big novels that followed, the hero takes high but solitary ground. A westerner, Christopher Newman, who has made a fortune in mining country, comes to Paris to find a wife. He is "a plain man but a fine fellow" who becomes engaged to the widowed daughter of a French patrician house. The tyrannical dowager who heads the family, Mme. de Bellegarde, finds a better match for her daughter with a wealthy English lord and disdainfully throws over the plebeian Newman. The daughter, Claire, is devastated and flees to a convent.

Newman then plans melodramatically to revenge himself. He has learned a terrible family secret of the Bellegardes; to reveal it will be to destroy them. Recapitulating the plot for himself, James recalls: "Then he [Newman] does the characteristically magnanimous thing—the characteristically good-natured thing—throws away his opportunity—lets them 'off '—lets them go." In the novel, Newman is a tragic hero, in a modest way; but for the Compton Comedy Company this will not do; he must be humorous and touching. In the play, therefore, James tells himself, he must still be magnanimous—"*but* get his wife."

From the novel James extracts a bare, simple tale with a happy ending, half comedy and half melodrama. Compton, of course, will play the handsome hero, and his wife, Virginia Bateman, the beautiful widow Claire, who is no longer in her first youth.

James was willing to accommodate himself to the marketplace and considered himself a student of this new medium. He was struck by the changes it imposed upon a novel. He was obliged to strip away much of the static conversation with which the novel was ornamented. On the stage, dialogue must always and only advance the action. By spring, he had written a play in four acts that, read aloud, ran about three hours; too long. He would have to make cuts, but that step would wait until rehearsals began. He had determined to submit himself to the discipline of the commercial stage, whatever that might entail, evidently separating it in his mind from his serious work, as he had done long ago when he had tried to be a newspaper writer, to support himself in Paris.

Every week or two, James spent a day with Alice in Leamington. She had been indoors all winter and spring, but her spirits were high. Her journal provided occupation and even a kind of company for her. It was not merely a daybook but a serious effort at self-expression:

I have an exquisite 30 seconds every day: after luncheon I come in from my rest and before the window is closed I put my head out and drink in a long draft of the spring—made of the yellow glory of the daffodils on the balcony, the swelling twiggery of the trees in front, the breathless house-cleaning of the rooks, the gradation of light in transition, and the mystery of birth in the air.

In March, Alice wrote, "Henry came on the 10th, and spent the day."

Henry the patient, I should call him. Five years ago in November, I crossed the water and suspended myself like an old woman of the sea round his neck where to all appearances I shall remain for all time. I have given him endless care and anxiety but notwithstanding this and the fantastic nature of my troubles I have never seen an impatient look upon his face.

Her old writing desk had been sent over from Cambridge, and in it Alice found a trove of old letters, including many from her father and mother, that brought back memories. It seemed as if Alice could at last forgive and part from her old parents, and she talked about them with Henry and wept over them for the first time.

When James's play was written, Balestier's partner, the publisher William Heinemann, set it in type and ran off copies for the acting company. On May 5, Compton came up to London to talk it over. Compton evidently was pleased with the play, and they discussed the production. James was gradually assuming the role of what a later generation would call the "director." He had the whole play printed in multiple copies for the cast, instead of the customary prompt copies, so that the performers could prepare their parts with understanding. He provided detailed stage directions for the actors' movements and gestures; he specified details of sets and costumes, and Compton seemed to welcome the direction and asked for more. When later in the year they began to plan a London production, James cast the parts, with Compton's agreement, attended the rehearsals, and gave notes to the actors. He confided to Alice even at this early stage that he thought he would have to "work over them" immensely.

As rehearsals proceeded, Compton began to speak more definitely of bringing *The American* to the West End, perhaps in the spring of the following year. Alice entered vicariously into the project with her whole heart, wishing perhaps even more than Henry did for a financial success that would make her dependence on him less burdensome.

On May 8, James carried a copy of the printed script out to Leamington for Alice. He found Alice at ease on her sofa, in the front room where she spent her afternoons, "placid and cheerful." Alice was alone, but she assured Henry that she would be all right. Her spirits were good, and the warm weather would come soon and bring the joy of outings in the lanes and fields.

Reassured about Alice and released from duty for a few weeks, he left a stream of happy letters trailing behind him, declining invitations and apologizing for his absence, and fled to Italy for a ten-week working vacation. He spent June in Venice, at the Curtises' Barbaro Palace, where he began and perhaps completed one or two more plays, a comedy for the Comptons' company (*Mrs. Jasper*) and perhaps a melodrama.

A letter from Wolcott Balestier reached him in Venice. Balestier had negotiated a favorable agreement with the Comptons that anticipated a successful London run for *The American*. The Comptons had asked for world rights to the play, so that they might tour with it abroad, and in return James was to receive 10 percent of gross revenues, once production costs had been met. After the London production there would be touring companies in America and Australia, as well as in Great Britain.

Greatly excited by the Comptons' enthusiasm and Balestier's confidence, he worked away at playwriting. The upstairs apartment at the Barbaro was an ideal place for work, and he settled into the glistening quiet of the library. "The peace and leisure of it, the exemption from 'pressure' are not to be said—they are blessings only to be devotedly inhaled." The Curtises were fond of him and offered to rent the upstairs apartment to him for a nominal forty pounds a year, so that it would be always available to him, and he thought that if his dramatic venture were a success he would accept their offer.

A letter from Alice too caught up with him in Venice, with more praise of *The American*. He replied at great length:

> I am ravished by your letter . . . which makes me feel as if there had been a triumphant première & I had received overtures from every managerial quarter & had only to count my gold. . . . I can do a dozen more infinitely better; & am excited to think how much, since the writ-

ing of this piece has been an education to me, a little further experience will do for me.

His brief submission to actualities was forgotten, and he now happily calculated the possible, the *probable* profits of his first venture on the stage. From the London run alone, he might expect £350 a month, "Which, as a steady thing, would seem to me a fortune." The revenues from touring companies in Great Britain, the United States, and Australia would be in addition. Of course, they had not yet performed the play for an audience; but "these castles in Spain are at least exhilarating."

A telegram from Alice asked him to hurry home, as she was ill once more. He hastened to her bedside in Leamington, traveling by rail without breaking his journey for rest and arriving in London early in August. Alice had been suffering from what at first seemed to be a digestive disorder. Rather ominously, she had lost her appetite for food, as their father had done in his last weeks, and Henry found her emaciated and weak. He immediately telegraphed Katherine Loring that the situation was grave. The physician whom Henry called in—an old friend from Florence, William Baldwin, who was visiting London—confirmed that in her present state, Alice might die (to which she responded fiercely, in her diary, "This most cheering to all parties!").

On September 2, Katherine arrived and immediately took Alice with her to the South Kensington Hotel, where appetizing food could be prepared to order. Under Katherine's care Alice recovered somewhat from her deep depression and was able to eat. The extraction of a rotten tooth helped matters further, and by October the danger seemed to have passed. But Alice remained terribly weak, as Henry dutifully reported to William: "Her weakness is utter & complete—such an effort as taking her breakfast, in bed, with every aid, prop & service, quite overcomes her." This, perhaps, was the dreadful progress of the heart ailment. Katherine settled in for the winter, and James did not think she would able to leave Alice alone again while she still lived.

A letter from Stevenson arrived with news of what was for James a great disappointment: "I must tell you plainly . . . I do not think I shall come to England more than once, and then it'll be to die." Even the subtropical climate of Sydney was too cold for him; England was impossible.

I was never fond of towns, houses, society, or (it seems) civilization. . . .
The sea, islands, the islanders, the island life and climate, make and
keep me truly happier. These last two years I have been much at sea,
and I have *never wearied*.

His next letter would be from Samoa. Months would pass before James
felt able to respond. Stevenson's "tragic statement" had silenced him.
When he did reply, he said that he could hardly fault the decision: "I
couldn't—I didn't—protest; I even mechanically assented; but I couldn't
talk about it." But missing Stevenson "was always a perpetual ache."

James's play was in rehearsals. He had so far spoken very little about his
new project, being unsure of its prospects and having a horror of newspaper paragraphs. Now he confided in Florence Bell, promised that he
would ask her to join him at a rehearsal of *The American* when she had
returned from the country, and sent her a printed copy of the play, accompanied by elaborate explanations. When she was at home again in
London, they began to discuss the casting of the centrally important part
of the villain, Mme. de Bellegarde, the wicked patrician.

Bell's friend Geneviève Ward seemed ideal for the part: past fifty, she
was the right age, she was an accomplished tragedienne with a magnificent voice and a classical manner, well able to carry off the part of an Old
World French aristocrat. James asked Bell to approach her and to lend
her a copy of the printed script. He waited anxiously for a reply: Ward
could be the making of the play. On October 14, James had still not
heard "the voice of the oracle," but he thanked Florence Bell for her
"promptitude and grace" in approaching the actress. A few days later, he
wrote to say that he would like to have his printed copy of the script returned, although he would be glad to leave it a little longer with Ward if
her convenience required it.

Bell finally advised James to see the actress himself: Ward had turned
down the play, saying rather strangely that the novel had been done before. "Many thanks for your note & all your trouble," he replied. "I *will* go
see Miss Ward . . . but, dear lady, is it not partly because with all her man-
ifest virtues she is essentially (let me write it in capitals but very small) a
GOOSE?"

James called on Miss Ward, read to her at least a portion of *The American*, and presumably reassured her that it had not been done before. She
continued to refuse, however, and James told Florence Bell that he

thought the problem was money; but it may also have been that at fifty-two Ward was not yet ready to play an old woman. James evidently saw that that was the true difficulty, for he sat down to write a new play with a more youthful role for her.

He was following the Compton company around the country, as it played a series of short engagements in seaside towns. From Yarmouth it went to Portsmouth for two days, followed by a week in Brighton and then a week in Northampton. Afternoons, its members would rehearse *The American*, and James would sit on the cold, unheated stage with the actors, making suggestions as to readings and gestures, commenting afterward—giving "notes," as one says now. He spent a good deal of time separately with Compton, talking through with him the character of Newman, on which the performance depended.

In the mornings, while the actors slept, James worked at the new play for Miss Ward. He took plot and characters ready-made from a French story that he had in memory: the tale of a middle-aged man who encounters the mistress of his bachelor years. It was to be called *Mrs. Vibert*, and the title role was to be a still youthful woman of middle age, who appears in the opening acts to be an unprincipled seductress, powerfully twisting men and women to her will, but who would prove in the denouement to be a noble figure, sacrificing herself for an illegitimate son.

He spun out this graceful little melodrama in about a month, and then the phase of collaboration began. He read it to Florence Bell and made revisions at her suggestion. He invited Geneviève Ward to tea at De Vere Gardens to discuss the play, and then read the first two acts of the play to Ward and her leading man, W. H. Vernon. The next morning, James sent Florence Bell an enthusiastic report: "the reading yesterday was a high success. . . . Miss W. is to take it immediately to *Hare*." John Hare was the most successful of the actor-managers and had his own theater.

In the midst of this bustle and intensity, William sent news that the book that he had been working at for a dozen years, his *Principles of Psychology*, had been published. Not long before, Wendell Holmes had published his own great work, *The Common Law*, in which he organized the data of the common law on scientific principles. In their shipboard conversations, William and Wendell had renewed their friendship; now William had constructed his own monument of scholarship, an effort to establish psychology as an empirical science, to stand beside Wendell's and Henry's books. He was at last able to meet his brother and his boyhood friend on an equal footing. Letters passed among the three men. Wendell wrote, "I have read your book—every word of it—with delight & admiration." But Holmes was careful to defend his own hard materialism against William's tolerant pluralism.

Henry dipped into William's massive work despite the urgent press of his own affairs and wrote his brother that he found much to praise in the "mighty & magnificent" work. He was glad to help in publicizing it, by reading a paper for William in Cambridge at a meeting of the Psychical Research Society.

The Principles of Psychology was nominally a textbook; it had grown out of the course that William had been teaching, but it was an enormous work unlike any ordinary text: fourteen hundred pages of small type in two clumsy, ill-bound volumes. A sustained monologue, it was a performance by William James as teacher: humorous, frankly confiding, self-revealing, argumentative. William had assembled a varied array of data—reports of laboratory experiments on animals, naturalistic observations, studies of other human beings, and years of introspection. It was an admirable, engaging book, and Wendell was right to say that it would establish William's reputation.

The book was quarrelsome, however, and William set himself apart from Henry by his choice of subject and his simple, direct style. He omitted entirely any discussion of pleasure or pain and did not treat of ethics or morality. William's was a psychology of consciousness and ego. To the question of sexuality, William devoted a single page to making the point that in "the higher vertebrates" the sexual instinct was under the control of the cerebral hemispheres and in humans subordinated to their unique consciousness:

> No one need be told how dependent all human social elevation is upon
> the prevalence of chastity. Hardly any factor measures more than this
> the difference between civilization and barbarism.

Yet, although William always seemed to be arguing, he, his brother, and Wendell all proceeded from common premises. Their studies were empirical, and their attention was turned to the solitary, paramount self and its powerful will. Holmes's addresses were a paean to the triumph of the will, and from the immense mass of data in William's book, as from

Henry's novels, there gradually emerged a sense of Self, consciousness mysteriously embodied in flesh.

The Compton Comedy Company went off for a last tour, during Christmas week, before settling in Southport for dress rehearsals and the opening of *The American*. James occupied himself with writing yet another play, perhaps a comedy for the Comptons. He had managed to avoid unwelcome press attention during the rehearsals of his play, but the secret was out now, and a leading theater critic, William Archer, wrote to him at Christmastime to ask about it. James replied promptly, cautiously:

> I am much obliged to you for your interest in an obscure & tremulous venture. It *is* true that a play of mine is to be produced at a mysterious place called Southport, which I have never seen, a week from tonight. . . . I won't deny that I should be glad to know that the piece was seen by a serious critic & by yourself in particular, but . . . the place is far, the season inclement, the interpretation *extremely* limited.

On December 29, James wrote to Florence Bell, anxiously asking her to join him at Southport to see the final dress rehearsal. Edward and Virginia Compton were both sick in bed, and James was growing apprehensive: "the curtain may never rise," and if it ever did it might fall on his "suicide."

The illness passed, the opening was not delayed, and William Archer answered in friendly fashion that he would like to see the play. He and the author agreed to go up together into the wilds of Lancashire for the premiere Saturday night, January 3, 1891. As the moment drew near, however, James decided to take an earlier train, so that he did not see Archer until after the performance. Florence Bell was in Yorkshire with her family for the holidays and could not attend. Only Wolcott Balestier went to Southport with James, who was in a high state of nerves.

Southport was a seaside resort in the new fashion, with amusement piers and bathing, on the Irish Sea ten miles north of Liverpool. James called it "the Brighton of Liverpool." On their arrival Saturday afternoon, James and Balestier checked into the Prince of Wales Hotel. James wrote letters, perhaps walked through the town, filling time until the performance.

When it was time, Balestier took a seat in the stalls, but James nervously went backstage and watched from the wings. He thought Compton was doing very well, far better than he had done in rehearsal, had risen to the occasion, and was acting most interestingly and admirably. After the first act, James flung himself on the actor and asked whether it was going.

"Going?—Rather. You could hear a pin drop."

After that, James thought he could feel and hear the audience responding. When the final curtain fell, the actors took their bows and there were cries from the audience for the author. James lingered in the wings, but the cast pushed him out onto the stage, where he stood beside Compton and took a bow. The applauding audience "emitted agreeable sounds from a kind of gas-flaring indistinguishable dimness." The audience applauded and, when Compton and James retired, called them out again, and then a third time. On the third curtain call, Compton turned to James, seized both his hands, and wrung them, smiling. James's intense nervousness had given way to a "simmering serenity." He remained on stage for a few moments longer, bowing and gesturing, and then retired.

Afterward, Balestier brought William Archer to their rooms in the hotel, and Archer eagerly gave detailed criticisms of the play; but James was wrapped in the glow of his triumph and paid little attention. Soon the Comptons came to the door and, bowing Archer out, James took the actors and Balestier downstairs to supper. Edward Compton and Virginia Bateman were radiant, and James was still serene. He felt as if they were victorious generals, celebrating after a battle. They talked of their plans; Compton hoped to make a great success with this play.

The next day, the company packed up and traveled to Birmingham for their next engagement. James and Balestier went with them, and later James fondly recalled the sociable, amused sense of participation in the traveling company's life that he and Balestier shared, in the slow-moving, halting Sunday trains, with frequent pauses in railroad stations, meals in refreshment rooms, and then another hotel suite in Birmingham.

On Monday, James, Balestier, and the actors talked again. The play was certainly going to London. The Comptons would lease an old theater in the Strand, the Opera Comique. Filled with confidence, Edward Compton wanted to take a year's lease, planning to open with *The American* in the fall. James had given him also a comedy, presumably *Mrs. Jasper,* that he had written in Italy, for Compton "to have in his pocket" for the season that would follow.

. . .

Shortly after his return to De Vere Gardens, James received a highly flattering letter from John Hare, who was having an enormous success of his
own as the actor-manager of the new Garrick Theatre. *Mrs. Vibert*, Hare
wrote, the play that James had written for Miss Ward, was a masterpiece
of dramatic construction, and within weeks an agreement was struck—
Hare was definitely to produce *Mrs. Vibert*, with Geneviève Ward in the
title role, as soon as the Garrick's stage was empty. The Garrick was the
preeminent theater of the season, where Arthur Pinero's hit, *Lady Boun-
tiful*, currently held the stage and where Hare wanted next to mount a revival. *Mrs. Vibert* would then follow. Hare spoke of James's play in the
warmest terms, and with a sure sense of what would please the author
best told him that it was meant for the Comédie-Française.

A few days after his return to London, on January 27, 1891, James went
with Florence Bell and Geneviève Ward to see a matinee performance of
A Doll's House. Matinees were the off Broadway of the London theater,
where experimental and foreign plays could be staged cheaply. Ibsen's
play had been performed before, in poor translations, but this new staging was said to show the qualities that were making him famous on the
Continent. James went to some trouble to attend, for tickets were scarce,
and he asked Ward to obtain one for him; she in turn asked Elizabeth
Robins, a young American actress who had a part in the play. His new
friend William Archer, who had grown up in Norway and was bilingual in
English and Norwegian—and who moreover knew the stage and had a
sense of what could be spoken—had done the translation.

Ibsen's was a new kind of realism, for which in truth the London stage
was not yet ready. Ibsen's plays were impolite and addressed questions
that were not proper. The plays did not resolve themselves into harmony;
instead, the action had the strange irrationality of the natural world. A
young lawyer, who has done everything that according to convention he
should and has preserved his honor, is shipwrecked. His young wife, with
the vigor of youth, smashes the structure of convention upon which their
lives have been built and escapes from their doll's house. As her husband
angrily says, the whole system of religion, duty, and honor is called into
question. Not only the position of women in marriage, but marriage itself
and the hypocrisy that it rests upon, make victims of all the characters
and spreads its destruction down through the generations.

Newspaper reviewers were divided in their reactions. For some, *A
Doll's House* was simply a play about the position of women, a lesson that

supposedly had been learned. Some critics saw its deeper radicalism and were troubled. Clement Scott, writing for *The Daily Telegraph*, said that Nora was a "socialist." Walter Besant, the guardian of the gates of art, wrote an attack on *A Doll's House*. James, however, was moved and interested by the performance, and set himself to learn more about the puzzling drama that was summoning up a new realistic style of acting.

Later that spring, after the revival of *A Doll's House*, there was a production of Ibsen's *Ghosts*, in which the theme of venereal disease was prominent and explicit. The lord chamberlain's office refused to license a public performance, but a club, the Independent Theatre was organized, the Royalty Theatre was rented, and subscriptions were sold for a nominally private matinee performance on March 13. James was among the subscribers.

There were two more Ibsen premieres that spring. James was abroad when *Rosmersholm* was staged for the first time in English, but he returned to London in time for the opening performance, in April, of *Hedda Gabler* at the Vaudeville Theatre. James called it the story of "an exasperated woman." Reviewing the performance and the play, James said that there was little action, little plot: *Hedda Gabler* was the portrait of an embodied personality, "the individual caught in the fact." Later, he would say that, like others of Ibsen's plays, *Hedda Gabler* had a mysterious quality. The published text seemed thin and abstract, but when performed it became a living thing, the characters on stage were like "lamps burning, as in tasteless parlors, with the flame practically exposed."

Florence Bell, and even Geneviève Ward, who had appeared with Elizabeth Robins in an early performance of Ibsen's *Pillars of Society*, did not care for Ibsen and were surprised by James's interest. It was their young friend, Elizabeth Robins, to whom the new plays spoke. James admired Robins's performance as Mrs. Linden in *A Doll's House*, and then later that spring as Hedda Gabler. He invited her to dine with him at De Vere Gardens. After dinner, he gingerly approached the question of her playing the part of a middle-aged housekeeper in *The American* that fall, a proposal she heard with some surprise. James evidently still thought of her as Mrs. Linden, but as he saw her reaction to his proposal he became aware of the attractive young woman in the armchair facing him.

With his first play well launched on tour and Katherine on duty, James fled the duties and distractions of London and settled into a hotel on the rue de la Paix for a month. This was extravagant, but he felt entitled to a treat after the long strain of rehearsals, and he thought that he would be able to do some work while he was in Paris.

His theatrical success, for all its promise, had not yet produced any revenue. *The American* was doing well on tour and had great successes in Belfast and Edinburgh; but having it in their repertory meant only that the Comptons would perform it once a week, on Friday nights. James's 10 percent share of the gate for that weekly performance was only about five pounds; for the effort to be more remunerative, he would have to wait for the London production. Until then, he would turn again to writing for illustrated magazines; not a serialized novel, for he had vowed not to undertake another, but short stories tailored to the narrow specifications of the new mass market.

Almost two years had passed since he had last published a short story, and he set to his task as if to a new medium. Fifty pages in a notebook, with 150 or 200 words to the page, he calculated, would make a short story of the right size for the illustrated magazines. A new journal had been launched in London, *Black and White*, and he had promised it a story; it was the first to which he turned his attention in Paris. The working title was "The Servant," a portrait of an elderly bachelor, "the most agreeable, the most lovable of bachelors," and young Brooksmith, "his butler and his most intimate friend," who lived together like an old married couple and together kept a salon.

And there was du Maurier's anecdote, ready to hand, about a genteel couple who have fallen on hard times and seek work as artist's models. The artist to whom they apply needs models to portray aristocrats to illustrate a magazine serial and takes them on. Their little tragedy is appealing and typical; but what will make it a story? The tale came to him "at a bound": why, the husband and wife will fail; they will be unable to represent their type but remain merely personal. A couple of Cockney models, talented performers, far outdo them as models for gentlefolk.

The third of the stories he sets down in quick succession is "The Pupil." It is another small scene: a family of Europeanized Americans, the Moreens, who live by not paying their bills, have hired a tutor for their eleven-year-old son, meaning to cheat him of his salary. The child, Morgan, is sickly and plain but supernaturally bright; the tutor comes to love him, and the boy returns his love. The tutor, Pemberton, is like the charming, foolish Hjalmar Ekdal in Ibsen's *Wild Duck:* he is tricked into staying on and on, in the Moreens' house, without being paid, for the sake of the child. At last the crash comes; the Moreens collapse utterly and ask him to take the boy. He pauses; his courage fails, but the boy is radiant at the possibility of living with his tutor. The child's emotion is too much for him, his frail heart stops, and he dies ecstatically in the tutor's arms.

These stories were, as James told himself they should be, "little gem[s] of bright, quick, vivid form." In two of the stories, he returned to love themes of his early success. Characters were rapidly, indelibly sketched; language was plain and precise, and there was a deep good humor behind even the tragic tales. Each picture composed itself as if in a dramatic scene, glimpsed within the small frame of the story, and owed perhaps as much to Ibsen as to Maupassant.

By early summer, he had written a half dozen of these short, confident, exuberant, realistic new stories. One could see, if one cared to, that the tales exemplified ideas James had expounded in his didactic novels and essays. Tutors, fathers, lovers, and husbands exercised their power over the young. In Arcadian gardens, charming heroes and heroines, having eaten of the "acrid fruit of the tree of knowledge," were freed to choose and to act. Artists of life, they chose well or badly, occasionally rising to the height of the sublime. One could see in the background the structural elements of morality and duty, if one cared to; the stories did not insist on them.

Alfred Parsons, Ned Abbey, and John Sargent had gone together to America the year before, to see whether they could exploit their considerable European success. They were accompanied by a friend, Gertrude Mead—a wealthy American a little older than they, who had become a patron of the Broadway painters. The four had now returned to England, and James was surprised to learn that Gertrude Mead was now Mrs. Abbey. She and Ned had been married in her father's house in Manhattan. At forty, tall, handsome, athletic, and strong-minded, Gertrude was both wife and patron. Blessed with inherited wealth, she was subsidizing big new projects for both Sargent and Abbey. The two young men were to provide murals for the new public library in Boston, a cathedral of the humanist faith. Abbey was to do a series of vast canvases, 8 feet high and 180 feet long, to decorate the walls of the "distribution room," on a subject of his own choosing. Sargent was to do another of the rooms, on the theme of the history of religion. It was understood that Gertrude would subsidize their projects.

Work on the scale required could not be done in the studios Sargent and Abbey had in Chelsea, and upon their return Gertrude rented Morgan Hall, an estate in Gloucestershire not far from Broadway, that could house both of the painters' new projects. Sargent went to Egypt for the winter, to immerse himself in the history of religions. James came down to have a look at Morgan Hall in November, as did Parsons, and each gave it his blessing. The house was a large, ivy-grown Tudor, surrounded by walled gardens and with ample level ground within the walls for construction of a studio.

While Gertrude superintended the renovation of the house and building of a new studio, Ned went to London and stayed at the Reform Club as James's guest. James often dined with him at the Reform or met him in the grillroom of the South Kensington Museum (the present-day Victoria and Albert), where Abbey was studying costumes. Abbey had chosen for his subject "the search for the Holy Grail"—a series of paintings portraying the birth of Romance. James looked on benignly, and when he came down to view the renovations of Morgan Hall, he twitted Gertrude on her extravagance. The new studio she was building beside the house was a steel structure, very modern, the largest studio space in England, perhaps in Europe—64 feet long, 40 wide, and 25 high—with three enormous skylights in the long northern wall. Sargent and Abbey would each be able to set up several canvases, Sargent at the east end and Abbey at the west—and pose their groups of models in period costume. Both their projects required what amounted to stage sets for the models, a panoply of props and costumes, arms and armor, architectural details and tapestries, a library of reference works, for all of which Gertrude made provision. By April 1891, the studio was ready. Gertrude and her bachelors, Sargent and Abbey, settled in to Morgan Hall; James was a frequent visitor, and Parsons took his own house nearby.

Alice, too, was now settled. The South Kensington Hotel, in which she had taken emergency quarters, was noisy and crowded, and Alice had grown fearful of dying in such impersonal surroundings. She and Henry agreed that when death seemed imminent, she would be carried to his flat. But she was better that spring, and Katherine found a tidy little house in Kensington for them, where James could easily make his daily calls and where Alice would not mind spending her last moments. "We are so absurdly happy in our decidedly silly little house," Alice told her diary. "The tone of the household is quite sublimated, full of a serene interchange of amenities."

Into this quiet moment came the news that a painful lump in Alice's breast was cancerous. Her physician, Sir Andrew Clark, after a thorough examination told her also that her heart ailment—probably the congestive heart failure from which her brothers would also suffer—was very serious. No treatment was possible for either disease. All that could be done was to alleviate the pain of the growing tumor and the periodic attacks of angina.

Years later, in *The Wings of the Dove*, James would describe at length a fictional heroine's experience as she learned of her fatal illness and was brought face-to-face with the ultimate fact. Alice was more succinct:

> To any one who has not been there, it will be hard to understand the enormous relief of Sir A. C.'s uncompromising verdict, lifting us out of the formless vague and setting us within the very heart of the sustaining concrete.

But Clark was reluctant to prescribe morphia for pain and was indeed vague about the likely course of the diseases, so that Alice soon was plunged once more into frightening uncertainty. She might die of her heart ailment in a week or so; but she might yet live for some months in great pain while the cancer spread. She became irritable and teased Nurse Bradford about her belief that Alice, although a Unitarian and not a communicant of the one true church, would yet enter Heaven.

There was necessary talk about funeral arrangements. Alice wished to be cremated, and Katherine inquired how to arrange for cremation at Kensal Green. Alice would also have liked to have a Unitarian minister perform a modest funeral service but feared she would end with the Church of England, Unitarians being scarce in the neighborhood. When her pain grew greater and Clark still declined to prescribe an opiate, James asked his friend and physician William Baldwin to intervene, and after examining Alice he prescribed morphine, which greatly relieved her pain. Katherine prepared a fatal dose that Alice could take if her suffering became intolerable.

James visited every day and preserved his cheerful demeanor, but the various strains upon him began to make themselves felt. A cold had persisted and deepened and showed itself for influenza. His lower back once again began to pain him badly.

By July, it had become clear that Alice would still have some months of life. James was tired and ill and longed for escape from the meshes of the Season, and perhaps from Alice's bedside as well. Feeling able to leave her for a time, he went up to Oxford for three or four days to visit with Constance Woolson, who had settled there. Oxford was quiet in the "delightful" long vacation—"emptiness and greenery"—but he soon picked up again and set off for Ireland.

Home rule for Ireland was the great topic of conversation again, and at first he thought he would go to Dublin. The storm of a divorce suit had broken over Parnell, just as he emerged from the collapse of the commission hearings, and the Liberal home-rule program seemed in ruins, with the threat of renewed violence looming. James once more thought of writing about the gathering revolution, the topic that was on every tongue. Wolseley was now commander of British forces in Ireland, Arthur Balfour was home secretary for the island, and both were in residence in Dublin; James would have the entrée to Irish affairs that he needed.

The ferry from Holyhead landed him in Kingstown (now Dun Laoghaire), a little English enclave, a port city just south of Dublin. The long arms of the East and West Piers enclosed the harbor, and behind the town rose low cliffs. He thought that when he had recovered fully he would visit Dublin and then tour along the coast southward to Queenstown, in the interest of journalism. The influenza dragged on, however, and he simply collapsed into his hotel and did not make any effort to visit Dublin or tour the troubled south. He walked in the mild sun, wrote letters, and thought about new stories.

The genuinely short story, written for a single number of a magazine, within a budgeted fifty pages of manuscript, was essentially a new form for him, as new as the stage play. These two forms were the medium in which he was now to have a second career, the small circular frames through which to capture his glimpses. Plays and stories seemed to fit together, to be part of the same general effort:

> I must hammer away at the effort . . . . I have done a ½ dozen [short stories], lately, but it takes time & practice to get into the trick of it. I have never attempted before to deal with such extreme brevity. . . . I must absolutely not tie my hands with promised novels if I wish to keep them free for a genuine & sustained attack on the theatre. That is one cogent reason out of many, but the artistic one would be enough by itself . . . the consideration that by doing short things I can do so many, touch on so many subjects, break out in so many places, handle so many of the threads of life.

James made a series of Xs here, to mark the passage of time. When he returned to the journal, he picked up the thread of his thought, as if he had been pursuing it while he walked on the cliffs over the bay.

> However, I have threshed all this out; it exists in my mind, in the shape of absolutely digested & assimilated motive—inspiration deep & clear. The upshot of all such reflections is that I have only to let myself go! . . . All life is—at my age, with all one's artistic soul the record of it—in one's pocket, as it were. Go on, my boy, & strike hard; have a rich & long St. Martin's summer. Try everything, do everything, render everything—be an artist, be distinguished, to the last.

He set to work on stories that for the most part were slight: glimpses of the superficial life around him, somewhat in the mode of Maupassant. But in one brief tale he seemed to honor his pledge to "let go."

"Collaboration" is enacted, like a play, in a single setting, a Parisian salon where on Sunday evenings guests relax on brocaded cushions, while cigarette smoke drifts up toward the high, frescoed ceiling. The principal characters are Herman Heidenmauer, a highly cosmopolitan and intelligent German composer, and Félix Vendemer, a French poet, who meet in the salon. Heidenmauer plays the piano and entrances Vendemer with his music and his conversation; they form a warm friendship and decide to collaborate on an opera.

The scene is a complex metaphor, and the story might stand for a little essay on the evils of nationalism. Art, like civilization, is a harmony of disparate elements: a collaboration.

The two principal characters and their cross-border friendship resembled that of the German-Jewish William Heinemann and the American Wolcott Balestier. Their collaborative art recalled not only James's experiences in the theater but the artistic collaboration of Sargent and Abbey in their happy ménage with Gertrude Mead; the other collaborations of writers and illustrators at Broadway that he had celebrated in essays; his own friendship with Balestier. For the first time, in this story, James allows the friendship of two men to dominate their affections and a male friend to displace a female rival.

Quietly, and with suppressed humor, James portrays the cosmopolitan world of art and contrasts it with the jingoism of national rivalries. The mutual embrace of the two men is contrasted with the bitter memories of those around them, of past wars and preparations for future wars in France and Germany. The two men are, to be sure, characteristic German and French national types; but their friendship will produce a new art form.

The world will not accept their intimacy. Heidenmauer knows that he will be condemned in Germany for collaborating with a Frenchman; Vendemer is aware that his friendship with a German is already being commented upon in Paris. But they are caught up in the enthusiasm of their affection. "You'll injure my career. Oh yes, I shall suffer!" Heidenmauer joyously, exultingly cries; and Vendemer exclaims, "And I as well!"

The narrator of the tale grows alarmed and warns Vendemer of being "deliberately perverse." But the Frenchman flashes out in his own defense. There is a moment of ambiguity as to what is meant, what sort of perversity he is being warned against. But Vendemer defends himself against all bigotries. The greatest crime that can be perpetrated against art is "the hideous invention of patriotism":

> In art there are no countries—no idiotic nationalities, no frontiers, no *douanes*, nor still more idiotic fortresses and bayonets. It has the unspeakable beauty of being the region in which those abominations cease, the medium in which such vulgarities simply can't live.

Disregarding convention, the two men go to Italy, where they live together and work at writing an opera. They are poor—Heidenmauer's family withdraws his allowance because of his "unnatural alliance" and tells him that it will not be restored until his "unholy union" is dissolved. But the narrator of the tale confesses that he has heard snatches of the opera and that it may be truly epoch-making.

> There are still other details which contribute to the interest of the episode and which, for me, help to render it a most refreshing, a really great little case. It rests me, it delights me, there is something in it that makes for civilization. In their way they are working for human happiness.

The narrator of the tale falls out of character and remarks hopefully, "Don't we live fast, after all, and doesn't the old order change? Don't say art isn't mighty! I shall give you some more illustrations of it yet."

Wolcott Balestier had gone to the Isle of Wight, where he had taken a house for the summer. In August, a few days after his return from Ireland,

James went out to join him. He and Balestier lingered beyond their time, despite repeated pleas from Balestier's office to return to London. Afterward, James would remember with particular fondness a sunny afternoon spent with Balestier, "as if it were a leaf out of an old-fashioned drawing book":

> It was given all to a long drive to Freshwater, much of the way over the firm grass of the great downs, and a lunch there and rambling, lazy lounge on the high cliffs (with the full sense of summer. . .) and a still lazier return in the golden afternoon, amid all sorts of delicacies of effect of sea and land. He [Balestier] loved the little temporary home he had made on the edge of the sea . . . and no season of his life, probably, in spite of haunting illness, had given him more contented hours.

They had been together a great deal during the year, from the time that Balestier had loyally accompanied James to Southport on that cold January night to provide moral support at his premiere. After their shared days and nights in Southport and Birmingham, Balestier had been a frequent guest at James's flat, and James had been a frequent visitor to Balestier's office. The few summer days they now spent on the Isle of Wight marked a deepening of their intimate friendship. Alice wrote in her diary, after that summer, that she hoped Balestier would be a lifelong companion, as well as a business friend, for James.

Rehearsals of *The American* and preparations for its London opening, now scheduled for September 26, were under way. The parts of the older women still had to be cast, and it was difficult to find actors for them; in the end, Virginia Compton's older sister was asked to play the villain Mme. de Bellegarde, the part that James thought would have been so well suited to Geneviève Ward. Virginia herself was now pregnant and would not be able to play the heroine, Claire de Cintré, as she had in Southport. Elizabeth Robins, who had reluctantly agreed to play a serving woman, Mrs. Bread, was promoted to the role of heroine. She was just shy of thirty years old, the right age for the part. But she was an American and, while handsome and charming, was neither the Old World aristocrat nor the great beauty for whom the part seemed to call. Yet she was sufficiently talented, James thought, to remedy these deficiencies. Robins was delighted and indeed left a more lucrative part in the West End for the chance to join James's little company.

When rehearsals began in London, James attended them assiduously, endearing himself to the cast by bringing hampers of sandwiches, prepared by Mrs. Smith, for the actors. He wrote to Florence Bell, who was in Yorkshire with her family, wistfully inviting her to return to London, to stay with him and assist with the rehearsals. With the experience of a dozen performances behind him and with a new cast, James began to make revisions to the play. The actors made notes of the blocking, and of revisions that James made, in their copies of the scripts. James and Virginia Compton began to choose costumes for the female characters, and he was able to amuse Alice with a swatch of the fabric from which the heroine's ball gown would be made.

The American was well in hand, but *Mrs. Vibert* would be delayed. Geneviève Ward had gone on tour in the United States, and John Hare was having difficulty finding another actress for the title role. When he repeated that James's play was really meant for the Comédie-Française, the compliment had an ominous note.

James believed in the art of the actor, the collaboration of author and performer, and his plays were filled not with stock characters but with highly individual personalities. Action and interest lay in the revelation of character. Even in this first play, *The American*, all depended on the hero's performance: the climax of the action occurred when he forswore revenge upon the vile Bellegardes. *Mrs. Vibert* was still more dependent upon the principal actor, the powerfully attractive mature woman, seemingly the villain of the piece, who was to be revealed in the last act as a nobly self-sacrificing heroine.

Such plays could not be cast out of inventory, so to speak: highly particular talents were needed for the principal parts. James was perfectly aware of this; it was the whole point of the theater to him and the principal reason actors sought him out. He was an actor's author, and his study of Ibsen had helped him to understand what an actor required; but to assemble the right actors and to find a stage for them was difficult and risky; rarely would all the needed components come together at one time. William Archer and others wrote of the need for a national repertory theater modeled on the Comédie-Française, where a troupe of highly trained actors could alternate leading roles among themselves. James began to entertain the hope that perhaps, with the success of *The American*, he and Compton might begin to build a company for his plays, attracting to it talented young actors like Elizabeth Robins. That fall he was at work on a new comedy for the Compton company, and he confided to Robins that he was writing the role of the heroine with her in mind. Compton had a theater, and they had only to build upon their first success.

James did not feel, it was true, as William Archer did, a personal calling to elevate the British theater. As he told Stevenson, to whom he confided more freely than to anyone else:

I am doing what I can to launch myself in the dramatic direction—& the strange part of the matter is that I am doing it more or less seriously, as if we had the Scène Anglaise which we haven't. And I secretly dream of supplying the vile want? Pas même [not at all]—& my zeal in the affair is only matched by my indifference.

If it seemed that he could do well by doing good, so be it. Yet he was not precisely indifferent, as he claimed, at least was not indifferent to success: he plainly enjoyed and welcomed the struggle. He spoke of his early successes in the theater as conquests on a field of battle and spoke in military metaphors. He savored his victories and accepted his defeats:

I find the *form* opens out before me as if there were a kingdom to conquer. . . . I feel as if I had at last *found* my form—my real one—that for which pale fiction is an ineffectual substitute.

But this was a little too strong, and he hastened to say that he had not abandoned literature, had not given himself over entirely to the lust for conquest of the public heart and purse. With a touch of self-mockery he added:

God grant this unholy truth may not abide with me more than two or three years—time to dig out eight or ten rounded masterpieces & make withal enough money to enable me to retire in peace & plenty for the unmolested business of a *little* supreme writing as distinguished from gouging.

Robins entered wholeheartedly into his theatrical plans, as did Florence Bell and Wolcott Balestier. As did Alice James, for whom Henry's stage career was an entrancing, vicarious excitement. She was growing weaker but was not less vividly alive. Henry reported to their brother Bob:

she is slowly dying of cancer in the breast—a form of it that would be dreadfully painful if it were not for the ineffable blessing of morphine.

She suffers a good deal, but much less than I feared at first, & it only brings out her extraordinary fortitude & her wonderfully unconventional individual view of life, death, pain & her whole situation. Her situation is very touching, but I can't call it tragic in the presence of her extraordinary mastery, as it were, of it, & superiority, as it were, to it. Katherine Loring's blessed presence, moreover, keeps it from this descent—she will not leave her now, so long as she lives.

William, informed of Alice's now-terminal illness, came over for a hasty visit, arriving in mid-September. He remained for ten days, just long enough to attend the opening of *The American*, and then hastened back to his classes. Florence Bell did not return to London in time for the rehearsals, but she did come back soon enough to help issue invitations for the opening night. James asked all his friends to rally to his support: Sargent, Parsons, and the Abbeys, the du Mauriers, the Smalleys, Rhoda Broughton, Lucy Clifford, Florence Bell, Geneviève Ward, Arthur Pinero. He invited the new American minister, Robert Lincoln, son of the late president, and every dignitary he thought would help to dress the house and give his play a warm welcome. Constance Woolson wrote about it to a friend:

A first night in London is like a reception. All the best seats are given to friends, to critics, and to persons of distinction; full dress necessary. I put on my best, and we looked well enough, but were nothing to the others! Pink satin, blue satin, jewels of all sorts, splendour on all sides of us. The house was packed to the top, and the applause great. . . . All the literary and artistic people were there, and many "swells" also.

James paced the Strand, looking into shop windows, when the performance began, but as before he could not remain away and went backstage and heard that it was going well. The tremendous nervousness of opening night, the accumulated tension of the weeks of rehearsal and preparation, again gave way to serene intensity, composure at high voltage. He went before the curtain and took his bow. This was a success in London.

When the performance was ended, and the actors had been called out, there arose calls of "author, author!" After some delay, Henry James appeared before the curtain and acknowledged the applause. He looked very well—quiet and dignified, yet pleasant; he only stayed a moment.

He went to the dressing rooms and congratulated the actors. When they had removed their makeup, he carried them off to a late supper in his flat with William, Florence Bell, and Wolcott Balestier. It was another triumphant dinner among friends, a celebration on the field of battle— there could be no mistaking the enthusiasm of the audience. The next morning, James sent a few notes to friends who had not been present. To Gosse:

I have had all the air of a success—even a great one. The papers, I believe, are very restrictive—very stingy I call it—very stupid *you* must. But the play goes—it went last night in an indisputable fashion.

12

THE LANDSCAPE IS
ALTERED BY DEATH

William Archer said that James's play showed the touch of a "born playwright." Other reviews were mixed. Compton's performance was objected to as a caricature; it seemed odd not to have cast an American in the part. Elizabeth Robins, an American cast as a Frenchwoman, was criticized for her nervous, realistic Ibsenish portrayal of Claire de Cintré. But James's friends confirmed his sense that the play was a sufficient success. The jurist Frederick Pollock, who had been at the opening, wrote to Wendell Holmes, "America in the divine person of Miss Robins has again captured the British stage, and *The American* is likely to survive its critics."

In October, when people began to return to London, the theater filled satisfactorily. James made some revisions, especially in the third act, which had seemed to drag, and critics were invited for a second opening. The royal household informed Compton that the prince of Wales would attend, and James marshaled his friends again to dress the house. By mid-November, the play had held the stage for two months, and there was a chance of its carrying over into the new year: "Whatever may happen now, I have had an honourable run—& it may become more honourable yet." Under James's encouragement and direction, Compton and Robins were proving to be fine actors. The two leads might be the nucleus of an acting company that would perform his plays and to whom he could provide the opportunity to develop their art. "Whatever *shall* happen [with the run of *The American*]," James pledged, "I am utterly launched in the drama, resolutely & deeply committed to it, & shall go at it tooth & nail."

Hare still had his second play, *Mrs. Vibert*. Geneviève Ward had returned from her tour but had joined Henry Irving's company and was fully occupied there, playing the classics, and no replacement for her had been found. But these were the ordinary vicissitudes of the stage. James had proven himself.

He had by no means abandoned the monthly magazines, however. Theatrical life and story writing were complementary, and James's commitment to the actors did not require him to abandon literature. Short stories were like plays, evocations of an extended moment, and experiments in one medium led to advances in the other. His novel *The American* had not been readily adapted for the stage, but, as for short stories and plays, "It is all one quest—in the way of subject—the play and the tale. . . the same attitude and regard." Nor did stories take him away from the theater for months at a time, as novels did; his new enterprises meshed together well. They were each glimpses through the small frame, as he told Stevenson: "I am busy with the *short*—I have forsworn the long. I hammer at the horrid little theatrical problem. . . [and] I shall soon publish another small storybook which I will incontinently send you."

Alice was growing visibly weaker, and at times when he made his daily afternoon calls she was not able to receive him. Morphine had quieted the pain in her breast, but she was unable to sleep; at William's suggestion Katherine brought an alienist, Charles Lloyd Tuckey, one of the pioneers of hypnosis therapy, to see her. Tuckey hypnotized Alice with great success: the hypnotic treatments soothed her anxiety and allowed her to sleep. He made three visits, and Katherine learned to administer this new treatment effectively—so long as she did not attempt Tuckey's solemn verbal suggestions, which only made Alice giggle. Alice recorded with sad amusement that only now, at the end, had an effective treatment for her anxiety and depression been found.

In the evenings, James kept up with his circle of friends, visiting Gosse once each week, seeing the Smalleys less often, sometimes supping with Ned Abbey and Sargent at the South Kensington Museum grill. Wolcott Balestier was his most frequent companion. Balestier had become his collaborator and intimate friend, and Balestier's wainscotted chambers in the Dean's Yard, under the tower of Westminster Abbey, were social and lively as winter descended. James often found a companionable group there well into the evening. It was a country of the young: Balestier was only twenty-nine, Carrie a year older, Josephine a little younger. Rudyard Kipling, who made Balestier's office his second home, was only twenty-six, and William Heinemann, Balestier's partner in new publishing ventures, was just short of thirty. They were, taken together, a cosmopolitan crowd: the little, plump Heinemann, with his waxed mustache, was distinctly exotic: the English-born son of a German-Jewish father, educated in Dresden, he had Continental manners; Carrie Balestier was the soul of New England; while Balestier himself, who had lived in Colorado, liked to talk about his life in the mining country of the West.

The Anglo-Indian Kipling, who was having an immense success, had evidently fallen in love with both Wolcott and Carrie Balestier. Wolcott arranged to have Kipling's first novel, *The Light That Failed*, published in America by Lovell and had a few copies printed in England to protect the copyright. He was collaborating with Kipling on a novel of East and West, *The Naulahka*, a melodramatic tale that Heinemann was to publish. Balestier was a skillful typist: he sat at the machine in his office, before the coal-fire grate, while Kipling paced, sometimes dictating, sometimes listening as Balestier read aloud.

James, approaching fifty, a throughly Europeanized Anglo-American, presided benignly over the intricate relations of the younger men and women. He read the early chapters of *The Naulahka* as they came from the machine and said that he was delighted by them, as he evidently was by the two authors.

Balestier and Heinemann between them had begun the English Library, a Continental publishing scheme to take advantage of the new copyright treaty. The young partners had lined up a long list of prominent English and American writers, whose work they proposed to publish on the Continent, competing with Tauschnitz's cheap editions. Balestier was acquiring world rights to novels in the English language, each to be published by Heinemann in Great Britain and the Commonwealth, by Heinemann and Balestier's English Library on the Continent, and by Lovell, Balestier's principal, in America. James happily agreed to join the English Library and have his early work reprinted by it, and he recommended Stevenson to do likewise. George Meredith, Hall Caine, J. M. Barrie, and Oscar Wilde quickly joined them, and from mere idea the English Library became in a matter of months a substantial enterprise. James twitted Balestier genially on his grandiose ambitions and his Napoleonic self-confidence.

Late in November, Balestier set off for Leipzig, where the English Library books were to be printed. James thought travel might be good for him, as Balestier had been ill. Everyone in London seemed to have come down with the Russian flu, and Leipzig was comparatively untouched. But Balestier worsened as he went on and was obliged to interrupt his journey in Dresden. Carrie went to him at once and found him very ill indeed, not with flu but with typhoid fever. She moved him to a private hospital, but on Sunday, December 6, 1891, he died, a few days short of his thirtieth birthday.

Responding to Carrie's urgent telegram, James and Heinemann set off immediately for the Continent, James carrying with him a box of flowers that Mrs. Gosse hastily provided. They were obliged to spend Monday night in Dover, immobilized by weather and tides; in the morning they resumed their cold journey, a rough crossing to Ostend, proceeding by rail to Cologne, changing trains there, and from Cologne across the breadth of Germany to Dresden. They arrived wearily on Wednesday night and settled in the Europaeischer Hof, thinking that they had missed the funeral; but it had been put off until Thursday morning.

Carrie had summoned her mother and sister from Paris; Heinemann had telegraphed to his own mother and sisters, who were in Dresden. The women had waited, and the two men now joined them. They were a sad little gathering. An English chaplain read the burial service, and they went in creaking black-and-silver coaches, with black-and-silver-uniformed footmen clinging on behind, to a suburban cemetery. James gave his flowers to the younger sister, Josephine, and she carried them to the brink of the grave and dropped them in.

Carrie asked James to ride back with her alone, as she wanted to talk with him. As he told Gosse afterward, "poor little concentrated, passionate Carrie . . . [was] remarkable in her force, acuteness, capacity & courage—& in the intense—almost manly—nature of her emotion." It appeared that Carrie and Rudyard Kipling had agreed to marry. Kipling was now on a journey to see his parents in India; he had planned to return by way of the South Pacific, calling on Robert Louis Stevenson in Samoa on the way, and making a complete circuit of the globe. But Carrie had cabled to him in Lahore: "Wolcott dead. Come back to me," and Kipling was already on his way back to London. He and Carrie would marry immediately on his return. Her father was dead, and her surviving brother was in the United States; she asked James to give her away. James was happy to oblige. "She is a worthy sister of poor dear big-spirited, only-by-death-quenchable Wolcott . . . she can do & face, & more than face & do, for all 3 of them, anything & everything that they will have to meet now."

Tired and ill from the months of sustained stress, James collapsed into his hotel before returning to London. He was stretched to the point of breaking by Balestier's death, which he had not yet absorbed, and the hasty winter journey. He remained in Dresden for a few days, resting and digesting what had happened. As if by a stroke of lightning, Wolcott Balestier was gone and the circle that had formed around him had broken and scattered.

On December 3, just before Carrie's telegram summoned James to Dresden, *The American* had its last performance at the Opera Comique. Honor was saved, as he told William, by a respectable run, and if the production had not made money, it had not lost any. "I have had success with the fastidious, and anything else I do will be greatly attended to."

Compton had another American drama, *The Mayflower* by Louis Napoleon Parker, rehearsed and ready to open at the Opera Comique after the first of the year, but he wanted a comedy from James to follow immediately afterward, one in which Compton and Robins could appear together. As soon as James could give him a play, he would begin rehearsals. On James's return to London, therefore, he immediately set to work. Compton had not cared for *Mrs. Jasper*, the play written in Italy the year before, so James began in all confidence to write a new comedy, with all his freshly acquired stagecraft at his command.

It was a mild and sunny winter, and there was little fog. London was quiet, in part because it was a plague city. The "Russian flu" was now acknowledged to be a great pandemic, sweeping across Europe from China, and those in London who were not ill remained indoors and avoided public gatherings. Kipling returned to London on January 10, 1892, at the height of the epidemic; he later recalled that "the undertakers had run out of black horses and the dead had to be content with brown ones. The living were mostly abed." James had had the flu the previous summer and was now healthy and immune, but his servants the Smiths were both ill. Alice and Katherine were spared, but their servants too were ill.

Only days after *The Mayflower* opened it closed, a complete failure. James reported the disaster to Florence Bell:

I *ain't* doing a comedy for the [Opera Comique]—I *was*—but the painful collapse of that establishment, in consequence of the production of an unspeakable horror called "The Mayflower," has thrown everything into pie. The theatre is closed & is not to open again under Comptonian management.

The failure may not have been entirely Compton's fault, as he had had the bad luck to open at the height of the influenza epidemic. But there it was: he had leased the theater for a year, full of optimism, but had not raised enough money to weather such a loss. The theater went dark, and after a fruitless search for new backing, Compton found another tenant to take over the balance of his lease. The Compton Comedy Company resumed its touring, and James's vision of a company and a London theater in which to develop his art was abruptly extinguished, at least for a time, by the meaningless chances of material life.

On January 18, 1892, James attended the wedding of Rudyard Kipling and Carrie Balestier at All Souls Church in Langham Place. There was only a small gathering: Mrs. Balestier and Josephine were both ill with influenza. Rudyard's parents were still in Lahore, and the Kipling family was represented only by a cousin, Ambrose Poynter. James, as agreed, stood in the place of Carrie's father and gave the bride away. William Heinemann, Edmund Gosse, Mrs. Gosse, and their little boy, Philip, made up the remainder of the subdued gathering. Carrie was not in mourning and wore a brown wedding dress, with buttons down the front. The four men were witnesses, and on the license Carrie gave her age as twenty-six, deducting three years to make her age the same as Kipling's. After the brief ceremony, the bride and groom separated, to the great scandal of the curate: Carrie went to her lodgings to care for her flu-stricken mother and sister, while Rudyard carried his cousin Ambo off to a bachelor wedding breakfast. It was a "dreary little wedding," James confided to William afterward, and he didn't in the least understand Kipling's marrying.

Before leaving London for his trip to India, Kipling had sketched out a poem, "The Long Trail," that appeared to be an appeal to Balestier to leave his partnership with Heinemann and embark with Kipling on his travels:

> Ha' done with the Tents of Shem, dear lad!
> We've seen the seasons through,
> And it's time to turn on the old trail,
> our own trail, the out trail. . . .

But Balestier was dead, and on Kipling's return to London he altered the poem, changing "lad" to "lass." Two weeks after the wedding, on February 2, Rudyard resumed his journey around the world, accompanied by Carrie. James saw them off.

Alice was weaker still. The pain in her breast had subsided somewhat, but her heart and her strength were ebbing away. Early in March, she developed a cough and a fever, perhaps pneumonia, that greatly added to her sufferings and that it seemed to Henry she could not survive. There was a new pain in her chest, perhaps her heart; Baldwin thought it another tumor.

On Saturday, March 5, the symptoms of pneumonia and her chest pain seemed to pass away, leaving Alice terribly thin and pale and longing for release. She asked that a cable be sent to her brothers and their families in America: "Tenderest love to all farewell am going soon Alice."

Katherine wanted Alice to rest, and so on Saturday afternoon James left her, although he felt the end must be near. On Sunday morning, he returned and found Alice sleeping after an uneasy, wakeful night. With Katherine and Nurse Bradford, he sat beside Alice's bed. Her breathing became loud and deep, almost stertorous. The doctor came to the street door late in the morning, and James went down to him and gave a circumstantial report, after which the doctor departed without seeing Alice. He said that he did not like to see his patients in their last suffering, when there was nothing he could do for them. Henry returned to the sickroom, living through each hour. When it was all over, he gave an account to his brother William, who was a physician, of Alice's dissolution:

> For about seven hours this deep difficult & almost automatic breathing continued—with *no* look of pain in the face—only & more utterly the look of death. They were infinitely pathetic &, to me, most unspeakable hours. . . . Her face then seemed, in a strange, dim, touching way, to become clearer. I went to the window to let in a little more of the afternoon light upon it (it was a bright, kind, soundless Sunday,) & when I came back to the bed she had drawn the breath that was not succeeded by another.

James spent much of the next two days with Alice's strangely dignified remains, until it was time for the cremation. In accordance with Alice's instructions, only he, Katherine, Nurse Bradford, and Alice's good friend from Cambridge days Annie Ashburner Richards, attended the simple

ceremony. A sweet-voiced young clergyman read the brief Anglican service. Alice's ashes were sent to America, to lie beside her parents and to
await her brothers in the Cambridge cemetery. Henry wrote his last
words for her, to William:

> Strange & rare was the force that she exercised in all her prostration &
> weakness—& strange enough it seems—in the little house that is now
> so senseless & void—that this force has, in an hour, been quenched.

> It is the last, the last forever. I shall feel very lonely in England at first.
> But enough.

Katherine remained in London for a few weeks. James helped her with
the now-familiar tasks: cabling and writing to friends and relations, in-
forming them of Alice's death; communicating the terms of her will to
the beneficiaries, replying to numerous letters of condolence, helping to
wind up Alice's affairs in London and to dispose of her personal effects.
Of the heirlooms, William was to have the silver, as well as the furniture
that he already had in his keeping. Henry would have a few pictures, including the portrait of their Scottish grandmother. Bob was to receive a
carefully calculated bequest of $10,000. Numerous smaller, specific be-
quests had been made; Katherine, Henry, and William were to share
equally in the residual estate. Katherine, who was executor, estimated
that each of the three would receive about $20,000.

There was the usual dispute. William complained that Katherine, who
in his view was not a member of the family, would receive as much as he
and Henry and more than Robertson; William was deeply troubled by
Alice's death, and this was perhaps an unfortunate expression of his unhappiness. Henry wrote at length to mollify him and to say that in any
case the will could not be changed now. William thereupon wrote, first to
insist that Henry set aside a portion of *his* income for Robertson during
his life and then somewhat inconsistently and unkindly to say that he had
better be careful to preserve all of the little capital he had received: "You
will need a good deal more than you are likely to have when your writing powers are cut short, as in the nature of things they must be some day
if you live."

But Henry's situation was more secure than it had ever been before.
Alice had been careful during her lifetime and generous in her will. He
would now receive, for the first time, his share of the income from their

father's estate, principally rents from the property in Syracuse (about $1,500 per year). His share of Alice's estate, still invested in the railroad bonds she had inherited, would produce another annual income of $1,000 or more, and with some modest sales of short stories he could plan on $3,000 or $4,000 a year, the salary of a college professor. This was not wealth, but it was enough to provide freedom from care and some as- surance for his old age, William's warnings notwithstanding.

Abruptly, then, he was become a man of modest private means, and for the first time since he left his parents' house he did not have to work to maintain himself. Pressure to write for the stage evaporated, and he had few deadlines to meet. He wrote an obituary for James Russell Low- ell, the friend of his youth, and a long, affectionate obituary notice for his friend Wolcott Balestier: "to the young, the early dead, the baffled, the defeated, I don't think we can be tender enough."

Although in mourning, James attended the theater often with Rhoda Broughton and Elizabeth Robins to see the new plays. Oscar Wilde seemed to be following in James's tracks and had written a stage comedy, *Lady Windermere's Fan*, that looked to be a popular success. With Robins, James saw Sarah Bernhardt perform; she was in London with her own company. He did not care for Oscar's or Sarah's plays, which were popu- lar, and in general was content now to be an observer of the theatrical season. His letters to Florence Bell took on a detached tone: he was at least for the moment an observer and patron of the art, rather than an ac- tive participant. He wrote a long affectionate letter to his brother Bob:

> I hope you are not without sources of happiness. I trust your children count for much among them—I must see your children. I shld like to borrow them, seriously, for 6 months—& one of these days I shall.

He renewed his regular visits to du Maurier, to whom he had once written that "I carry everywhere in my heart an interest, affectionate even perhaps to indiscretion, in your concerns & affairs," but whom he had somewhat neglected that winter. Du Maurier had published his first novel, a graceful fantasy called *Peter Ibbetson*, which James had liked and praised. This was the book begun that evening, three years earlier, when James had urged him to write. Du Maurier was encouraged by the criti- cal reception for his book and by James's words of praise. He had begun a second novel, based on the plot he had told to James that same night, the story of the Jew who hypnotizes a young woman and makes her sing beautifully. It was to be called *Trilby.* Du Maurier's sight was failing, and he hoped to make a second career as an author.

In the early spring, William and his Alice wrote to James separately, discussing from their different perspectives William's plan of coming to Europe. His term at Harvard would end shortly; now that his big book on psychology was finished he proposed to take a sabbatical year traveling in Europe, and for once he asked his wife to accompany him. Sister Alice's generous bequest would make this possible. William's Alice was willing to make the journey, although she told Henry she had some qualms about spending a year in Europe with four small children: "I confess the undertaking looks formidable but I have a good nurse and I am a fair sailor myself." James was pleased to think he would have an opportunity to become acquainted with his young nephews and niece, and his sister-in-law happily assured him, "I long to have the children know you." William delayed making any definite plans, however, beyond saying he thought the trip would be good for Alice, a vacation for *her*, and the whole matter remained in suspense.

That winter, James received another reminder of their shared youth: Wendell Holmes sent him a slim volume of speeches, beautifully printed and handsomely bound in white calf, that recalled the Civil War years in which they had first formed their friendship. The book was warmly inscribed to James.

Holmes had arrived at a kind of philosophic realism, and his essays were not far removed from the efforts of Henry and William, empirical studies of a kind. Holmes had tried to give an objective account of the society around him, taken in brief glimpses and written in precise, deeply poetic images. His addresses were, moreover, texts to be read aloud, to be performed, and were drenched in nostalgia for the young men who had died in the Civil War. James responded to the little volume promptly and in effusive, affectionate terms:

> Nothing for a long time has gratified me so much as to see yesterday that you had judged me worthy to receive the slim but precious volume of your beautiful, noble speeches. They have been but a day in my house, but I have read them & re-read them, chanted & cherished them, learnt passages by heart & praised them to myself with an eloquence almost caught from their own . . . . The first five of them seem

to me absolutely perfect things in their kind—& you know better than I (vividly as you make me feel it) that the kind is great—greatest perhaps of all. These addresses are, to my sense, equally faultless in spirit & form—and more high & beautiful than I can say. . . . They recall for me the dearest of far-away hours and revive a hundred noble emotions.

The Palazzo Barbaro was a wonderful haven of refuge: the great salon's windows faced south across the wide mouth of the Grand Canal and filled the room with sunshine. Turkish carpets were spread on the cool marble floors, and cigarette smoke disappeared into the high shadowy recesses of the room. After a month's rest in Sienna, visiting the Bourgets and awaiting word of William's plans, James went on by rail to Venice and settled into the fantastic, familiar palace and its leisurely, unintrusive life.

Although financial pressures were in abeyance and the theatrical venture seemed over, he had by no means ceased to work. In the fall and winter he collected tales of men's friendships into a slim volume, *The Lesson of the Master*, of which he had spoken to Stevenson. Macmillan brought it out in a relatively cheap, six-shilling edition in Great Britain and a one-dollar volume in America. It contained some of the best work he had ever done.

He wrote also a new story that he had promised to a popular newspaper, *The Graphic*. Just before leaving London, he had made a brief note in his journal: perhaps in part because of Holmes's speeches, he was thinking of the young men who had served in the American Civil War. He was prompted also "a little" by his reading that spring of General Jean Marbot's newly published memoirs of his service in Napoleon's armies. James imagines a young heir of a military family, a charming youth like Marbot, who is, as it were, a hereditary soldier but who declines to serve, who rebels against the barbarity of war. This young man—"Owen Wingrave"—chooses instead to be a man of letters. To refute an imputation of cowardice, however, he resolves to face the ghost of his martial ancestor. He locks himself overnight into a haunted room, faces the ghost—and dies.

The story remained in the back of his mind, unrealized, until one afternoon on the eve of his departure when James seated himself on a bench in Kensington Gardens to enjoy the early summer weather. While he sat under a great tree, a "tall quiet slim studious young man, of admirable type" sat down beside him "and settled to a book with immediate gravity." The slender, attaching figure in the park seemed to bring this new story to life; it seemed as if the spirit of Owen Wingrave descended upon the quiet figure in the park. Tender memories and the intensity of the moment fused. James felt for the figure beside him in Kensington Gardens all his tenderness for Balestier and Stevenson, for brave Alice, for the young Holmes, for the boys he had known who had died in the American war: "the young, the early dead, the baffled, the defeated."

Now in Venice, he wrote out this story for *The Graphic;* years later he would rewrite it as a play. He would return three more times to this theme of the warrior and his peaceful alter ego, in another story that was more explicitly autobiographical, in an uncompleted novel, and in a long-meditated work on the Bonapartes that he began only on his deathbed.

On the eve of his departure for the Continent he had jotted down several further ideas for short stories, one or two of which, like "Owen Wingrave," he now fleshed out in leisurely fashion in the library of the Palazzo Barbaro. He worked in the mornings, as always, writing or reading proofs, answering the many letters that followed him to Italy. The palace remained cool, despite the hot weather, and in the afternoons and evenings he allowed himself to be rowed into the lagoon by the Curtises' gondolier, or slipped comfortably into the polyglot society of Venice.

He had been persuaded to make a prolonged visit to Venice partly because he expected to find there Paul Zhukowsky, whom he loved and to whom he had pledged lifelong friendship. The unhappy memories of their parting more than fifteen years earlier, which had contributed to James's flight from Paris, had long ago subsided. The two men remained friends, albeit widely separated. Zhukowsky, still a bachelor, had returned to Saint Petersburg and joined the court of Alexander III, with whom he had been raised. His father had been Alexander's tutor, and he himself had been a member of the corps that waited upon the young prince. Now Zhukowsky was court painter to the young czar. James was glad to be able to make his own visit to Venice coincide with Zhukowsky's—there had been so many failed plans to meet in years past.

Zhukowsky was at the Palazzo Dario, at that time a *pensione*, directly across the Grand Canal from the Barbaro. One had only to stroll across the Accademia Bridge. The weeks went by quickly and happily. Zhukowsky said later that when he returned to Venice alone, James's absence cast "a constant and painfully felt shadow."

• • •

After many changes of plans, of putting his boys in school and then abruptly taking them out again, reminiscent of his father's tyrannical whimsies, William took his family to Switzerland. Alice, with the two youngest children, a governess, and a nursemaid, settled in Lausanne, while William visited scholars in Germany and France. The two older boys, Harry and Billy (thirteen and ten, respectively) boarded with local clergymen for the balance of the summer, to learn French. With these arrangements in place, William at last wrote to his brother inviting him to visit.

Henry thereupon went to Lausanne and took rooms in the hotel where William's family was staying, for a leisurely visit. But William went off on a walking tour, leaving Alice to care for the children and play hostess to Henry. The older boys came to the hotel to meet their uncle, and he was glad for the chance to become better acquainted with his nephews.

When Harry and Billy returned to their pastors, James spent a quiet week visiting with their mother, sister, and baby brother. Alice and he cemented their friendship. He was not greatly interested in the baby boy, in babies generally, but he thought five-year-old Peggy a charming little girl. He found that he greatly enjoyed uncledom, and before leaving Switzerland he paid another visit to the two older boys, picking up Billy and taking him along on a visit to Harry in Montreux.

By the middle of August, he was back in his flat in London, without having seen his brother.

James had grown stout in his months of leisure and was somewhat depressed in spirits. Elizabeth Robins, when she had a cold and was feeling sorry for herself, said she was "feeling a little Henry James-ish." He was enmeshed in London again, and the theater was making its demands. He ran down to Brighton in miserable weather for a few days, to see Robins reprise her role as Mrs. Linden in a revival of *A Doll's House*, and wrote a careful critique of the production (which was poor) as well as of Robins's performance (excellent) to Florence Bell. In addition to his labors for young friends in the theater and almost daily conversations and correspondence with Florence Bell and Elizabeth Robins, he now entered into discussions with a very different sort of repertory company, hoping to be rescued from his leisure.

An American, Augustin Daly, manager of a successful New York company, had begun construction of a new theater off Leicester Square,

Daly's Theatre, at the immense cost of £40,000. The foundation stone had been laid with great publicity by his leading lady, Ada Rehan, a charming Irish-born Brooklyn girl. The theater was to open early in 1893, and Rehan had sent a message to James by a mutual friend, during the run of the *The American*, praising his play and asking if he might not have one for her. James responded warmly, saying that he would like to sit down with her and discuss a play he had written (probably *Mrs. Vibert*). Rehan was evidently interested but returned to New York before the promised conversation could be held. Daly was still in London, however, and on James's return from the Continent he now resumed the discussion.

Daly wanted a comedy, not a melodrama, for Rehan, and James sent him the first comedy he had attempted, *Mrs. Jasper.* The program of Daly's Theatre was not unlike that of the touring Comptons—light, popular fare—and *Mrs. Jasper,* written with the Comptons in mind, seemed to fit. Daly was not satisfied with it in its present form but said he would like to talk about revising it. James had no illusions about the merits of this maiden effort and replied that he would be very happy to discuss how it might be improved. They talked, James went to work, and Daly spoke of producing the revised comedy in New York with Miss Rehan in the title role, perhaps very soon, before bringing it to the new London theater.

James was again writing for the Compton Company, as well. It was touring, performing *The American* regularly on Friday nights, with Virginia Compton restored to the role of heroine. Compton asked whether James would not rewrite the fourth act: months of performing for country audiences had persuaded him that the final act, with its deaths and renunciations, was inconsistent with the generally light tone of the play and accordingly a letdown for the audience. James obligingly—and deftly—turned the denouement of the story into a light comedy finish, with reconciliations and marriages all around. This was bread-and-butter theater, not drama.

As the holidays drew on, he discarded his mourning and the black-bordered notepaper he had used since Alice's death. William and his family were now in Florence, and James thought of returning for another visit after the first of the year; Bourget wrote to ask him to spend another month with him at San Remo, where he was wintering; his sisters-in-law Mary Holton James and Carrie James were both in Europe with their children, Mary in Dresden and Carrie in Paris, and were all converging on William in Florence; it seemed he must go over to join this gathering of family and friends, but there was simply no time to spare. He abandoned Florence Bell's tea-and-theater parties and began again to refuse dinner invitations upon the plea of work. It was difficult to resist the renewed call of the stage, the possibility of a commercial success and real prosperity.

Gosse and James had their customary end-of-year dinner, and their talk became intimate, at least on Gosse's part. He spoke of John Addington Symonds's privately printed booklet *A Study in Modern Ethics*, a polemic against the Criminal Law Amendments Act of 1885, which made all intimacies between men a crime.

Early in the new year, James went to Gosse's office at the Board of Trade to borrow the pamphlet. Not finding Gosse in, James went home, and next morning Gosse came to De Vere Gardens with the book in hand. James read it the same night and carried it back to Gosse's office the next day with a brief note of thanks for "those marvelous outpourings."

James spoke of the book's subject without evident self-consciousness and with some apparent sense that it had a personal application. In half-joking fashion he remarked that his "natural modesty" had been "strangely impaired since yesterday p.m.!" when he had read the tract.

Gosse had responded very warmly to the little book, as well as to some autobiographical musings that Symonds had shown to him, and had written to the author as perhaps he spoke to James:

> I know all you speak of—the solitude, the rebellion, the despair. Yet I have been happy too; I hope you also have been happy . . . Either way, I entirely and deeply sympathize with you.

James himself now wrote to Gosse with caution but with evident sympathy:

> I don't wonder that some of [Symonds's] friends and relations are haunted with a vague malaise. I think one ought to wish him more *humour*—it is really *the* saving salt. But the great reformers never have it—& he is the Gladstone of the affair.

As his fiftieth birthday approached, James was subjected to undignified reminders of mortality. He began to suffer from gout, a painful condition that made his feet swell; aside from the pain, he was subjected to the humiliation of wearing enormous shapeless galoshes instead of shoes, a trial for a man who was so careful of his appearance.

Fanny Kemble, his oldest London friend and mentor, was dying. For two or three years past, weakness and a deepening dementia had kept her from going out or seeing visitors. James had ceased his weekly calls, and he had missed her vigorous conversation, her gossip about the vanished epoch of her youth, and her stern judgments on her contemporaries. Her daughter Frances Leigh had come to sit at her bedside, but as Kemble seemed to rally Leigh went off on a planned visit to her sister, Sarah Wister, in America. James alone was with Fanny Kemble when she died:

> She had been on her bedroom sofa, sleeping—after some bad days, during which she refused food—and her maid was at her request—very distinct and comparatively cheerful—helping her back to bed. As she reached the bedside she gave a little "Oh!" and, with a drop of her head, all was over. She had died in that second—so enviably! . . . it is almost impossible to feel—to believe—that such a quantity of being, such a force of nature, as it were, is extinct and ended.

Kemble had outlived the friends of her own generation, and both her daughters were in America at the moment; James was left to perform the familiar tasks, to answer the questions of newspaper reporters, and to write yet another obituary for a friend. He was saddened to find that she who had been one of the public figures of her day, a leading actress, a great antislavery campaigner and the author of bestselling memoirs, was now all but forgotten. Newspaper reporters were surprised to find that she had only just died, and James was reminded once again of how quickly in London the dead disappear from sight and remembrance.

At some point that winter he wrote a story about the death of an author. "The Middle Years" was a portrait of a middle-aged writer, Dencombe, alone and ill at a seaside resort. In the story, Dencombe has written his novels and now longs for a second period of life in which to make a new start, to show what he is really capable of doing. He is dying, however, and he will not have, as James is having, a second debut. Hugh, a young doctor who loves and admires him, takes up his care, and through the doctor's affectionate eyes the dying man sees that he has already done what he hoped to do, "that he has put into his things the love of perfection and that they will live by that."

James wrote the story out for *Scribner's Magazine* and struggled to keep it within the meager six thousand words allotted him. He was pleased with the result: as with his plays, the struggle to achieve concision had forced him to reduce his tale to a few powerful images. As he wrote, James put a good deal of himself into the dying novelist, made him almost an alter ego: James as he would have been, without his second start. The doctor became a handsome representative of the younger generation, a scientist with a taste for letters: his admiration for Dencombe's work is a promise of a future life for the books he has already written. Hugh's love reveals to the author that his longing for success has been a delusion: the true glory is simply to have lived fully.

It *is* glory—to have been tested, to have had our little quality and cast our little spell. The thing is to have made somebody care. . . .

"You're a great success!" said Doctor Hugh, putting into his young voice the ring of a marriage-bell.

Dencombe lay taking this in; then he gathered strength to speak once more. "A second chance—*that's* the delusion. There never was to be but one. We work in the dark—we do what we can—we give what we have. Our doubt is our passion and our passion is our task. The rest is the madness of art."

13

RENEWED EXPERIMENTS

Elizabeth Robins was tall and wore her luxuriant chestnut hair swept loosely up, in a way that bared her neck and emphasized her height; dark, penciled brows framed her widely set blue eyes. She was intelligent, forceful, and charming and, after a disastrous, youthful marriage to an actor that had ended with his suicide, was determined not to marry again. With a kind of masculine freedom she had become a central figure in the introduction of Henrik Ibsen to the English-speaking world.

She had allies among James's friends. William Heinemann, in his joint project with Balestier, had acquired the English language rights to *Hedda Gabler* by making a generous advance payment to Ibsen. Ibsen's plays were not popular with a wide public, and a printed edition was not likely to be profitable, but he bought the rights to Ibsen's plays for Elizabeth Robins, with whom he was very visibly in love. He did not know that she was conducting a love affair with William Archer.

Robins and her friend Marion Lea had formed a production company, Robins-Lea Joint Management, and spoke of establishing a permanent repertory company to perform superior plays, Ibsen's among them. They put on a well-received matinee performance of a Swedish play, *Karin*, in Florence Bell's translation, and hoped to bring other European plays to London. James happily joined their discussions and helped them secure the English-language rights to Alexandre Dumas's *Denise* and search for other properties suitable for the London stage. They talked of producing a stage version of James's early novel *Roderick Hudson*.

But Ibsen was the central figure. Robins, who was to perform the title role, persuaded a reluctant lord chamberlain to license the first public performance of *Hedda Gabler* in London. She then mediated a dispute among William Heinemann, Edmund Gosse, and William Archer over the rights to the English translation. Heinemann ran off copies of Gosse's translation, and Robins enlisted Archer to assist her in revising the awkward and inaccurate text. Gradually, as rehearsals progressed, Gosse's translation gave way to Robins and Archer's more accurate and playable version.

When the play was performed for the first time in English, the character of Hedda Gabler was intimately Robins's creation: she felt as if she and the playwright had collaborated. Archer, whose connection with the production had been kept secret, wrote a review for *The World* praising her performance, and despite violent denunciations of the play by other newspapers the matinee performances were eminently successful. The manager of the theater shifted them to evenings, for a month of packed houses; Robins's *Hedda Gabler* was a success, and Ibsen was launched on the English stage.

Now Heinemann secured for Robins, with another generous advance, the rights to Ibsen's next play, still in preparation, a play that would be known as *The Master Builder.* Ibsen sent pages of the play as they were printed in Norwegian, and an excited little group began meeting at Robins's big, shabby flat in Dorset Street—Robins, Gosse, Heinemann, and Archer—Robins reading aloud rough translations of the advance sheets. James sometimes joined the group and faithfully sent comments on the first translations from the proofs. When Florence Bell returned to town, James often invited her and Robins to join him at De Vere Gardens for further discussions of the play and the repertory plan.

As the sheets of the fragmentary *Master Builder* emerged, they seemed strange, disturbing. The central figure was an architect, an old man of Ibsen's age, and the principal female character, with whom the old man falls in love, a very young and innocent woman, hardly a part for the thirty-year-old Robins, although surely the play was intended for her? After a long visit with James, Robins wrote to Bell expressing her dismay; she thought the old man was mad; Heinemann came in and demanded that the latest bits of translation be read to him, and then Archer came in—a good deal puzzled, like the others. James told Bell that he was "utterly bewildered and mystified":

> It is like an uncanny trick of the hard and shrewd old Norseman, safe in his far-off Christiania with his splendid bargain. That at least is what it *looks* like as yet—of course it's too soon to be wholly sure. But this

week—the next 2 or 3 days—will settle the awful doubt. . . . It is all most strange, most curious, most vague, most horrid . . . and alas most unpromising for Miss Elizabeth.

Robins had deep qualms about going forward, but once the whole play was in hand she decided to accept the part of the girl, Hilda Wangel. Heinemann proceeded to secure the international copyright by arranging a "performance"—a reading of the play in Norwegian—renting the Haymarket Theatre for an afternoon for the purpose. Elizabeth Robins, Gosse, and Heinemann were in the improvised cast, and they read the play aloud to an audience of four. "I am Hilda Wangel," Robins told Virginia Woolf many years later. "I'm the person it was written for."

Her collaborator Marion Lea, meanwhile, had married and returned to America, leaving Robins in sole charge of Robins-Lea Joint Management. Robins thereupon took the burden alone of producing the play. She asked Herbert Waring to play the title role of the master builder, Solness, and he in turn helped her to find a financial backer. They rented the Trafalgar Square Theatre for a week of matinees, hoping the play would find additional backers and a better venue once it had been seen. Rehearsals began, with Archer in constant attendance, making notes and giving them to the actors. James looked in often and added his comments; as the play began to take shape, he wrote a friendly advance notice for *The Pall Mall Gazette.* He reassured his readers that "In spite of its having been announced in many quarters that Ibsen would not do," Ibsen was returning to the London stage with a new play that was not at all shocking, a play to which "a young lady, as they say in Paris, may properly take her mother." The female lead was not a Hedda Gabler, James said reassuringly; indeed, she was the healthy, positive, beneficent *opposite* of the troubled Hedda.

The advance publicity he and Archer arranged was successful: the first matinee, on February 20, 1893, was performed to a full house, and as many as one hundred ticket seekers were turned away at the door. Elizabeth Robins was lifted above herself by the part, and the audience was enraptured. The newspapers next day were politer to Ibsen than they had been in the past and were even enthusiastic about Robins's performance. James sent her an effusive note:

The freshness, the brilliancy, the variety and the intelligence and power and charm of your creation there was but one voice yesterday to recognize, as there is but one result of it all for you to look for—the biggest

lift to your professional position. You have had in other words a great
and delightful success.

Their one-week run at the Trafalgar Square Theatre was extended for
a second and then a third week of matinees, and the play was taken up
for an evening run at the Vaudeville Theatre. James brought George
Smalley to see *The Master Builder,* and Smalley wrote an enthusiastic review for his *New-York Tribune* audience, preparing the ground for Ibsen
in America.

With *The Master Builder* launched and his obituary of Fanny Kemble
completed and delivered to the printers, James treated himself to a
month's holiday in Paris, and on April 15, 1893, he celebrated his fiftieth
birthday there.

In Paris, he found another generation of young Americans who reminded him of his own youthful self. A brief entry in his notebook: "Said
in defense of some young man accused of being selfish—of self-love: 'He
doesn't love *himself*—he loves his *youth!. . .*—and small blame to him!'
"The most beautiful word in the language?—Youth."

He had planned to visit William and his family in Florence, but William
again had shifted his plans. He took his eldest boy, Harry, out of the English school in Florence, placed him in another establishment in Munich,
and wrote that he planned to leave Florence shortly for Switzerland.
James happily lingered in Paris until early in May, waiting for them to settle, and then joined his brother's family near Lucerne, where Henry had
a pleasant, leisurely visit with William and the younger children. Alice
had gone off briefly to be with Harry in Munich for his fourteenth birthday, and William played host. He was at last well established in his profession, and Henry was a man of leisure. They walked and talked and
wept a little over Wilky. Henry took the children off William's hands a
good deal and cemented his friendship with them.

When Alice returned, Henry invited his brother and sister-in-law to
visit him in London for a couple of weeks. He urged them to leave their
children behind in Switzerland and give themselves a grown-up holiday.
To Alice's delight, William agreed, and in May, Henry went home to London to prepare the way and to see Augustin Daly, whose new theater was
now after many delays, nearing completion. James's comedy was nearing

its debut: Daly had abandoned plans for an American opening, and that summer, sets and costumes had been designed for the London stage; rehearsals were to begin in the fall.

George Alexander was the actor-manager of the St. James's Theatre, one of the great venues of the West End. He was a tall man, handsome in the style of the matinee idol—wavy chestnut hair, widely set blue eyes, square jaw, and cleft chin—and had been successful in light comedies and teacup-and-saucer dramas. He was a member of Aïdé's and James's circle and had made a success of a farce adapted for him from the French by Aïdé and another with Oscar Wilde's *Lady Windermere's Fan*. He now was putting on for the first time a serious play, Arthur Wing Pinero's *The Second Mrs. Tanqueray*. Pinero, too, had made a success principally with light comedies, and this was his bid, as well, to be taken seriously.

The story was simple and not unlike that of James's *Mrs. Vibert*. The second Mrs. Tanqueray had been a courtesan in her first youth. A widower, Aubrey Tanqueray, married her with full knowledge of her past. His prudish daughter from a first marriage disapproves of her, however. When the second Mrs. Tanqueray meets the daughter's fiancé and realizes that he is one of her former lovers, that her very existence threatens her stepdaughter's happiness, she commits suicide.

The subject matter was daring for the London stage, especially as the treatment of the courtesan was sympathetic, and there was some question as to whether it could be licensed. Comparisons with Ibsen were inevitable, after *Hedda Gabler*, and indeed Alexander considered Elizabeth Robins for the part, thinking of Hedda. But Mrs. Tanqueray was not, like Hedda, an enigmatic Salomé wreaking destruction in suburbia, but only an attractive woman in a difficult situation; in the end she was played by a neophyte, Stella (Mrs. Patrick) Campbell.

Thin and pale owing to a recent bout of typhoid fever, with enormous dark eyes, Stella Campbell came on alone in the first act, sat down at a piano, and began playing very beautifully a Schubert étude. George Bernard Shaw, reviewing the play, fell in love with her. The young Alexander Woollcott, who was present, still remembered many years later her entrance: "a slim, Italianate and quite inexperienced young woman. . . . She was, I think, as disturbingly beautiful a woman as ever stepped through a stage door . . . tempestuous, undisciplined, and inexpert." She played her part with instinctive talent, and in the small gaslit theater, each member of the audience was in the drawing room with her.

The news of her offstage suicide fell like a blow at the final curtain. There was a long silence, and then the audience burst out in a storm of applause that did not subside until after repeated curtain calls. Men and women stood and waved their handkerchiefs; Pinero came out, and the audience crowded up onto the stage. Stella Campbell fled to her dressing room, frightened by the uproar. It was a complete triumph, one that echoed through the newspapers: England had no need of Dumas fils or Henrik Ibsen, now that it had its own Arthur Wing Pinero!

James sent a note of congratulations to Pinero, whose guest at the opening he had been, and Pinero answered warmly, praising one of James's recent stories and suggesting that it would make a good property for the stage. Shortly thereafter, James was in discussions with George Alexander, who was now securely launched as a serious actor and who wanted a play from Henry James.

In the United States in the spring of 1893, there were uneasy reports of a run on banks, but prosperous Americans nevertheless came in enormous numbers to Europe, on the competing White Star and Cunard lines, and many had letters of introduction to James, who was both a celebrity and a gatekeeper of society. Europeans bound westward came to him as well. Émile Zola was in London, and James managed to have lunch with him before he departed. Paul Bourget passed through en route to America, where he was to make a lecture tour, and James gave him a letter of introduction to Wendell Holmes.

On June 17, after many delays, William and Alice arrived in London. Henry put them up in his own flat and took lodgings for himself in Ramsgate on the Strait of Dover, one of the newly popular seaside resorts, of the bathing-machine and German-band sort—the noise of hand organs in the street disturbed his composure—but it was cheap and convenient on short notice. He left William and Alice in happy possession of his flat in London, waited upon by his servants, and came up to town once a week "for a few hours, to look after them."

This was Alice's first true vacation away from the children, and James was glad to make it possible. He provided Alice and William not only with a flat and servants but with an introduction to intellectual and artistic London. Alice told him that she was "enjoying life to a degree that is little short of unprincipled. And after all it is your kindness which makes London such a paradise."

He left William and Alice to their own devices, however, for he was deeply engaged in writing new plays and stories, and on his weekly forays into London he was enmeshed once more in the world of theater, into which his brother, three sisters-in-law, nieces, and nephews could hardly enter. "Dear Mrs. Bell, I am engaged to go to 4 different places this afternoon between 5 & 6:30, & to do, besides, 17 other different things."

The theaters were busy at the height of the Season, and he struggled to keep abreast, attending plays with Lucy Clifford, Rhoda Broughton, and Florence Bell. Eleonora Duse was in London, playing the classics in a new, realistic method, drawing on her own sense memories and feelings rather than on a repertoire of formal gestures. With Rhoda Broughton, James saw Duse in *Antony and Cleopatra*, and he came away astonished at the effect Duse could produce without makeup, elaborate sets, or costumes.

Oscar Wilde had written a play in French, telling the story of Salomé, and had given it to Sarah Bernhardt to perform; Bernhardt was, of course, denied a license to perform the play in London—even aside from its sexuality, it was a Bible story and so barred on that ground alone from the British stage. As the lord chamberlain had no jurisdiction over the press, however, Wilde arranged for John Lane to publish the play in London, in an English translation prepared by his young friend Alfred Douglas. Lane provided suitably fey illustrations by the heretofore unknown Aubrey Beardsley.

Salomé in its French edition was well received in Paris, and while still there James had written to Florence Bell with intense curiosity to inquire about the English edition, asking for "any crumbs of information on these thrilling themes that you could flick toward me with an idle finger." Back in London, James saw Wilde's other new play, *A Woman of No Importance*, which he thought thin and cynical; it was a comedy of manners in which the effete Lord Illingworth, an extension of the Wilde–Dorian Gray persona, exhibited the corruption and hypocrisy of Society. At the debut, Wilde came on stage to take his bow wearing a white waistcoat and a bunch of lilies in his buttonhole: Illingworth personified. There was applause from the boxes but hoots and hisses from the gallery. Wilde seemed upset by the uproar and after a moment withdrew behind the curtain.

There were a great many things for James to consider quietly in Ramsgate, freed from the distractions of London. Compton had asked for a comedy to add to his repertoire. James wanted also to have a second play in hand for Daly, another light comedy, in the event that *Mrs. Jasper* was a success. Most demanding of all, however, was George Alexander's request for a serious play, to follow the success of *The Second Mrs. Tanqueray.*

James distinguished in his notes made at this time between "drama" and "the theater." Drama was an art whose forms he had begun to master and in which he took great pleasure. The pressures of the marketplace had forced him to learn that the same method of attack was needed for both short stories and plays: "this frequent, fruitful, intimate battle with the particular idea, with the subject, the possibility, the place," within the narrow constraints of the small frame, the strict allowance of time and space. Literature of a particular moment, the drama and the short story— rather than the great architectural works and landscapes of the serialized novel—seemed to him his true medium. In the midst of his efforts to storm the commercial theater, therefore, he reminded himself:

> that literature sits patient at my door, & that I have only to lift the latch to let in the exquisite little form that is after all, nearest to my heart & with which I am so far from having done.

"Hew out a style," he told young Fred Benson at this time, "it is by style we are saved." He evidently meant more than the choice of words. "Style" was what separated him from Howells, style was everything that mattered: the window through which he saw, the frame within which he composed his embroideries; it was the balance of light and dark, the composition and the brushwork.

Having abandoned the serialized novel, James had undergone a sort of literary conversion. The big novels and the studies that had led up to them—"All my previous work," he said, exaggerating—have "been subaqueous; now I have got my head above water." In the noisy privacy of Ramsgate, he filled his notebook with ideas for short stories and plays; began sketching plays based on already published stories; set down story ideas that would become the plays *Guy Domville* and *The Other House,* the latter of which would in turn become a story as well; made preliminary sketches for what were conceived as short stories and would become his great novels *What Maisie Knew, The Spoils of Poynton, The Sacred Fount,* and *The Golden Bowl,* planting seeds that would flower into his work for much of the next ten years.

This revel in drama was quite separate from his experiments in the theater, in the successful production of commercial properties, which had their own place in his economy and education.

By the middle of August, when by tradition the shooting of grouse could begin, the Ten Thousand had abandoned London for the countryside and the Continent, American visitors had also fled, alarmed by the news of a spreading financial panic. A bubble of speculation in railroad securities had burst, and a vast invisible structure of debt was collapsing. Depositors and creditors lost confidence in paper instruments and demanded to be paid in silver or gold; banks that were unable to meet these demands began closing their doors, brokerages collapsed, bankruptcies and defaults spread, further fueling the panic. James was not affected, the family investments were principally in Syracuse real estate, which was free of debt, and their own railroad bonds seemed secure; but Henry Adams went home hastily. William and Alice returned to the Continent to gather up their children for their voyage to Boston and Cambridge, where William was to return to his teaching duties.

One Sunday afternoon the following winter, Henry Harland and Aubrey Beardsley came to James with a plan for a new sort of illustrated magazine, a fat quarterly, self-contained and bound between hard covers like a book. Each number would be newly designed to suit its contents. Harland and Beardsley proposed to bring together the best of modern designers, writers, and illustrators in a cooperative venture.

The project seemed made to order for James. There would be no serialized novels; instead the editors would give ample space to short stories and novelettes. The discipline of fitting his tales within rigidly defined spaces had forced James to write some of his best work, masterpieces of concision, but he hated the restraint. Here was an opportunity to free himself from these fetters, to allow each idea to expand to its natural form, without retreating to the serialized novel.

The proposed design of the magazine was also attractive. Monthly illustrated magazines had the ugliness of the machine-made; but this new magazine would be, as it were, handmade, produced with all the care that was customarily lavished on the three-decker novel but sold at an annual subscription of one pound.

Recalling that Sunday afternoon many years afterward, James saw in a kind of golden light these fragile young men, both suffering from tuberculosis. Harland was an American, a Brooklyn boy who had attended the City College of New York, who had worked as a freelance writer before journeying to Paris. He was tall, painfully thin, and pale; his long hair, winged mustache, and Vandyke beard gave him an exotic air, and he allowed people to think that he was born in Saint Petersburg and had studied in Rome. He greatly resembled the young painter John La Farge of James's fond remembrance, who had introduced James to art and literature. Like La Farge, he was severely nearsighted and depended on ugly spectacles that he disliked wearing.

James was charmed as well by the young man who accompanied him. Aubrey Beardsley and James had met before, but this was their first extended conversation, and James would recall the encounter fondly: "This young man, slender, pale, delicate, unmistakably intelligent, somehow invested the whole proposition with a detached, a slightly ironic, melancholy grace."

Harland was to be fiction editor, Beardsley art editor and chief illustrator, and John Lane would publish the magazine. As it was a cooperative venture, the authors and illustrators would all share in the profits, which would be immense. There would be editions in Great Britain, America, and the Commonwealth. James was urged to become a founding member and a regular contributor to the somewhat vaguely defined enterprise. This was to mark an epoch in his career, as he would recall many years later:

> I was invited, and all urgently, to contribute to the first number, and was regaled with the golden truth that my composition might absolutely assume its own organic form. . . . For any idea I might wish to express I might have, in other words, the space to express it.

James suggested practical difficulties, but Harland turned them aside with a laugh, and James became thoroughly engaged. He would contribute a story for the first issue, would happily associate his name with the new venture, would become a regular contributor. The project seemed to open up a "millennium," or at least a new century, to the short story.

The nominal business offices of the magazine were at Lane's Bodley Head, on Vigo Street, but in practice were in the flat Harland and his wife, Aline, had taken on Cromwell Road, Kensington. The editors had appropriated one small room of Harland's flat, down a short flight of stairs from the other rooms, and nearly filled it with a big writing table. Harland had a revolving chair at a small desk beside the fireplace, where he was often bent over proofs but could swivel about to face the room and his visitors. This office was in its way a replacement for Balestier's congenial rooms in the Dean's Yard. *The Yellow Book* not only opened a new era for James's fiction writing, it formed a center for his young friends. Harland and Gosse now became better acquainted, and Gosse became one of the regular contributors, as did the young Arthur Benson and Max Beerbohm. The old Broadway circle was drawn in, and Sargent contributed the pencil portrait he had done of James at Broadway, four summers before; or rather, James obtained Sargent's permission to submit it, inscribed to him by the artist as it was.

Early in December 1893, Daly held a perfunctory walk-through with scripts in hand of the revised *Mrs. Jasper,* with Ada Rehan reading the title role, and afterward wrote to James saying that, as it stood, the play would not do, at least not without further extensive revisions.

James replied angrily, having worked hard in reliance on Daly's assurances; his angry letter charged Daly with bad faith, with having held the play for a year and having then dropped it; the walk-through was a mere pretense for dismissal. The inaugural season in Daly's expensive new theater had gone very badly, and now with financial hard times Daly was evidently trying to pull back from his ambitious venture. James wrote a stern, contemptuous letter. Far from offering to make further changes to salvage the play, he concluded, "I withdraw it from your theatre without delay & beg you to send me back the MS."

Daly responded somewhat defensively—he had designed and ordered sets and costumes for the play, which hardly showed bad faith—James would have been free to revise his text on "subsequent rehearsals." But James shrugged and moved on. ("Oof!—it's a relief to be able to stop so painfully pretending (for good manners) that one takes the poor blundered & muddled Daly enterprise seriously.")

Daly had behaved badly and his venture had failed, but James's comedies had not inspired much enthusiasm among other producers. James was too good-natured for the medium; his comedies lacked edges, had no violent overturnings of expectations or conventions, nothing startling or outrageous; they provoked smiles rather than laughter. But unwilling for the poor things to die unseen, James arranged for publication of all his unacted plays. *Mrs. Vibert* and *Mrs. Jasper* (renamed *The Tenants* and *Disengaged*, respectively, now that there were no actors to flatter) were printed as a single slim volume, *Theatricals.* Two unacted comedies, *The Album* and *The Reprobate*, were to follow in the fall. James wrote for the first volume of "theatricals" (evidently not "dramas") a brief preface that still bore the marks of his anger, but for the second volume he recovered his good humor and wrote a longer and more thoughtful note, summing up his early experiences in the theater. He had come to the stage from a career as a novelist but had very quickly learned that a "big" subject could not be handled in two and a half hours of performance. The lessons for a novelist to learn were those of brevity and simplicity, and that a play was a collaboration.

In the new year, winter descended with unusual force: black, fiercely frozen days, water pipes congealing and then bursting. The financial panic had deepened and spread to Great Britain; coal miners had been on strike for months, threatening real hardships for the miners and for a city without coal in winter. James's friend Lord Rosebery was attempting to mediate the strike.

Gladstone, seemingly as vigorous as ever at eighty-four, had returned as prime minister and had forced through the House of Commons a bill that granted limited home rule for Ireland within a British commonwealth. Arthur Balfour spoke against it, with great effectiveness. There was violent opposition to the home-rule bill from English landowners in Ireland, and it seemed likely to die in the House of Lords.

James might have observed from the center of affairs, if he had cared to, as the principals in these great dramas were his friends; but he did not. He was in the process of letting go. On Christmas Day, James dined with the George Smalleys, as he did nearly every year, but he was glad to avoid the annual visit to the Roseberys at Mentmore or any country-house celebrations of the holiday, with their "forced hilarity." On December 26, he opened his notebook:

> I have been sitting here in the firelight—on the quiet afternoon of the empty London Xmastide, trying to catch hold of an idea, of a "subject." Vague, dim forms of imperfect conceptions seem to brush across one's face with a hint of suggestion, a flutter of impalpable wings.

He marked the end of the year by having dinner with the Gosses and writing letters to family and friends scattered across two continents.

Early in January 1894, he held one of his little dinners for six. Margaret Brooke, an old friend to whom he had recently grown closer, was there. She had left a quiet rural English home to marry the buccaneer James Brooke, the conqueror of a tropical kingdom in Borneo who had been named rajah of Sarawak by its Malayan governor. Margaret Brooke was a woman of James's own age who had lived a strange life in Brooke's jungle palace, among his concubines, and had vivid stories to tell. When Margaret seemed to be taking too much interest in a Malay servant, Brooke wrung the necks of her pet doves and served them to her in a pie. She set off with her sons, for England.

Now the ranee—she signed herself "Margaret of Sarawak"—had a house at Ascot and another at Nervi, near Genoa. Her principal interest was in securing the succession to the throne of Sarawak for her eldest son, Charles. She and James had long been acquainted but became close friends when Charles fell gravely ill and James entered in his sympathetic way into her concerns. The tall, spare, regal, and intimidating Brooke was thereafter fiercely devoted to him and supported his theatrical projects with enthusiasm.

Into his winter London quiet fell a telegram telling him that his dear friend Constance Woolson was dead. She had been living in Venice when she died—James had only the other day received a letter from her there. The telegram came from Woolson's cousin Grace Carter, who had been summoned from Munich; the only close relative, a married sister, was in America and would not arrive for weeks. James was for practical purposes Woolson's nearest relation in Europe. Nothing was said as yet about the cause of her sudden death.

Woolson's death was a blow: she had been a good friend for many years, and he had been her mentor artistically and personally; she was one of a very few American writers with whom he felt artistic kinship, of whom it was said that she was of his school. He had introduced her to the Europe in which she had settled, his friends had become her friends. The deaths of Elizabeth Boott and Alice James had hit her very hard and had left her even more alone. James was named one of the executors of her will: he now turned his attention to the familiar duties that followed such a death.

Woolson had often expressed her wish to be buried in the Protestant

Cemetery in Rome. James cabled to John Hay, whom he knew to be in Rome, and asked his help in making arrangements. Woolson had died on Wednesday, January 24, and the funeral was to be the following Wednesday. James hastily made preparations for departure and went to Cook's for railway tickets. It would be just possible, if he set off on Sunday morning and made all his connections, to arrive in Rome in time for the burial. He bought his tickets, but returning to De Vere Gardens he found a note from a friend who had just returned from Venice, enclosing a clipping from a Venetian newspaper, a paragraph that contained what was for James an appalling account of Woolson's death. It appeared from the newspaper that she had committed suicide. This news deepened his distress still more. An invitation from Margaret Brooke was awaiting his answer, and he wrote to her very hastily:

> A close & valued friend of mine—a friend of many years with whom I was extremely intimate & to whom I was greatly attached (Miss Fenimore Woolson, the American novelist, a singularly charming & distinguished woman), died last Wednesday, in Venice, with dreadful attendant circumstances. Ill with influenza, aggravated by desperate insomnia, she threw herself out of the upper window of her house & died an hour later! It is too horrible to me to write about it—I mention it really only to tell you that for the present I *can't* write.

There was another telegram, from John Hay, offering every assistance and passing along a word from Robert Nevins, the pastor of St. Paul's Within the Walls, the American church in Rome, assuring James that arrangements had been made for Woolson's burial in the Protestant Cemetery. After reading Hay's telegram, which assured him that his presence was not required, he cabled Grace Carter to say that he was not coming, after all. He was not needed and could not face an exhausting and sleepless two-day rail journey simply to stand beside Woolson's grave. He cabled to Hay that he was not coming and wrote a letter to explain:

> Miss Woolson was so valued & close a friend of mine & had been so for so many years that I feel an intense nearness of participation in every circumstance of her tragic end & in every detail of the sequel. But it is just this nearness of emotion that has made—since [reading the newspaper account] yesterday—the immediate horrified rush to personally *meet* these things impossible to me. . . . But what a picture of lonely unassisted suffering! It is too horrible for thought!

He had written stories in which suicide was portrayed without moral condemnation, as an ultimate sacrifice, or as an escape from suffering. But Constance Woolson, whom he had loved in his way, seemingly had merely given her life up, giving way to depression and the temptation of self-murder. Or so the newspaper claimed. It was only too easy for him to imagine her alone and ill, suffering from depression and surrendering at last to weariness. He was upset for several days and, for once unable to conceal his feelings, was obliged to explain the cause of his unhappiness to his friends. To Rhoda Broughton he wrote, putting off an engagement:

> I have been terribly overwhelmed by some shocking news—the death of my old and dear friend Miss Woolson in Venice—with deplorable attendant circumstance. . . . You will easily see how miserably spent I have been—(the whole event is unspeakably tragic; which is why I haven't written to you [sooner].)
>
> The tragedy of Miss Woolson's death remains—till I have more light (I have none yet,) terribly obscure—as obscure as it is shocking. It is explicable only on the hypothesis of some sudden explosion of latent brain-disease. But it is unspeakably sad & pitiful.

He wrote to Gosse ("what an overwhelming, haunting horror—& intolerable obsession of the ghastly, pitiful *fact!*"). Arthur Benson kindly kept him company on the day of the funeral, "a day of despair," but he otherwise ceased seeing people for several days. He lived through his anger, sadness, and distress of the moment, faced it, and was shortly at work again.

It was February, and the first number of *The Yellow Book* was scheduled for publication in April. He had promised to provide a short story for the inaugural issue, and in a sleepless night just before receiving news of Woolson's death, he had made some notes of ideas for stories, but none had crystallized. He had wanted to write about a writer's death, before he had learned of Woolson's; it was a theme that had interested him since about the time of his fiftieth birthday and that he had already addressed in "The Middle Years." He now returned to the pairing of youth and age, love and death. He wanted to treat this question from the perspective of the dying writer himself, somehow to divide the writer's consciousness or supply him with an alter ego, but no image of how this could be done had yet appeared to him. On the Saturday after Constance Woolson's burial, having cleared his calendar, James sat down to his writing desk and pursued his earlier thought:

> Could not something be done with the idea of the great (the distinguished, the celebrated) artist—man of letters he must, in the case, be—who is tremendously made up to, fêted, written to for his autograph, portrait, etc., & yet with whose work, in this age of advertisement & newspaperism, this age of interviewing, not one of the persons concerned has the smallest acquaintance? It would have the merit, at least, of corresponding to an immense reality—a reality that strikes me every day of my life.

He began to sketch out a story, "The Death of the Lion," a comedy tinged with melancholy: just the tone for the new end-of-century magazine. Neal Paraday is a novelist who has had a sudden vogue and is harried, literally to death, by hostesses in pursuit of the latest fashion. It could be a little play: Paraday lies dying in an upstairs bedroom, forgotten, while his hostess chatters with her guests downstairs about his latest masterpiece. Among the guests are "Guy Walsingham," the author of *Obsessions,* who is in reality a Miss Collop, and "Dora Forbes," a bluff mustachioed fellow who writes romantic novels. Paraday dies; he has lent the draft of his last great work to one of his fatuous hostesses, who has lost it, and it vanishes along with him.

A pressing request from Henry Harper: to write once again about George du Maurier, whose second novel, *Trilby,* was beginning its run in *Harper's New Monthly Magazine.* Would James please write a notice—a puff—for the weekly?

James had already written three admiring essays on du Maurier's work as an illustrator, and he was pressed for time, but he did not like to say no to Harper, especially when a favor was asked for his friend, and so despite the press of other work he looked into the proofs of *Trilby* and hastily wrote a gorgeous, joyous, and uncritical notice praising his friend's two novels. They genuinely touched a chord for him: each was "intensely a vision of youth and the soul of youth. . . . Everything and every one is not only beautiful for him, it is also divinely young."

James had encouraged du Maurier to write, and these first efforts visibly reflected their conversations and their shared fondness for France. The early chapters of his first novel, *Peter Ibbetson,* had been a reminiscence of du Maurier's childhood in Passy; the early chapters of *Trilby* now recalled his years as an art student in Paris. James cheerfully set aside his own memories of Paris and immersed himself in du Maurier's; their memories would soon mingle again in his own novel *The Ambassadors*.

Du Maurier was illustrating the serial himself. His drawings portrayed a circle of young men sharing a studio in Paris, intensely enjoying one another's company. He vividly evoked the lovable, doomed artist Little Billee—the name was from a ballad, a favorite of du Maurier's—who greatly resembled du Maurier himself. Trilby, a girl not yet out of her teens, poses in the nude for the artists and takes casual lovers from among them. Trilby is a picture of innocent sensuality from whom Little Billee turns in alarm, while the villain Svengali "capers like a goat of poetry, and makes music like the great god Pan."

With his story in Harland's hands, his essay on du Maurier and two plays at Harper's awaiting publication, on March 20 James set off for Italy. He planned to be away until July, avoiding most of the Season in London; he promised himself a long and leisurely visit to Venice.

He went first by rail to Paris, stopping briefly there to see old friends, and then embarked on the long journey by rail into Italy. His destination was Venice, but he broke his journey in Genoa and went out into the country to visit with the ranee in Nervi for a few days. Back in the cars, he continued across Italy to Venice for a long stay—"I am making love to Italy as hard as I can—it's the only way to treat her." He was rapidly recovering from the downturn in health and spirits that always followed a period of high-pressure work.

James took lodgings in Venice. The Curtises' son, Ralph, was with them at the Barbaro, occupying James's usual apartment; he did not want to inconvenience the Curtises, and in any case did not want to be a house guest, with obligations to his hosts, for a period of months. He took rooms in the Casa Biondetti, near the great mouth of the Grand Canal and a short walk from the Casa Semitecolo from whose windows Constance Woolson had plunged to her death. There was still the matter of her estate to deal with.

Woolson's sister Clara Benedict and her daughter, Clare, had arrived and were lodged in Woolson's rooms in the Casa Semitecolo, sorting through Woolson's papers and belongings. James helped to carry out Woolson's wishes as well as he could. He was glad to hear Clara Benedict's firm opinion, which he accepted, that Constance had not thrown herself from her window but, feverish and confused, had fallen accidentally.

James found himself much in demand in Venice: by the Curtises, by his old Bostonian friend Mrs. Bronson, who insisted on his visiting her new summer house in Asolo; the aged Countess Pisani, the once-lovely daughter of Byron's English physician, who had introduced him to the old cliff dwellers of Venice in former years. These were not onerous obligations; he spent a very pleasant day with Ralph Curtis, forming a lasting friendship with the languid, talented youth. On his return to London he would begin a lifelong correspondence with "My dear Ralph," signing himself, "Yours forever." Through Ralph, he met another young American painter attempting to make his way in Europe, John Briggs Potter—"he is so young, so clean, so sincere & ingenuous, with such a charm in his face, such a beauty of a curious sort, in his delicate talent, & such an absence of fortune at his elbow, that he interested me"—to whom he gave letters of introduction to friends in Paris, something he rarely did.

Although he had plainly recovered from the shock of Woolson's death, his labors at the Casa Semitecolo were considerable and kept him from either work or rest. He made funny, self-deprecatory anecdotes about the sad business of disposing of Woolson's belongings. One evening at the Countess Pisani's, he told a story of carrying out Woolson's instruction to dispose of her personal things. A lady who was present remembered long afterward his saying that Woolson's instructions obliged him to take some of her personal belongings out in a gondola and drown them in the lagoon:

> He made a frightfully funny story, I thought, of it, because he said he took all these things out into the laguna and there were a lot of clothes, a lot of her black dresses, so he threw them in the water and they came up like balloons, all around him, and the more he tried to throw them down . . . the more they came [up] again, and he was surrounded by them.

He was struggling to read proofs, to write another long story for the second number of *The Yellow Book*, and to deal with the voluminous correspondence forwarded to him from De Vere Gardens ("Dear Lady Carnavon, I very greatly regret that your invitation to dine on May 24th should find me so far from England.") Some of his letters concerned

Trilby, which was having a scandalous success in the United States. The young heroine's innocent sensuality and du Maurier's anticlerical diatribes were disturbing some readers. Du Maurier, far from condemning Trilby's behavior, had interpolated into his novel a little essay in praise of nudity and extended his approval even to her casual love affairs. In his illustrations Trilby appeared in a sort of halo, in bright contrast to the villain Svengali, whose dark and greasy Semitic features were made literally devilish. The magazine serial created an uproar, echoes of which reached James even in Venice. He found among his forwarded letters one from an American lady who denounced him for having praised *Trilby*. He sent it along to du Maurier with an amused little note: "Only see . . . to what my thick-and-thin espousal of your genius exposes me."

The first number of *The Yellow Book* appeared in April as scheduled, and prompted another uproar. The book was elegantly designed by Beardsley, in stark black-and-white line drawings, a new kind of design that seemed to look forward to an age of machines. The drawings were in the style of his *Salomé* illustrations, and they seemed somehow perverse. In that first issue, twenty-one-year-old Max Beerbohm, still at Oxford, had written a sub-Wildean essay in praise of cosmetics, comparing the present age to the declining years of the Roman Empire and referring archly to "many men in a certain sect of society" who painted their faces and "lay among the rouge pots." The new century that was coming, he forecast, would be a postfeminist world in which innocence was lost, in which young women would give up the bicycling and typewriting for which they had fought and devote themselves to seduction: "For behold! The Victorian era comes to its end."

This first number of the quarterly was a great success and went through three further printings (each sold as a collectible "first edition"), its success fanned by cries of outrage from reviewers. The conservative *Westminster Gazette* called, in all seriousness, for an act of Parliament to prohibit such drawings as Beardsley's. Violent attacks were aimed at Beerbohm, and the whole enterprise was lampooned in *Punch;* altogether the editors could hardly have asked for a better reception.

James's mildly comic, fey, and faintly autobiographical story opened the book, and he seemed to spread his benevolent cloak over the fun. He was happily at work on a story, really a novelette (he preferred the French term *nouvelle*), "The Coxon Fund," for the second issue, and was reveling in the ample space Harland was giving him. But he did not send a copy of this first issue to his brother William, as he had usually done with his published work.

With deadlines met and Constance Woolson's estate in order, James spent a month as a tourist in Italy. He went first to Rome, planning to stay only a few days and then go on to a cooler climate, but Rome proved to have unexpected attractions, and the few days extended themselves through the month of June.

He was at relative leisure, and while in Rome he read his late sister's remarkable diary, whose existence he had not until then suspected. Katherine Loring, Alice's heir, had had duplicates made for the three surviving brothers and herself in the only practical way, by having it set in type and printing off four copies; his had found him in Italy. Katherine evidently had no plan to publish the diary and so had allowed everything in it, personal references and disclosures included, to stand.

The diary Alice had kept in her final months was an eloquent and forceful document, a unique record of her personality and of her dying. James read his copy with great pleasure, mitigated only by his fear that the diary would not remain within the family. They were all public figures, under constant scrutiny by the newspapers, and both William and Robertson were capable of showing the diary to neighbors or even to a newspaper reporter. Indeed, gossip had already begun: while still in Venice, James had been startled by the remark of a Miss Wormley, who had made him jump by saying, "I hear your sister's letters have just been published, and are delightful." Much of the diary was devoted to him, to his conversation and his highly colored anecdotes about friends; Alice with her sharp pen had drawn numerous unflattering portraits of his friends, whose names were given.

The great pity of Katherine's thoughtlessness, as it seemed to James, aside from the risk of embarrassment, was that she had printed a few copies of the diary, but in a form in which it could not be made public. This was a great loss, for the diary not only was a fine work in its own right but kept alive Alice's "extraordinary force of mind and character, her whole way of taking life—& death." As he told William when he had finished reading it:

> I have been immensely impressed with the thing as a revelation & a moral & a personal picture. It is heroic in its individuality, its independence—its face-to-face with the universe for-&-by herself—&

the beauty & eloquence with which she often expresses this, let alone her rich irony & humour, constitute (I wholly agree with you,) a new claim for family renown. . . . Her style, her power to write, are indeed to me a delight.

James wished that Katherine had substituted blanks or initials in place of a few of the names; the diary could then have been published. But Katherine was Alice's heir, the diary was Katherine's property, and she had done all that she meant to do. She would leave to a later generation the task of preparing it for publication, and its long suppression was wrongly thought to be owing to James's sensitivity.

Rome had changed greatly since the day twenty-five years earlier when James had first gone reeling and moaning through its streets. He lived as much as ever in his senses, in each moment, but the atmosphere of ancient greatness that had so excited him in his youth was dissipating. New boulevards were being cut through the city; monuments that had stood outside of time were being briskly brushed up and cleaned or were giving way to ugly statues of King Victor Emmanuel II and raw monuments to a new Italy. The flickering candlelight and flaring torches of the old papal Rome had vanished in the harsh glare of the new nationalism; and if Rome was no longer old, James himself was no longer young. But he settled into the familiar Grand Hotel and a little at a time began to recover some of his pleasures and to find again an atmosphere of aesthetic sensibility.

Joseph Primoli helped reconcile James to Rome and persuaded him to extend his stay. James and Primoli had kept distantly in touch since their first cordial meeting in London, and their paths had occasionally crossed, but this was James's first visit to Primoli at home in Rome. The Palazzo Primoli, a picturesque sixteenth-century house on the Tiber, stood at the foot of Via Tor di Nona (now Via Zanardelli), opposite the garrison at Castel Sant'Angelo, overlooking vast uncompleted and half-abandoned earthworks, embankments, and highways along the river. Primoli was a bachelor and lived in the little palace with his mother and his younger brother, Louis.

Passing through the old entrance to the palace on the Tiber, one stepped out of modern Italy into the candlelit Rome of James's memories. Little rooms led into one another, every surface and corner filled with pictures and mementoes of Primolis, Borgheses, and Bonapartes and photographs of the new royalty and artistic elite of Rome. Louis Primoli was an enthusiastic photographer and had set out to document his age in photographs; Joseph had recently taken up the art from his younger brother, and they had accumulated a remarkable collection of pictures, some taken secretly with small new cameras that could be concealed within a coat or under a tall hat. There were numerous formal portraits of the contessa's father, Prince Charles-Lucien Bonaparte, and her brother Cardinal Luciano Bonaparte. There were mementoes of her grandfather, Joseph Bonaparte, who had briefly been the king of Spain; of princes whose principalities no longer existed.

Primoli was a mild, plump, and amiable man, devoted to the care of his mother. He had grown up in the courts of the Second Empire and of the Bonapartes in exile, and his easy, graceful manners and his easy hospitality made the Palazzo Primoli a gathering place for a literary set. Primoli was happy to introduce James to his friends and their work: Gabriele D'Annunzio, who was a great personal friend, as was Matilde Serao—"a wonderful little burly Balzac in petticoats," James said—"full of Neapolitan life & sound & familiarity." Gradually, James recovered some of the happy spirit of his first visits to Rome.

On his return to England, James was struck once again by the contrast with the Continent, but on the whole he was glad to be back among the "Protestant . . . sea-girded, Eton-bred & beef-fed & matutinally tubbed" English—he was none of these, he said, except the last (he loved the tub of butter at breakfast)—but after all it was not a question of preferring either England or the Continent but of enjoying the contrast. He renewed his visits to Morgan Hall, his favorite window on rural England, where Abbey and Sargent were happily at work in their vast new studio. Canvases leaned upon immense easels, the walls were covered with tapestries and ornaments evoking a fantastic world; models in dishabille lounged on chairs or were posed upon the two theatrical stages in period costumes; heaps of costumes and backcloths were everywhere. James luxuriated in the theatrical atmosphere and the hospitality that Gertrude Mead supplied, enjoying especially the fresh eggs and butter that marked the excellence of the English countryside. James admired the butter and eggs so much, indeed, and complained so pointedly of the difficulty of obtaining fresh eggs in London, that Gertrude obligingly arranged to have eggs from Morgan Hall sent to him. She had a box specially constructed and had a servant carry it to London. Mrs. Smith sent it back empty, and lo! it promptly returned again, filled with another week's supply of eggs.

"The arrival of the eggs makes me believe in better things, " James said in his thank-you note. "I don't mean better than eggs—there is nothing better." When the supply of eggs ceased in the fall, he wrote to inquire:

> We are very unhappy at the non-arrival of our eggs and are full of delicacy, at the same time, as to inquiring about them. Is the egg crop failing? Have the animals struck? Are we and they all victims of agricultural depression? I feared it, and if the disaster is at last upon us, won't you very kindly let me know the worst. . . . May we at any rate have news. News would be good, but eggs would be better.

He was determined, now, to achieve his long-standing ambition to have an enclave of privacy of his own. In late summer, James went in search of a country house. He visited the Thomas Huxleys in Tunbridge Wells; spoke with them and asked for their advice about a house, perhaps one nearby, convenient to London but close to open countryside: "I particularly envy you the resource of Sussex downs & the ventilation of Sussex air" where there was "no black phantom [of depression] you can't walk away from." Aside from wanting a retreat for himself in summer, he wanted more room for visiting sisters-in-law, nieces, nephews, and intimate bachelor friends.

James thought that he might like a seaside town on the mild south coast, warmed in winter by the Gulf Stream, and went for a long tour of Cornwall, where he paid a visit to Leslie Stephen, and of Devon. In Torquay, he struck up a warm friendship with William Norris, a lawyer who as "W. E. Norris" wrote popular and successful novels; but he did not find quite what he wanted.

On his return to London for the winter, his spirits were somewhat depressed. He would write a short story for every issue of *The Yellow Book*, but the cooperative scheme had collapsed and the promised profits had not materialized. John Lane had taken over management of the enterprise, and payments to authors were meager. James now had few other outlets in Britain. He felt that a new generation, whom he knew not and prized not, had taken possession, and in gloomy temper he wrote to Howells, inquiring about markets for his work in the United States.

· · ·

The visits of William and Alice, perhaps, as well as the advent of friends of a new and younger generation, had made him conscious of how dingy the walls of his flat had become, and while searching for a country house, he also made arrangements for his flat to be painted, repapered, and wired for electric light.

A long, charming letter came from Louis Stevenson in Samoa, but James complained to Sidney Colvin that there was nothing about Stevenson himself, his health, or his plans, except that he was "bad in the head and languid in the heart."

> This was a mood I take it—he says himself it would probably lift at any hour, but it effectually cut off, in the letter, everything else one wanted to know. I shall be as communicative as possible in reply—to heap coals on his head—Meanwhile any direct word from him gives me joy, as hinting that he hasn't forgotten a fellow—and sacrificed one wholly to cannibal friendships.

Although James had seemed to make his peace with the stage and, like the dying author of his tale "The Middle Years," had renounced the struggle for glory, when George Alexander asked for a play James rose once more to the lure. James gave Alexander a choice of three plays for which he had prepared outlines. Alexander chose a play whose working title was "The Hero." It had begun as a note for a short story, two years before, an anecdote picked up in Venice:

> Situation of that once-upon-a-time member of an old Venetian family (I forget which), who had become a monk, & who was taken almost forcibly out of his convent & brought back into the world in order to keep the family from becoming extinct . . .—it was absolutely *necessary* for him to marry.

As it first appeared to him, the masculine protagonist's heroism would consist in submitting himself to marriage. Perhaps because this might seem just an old joke about George Eliot and her young husband, he decided to give the story a turn.

The protagonist, Guy Domville, was to be lured back from a convent and introduced to the pleasures of the world, but then—for some reason—he must refuse the marriage that is offered to him and now, in full knowledge that he is giving up love and life itself, must condemn himself to celibacy. It was the part James had written for Isabel Archer in *The Portrait of a Lady* and for Claire de Cintré in *The American*, and in a way it was also the part Pinero had written for Stella Campbell in *The Second Mrs. Tanqueray*. Now George Alexander would play the lead, would be beautiful, and would sacrifice himself for others.

But it was a difficult question, how to translate the essentially Continental and Catholic story to modern, Protestant, beef-eating England; how to adapt it "somehow or other to today." James thought he could solve the problem by setting the play in the eighteenth century, in an old country house where an English Catholic family might evoke echoes of Thackeray's historical novels, rather than popish Italy.

He placed the play indeed in the same house in which he had put his *The Portrait of a Lady*, one that had been the estate of an old English Catholic family, and the play opened as the novel did, in "the garden of an old house . . . behind the house, away from the public approach." Into the garden once again stepped the tempter, Lord Devenish, a corrupt aristocrat.

It is Devenish who tries to ensnare Guy Domville in a loveless marriage. After escaping from one scheme, Guy considers marrying the widowed lady of the house, Mrs. Peveral, with whom he has fallen in love. But this marriage too would require him to submit to Lord Devenish's schemes, and he refuses as honor requires. The play ends, as *The Portrait of a Lady* did, with the hero poised to leave the scene of his temptation, his hand on the door, intending to follow the straight path of duty and sacrifice, while love seeks to call him back.

The clarity of James's idea, his "Portrait of a Gentleman," was obscured by the plot devices required for Guy Domville to make his double sacrifice within the space of an evening's entertainment.

The story had expanded to take necessary characters and events into account and took on some of the architectural quality of James's big novels. He began to complain about the constraints of the London stage, the two and a half hours to which he was strictly limited, when in Paris a play might run for three or even four hours. Now that he was largely freed from the constraints of the marketplace, James set aside the lesson of the commercial theater, the lesson of selection that he had celebrated and that had led him to produce some of his best work, and hoped for a success in drama as well as the theater.

Alexander liked the play and evidently shared James's ambition for it. He asked that James call it *Guy Domville* for the leading character that he would portray. He had sets and costumes designed for an opening in January, to begin his first season at the newly refurbished St. James's Theatre, where electric lighting had been installed. His character would be on stage for nearly every scene, and the story would show him emerging from youthful innocence into gaudy worldliness. During the course of the play he would acquire a manner and make an entrance in the second act transformed by the beautiful clothes of the peacock dandies of the Georgian era—in powdered wig, cutaway coat, snug velvet knee breeches, silk stockings, low-cut buckled shoes—the costume that Oscar Wilde had once tried to approximate.

The eighteenth-century setting, aside from providing gorgeous costumes, allowed James to speak more frankly of sexuality than would have seemed appropriate in the Victorian world. The play would be a virtuous revel in sensuality and could hardly have provided a better part for Alexander. But when the first reading of the full play showed how long it had grown, he insisted that James cut it back to the usual two and a half hours, and James began to fear that this was simply not adequate to his idea. He would have to cut a whole act from the middle of the play, one that might have allowed him to portray a needed lapse of time.

When daytime rehearsals began, James was in daily attendance. (Another play, Henry Arthur Jones's *The Masqueraders*, was being performed in the evenings.) Alexander had assembled a fine cast and was proving himself to be a talented actor, as James was happy to see. The sets and costumes for James's play were elaborate and realistic, and James devoted much attention to them, as in times past he had worked with illustrators over their drawings. The scenes in the garden were particularly elaborate, with a living tree espaliered against a sunny back wall. In December, the theater closed in order for the sets to be put up, and evening rehearsals began.

In the midst of these consuming preparations, newspapers reported that Robert Louis Stevenson had died in Samoa on December 3, 1894. James first read a report of Stevenson's death on December 17, and he broke off a cheerful letter to Florence Bell—"Since I wrote this 2 hours ago—has come the most unspeakable news of R.L.S.'s death."

Although Stevenson's death from tuberculosis had long been expected, the news fell upon James, as Gosse later recalled, "with a shock which he found at first scarcely endurable." To Gosse he wrote immediately:

I meant to write to you tonight on another matter—but of what can one think, or utter, or dream, than save of this ghastly extinction of the beloved R. L. S.? It is too miserable for cold words—it's an absolute desolation. It makes me cold & sick—& with the absolute, almost alarmed sense, of the visible material quenching of an indispensable light. That he's silent forever will be a fact hard, for a long time, to live with. Today, at any rate, it's a cruel, wringing emotion. One feels how one cared for him—what a place he took; or as if suddenly into that place there had descended a great avalanche of ice. . . . I can't write of this.

For a long time afterward he could not bring himself to mention Stevenson's name without distressing agitation. As Christmas approached, there was still no direct word from Fanny confirming the death, and James had a flicker of hope that the newspaper stories were wrong. But Stevenson had in truth died, and confirmation came soon.

In the midst of his troubles, a letter came from Howells, answering a little belatedly James's discouraged note in the fall. American magazine editors would leap at the chance to publish James's short stories; why did he not send them? If he should write stories of the quality of those he had been sending to British journals, he would address a larger public than he had ever reached before. New magazines were starting up—the field was widening, he had only to occupy it. As to his fears for the younger generation, "You must know, you are very modern." Howell said that his daughter, who was very twentieth century in her tastes, had joy "in everything you do." James did not respond immediately, but it was a reassuring letter to receive just then.

14

CLOSING THE CHAPTER

Dress rehearsals for *Guy Domville* began on New Year's Eve, the cast performing in costume for the first time, in an empty house with James their sole audience. Costumes, sets, and blocking required adjustment and modification, and James fretted and slept badly through the three nights of dress rehearsals and last-minute changes.

The opening was scheduled for Saturday, January 5, 1895, four years almost to the day since his first opening in Southport. In the last few weeks of preparations, James had again attended to the business of dressing the house: a stream of letters of invitation had to be sent; anxious inquiries from friends to be answered. "My dear Gosse: It will be all right. . . . None of the seats have been sent out yet. Those you will receive are not to be paid for—they are direct from the author." William Norris was coming up from Torquay, in the midst of winter, to be present, and James tried to arrange a box for the Gosses that Norris could share. Many other friends had inquired or told him of their plans to attend: the advance publicity had been excellent, and Alexander informed him that advance sales were good—lending libraries that acted also as ticket agents had purchased £1,600 worth—and James's friends once more rallied around him: Florence Bell and Elizabeth Robins, of course; the Gosses; Sargent, Abbey, and Parsons; the Frank Millets; Mary Ward and Lucy Clifford, with their escorts; the du Mauriers; the Smalleys. There were negotiations to conduct with the theater management over the boxes and stalls he would be given, surrogate hosts asked to arrange to fill the boxes. Hugh Bell was to be in charge of one box of six, Florence Bell and Elizabeth Robins had stalls but "Forgive the uncontrollable accident if you have received from the box office of the theatre a stall you will have had to pay for, instead of receiving it from my hands and gratis."

All of this had to be done despite the awful fact of Stevenson's death. A telegram from Stevenson's lawyers in Edinburgh informed James that he had been named Stevenson's literary executor and asked him to reply immediately by telegram whether he would accept the appointment. In the midst of his hurry and anxiety he telegraphed back that he must decline. He had repeatedly been through the exercise of administering an estate and was not willing to undertake what seemed likely to be a still more daunting one. He was not a man of business, and his circumstances would not allow him the leisure or the means to handle any of Louis's business affairs. It was still dimly possible that the reports from Samoa were wrong; but then at Christmas came the telegram from Fanny confirming absolutely that Louis was dead. James sat down to write a long letter of condolence and apology for having refused appointment as executor.

He had not had the luxury of taking a day or two to absorb what had happened, as he had with the news of Woolson's suicide, but was obliged to go on with his work, and, as he confessed, "The ghost of poor R.L.S. waves its great dusky wings between me & all occupations," crying out for his undivided attention.

There were intense discussions among James's and Stevenson's mutual friends as to who should take up the nomination that he had refused. Sidney Colvin pleaded with Gosse not to take it, as it belonged properly to him, Colvin. Each asked James for support, but he stood aside from the quarrel, and the chaos of material life asserted itself. Louis had made another will in Samoa, naming no executor at all, a will of which the Edinburgh lawyers knew nothing but that displaced the one they had in their keeping, so that James's refusal was not needed and could only be hurtful, and the poisonous quarrel between Gosse and Colvin was wholly unnecessary.

Opening night for *Guy Domville* drew on. James decided to stay away from the theater, as he was too anxious and restless to sit quietly through the performance. He at first planned to spend the evening in a pub. Everyone he knew well enough to keep him company was either in the theater audience or out of town, however, and not wishing to sit alone in a pub, and perhaps with a vague idea of seeking company, he bought a ticket for Oscar Wilde's rival play, *An Ideal Husband*, which had opened just two nights before at the Haymarket Theatre, across St. James's Square from his own theater. This was a curious thing to have done; he seemed drawn to Wilde's play by that mixture of interest and repulsion that characterized all his relations with the man.

He did not care very much for Wilde's teacup-and-saucer drama but thought it went over well and was likely to be a success; which made him wonder whether the same audience was likely to approve his own effort. At the interval, he walked back from the Haymarket across St. James's Square and went into the wings.

At the final curtain for his play there was enthusiastic applause but also some hissing and shouting from the back of the house. When the actors had taken their bows, there were the usual calls for the author, although the uproar in the rear of the theater continued. He went out with George Alexander to stand before the curtain, the familiar golden haze of the footlights shrouding the chamber. The well-dressed men and women in the boxes and stalls at the front of the house applauded him warmly, but the uproar from the rear increased. James thought it came entirely from the gallery, from some young men there hidden in semidarkness. Some of the well-dressed people in boxes and stalls turned in their seats and applauded *at* the gallery, whereupon the noise from the back of the house redoubled, angrily. As James reported afterward to his brother:

> There followed an abominable 1/4 of an hour during wh. all the forces of civilization in the house waged a battle of the most gallant, prolonged & sustained applause with the hoots & jeers & catcalls of the roughs, whose roars (like those of a cage of wild beasts at some infernal "Zoo") were only exacerbated (as it were!) by the conflict.

Frances Burnett remarked afterward that it broke her heart to think of James being subjected to such stress. But he did not try to escape or to detach himself. James "stood before the curtain looking like a man who had steeled himself to *anything*—to *everything*," she said. When his moment had elapsed, he turned from the audience with an angry gesture of dismissal and went backstage. Alexander remained and, apparently losing his head, said a few words that had an air of apologizing and deferred to the rumpus as "the opinion of the public."

Despite the uproar, "a charming scene, as you may imagine, for a nervous, sensitive, exhausted author to face," and his anger at Alexander for pandering to the mob, James gave his customary dinner for the principals in the cast. As he wrote to Margaret Brooke the next day, "No one after the thing could have suspected any dejection in my attitude. My supper went off quite gaily & you would have been proud of your friend."

He thought the rowdies were probably a claque, put up to make trouble. George Alexander reported at dinner that a telegram wishing him a cordial "failure" had been delivered before the performance, which pointed in the same direction. Hired claques were by no means unknown, although the uproar had seemed to spread among the young men of the pit and the gallery, beyond any likely claque. But the evening was a success for the actors: Alexander had done very well, and Marion Terry, who played Mrs. Peverel, had made a great success, as the newspapers would soon confirm.

After the supper, James walked off the excitement and agitation of the evening. His dominant emotion seems to have been anger at the indignity to which he had been subjected, coming at a time of extreme nervousness and vulnerability. He was angry at the ignorant mob at the back of the hall, and it was to a degree a cleansing anger. They—the great anonymous public—did not care about his subject; they didn't care about his play. He resolved to abandon completely his on-again, off-again siege of the West End, finally to have done with the theater and with his quest for popular success. "I swore to myself an oath," he later told Virginia Compton, "never again to have anything to do with a business which lets one into such traps, abysses and heart break." He began to feel a certain liberation.

The following morning, Gosse came in early and found James cheerful. Gosse later recalled, "I was astonished to find him perfectly calm; he had slept well and was breakfasting with appetite. The theatrical bubble . . . was wholly and finally broken, and he returned, even in that earliest conversation, to the discussion of the work he had so long neglected."

Guy Domville prompted more messages of praise and support than anything he had written before. "All *private* opinion is apparently one of extreme admiration—I have been flooded with letters of the warmest protest & assurance." On Sunday, Florence Bell and Elizabeth Robins came in for tea and "to gossip a bit." William Norris, too, looked in, as did others who had attended the play. All praised it and condemned the rowdies.

Monday's morning papers carried the first reviews. Although in later years a fable would develop that James had been driven from the stage— a fable that would be fueled by his own expressions of disappointment— the principal critics, Clement Scott and William Archer, as well as some of the younger men—George Bernard Shaw and the young H. G. Wells— approved the play, taking it more or less as intended. Shaw admired what seemed to him an effort to raise the artistic level of the commercial stage:

> "Guy Domville" is a story, and not a mere situation hung out on a gallows of a plot. And it is a story of fine sentiment and delicate manners, with an entirely worthy and touching ending . . . it relies on the performers, not for the brute force of their personalities and popularities, but for their finest accomplishments in grace of manner, delicacy of diction, and dignity of style. It is pleasant to be able to add that this reliance, rash as it undeniably is in these days, was not disappointed. Mr. Alexander, having been treated little better than a tailor's dummy by Mr. Wilde, Mr. Pinero, and Mr. Henry Arthur Jones successively, found himself treated as an artist by Mr. James, and repaid the compliment.

For the most part, newspapers (like James's friends) condemned the rowdy audience and criticized Alexander for his little speech of apology. Only *The Times'* anonymous reviewer said the uproar at the end was a "chorus of popular dissent," provoked by the applause of James's friends in the boxes. Whether the "public" objected to the play or to George Alexander in his velvet knee breeches; whether they hissed James, as they had hissed Oscar Wilde or even *The Yellow Book;* or whether (as Shaw was to speculate) it was a premonition of a coming class war, no one could say. Perhaps all were true.

James, in any case, was by no means finished with his play. On the Monday after the opening, he agreed to remove a scene from the second act that had been much criticized, and the performance that night went along very briskly. He took a seat himself in the gallery, to quell any rowdies, and the audience was extremely well behaved. The house was full, the seats filled by paying customers, and the play went singularly well. The applause of the front rows was not answered by any noise from the rear, and the play seemed to be a great success, so far as that evening's performance went. James thought it might succeed commercially in the end, if it could only hold the stage until his audience returned to London in February. The question would hinge on continued advance sales in the coming week; *Guy Domville* was an expensive play to mount, and Alexander might want to cut his losses without waiting for the Season.

James had now an enormous volume of correspondence and calls to answer—it seemed that everyone who had attended the play, all those he knew and many whom he did not—wrote to him. "My dear Norris. . . . Your letter makes me too glad for me to hold my tongue over it. . . ." "My dear Ralph [Curtis], Please believe that I greatly appreciate the graceful & generous instinct that led you to write to me." "My dear [Sir George] Henschel. I am touched by the kindness of your letter. . . ." "My dear Squire. I can't do more than in a very few words thank you for your so friendly letter." "Dearest Miss Etta . . . I rejoice in the warm glow of your friendship & of your indignation." William and Alice sent their congratulations and condolences and conveyed Wendell Holmes's love, at his particular request. There were more invitations to issue and requests to honor: "Dear Miss Phillips. . . . Is there any evening for which you would gracefully consent that I should send you a couple of stalls?" "Dear Rhoda Broughton, Will it come within the compass of your convenience to accept a box—or a couple of stalls—for my little play?"

Ordinary obligations continued to accumulate as well. Ned Abbey had completed his first canvases for the Boston Public Library, and Lawrence Alma-Tadema had arranged for them to be exhibited in London, before being shipped to America. A catalogue was needed, to describe the project and the individual works; Gertrude Mead asked his help in preparing it, and James was happy to give it; despite the crush of events he had no writing projects in hand. As he told Gertrude later, he was glad to be doing productive work, and he was very pleased to see his friend's pictures—the first paintings of the Holy Grail frieze—happily displayed.

The second Lord Houghton, the son of his old friend, wrote to invite him to spend a few days in Dublin Castle. The government was being boycotted by English landowners in Ireland, and Houghton as lord lieutenant was trying to maintain appearances by filling the castle with guests from England; James had refused an earlier invitation but now felt obliged to accept. He wrote to Louisa Wolseley, who also had been rather insistently inviting him, saying that he would be at Dublin Castle for a week and would very gladly join her and Lord Wolseley at his headquarters in the Royal Hospital.

On the Thursday after his opening, he had dinner and spent the night at Addington, the archbishop of Canterbury's country house. James by then was an old friend, almost one of the curious and vivid family. Addington was pleasant and quiet, with only Arthur of the children at home and no other guests but Edmund Gosse. After dinner, the archbishop told a curious story that struck James as a tale that he could use:

the story of [two] young children . . . left to the care of servants in an old country-house, through the death, presumably, of parents. The servants, wicked & depraved, corrupt & deprave the children; the children are bad, full of evil, to a sinister degree. The servants *die* . . . & their apparitions, figures, return to haunt the house & children, to whom they seem to beckon.

By late January, it was clear that James's play would not be able to hold the stage until the sitting of Parliament and the return of the Ten Thousand. Alexander informed him that *Guy Domville* would be taken off after only four weeks' run to make room for something else that might have a better chance of making a hit in the Season. Alexander had arranged to put on Oscar Wilde's latest, *The Importance of Being Earnest*, in its place. James went down to see what he thought would be the final performance of *Guy Domville*, and to bid farewell to his cast, on February 2.

The previous fall, Alexander had refused Wilde's offer of a play and had chosen to go ahead with *Guy Domville* instead. Now Alexander had asked to have Wilde's play back, and his company began rehearsing *The Importance of Being Earnest* in the afternoons, while they performed *Guy Domville* in the evenings. Wilde was understandably pleased with himself: his drama *An Ideal Husband* was a success at the Haymarket, and now that James's play was being taken off, his own farce would replace it. He could expect now to have two plays running, perhaps two hits, facing each other across St. James's Square. When a reporter approached him in mid-January for an interview, he seemed partly to be addressing James, in triumph. Wilde had rejected the classical form of the drama, the form that James had labored to master. *The Importance of Being Earnest* was something new.

"What sort of a play are we to expect?"

"It is exquisitely trivial, a delicate bubble of fancy, and it has its philosophy."

"Its philosophy?"

"That we should treat all the trivial things of life very seriously, and all the serious things of life with sincere and studied triviality."

Wilde attended rehearsals for a time but argued so much with Alexander that at last he was asked to stay away and went off to Algiers with his young friend Lord Alfred Douglas.

• • •

Guy Domville was extended for a few final days, and then at last, on Saturday, February 5, the St. James's Theatre was closed, *Guy Domville* was taken off, and evening rehearsals of *The Importance of Being Earnest* began. James may have seen one of the rehearsals and most likely read Wilde's interview, for he wrote indignantly to friends about

> the withdrawal of my beautiful (though I say it who shouldn't) & ill-fated little play in its 5th week: to make room for a new drama by Oscar Wilde called "The Importance of Being Earnest"—the subject, I believe, of which is that the young hero's real name is Ernest, but he thinks it isn't! The pun halts for want of a letter—but the stern moral is scarcely less good.

Wilde's play was by far his best and would live, one of the finest light comedies in English. It was a glimpse of the future, for better or worse, but James could hardly be generous or even fair. He began to speak bitterly even of George Alexander, whose performance he had at first praised. But his bitter mood quickly passed. Almost from the moment at which he knew his play would not succeed, he turned with new energy to fiction.

James's story for *The Yellow Book*, "The Coxon Fund," had expanded to novelette length; even more than the twenty thousand words he had planned, roughly the length of the dime novels that were being sold in paper covers, in great numbers, in America. Why not publish directly in book form, without struggling through the magazines first? Short novels had a market in France and America, and even in Great Britain inexpensive one-volume editions were beginning to appear. William Heinemann had caused an uproar the year before, by bringing out a Hall Caine novel in a single cheap volume, without first publishing a three-volume edition for the lending libraries. James renewed his relations with Heinemann and agreed to supply him with two short novels that would be published in single-volume editions without prior magazine serialization.

On January 22, after these arrangements were made, he sat down to answer Howells's letter of December, the letter in which Howells had encouraged him to write for the American market. James's tone was cheerful ("I sent you only last night messages of affection by dear little Ned Abbey, who presently sails for N. Y. laden with the beautiful work he has been doing"). He had felt discouraged in the fall, he now admitted, especially by the younger generation's seeming lack of interest in his work, but he reflected that he had not been writing very much fiction in the last year or so. "I did say to myself, 'Produce again—produce; produce better than ever, & all will yet be well.' " Now he was bursting with ideas and subjects for stories that would be allowed to find their own length, and he was grateful for Howells's encouragement. "I shall never again write a long novel; but I hope to write 6 immortal short ones—& some tales of the same quality." The following morning, he opened his notebook and wrote:

> I take up my own old pen again—the pen of all my old unforgettable efforts & sacred struggles. To myself—today—I need say no more. Large & full & high the future still opens. It is now indeed that I may do the work of my life. And I will.

When he next reopened his notebook, he marked a delay with a line of crosses and began a new entry: "I have only to face my problems." He broke off there and after marking another delay continued, apparently referring to his "problems" and using language that he reserved for personal relations too intimate to record even in his journal: "But all that is of the ineffable—too deep & pure for any utterance. Shrouded in sacred silence let it rest."

February 5, the day of the last performance of *Guy Domville*, he called on Ellen Terry, perhaps the leading actress of her day, who had seen *Guy Domville* and had sent him a note with words of praise and a suggestion that he come to see her. Would James write a short play for her, a light curtain-raiser that she and Henry Irving could take with them on a forthcoming tour of America? James expressed his willingness and shortly began to make notes for yet another small subject, his vow to abandon the theater already forgotten.

Oscar Wilde returned from Algiers with his young companion, known to his friends as Bosie, in time for the opening of *The Importance of Being Earnest*. The opening was somewhat marred by the presence of police officers at all the doors, posted there to keep out the Marquis of Queensberry, Bosie's irate father, who had threatened to disrupt the occasion. The play was a success with the opening-night audience, and Wilde was present, but he did not take a bow. Queensberry had begun to follow and harass Wilde, and a few days later he left an insulting message for Wilde at his club. On March 1, hoping to put a stop to this harassment, Wilde swore out a warrant for Queensberry, who was shortly thereafter arrested on the charge of publishing a criminal libel and as quickly granted bail.

Queensberry was bound over for trial in the criminal courts, and the trial itself began on April 3, in a dingy courtroom of the Old Bailey. The trial was brief. Queensberry's message had accused Wilde of "posing as a sodomite." Wilde as the prosecutor of the libel charge testified ably, and sparred wittily on cross-examination with Queensberry's counsel. When the defense put on its case, however, it was devastating. A procession of working-class men and boys testified that they had received money from Wilde in exchange for sexual favors. It was shown that he had patronized a house of prostitution very much like the infamous address on Cleveland Street. His aristocratic demeanor, his negligent sarcasm, told against him: it was another case of the gentleman corrupting boys of the working class. The jury brought in a verdict for Queensberry of "not guilty," the defendant's statements having been proven to be both truthful and justified, without leaving the box.

Nor was that the end of the matter. The testimony of the boys showed that Wilde had violated the Labouchère Amendment of 1885, in just the sort of case in which it was intended to apply. The public prosecutor was obliged to take notice. Wilde's friends urged him to flee the country, and indeed even Queensberry expressed a willingness to let him flee. But he remained in a London hotel, seemingly immobilized, until he was arrested and charged with committing indecent acts. (Later commentaries suggested that it was Bosie who persuaded Wilde to remain, to carry on the quarrel with his father.)

The prosecution and publicity made Wilde an emblematic figure, to which all sorts of feelings were drawn. The hooting of rowdies at Wilde's and James's plays now seemed an ominous precursor of larger upheavals. A crowd gathered at night outside the Bodley Head offices, where *The Yellow Book* was published, and the windows were smashed. Beardsley's drawings for *The Yellow Book* had created an impression that the magazine was somehow connected with Wilde. To make matters worse, when Wilde was arrested, he was reading a yellow paper-covered novel, and the newspaper placards the next morning proclaimed: ARREST OF OSCAR WILDE: YELLOW BOOK UNDER HIS ARM.

John Lane struck Wilde off the list of Bodley Head authors and fired Beardsley. The Haymarket Theatre and the St. James's Theatre went dark, and there was an uneasy feeling abroad that the scandal would spread. The rent boys who had testified against him had more clients than Oscar Wilde. James's friend Lord Rosebery was now prime minister, the aged Gladstone having resigned, and Rosebery's name had appeared in the evidence. Bosie, too, had a wide acquaintance; he and Fred Benson had spent a week together abroad, as James well knew. Gosse was an intimate friend of Wilde's former lover Robert Ross. When Wilde's trial began, James reported to his brother William that "there are depths in London, & a certain general shudder as to what, with regard to some other people, may come to light."

James did not feel the need to absent himself, as he had at the time of the Cleveland Street scandal; but his association with *The Yellow Book* was enough to mark him publicly as a member of the suspect circle. He had written stories for the first two numbers of *The Yellow Book* and was prominently associated with it. In later trials for "homosexualism," a defendant's interest in James's novels was enough to arouse suspicion. But he had promised an article for the next number, and he now stolidly finished and delivered it, for publication in the July issue. He had been a public figure all his life, and while he had once felt bad reviews and personal attacks deeply, they were an old story now.

Others stood with him. William Heinemann brought out a volume of James's *Yellow Book* stories in the midst of the turmoil, and Margaret Brooke, with her customary courage, took Wilde's two sons into her own home. But Gosse was alarmed by the uproar and broke off relations with Wilde's family.

When his trial began, Wilde defended himself with dignity, Queensberry managed the prosecution ineptly, and a brief trial ended with a hung jury. The trial judge refused to grant bail, however, and Wilde remained in jail until he could be tried again. He was then tried together with the ponce Alfred Taylor, and the second trial proceeded quickly and inevitably to conviction. Tainted by the evidence given by boy prostitutes against Taylor, Wilde was given the terrible sentence of two years at hard labor. James wrote to Gosse about the seemingly self-inflicted disaster:

> Yes . . . it has been, it is, hideously, atrociously dramatic & really interesting—so far as one can say that of a thing of which the interest is qualified by such a sickening horribility. It is the squalid gratuitousness of it all—of the mere exposure—that blurs the spectacle. But the fall—from nearly 20 years of a really unique kind of "brilliant" conspicuity (wit, "art," conversation—"one of our 2 or 3 dramatists &c.,")

to that sordid prison-cell & this gulf of obscenity over which the ghoul-ish public hangs & gloats—it is beyond any utterance of irony or any pang of compassion! He was never in the smallest degree interesting to me—but this hideous human history has made him so—in a manner.

It was natural to think of poor John Addington Symonds, who had died only weeks earlier and whose vigorous defense of homosexuality he had praised. After sealing this letter, James wrote on the flap of the envelope (in French, for the sake of privacy): "What a pity—but how fortunate—that J.A.S. is no longer of this world!"

Gosse replied by lending James a copy of Symonds's unpublished au-tobiography, an explicit collection of memoirs of his sexual life that Symonds had planned to publish jointly with the young Havelock Ellis. James read it promptly and returned it to Gosse at his office in Whitehall with a brief note thanking him for these "fond outpourings of poor J.A.S."

James had managed to preserve an island of quiet and solitude at De Vere Gardens, and he opened his notebook to return to his proper work. *The Yellow Book* was not profitable, and British magazine markets had gener-ally failed him; perhaps it was time to close another chapter and return to the novel—if not to the big architectural, monthly serial novel, at least to the novelette. He had profited artistically by experiments in the short form and perhaps was ready to return refreshed to full-length fiction. The public uproar in the weeks following the opening of *Guy Domville* seemed in a way to have freed him to be himself.

I have my head, thank God, full of visions. . . . Ah, just to let one's self go—at last: to surrender one's self to what through all the long years one has (quite heroically, I think) hoped for & waited for. . . . One has prayed & hoped & waited, in a word, to be able to work *more*. And now, toward the end, it seems, within its limits, to have come. That is all I ask. Nothing else in the world. I bow down to Fate, equally in submis-sion & in gratitude. This time it's gratitude; but the form of the grati-tude, to be real & adequate, must be large & confident action—splendid & supreme creation.

15

⟡

THE LESSON OF THE THEATER

James once again remained in London for the Season. He spent Easter week at home, nursing a gout-swollen foot, sore back, and sore throat, struggling with an accumulation of correspondence. Among his letters and journals was a book of poems, *Lyrics*, that Arthur Benson had sent him with a very warm inscription. "I am singularly accessible to demonstrations of regard," James replied, "and welcomed the book almost as much as if you had written it on purpose for me." On April 15, his fifty-second birthday, he received a gift from Florence Bell, who was in Yorkshire, and a visit in person from Elizabeth Robins, who found him sitting by his fire with his throat wrapped up. Exhausted by his theatrical adventure, he yearned to escape from London and planned to spend the summer at the Devon shore, writing and looking about for a country house of his own; but he was bound to De Vere Gardens by duty. Alphonse Daudet, who had kindly played host to him at the time of the Cleveland Street scandal, was visiting England with his family, and James felt called upon to return his hospitality. For three weeks, he exhibited his England to the Daudet entourage—seven family members, including Georges Hugo, a grandson of Victor, who had married Daudet's daughter, plus servants. Daudet was in the final stages of his painful illness, unable to walk, wasted, heavily dosed with morphine and chloral, yet charming, interested, sensitive. James carried him and his family out to Oxford, Eton, and Windsor to view Windsor Castle (but not to meet the queen), to Box Hill to meet George Meredith, and then to Lambeth Palace to dine with the archbishop of Canterbury. But Daudet seemed to enjoy a visit to Arthur Benson's picturesque cottage at Eton more than the palaces: "Ah, if you knew how I amuse myself in these little corners of England!"

Mrs. T. P. O'Connor had a house in Chelsea and, exercising a claim as a fellow American summoned James to a tea party in her garden, where he chatted with Aubrey Beardsley, who was visibly succumbing to tuberculosis, Walter Besant and the novelists Pearl Craigie, Marie Corelli, and Arthur Conan Doyle. There were familiar faces from the stage: Richard Le Gallienne, Geneviève Ward, Bernard Shaw, John Hare. A middle-aged American woman, Gertrude Atherton, attached herself to his arm and told him a long story about her enthusiasm for his work when she was a girl. She and her sister, Helen, had had a craze for *The Portrait of a Lady* and argued over which of them was most likely to attract the affection of its author. Helen for some reason had won the argument, and Gertrude smiled at James, perhaps hoping to hear a protest. James too smiled and tried to frame an appropriate response. Atherton stared at him in silence as he unfolded a laborious reply to her flirtatious tale.

Mary Ward and Frances Burnett, the reigning queens of popular fiction, were both in London. Burnett had settled in London with her companion, Kitty Hall, and an entourage of family and friends that included Hamilton Aïdé and Bernard Berenson. These two successful ladies, both James's friends, were entertaining energetically and competitively, and while in London James felt obliged to visit both.

Ellen Terry wrote, praising his little volume of published plays and reminding him that he had promised to write one for her. She would be going on tour in America shortly, and it would be charming to have his curtain-raiser there. He replied, a little harassed, that "Yes, I will finish the play, & when I get at it, I shall probably go pretty fast." But he warned her that there would be a slight delay.

One of the few social obligations that was not burdensome was James's regular Sunday afternoon walk with George du Maurier, followed by dinner with his family. *Trilby* had finished its run in *Harper's New Monthly*, the book edition in the United States was an immense best-seller, and a hit play based on the novel was playing to packed houses in New York. The excitement was as yet principally American; the novel had not been serialized in Great Britain, and the English three-decker edition of the book had been published without illustrations and to poor reviews.

On his regular visits, James found his old friend in failing health and greatly oppressed by the distractions that *Trilby* was creating. Reporters from America besieged him and traded on his politeness; one managed to insinuate himself into the household, gained introductions to du Maurier's friends, and then wrote a terrible account of their daily lives, accurate in detail but false in every way. Fan mail poured in and was dutifully answered; he was asked to endorse "Trilby" songs, "Trilby" shoes, even a

"Trilby" kitchen range. He had sold the book to Harper for a flat fee, against James's advice, and had sold the theatrical rights as well, so that the unexpected wide sales and celebrity of his tale were of no direct benefit to him. A princely sum was promised to him for his *next* novel, however, and upon this he had dutifully begun work, although he was in poor health. He was oppressed by the feeling that he was not up to writing another tremendous success, a novel that would meet the exaggerated expectations of his audience.

The success of the stage version in New York attracted the attention of Beerbohm Tree, and du Maurier was drawn that summer into casting and staging a London production that would bring the storm of publicity to Great Britain. As James recalled:

> The whole phenomenon grew and grew until it became, at any rate for this particular victim, a fountain of gloom and a portent of woe; it darkened his sky with a hugeness of vulgarity. It became a mere immensity of sound, the senseless hum of a million newspapers.

James and du Maurier spent an afternoon talking over the remarkable success of *Trilby* and puzzling over how du Maurier was to follow it. Du Maurier was a raconteur, he wrote as he spoke, and the conversational style of his novels was like an extension of his talks with James. He had perhaps learned from James to clothe fabulous tales with his own vividly recalled memories, giving them the air of reality. He began each of his novels in an Eden-like enclave, as James often did. In *Trilby*, the heroine literally learned to be ashamed of her nakedness. Gaining the knowledge of good and evil, she rose above her instincts and chose wisely, sacrificing herself magnificently. Her gray eyes were repeatedly said to be dovelike, and her glance like the brush of a dove's wing, reflecting a favorite image of James's.

In his final novel, du Maurier now brought his old friend Henry James bodily into the story, an imaginary biography of "the greatest literary genius this century has produced":

> the most affectionate and good-natured of men. . . . Generous and open-handed to a fault, slow to condemn, quick to forgive, and gifted with a power of immediately inspiring affection and keeping it forever.

The story of this great literary genius, affectionately made tall and blond, was a fable taken from Balzac's novella *Louis Lambert*. The narra-

tor of the tale and the great literary genius who is the subject of his supposed biography are boys at school together in France. As in Balzac's tale,
the school is a walled enclave, within which the boys have a charming, innocent, romantic friendship. The narrator is utterly devoted to his friend,
who shows early signs of his future greatness, a powerful imagination
that is like a compass, showing the true north.

The source of the friend's greatness proves to be the spirit of a woman
that inhabits his manly frame and that confers her womanly virtues and
her imagination upon the great novelist; it is she who dictates his novels.
This female genius speaks to the novelist through his dreams. She says
that she has paused on her journey to the sun and immortality. This female spirit gives him "a very deep insight into woman's nature . . . all his
perceptions [are] astonishingly acute, and his unconscious faculty of
sympathetic observation and induction and deduction immense." Her
message was cloaked in an elaborate science fiction fable of spiritual immortality; she claimed to be a Martian but at bottom was simple and
Jamesian: "There is no longer despair in bereavement—all bereavement is
but a half parting. . . . Whatever the future may be, the past will be ours
forever."

The Wolseleys were in London, entertaining again. The commander in
chief, the duke of Cambridge, who had been hostile to Wolseley's reforms, was in his final illness and had retired. Wolseley hoped for promo-
tion, and after some vacillation on the part of the queen, who disliked
Wolseley, some backstairs maneuvering, and a clamor in the press, he returned from a brief diplomatic appointment to Germany to become
commander in chief of British forces.

A new epoch in James's life can be marked from the beginning of his romantic friendship with Arthur Benson, whose book of poems initiated an
exchange of letters and visits. Benson, as a housemaster at Eton, had an
ivy-covered cottage of his own that Daudet had much admired, and he
invited James to dine. After juggling other obligations, on June 6 and still
suffering from an attack of gout, James went out to Windsor to dine with
Benson and four other guests, bachelors all, in Benson's quiet, peaceful
refuge. The evening was extraordinarily pleasant, in part because James
saw his young friend in his own element for the first time, host at his own

table. The dinner was the beginning of lifelong intimacies with Benson and James's entrance into what would be for him a precious circle of intimate friends.

Benson presided gracefully: he had a capacious and accurate memory, a fund of vivid anecdotes, an acerbic wit, and a way of bursting out in uproarious laughter that was charming. He had spent his happiest years at Eton and after King's College had returned to Eton to teach. The atmosphere in his cottage that evening was tinged with gold, a kind of summer afternoon gleam. His guests were men who had been students at Eton and who had fondly returned to it: the new vice provost, Francis Warre-Cornish; Howard Sturgis, who had settled in the neighborhood; Sturgis's intimate friend Arthur Ainger, his former tutor; and H. E. Luxmore, who was like Benson a housemaster. They were a superlatively intelligent and congenial company of bachelors, among whom James felt thoroughly at home.

James had met Howard Sturgis almost twenty years before, in his first years in London, when Howard was still a boy. Sturgis was now a stout, six-foot-tall young man, who wore a walrus mustache and whose prematurely white hair was parted down the middle: a big, hearty figure with a frequent smile on his broad, open face. He had lost both his parents, to whose care he had been devoted, and was in possession of a considerable fortune derived from his father's share in the transatlantic bank Baring Brothers. He had settled at Windsor to be near Eton and his old tutor Ainger.

James had once been critical of men who chose to remain in the company of other men and boys, in a kind of suspended adolescence. He had written in especially critical terms of effeminate men, calling them "cads," who sometimes made him uneasy. But he now seemed to have suspended such judgments and to have entered into the genial spirit of the evening, and indeed he would soon write a fanciful story—"The Great Good Place"—full of nostalgic yearning for an escape to such a refuge. It was a glimpse of a world that had been closed to him, where—whatever its faults—one found an ideal of leisure, of intellectual life infused by gently restrained affections.

Despite his considerable wealth, Sturgis's house was a modest, modern brick villa (with the incongruous Tudor half-timbering then popular), on a single acre near the Great Park adjoining Windsor Castle, that with a touch of humor he had named "Queen's Acre," soon abbreviated by his friends to "Quaker," which too was suitable in its way. He was gentle and democratic in his views, somewhat embarrassed by his wealth, and disliked every form of hierarchy or injustice. His principles and his generous spirit combined to make him an openhanded host, a collector of strays, and his house was often filled by visiting American friends and relations who drew upon him freely. One young American cousin of whom he was fond, William Haynes Smith, had settled in as a more or less permanent guest and to earn his keep served as majordomo to the household.

Sturgis had taken up needlework as a boy, and he generally had his workbasket beside him at Queen's Acre. His manner was a mixture of Victorian dowager and sharp-tongued schoolboy; but his size, his composure, his assured manner, and his charm disarmed any objection to his feminine mannerisms. Within days of the happy dinner at Benson's, Sturgis invited James to Queen's Acre, to dine in company with Arthur Benson and their mutual friend Edmund Gosse, and on July 17 James again journeyed out to Windsor and found his way to Sturgis's villa.

The dinner was evidently arranged by the benevolent Sturgis for his friend Arthur Benson's benefit, to bring him together with James, and was somewhat awkward and pointed. The dinner was ample and prolonged, and speaking of it afterward James called it "almost violently supererogatory," presumably because it was so extravagantly generous; still later he joked with Benson about the awkwardness of the "hideous repast." But excessive and embarrassing as it may have seemed, it served its purpose, and afterward Benson made a brief note in his diary: "Henry James, whom I met at Quaker, very affectionate. I love him very much."

Shortly afterward, James—released at last from duties in London—fled to the Devon shore; but he wrote quite soon to Benson from his hotel in Torquay, saying that he wished Benson could join him, and they kept up a very steady correspondence, exchanging letters every few days through the summer. In the fall, Benson published a book of essays that he dedicated to James, who thanked him very warmly and invited him to visit De Vere Gardens in the winter vacation, for their first overnight visit.

The "safety bicycle" was having effects, as profound in its way, as dynamite. The older high-wheelers had been popular with athletic young men, but only an athlete could ascend to the seat, and big-wheeled bicycles had a distressing tendency to pitch their riders forward—make them "take a header" as the expression went. The new "safety bicycle," by contrast, was a low-slung affair with two wheels of equal height and pedals linked to a gear on the rear wheel, rather than directly to an enormous front wheel, and consequently one could move rapidly and easily, without great effort. The safety bicycle, compact and portable, was now being cheaply mass-produced. Working men and women took up the bicycle as a mode of transportation, and adopting "sensible dressing," without corsets or bustles, middle-class women also took to the roads. The bicycle was a benign, civilizing, democratic innovation.

James, in Torquay that summer of 1895, bought a bicycle and learned to ride, just as his old friend Wendell Holmes was doing at the same moment, on the other side of the Atlantic. An "astounding experience," Holmes said.

> I have got over the first general black & blue color of my person—my ankle & wrist are no longer twisted, to speak of, & after I have got on, which I do not do with infallible ease & grace I powder ahead at a comfortable judicial speed which gives me much pleasure. I take about five miles of an afternoon—get pretty warm over it & feel like a bird.

In Torquay, there was a bicycle "academy" where lessons were given and where a bicycle track had been laid out, a quarter-mile oval on which ladies and gentlemen cycled gently. James spoke of the experience of learning to ride very much as Holmes had—his "poor legs" were "blue and green and yellow and black, and flaming scarlet," as he acquired the rudiments, but James, like Holmes, was enchanted with the new sport, with the discovery that he could tumble off and remount, like a boy, and as he gained skill he found that he could leave the level track and cycle about the town and into the countryside.

Torquay was a resort of an old-fashioned kind, not one of the new seaside amusement parks but a watering place, vaguely Continental, where heated seawater baths could be taken. The town lay on a little peninsula on the northern margin of Tor Bay. Along the margin of the bay, red sandstone cliffs rose sheer from the sea, cut here and there by streams emptying into comfortable little coves. White houses stood shoulder to shoulder in little crescents in the town, white Italianate villas were scattered in the undulating hills that rose behind the harbor. James took rooms in Osborne Crescent, on the top floor of a hotel; his windows opened onto a little balcony, shaded by an awning, and looked out on the blue, blue bay. He looked into leasing a villa, hoping to find a "small house with a small garden." But prices were high, he was short of cash, and the desirable villa did not present itself immediately.

After a distracting spring, James was worried about money again. He had a modest private income, but since becoming a rentier, James had spoken and thought more often about money than ever. To maintain both his flat in London and a country house would require more cash than he could count on from his private means. American magazine editors, as Howells had promised, were receptive to his proposals for short stories, however—perhaps he should not abandon the short form yet— and Heinemann was happy to consider short novels for single-volume publication. Torquay now provided a "much needed bath of silence and solitude," in which he was able to return to work, to produce, and to refresh his income.

But first, there was the ever-present accumulation of correspondence. Holmes had not only written to him but had sent a printed copy of his latest address, "The Soldier's Faith," of which Holmes was proud. The speech was a bleak commentary on the time and a passionate demand for fealty to older martial virtues in a degenerate modern age:

> [I]n the midst of doubt, in the collapse of creeds, there is one thing I do not doubt, that no man who lives in the same world with most of us can doubt, and that is that the faith is true and adorable which leads a soldier to throw away his life in obedience to a blindly accepted duty.

The address had come to James while still in London, and he had read it immediately but delayed answering until he had a moment of leisure. He in truth had some reservations about Holmes's message, about which there was something meager, abstract, and theoretical. When he at last wrote from Torquay, he was not so effusive as he had been when Holmes sent his first volume of speeches but spoke simply out of friendship and affection:

> I've told you before what beauty I think you put into these things . . . . You have the genius of romantic eloquence & what is more, you have the genius of romantic feeling. And then your form is of a chastened nobleness. But why do I talk of your form? for what do I know about it, when I've not gazed up at your rostrum . . . . Come back [to England], come back, & bring your bicycle with you: we will spin away together, into the land of friendship.

And Ellen Terry's one-act play was waiting, for which she had promised a generous advance. Once he sat down to it, the play—*Mrs.*

Gracedew—indeed went off very quickly. Terry had been tempted by the idea of playing an American woman, and James accordingly gave her a one-act curtain-raiser about a charming American woman of a certain age, Mrs. Gracedew, who rescues an improvident English family.

All through the distractions of the spring he had been ruminating upon the work that was to be done now that the theatrical experiment had failed to make money and he was at comparative leisure. He was still somewhat bitter over his own commercial failures, and he dwelt for a while on the theme of the loss of standards, the cheapening of values, in the new democratic age. In notes he made at this time, the women who had succeeded in the marketplace, the Mary Wards and Frances Burnetts, came in for special animus: one of the themes of a satirical novel he contemplated was to be the "masculinization of the women . . . their *concurrence* [in vulgarity,] the fact that, in many departments & directions, the cheap work they can easily do is more & more all the 'public wants.' " He would portray the invasion of London by American women in the Season, the

insane frenzy of futile occupation imposed by the London season . . . this overwhelming, self-defeating chaos or cataclysm toward which the whole thing is drifting. . . . The Americans looming up—dim, vast, portentous—in their millions—the gathering waves—the barbarians of the Roman Empire.

But this was a passing mood, and these notes were never expanded.

For the sake of ready cash, he turned again to the very short story that the illustrated monthlies most wanted, five to seven thousand words for a single number: a single incident, an extended moment or scene. He felt he had mastered the form. With remarkable speed he wrote out a story, "The Next Time," which he had promised *The Yellow Book* during its tribulations, a lightly comic piece about a novelist who greatly resembled Mary Ward, who wanted to write something "artistic" but who could turn out nothing but bestsellers, and her hapless Jamesian friend, Ralph Limbert (a name that echoed Balzac's and du Maurier's Lambert), who promised himself a popular success but could write nothing but another unsuccessful masterpiece. Limbert dies, brokenhearted, but the ending is black humor rather than tragedy, and James writes with the note of confidence he has struck repeatedly in his journal since the closing of *Guy Domville*. The anger in his earlier notes has quite disappeared.

He had begun to rethink the question of the novel. In his earliest essays he had classed the storyteller as a "bard," a simple and even primitive figure standing beside a fire, telling his tales. Such figures had appeared in James's fiction as the narrators of ghost stories. He placed Stevenson among the bards, with Scott and Tennyson.

James had never considered himself a bard. While he had written novels that followed a traditional pattern of conflict and resolution, James's plots were more often accounts of unfolding and discovery. His big novels were composed like painted landscapes, with seemingly natural elements that made a large harmony within the frame he had devised. Such novels were like old tapestries slowly unrolling, in which the reader was invited to follow along and at last to see the landscape as a whole, from the eye of omniscience, as the author had seen it.

The short story required a different structure; there was not room for unfolding a realistic landscape populated by fully realized characters. Working within a small frame, the glimpses that it allowed were tantalizing in their way. He recalled his idea for a short piece, jotted down years earlier, of a wealthy, dying girl—an American. Suppose he were to expand it?

May I not instantly sit down to a little close, clear, full scenario of it? As I ask myself the question, *with* the very asking of it, & the utterance of that word so charged with memories & pains, something seems to open out before me, & at the same time to press upon me with an extraordinary tenderness of embrace. Compensations & solutions seem to stand there with open arms for me—& something of the "meaning" to come to me of past bitterness, of recent bitterness & that otherwise has seemed a mere sickening, unflavoured draught. Has a *part* of all this wasted passion & squandered time (of the last 5 years) been simply the precious lesson, taught me in that roundabout & devious, that cruelly expensive way, *of the singular value for the narrative plan too* of the (I don't know *what* adequately to call it) the divine principle of the Scenario? . . . I almost hold my breath with suspense as I try to formulate it; so much, so *much*, hangs radiantly there as depending on it—this exquisite truth that what I call the divine principle in question is a key that, working in the same *general* way fits the complicated chambers of

both the dramatic & narrative lock. . . . Let me commemorate here, in
this manner, such a portentous little discovery, the discovery probably,
of a truth of real value even if I exaggerate, as I daresay I do.

The value of this discovery, "how much of the precious there may be
in it," he could tell only by trying. In the quiet of Torquay, he began to explore his notion, the solution perhaps to the problem of form. Instead of
a branching, meandering series of relations among his characters, slowly
unfolding, a story or novel could be a series of scenes—each portraying
an action—playing out a drama to its climax. It was a curious notion, one
that would have surprised a stranger and that would continue to puzzle
readers and critics: the idea that a story should be a succession of more or
less static scenes. But as he grew accustomed to the idea, it continued to
seem right.

He began to explore this new notion more fully, not yet in the tale of a
dying American girl but in a story that at first he called "The House Beautiful," borrowing the title of Oscar Wilde's magazine and popular lectures, and that at first he imagined would be one of three short stories he
had promised for *The Atlantic*. It began with an anecdote recorded in his
notebook more than a year earlier: a widow lived unmolested for some
time after her husband's death in their rich old house, filled with the
beautiful old things—pictures, china, lace, furniture—they had collected
together. But the eldest son was heir to the estate. He married, and the
young couple decided to put the widow out of her old home and into a
meager dower house, as they had a legal right to do. When son and
daughter-in-law came to take possession of the estate, however, they
found the widow had taken all the beautiful old things with her. A
hideous public quarrel and scandal followed. The widow at last tried to
force her son out of the paternal inheritance by publicly stating that he
was illegitimate, and this was the point of the anecdote as told to James.

The public name-calling did not interest James as the subject for a
story; what interested him was the original situation, the unfair treatment of the widow and her assertion of her moral right: "the situation of
the mother *deposed*, by the ugly English custom . . . the rebellion, in this
case . . . of a particular sort of proud woman—a woman who had *loved*
her home."

This was what he called the *essential* drama of the anecdote: not the
long, ugly conflict between mother and son, mere platitudes of fact; but

the single act of the mother's rebellion, amid characters and in a setting that gave it meaning: what interested James was this *scene*.

At Torquay, he now decided to expand this anecdote into one of the stories he had promised Horace Scudder for *The Atlantic*. It was an eminently dramatic story, he thought, and he quickly wrote out four brief chapters, the first act of the drama and the opening scene of the second act.

The story opens with the heroine of the original anecdote, the widow, whose name, it appears, is Adela Gereth: a stout, strong-minded woman of fifty, dressed elegantly in mourning. She steps into the garden of a country house, where she is a guest, and immediately reveals herself to be a rather Wildean aesthete. She says that she has been kept awake for hours by the wallpaper in her room. As she comes into the garden she carries on an audible monologue about the horrors of the decorations.

A young woman is already onstage, in the garden, when the curtain rises: Fleda Vetch, a slender dark-haired girl whose simple clothes speak of good taste and poverty. "Horrible, horrible," Mrs. Gereth exclaims to Fleda, sensing a kindred spirit; and Fleda smiles in sympathy.

Scrambling in like a couple of puppies, Mrs. Gereth's son Owen enters accompanied by Mona Brigstock, the daughter of the house. They are healthy, vigorous, and stupid. Mrs. Gereth confides to Fleda her fear that Owen will marry this strong-willed girl. If only he would find an intelligent, sensitive young woman—someone like Fleda, perhaps—who would care for the old house and its treasures, the estate to which Owen is now heir. Fleda thinks that Owen is quite beautiful, even if he is stupid, and that she herself might be intelligent enough for the both of them. So ends the first scene, with the characters and situation established with all the economy of the stage.

Scene followed scene, and James had written about seventy pages and more than ten thousand words, the utmost length that Scudder would allow him, for these opening scenes. Yet he paused to think through what must happen next. He had established the situation and the characters of "The House Beautiful" with skill and considerable economy; the style was highly compressed but clear, and the situation was full of interest. He communed with his journal: "What then is it that the rest of my little 2d act, as I call it, of *The House Beautiful*, must do?"

James decided to write out a scenario for the balance of the tale: to summarize in such a way that he could move, scene by scene, to a climax, picking up each piece of the mosaic in its proper order.

When I ask myself what there may have been for my long tribulation, my wasted years. . . of theatrical experiment, the answer, as I have already noted here, comes up as just possibly *this:* . . . mastery of fundamental statement—of the art and secret of it, of expression, of the sacred mystery of structure.

And so it was that for "The House Beautiful," which would be published as "The Old Things," and then republished in its final form as *The Spoils of Poynton,* he wrote out his first scenario for a work of fiction.

At the pace at which he was working, the completed tale would be roughly thirty thousand words: "a production that [Scudder] doesn't want" and that would be difficult to place elsewhere. It was no longer a story but a novel. Yet he did not want to question the "the larger manner" that seemed to impose itself upon him—the detailed description that was needed for the vivid evocation of a series of living scenes. He set aside "The House Beautiful." Perhaps it would serve as one of the short novels promised to Heinemann.

He told himself to hold his new discovery in abeyance and to write short stories of the allotted length and in his former manner for the magazines, for the sake of his income. "I've been too proud to take the very simple thing . . . the single incident." He rehearsed for himself the series of little short stories he had written, early in his playwriting experiment, brief treatments of single episodes—one-act curtain-raisers, as it were. He must return to such efforts. There was an idea, for instance, that had made him think of Maupassant, of a beautiful woman who refused to wear spectacles and allowed herself to go blind. "It has the needed singleness, hasn't it? Surely, if anything *can* have."

He was turning over in his mind several story ideas, more or less simultaneously. He had just completed "The Next Time," for *The Yellow Book* and thought of writing a story about a novelist whose works were misunderstood—"The Figure in the Carpet"—for the new American illustrated magazine *Cosmopolis,* even as he continued to tinker with the scenario of "The House Beautiful." They were all stories about artists, in one way or another: or perhaps it would be better to say the madness of art. Mrs. Gereth, who was obsessed by her beautiful things; the heroine of "Glasses," whose own beauty was her art and her ambition; the obsessed novelists who were the protagonists of "The Next Time" and "The Figure in the Carpet."

As he developed each of these stories, he found that each scene required an observer, someone to stand in the place of a perceptive audience and report the subtleties of the performance. Novelists were observed by critics; the young woman who went blind was observed by a portrait painter. The principle of the scenario was coupled in James's mind with this corollary, that there was always a witness of the scene, an exquisitely sensitive recorder, a kind of motion-picture camera.

James sat down at his desk in Torquay and wrote out "Glasses," from first word to last. He spoke in the first person, and while he made himself a painter rather than a writer, he was speaking in his own voice. He worked very hard at this story, painting each of its successive scenes, advancing the action through dialogue alone, yet trying to keep the whole effort within his small frame. He took the manuscript up to London to his typist and then carefully revised the typescript, cutting and cutting. He brought it down to seventeen thousand words and sent it off to Horace Scudder with apologies for its length. He thought it a slight effort and did not include it in the New York Edition of his collected works, but it was a polished gem. Scudder placed it at the head of his magazine in February, pushing aside Sophia Hawthorne's reminiscences of her father and holding until the following month the second installment of Sarah Orne Jewett's serial, *The Country of the Pointed Firs*, to make room for James's story.

The corollary to his principle of the scenario, the necessary principle of an acute observer, continued to show its importance and indeed began to displace in importance the original motive of some of his stories. When James returned to "The House Beautiful," he began to pay more attention to the observer, Fleda Vetch, who at first had been no more than a convenient confidante to whom Mrs. Gereth could explain herself. He became increasingly absorbed in the interesting task of portraying Fleda's perceptions, her deepening understanding of the complex situation around her. The observer's consciousness became the center of the tale, and James was well on his way toward a new kind of fiction.

Young Jonathan Sturges came to visit and stayed for ten days. Sturges was a frail, pale American of thirty, handsome, clean-shaven and curly-haired, with wide blue eyes and a charming manner. He had a beautiful face but a frail body disabled by polio in childhood. He was the son of a New York merchant family (not related to the Sturgis banking clan), a bachelor of ample means who had settled in London and was a good friend of their fellow countryman James McNeill Whistler, as well as of Oscar Wilde. He and James had been casual friends for several years; James had written a preface for his translation of thirteen Maupassant stories, a book that had just been reissued. In letters, James had addressed him in sturdy, comradely fashion as "Sturges," but their long visit in Torquay marked a new intimacy in their relations, after which the younger man would always be "dear Jonathan," an intimacy that presaged regular visits and long stays in James's house. Sturges was one of those to whom James offered a lifelong friendship in these expansive years—"Oh the old full De Vere Gardens days!"

At the end of October, as Sturges's visit was ending, James made a note of a brief anecdote: hardly even that, James recalled, the briefest of moments, but it seemed to give him a glimpse of a story, even a short novel. His old friend William Dean Howells had visited Paris the year before, almost for the first time in his life. On the threshold of old age, Howells had been to see his son, who was studying painting there. Sturges had come upon Howells in Paris, at a party, where Howells was sitting on a bench, rather sad and brooding. Responding to some remark, he laid his hand upon Sturges's thin shoulder and said as if giving advice to his own son:

> "Oh, you are young, you are young—be glad of it: be glad of it & *live*. Live all you can: it's a mistake not to. It doesn't so much matter what you do—but live. This place makes it all come over me. I see it now. I haven't done so—& now I'm old. It's too late. It has gone past me—I've lost it. You have time. You are young. Live!"

The fall was oppressively hot, and Sturges was ill. James accompanied him to London and saw him into a nursing home in Upper Wimpole Street, where for the balance of the autumn he paid regular, almost daily visits, as he had once visited his invalid sister. They spoke of Oscar Wilde's situation, and Sturges asked James to join in a petition to the government to ease the conditions of Wilde's punishment. A sentence of two years' imprisonment with hard labor was one of terrible severity. It was in theory less harsh than "penal servitude," reserved for more serious felonies—"hard labor" was frequently meted out to those convicted of political crimes in Ireland—but a committee on prison reform had recently reported that it was in practice a brutal system, and often amounted to a death sentence. Prisoners spent their days in solitude, working alone on the treadmill or in their tiny cells doing the useless and debasing work of "picking oakum"—picking apart hard ropes into loose fibers with their fingers. One hour a day was allowed for outdoor exercise, and talking with other prisoners was forbidden. The committee had found poor and inadequate diets, and the unheated, poorly ventilated cells were profoundly unsanitary, so that prisoners sentenced to do hard labor were debilitated in body and mind, broken rather than reformed through labor.

When Wilde's harsh sentence was handed down, James expressed to Paul Bourget his feeling that it was cruel; James knew the work of the parliamentary committee, and he thought that imprisonment alone, without hard labor, would have met the popular outcry for punishment. After three months of the systematic sadism of the hard-labor system, Wilde had lost more than thirty pounds; he was suffering from dysentery and had been injured by a fall onto the stone floor of his cell. Newspapers reported not only his ill health but that he was going mad.

Wilde's debilitated state was displayed in October, when he was dragged in chains before a bankruptcy court, a proceeding forced upon him by Queensberry's relentless demand for £600 in legal fees awarded to him in the disastrous libel proceedings. Wilde had been unable to testify, and his friends were circulating a petition, drafted by Bernard Shaw, asking for his early release; it was for this that Sturges asked James's help.

The first step James took was to inquire of Robert Haldane, a Liberal MP who had been a member of the committee on prison reform and who had visited Wilde in Pentonville Prison. Wilde's state of collapse was so severe that the authorities had taken measures to mitigate the conditions of his confinement, Haldane told him. Wilde was presently in an infirmary, where he would remain for some time, and he was likely to be allowed to serve out the remainder of his term in relatively easy conditions.

Haldane may also have told James what the chairman of the prison commission had told Frank Harris, when he too proposed such a petition: a question would certainly be asked in Parliament if Wilde were treated differently from other prisoners, and as Wilde was not eligible for parole on the usual grounds it would be difficult to justify an early discharge.

James thereupon told Sturges that he thought a petition would be futile and advised against obtaining signatures from Zola and Bourget, whose support in any case would be counterproductive. A petition would not have the slightest effect and "would only exist as a manifesto of personal loyalty to Oscar by his friends, of whom he was never one." James's dislike for exposing himself to publicity, especially in such a case, undoubtedly also played a part in his refusal. He was aware from Haldane that private interventions were having a better effect, but his message to Sturges still seemed meager. Surely there would have been some intrinsic value in a protest? The sponsors of the petition failed to obtain signatures from any other prominent figures, however, and soon afterward they abandoned the effort.

Horace Scudder had liked and accepted the tale of the woman who would not wear spectacles, despite its length, and James ventured to have the opening chapters of "The House Beautiful" typed and sent to Scudder as well, apologizing for the length to which this second tale was growing. Scudder somewhat ruefully accepted it as well and began running it in April as "The Old Things." Henry Harper expressed an interest in bringing out the completed tale as a short novel. *Cosmopolis* happily accepted another story in the new manner, "The Figure in the Carpet," and ran it simultaneously with his stories in *The Atlantic*.

James was at home again in De Vere Gardens for the winter. London was darkly charming and comfortably social, and he settled into his familiar routine, writing in the mornings and paying calls at teatime, entertaining or dining out in the evenings. He continued to ask about country houses. The experiment of spending the summer in the country, freed from the ladies of the Season and able to work and entertain his bachelor friends, had been a great success. The summer had been both comfortably social and one of his most productive. Torquay was too dear, however, and too far from London for friends to visit easily, but the architect Edward Warren invited him to spend some time the following summer in Sussex, which was closer and cheaper, where he might again look for a house of his own.

Arthur Benson's new book of essays was waiting for him in London, and he read it with great pleasure. The book, beautifully printed by Heinemann, was again dedicated to him. It was a book of brief biographical essays, portraits of scholars and literary figures of the past. In a brief epilogue, Benson quoted Henry James on moral realism and showed himself to be a follower. This was very moving indeed, and the older man replied:

> my dear Arthur . . . I can't in the least criticise your book, nor give myself up to the process of judgment about it. I read it affectionately, even romantically—liking it almost as much when I didn't like it best as when I did! I liked you for writing it—and I liked it for being yours. . . .
>
> [I]t's hideous that we're both so busy—so engulfed. Perhaps the Xmastide will bring you an hour or two that you can give me. . . . You must be full of great affairs—I delight in knowing it. Life's nothing—unless heroic and sacrificial. There are things of art—of perfection we'll talk about. . . . You must really, on some evening of the imminent season, come and dine with me and sleep—

Arthur did come to dinner one Saturday during his school holidays, and although he had Lambeth Palace at his disposal during his visits to London, he stayed overnight and remained until Monday at De Vere Gardens, where, as James assured him would be the case, no one else was in the house but the servants and Tosca. It was the first of many overnight visits and marked a new stage of intimacy in their relations.

James did not have his usual holiday dinner with the Smalleys: George Smalley, who had been London correspondent for the *New-York Tribune* since James's first days in London, had returned with his family to America, to be New York correspondent for the London *Times*. James remained in London and was not sorry to be alone. He was steadily at work again, writing at a furious rate. The constraints of the theater and the "scenic" form had turned him back to the popular themes and subjects of his earlier work, the warm and powerful forces that drew men and women together. "The House Beautiful," renamed "The Old Things," was running as a serial in *The Atlantic*, and James pressed to stay ahead of the monthly installments. He wrote another story for *The Yellow Book* and a review essay on the work of Dumas fils for American newspapers; still another short story, "The Way It Came," for *Chapman's Magazine of Fiction* and the American *Chap-Book*; began yet another serialized novel for the weekly *Illustrated London News*.

This new novel was *The Other House*, which James had first conceived as a play for Edward Compton. It was a melodrama of two women, rivals for the love of a young widower. The "bad heroine," as James called her in his notes, plots to poison the widower's little daughter, freeing him to marry her, and contrives to throw suspicion on her rival, the "good heroine." In the end, the bad heroine resists the temptation to commit murder, and all ends happily. This was just the sort of thing Shorter wanted for his mass-circulation weekly, and James turned his play scenario into a short novel. It would do double duty: Heinemann had agreed to publish two of his short novels, of which the putative short story, "The House Beautiful," would be one; the second would be *The Other House*.

James was producing prodigiously and was once again at the forefront of fiction in America and Great Britain. His stories were running in the leading magazines—from *The Atlantic*'s staid double columns of type to the outrageously illustrated *Yellow Book*, from the new monthly *Cosmopolis* to illustrated weekly newspapers in Boston, New York, and London. His new short novels were to appear in the popular, single-volume format. There was less money in all this, perhaps, than he had once commanded in his first success as a novelist, but his standing and celebrity had never been greater, he had gained a new circle of young admirers on both sides of the Atlantic, and he was conscious of having made yet another debut.

After his long absence from the magazines, however, James had no literary agent and was plunged into a flurry of correspondence with editors, arranging for all these magazine publications, arranging for a collection of his new short stories (*Embarrassments*) to be published in England by Heinemann and in America by Macmillan. He began looking for an American publisher for the serial and book versions of *The Other House*. It would have to be serialized in a weekly, but Henry Harper, who had both a weekly magazine and a book-publishing house, turned it down. James proposed it to *The Saturday Evening Post*, but it too declined. There were few quality weeklies; he wrote to George Brett, Macmillan's representative in New York, proposing that it publish at least the book edition in America and asking if Brett had any further notions about weekly serialization. Macmillan did publish the book in America, but Brett could not find a weekly to serialize it there. He suggested that, to protect the copyright of the magazine version from piracy, James should send him the proofs from *The Illustrated London News* so that Brett could register the serial version for American copyright, which James dutifully did.

Although writing as furiously as in his youth, James was not a novice making a name and an audience for himself but a public figure, a man who stood at the intersection of many lines. He agreed to serve on the committee to create a memorial to Robert Louis Stevenson; declined insistent invitations from William Archer and Elisabeth Robins to serve on the board of the New Century Theatre. He accepted an invitation to join the Omar Khayyam Club and was elected one of the first members of the American Academy of Arts and Letters. He wrote reviews in the leading journals of Great Britain and the United States and was thought able to help a young writer's career. He was in some ways powerful but also attracted the animus that always attaches to a public figure. He became the target of remarkably bitter sneers from men like Frank Harris, the new editor of *The Fortnightly Review,* to whom Margaret Brooke had introduced him. Harris privately accused him of effeminacy, of being part of a shadowy conspiracy of homosexuals. "The admirers of James . . . were all people of no importance as judges of literature," Harris said afterward; they were "would-be geniuses . . . or society women." There was something almost racist in his malice: "[James's] well-formed, rather Jewish-looking nose was the true index of his character."

A curious example of the power James's position gave him and the virulence of the attacks it prompted was given by the publication of Stephen Crane's novel *The Red Badge of Courage.* This was a sort of fiction new to America: rough, direct, colloquial, and naturalistic in the manner of Zola. Though the reviews were good when it appeared in October, in New York, it did not sell. Heinemann brought it out in London that winter, and James read it. The twenty-four-year-old Crane's work struck him as very able, and an anonymous and strongly favorable "comment" on the new book soon appeared in *The Atlantic.* Evidently hoping to help the book, James also spoke of it to men who wrote for New York newspapers, including his friend George Smalley and the London correspondent of *The New York Times,* Harold Frederic. These men wrote about the book, and praise from London had a great impact in America. Frederic's letter to the *Times* was particularly effective, and sales of the novel prospered. But Frederic could not bear being indebted to James, whom he gratuitously savaged:

> Henry James is an effeminate old donkey who lives with a herd of other donkeys around him and insists on being treated as if he were the Pope. . . . Mr. James recommended Mr. Crane's novel before me in the house of our one mutual acquaintance and I was deterred from reading it for some days for that reason.

The crowd of "donkeys" and "would-be geniuses" around James included a number of young men of letters—Jonathan Sturges, Edmund Gosse, Max Beerbohm, Arthur Benson, and Morton Fullerton—who admired him and hoped for his help and influence. In his last, unfinished novel, *The Ivory Tower*, James would reflect upon the pleasure a powerful older man might take in the perfectly sincere affection of such young men. He treated Fullerton with elaborate gallantry; Gosse had become an intimate friend; but it does not appear that he was diverted from his work by the temptations they offered. In the midst of his struggle to establish himself on a new footing, professionally and financially, the only affection he seemed to return vigorously and passionately was Arthur Benson's.

On January 6, after their weekend together, Benson left to join his family at the archbishop's country seat Addington, and almost immediately sent James a long and affectionate letter. (In his diary, Benson said of the weekend only, "I love him.") James then received an invitation to join the Bensons at Addington. On the eve of this visit, in the midst of hurry and bustle, he wrote to Arthur; he apologized for not writing sooner about their lovely weekend together: he was "panting" to see Benson in person and so was "taken up with living in the future and in the idea of answering you with impassioned lips," and he signed himself "Yours almost uncontrollably."

But Benson was tied to Windsor and James to London. Each of them was burdened with work and social obligations that could not be neglected, and their meetings were brief and infrequent. They were both victims of their "devouring age"; but, as James wrote after their holiday visits:

> if I can pick your bones before the last scrap of you—and of me—is gobbled up, I suppose I shall be entitled to say that I have known friendship and intimacy in what they have of most intense and abandoned. *Pazienza*. . . . Consign to no deadlier limbo than you can help, the pale phantom of our intercourse. There *is* no life, but I am if not for time at least for eternity, Yours. . . .

Although the conventions of the day allowed what later would seem to be startling expressions of affection between men, James's references to "impassioned lips," to "intense and abandoned" intimacy, his later invitation to make an overnight visit in which he promised to embrace and enfold his visitor were well out of the ordinary. A minimum of discretion was observed, he wrote in double entendres, but he was reassuring Benson of his love and his language could hardly be misunderstood.

The Smiths had drinking problems, which seemed to have grown worse during the holidays: they were better when they were busy and grew especially bad when James was away. He feared that their downward course would soon be completed, but there was nothing he could do.

He had tea once or twice with Augusta Gregory, who would be remembered for her efforts to preserve Irish folktales, her benevolence to Irish letters, and her patronage of William Bulter Yeats. She noted in her diary how fond she was of James's "benedictory" talk. She asked his help with her adopted son, Paul Harvey, whom he knew. Paul was the orphaned nephew of James's old friend Blanche Childe, beside whose deathbed in Paris he had patiently sat. Mme. Childe had adopted Paul after his mother's death, and he had been orphaned a second time by her passing. Lady Gregory had been a great friend of Mme. Childe's, and had stepped into her place as adoptive mother to young Paul. Now he had graduated from Oxford and was getting a promising start in the civil service but was enmeshed with a hard young woman who had inveigled him into an engagement, or so Lady Gregory viewed the situation. She was highly upset and had some difficult conversations with Paul. They agreed that Paul would take Henry James's counsel. One evening that winter, accordingly, after a stormy dinner with his adoptive mother, Paul went to James and told him the whole story. The next day, Paul reported to Lady Gregory that he had found Henry James "a more comfortable guide" than his anxious, jealous adoptive mother. "And what did Henry James say?" "He just said it was impossible, and that I must put it out of my head."

Ellen Terry didn't use *Mrs. Gracedew*, the play he had written for her, on her American tour, and he complained bitterly to the Gosses (who often heard his complaints about the theater). "Perhaps she didn't think the part suited her?" Mrs. Gosse ventured. "Think? *Think?* How should the poor toothless chattering hag *think*?"

A friend of Edward Warren's had a cottage in Sussex, Point Hill, that was available for three months that summer. It was a modest brick cottage with a sharply pitched tile roof—James called it "a grubby hovel"—but it was cheap, it was just over two hours from London (with two good trains every day), and it had a spare bedroom for guests. He arranged to take it, and on the first of May, after a hasty round of visits, he fled London's tangled obligations for the picturesque quiet of the country.

The advantage of the house was that it stood near the crest of a hill. A little flagstone terrace behind the house faced south and was shaded by an ancient weeping ash that drooped its leafy branches over the terrace like an awning, down almost to the stone parapet, casting a pale green high-summer shadow. The parapet projected into space like the prow of a ship sailing through the air, and spread out before it was the flat margin of the Sussex coast, reclaimed from the sea, like a richly laden table, with the Channel itself visible on the horizon. In the mornings, James sat at his little table under the ash tree, with his notebook open before him, and gazed out at the spacious view. In the middle distance, off to his right and perfectly composing the landscape, another little hill rose abruptly from the flat plain. A wide, shallow, meandering stream came up to the foot of that hill, and formed a busy little harbor. The town of Rye crept up its sea-rock hill from the harbor, and from James's eminence he saw the town as a mass of brick-red tile roofs, capped by an ancient church with a queerly truncated, battlemented tower. In the evening, when the valley filled with shadow, a copper weathervane on the distant church tower gathered the yellow-red light of the setting sun into a single intensified point, like a beacon.

The flat countryside was ideal for bicycling and walking—miles and miles of perfectly level, wandering paths along dikes and on the margin of the sea itself. It was characteristic of James, searching for a seaside house, to settle in a town that *once had been* a seaport, where the sense of the sea and the invading French lingered. He bought a bicycle, a Humber, and began to explore this new place, cycling immense distances along the coast and returning to his cottage exhausted and happy.

Edmund Gosse came down to Sussex and stayed with him at Point Hill for a weekend in June, and then again in September. Gosse remembered that summer as a particularly happy one for James. He had always before found James reserved and quiet, withdrawn behind his mask, and in recent years had seen him only in London, where he was under stress, depressed, and often fretful as he struggled with the problems of the stage. Now, in Point Hill, James seemed to have emerged figuratively as well as literally onto a sunlit plateau. Clouds had ceased to brood over him, and Gosse was surprised and delighted to find that they left behind:

a laughing azure in which quite a new and charming Henry James stood revealed. The summer of 1896 . . . rests in my recollection as made exquisite by his serene and even playful uniformity of temper, by the removal of everything which had made intercourse occasionally difficult.

In this sunny moment James was enjoying his role as host and reaching out eagerly to his friends. Arthur Benson was engaged elsewhere for much of the summer, and travel was difficult, but James hoped to secure him for at least a brief visit; they exchanged letters every week or two and talked of possible dates:

> My dear Arthur, A charming letter from you . . . to hear of you, in your habit as you live, peoples, for the day, animates and most agreeably, as it were, odorizes, my successful little solitude. . . . I like not being in the madding crowd in these months . . . just Platonically wishing that some of my friends were with me. (The platonics, in some cases, I admit, become highly acute.)
>
> Is it the wildest of dreams to wonder in the dimmest of ways whether, by a matchless miracle, you would be free and disposed to come down here for any Sunday before I go away? . . . I could put you up not discomfortably and the little place has a small old-world charm. I should furthermore delight to behold—to enfold you.

Although he spoke in his letters of the "solitude" of Point Hill, he filled his spare room every weekend and ran up to London regularly during the week. When Holmes wrote to tell him of a planned visit to London, James answered promptly, inviting him to come down:

> my little hovel (near Rye in Sussex) is only 2 hours 40 minutes from Charing Cross: & it has a spare room calculated with the subtlest foresight for your immediate dimensions, if not for your general greatness. Your presence there will be expected at an early—at the earliest day; & the warmth of my affection may blind you to the modesty of my hospitality.

Holmes was in London alone, as Fanny was recovering from an illness and had sent him off for the summer. James's invitation was not at first answered; Holmes was energetically renewing his acquaintance with Lucy Clifford, Alice Green, and other young married women and widows to whom James had introduced him on earlier visits. After a delay, James wrote again to Holmes at MacKellar's Hotel in London, renewing his invitation, and Holmes eventually came down for a Sunday visit, which for James was "a very great pleasure." Wendell was "in admirable youth, spirits, health & form" and spoke engagingly of the social successes he was having in London, "as vivid & beautiful as ever about them," although his naive pleasure in the Season made James feel a hundred years old.

Holmes agreed to come back for a full weekend, but both their calendars had filled up by then and it was difficult to fix a date. James offered a weekend in August and wrote at fussy length about railroad connections and suitable clothes; then wrote again, the same day, enlarging on his directions (convenient trains left Charing Cross station at 11:00 and 4:30), but on the Friday before Holmes was to arrive James sent a telegram canceling the visit and followed it with an abject letter of apology:

> My dear Wendell, I was heartbroken & desolate at having, an hour ago,
> to send that monstrous telegram; but it was—it is—the only course
> that was open to me. I never had anything harder to do!

The difficulty was caused by the last serial installments of *The Other House* for *The Illustrated London News*, which James had been struggling to keep within the strict allowance of five thousand words each week. Clement Shorter had been increasingly irritated by the length of the installments and the delays, and both printer and illustrator were complaining that they did not have sufficient time to prepare them for publication. James had now received a telegram that imposed an absolute deadline. He could not risk missing it. Difficulties multiplied; as he confessed to Gosse, although he had long ago made a scenario for it, writing the novel itself was another matter:

> I began to pay the penalty of having arranged to let a current serial
> begin when I was too little ahead of it, & when it proved a much slower
> & more difficult job than I expected. The printers & illustrators over-
> took & denounced me, the fear of breaking down paralysed me, the
> combination of rheumatism & fatigue rendered my hand & arm a tor-
> ture.

Heinemann's book edition was scheduled to follow immediately upon conclusion of the serial and had already been announced. Delay of that book would also have meant delay in publication of *The Spoils of Poynton*, which was to follow and had also been announced. A large part of James's income and prospects therefore were implicated. He could not explain all this, could only tell Holmes that he was faced with a "disaster" unless he did "heroic work for three or four days."

> Forgive me . . . I will try & propose something else—get at you *some-how*, after the next 3 days. It makes me sick—it makes me ill—& to have to write in this mood is tragic. Kick me! Ever abjectly yours . . .

On Monday, the last of *The Other House* safely with the printer, he wrote again: "I launch this note into the void to reiterate my desolation . . . Is there any hope or possibility of your being able to come for next Sunday . . . or *any night this week*? If I don't see you I will take it cruelly hard." Holmes declined to make the journey, as on Sunday he was booked for a visit to Lady Castletown at her Irish estate; he would depart from Ireland for home. But he invited James to dine with him at his hotel on Saturday. James replied eagerly, "I jump at the chance of see-ing you. . . . Only I shall not dine with you, <u>please</u>; but you, quite dis-tinctly, with *me*. I will call for you at 7.45, at MacKellar's & take you by the arm."

They dined at De Vere Gardens, evidently cordially, on Saturday, and on the following Sunday James had tea with Holmes at his hotel and saw him off to the train. Sometime later, when Holmes had sent him a recent photograph, James thanked him, and said that it recalled for him their meetings that summer:

> Standing before me while I write . . . [the framed photograph] makes me feel as if I were talking to you now & you were bearing with me as patiently—in spite of your so handsome high haughtiness—as you have often done before. Thereby you give me ease, as well as, by this public possession of you, glory & grace.

Although James would dismiss the two novels he wrote that summer as "potboilers," he had meditated *The Spoils of Poynton* carefully, and in the preface he wrote for it, he recorded the great discovery that he had made in putting Fleda's awareness at the center of the tale. Only "fools," he said, cared passionately for *things*; he sneered at the widowed Mrs. Gereth, who had begun as the heroine of the piece. James's passion was now reserved for the mind of his beloved observer. The beauty of his tale lay not in the old things to which the foolish characters were so passionately attached but in Fleda's intelligence.

James was not a storyteller, a bard; nor was he a poet. His language was sometimes surprisingly awkward and resistant to quotation; he had a fondness for Latin roots and French expressions that made his prose seem affected and foreign. But he set his scenes carefully, and the slow, cumulative effect was of remembered experience itself. His artistic struggles had taught him to work in this medium as it were directly. He had only begun; in the years ahead he would fashion a style that would match this new form.

His new effort in fiction was so ambitious that perhaps it merited James's description as the madness of art. But what a reward was promised—the alchemy of creation:

> There can be for him [the artist], evidently, only one logic for these things; there can be for him only one truth and one direction—the quarter in which his subject most completely expresses itself. The careful ascertainment of how it shall do so, the art of guiding it with consequent authority . . . renews in the modern alchemist something like the old dream of the secret of life.
>
> Extravagant as the mere statement sounds, one seemed accordingly to handle the secret of life in drawing the positive right truth out of the so easy muddle of wrong truths.

James's ability to evoke the richness of conscious experience, which for him was life itself, would lend to all his work a depth that future generations would continue to find beautiful. He would pursue his discovery of a new form for fiction until he had learned to convey with startling immediacy the very touch and odor of conscious experience.

He had labored at *The Spoils of Poynton* for more than a year, making notes for the scenario, drafting and redrafting. He had given more pages in his notebook to this story than to any other work. It remained slight, but it marked a beginning, and his young friend and follower the novelist Ford Madox Ford later insisted that it was a "wonderful book," one of his "great and impeccable" masterpieces. James was conscious of entering a new phase, of beginning to harvest the fruit of his labors in the confines of the stage.

. . .

Despite Clement Shorter's complaints, *The Other House* was reasonably popular, and early sales of the book "showed symptoms of being the most successful thing I have put forth for a long time," James told his brother (and added, "If that's what the idiots want, I can give them their bellyful"). Heinemann delayed publication of *The Spoils of Poynton* so as not to interfere with sales of *The Other House* in its one-volume edition. Actormanagers would ask to have *The Other House* rewritten as a play, the form in which it had first been conceived. James had succeeded modestly in the marketplace and had also embarked on a great new artistic enterprise.

Some years later, writing a memoir, he recalled a dream from which he had awakened on a summer morning. It had begun as a nightmare: some nameless awful creature or presence was creeping toward his closed bedroom door. In the dream, he started wildly from his sleep and hurried to the door, pressed his shoulder against it, felt the hard pressure from the other side. After a long moment of thus abjectly defending himself, in unutterable fear, with a sudden clarity of thought and lifesaving energy he flung the door outward and open. A dimly descried figure retreated in terror before his rush, and as it retreated swiftly into the corridor outside his room he pursued it. The creature vanished into the distance, frightened in turn, and now victorious and alone he found himself in a long gallery of the Louvre, the Gallery of Apollo, that he vividly remembered from his childhood in Paris. A thunderstorm had broken outside, and the long gleaming gallery, illuminated by lightning flashes, was ornamented with the symbols of Napoleonic empire. In that gallery, he remembered, he had first inhaled the sense of *glory* and felt a premonition that it would be his.

Later that year he wrote to Arthur Benson:

I never had more intentions—what do I say?—more ferocities. . . . In short I propose to win my little battle—and even believe, more than hitherto, that I may annex my little province. . . . It's *all* a fight. . . . Let us then fight side by side, never too far out of sight.

BOOK III

Artist of Experience,
1896–1904

16

RYE

Point Hill, with its beneficent shaded terrace, was just the house for which James had been searching. He had been able to take it for only three months that summer, however, as the owners wanted it for themselves thereafter, and so in August, in the midst of his struggle with *The Illustrated London News'* weekly demands, he was obliged to shift to other quarters.

Hoping to find another house with the same wonderful distant views, he walked across the intervening plain and up the steep-sided hill on which was perched the town of Rye, through the fourteenth-century "land gate," up a cobbled way to the top of the hill and the much-amended old stone church with its squat tower. Facing the church, at the end of a cobbled way, was an old brick house. It stood a head taller than the little half-timbered cottages that lined the street and evidently had a magnificent view of nearly the whole horizon. Beside it, a miniature Georgian house was perched in the garden wall, making a cozy corner. The cobbled lane, just wide enough for medieval carts, made a sharp right turn at the door of the house and ran down the hill to the high street.

The setting was curiously similar to the vividly remembered village of Albany of his childhood, where his paternal grandmother, the head of the James family, had lived. In those early itinerant years his grandmother's house was the center to which his family had regularly returned. Albany was then a little brown village, whose old Dutch houses gave it a medieval air, and like Rye climbed up a low hill from a busy riverside harbor.

The tall, distinctive brick house in Rye had a plain facade, but the front door was framed by an ornate Georgian pediment. The oversize front door, at the top of a little flight of stone steps, was oddly like the front door of his other grandmother's house, in Washington Square, as a child might have remembered it. Whether conscious of these resemblances or not, James fell in love with the house in Rye without ever having entered it and made inquiries about it in the shops. He learned that it was called Lamb House, after the family that had occupied it in the eighteenth century, and that it had always been the house of the principal citizen, the mayor of the city and baron of the Cinque Ports. Its present owner was handsome old George Bellingham, who was pointed out to James on the high street.

Was the house ever rented out in the summers? A loquacious ironmonger was helpful but not encouraging. Bellingham lived there with his wife and grown son; he was an old man, but the wife and son were likely to keep the house when he died. In short, there was little prospect of its ever being let or, even if it were, of being within James's means.

He continued to walk over "to make sheep's eyes" at the house, as he smilingly told William's Alice, but he made up his mind to renounce it and for the balance of the summer found another place nearby, a former vicarage that stood between the church and Lamb House. The vicarage was small and shabby, but it had a little garden behind, from which he had much the same sweeping view of the surrounding countryside that had been the charm of Point Hill, where he could take his meals and enjoy the coolness of the breezy hilltop. He settled there happily enough until the end of September, growing still more fond of Rye, which was not at all a resort but only a rather quiet country town—very much, he thought, like a large family.

He was, remarkably, well along in writing a third novel that summer. He had been impatient with *The Spoils of Poynton* and *The Other House* as these melodramatic potboilers bubbled on, keeping him from what he considered more serious work. Now in the old vicarage he set down the first chapters of a novel for which he had better hopes, *What Maisie Knew*. When he returned to London in October, he wrote out a detailed scenario with which to continue.

"I have been living in the midst of death and woe," he told Daniel Curtis shortly after his return. "I stood yesterday by my dear old friend George du Maurier's grave—& 3 days since died the Archbishop of Canterbury."

Du Maurier's funeral was held on Tuesday, October 13, 1896, modestly, in the parish church in Hampstead. His remains were cremated in accordance with du Maurier's instructions, and the urn containing his ashes buried in the churchyard. The service was read by his friend and neighbor Canon Alfred Ainger, and James found the familiar words deeply moving.

Archbishop Edward White Benson, too, had been both an old friend and the head of a family that had opened its arms to him. His funeral was an affair of state, in Westminster Abbey, however, and James attended the two days of obsequies. Mrs. Benson would have to leave Lambeth Palace, of course, but for the moment she had no notion of where she would live in future. Arthur came down from Windsor to help her sort through their furniture and papers.

The usual heaps of letters, journals, and books greeted James at De Vere Gardens. Daniel and Ariana Curtis wrote from Venice, inviting James to visit and offering him the use of a house on the Zattere, as they had once offered him an apartment in their palace. James thanked them very warmly, but he no longer wished for a perch in Venice; he had grown older and more reluctant to travel, and his "alternative refuge" must be closer to London and De Vere Gardens, to which, as a "fundamental habitat, I fear I must always cling."

William, at fifty-five, was becoming a celebrity, at least in academic circles. His hard-won eminence seemed to make his relations with Henry easier, and the brothers corresponded with affection and at great length. Their cousin Kate Gourlay had died, and perhaps there would be a bequest, and certainly heirlooms to allocate; Henry put in a request for Grandmother James's portrait from the house in Albany. Bob was doing very badly, William reported, with severe outbreaks of his illness, exacerbated by drink. Evidently there was a woman involved, and Mary was deeply distressed.

Henry was an uncle many times over, and the nieces and nephews were grown and kept up their own correspondence with him. Bob's daughter Mary was in Europe that summer. Henry was not in London when she was passing through, but perhaps if she stopped for a while in Saint Leonard's, on the Sussex coast, as she thought of doing, he could easily run over from Rye to see her there? But he counseled her against staying in Folkestone: "I doubt if you would find any comfortable accommodation there at all. It is fashionable (for Jews, etc.) in Aug & September."

In the background, all that winter, were depressingly regular reports of massacres in Turkey. Sultan Abd al-Hamid II had abolished his Parliament, had abandoned the reforms and the policy of toleration that Turkey had pledged at the Congress of Berlin, and was imposing a vast tyranny on the nations of the Ottoman Empire. To punish Christian Armenia for its rebelliousness, he undertook a systematic murder of Armenians in Turkey and had just conducted a vast slaughter in Constantinople.

Armenia was the first Christian state, and the Armenian church traced its founding to the Apostle Bartholomew. The systematic murder of Christian Armenians, in pogroms backed and assisted by the troops of the sultan, aside from its intrinsic horror, seemed the most direct and appalling challenge to European civilization. James's Liberal friends in England and America were making strenuous efforts to assist the beleaguered Armenians, as twenty years before they had rallied to the cause of Christian Bulgarians; but the horrors in Armenia were far worse than anything that had yet been seen—the sultan seemed bent on destroying an entire nation, a crime for which there was as yet not even a name. James Bryce, a good friend, hastily republished a scholarly study of Armenia, adding a new chapter on the atrocities being committed by the sultan. *The Dial*, one of James's new venues, reviewed it prominently that winter:

> During the past few years, nearly two hundred thousand Armenians have perished by sword, torture, fire and famine; and this enormous destruction of life and of property as well, is distinctly traceable to religious fanaticism, that inspired diabolism which still continues to drench the world with blood. The effort of the Sultan to extend his Kaliphate, or spiritual leadership of the Ottoman Turks, to the entire Mohammedan world, from Morocco, through inner Arabia and Persia, to India, has stimulated the religious passions and intolerance of the Mussulmans, and they have proved to be a willing instrument in persecuting the Christians. The proximate cause of the persecutions is, however, political. . . . Remembering the loss of Bulgaria, [the sultan] resolved upon a policy of conversion or extermination.

Yet Turkey was a tacit ally against Russia, and England was officially silent. James, who had believed in Britain's civilizing mission, was appalled by "the hideous cowardice & baseness of Europe in the face of the Turkish massacres" and burst out to William:

> This has been more disillusioning to me on the question of the "progress of the race" than anything that has happened since I was born. England is only ashamed of herself—but it doesn't go farther

than that. . . . I wish to the "most high God" she & the U.S. wd. do something TOGETHER.

There wd. be *something* for the civilization of the future worth talking about. It's all, over here, a most sickening consciousness of something hideous that one seems *one's self* to participate in.

He did, indeed, feel quite personally the need for gradual linking of the two great English-speaking empires, carried out in part through numerous individual alliances, marriages, and business arrangements and in part through diplomacy, in the name of civilization. That linkage was part of a still larger system, the cosmopolitan world, in which Americans and Europeans could meet without abandoning their national characters, a peaceful globalization in which James felt that he had himself " 'assisted' from far back." He was glad to learn, soon after the new American president, William McKinley, was inaugurated, that John Hay would be ambassador to the Court of St. James's. George Smalley made the announcement with pleasure in the *Times*. Like James a friend of Hay's, he too had been lecturing Americans on the importance of alliance with England. The appointment of Hay showed that the new Republican administration was very much of their mind, determined to cultivate the Anglo-American alliance that the Democrats Grover Cleveland and William Jennings Bryan had attacked. James foresaw being able modestly to assist his old comrade and mentor, the new ambassador, as he had assisted his old friend James Russell Lowell, in the task of building a friendly alliance. He wrote promptly to Hay on seeing the newspaper story:

> This is tremendous and delicious, and my emotion overflows. . . .You make the plot of existence thicken more delightfully—even across the hiatus of the Atlantic—than anything I can manage on paper this morning, at least until I have embraced you. I long for the hour when I shall come as near as I dare to laying hands with that intent on your inviolable ambassadorial person. You change the whole prospect—you light it up. . . . Your opportunity to make for righteousness here—I use that word because it sounds priggish to say make for civilisation—will be so ideally beautiful, and is a theme so rich and inspiring, that I won't pretend yet even intelligently to hint at it.

James signed himself, "yours, rejoicingly, restlessly, impatiently, devotedly."

In April, when Hay arrived in London to take up his post, James greeted him with "a hundred thousand welcomes," and letters and telegrams carrying invitations began to fly between them. Despite the pressures of time, the two men confabulated about tactics. Later, when Hay returned to the United States as secretary of state, they continued their friendly alliance. Mutual friends from Boston days, Henry Adams and Wendell Holmes, were among those whom Hay drew into his efforts and who shared his aspirations. Adams would later say of this time that "for the first time in fifteen hundred years, a true Roman pax was in sight."

James had established himself once again as a fiction writer, primarily of short stories and novelettes, for the better illustrated magazines. James's income in 1896, from books and magazines, was roughly £1,000, or $5,000; with his investments in America his total income was about what he had earned at the height of his popularity as a novelist.

The discipline of writing in the short form had been salutary and had prompted him to experiment. But after the stress of his extraordinary productivity of the past two years—seeing two volumes of short stories through the press, writing out two completed short novels and a large part of a third, correcting magazine pages for the American editions of the two novels, and then correcting proofs again for the English magazine and book editions, with the unrelenting burden of his correspondence added, his right hand was swollen and painful, and his handwriting had grown nearly illegible. Yet, on his return to London, he was pursued with offers to write still more. The faithful Henry Harper suggested he write a regular letter from London for *Harper's Weekly*; Elizabeth Robins asked him to write about Ibsen's newly translated play, *John Gabriel Borkman*, which she hoped to produce. He reviewed, as an obligation, Ellen Terry's performance in *Cymbeline*, flattering the middle-aged actress outrageously, almost insultingly: "Her performance . . . has delightful grace and youth. Youth above all—Miss Terry has never, without effort, been so young and so fresh. Short-skirted and free, crowned with roses."

This was the last straw; his hand was crippled, and he could write no more. His old friend William Baldwin was in town, having been summoned from Italy to attend a royal patient, and he bandaged James's hand and prescribed rest. For about two weeks in December, James was unable to write at all, ceasing even to write letters or to make entries in his journal. This was not a serious lapse at first, as he had already completed the opening chapters of *What Maisie Knew*, which was to be serialized in the *The Chap-Book* beginning in January, and shortly thereafter in *The New Review*. After some much-needed rest, his hand seemed to recover.

Late in December, when the weather was mild and gray, he began writing again and resumed his correspondence with his usual year-end letters. To Arthur Benson, who was in the country for the holidays, he wrote a particularly long and effusive letter, responding to one over which Benson confessed he had hesitated and thought of burning.

"Burn" it, quotha!—it wouldn't have burnt, I would have you know: it would have flown straight up the chimney and taken, unscathed as marble, its invulnerable way . . . You say to me exactly the right things, and you say them to exactly the right person. I can't tell you how glad I am for you that you have all that highest sanity and soundness (though it isn't as if I doubted it!) of emotion, full, frank, and deep . . . Let your soul live—it's the only life that isn't, on the whole, a sell.

But his arthritic hand rapidly deteriorated once more, just as the burden of work and correspondence grew heavier still. His business dealings with editors on both sides of the Atlantic were as complex as they had ever been. Early in 1897, James therefore again turned to a literary agent, a young man named James Pinker who had just set up shop. Pinker was a short, round-faced young man with a pugnaciously protruding underlip. Like Balestier, he planned to represent authors in both the American and British markets and was rapidly signing up Balestier's former clients. With a sigh of relief, James turned over his financial dealings with publishers to Pinker. James also took a step that he had considered and discussed in recent years—he hired a stenographer, one William MacAlpine, to take down his dictation in shorthand and turn it into neatly typewritten copy.

MacAlpine was a sinewy, inexpressive Scot who appeared regularly each morning at De Vere Gardens with his shorthand notebook. James dictated in the morning, and typed copy appeared next day. Impatient with even this delay, he purchased a typewriter and MacAlpine began to take dictation directly on the machine. James could then dictate in the morning and revise in the afternoon and evening while MacAlpine typed and retyped. The pages flew with a wonderful celerity. He began to dictate letters as well, although he apologized to his correspondents for this interposition between them of a third person and a machine.

James reserved his handwritten communications for his journal. There he renewed his commitment to the scenic method, "the march of an action"; reading Ibsen's splendid *John Gabriel Borkman* had brought the importance of it home to him:

> The author who at the age of seventy . . . turns out *John Gabriel* is frankly for me so much one of the peculiar pleasures of the day, one of the current strong sensations, that erect as he still seems to stand, I deplore his extreme maturity and, thinking of what shall happen, look round in vain for any other possible source of the same kind of emotion.
>
> If the spirit is a lamp within us, glowing through what the world and flesh make of us as through a ground-glass shade, then such pictures as Little Eyolf and John Gabriel are each a *chassez-croisez* of lamps burning, as in tasteless parlours, with the flame practically exposed. There are no shades in the house. . . . The author . . . arrives for all his meagerness at intensity.

In *John Gabriel Borkman*, an intense and incestuous family group revolves about a child, competing for his affection. In the background is the corruption of the new capitalist order, the collapse of the old aristocracy; but in the foreground are young people who insist on life. Scene by scene, flames flare up and are extinguished.

If there are to be scenes, James had learned, an observer is required, and James had found a perfect, innocent eye to turn upon them. The novel upon which he was now at work, *What Maisie Knew*, was being written from the perspective of a small child. This would be the first of his works of fiction in which subject matter and a new, evocative style fuse into unity. Little Maisie will see the action of the novel as if she were at a play performed for her alone, and through her innocent eyes the reader will see a great deal more than she can at first understand. The purity of her innocence will be conveyed, magically, through precisely detailed recreations of sense memories. The reader will share the intensely lived, moment-by-moment experiences of a child.

What Maisie Knew began, like all of his later novels, with the germ of a short story or play, an anecdote recorded in his notebook: a divorcing couple with one child fight over the girl's custody. A court decides that the child should be shared between them, spending some fixed period of time, a month or three months, with each parent. This was still a novel situation, one that struck James as dramatic. The child, thrown back and forth between her parents like a shuttlecock, interested him, but the situation did not quite amount to a story. Ruminating over it in his notebook, it occurred to him that the divorced parents would remarry and resume their infidelities.

There was an odd resemblance in this germ of an idea to Ibsen's *Little Eyolf,* which he had just read, in which an incestuous triangle of adults revolves around the pale, intelligent child. If James was aware of the similarity, he did not remark upon it. Ten years later, writing his preface for the novel, he would remember only the pleasure he felt at this development of the story, his sense of grasping "the torch of rapture and victory."

The story of the child shuttled between divorced parents, who each would remarry, was a story that could be told in a succession of scenes and was almost a dance in formal figures. The original parents separated and found new partners; the new pairs broke apart, betraying each other, and the newest arrivals came together at center stage. The affection of her two new stepparents for the child, their illicit relations with each other, held within it the chance of happiness for her, the promise of a family.

He thought first of writing the short story for a number of *The Yellow Book.* As he sat down to it, however, in the late summer of 1896 at the vicarage in Rye, and felt his way into the incident, it outgrew the limits of a short story. Nosing into the idea, the more he penetrated, pursuing the buried scent, the more interesting it became, until he reached the center of the tale, the child's own consciousness.

The "small expanding consciousness" was what interested him most, what attracted his affection. Maisie not only would be a register of impressions, like *Poynton*'s Fleda Vetch, but would rise to the situation and become an actor rather than a victim. Rather than submitting and being coarsened, she would be a catalyst, a wonder-working agent who would create fresh elements of order.

A reader would see through her eyes the complex figure of the dance of the four divorcing, remarrying, and yet again recombining parents; not limiting oneself to what the child could understand or express but portraying fully what she *saw* and feeling the emancipation of the child, her precocious understanding. The lessons of his short-story and playwriting experiments, and the elements of a new style, had now come together.

It was to be the fate of this patient little girl to see much more than, at first, she understood, but also, even at first, to understand much more than any little girl, however patient, had perhaps ever understood before. Only a drummer-boy in a ballad or a story could have been so in the thick of the fight. She was taken into the confidence of passions on which she fixed just the stare she might have had for images bounding across the wall in the slide of a magic-lantern. Her little world was phantasmagoric—strange shadows dancing on a sheet. It was as if the whole performance had been given for her—a mite of a half-scared infant in a great dim theatre.

The background of the tale was the coarsening and vulgarization of the upper class. Maisie's parents are selfish, mercenary, and promiscuous as goats. They are handsome in a new fashion, photogenic rather than beautiful—Ida Farange is six feet tall and exquisitely thin, all arms and legs and wide blue eyes; Beale Farange too is tall and slim, and sports a luxuriant blond beard. They wear their expensive clothing as one carries luggage; they visit Folkestone and mingle promiscuously with the "Jews, etc.," and take their illicit affairs across the Channel to Boulogne. They speak with startling vulgarity and have not hesitated to accuse each other of infidelities in their very public divorce proceeding. They now selfishly use Maisie in their continuing quarrel. Six-year-old Maisie shuttles between them, and her child's eye records the scene for us. James gives us the mind of a child from within:

> In that lively sense of the immediate which is the very air of a child's mind, the past, on each occasion, became, for her, as indistinct as the future; she surrendered herself to the actual with a good faith that might have been touching to either parent. . . . She was at the age when all stories are true and all conceptions are stories. The actual was the absolute; the present alone was vivid.

We see Maisie forming an idea of herself, little by little, and an image of how she appears to others:

> Some of these gentlemen [who came to see her father] made her strike matches and light their cigarettes; others, holding her on knees violently jolted, pinched the calves of her legs . . . and reproached them with being toothpicks. The word struck in her mind and contributed to her feeling from this time that she was deficient in something that would meet the general desire. . . . [S]he was impelled perpetually to look at the legs of other children and ask her nurse if *they* were tooth-

picks. Moddle was always terribly truthful; she always said, "Oh, my dear, you'll not find such another pair as your own!"

Maisie learns to store away her impressions for later scrutiny and understanding. She feels an atmosphere of danger around her and begins to conceal her thoughts, to keep secrets; this is the beginning of her sense of self. When she is given an illiterate servant who loves her, Mrs. Wix, to serve as governess, she feels that the old woman represents safety and comfort, and their mutual love is expressed in shared secrets. Both Maisie and Mrs. Wix conceive a passion for Sir Claude, Maisie's stepfather, who wishes her to provide an air of respectability to his affair with her stepmother. But Maisie declines to be used in this way and takes Mrs. Wix back to England.

Maisie's dawning awareness of different kinds of love and the power that they confer: Sir Claude's fascinating hands that so often rest on her shoulder or arm; his weakness in the face of his desire for women; the dangerous, enveloping embraces of the stepmother; even Mrs. Wix's helpless surrender to Sir Claude, all become clear to her. Above all, she becomes aware of her own feelings, which she must manage and master. The books ends, as so many of James's stories had, with young Maisie's departure from a promised garden of delights, but with the great world all before her.

The child's story was not, of course, James's own; it grew in his mind as he wrote and took its familiar shape. It was a story that had the truth of legend, "the blue river of truth" that ran through fables and Bible stories he had listened to when a child and that Mrs. Wix had told to Maisie. But James was able to give the child's perceptions and emotions startling immediacy by rummaging among the vivid memories of his own childhood: the strange, abrupt disappearances of the young female servants, the uneasy fears that lead a child to keep secrets, her secret loves for tutors and governesses. Mrs. Wix's eyeglasses, her "straighteners," were much like his father's eyeglasses, with which years before he had equipped Miss Birdseye, a metaphor for the moral sense. He gave Maisie his own vivid memories of going to the dentist; of making adults laugh with his questions; of a dawning awareness of sexuality. The Boulogne that Maisie visited was the Boulogne of his own awakening, and Maisie, like James, remembered the red-legged French soldiers there and the women wading into the surf with flashing bare legs.

· · ·

The three novels that he had written over the past year and a half tumbled over one another in haste. Each opened with a little prologue and then progressed through numbered scenes in the manner of a French (or Ibsen) play: in each scene, the unities of time, place, and action were preserved. Stage settings were each precisely located in the social and cultural matrix of Europe. In each novel, the narrative was told by an observer within the tale, although in *The Other House* the point of view shifted from one heroine to the other and sometimes shifted again to a member of the audience. In *The Spoils of Poynton* and *What Maisie Knew*, the observer's intelligent awareness became the center of the story, and James struggled to portray both observer and observed, with a consequent density of style.

There was a clear line of development through the three books, and in the three acts and thirty-one numbered scenes of *Maisie*, James's new method found its first full expression, and James properly began his new style. As Rebecca West would remark a few years later, *Maisie* heralded a new theme: "blessed are the pure in heart." Maisie's clear eyes show us a scene with clarity and Zen-like immediacy of feeling. Her affections are virtuous because her perceptions are clear. Later critics would call *Maisie* a "portrait of the artist as a young girl." The story was not autobiographical, in the ordinary sense, but James was able to re-create the universal quality of childhood by dressing the tale with his own memories. James, who had made a personal religion of living in and experiencing the moment, had found a medium in which to create memories of passionate moments as if they had been truly lived.

These three novels are books of social commentary, as well, and the child's innocent gaze gives a particularly damning view of the selfish adults around her, members of a prosperous English middle class cutting themselves off from tradition and restraint. The only American who appears is a mongrel, deracinated "countess." But a hundred years later, the social criticism will be less interesting, the failings of the adults will appear more as individual faults than reflections of a new social order. Maisie alone interests us now, and the magic by which the particularity of her experience, its unique human feeling, becomes a universal history. More than a century later, a critic will remark that it is "the wonderful beginning of James's 'second go.' "

A drawback of the method James had worked very hard to find was the increasing complexity of his style. He had trained himself to analyze his own memories into their original, constituent units, breaking down his own remembered perceptions into abstract elements, very much as a painter abstracts from his model a line drawing and a selection of pigments, which he then assembles artfully in a manner that will create the illusion of reality.

This study and practice were a part of his life, and James's speech and letters began to reflect the analysis he constantly performed. He was, as it were, constantly dictating. When a neighbor's door opened and he was surprised by a barking dog, James said that from the dusky entry there emerged "something black, something canine." The elements of his description fuse in the reader's imagination, as an Impressionist's brushstrokes fuse in the retina of an observer, with the force of an immediate impression. His sentences became more elaborate, with a habitual reliance on double negatives—reflections within the shadow.

Over the years, ordinary nouns and verbs would slowly drop from his writing. He preferred proper nouns—names of unique entities—and concrete images, each of which would quickly give way to a pronoun. A cloud of descriptive nouns, adverbs, and adjectives would surround the pronoun like a skein of metaphors—coalescing in the reader's eye. The scene itself then seemed to appear magically, as if illuminated and framed by a proscenium. James's characters and their relations to one another, described in this way, would take on a uniquely persuasive reality. It was impossible, in the end, for a reader to believe that James's characters were invented or that he had not shared their experiences. His friend Edith Wharton years later described the effect of one of the matchless monologues which resulted from his constant practice:

> I remember in particular one summer evening . . . one of us suddenly said to him (in response to some chance allusion to his Albany relations): "And now tell us about the Emmets—tell us all about them."
>
> [F]or a moment he stood there brooding in the darkness, murmuring over to himself, "Ah, my dear, the Emmets—ah, the Emmets!" Then he began, forgetting us, forgetting the place, forgetting everything but the vision of his lost youth that the question evoked, the long train of ghosts flung with his enchanter's wand across the wide stage of the summer night. Ghostlike indeed at first, wavering and indistinct, they glimmered at us through a series of disconnected ejaculations, epithets, allusions, parenthetical rectifications and restatements, till not only our brains but the clear night itself seemed filled with a palpable fog: and then, suddenly, by some miracle of shifted lights and accumulated

strokes, there they stood before us as they lived, drawn with a million filament-like lines, yet sharp as an Ingres, dense as a Rembrandt.

The Season descended with unusual force in the year of the queen's Diamond Jubilee—the sixtieth of her reign, the longest in British history. James was anxious to be out of the way. He considered taking up the Curtises' invitation to Venice, stopping in Paris on the way as in earlier times, but he was short of cash. His hand was much recovered, but he was not willing to return to the drudgery and pain of manual labor, and the click of the typewriter had become a welcome accompaniment to his thought and his deliberate speech. He could not take so long a vacation from work, but traveling with a stenographer and a typewriter was not practical, and the unwanted company would interfere with much of the pleasure of a visit to the Continent.

Louisa Wolseley, although much taken up with preparations for the jubilee, invited him to Sussex to see a neighbor's house that she thought might do as a retreat for him. James was inclined toward Sussex, but the house and its decorations were not in James's taste: "the whole thing . . . [is] far too Germanic, too Teutonic." He refused Augusta Gregory's invitation to dinner to meet her protégé William Butler Yeats, to whom she was again trying to introduce James; he much regretted "the loss of the occasion to meet your interesting Celt." Instead of accepting any invitation, he spent June and July in lodgings in Bournemouth, which had few visitors in the summer months, accompanied by MacAlpine, who was taciturn and not very good company at meals. James bought a bicycle for him and they went considerable distances in the afternoons, however, and it was good to have even silent company on these long jaunts.

He and MacAlpine moved in August to the seaside village of Dunwich, in Suffolk, where James planned to spend a month with his cousin Ellen—formerly Ellen Temple, of the Emmet and Temple cousins, now Ellen Hunter—and her daughters. To James's great satisfaction, he and MacAlpine were able to bicycle the unpaved roads and to explore the Suffolk downs for long distances, stopping for tea in the parlors of village inns. Edward Warren, who had first pointed him toward Rye, joined him for a while and replaced MacAlpine as his cycling companion. They rode together on the lanes of the downs, taking tumbles but raggedly struggling to ride abreast. James spoke of his fondness for Point Hill—he would like to take it again the following summer—and his yearning for the lovely, unattainable Lamb House.

This Dunwich interlude was interrupted by a tedious journey back to London. A cousin on his father's side whom he knew only slightly, Howard James, had appeared without warning at De Vere Gardens. James had heard a little of this cousin and his financial difficulties from William and had contributed to the cousin's support. Now, however, young Howard had taken possession of James's flat and announced that he would stay until James returned to London (which was not to be for three weeks); he borrowed money from Smith, got drunk, and kept the servants up all night. Smith wired in desperation to James, who answered promptly that Cousin Howard must find other lodgings. Smith managed to get him out of the flat and down to the East London docks, where Howard claimed that he would embark for America.

James came up to London and found the damage to the flat considerable. He remained long enough to see it put to rights. Cousin Howard had disappeared with the Smiths' money, which James immediately made good. He thought of hiring a detective to find the young man and did consult the police, but he was not willing to charge his cousin with a crime; and so the matter passed over.

When he had restored order, James set off for Dunwich again, and Smith accompanied him to the railroad station. Just as the train was getting up steam, the butler fell to the platform in an epileptic fit. There he lay, writhing, as a crowd gathered around him. James was just able to throw his bags out of the train and jump down after them. He got Smith into a cab, carried him home, and remained with him for another night. The next morning Smith was much recovered, and James was able to return to the seaside.

Almost nothing now is known of the Smiths, nothing of their family or circumstances, not even their first names. The good, unimaginative Mrs. Wix, Maisie's working-class governess, the good unimaginative Mrs. Grose, the housekeeper in *The Turn of the Screw*, perhaps are memorials to Mrs. Smith. Of her husband little is known except that he was an excellent butler, that he drank, that he was ill, and that Henry James brought him home one night when he had fallen down.

James had twenty-one first cousins on his father's side alone—some, like Howard James, he knew only slightly—among whom was a branch of the family that had included the famous Anglo-Irish revolutionary Robert Emmet and that had extensively intermarried with the Temples. Of all his cousins, he had been closest to Ellen and Mary Temple, orphaned cousins on his father's side. He and they had been children together in their grandmother's house in Albany.

Mary, known in childhood as "Minny," was the eldest and the most charming of the four Temple girls. William James, Wendell Holmes, and John Gray had each at various times been in love with her. She had died of tuberculosis in 1870, twenty-seven years past. Two of her younger sisters had married Emmet cousins, extending and ramifying the vast Temple and Emmet cousinage. Ellen Temple had married her cousin Richard Emmet and moved to San Francisco with him. She was widowed and remarried now, with three grown daughters from her first marriage. Her niece Jane Emmet had come over from America for a visit and was spending part of the summer with them in Dunwich.

James spent as much time as he could with Ellen and the four young American women, who were in their early twenties, the age at which he remembered their mother and aunt so fondly. He thought them "full of life and humor and sentiment and intelligence." They for their part found him "the nicest thing," although he did nag them about their American accents. He and the middle daughter, Ellen, known as "Bay," hit it off particularly well, and she happily called him "the *silliest* man that had ever existed." Their meeting and renewed relation would bear fruit in a new prose portrait of Mary Temple in *The Wings of the Dove.*

James's return to the novel was widely and for the most part favorably reviewed. *The Other House* was admired in both England and America, and while James's new style was often taxed for obscurity, reviewers were glad to have him tell an exciting story. *The New York Times* called it a "masterpiece," and while English notices were more restrained, they were favorable and even understanding. *The Saturday Review*'s anonymous reviewer was respectful—"whatever Mr. Henry James does is of importance to literature"—but did not entirely accept the "cultivated indirection" of his new style. But the reviewer acknowledged that "a curious thing happens":

> The reader unexpectedly finds that the printed page has faded away; he looks in retrospect over the footlights instead, and the murderess of "The Other House" becomes a great tragedienne, the central figure in a dramatic situation of commanding intensity of force. There is no gainsaying the grip of the effect which Mr. James secures at the finish.

The book edition of *The Spoils of Poynton* appeared only a few months later and prompted puzzled and often negative reviews. Confronted with the new style but without an exciting drama to carry the reader along, readers were respectful but unenthusiastic. In the United States, James was compared with George Meredith, whose heavily mannered style was more often admired than read. In England, *The Athenaeum* complained about the difficulty of his new style, especially his trick of giving the reader a series of descriptive terms instead of a simple noun:

> If you debar yourself from the use of "spade" . . . it is not always easy to find an English phrase that will legitimately denote the article, and when you do find one the chances are that your reader will not . . . be able, without conscious effort, to proceed from it to the idea of that object. And conscious effort is just what the novel-reader does not want.

"Conscious effort" was exactly what James demanded from his readers, however. He wanted them to do their part in the process of creation.

In September, Heinemann issued *What Maisie Knew*, James's third short novel in twelve months. "Considering their nature and workmanship," *The Athenaeum* remarked dryly, "Mr. James's novels appear with a frequency that is little short of surprising." The book was generally praised: the success of James's audacious experiment, re-creating the sensibility of a child, was widely admired. *Book News*, summarizing the American reviews, called it one of the most remarkable novels in English for many years: "It triumphs over its faults and glories in them." Nearly every reviewer remarked upon the difficulties of James's style, but most forgave him for them. *The Boston Critic* wrote, interestingly, that "The book is a piece of alchemy rather than a novel."

The British reviews were still mixed, but the old irritation at an American author portraying English manners had dissipated. James was given leave to criticize his hosts, and the characters he portrayed were accepted as brutally, vigorously true. Not everyone cared for his choice of subjects, but all seemed to agree with *The Saturday Review* that

> The vulgar, selfish, beautiful [English] people are presented with an amazing realness: now they themselves reveal their depths, in wonderful phrases that ring with the cold truth, in actions of an astounding meanness.

His portrait of the working-class governess, Mrs. Wix, a modest heroine, was held up for particular praise as a sympathetic and realistic portrait. And *The Pall Mall Gazette* wrote, gratifyingly, that James

> holds a high and distinctive position among novelists of the English-
> writing races. He stands in the van with one or two compeers, and no
> more. Bit by bit, piece by piece, he has accumulated his dignity. . . . This
> latest novel from Mr. James's pen seems, beyond doubt, to touch his
> highest point. . . . This is a work of genius, as much as Mr. Meredith's
> best work.

Such praise, and such a comparison with the greatest living English
novelist, in an English review, would have been unimaginable in James's
first novel-writing period. At this time, in a gesture of acknowledgment
of his hard-won stature, James was elected by a committee vote to membership in the Athenaeum Club, cutting short the usual waiting period of
twenty years.

He had several reasons for thinking about literary biographies. He was
feeling old and had been occupied with writing obituaries for his friends
Alphonse Daudet and George du Maurier. A friend and fellow member
of the Reform Club, James Payn, had just passed through his last illness,
and James had called and sat beside his sickbed. Payn was one of the great
fixtures of Victorian publishing, had written a hundred popular, sentimental novels, and had succeeded Leslie Stephen as editor of *The Cornhill Magazine*. Payn's passing seemed a sign that the Victorian era itself
was drawing to a close. *The Illustrated London News* devoted its front
page to his portrait and the next two pages to tributes from leading popular authors of the day. Clement Shorter asked James to add his tribute to
those of Walter Besant and Arthur Conan Doyle, which James was glad
to do.

> Even to the end of his sad last few years—in perpetual confinement
> and pain—Mr. Payn gave me the impression of the command of an
> independent faculty of laughter and sighs, a blessed chamber of the
> brain that could remain clear, show at least, at the top of the light-
> house, the lamp trimmed and the spark red, while darkness crept
> steadily on. . . . He wrought, like a good workman, to the latest hour,
> and as the world shrank more to what was devotedly close to him, he

had more and more affection to take and more and more gentleness
to show.

The Yellow Book published its last number in July and quietly disappeared, the indirect victim of Oscar Wilde's terribly public downfall.
Arthur Benson sent James a notebook in which he had begun an exhaus-
tive diary, one that he intended to leave behind him as a record of his
time. James appears to have been the only person with whom Benson
shared the diary, otherwise intended for posthumous publication. Benson
asked the older man's opinion and also, perhaps, wished to reassure him.
Omitted from this formal diary were the confessions of his love for James
recorded in his more purely private journal; entirely omitted indeed were
the more intimate aspects of his private and personal life. James was
pleased to have the diary opened to him and wrote to Arthur thanking
him: the diary had deepened their intimacy, had given him a sense of getting a little behind Benson's door. He had only one complaint: the omission of Benson's private life. "At any rate, I welcome it as a document, a
series of data, on the life of a young Englishman of great endowments,
character and position at the end of the 19th century."
    This was duly recorded in the diary upon its return: "Henry James . . .
has gallantly read it & writes me a priceless letter. . . . I don't know anyone like H.J. for throwing a halo, restoring one's sense of dignity."

James's reflections on literary biography, colored by his knowledge that
in the not-distant future he himself would be the subject of such biographies, found their way into The Yellow Book. James was faithful almost to
the last page of the quarterly and wrote a review for it of a volume of
George Sand's letters to her lover Alfred de Musset, just published in
France. Sand had been a great figure to James in his youth, and this revival of ancient scandals touched him with nostalgia. Sand and Musset
had displayed in public, all but literally, their dirty linen, and Mme. Sand
had written a novel frankly portraying the affair and its breakup. The
publication of her letters to Musset posed for James the highly interesting question of the step from fact to fiction, of "the process by which private ecstasies and pains find themselves transmuted in the artist's
workshop into promising literary material." The fundamental question of
the alchemy of art required such a peep into the diaries and private correspondence of the artist; but legitimate interest in this essential question
was always at war with the artist's privacy. This was

the greatest of all literary quarrels . . . the quarrel beside which all others are mild and arrangeable, the eternal dispute between the public and the private, between curiosity and delicacy. This discussion is precisely all the sharper because it takes place for each of us within as well as without. When we wish to know at all we wish to know everything.

How was the artist to respond, to prepare, for this interest in his private affairs? Émile Zola had allowed his physician to publish a complete inventory of the author's physiology. This was evidently going too far:

[the] marvelous catalogue of M. Zola's inward and outward parts . . . leaves him not an inch of privacy, so to speak, to stand on, leaves him nothing about himself that is *for* himself, for his friends, his intimates, his lovers, for discovery, for emulation, for fond conjecture or flattering deluded envy.

The difficulty with such prosy self-revelation was that it dispelled the mystery and magic that were essential to the feelings of lovers and readers. "When we meet on the broad highway the rueful denuded figure . . . mystery has fled with a shriek."

The biographer is a sleuth, and the celebrated author is obliged to bear in mind that letters will be examined, notebooks opened. One response to the problem might be utter secrecy. Matters that should be kept for privacy and silence—the secrets of the sexual life, of "the natural and instinctive man"—perhaps could be guarded by the author with the same assiduity with which the reporter pursues them. But only by absurdly drastic measures could the fearful author be sure of preserving his privacy:

the pale forewarned victim, with every track covered and every paper burnt and every letter unanswered, will, in the tower of art, the invulnerable granite, stand, without a sally, the siege of all the years.

George Sand was not one of this fearful sort. She had left behind these frank letters to Musset, as well as their transmutation into art. But her letters were not the exhibition of Zola's nudity by his physician; they had the legitimacy Sand's artfulness had given them. They were not photographs but paintings; they had the truth not of bald fact, to which she did not scrupulously adhere, but that of art and legend.

Nothing, in short, is forbidden in itself to be disclosed so long as the disclosure is artful. A love affair, when described with self-restraint and treated with tact and taste, is capable of taking its place as "one of the triumphs of civilization." To transform physiology into great art, all that is required is genius. Sand lived every moment with all her perceptions and in all her chambers, James tells us. Her letters of self-revelation accordingly are as much works of art as her novels, and indeed have better stood the test of time. Her "tone" is the solution, the secret for saving not only her reputation but her life—the life of her soul.

James soon returned to the question of literary biography in a short story, "John Delavoy." In it, a critic has written the biography of a recently deceased novelist, one whose principal subject is the relations between men and women. The biographer necessarily includes reflections upon sexuality in his portrait of the great man. The editor of the leading journal of the day firmly rejects the biography as indecent. With "the question of sex in any degree," the editor solemnly pronounces, "we have nothing whatever to do." Instead of intelligent reflections upon sexuality, the editor wants a report of the author's household, diet, and domestic habits, the sort of vulgar intrusion that du Maurier had suffered. James's critic declines to write such a study and sends his truthful portrait to another, more obscure journal, where it is printed for the few who care for it.

In another of James's stories about the alchemy of art, "Paste," there is a charming image of an actress. A string of pearls found in a trunk of costume jewelry and thought to be paste turn out to be real, the fruit of an illicit liaison. The pearls glow when the actress proudly wears them, brought to life by the warmth of her skin, beautifully confessing their origin.

Pinker was doing his best for James and introduced the innovation of an auction for his work. Instead of offering a story to a single publisher and waiting in gentlemanly fashion for a verdict, he sent it to several and asked for bids. The advances he obtained for James's three novels during 1896 could not be repeated in the following year, however, and even with James's manic pace of composition—or because of it—the sales of individual book titles fell below hope and expectation. Without new magazine serials his income dropped precipitously. James suspended his search for a country house and set to work on the first of a pair of short novels that were to be published by Heinemann as a single slim volume, pure potboilers. The first of the tales, *The Turn of the Screw*, was to be serialized (it had outgrown the bounds of the requested short story) in an American weekly, *Collier's*. The editors had asked him for a traditional ghost story for the Christmas season, and James bethought himself of the archbishop's holiday story of two children left in the care of servants, corrupted, and then lured to their deaths by ghosts. *The Turn of the Screw* and its approaching deadlines filled James's hours of dictation that summer, as he gleefully set out to write his first horror story, a perfectly irresponsible tale, as he said later; an old-fashioned ghost story that had no purpose but to entertain.

> The thing as I recall it, I most wanted not to fail of doing, under penalty of extreme platitude, was to give the impression of the communication to the children of the most infernal imaginable evil & danger—the evocation, on their part, of being as *exposed* as we can humanly conceive children to be. This was my artistic knot to untie.

This story was immensely successful. Readers appeared not to notice that James had deployed all the devices of his new style, and that considerable conscious effort was required from the reader. Reviewers were enthusiastic: here at last was a story that carried them along, one that kept them exercising their imaginations. "The . . . definite outlines of the plot are never blurred, but stand out distinct in the masterly narrative," proclaimed *The Athenaeum*, which otherwise detested his new manner. James "has rarely written anything so subtle, so delicate in workmanship, so intense in feeling, so entirely artistic," proclaimed *The Illustrated London News*. American reviewers were more enthusiastic still. When the book edition was published in the United States, the cover carried a quotation from an early review: "The sense of irresistible forces sweeping against and overturning divine innocence of heart, in the downfall of the physical under the fierce assault of the spirit." James's potboiler, written (like some others of his best work) under constraints of time and money and scorned by him as mere amusement, would become a classic.

Waiting for him on his return from Dunwich to London was a wire from the loquacious ironmonger in Rye. Lamb House was to be let after all! Old Bellingham and his wife had died, and the son was not going to live in Lamb House; he was setting off to make his fortune in the newly discovered Klondike goldfields. (The ironmonger was mistaken in one respect—the goldfields in question were in the Transvaal, not the Yukon; young Bellingham had joined a gold rush that would soon lead to war.)

This abrupt and unforeseen realization of a dream was "a little like a blow to the stomach" and took James a few hours to absorb. He wrote to Edward Warren, with whom he had just been discussing Lamb House without any hope of getting it; he explained what had happened and that he couldn't think about actually taking the house without seeing the interior. He asked Warren to accompany him to Rye.

The two men hurried down and looked the house over. The rooms were small and dark, but the detached banquet hall in the garden was roomy and would make an admirable study, with space for a secretary and for pacing. Warren pronounced Lamb House structurally sound. The rent was seventy pounds, more than the fifty James had calculated he could afford but still cheap. There would be considerable added expense, however—the house needed repair and redecoration; James did not have nearly enough furniture for two establishments; he would have to keep on the Bellinghams' gardener, and the Smiths would probably require additional help. Despite all these difficulties he did not hesitate a moment. He signed a lease for twenty-one years and began to plan for the entire upheaval of his settled household. After a nomadic life and years of searching, he had found a home in which he would be precisely located, socially and geographically, in a house on a hill, with a walled garden beside it, and with ample room for the visits of intimate friends and relations. From his writing desk in De Vere Gardens, with the lease still before him and the pen still in his hand, he wrote out a letter to Arthur Benson:

> I am just drawing a long breath from having signed—a few moments since—a most portentous parchment: the lease of a smallish, charming, cheap old house in the country—down at Rye—for 21 years! (One would think I was *your* age!) But it is exactly what I want and secretly and hopelessly coveted. . . . [It] has a beautiful room for you (the "King's Room"—George II's—who slept there;) . . . Come down to Lamb House . . . my dear Arthur, to yours very eagerly,
>
> Henry James

17

LAMB HOUSE

Invitations were premature, however, as a good deal of work first had to be done. After signing the lease, James went down to Rye again with Warren, who had agreed to take charge of the renovations and had already begun to map them out. Alfred Parsons joined them on this journey and walked through the garden with them. James happily reported to his sister-in-law Alice that

> Parsons, best of men as well as best of landscape-painters-and-gardeners . . . revealed to me the most charming possibilities for the treatment of the tiny out-of-door part—it amounts to about an acre of garden & lawn, all shut in by the peaceful red brick wall . . . on which the most flourishing old espaliers, apricots, pears, plums & figs, assiduously grow.

London was at its worst in December 1897, damp and cold, with an impenetrable choking fog over all. James walked, coughing, on Christmas Day to see Jonathan Sturges, who was again very ill, at his nursing home on Wimpole Street and then dined with John Hay and his wife and daughter at the U.S. Embassy. It was a cheerless holiday, haunted by ghosts, and James wrote yearningly to Daniel and Ariana Curtis, promising that soon, soon he would accept their repeated and so generous invitations to visit them again in Italy, where the sun shone. "We are here simply on another planet, a planet worse even than Mars, which has no atmosphere at all. That is better than an atmosphere of smutty cotton-wool."

In the midst of this dreary holiday season, his brother Robertson arrived unannounced and paid James a visit until after the new year. As he told Mary afterward in a handwritten letter, Bob left behind him

> impressions of his condition & future (as you may well believe,) too strange & too numerous—as well, many of them, as too painful—to . . . relate. He struck me of course as in many ways absolutely *insane*—but as weakening, progressively, in respect to some of his old impossibilities, so as to tend to become more tranquil & more manageable.

A mountain of letters awaited reply: invitations, requests to subscribe to various benefits, holiday greetings. He dictated his replies and his end-of-year letters to the click of MacAlpine's Remington, apologizing to his correspondents as he did: "When once one has mastered the difficult art of dictation it has, by force, to impose itself." John Hay invited him to join a winter vacation on the Nile, an invitation he could not afford to accept. Waldo Story, the son of his old friend the sculptor William Wetmore Story, the year before had very insistently asked James to write his father's life. James had reluctantly agreed; had then pleaded the press of other obligations and asked to be released from his promise. Waldo now insisted that delays were of no consequence, and once again James made "vague, but scarcely the less terrible, promises" to complete the long-delayed project. Perhaps when he had visited Rome again and refreshed his recollection of the scene.

He soon heard another voice from the past calling him to Rome. James wrote a New Year's letter to his friend Paul Zhukowsky, renewing their correspondence after one of its periodic lapses. Zhukowsky had never visited England, and almost six years had passed since James's last visit to the Continent. The days in which they might hope to meet in Europe were seemingly past, but they continued to correspond and to speak of meeting again. James now wrote in a hopeful vein, speaking of the success of his return to the field of fiction, apologizing for his long silence, explaining that his new success kept him terribly busy. Zhukowsky's answer was not long delayed:

> My very dear friend! . . . certainly the interruption of our correspondence gave me pain, but it has not in the least altered my feelings for your dear person, for I explained it to myself just as you have in your letter of January 1, for which I embrace you as I love you, that is, with

a great, solid and unshakeable affection. I am quite delighted that your silence was caused by nothing else than an excess of work, that is, of happiness and contentment.

A commission to design decorations for a memorial to the martyred Alexander II had kept Zhukowsky in Moscow more than he liked, but the great work was completed at last and the dedication of the memorial would be in August. "Will you come, dear friend? Give it a bit of serious thought." Now that his time was his own again, Zhukowsky planned to establish himself in Rome and visit Moscow only when the weather was pleasant. He hoped that James had not renounced Italy forever and that they would meet again there from time to time. "Now let me embrace you most affectionately and beg you to write, even if only two lines, to tell me how you are."

James was anxious to leave London for his new country house. It was just twenty years since he had settled in London. Many of his old friends were gone, and the older generation who had welcomed him had passed away. He was a celebrity now, and even in winter he was obliged to respond to a stream of invitations from eager hostesses. At a tea party he could not refuse to attend, he met a young American woman, Emilie Grigsby, whose wealth and Kentucky antecedents were shrouded in mystery, who was conducting her own siege of London and in the process cultivating his acquaintance. He met her periodically at dinners and after repeated invitations called upon her at the Savoy Hotel. In time, American newspapers carried rumors that they were to be married, and Miss Grigsby let it be known that she was the model for one of his fictional heroines, which James did not trouble to deny.

He called, also by invitation, upon another of the reigning beauties of London, Vera Campbell, known by courtesy as Lady Colin Campbell, whose bitterly contested divorce had been one of the great public entertainments of recent years. Vera Campbell was tall and well made, with striking, often-photographed features, and might have sat for a portrait of Maisie's mother—as perhaps she had. She was a lion hunter, in pursuit of the famous novelist. When James arrived he found her dressed as if for an assignation. Gertrude Atherton was the only other guest, and she excused herself quickly. Atherton—whose own overtures of two years before had met with so little response—recalled that "Vera had oriented herself to the role of siren, but I couldn't see Henry James making love to any woman."

The depression of the economies of Great Britain and America had not lightened; but the well-to-do were more prosperous than ever. A new web of electrical communication linked them in a cosmopolitan realm of their own. Telegrams could be purchased from Her Majesty's postal service, at wickets tucked into corners of groceries, and the cages in which clerks sat were a metaphor of poverty amid wealth. James vividly recalled from his Bolton Street days the almost daily visits, the lines of impatient young gentlemen at certain times of day, the servants carrying their masters' letters, the occasional well-dressed lady evidently sending a private message, and the weary clerk behind the wicket. It struck him to write a story from the perspective of a young clerk in a cage, with the whole traffic of communications, laden with secrets, passing through her hands: the whole corrupt and luxurious world of London visible to one who had the imagination to piece together the clues. As a perceptive reader would later remark, in James's story the clerk's perspective is the artist's, seeing through a limited aperture but imagining the larger world that she "feels burningly in this one focus."

The clerk's cage is in a dark corner of a small grocery in Mayfair, a construction of wood and wire mesh within which she sits like a tame bird or a guinea pig; gentlemen and ladies thrust their letters and telegraph forms at her through the narrow opening. Without looking up at their faces, the clerk takes their letters and weighs them, answers stupid questions, doles out stamps, makes difficult change from five-pound notes (which speak in themselves of unattainable, almost incredible freedom). The telegram forms are numerous and burdensome: she must count the words, at a penny each. Her forearm aches with rubbing across the counter from morning to night. The other clerks crowd against her, a sharp elbow against her arm, foul breath beside her ear. The young men at the grocer's counter flirt with her clumsily and sometimes rudely. The shop is pervaded in winter by the sulfurous smell of coal gas and at all times by the odors of hams, cheese, dried fish, soap, varnish, kerosene, and other smells whose source she does not know. Poverty is physical constraint and material ugliness. But the place is quiet in the early afternoon, when the ladies and gentlemen are at lunch. On a rare October afternoon, the slanting sun casts a patch of light on the floor and strikes bright colors from bottles of syrup.

There is to be no rescue; this is a realistic tale, and, despite her hopes for love and freedom, her artist's imagination, the telegraph clerk's fate is marriage to a grocer's clerk, Mudge, who has risen to partnership in a grocery shop in Chalk Downs, where she will exchange one cage for another.

Edward Warren happily took charge of the renovation and restoration of Lamb House. He and James studied the history of the house and the town. Rye in ancient days, when it was still a seaport, had been one of the Cinque Ports, eventually seven in number, with a charter that dated back to the fourteenth century. Over the slow centuries, siltation had extended the fringe of the coast, leaving the village stranded on its hill. James's house dated from a later period of prosperity; it was built in 1705, in the reign of Queen Anne, in the plain style of that time. The Lambs had completed the house in 1723, making additions in the new Georgian style. The house was built upon cellars and an old kitchen with a wide fireplace that were much older, dating back to the Tudors. The "banqueting room," what James would call his Garden Room, and the high, green-painted, canopied front door that had so taken his fancy were Georgian, and he decided to restore the whole house to the eighteenth-century era of its greatest glory. Ugly "gasoliers" were to be removed, paper stripped from the paneled walls. The front bedroom (the "King's Room") and the front parlor had lovely floor-to-ceiling oak paneling that was to be left exposed; the paneling in the other rooms was to be painted green or white throughout the house. James looked for Georgian oak paneling for the dining room, where it was lacking, and hunted for "not too delusive" Sheraton and Chippendale furniture—"old mahogany and brass."

Margaret Warren, Edward's wife, was caught up in the general enthusiasm and agreed to take charge of the window treatments on the first two floors; the top floor and the dormer windows under the roof looked out over the tops of neighboring houses and would be left without curtains.

The outdoors was under Parsons's supervision, who recommended against a flower garden, which would be troublesome to maintain. The ancient mulberry in the center, perhaps older than the house itself, would be surrounded by a sweep of lawn, with perennial borders and flowering shrubs under the walls.

Changes in the house required young Bellingham's permission, which was sought via his local solicitor, as Bellingham himself was in South Africa. James wanted to put French doors, opening onto the garden, into the otherwise dark dining room. A large greenhouse that filled that corner of the garden would have to be removed; James promised to replace it with a smaller greenhouse near the gardener's cottage. The kitchen would have to be modernized, of course, and an upstairs bathroom with running water would have to be added.

Bellingham's solicitor agreed to all these requests, and the planned work grew ever more elaborate and expensive. James made hurried visits to Rye to supervise, staying at the Mermaid Inn around the corner and asking Rye neighbors for reports when he was absent in London. The work went more slowly than he had hoped, and when Easter came around he was still in London and the renovation was still in progress. He had hoped to rent De Vere Gardens for the Season to defray some of the unexpected expense, but after Easter it would be difficult to find a tenant. Not until the first of June, however, could he begin to send some furniture into his new home.

He was conscious of moving into not only a house but a village. Since his first summer in Rye he had become acquainted with some of the townspeople, the shopkeepers, and the postman. John Adams, the stationer, and he became particularly well acquainted and it was from Adams that he happily ordered Lamb House notepaper long before he actually moved to his new address. Rye was in some ways like the vanished London of his early memories, a tight little community with its back turned to the world.

> Rye society in those days consisted of perhaps a score of households beside the local shopkeepers and tradesmen. There were one or two writers and artists, but the majority of the residents were retired folk, soldiers, sailors and civil servants, besides whom there was the usual run of professional people to be met with in any English country town, such as lawyers and doctors, not to mention various old ladies. The principal industry, indeed the only one, was fishing.

Once he began properly to settle in, as he told Alice, "the special note of Rye, the feeling of the little hilltop community, bound together like a very modest, obscure and impecunious, but virtuous and amiable family, began most unmistakably to come out." He quickly made friends with his neighbor, the bachelor travel writer Arthur Bradley, and with George and

Fanny Prothero, summer people like himself, who had taken Dial Cottage on a long lease. James joined the golf club, although he did not play golf, and often stopped there for tea after a long walk. At other times, he went into the bar at the Mermaid Inn for an evening drink, and he became well acquainted with the leading men of the town. He exchanged invitations to tea with the ladies. He was good-natured and not at all averse to gossip, which was always a point in his favor.

At last he was able to tear himself away from London. A dinner with Rosebery, who was now leading the Liberal opposition; tea at the American embassy; and then in the middle of June he brought the Smiths, Tosca, and MacAlpine down to Rye. MacAlpine found lodgings nearby, and the Smiths—with the gardener George Gammon's help—set to work putting the house in order. James returned briefly to London, but in a few days he was back in Rye. De Vere Gardens was rented, and he planned to remain in Lamb House through the Christmas season. He expected to remain in the country until after the new year, if Lamb House proved to be comfortable in cold weather, and then to depart for Rome to join Zhukowsky and begin his biography of Story.

As soon as he was installed in Lamb House, a stream of guests came to him: Arthur Benson, of course; the Gosses. His nephew and namesake, Harry James, Alice and William's eldest son, came over on summer vacation from college, accompanied by a Cambridge aunt, Margaret Gibbens, and brought with him a set of china, a house gift from Alice. Harry arrived while the Gosses were still at Lamb House, and James was pleased to be able to put them all up at once. Paul and Minnie Bourget visited briefly; Edward and Margaret Warren; the Godkins, who were spending the summer in England again. Annie Fields and Sarah Orne Jewett, visiting from America, came down from London for a day, and if they had ever resented his intrusion into their household for *The Bostonians*, the incident was long forgotten. Annie Fields recorded the pleasant visit in her diary:

> He was waiting for us at the station with a carriage, and in five minutes we found ourselves at the top of a silent little winding street, at the green door with a brass knocker. . . . Mr. James was intent on the largest hospitality. We were asked upstairs over a staircase with a pretty balustrade and plain green drugget on the steps; everything was of the severest plainness, but in the best taste. . . . The dominating note was

Mr. James's pleasure in having a home of his own to which he might ask us.

Wendell Holmes was in London, and after an exchange of messages about possible dates and train schedules, other guests, and the possibility of dressing for dinner, he came for a weekend at the end of July. This was again a very pleasant visit, and they spoke of meeting again. But Holmes was engaged to spend a few days with Lady Castletown at Doneraile, her family's estate in Ireland, and caught his ship at Queenstown without returning to England.

Frances Hodgson Burnett was at Rolvenden, a few miles away, and she sent James a welcoming basket of fruit from her own little walled garden, the "secret garden" abandoned and overgrown, in which she would soon set her tale. A scattering of younger artists and writers were also finding their way to the coast: Ford Madox Ford (Hueffer, as he was then), Stephen Crane, Joseph Conrad, and H. G. Wells.

Later in the summer, Jonathan Sturges came down from London for a fortnight and remained until the new year. Sturges was good company, and during the holiday season Arthur Benson joined them. The house, in short, was filled with company, as it was meant to be. James began characteristically to complain of the burden of his social obligations. He pleaded a press of engagements when refusing Vera Campbell's renewed invitations, and he declined Augusta Gregory's invitations to dinner. Even James's sacred mornings were somewhat broken in upon, as he was obliged to have more protracted conferences with Mrs. Smith to plan the days; but he hired additional help for her, and despite the stream of guests coming down from London, the house ran quite smoothly.

His working space for the summer months was ideal: the big, beautifully proportioned "Garden Room," quite separate from the main house. A little flight of seven steps led up to it from the garden. It was a long, high-ceilinged space. The bow window at the north end was quite high up, when seen from the street, but from within made a comfortable window seat. There was a fireplace, with a coal grate, at the opposite end of the room. Ample windows on the west wall gave a pleasant view of the house and garden, and with so many windows the room was filled with cool, indirect light. The furnishings were still very sparse: a writing table for James and another for MacAlpine; the Remington typewriter on its stand; a few books. James had a wicker chair placed in the garden under the mulberry tree, just outside the garden room, and in the afternoons and early evenings, he would often sit there with a book.

He wrote a short novel that summer, *The Awkward Age*, which was to be serialized in *Harper's Weekly*. In it, he pursued his notion of the decline of the upper class, the decline that seemed so visible in London. Feeling old as he was, he could not help recalling what seemed to him a more tranquil time, the age of the "early Victorians" whom he had known on his first visit to London almost thirty years before. He imagined an old man, a Londoner who had been living in the country for thirty years, a sort of Rip Van Winkle figure who now arrived in the marketplace that London had become. "Mr. Longdon" embodied Old World friendship and family, still preserved in his rural village; his house and garden were recognizably James's Lamb House. His little family seat made a contrast to modern London society, the market in which uprooted young men and women were bought and sold; his adult but innocent eye gave the reader her camera lens.

James had returned, in short, to the novel of social commentary, albeit within the scenic structure of the shortened form. The conflicts of young and old, of democracy and the old order, were fought once again by passionate, intelligent, and powerful women. Instead of observing the conflict of class and nationality from above, from the eye of omniscience, however, James pursued his new and more congenial method and looked about him through the innocent eyes of Mr. Longdon. Scene after scene assembled itself in the reader's imagination, detail by detail, brought to life by conscious effort.

The author provided almost no explanation, however, and the action proceeded entirely through fragmentary dialogue. The central character, Mrs. Brookenham, maneuvered with real brilliance in her efforts to marry her daughter to a vulgar but decent businessman. The lovely young daughter, Nanda, just eighteen years old, has been soiled by her exposure to the loose manners of her mother's set, and a more suitable marriage to the man she loves is not possible. Instead of accepting the meager compromise her mother offers her, however, Nanda retreats from the marketplace and joins old Longdon at his country retreat.

Like Maisie, like James's American girls, Nanda is freed by her knowledge of adult affairs. She chooses generously at the end of the drama to confer on a friend the wealthy husband that her mother has provided. The story is meant to have a light tone, a gentle air was to blow upon it from France, and the spirit of "Gyp's" light Parisian novels in dialogue was invoked. The tale was elegant and well written, and, as James later claimed, he succeeded in fusing the forms of the drama and the novel. He wrote in a high good humor.

But the scenic plan, and the limits of a short novel, made it difficult to show Longdon's world, his house and village. His friends and private circle remained invisible, and he had only his memories of youthful love, so that Longdon appeared to be a recluse, and his disapproval of the modern marketplace seemed little more than innocent prudishness. The dialogue was realistically full of gaps and jumps and was written in James's increasingly impressionistic style, so that a reader was obliged to struggle through each conversation and to supply the needed continuity and references. Mrs. Brookenham's maneuverings among a large and varied cast of characters were difficult to follow, and interest was difficult to maintain, especially with so little story to pull the novel along, and although an artistic tour de force, the book was not popular then or later.

James did not then see these difficulties, his own imagination evidently supplied the deficiencies, and he saw only that he had portrayed living characters in genuine relations to one another, in a situation that exemplified modern dilemmas. As it was to appear in an American weekly, he offered *The Awkward Age* to *The Illustrated London News,* but Shorter turned it down, and no other British venue was found for the serial.

Nothing seemed to result either from three short stories he had written that summer and asked Pinker to place. He wrote to Pinker in a fit of depression, asking to have the stories returned, but Pinker reassured him, and eventually the novel and tales were all published.

France and Russia were allied, the German and Austrian emperors were allied; England stood alone in Europe, and General Wolseley warned that it relied too much upon its navy. Wolseley made little progress in his argument for a large, standing army, but he was able that summer to preside over a triumphant, vengeful return to Khartoum. He had been preparing the ground for two years, building a flotilla of steamships on the Nile and a railroad across the desert into the Sudan. Illustrated newspapers were filled with stories of troops on maneuver, on their way to the campaign that had now begun, illustrated with drawings of the elite mounted regiments leading British and Egyptian troops to Omdurman.

London newspapers gave almost as much space to America's war with

Spain. American battleships had destroyed the aging Spanish fleet off Santiago, Cuba, and Spain had sued for peace, had surrendered the Philippines and Guam. The United States, now a global power, was garrisoning its new island possessions. The "splendid little war," as John Hay called it, was accompanied by a triumphant assertion of his program of alliance with Great Britain. Hay was summoned home from Egypt, to join the president's cabinet as secretary of state, and James bade him farewell. Hay came down with his wife to Surenden Dering, in Kent, to say good-bye to his hosts there: the newly retired Senator J. Donald Cameron, a great Republican chieftain, and his charming wife, Elizabeth. Henry Adams and his brother Brooks were there, and James ran over from Rye to join them for the extended family gathering.

Winter came early, and on a gray, gusty, lonely Sunday, a "perpetual gale" seemed to be blowing. James took refuge in his upstairs paneled study, freshly painted green, where Smith kept hot the little coal grate in the fireplace. Here he had a writing table, a bookcase, and the oil lamps with which he had replaced the gas fixtures. Cold winds outdoors made the study seem all the cozier, although "the wail of the elements starts up—in my solitude—all ghosts & memories."

The house was nearly empty of guests, after the friendly siege in summer and fall. Nineteen-year-old Harry was back at Harvard, after a long stay. His visit had been most pleasant for both uncle and nephew and had laid the basis of a genuine friendship between them. Only Jonathan Sturges had remained; he had proven himself a congenial guest, and his visit had extended itself until the first of the year.

Christmas in Rye was not elaborate, and the simple feudal quality of the celebration was much to James's taste. By taking Lamb House he had in some degree succeeded to the social position of a baron of the Cinque Ports. Children who came to the door were given coins, and workingmen were given a drink in the kitchen.

After the first of the year, he accompanied Sturges back to London. They agreed that the younger man would return in the spring and keep the house lively with guests while James was in Rome. James spent a few days in London. He ran into Howard Sturgis at a museum, and they fell to talking about *The Awkward Age*, which Sturgis admired—but declared that he was one of the very few people who would care for it. "I greatly applaud the tact with which you tell me," James replied, smiling, "that scarce a human being will understand a word. . . . I tell *myself*—& the 're-

views' tell me—such truths in a much cruder fashion. But it's an old, old
story—& if I 'minded' now as much as I once did, I should be well beneath the sod."

The conversation in a museum prompted an invitation to Queen's
Acre, and after paying that visit, James sent his host an inscribed copy of
The Awkward Age; this in turn opened a correspondence that they carried
on through the summer. James extended vague invitations to visit Lamb
House.

He decided to sublet his Kensington flat for the balance of his lease.
Lamb House had proven itself habitable through the winter, and while
he did not want to give up London entirely, all he really needed was a
foot on the ground there. He put his name down for a bed-sitting room
at the Reform Club, which he thought would be sufficient for his winter
visits.

Back in Rye, now solitary and a little depressed, he opened his notebook for the first time in eight months. *The Awkward Age* had finished its
run as a serial, and he was correcting the pages for book editions in the
United States and Great Britain; but he had no new project yet.

> George Alexander [the star of *Guy Domville*] writes to ask me for Cov-
> ering End, for "him & Miss Davis" to do, & I've just written to him the
> obstacles & objections. But I've also said I *would* do him a *fresh* one-act
> thing, & it's strange how this renewal of contact with the vulgar theatre
> stirs again, in a manner, & moves me. . . .
>
> The wind booms in the old chimneys, wails & shrieks about the old
> walls. I sit, however, in the little warm white [downstairs] study . . . &
> feel the old reviving ache of desire to get back to work. This note of
> Alexander's is probably the germ of something. . . . Ah, the one act! Ah,
> the "short story!" It's very much the same trick.

He made a series of notes over the next few days, of anecdotes that
might give rise to more of the short stories that were providing half his
bread and butter now. But he was tired, and the trick had been mastered
and was beginning to weary him. The one-act play and the short-short
story were single scenes, extended moments. Short novels, "nouvelles,"
were like full evening-long plays, but even these were cramped by the
limitations of the form. He began to think of returning to the big novel:

> How, through all hesitations & conflicts & worries, *the* thing, the desire
> to get back only to the *big* (scenic, constructive, "architectural" effects)

seizes me & carries me off my feet: making me feel that it's a far deeper economy of time to sink, at *any* moment, into the evocation & ciphering out of *that*, than into any other *small* beguilement at all.

He would do a short, strong piece for the magazines now, he decided, but would take a winter vacation in Rome, to which Story and Zhukowsky were calling him. He would bring with him the notion of writing once again a big novel, to commune with it at leisure: "I must have a *tête à tête* with myself, a long ciphering bout, before I really start."

Sunday, February 26, the night before his departure, struggling to clear up his correspondence before leaving the country, he sat up late in the green-paneled study. While writing his last letter, to a friend in Rome, Antonio Fernando de Navarro, he gradually became conscious of a growing odor and, looking up from his work, saw wisps of smoke coming from between the floorboards, beyond the margin of carpet and rugs. He went upstairs and woke Smith, who found some tools. They pried up two floorboards and found that the old beam beneath the hearth in his study was smoldering. Heat from the new coal grate had kindled the ancient wood beneath. The two men put out the fire, as they thought, with soaked sponges, and James returned to his writing desk. But the fire was not extinguished. Seeing smoke once more, he roused Smith again and, as he told Warren the next day,

> We rushed for fire and police brigade, and they arrived with very decent promptness and operated with intelligence and tact. . . . The brave pumpers departed with the early dawn. But I was sickened by the little desolation and defacement—the house befouled and topsy-turvy—and couldn't sleep.

The fire had spread down into the dining room below, and while the smoke and water damage was not extensive, the disorder and mess were considerable, and neither dining room nor study could now be heated.

James telegraphed Warren early Monday morning, sending a longer letter of explanation to follow, and Warren hurried down the next day. The chimney and flues that served the dining room and the green study above it would have to be rebuilt and the thin tile hearths replaced with heavy stone. The fireplaces throughout the house ought to be remodeled in the same way and would in the end be both safer and more attractive, with properly installed grates and, in the dining room, a newly designed mantel; Warren would be able to put some badly needed bookshelves into both dining room and study while he was at it. He would take complete charge of the renewed renovations.

When they had finished their tour and assessment of the damage, James sat down and completed his letter to Navarro—"My dear Tony, you are literally my saviour." If James had not been sitting up late to finish his letter, he might not have discovered the fire in time and might have lost his house and even his life. As it was, the damage was fully insured; Warren's renovations would be improvements, and while James's departure for the Continent was necessarily delayed, he went to France and Italy with an untroubled mind.

The unexpectedly rapid American victory over Spain, and the far more violent British victory in the Sudan, were almost equally celebrated in England on placards, in the press, and by shouting newsboys in the streets. James at first had joined in the general good feeling, but this had given way to uneasiness. The slaughter of tens of thousands wreaked by British machine guns at Omdurman was horrific and pointless: the Sudanese regime was not a threat to Great Britain. The American war was even more disturbing. Its stated purpose was to free island colonies from their Spanish masters; but the Filipinos had rebelled against their new American occupiers, and the McKinley administration had responded with force and begun a long war of repression.

James had accepted the arguments for the British Empire in Africa— ending the slave trade, civilizing and liberating subject peoples in Muslim and black African empires—had accepted even the newspaper's view that Sudanese "dervishes" were "devils," but he was uneasy about the new, more frankly selfish imperialism: the United States' occupation of the Philippines, Britain's adventures in South Africa, its grab for the gold of the Transvaal. He and William exchanged sympathetic notes. William remarked that "the old human instincts of war-making and conquest sweep all principles away before them," and Henry agreed. The repression of the Philippine rebellion made him, for the first time, regret his own nationality:

> We have ceased to be, among the big nations, the one great thing that made up for our so many crudities, & made us all superior & unique— the only one with clean hands & no record of across-the-seas murder &

theft. *Terminato—terminato!* One would like to be a Swiss or a Montenegrian now.

James as usual broke his long rail journey into Italy with a stop in Paris, where he said hello to a few old friends—but "my old circle here has faded away into *Ewigkeit.*" He spent some time with Ellen Hunter, née Temple, who was staying with two of her daughters at Giverny; a visit that again recalled for him the young Temple sisters and his own youthful prime. He clasped the hands of some of his younger friends—Morton Fullerton, Ralph Curtis. He met, for the first time, young Maurice Barrès, whose books he had been reading with mingled admiration and horror. Barrès had coined the term "nationalism," now the slogan of a movement. The old regime had been "cosmopolitan"—aristocracies were international—but the great force in the modern, democratic world was the new nation-state, expressing through a heroic figure like Napoleon the character and will of a people.

The imagery of mingled race and nation, the fantastic idea that France was a single entity with a single character and a single will, was terribly compelling. Barrès and others gave it rational, analytic expression, gave it what seemed to be a factual, scientific basis, drawing upon the studies of Ernest Renan that had been so admired in the James household. Barrès and Bourget were among the intellectual founders of this new, more radical nationalist Right. "Have you seen Maurice Barrès's last volume?" James asked Gosse. He thought it "exquisite in its fearfully intelligent impertinence and its diabolical Renanisation." The new movement was gaining strength, and "France . . . will presumably soon have its new Caesar—by acclamation—in the person of the younger Bonaparte princes."

James continued his journey by rail into the south of France. The Bourgets were not in Paris but in the country house they had recently acquired in Costebelle, on the Riviera, and James joined them there for a few days. James thought the place, on a terraced mountainside with "exquisite views inland and to the sea," a "precious and enviable acquisition." The visit was strained, however. Bourget was deeply immersed in the new nationalist movement, but James did not like to disagree with his host; he ducked his head and passed by in silence.

With his journey delayed by the fire in Lamb House and the obligatory stops in France, James had missed finding Zhukowsky in Rome. The Russian had followed his emperor to The Hague, where the young czar had convened an international peace congress; he and James agreed to meet in Florence instead, in June.

James accordingly first went eastward by rail through Genoa and across Italy to Venice, accepting the insistently repeated invitations of Daniel and Ariana Curtis to be their guest at the Palazzo Barbaro. They were away but urged him to make himself at home in the Barbaro, where another guest was already in residence, a Miss Jessie Allen, with whom he promptly formed a cordial friendship. James took his old familiar apartment upstairs, worked in the mornings in the library, and reacquainted himself with Venice in the evenings, making free use of the gondola piloted by an old friend, the gondolier Angelo, whom the Curtises put at his and Miss Allen's disposal.

His recently renewed friendship with Ellen Temple Hunter and her daughters, refreshed by their cordial visit in Paris, brought with it reminders to him of long-ago days, of her sister Mary and his first venture to Italy thirty years earlier. On the eve of that first sojourn in Europe his dear cousin Mary Temple, already dying of tuberculosis, had yearned to accompany him, and when he was in Italy she had written to him touchingly, "Think, my dear, of the pleasure we should have together in Rome. I am crazy at the mere thought." But she was then already too ill to travel.

At work in Venice, as James began to nose his way into a new novel, a big architectural work of the kind he had thought never to write again, the image of young Mary Temple clutching at life as it slipped away lifted itself in his imagination. Now, she remained in memory as he had last seen her, tall and slender, with disordered, luxuriant red hair, gazing at him with mingled sadness and defiance. Now she had come to Venice after all, to the Palazzo Barbaro of marble floors and old ceilings, seeing it with innocent, hungry eyes.

From Venice he went on to Rome, although Zhukowsky was no longer there, to begin work on the life of William Wetmore Story that he had promised. Rome was greatly changed, and he could not help comparing the nationalist, republican Rome of the present day with the papal, cosmopolitan city of his first visits and fondest memories. He spent a good deal of time with Waldo Story, who had inherited his father's studio, his "vast marble-shop," going over old papers and seeing old sites, and he was necessarily plunged into memories of earlier days. The month he spent in Rome, from the middle of May to the middle of June, despite the increasing heat and the absence of Zhukowsky, he spent pleasantly. He also entered into a friendship that would prove to be profoundly important.

He had called upon old friends, among whom was Julia Ward Howe's daughter, Maud, who had married a painter, John Elliott, and had settled in Rome. The Elliotts had a charming apartment in Trastevere, on the upper floor of the Palazzo Rosticucci, and kept a modest salon there for the American colony. James remembered Julia Ward Howe fondly from his earliest days in Rome and was amused by her daughter's account of the aged Julia's visit the previous winter. Julia Ward had been rather plain as a young woman and had not shone in society, but in her old age she had been a great hit in Rome, and all the artists raved about her: "the most picturesque, striking, lovely old (wrinkled and *marked*) 'Holbein.' " James would make a short story of the incident.

One Sunday afternoon at the Elliotts', on their cool terrace, he met a young expatriate American sculptor, Hendrik Andersen: tall, with broad shoulders but a rather delicate build, flaxen hair, a fine aquiline profile, and an open, frank manner. His family were Norwegian immigrants who had settled in Newport, Rhode Island, where Hendrik had been raised. He had left home to study in Europe and had been trying to maintain a studio in the Via Margutta for the past two years. Andersen had been the protégé of Lord Ronald Gower but had recently been supplanted in Gower's affections by another young man, James's friend Morton Fullerton. He was now at loose ends, trying to make his way by modeling portraits—he was one of the artists who had asked Julia Ward to sit—but was having little luck in obtaining commissions.

Andersen was twenty-seven years old, sensitive and unsure of himself, and James gathered him up. He visited Andersen's studio, where he saw the larger-than-life nude marble figures, in monumental groups, carved under Lord Gower's patronage—"giants," as James called them. He admired Andersen's portrait of Julia Ward Howe and made his first modest gesture as patron by purchasing a small terra-cotta head of a boy, Count Alberto Bevilacqua.

Lacking clients or a new patron, Andersen had decided to abandon Rome and to return home to America, and James invited him to make a long detour, to travel by rail across Europe to pay a visit to Lamb House before sailing for America.

· · ·

A photograph of Henry James: he stands on the steps of the Borghese Gallery, doffing his hat to the photographer and squinting a little in the bright sunlight. The photograph is a memento of James's visit to Joseph Primoli in that summer of 1899. The Borghese Gallery was in a manner of speaking a Primoli family archive. The art collection of Cardinal Scipione Borghese had passed into the hands of Primoli's great-uncle, Camillo Borghese, who had sold part of the collection to his brother-in-law the Emperor Napoleon with which to decorate the Louvre Palace. A charming gesture of Primoli, to have brought James to the gallery; the memory of the visit would enrich the imagery of his last incomplete work of fiction.

The Villa Borghese was a shrine to the sublimity of love. At its center was Canova's life-size portrait of Camillo's bride (Primoli's great-aunt), Pauline Bonaparte, in milk-white marble, reclining, her arms and torso bare, leaning on one elbow, her head lifted regally. She had been a great beauty, and this all-but-nude portrait had been conceived by the sculptor to be viewed by candlelight, so that the illusion of life would be almost perfect.

The portrait of Pauline was almost synonymous with the gallery, but the most famous painting there was Titian's *Sacred and Profane Love*, a gift to celebrate the marriage of Nicolò Aurelio and Laura Bagaratto. The auburn-haired bride sits demurely in white beside a sarcophagus that lends solemnity to the moment. Assisting her is a magnificently nude Venus, who flatteringly resembles the bride. One could hardly have a better celebration of the sublimity of love. A later and more prudish generation labeled the picture "sacred and profane," but the question was always slyly asked: Which figure is sacred, which profane?—a question that would be echoed in the title of James's wickedly satirical novel *The Sacred Fount*.

James began his return to the north with his long-delayed visit with Zhukowsky in Florence, a visit that extended itself from the original plan of ten days to three weeks. He then crept back overland to Paris and home, answering en route a letter from Howard Sturgis that had been pursuing him across Europe: "I crawl, depleted as to purse, wan though bloated as to person, back to my little hole in the sand at Rye, there to burrow & burrow during an indefinite future."

James's return from Italy was even more of a letdown than usual. A mountain of unanswered letters awaited him. Business dealings with publishers were in Pinker's hands, but the editors and publishers were accustomed to dealing directly with James and didn't like to bargain with an agent. James had given William Heinemann first refusal of his books in the United Kingdom, but when Pinker began sending proposals, Heinemann refused to answer. James was obliged now to intervene. He had also promised George Brett of Macmillan first refusal of American rights for his next book, and this had to be communicated to Pinker and dealings with Macmillan shifted into the agent's hands as well.

James's beloved Tosca had died while he was abroad, and Gammon had buried her at the foot of the garden, in a corner of the wall beneath a walnut tree. James had been too fond of her, despite their enforced separations, to think of replacing her so soon, and the house seemed empty. The Smiths, who were growing older, showed even more than usual the debilitation of drink. The fire and consequent renovations had kept Jonathan Sturges away, and the Smiths had been idle and demoralized. Lamb House on his return was a lonely and disordered place, and James himself after his long journey was tired, overweight, and worried about money. In a deep depression of spirits he began to put his household in order.

Among the accumulation of books, journals, and letters that awaited him were reviews of his novel *The Awkward Age*, which had appeared in Great Britain without prior serialization and which had called down there a torrent of resentful criticism. A note from Heinemann prepared him: "I've never in all my experience seen [a book] treated with more general and complete disrespect."

Part of the difficulty evidently was his new style, which was not supported in this case with a story of adventure or youthful romance. Scene followed scene, each casting a new light on the developing situation of mother and daughter, but there was no obvious narrative. Reviewers responded with remarkable uniformity, with the anger of men who suspected that they were missing the point of a joke. *The Pall Mall Gazette* headed its review "Mr. Henry James Exasperates," and *The Manchester Guardian* reported with irritation that the tale was an "enigma, the very quintessence of a riddle." Even the few reviewers who liked the book found it puzzling and difficult:

A charm, sometimes a snare, of Mr. James's method is that no such thing as an explanation is ever vouchsafed. . . . You over hear and interpret as you can, but nothing is said for your benefit. Therefore the need for an intelligent attention to every shade and half-shade in intonation and manner. If you have to strain an ear for what is said, you must do it still more for what is only implied. Many people will think that for all this trouble they get no adequate return.

"You must take time and trouble," *The Bookman* warned, speaking the condemnation of the new consumer age. "The honest reader in search of a story will stare dazedly through perhaps a third of Mr. James's new book, and then shut it with a snort."

Never had he suffered such uniformly bad reviews or so complete a commercial failure. "The book has done nothing to speak of," Heinemann told him. The loss of income was distressing, but James's belief in his own work was not disturbed. "Nothing I've ever done is better—firmer, fuller, more unbrokenly sustained, in every way more expert & mature," he told Howells. Mrs. Brookenham and Nanda were rich and deeply understood characters. For the reader who could hold the successive scenes in memory and follow the mother's intelligent maneuvering and her daughter's final emancipation, it was a vivid satire of a greedy, aristocratic circle among whom privilege did not imply duty, where there was no place for a generous spirit. James angrily called the reviewers "thick-witted" and never ceased to defend his book. He included it in the definitive New York Edition of his work, and in the preface he wrote for it he continued to praise it.

The central feature of the book that reviewers seemed uniformly to miss was the character of Mrs. Brookenham, the moving force who set the machinery of plot going and to whose maneuvers all the characters responded. Mrs. Brookenham was one of his wonderful middle-aged women, dealing as well as she could with the constrained realities of her situation; to reviewers she seemed invisible.

The only bright note on his return was the success of the renovations of Lamb House. Warren had faithfully superintended the repairs of damage done by fire and smoke and had improved the safety and appearance of fireplaces and chimneypieces; the new bookshelves were a treasure.

James had hardly assimilated these changes when, shortly after his return, he received a letter from the Bellinghams' solicitor. Arthur Bellingham had died, and his South African widow did not wish to keep Lamb House. In accordance with the terms of the lease, James had first refusal of the property. Would he be interested in purchasing it outright? The parcel would include a little brick building on Watchbell Street, a former

Wesleyan chapel that overhung the far wall of the Lamb House garden, that old Mr. Bellingham had purchased to protect his privacy and that his son had converted into a studio.

The price asked for Lamb House itself, the garden, and the studio on Watchbell Street was £2,000, which was more than James had ready to hand, but he thought it possible to borrow at least a portion of the purchase price. He wrote at once to William, overflowing with pleasure at this unforeseen and unhoped-for turn of events. The more deeply settled into Lamb House he had become, the more troubled he was by possible disturbances. If the house should now be sold to a new owner, or if the widow should remarry and claim the property, he might lose his lease. Aside from these practical considerations, there was the sense of owning land, of being rooted in place: "It fixes me, in security, *ideal* suitability & safety, for life, in a blessed little home."

He ran up to London to consult his bankers, Brown Shipley & Co., about the possibility of borrowing against the security of the house itself. Purchase-money mortgages were still unusual, but James was aware of the possibility; on further investigation however he found that Lamb House was already encumbered with two mortgages amounting to £1,250, which James could take over if he wished, obviating the need for a new loan. The purchase would then require only £750 in cash, and payments on the assumed mortgages would be less than the rental he was already paying. If he succeeded in getting rid of the remaining five or six years of his lease on De Vere Gardens, he would end by reducing his living expenses substantially and creating a safe haven for his old age. He put the proposition to his landlords at De Vere Gardens, and they happily agreed to seek a new tenant (undoubtedly at a higher rent) for the balance of his lease.

While these hasty arrangements were in train, James wrote to William in Bad Nauheim, where he was taking the waters in hopes of ameliorating his heart trouble. The illness had come upon him that summer, with a painful heart attack, and was proving to be a chronic condition, but not one that he yet thought to be life-threatening. William replied in one of his unfortunate spells of wishing to be Henry's wiser, older brother. He sent a first hasty note that advised him to exercise caution over Lamb House and bargain down the seller's asking price. He sent a second letter the same day, after talking with their mutual friend and physician William Baldwin, who was also at Nauheim, saying not only that the asking price seemed high but that the purchase seemed a risky speculation— a long-term lease was far safer.

Then Alice wrote as well, explaining that since the property was subject to his lease, its value could be imputed from the annual rental he was paying and by that measure the asking price was high; "I don't wonder you want to own the place and the joy of possession is well worth paying for, but they ought not to make you pay too much!" James replied at length and in some irritation:

Your . . . letters make me feel that I have disquieted you more than I meant & drawn upon myself & my project a colder blast than I could apprehend. But I beg you to be reassured. I do, strange as it may appear to you, in this matter, know more or less what I'm doing.

He had consulted Edward Warren, who thought Lamb House and the Watchbell Street studio might be rented for £100 or £120, which even at the lower estimate would represent a return of 5 percent on James's investment, rather than the 4 percent on which such calculations were usually based. On that basis, the price Mrs. Bellingham offered was a great bargain. The decision, in any case, had been made. The weather was very hot, and he had been under extreme tension for the past few days; he allowed himself to run on:

I *may*, of course, have made a mistake. . . . But all I can say is that if, feeling as I have felt, consistently, from the first, I had let this present opportunity pass instead of *acting*,—for the very joy of it—I should have had to sit down, in utter depression, as without faith in myself. . . . My joy has shriveled under your very lucid warnings, but it will re-bloom. My misfortune, & it's a great one for occasions like this, is that, as an individual of imagination (& nerves) all compact. . . . I am temporarily accessible, in an extreme degree, to "suggestion" . . . though all the while, in the background, my own judgment waits in limited—partial— eclipse, absolutely certain to reappear, the other influence launches me on a sea—a torment—of sickening nervosity. . . .

   It's such a rare boon for me to want anything so simply & singly as I've wanted L.H. that, for myself, it seemed (the nature of the want) just a rare bird to be caught. Never to catch it means a life without *any* joy!

In the midst of these complexities, just as he returned from making arrangements with his bankers in London for the purchase of Lamb House, a throughly wrapped and corded package arrived with Hendrik

Andersen's clay portrait of little Count Bevilacqua. It had traveled intact from Rome, and James placed it on the new chimneypiece in his dining room. He sat down now to answer Andersen's earlier letter, mistaking his name and addressing him as "Hans Anderson." The bust had arrived safely and without damage and been installed in a place of honor where it would be seen, "and where, moreover, as I sit at meat, I shall have him constantly before me as a loved companion & friend. . . . I foresee it will be a lifelong attachment." He hastened to add that

> I am by this post writing to my bankers in London for a draft on Rome of the amount of $250—that is Fifty Pounds—which will immediately reach me & which I will instantly, on its arrival, transmit to you.

Andersen needed the money, nominally payment for the bust, for the expense of his journey. Two days later James sent a draft for fifty pounds drawn on Sebastiani's, writing in the most friendly way but again misspelling Hendrik Andersen's name.

Andersen was evidently eager to pursue his acquaintance with the famous author and possible patron, and, thus encouraged, he wrote that he soon would leave Rome and would accept the invitation to visit Lamb House en route to America.

The young sculptor spent three days in Lamb House in the middle of August. James met him at the station and walked up the cobbled streets with him, while George Gammon followed with Andersen's bags in a cart. James had given up his own oak-paneled bedroom to his guest. That evening, Andersen wrote to his parents in Newport, "I will spend a few quiet days with Henry James, who is kindness itself and whom I care very much for."

The visit was brief but intensely satisfactory. They bicycled through the countryside and returned to Lamb House for dinner, and a quiet evening together. Afterward, James found himself reminded, whenever he passed a certain corner, of the "charming spin homeward in the twilight" and the walk up the hill to Lamb House. But James had other guests coming and work to do, Andersen's departure was fixed, and the weekend could not be extended. They walked rather sadly to the station together on the morning of his departure, Gammon again following with the luggage. Their parting was public and hence somewhat distant; Andersen turned away, and James walked alone back up the hill, feeling more lonely than he should have thought he could after only three days of companionship. But he soon received a charming note of affection and thanks from Andersen, in New York, who asked if he might return to Lamb House the following summer, and when James replied he addressed him with what by now had become a pet name:

> My dearest little Hans: without prejudice to your magnificent stature! Your note of this morning is exactly what I had been hoping for, & it gives me the liveliest pleasure. I hereby "ask" you, with all my heart. Do, unfailingly & delightfully, come back next summer & let me put you up for as long as you can possibly stay. There, mind you—it's an engagement.

Visit would follow visit, and Andersen would be a most intimate friend.

18

CENTURY'S END

James's return to Lamb House from Italy had marked the end, as it then seemed, of a long period of cosmopolitan life and European travel. Rootless no longer, he turned his attention and his considerable energy to home, friends, family, and work. The center of his life was at Lamb House; as he told Louisa Wolseley on his return from Italy, apologizing for the long silence during his absence abroad:

> Lamb House . . . blushes with me, in every old purple brick, for my bad manners. . . . This is the sign of our intimate union—Lamb House's & mine. It is the jog-trot of matrimony to which we have settled down—none, I think, will ever put us asunder.

An urgent first necessity on his return was once again to make money. He was anxious to meet the required payment of £800, due in February, for the purchase of Lamb House without further depleting his savings, upon which he had already drawn heavily for the expenses of renovation, furnishing, and his happy but exhausting summer. His bank accounts in England now amounted only to about £1,000, and he did not want to deplete them further, nor did he want to draw on his investments in the United States. The book edition of *The Awkward* Age had absolutely failed to make any money, and after a summer without writing anything new he was obliged to refresh the sources of his income rapidly.

He accordingly flung himself into another of his remarkable bursts of production. First were potboilers for magazines, and he fired off short essays on France and Italy, plus several short-short stories that Pinker placed in weekly and monthly magazines without trouble and that would fill out the volume of stories he had promised Macmillan. Among these was "The Great Good Place," a happy little fantasy about a man like himself, coming home to a vast accumulation of work and social obligations, being magically transported to a heavenly country house where all the guests were congenial men, mirror images of himself, and there were no duties to fulfill.

Next he filled the pipeline for future royalties by proposing two novels for serial publication. The first of these was a scenario for the novel, eventually to be called *The Wings of the Dove*, on lines he had laid down while in Italy. The core of the idea for the novel was the image of Mary Temple, a dying girl, grasping for what she could have of life. She is in love with life and clings to it with passion. The dying girl—she is wealthy—meets a young couple who are secretly engaged but poor and so unable to marry. The young man is kind to the dying girl, who falls in love with him, and the idea of inheriting her money dawns upon him. His fiancée colludes in the scheme. . . . As James ruminated in his notebook, the plot began to open up to his gaze:

> It has bothered me in thinking of the little picture—this idea of the physical possession [of the dying girl], the brief physical passional rapture which at first seemed essential to it; bothered me on account of the ugliness . . . of the man's "having" a sick girl. . . . "Oh, she's dying without having had it? Give it to her and let her die"—that strikes me as sufficiently second-rate.

Better to offer her not sex but love. Perhaps she loves the young man and he can kindly let her think that her love is returned, that they might have married. She grows in stature as James examines her. She is an American heiress, a princess, the embodiment of the American spirit, heir to all the ages. She rises almost to divine heights, and her eyes brush one like the wings of the dove—the traditional image of the Holy Spirit. She will learn that she has been deceived, but dying will confer the gift of freedom on her beloved betrayers.

His second proposal for a novel was written in response to Howells's suggestion that he combine two of his most popular genres and write a transatlantic ghost story. The idea tickled James. It made him think again of his old theme, of a peaceful young man who is the heir of a military tradition. Perhaps a modern American heir of the older martial, Napoleonic, Byronic age. He imagined a man like himself changing places with a martial English ancestor, each appearing like a ghost in the other's nation and time. He sketched out a proposal. He would call the novel *The*

Sense of the Past, and he sent the proposal to an American publisher, as Howells suggested.

But the tale of the dying girl interested him most, and he set to work on the opening chapters without waiting for either proposal to be accepted.

James also began work on the biography of William W. Story that he had promised to Story's son Waldo. While in Rome he had made notes to give himself a start; it would be a difficult enterprise. There was no obvious narrative in Story's life, and James had not known him very well; what they had shared was the old papal city of Rome. Perhaps that would be enough. He sketched a beginning:

> The writer of these pages—(the scribe of this pleasant history?) is well aware of coming late in the day . . . BUT the very gain by what we see, *now*, in the contrasted conditions, of happiness of old Rome of the old days.

He would write, in other words, about their shared youth in Rome, putting Story in lightly against a background of candlelit palaces, seen nostalgically from the very changed conditions of the present day; avoiding in this way difficulties created by his lack of material and the meager interest of what he did know of Story.

By the end of the year, a half-dozen essays and stories had been written and placed in magazines, and he was well along in completing *The Soft Side*, the collection of stories that went to Macmillan for American publication. Heinemann continued to refuse to deal with Pinker, to his distress, and so James reluctantly abandoned Heinemann; British rights went to Methuen. He began to sketch out a one-act play, and some new stories. One of these began to expand beyond the bounds of the small frame, however, and soon became a proposal for another novel, *The Sacred Fount*.

It began as a joke. Years before, there had been gossip about George Eliot's late marriage to a younger man: the older wife flourished and became youthful, while the young bridegroom rapidly tired, aged, and died—exhausted by the "intellectual effort." An acquaintance in London, Stopford Brooke, recently had offered James another such anecdote, but it was rather trite. James returned now to the idea, slowly transmuted in memory, of a liaison that betrayed itself by the transfer of qualities, of beauty or intelligence. As he set to work, the story became a still more wicked joke.

The center of the tale would be another incarnation of his magnificent middle-aged villainess-heroine who possessed so much of his own intelligence and force, and who had first made her appearance as Madame Merle in *The Portrait of a Lady.* Her most recent avatar was Mrs. Brookenham of *The Awkward Age.* Now she would be called Mrs. Brissenden—a middle-aged married woman having a love affair with a younger man. The affair with Gilbert Long (his name is part of the joke about sacred founts, one supposes) gave her renewed youth and the beauty of youth, while her lover acquired some of her intelligence and maturity. He seemed to grow more clever as she grew younger and more beautiful. The transfer of qualities was the entirely beneficent effect of their drinking at the sacred fount.

In the opening pages of the story, the scene is set: it is the milieu of *The Awkward Age.* Wealthy people are engaged in complex love affairs; acknowledged lovers are invited to country houses for weekends together and travel from town "in the wondrous new fashion" with their luggage and their servants, "like a single household—starting, traveling, arriving together."

Mrs. Brissenden is on her way to such a house party with Gilbert Long. Her husband is going up separately, with the woman we must presume is *his* lover, the appalling Lady John. He and his wife will be tactfully placed in different wings of the country house, with their paramours rather than their spouses.

This is recognizably the opening scene of a farce. The humor will be provided principally by the stumbling of a clueless, middle-aged person who has been invited to balance the dinner table and who accidentally encounters Mrs. Brissenden and Gilbert Long at the railroad station in London, en route to the house party with their luggage. The clueless person fails to understand the nature of their relationship, intellectualizing instead of perceiving. He is, in fine, a critic, the sort of person who lives among doctrines and theories. We are to be amused by this person's constant tripping over the obvious.

He has so little character that he is not even given a name, and the story is far along before we learn his gender. When this disembodied intellect meets Grace Brissenden and Gilbert Long at the railroad station, he begins clumsily to speculate about the source of each one's transformed appearance. Surely these are the effects of love affairs? Mrs. Brissenden puts him off the track easily, by confiding to him that Long indeed has a lover. The nameless critic does not imagine that she is the lover; he assumes that her own youthful bloom is only the effect of a happy marriage.

At the country house, the nameless man discovers that her husband, Brissenden, seems drained and haggard, and in his callow way the critic imagines that demands made by his blooming middle-aged bride must have drained him. It is the old joke about George Eliot's unfortunate husband. The nameless critic evolves a sad little theory and imagines that one lover, like a vampire, must always drain the vitality of the other.

The nameless and solitary man wanders through the country-house weekend. His encounters with other guests are increasingly ludicrous. He asks them awkward questions and propounds his theory, and they are angry or embarrassed or bored, depending upon whether he has accidently trodden on their unperceived affairs. He wanders through the house and through the misty, mystical intellectual fashions of the fin de siècle. The atmosphere is early Maeterlinck, the English country house seems to him a mist-shrouded castle, where he imagines suicides make splashes in the pond and a mad, solitary king has ordered Wagner's music to be played. A mysterious painting is reminiscent of the picture of Dorian Gray.

The house party in reality, of course, is a gathering point for flirtations and love affairs, where innocent-seeming flirtations screen the less-innocent affairs. There is talk of red herrings drawn across trails, to throw the hounds of scandal off a scent. The nameless man revels in the complexities; he has the true theorizing spirit. But his clumsy inquiries threaten to expose, all unknowingly, a love affair that provides convenient cover for Grace Brissenden and Gilbert Long. She goes to the nameless man and asks him to cease his inquiries. When he persists, she puts a stop to his investigations by crushing him with facts and heaps scorn on his absurd theory. The poor man realizes that in some fashion he has been made sport of but, alas, still fails to understand what has happened. It wasn't that he lacked method, he thinks; "What I too fatally lacked was her tone." And with that enigmatic statement the curtain falls on the bewildered critic.

The story is told by the clueless, nameless man. Writing in the first person, performing with great relish the part of the innocent, clueless bachelor, James adds no explanations to his narrative. The effect is ludicrous in the extreme—unless the reader, too, is captivated by doctrines, deceived by theories, and fails to see the humor. Some of James's literary friends, and many critics then and later, were puzzled by the tale when it appeared. His repeated assurances that it was only a joke did little to comfort them.

• • •

The furniture from his big, modern, high-ceilinged London rooms would have to be fitted into the smaller, albeit more numerous, rooms of Lamb House. Thousands of books and enormous masses of paper, too—notes, drafts, letters, and telegrams—had accumulated in De Vere Gardens. It was impossible to think of moving all of it to Lamb House, and a great many papers went into the fire instead. As he said later, "When . . . I broke up my London existence, I committed to the flames a good many documents, as one does on the occasion of the great changes & marked dates & new eras, closed chapters, of one's life."

James was obliged to consider the question of companionship. In summer and fall he evidently could count on a steady stream of young visitors to Lamb House, but there was the long lonely period from November to April to think of. Even if he went up to London in the winter, without a flat of his own he could hardly expect to entertain overnight guests. Jonathan Sturges had admirably helped to fill the gap the previous year by joining him in Rye, and James invited him to spend the holiday season with him again; but Sturges was so often ill, and so comfortably settled in his own London circle, that this did not seem likely to be a stable arrangement.

Hendrik Andersen's visit had been joyous and Andersen's departure left him feeling lonely, but the young sculptor was in New York trying to obtain commissions for portraits and would not return until the following summer, at the soonest. James urged him to persevere in this effort, although it kept them apart. He invited Arthur Benson to visit Lamb House and had conversations about companionship with other friends, but for the moment without results.

Not only could he count upon a steady stream of family visitors in summer, but at Lamb House he could help his invalid brothers find their way to European treatments, help nieces and nephews complete their educations, help his talented and ambitious niece Bay to make her way as a painter of portraits, help his nephew Harry—so much like him—to find his place in the world.

William was grateful for the welcome that Henry provided. He had begun to suffer more severely from the chronic heart condition that had manifested itself the previous summer. The baths at Bad Nauheim again helped him to feel somewhat better, and in the summer of 1899 William went from Bad Nauheim to Lamb House to be cared for and helped along the way to recovery while he prepared a set of lectures to be delivered at the University of Edinburgh. William had been asked to give the Gifford Lectures on "natural theology" early in the new year; his subject was to be "The Psychology of Religious Experience." The breakdown of his health had been particularly distressing, as it had threatened to jeopardize these long-sought lectures.

William sent four large packing cases filled with books ahead to await his arrival. Henry now forwarded one of the cases to Bad Nauheim, ordered a newspaper William had requested, and looked into a suitable school for his niece Margaret Mary, always known as Peggy, who was then twelve years old. William's three boys were to spend the coming year in school or with relatives, but little Peggy was carried along with her parents to Europe.

William, Alice, and Peggy arrived in London early in October and put up at De Vere Gardens—now somewhat bare of furniture and with curtainless windows but fortunately not yet taken by another tenant—while William consulted a cardiac specialist. William, Alice, and Peggy wrote happily from De Vere Gardens, thanking Henry for "the luxury, the beauty, the perfectly *charming* greeting of this place which we are to treat now as our own, when it opened its sunny chambers to us." De Vere Gardens was to be let in November, but they were all then to come to Lamb House.

That visit was once more postponed. William, on doctor's orders, went for further treatments at Malvern, the English watering place that his father and brothers had all visited in years past. From Malvern, he was to come at last to Lamb House. The Edinburgh lectures were indefinitely postponed, and a much desired invitation to lecture at Oxford had to be declined. "It is all sad work," Henry reported to his sister-in-law Mary.

There were other distractions. As James confessed to Mary Ward, instead of shutting himself up in his workroom, "I sit in the garden & read l'Affaire Dreyfus." A court of appeal had reversed an earlier court-martial verdict against Captain Alfred Dreyfus for passing secret information to Germany and ordered a new trial that was now the focus of French political life and was being watched all through Europe and North America. The future direction of France seemed to hinge on the outcome. The radical nationalist movement of Bourget and Barrès had taken up the anti-

Dreyfus cause: the man was a Jew from German-speaking Alsace and, according to Barrès and his party, was "racially incapable" of loyalty to France.

Yet the charges against Dreyfus were plainly based on forged evidence. A French intelligence officer, Major Hubert-Joseph Henry, had confessed to having used forged documents to strengthen the earlier case against Dreyfus; he was found in his hotel room with his throat slit, an apparent suicide. Rumors that he had been murdered were immediately reported. A strange figure, Major Charles Esterhazy, was thought to be the actual spy who had implicated Dreyfus in order to divert suspicion from himself. Esterhazy too was tried at court-martial but acquitted. He fled to England, and now he admitted to having forged the documents used to strengthen the case against Dreyfus.

This was high drama, and as the second trial of Dreyfus opened, James spent each morning in the garden with his newspapers and became somewhat excitable on what he called these "Dreyfus-mornings." He spoke to William of "this almost intolerable suspense of Dreyfus!":

> I confess I live in the great shadow of Dreyfus. . . . The wretched Alfred is, to one's haunting apprehension, condemned—a victim inexorably appointed; for if he be acquitted (& the Ct. Martial will perish 1st!) he will be assassinated the next moment. . . .
>
> [The Dreyfus Affair] darkens our days & poisons the gentle summer.

On September 9, 1899, the second court-martial of Alfred Dreyfus delivered a verdict against him, seemingly a political rather than a legal judgment. Liberal opinion was outraged, and there were protests in the newspapers. Demonstrations were held throughout France and in Antwerp, Milan, Naples, London, and New York. To defend the verdict, gangs organized by Action Française and the Anti-Semitic League appeared in the streets, breaking shop windows and terrorizing Jews and other cosmopolites.

That fall, in South Africa, war with the Boers had begun. Garnet Wolseley was commander in chief of the armed forces, Wolseley's generals were in the field, but the first battles with the well-armed and -prepared enemy were unexpected defeats for the British. James watched from his perch at Lamb House and wrote sympathetically to Louisa Wolseley, "This miserable murderous war (so abject a man of peace am I,) makes me think of you, with deep compassion." James had disliked the agitation for war, disliked the greed for the gold mines of the Transvaal that seemed to prompt it, as much as he had disliked the American war in the Philippines. But once the war was on, his patriotism asserted itself:

> There is something sinister in this S.A. disaster—so *big* a surrender—& it scatters gloom, & these next days, or weeks, will be nervous. But such things make me very British, & I cultivate the British faith.

When the news of British defeats began to arrive, Wolseley's protégés were pushed aside, a veteran of Indian campaigns was placed in command, and the administration began to mobilize a force of 400,000 troops. James set aside his doubts about the manner in which the war had begun: abandoning it would be a still worse mistake.

> The war drags its daily gloom along & we hóver, every week, on the eve of refreshments that never come. Yet, strange to say . . . one feels that the nation has taken up the job only to *do* it & *will* do it . . . giving-up has now got to seem quite like chucking up the very sponge itself of the B[ritish] E[mpire]—& that feeling . . . will see the country through.

He was lonely but not solitary. Sturges, Benson, and Gosse paid visits; many Londoners were in the country for the Christmas holiday. Ellen Terry called with a gaggle of her colleagues, and James was polite, but when Gosse asked him if any of the actresses was pretty, James "turned up his eyes & held up his hands in speechless horror." Stephen and Cora Crane had rented Brede Place near Hastings, a modest house dating from Tudor times, picturesque and inconvenient, and it was a gathering place that summer for aspiring authors who had found cheap lodgings in the area. James was glad occasionally to join their parties. He attended a fête at Brede Place shortly after returning from Italy and met some of the young men—Joseph Conrad and Ford Madox Ford—as well as the Cranes themselves for the first time.

William and Alice returned to stay with him. Malvern had not helped William very much, and William was ill and depressed. The Gifford Lectures had been put off, and it was not clear whether William would ever be able to give them. He had asked for and been granted another year's leave from Harvard, and it was uncertain when or if he would be able to return even to his teaching. He was heavier than Henry remembered him, his blue eyes were less fierce, his beard was now iron gray, his energy much subdued. In the brief intervals of sun, William sat bundled up in the garden unless relentless wind and sporadic rain drove him indoors.

Peggy came to join them for the school holidays, and Henry, Alice, and Peggy would take a stroll in the village at twilight, before dinner; long afterward, Alice still remembered the glimpses of families gathered around their fires, taking tea, and Henry's steady stream of amusing, rambling anecdotes.

The two brothers were close now. James worked in the mornings as always but set aside his afternoons for William, and their letters after this visit were warmly affectionate. They spoke of séances that William and Alice had attended in London, where a medium had given them communications purporting to be from their lost son, communications about which William kept an open mind. Henry had no belief in spirit manifestations, but he thought it possible that the medium had in some fashion perceived William's and Alice's thoughts and feelings, perhaps by a sort of telepathy, a wonderfully heightened faculty of imagination.

Hendrik Andersen had written from New York City, but James had not been able to respond immediately. Now he wrote with affection:

> May these words bring you my tender good wishes for the dawn of a good New Year! I gather that your installation & start in New York are a grimmishly up-hill matter & I think of you with infinite sympathy & understanding. Hard conditions & rough & cold & ugly much of the way. But throw yourself on your youth, your courage, & your genius. . . .
>
> These are cold, dark days—though this ripe little old corner has its small secrets of winter beauty as well as the friendly brightness & homeliness that you saw—that you must see & like again soon.

The James family spirits picked up a good deal after the first of the year. William's health and spirits improved; the Gifford committee elected him lecturer for the following two winters, when his health might be still better, and a friend lent him a villa in Costebelle, near the Bourgets, for the coming months. He would be able to prepare his lectures in a warm climate, at his leisure. Peggy was sent to live with friends where she could attend a day school near London, and Henry accompanied William and Alice to Dover. "This house is sadly shrunken & solitary, in the wet storm, without you; & tea, this p.m., was doleful & spectral."

· · ·

The round number 1900 had an ominous quality, as if to signify a break with the past. The hundredth year was the last of a century, but it began a new numerical series, and people were "fighting like cats and dogs," James said, as to whether it marked a beginning or an end. He sided with history and counted it an ending, one without promise. He feared the next century. The American war in the Philippines was, like the war in South Africa, relentlessly brutal. These American and British wars of conquest had been wrongly begun, and neither victory nor failure would bode well. Britain had suffered its worst defeats in memory in South Africa and at the end of the year had seized a German steamer, the *Bundesrath*, that was suspected of carrying volunteers and munitions to aid the Boers. Early in the new year, several other vessels were seized, and there were trepidations of war with Germany. In his New Year's letters, James was apprehensive: "This dreadful gruesome New Year, so monstrously numbered, makes me turn back to the warm & coloured past & away from the big black avenue that gapes in front of us."

The economic depression had at last lifted, but the little journals of experimental art and literature that had been pleased to cloak themselves with James's prestige had not survived; *The Chap-Book* had followed *The Yellow Book* into oblivion. A consumer-driven economy was emerging from the ruins of the crash. Mass-circulation illustrated newspapers and magazines, produced on new high-speed presses, were sold cheaply and supported by advertising revenues. They were so many mechanisms for assembling a mass audience of consumers. The great new events in publishing were the crowd-pleasing *Daily Mail, Saturday Evening Post,* and *Ladies' Home Journal,* which had readership and impact comparable to the television networks of fifty years later. The Harper publications were reorganizing to adjust to the new economics; even *The Atlantic*'s new editor, Bliss Perry, was concerned with raising his circulation figures; the most faithful of James's media were turning away from him. He had a sense of the disintegration of the old world and an uneasy anticipation of what was to come.

He greatly missed London, and with the departure of William, Alice, and Peggy and the disappearance of holiday visitors, Lamb House in deep winter was intensely solitary. He kept in touch with his London friends by patiently writing letters in the evenings after dinner, often writing until the early hours of the morning. Augusta Gregory had at last succeeded, after several attempts, in introducing James to her Celtic protégé, but unless he were to return to London the acquaintance could not easily be pursued: "I have met Mr. Yeats (just too little), & found him interesting & individual & am very sorry not to be able to profit by your help to see him again." He spent morning hours with MacAlpine, dictating to the clacking rhythm of the Remington. They had lunch together in the dining room on most days, James keeping some conversation going despite MacAlpine's taciturnity. After lunch, more work. In the early evening, James had tea with one of his neighbors or a drink at the Mermaid Inn. Dinner was often solitary, and at night he sat in his white downstairs parlor, where writing materials were conveniently arranged, answering letters. The dark mornings were given over to dictation in the green parlor, where there was a fire and the lamps were lighted. Bleak weather and early dusk kept him indoors in the afternoons, and he was deprived of the exercise that helped stave off depression. He gained weight and surrendered himself to the gloom. Sara Jeanne Duncan, an American who had written a novel as "Mrs. Everard Duncan," sent him a copy of the book, and he burst out to this perfect stranger:

> [T]here is nothing cheerful to talk of. South Africa darkens all our sky here, and I gloom and brood and have craven questions of "Finis Britanniae?" in solitude . . . the stillness ministers to fresh flights of morbid fancy.

He refused an invitation from Margaret Brooke—he had let his flat for the year and so would not see her in London: "How I wish, dear lady, that I could see you, hear your voice, take your hand, & have at least that lift out of depression. We are too separate—too impeded."

Lacking exercise, his sovereign remedy for depression, his back also troubled him and produced severe pains down his left leg, a problem he referred to as "sciatica" and that made walking difficult, even when the weather allowed him to go out. He was obliged to adopt a sort of goose step, advancing his left leg stiffly, when he walked. Friends and neighbors nevertheless continued to make their usual good-natured demands on his time, and he went down to Folkestone for a couple of days to call on H. G. Wells, who was ill. James feared falling more gravely ill himself, alone as he was, and began to ask himself, "very simply and blankly," who would be at his side when he was unable to care for himself.

He struggled against depression to write the opening chapters of *The Wings of the Dove*, although he had not heard back from Pinker about it. He picked away at his biography of William Wetmore Story as well and wrote a scattering of short-short stories, essays, and reviews to keep his pot boiling.

Arthur Benson, on an overnight visit in January, found him pale, rather tired, and looking older. They walked together for a little while to enjoy the early sunset, watching it flame red over Winchelsea; the river blazed as it meandered across the plain. They reached the golf club in time for tea and a quiet, solitary talk. They dined at Lamb House, the fare quite simple and modest (for which James made unnecessary apologies). He told Benson all his news, spoke of having purchased Lamb House—it was just what he wanted. He spoke of working very hard and being pressed by deadlines, of his old friend William Heinemann refusing to deal with his literary agent, and Benson noted in his diary that night that James had spoken with hatred of the money-getting side of his work. *Art* was nearly dead among English writers.

James's talk for the most part reflected his low spirits, but Lamb House continued to be his one happy theme, and he evidently urged Benson to think of moving to Rye. The next morning, when Benson came down to breakfast in the dining room he was amused to see James in the garden, wearing a black velvet coat and a curious square medieval-seeming velvet cap, scattering crumbs for the birds. James came inside to join his guest at breakfast, and they spoke of the war, which seemed to hang in suspense, besieged British troops isolated in the hostile African countryside; the morning papers had brought no news. A canary sang loudly and incongruously in its alcove while they ate and talked, and then James withdrew with apologies: he would have to join his secretary up-stairs. He offered his guest the white parlor, and Benson settled himself at the writing desk to make an entry for his formal diary:

> H.J. works hard; he establishes me in a little high-walled, white parlour, very comfortable, but is full of fear that I am unhappy. He comes in, pokes the fire, presses a cigarette on me, puts his hand on my shoul-der, looks inquiringly at me & hurries away. His eyes are *piercing.*

After lunch with Benson and MacAlpine, James interrupted his work to accompany his guest on a walk; he took Benson to look at a house, Whitefriars, that was both inexpensive and charming. As they walked back to Lamb House, they were obliged to stop frequently, and that evening, Benson made another diary entry:

> He seemed to know everyone to speak to—an elderly clergyman in a pony-carriage, a young man riding. Three nice-looking girls met us, two

of fourteen & fifteen, & a little maid of seven or eight, who threw herself upon H.J. with cooing noises of delight & kissed him repeatedly &
effusively, the dogs also bounding up to him. He introduced me with
great gravity. . . . I said that his simulated reclusion was all a fiasco. He
knew everyone; passed the time of day with clergy, & young ladies threw
themselves into his arms. He smiled & said he didn't really know them.

Benson would not join him in Rye, however much the town and James
attracted him; once again James had missed the chance for settled intimacy. But the younger man said that he thought Howard Sturgis would
be more "accessible" and encouraged James to invite Sturgis to visit Lamb
House.

At the end of January, to ameliorate his solitude, James found a dog to replace the departed Tosca, a lively puppy he named Timothy, that howled
when locked into the cellar at night.

James did pursue his invitation to Sturgis, and after a flurry of letters
about dates and train schedules, on Friday, February 16, Sturgis came for
a leisurely weekend visit. He had proposed to stay through Sunday, and
James had responded happily, "You will stay over, I trust, not only 'Sunday' but many, many, days."

James met him at the station and greeted his guest warmly; he had to
reach up a little to put a hand on the younger man's shoulder. They
walked up the hill together. Sturgis himself had a house full of guests; he
had come to escape them, he said cheerfully. The excuse he had given
was the need to pay a visit to an elderly female relation, a Miss Perry, who
lived in Hastings and was ill. Sturgis had come to Rye from Hastings and
would return to Queen's Acre by the same route.

Dinner was less frugal than that served to Benson, and in the evening
Sturgis sat with James in the little green study upstairs, where they read
aloud to each other from their works in progress. Sturgis read parts of a
novel he had begun, *Belchamber.*

Sturgis's novel, what James called the egg he had brought to hatch at
Lamb House, was the story of a man, the heir of a corrupt aristocratic
family, who disliked the position into which he had been born. He was
Lord Saint Edmunds, called "Sainty": a generous young man of radical

principles, whose Christian morality put him at odds with the established Church, a man who had the misfortune not to like girls or games or any of the things that he was expected to like. James praised the bits that Sturgis read to him and read aloud some of his own work in progress. The two men spent several days and nights together, excepting only the mornings, which were sacred to work. To James, the visit promised a great deal. Finding Sturgis so congenial, compatible in intimacy, he proposed that they live together.

Sturgis gently avoided the proposal. After the visit, he sent a friendly note and followed it with a personal gift, a cushion for James's bedside table on which to keep his pocket watch while sleeping—a specimen of Sturgis's own needlework. James replied promptly with a letter of his own, to repeat his invitation:

> Your good letter . . . prolongs a little the pleasure of [your] presence. . . . You were a most conformable . . . & delightful guest. I repeat, almost to indiscretion, that I could live with you. Meanwhile I can only try to live without you. It has been going quite hard til now. No one to listen to my lucubrations—no one to forgive my [illeg.], no one to admire my Timothy.

This proposal, too, was gently rebuffed, but with assurances of a continued relation. Whatever Sturgis found to say, it was evidently enough to make James happy. He sent a book he thought Sturgis would find helpful for *Belchamber* and in the covering letter made a happily salacious pun, in the manner that allowed him to make sexual references under the eyes of servants and editors: the gift would commemorate the "success" of their "congress":

> our so-happy little congress of two—a real peace congress, & highly superior, it would surely seem, so far as effects, or non-effects, go, to those lately held. Usually, I believe, a medal is struck or a picture painted; but for the congress of Rye an extremely dilapidated (though most interesting,) volume is given.

Sturgis would not live with him, but he would often thereafter escape from his own household of guests and dependents, ostensibly to call on the aged Miss Perry, and would run over from Hastings to Rye for a leisurely visit. James became an equally frequent caller at Queen's Acre;

they would exchange long visits and friendly letters for the rest of their joint lives.

The remainder of the winter was remarkably busy, even for James. He was writing almost desperately to meet his obligation to the Storys, to refill his pockets, and to pay his debts for the purchase of Lamb House. He sent off several short stories to Pinker for magazine publication and later inclusion in the volume promised to George Brett for Macmillan; of the dozen stories included in the book, all but three found homes in weekly or monthly magazines.

Of his three still outstanding proposals for novels, only the one for the satiric *Sacred Fount* was accepted by a publisher, Methuen. James asked to have the proposals for *The Wings of the Dove* and *The Sense of the Past* returned to him. He set aside the work he had done on the opening chapters of *The Wings of the Dove*, which had not attracted any publisher's interest as yet. Methuen had offered a handsome advance against royalties for *The Sacred Fount*, and Pinker hoped for a profitable sale of that novel in the United States as well (Scribner's indeed would soon match Methuen's advance). *The Sacred Fount* was to be a short novel in a single volume, to be published without prior serialization.

These short stories and proposals for novels clustered around common themes, as often happened when he was writing rapidly. He was approaching sixty. His nieces, nephews, and godchildren had grown to adulthood, were marrying and having sons and daughters of their own. James quite naturally found himself thinking about the lapse of time, of descent in families. Lamb House, or perhaps more precisely the move from London to Rye, seemed to be at the center of his thought. Revolving in his imagination were images of fathers, ancestral ghosts, and their modern heirs. Some of the children too were ghostly, echoes perhaps of William and Alice's séances with the spirits of their departed son. In one story, a woman asks to have a painting made of her imaginary husband; in another, a childless couple asks to have a painting made of an imaginary child; in still others, a married couple imagines that their dead daughter continues to live and an old woman in Cambridge blights the lives of her daughters, who yearn to flee to Europe. In the opening chapters of *The Wings of the Dove*, the heroine is the heir of a great fortune and her rival the daughter of a corrupt and selfish man. In *The Sense of the Past*, there is to be a pair of protagonists, one the distant heir of the other, who change places in ghostly fashion. Perhaps the most gently pointed of all was "The Third Person," about a pair of maiden ladies, cousins who between them were a reasonable representation of James—one had returned from travels on the Continent and the other had sacrificed her place in London society, in order to accept and live in an inherited house that was clearly Lamb House:

> The wind . . . was often high, as was natural in a little old huddled, red-roofed, historic south-coast town which had once been in a manner mistress, as the cousins reminded each other, of the "Channel," and from which high and dry on its hilltop though it might be, the sea had not so far receded as not to give, constantly, a taste of temper.

The house was filled with ancient memories; two hundred years of history filled the brown, paneled parlor, creaked patiently on the wide staircase, and bloomed in the red-walled garden. The house with its walled garden seemed to the cousins to be England itself.

Beneath the house, the women found cellars excavated centuries before by smugglers who had founded the fortunes of the town. The two peaceful, faintly silly old women discover that they are heirs of a violent past. Their house is haunted by the ghost of a distant common ancestor, a smuggler who hid his treasures in the cellars and was hanged for his crimes. The ghost appears and demands something of them, which they cannot at first make out, until at last the lively cousin returns to the Continent and smuggles back into England a Tauschnitz edition of an English novel. The ghost is appeased and thereafter is quiet.

With a good deal of work behind him—he had done in the past twelve months enough to fill three volumes—his promised book of short stories at Macmillan, and no serial deadlines to meet, in March he fled his relentlessly windy hilltop and went to London. He stayed at the Grosvenor Club, where he found his little room damp and unpleasant. The bed-sitting room for which he was waiting at the Reform would not be available until the following year, which was a disappointment. He was glad to be away from his lonely perch in Rye and in London among friends, but his spirits were slow to recover.

Thirteen-year-old Peggy James came into town for a visit, and James was glad to see that freed from her boarding school she had gained weight, health, and self-confidence. They were great chums now, and he took her, with the Clarke children, with whom she had been staying, to see the new sensation—motion pictures—at the Alhambra. The new biograph films were a novelty and amusing, but as yet he saw no great potential in them. The films they saw on this occasion probably included jerky footage of Alfred Dreyfus being released from prison; early battles of the Boer War, showing British heroics; and an ominous sequence of a new German battleship, the *Odin*, firing its immense guns. Afterward, Peggy announced that she was thoroughly pro-Boer and was surprised to find that her uncle Henry was not.

Sargent and Abbey were both in London, working in their winter studios in Chelsea. Sargent's portraits of some of the Souls, who had in a manner of speaking been the subject of James's most recent novels, were at the Royal Academy and the New Gallery and were drawing mixed reviews for their sensuous and impressionistic quality; but *The Times* thought his portrait of the Wyndham sisters the best painting that had been seen at the Academy in years. James went to see that painting and felt "quite weak & foolish" with astonishment as he stood before it. He and Sargent then went down to see Ned Abbey in his new Tite Street studio in Chelsea, where he was at work on a vast historical painting, *The Trial of Queen Katherine*.

At the end of March, James brought Sturges back with him to Rye for an indefinite visit. Sturges remained with him until May. Cared for by the Smiths, he made himself at home at Lamb House, staying behind when James paid visits to other houses.

The news from South Africa was better; the siege of British troops at Ladysmith was broken by a relief column; the balance of combat had plainly shifted. The report from Ladysmith prompted a holiday in Rye, where church bells chimed and shops were closed. But the war was just beginning. Guy du Maurier came for a weekend from Dover, where he was marshaling his Indian regiment on its way to South Africa.

Timothy's nocturnal howling did not abate and disturbed James's sleep and that of his guests; sadly, the dog had to be put down. Timothy was replaced by "a little jumping dog," a puppy that James named Peter. The days were growing longer, the weather and his health were better, and he was able to resume his habit of walking. Sturges of course remained behind, but Peter ran along with him, and they stopped often while James rolled little stones for the dog to chase. He celebrated his fifty-seventh birthday at Lamb House with Sturges, and, as if to complete the profound changes in his life, he shaved his beard for the first time in more than thirty years,

> unable to bear longer the increased hoariness of its growth: it had suddenly begun these last 3 months since, to come out quite white—& made me *feel*, as well as look so old. Now, I feel forty—& clean & light.

A letter from John Hay, on the engraved letterhead of the Department of State, inquired after him and spoke highly of his recent work. Hay evidently wanted to maintain ties both personal and professional—he asked for a report on how the new ambassador to the Court of St. James's was getting on.

On May 17, the last of the besieged British forces in the Boer republic was relieved. Colonel Robert Baden-Powell, commander of a small force trapped in Mafeking, had become a celebrity in seven months of siege, issuing terse, widely reported bulletins. A British defeat at Spion Kop with heavy casualties had been widely reported and photographed. Biograph motion pictures of the corpse-littered battlefield had been shown in London, and London accordingly rejoiced when the siege of Mafeking was broken. There was to be no repetition of the murder of General Gordon. Celebrations lasted for five days and would not be equaled until 1918; the *Daily Mail* reported that in London, "Women absolutely wept for joy, and men threw their arms about each others' neck."

Wolseley had not been closely engaged in the recent developments. Field Marshal Lord Frederick Roberts of Kandahar, a veteran of the recent brutal war in Afghanistan, had methodically built up the large force that was needed, largely with Indian troops, and with merciless method had destroyed the regular Boer forces. On June 5, he hoisted the British flag in Pretoria, the capital of the Transvaal. Wolseley's term as commander in chief was almost up, and Roberts would succeed him.

James was in regular correspondence with the Wolseleys through this trying period; he visited the Wolseleys at Glynde and invited them to Lamb House. Early in June, with the war going well, the Wolseleys accepted his invitation and came for lunch. Their presence in Lamb House quickly became known, and a little crowd gathered in the street; Wolseley went out on the front step and received an ovation from the gathering.

· · ·

Bay Emmet was in England that summer and came to stay with her uncle Henry for a good part of it, arriving after Jonathan Sturges's departure and staying until August. She was a delightful guest, and James enjoyed playing host. He turned over his bedroom to her, and she painted the view, from his bedroom window, of the little cobbled street with the crooked chimney of Gammon's cottage in the middle distance and the old church at the end of the perspective. Her mother and sisters arrived and stayed briefly for a time as well, and James was reminded again of the charming Temple girls of his own generation. He happily commissioned Bay to paint a portrait of himself, with his newly shaven and expressive actor's face revealed, and reported to William his pleasure in Bay's talent (if not in the portrait itself).

After his winter in the south of France, William had returned to Bad Nauheim for another course of baths; but his heart ailment grew no better. He experimented with a variety of treatments, ranging from magnetic healing to a "mind cure"; but after a laying on of hands by a magnetic healer, he broke out mysteriously in painful boils and abandoned all further experiments. William and Alice returned to England, planning to join Henry at Lamb House. But William suffered a new bout of pains in his chest and fled back to Germany and the healing waters. He thought of going to Egypt when the weather turned cold and proposed that Henry and Alice accompany him. But this did not seem practical, and William soon had a new plan: he would go to Rome, with Henry and Alice to keep him company and care for him. Henry demurred to this, and Alice hesitated.

William's further plans remained in suspense. From the middle of August to the middle of September, therefore, while William lingered in Germany, Alice and Peggy lived with Henry James in Lamb House. They were a comfortable little family. James worked in the mornings as always and on most days lunched with MacAlpine, Alice, and Peggy. Some or all of them accompanied James on his afternoon walks. In September, Peggy went back to school. Alice went to Bad Nauheim to join William, and together they went on to Rome for the winter. Henry was alone in Lamb House for the first time in months.

Despite demands of friends and family, James had continued to produce. In the remaining weeks of the summer he had corrected the proofs of his volume of short stories, *The Soft Side;* completed his novel *The Sacred Fount* (which as usual had grown far longer than planned); and written a detailed prospectus for a new novel, which was to be called *The Ambassadors*, and sent it off to Pinker, with the suggestion that it would be suitable for monthly serialization.

After the hard work of the summer, MacAlpine took a week's vacation to see the Paris exposition. James was annoyed with MacAlpine, perhaps unfairly, as he himself did not feel able to take a vacation in Paris, much as he would have liked. MacAlpine was not very good company, and he was expensive; James privately decided that when he went up to London that winter he would terminate the relationship and hire a less expensive and more amenable stenographer.

In Rome, William was now under the care of William Baldwin, who recommended injections of an infusion of goat glands, which he himself had received and now highly recommended. Alice patiently administered the injections, but William reported that there was little change in his heart condition, at least at first.

Lamb House seemed particularly empty after the guests of the summer. Adding to his solitude, James's admirable little puppy, Peter, died one Sunday in September, "fondly attended by the local 'canine specialist,' " after three days of a vile illness, and his remains joined those of his predecessors at the foot of the garden.

Hendrik Andersen had been ill that summer and had not come to Europe as James had hoped; but he wrote now to say that he could not spend another winter in New York and would be going to Rome himself again for the winter, where he would work at a commission for a civic monument to Abraham Lincoln. Might he come by way of Lamb House? James replied:

> This is brave news indeed & I highly, I exceedingly, rejoice in it. It will be delightful to see you & I shall pat you lustily on the back. I count on your coming straight down here [from Liverpool] & staying with me as many days as you can possibly spare from your naturally feverish impatience to get to Rome, work & glory.

James and his protégé had again a very happy visit, and when Andersen departed, James gave him William and Alice's address in Rome. He had not introduced William to his own circle of bachelor friends since the unhappy time, thirty years earlier, when William had visited him in Italy, but the brothers were on a better footing now.

His year-end letters were far more cheerful than those with which the year had begun. Lord Wolseley had retired from his burdensome post, his term as commander in chief having ended; when James wrote to Louisa, he said that he was not sure whether to congratulate or condole. His young nieces and nephews opened vistas for him into an optimistic future. Bob's son, Edward, had a daughter now, Olivia, making James a great-uncle for the first time—he had some trouble conceiving that he was now another generation removed from youth and was among the grandparents. His niece Mary was in Seattle, in a new world: "I much envy you," he wrote, "*your* young chance of seeing such fresh & interesting aspects of our roaring great country—to me so unknown."

The secretary of the Reform Club wrote to say that a bed-sitting room was available, and James ran hastily up to London. The room faced south over Carlton House Terrace Gardens and was "tranquil, utterly." It was let unfurnished for a year at a time, and he would be able to keep it as long as he liked. Long and narrow, the room had enough space for a typewriter and typist; he hesitated only until he was sure that he would be able to bring a female stenographer there and then took the room. The club staff would provide excellent service, and instead of the large and expensive establishment he had maintained at De Vere Gardens, he now had an economical and efficient perch in London to which he could come without servants. He began to inquire at an employment agency for a new stenotypist.

He returned to Lamb House for the Christmas holiday, however, because he had promised Peggy to spend it with her there, and after making his arrangements at the Reform he hastened back to Rye.

Peggy was a good companion, despite her young years. A white sea fog closed them in, but James and his niece walked down to the golf links for tea and took the tram back to Rye. In the quiet time after tea and before dinner, uncle and niece sat in the white downstairs parlor, and Peggy read a book while he wrote his year-end letters: "the clock ticks & the fire crackles . . . the young niece . . . sits near me immersed in *Redgauntlet*."

Just before returning to London, James sat up late writing the last of these letters and found that his friend Tony Navarro, to whom he had written on the eve of his departure for Rome two years before and who had then in a manner of speaking saved his life, was among those still to be acknowledged. With a little rush of pleasure he thanked Navarro for a gift and almost for his happy home as well: "Here by the Xmas fireside . . . I greet you and Mrs. Tony very constantly; I wish you a big slice of the new century."

19

THE MAJOR PHASE

The first winter of the new century he spent productively in his bed-sitting room at the Reform Club, working as always in the mornings, visiting friends at teatime, and sometimes dining out. "It's a very dusky, dingy, fog-smothered town," he told Hendrik Andersen. Trains to Windsor were excellent and frequent, however; he went to Queen's Acre for a visit with Sturgis, and on parting they promised each other frequent return visits. Invitations from his old, somewhat diminished circle of London winter friends arrived, but James was cautious about accepting them and stayed away from theater people. His closest theater friends were away, in any case: Florence Bell was in Yorkshire, and Elizabeth Robins had given up the stage and was traveling in North America.

The news and gossip alike were gloomy. The Boers had begun a guerrilla war against their British occupiers. A new British field commander, Horatio Kitchener, undertook to cleanse Boer territories of resistance, sector by sector, destroying homes of those suspected of subversion, burning the fields. Thousands of homeless civilians were herded into "concentration camps," a new term. As the resistance continued, however, casualties and costs of the protracted war mounted. British income taxes doubled, largely because of the war, and James was obliged to write to William for advice on how he might draw a thousand dollars from the Syracuse accounts.

Queen Victoria died on January 22 in her winter home on the Isle of Wight, after a long decline into illness and, as James was told, disheartened by the war in Africa. With the queen's death, most public and private entertainments ceased for a time, but gentlemen's clubs filled with political men summoned back to town. James dined one evening at the Reform with some members of the Privy Council and was glad to hear that the prince of Wales, of whom James thus far had known little to the good, seemed to be acquitting himself well. *Speriamo*, he said to himself.

Quiet, mourning London was ideal for concentrated work. He had given his secretary tentative notice, but MacAlpine good-naturedly stayed on until James's return to Lamb House in the spring. An employment agency sent a candidate to be interviewed, Mary Weld, who was young, inexperienced, and not in the least literary. She was a skillful typist, however, inexpensive and far less demanding than MacAlpine, and James offered her the job. She agreed to come down in April to Rye, where she would find lodgings near Lamb House, and James happily engaged her. For the balance of the winter, he dictated to MacAlpine. He was at work on *The Ambassadors* and did not want to disrupt that work. Pinker had submitted the prospectus to Harper and Brothers for their monthly magazine, and there it mysteriously languished; but James was absorbed in the novel, and despite uncertainty about its eventual home he was happily writing it in segments suitable for monthly serialization.

The center of the novel, the germ from which it continued to unfold, was the scene that Jonathan Sturges had described to him and that brought so many memories to mind, Sturges's anecdote of his encounter with William Dean Howells on a summer Sunday afternoon at a party in the Faubourg Saint-Germain. James had visited the self-same garden as a young man and readily imagined Jonathan Sturges, a young American artist in Europe, in his place. Sitting beside him in the garden is Howells, the friend of James's young manhood, who married early, became a father and worked in an office, remained in America and earned his salary and lived quietly while James went abroad.

Howells found the atmosphere in the garden, its beautiful young people and the remarkably accomplished elders, both a challenge and a reproach. Complex attractions bound these disparate, accomplished cosmopolites together and drove them apart. They were artists, diplomats, aristocrats. Passions were the more intense for the differences among them, like the attraction between poles of a magnet. The love of an older Frenchwoman, an aristocrat of the Old World, for a very young man from Woollett, Massachusetts, is the heart of the scene as James imagines it. Howells is dimly aware of the liaisons and rivalries among those around him and acutely conscious of their beauty. He had lived in dull, flat, uniform America but now was plunged into the heart of the great world, where accomplished elders were artists of life, managing and composing the strong forces of youth. What had he lost by his unaccountable passivity, by remaining at home? He was too far down one path to imagine entering now into the other:

> This rather fatigued and alien compatriot, whose wholly, exclusively professional career had been a long, hard strain, and who could only be—given the place, people, tone, talk, circumstances—extremely "out of it" all . . . watching the situation in rather a brooding, depressed and uneasy way.

After an uncomfortable interval, Howells puts his hand on Sturges's slight shoulder and says a few words that speak volumes: "Oh, *you're* young, you're blessedly young—be glad of it and *live.*"

Be glad and live! The intense yearning of this phrase was to be the heart of the novel. The garden had been Mme. Mohl's and was now Whistler's, a setting James had visited in his youth and remembered well. James, on the threshold of old age, was able to revisit in memory, to observe and even advise, in a manner of speaking, his own young self. The afternoon light in the walled garden evoked an old man's regret for a vanished time, the prime of life, of the unclouded senses of youth, never to be repeated, when one lives most intensely and fully.

Describing the scene in his prospectus for the novel, James spoke with the mingled affection and self-regard that infuse one's memories of youth, and also with the feeling of a father for a son, of a lover for the beloved: the quality that a same-sex relation necessarily has, the sensation of facing someone who is both same and other.

Like all his late novels, *The Ambassadors* trembles with sexuality and with some deeper note that is more difficult to put into words. One senses the profound force that holds the human world together against all jealousies and violence. In the civilized gardens of the great world it was fully expressed, for there one found the differences, the selfishness, violence, and jealousies against which it exerted itself most powerfully. Only in the great world could one find a place for every form of love: for religious ecstasy, for sexual passion, for lifelong friendship, romantic love, and the moral sublimity in which all were fused.

James, like Balzac before him, shows us a woman of thirty, a passionate marquise. She falls in love with a young American, and his beauty and intelligence are brought to life by her passion. She loves him to the roots of his hair, and their realized love is virtuous, however wrong it may seem in the eyes of Woollett, Massachusetts.

James plays all the parts and speaks as one who has drunk from the sacred fount, but there is still in his voice a note of yearning, of regret. He is a bachelor, now growing old, although like the fictional Mme. de Vionnet he has loved across wide gulfs and been loved in return.

Sturges, who had told him the story, was in his thoughts. George du Maurier was there as well; the anecdote evoked du Maurier's Parisian youth, so like James's own. In *The Ambassadors*, the Sturges character is a "little artist man" called "Little Billham," who greatly resembles Little Billee, du Maurier's self-portrait as a young artist in *Trilby*.

The Howells character, who is the hero of the tale, is called Lewis Lambert Strether, another reference to du Maurier and the affectionate caricature of James himself drawn by du Maurier in his last novel. James accepted the picture of "Louis Lambert" with a good deal of self-conscious humor. His protagonist is nearly overwhelmed by his own intense imagination, like Balzac's and du Maurier's heroes, and like du Maurier's "Louis Lambert" is possessed by the spirit of a woman, "generous and open-handed to a fault, quick to forgive, and gifted with a power of immediately inspiring affection and keeping it forever after."

Imagining himself back into the enclosed garden in Paris, his older self observing his younger, James filled it with memories drawn from the whole span of his adult life and with ghosts of friends and images of alternate futures. Primoli's Napoleonic mementoes furnish Mme. de Vionnet's apartment; the ghosts of Francis Boott's and George Smalley's mill town belongings give rounded life to the representative of New England manhood, Waymarsh. In the background one glimpses the Cambridge from which James escaped and the Paris to which he fled. In the foreground: young Chad, the object of Lambert Strether's mission, beloved by men and women alike.

Working at high speed and with intense concentration, hoping to complete the novel while still in his London retreat, James nevertheless strikes a pure and consistent tone. His prose is adapted to the subject matter, the reader sees and feels with Lambert Strether's senses:

Chad raised his face to the lamp, and it was one of the moments at which he had, in his extraordinary way, most his air of designedly showing himself. It was as if at these instants he just presented himself, his identity so rounded off, his palpable presence and his massive young manhood, as such a link in the chain as might practically amount to a kind of demonstration. . . . What could there be in this for Strether but the hint of some self-respect, some sense of power, oddly perverted; something latent and beyond access, ominous and perhaps enviable?

Mme. de Vionnet's love for Chad is palpable, James's own. Reading, we feel it and share it. Temporal and spatial elements—theory and experiment, melody and harmony, story and picture—fuse beautifully, as in the imagery of a poem. Sentences dissolve in the intensity of James's remembrance; punctuation and ordinary syntax drop away. The sentence indeed is no longer the unit with which James works; he makes impressionistic images rather than statements, patiently creates moments that seem to belong to the reader's own memories. Shadows are not black but infused with color: double negatives take the place of bare assertions—each quality that is denied adds a dimension to one that is affirmed. Strether "was not wholly disconcerted . . . his relation to his errand might prove none of the simplest. . . . There was detachment in his zeal and curiosity in his indifference." Lambert Strether's half-puzzled, half-surprised joy in the moment is not so much seen as felt:

> How could he wish it to be lucid for others, for any one, that he, for the hour, saw reasons enough in the mere way the bright clean ordered water-side life came in at the open window?—the mere way Madame de Vionnet, opposite him over their intensely white table-linen, their *omelette aux tomates*, their bottle of straw-coloured Chablis, thanked him for everything almost with the smile of a child, while her grey eyes moved in and out of their talk, back to the quarter of the spring air, in which early summer had already begun to throb, and then back again to his face and their human questions.

Here is Strether on the balcony of an apartment in the heart of Paris, alone in the warm night air:

> He felt, strangely, as sad as if he had come for some wrong, and yet as excited as if he had come for some freedom. But the freedom was what was most in the place and the hour; it was the freedom that most brought him round again to the youth of his own that he had long ago missed. He could have explained little enough to-day either why he had missed it or why, after years and years, he should care that he had; the main truth of the actual appeal of everything was none the less that

everything represented the substance of his loss, put it within reach, within touch, made it, to a degree it had never been, an affair of the senses. That was what it had become for him at this singular time, the youth he had long ago missed—a queer concrete presence, full of mystery, yet full of reality, which he could handle, taste, smell, the deep breathing of which he could positively hear. It was in the outside air as well as within; it was in the long watch, from the balcony, in the summer night, of the wide late life of Paris, the unceasing soft quick rumble, below, of the little lighted carriages.

Realism of this sort evokes both the surrounding scene and the emotional quality of the observer's perceptions. It is what Gertrude Stein would call "cubist" writing and Seamus Heaney "the utter, self-revealing double-take of feeling." We have no conventional name for this style, but using the vocabulary of James's time we might call it "moral realism." In the preface of his definitive edition, James would say that *The Ambassadors* is the best, all round, of his novels. Mary Ward, like many others in the century following, would say that it is the masterpiece of his later work. One can hardly credit that this rich and complex novel was dictated with only minor revisions straight through from its famous opening words, "Strether's first question," to the triumphant conclusion in James's own voice: "Then there we are!"

James did not succeed in completing the novel in London and was obliged to take it with him to Rye. *The Ambassadors* was the first big book he dictated to Mary Weld, but he maintained his steady pace. When Miss Weld came to Rye, she found lodgings near Lamb House. She was quick and bright, and James soon accustomed himself to the new rhythm of her typing on the familiar Remington. He had always framed sentences carefully in his mind before speaking, a lifelong habit first imposed upon him by his stammer and cultivated over years of writing rapidly for publication; it was not difficult for him to spell unusual or foreign words as he went along, something that had not been necessary for MacAlpine. Miss Weld adapted herself perfectly to his habits; she soon learned to bring along knitting with which to occupy herself while James paced, moaned, and searched for a word. He told William that she was "a gem."

Years later, composing his preface for the definitive edition of the novel, he would recall the "absolute conviction and constant clearness" he had felt while dictating *The Ambassadors*. In his mind's eye he assembled the central characters who had populated nearly all his big, architectural novels: the two women, good and bad heroines, who were rivals for the love of the handsome young man; the young man himself, passive and beautiful; and a fourth figure, a mentor, who is passionately engaged with the others but who tries to manage the situation selflessly, like a benevolent parent. These characters had grown and, so to speak, matured over the course of twenty years; James had only to describe the new costumes and settings in which he had now placed them. He, of course, played all their parts with relish. Chad, however, was seen solely from the outside, the object of desire.

Chad was as young and beautiful as ever. The women were older now, as was the mentor, Lambert Strether. For the first time, James used his own mature intelligence and imagination as his camera lens. The benevolent mentor himself experienced the slow growth in understanding that was the principal action of the novel, and an epiphany when he experienced—albeit only vicariously—the life-altering truth of embodied love. The older man's affection for the younger now had a curious overtone of self-love and longing.

Watching the familiar characters in their latest costumes, seeing through his own eyes, the novel flowed on without interruption, "like a monotony of fine weather." With remarkable speed and little revision, he dictated through from beginning to end and sent the completed twelve "books," or monthly installments, like twelve acts of an immense drama, to Harper and Brothers; but they remained silent.

Peter was succeeded by Nick, a terrier puppy. This new pet was badly behaved and noisy and had an evil tendency to chase chickens and sheep; his care was left largely to the Smiths, who indulged him terribly. They, too, found winters in Rye difficult, and in James's absence their drinking had grown worse. On James's return early in April he found the household in serious disarray, the dog's messes in the kitchen, and the Smiths unable to function. This was a grave matter, not only because of the distraction from work but also because William and Alice were on their way from Rome. The house had quickly to be put to rights. William's long-postponed Gifford Lectures were to be given in Edinburgh, from mid-May through September, 1901. More packing cases filled with books had arrived at Lamb House and were followed by William and Alice themselves early in April. Peggy joined them, and by the first of May, Harry came over to hear his father's lectures and joined them all at Rye.

Henry and William James were seemingly different in every detail. William was thin and bearded and had his mother's beauty and her furious blue eyes. Careless of his appearance, restless, exuberant, he was constantly in motion. Henry was stout, self-contained, careful in dress, and had a manner of conscious repose. They had followed different courses in life yet had a common history, had grown up in the same New York world of Scottish, Scots-Irish, and Dutch Calvinism, had fled with their father to Europe; they shared intimate memories and a troubled inheritance of illness; they had by now arrived at something like the same attitude toward life and work. Their points of view had converged; William had begun to call his method "radical empiricism," and the results of his studies in psychology were the foundation of what he now called philosophic "realism," a view not unlike his brother's. The world could be seen only through human eyes, by an embodied consciousness; one looked out one's own window.

There was a mysterious constancy in human experience, however: at all times and places, sensitive persons reported spiritual experiences that seemed strangely similar, experiences of submerging one's small self in a larger one. So William had earlier understood his father's yearnings. Such experiences were themselves important facts, hinting at a larger, dimly perceived spiritual reality. One saw shapes and colors solely through the medium of sense, and so too the spiritual realm was perceived through the nervous system. People reported "healthy-minded" experiences or were plunged into a nightmare realm. Good and evil were as much the data of experience as were sound and light.

In Cambridge, William had pursued experimental studies of spiritual phenomena, had encouraged his students to investigate them, and had founded the first laboratory of experimental psychology in America, following the lead of German scientists. Now, like his Cambridge friend Frederic W. H. Myers, William hoped to find correspondences between mystical experience and an objective, spiritual realm in which—perhaps—the personality continued to survive after its physical existence was ended. A young woman named Gertrude Stein, one of his students, had submitted to him her report of an experiment in "automatic writing," an effort to gain access to the subliminal realm, the spiritual world that lay beneath the threshold of awareness. Stein found herself more interested in the unique individual character of her subjects, however, than in the theoretical investigations; although she was William's student, she would later call herself Henry's successor.

These experiments, and the philosophic conclusions to be drawn from them, had opened for William a path into philosophy. He wrote of the human importance of religious experience, experience that was as real and important in its way as the data of physical science. William noted that Immanuel Kant's transcendental idealism and orthodox Christian theology were equally consistent with the experimental data; indeed, the shared mystical experiences of humanity seemed to be the ground and basis of religions in all their variety. The importance of religious experiences lay not in dogma but in themselves. Religious experience was the heart of passionately realized life.

> Not God, but life, more life, a larger, richer, more satisfying life, is, in the last analysis, the end of religion. The love of life, at any and every level of development, is the religious impulse.

William's Harvard colleague Josiah Royce had preceded him in Edinburgh, but Royce's reworking of Continental philosophy had not generated much interest or excitement. As he generously told William, "Everywhere they ask about you, and regard me only as the advance agent of the true American Theory. *That* they await from you."

While Henry dictated in the mornings in the garden room, William sat in the garden and read or made notes for his lectures. In the afternoons, William dictated to Miss Weld and Henry took walks with Alice and Peggy, the new terrier, Nick, racing ahead. Once they were well out into the country, Nick gleefully chased terrified sheep to the far ends of their dyked pastures. Fourteen-year-old Peggy reported with amusement to her brothers at home that Uncle Henry would shout after him, "Oh! oh! oh! oh! oh! you little brute! you little brute! you beast! oh! oh!"

He took Alice and Peggy on outings to Winchelsea and Hastings, where they shopped for books. They copied curious inscriptions in the churchyards; they visited ruined Norman castles dotted along the coast. They went to Brede, where they showed themselves around. The owners, Moreton Frewen and his lovely American bride, Clara Jerome, were away, and the onetime tenants had departed. Stephen Crane had died of tuberculosis while abroad, and Cora had not returned. Henry showed his guests around the empty old house, with its ill-assorted gables and chimneys, its incoherent additions and overgrown gardens. He gossiped a little about Clara Frewen, one of three sisters who had grown up in the rural Bronx and had all married titled British husbands.

Clara's young nephew Winston Churchill was a newspaper reporter, whose escape from a prisoner-of-war camp in South Africa had made a stir.

William, Alice, Harry, and Peggy departed for Edinburgh on May 13, remained there for the six-week course of William's lectures, and returned to Lamb House flushed with victory. This first series was a great success. William thought he would return to Edinburgh the following summer for a second series. His heart fortified by daily administrations of digitalis, William was in his most elevated and energetic mood. He began to plan a new book in which he would propound a complete system of thought: a purely empirical system, leaving behind the metaphysical arguments of his youth, cleaving close to experience.

In September, when William and his family departed for America, the Smiths suffered a general collapse. After their busy summer and with the house at last empty of guests, Mrs. Smith went slack and Smith drank heavily. There was a sudden uproar; the police were called—perhaps there was a complaint by a young woman—and in forty-eight hours the Smiths were gone as if hurled into outer space.

James dined at the Mermaid Inn for several weeks while he made new arrangements. He decided to forgo the expense of a butler and consulted an employment agency about hiring a cook-housekeeper. It recommended Joan Paddington, who came with very good references. Her last position had been with the pompous and undistinguished poet laureate, Alfred Austin, who also had a house in Sussex. She was hired and proved herself a far better household manager than Mrs. Smith.

Mrs. Paddington had a feudal view of her place in the scheme of the household; she curtsied when she came into the room and taught the housemaid, Minnie Kidd, to do likewise. For tasks that required a male servant, James hired a local lad, Burgess Noakes, then just seventeen years old, who at first lived at home but soon had a room of his own under the eaves of Lamb House.

Paddington took hold, very firmly, of a house that was in great disorder. The puppy Nick, a great favorite of the Smiths', had been allowed to spend his days in the kitchen eating table scraps and making messes in the corner. Young Noakes took over his care but did not improve his behavior, and Mrs. Paddington insisted that the dog be removed. The dog's habit of chasing livestock, a serious matter, certainly contributed to the decision. To Noakes's shock and regret, James accepted the necessity and asked the boy to bring Nick down to the local veterinarian to put the dog down. Noakes still remembered many years later carrying the corpse back in a bag, much distressed. Gammon buried it in the garden beside those of Tosca, Tim, and Peter.

The Smiths were gone, and the house was filled with strangers. James was embarrassed to find, when a vaguely familiar woman crossed to meet him as he walked down to the high street, that he did not know who she was. But when she opened the conversation by saying, "I've had the rest of it turned into rissoles," he recalled that she was his cook and was speaking of last night's leg of lamb.

In the midst of these excitements, after the Smiths had departed but new arrangements were not yet in place, Hendrik Andersen arrived for what was meant to be a long visit of friendship and consolation. Hendrik had been obliged to bring his alcoholic father to Europe that winter and provide him a modest pension; his mother in America was greatly distressed; his brother was ill; and to cap all, the city of Buffalo had rejected the monument upon which he had lavished much thought and labor. His seated Lincoln was to be surrounded by symbolic nude figures, whose nudity the city fathers could not accept. Upon receiving Andersen's anguished letter reporting this latest disappointment, James answered immediately with an invitation, half parental and half erotic:

> What a sad & sorry upshot of a whole winter's work—of so many months of high hope & good faith! It is odious, it's utterly upsetting & I don't know—or scarce—what to say to you about it that won't seem too poorly comforting. Patience & courage you have in high measure—& one can only feel sure that you are throwing yourself upon them. Do that, my dear Boy, as hard as ever you can . . . but press also, I beg you, with no less intensity, on my affectionate friendship—let me feel that it reaches you & that it sustains and penetrates. . . . Lamb House . . . opens, from tonight, to its utmost width to you, & holds itself open till you come.

Andersen happily accepted the offer and arrived at Lamb House just after the Smiths' departure. He remained only for a pleasant week, however, fearing that a longer visit would be a burden in the circumstances. He was deeply anxious about his father but evidently returned to Rome with renewed optimism, and James bade farewell to him with great reluctance:

> Now that you're the young priest within the great temple again, with the flame glowing on your altar . . . I feel easy & glad for you, I like to think of you so "fixed" for the long, soft Roman winter, & I wish you,

my dear, dear Boy, such a high tide of inspiration & execution as will float you over every worry. . . . Addio, caro—buon riposo. . . . I hold you close & am ever your affectionate old friend.

In time, his new household settled down. James found a new and highly satisfactory dog, a well-behaved and affectionate dachshund who took no interest in the neighborhood sheep and whom he named Max. The Smiths had departed, MacAlpine was gone, the house was empty of guests, and James's last links to his London home were broken, but order and economy had been restored to his home. He promised Hendrik Andersen that he would come to Rome to return his visit, soon, and William that he would come soon to America.

His renewed friendship with William, after years of estrangement, was a firm tie to America and was maintained, as it had been in their youth, by exchanges of confidences regarding their shared illnesses. James discussed with his brother his recent bowel disorders, his struggle to keep his weight down, his distaste for eating. William replied that in Rome he had met a kind of guru, Horace Fletcher, whose works he had quoted in the first series of Gifford Lectures. Shortly after his return to America, William sent the latest edition of Fletcher's book *The New Glutton or Epicure*, which prescribed a Methodist yoga of nutrition. Meals were to be simple, chewing and swallowing were to be slow and mindful; eating was to be a conscious pleasure. Excess weight would fall, the bowels would be regulated naturally, health and vigor would be restored. William reported that he was trying the method, and he recommended it to Henry for their shared ills.

Horace Fletcher's self-help books, which William had praised in his lectures as examples of "healthy-minded" religious experience, were a twentieth-century American mingling of yogic practice and Protestant optimism. The original title, *Glutton or Epicure*, was a reference to John Wesley's discourse on the afterlife, in which he said of Paradise, "There is no miser there . . . nor is there any wasteful glutton or epicure." A revised edition, *The New Glutton or Epicure*, was a runaway bestseller. A newspaper reported that the dinner tables of America had fallen silent, except for the sound of chewing.

Money was a constant preoccupation. James's modest fixed income did not free him from concerns about money but instead seemed to fix his attention on it. Joan Paddington was an excellent household manager, and they went over the tradesmen's bills each week together; she kept strict account of expenditures, but playing host to friends and family for months at a time, together with the costs of the upheavals in his domestic arrangements and of the travel to Italy and America that he had promised, now required a redoubling of efforts to earn money from his writing. Harper had given no word as to when *The Ambassadors* would be serialized and payment made. With this great question hanging over his income, he set to work immediately to complete the Venetian novel that he had begun two years earlier and had set aside when it met with little interest from magazine editors. Pinker had found a book publisher for it, Arnold Constable, and it would appear without prior serialization if he were able to complete it quickly.

James had begun his sketch of the still untitled novel that would become *The Wings of the Dove* at the Palazzo Barbaro with an image of young Mary Temple—"Minny," as she had been called in the family when they were children—she who had so longed to go with him to Europe. He imagined her, renamed "Milly Theale," coming to London and Venice before she died. He assembled his repertory cast: Milly was to be the good heroine and would be befriended by a bad heroine, Kate Croy. Between them would stand a beautiful, passive young man, Merton Densher. The benevolent mentor, in the first version of the story, was to be an older woman companion of Milly's, a Bostonian.

James had promised to deliver the typescript in the fall of 1901, for publication early the next year. It was an old project, and he was anxious to be done with it and to get on with other tasks—with his long-promised biography of William Story, for which he had already been paid, and newer projects that would keep the flow of advances going. He did not finish *The Ambassadors* until the middle of May, however, and even though he had already made a substantial beginning on *The Wings of the Dove* and picked it up again the day after he completed *The Ambassadors*, he could not expect to finish for many months. The usual procession of visitors arrived at Lamb House in the summer and fall, and he had his own obligatory visits to make. Holmes came over for the Season. Another old friend, E. L. Godkin, one of the first editors to accept his work, came to Bournemouth to die, and James went down the coast to sit at his bedside. But he worked when and as quickly as he could.

In the fall, with the book only half done, James pleaded with his publisher for an extension of time to the end of the year. The extension was granted, but he missed the new deadline as well. After the first of the year, he spent the winter in London at the Reform Club, dictating to Mary Weld, but soon fell ill with a new bowel complaint, perhaps a type of influenza, and his work was interrupted once more. Miss Weld remained on call, receiving her weekly salary while she waited for the summons to resume work.

A full year after he resumed the interrupted task, in May 1902, *The Wings of the Dove* was at last completed. Taking no account of the opening chapters that had been dictated to MacAlpine, Weld noted in her diary that finishing the book had taken six months of dictation, spread over the course of twelve. In the final weeks, James had once again been obliged to dictate the closing chapters of a novel after the opening chapters were already set in type.

When he was able to work, he found that the story flowed easily. His accurate visual memory and his mastery of language, his habit of framing long passages in his mind before speaking, allowed him to dictate steadily. He was writing in haste, and there was the added difficulty that during the two years in which the novel had been set aside he had destroyed the original scenario and in the interim had written another ambitious novel that had moved his art onward another step. His enthusiasm for the original conception of *Wings* had cooled and perhaps to a degree had been forgotten.

The novel opens in Lionel Croy's lodgings on Chirk Street, on the wrong side of the Thames: dreary, furnished rooms on a street of soot-blackened lodging houses. We see that Croy, a gentleman, has slipped and is on the verge of an abyss. As the curtain rises, we see his daughter, Kate, in her father's shabby lodgings. Dressed for the outdoors, she has evidently just arrived. By her genteel clothes and manner, we see that she is out of place here.

The father enters. He is handsome, unscrupulous, a genteel villain who spent his wife's little inheritance and left her to die. The situation is quickly established: his last hope of salvaging his fortunes is to sell Kate into a mercenary marriage. An aunt, the dead mother's sister, also wishes to trade on Kate's beauty and tacitly colludes in this betrayal. To advance her own social ambitions, Aunt Maud has promised to find for Kate an aristocratic husband. She will provide the cash needed for the effort, if only Kate will allow herself to be sold into a suitable marriage that will justify the investment. Aunt Maud has given the calculating father the means to exploit Kate's beauty and charm.

Kate resists the pressures of her family and her own longing for wealth. She offers to live with her father and keep house for him. We understand that this is a desperate attempt to avoid a mercenary marriage. She will work and support them both if only she is not obliged to prostitute herself. Her father refuses her offer; he will not share a life of poverty with her. He insists that she marry well; she must allow her aunt to arrange a suitable marriage and rescue them all.

Kate's stubborn resistance is not entirely virtuous; as scene follows scene, we will find her in love with a poor newspaper journalist, a handsome and passive young man, Merton Densher, who has no hope of prosperity. Kate will not make a mercenary marriage, but neither will she marry into poverty. She lingers in her dilemma.

A chance of escape appears. A wealthy young American woman, Milly Theale, innocent and generous, arrives in London and is taken up by Aunt Maud. Kate befriends the heiress—if she could only share in her riches!—and discovers that Milly is dying. Kate slowly forms her plan, and circumstances conspire with her: Milly must fall in love with Kate's young journalist; perhaps she will leave her money to him.

The opening chapters are an urban landscape, James's beloved London of lights and shadows. We see, as if from the windows of Croy's parlor, the immense, smoky landscape of London. Chirk Street and its working-class neighborhood: ragged figures gather in the streets. Indoors, Lionel Croy's ugly lodgings are a "privacy," a sadly complementary little world of meager social relations. In the innermost sphere, in Croy's parlor, Kate looks at her own image reflected in a tarnished mirror on the chimneypiece. She turns to this image, whose charm is produced by some inner force, as a refuge and partial escape from the meanness of her surroundings. It is a reminder of her constant innermost and secret realm of being. Her world is a set of nested spheres, from public to private; in the innermost sphere is her secret.

James follows Kate's movements as if with a motion-picture camera. We fly westward with Kate to Chelsea, a notch up in the social scale: a lower-middle-class refuge. Then north, over the expanse of the West End and Kensington Gardens to Lancaster Gate, where Aunt Maud presides over a suitably prosperous house—a high, bow-windowed white Victorian row house in a solid upper-middle-class block, looking across Bayswater Road to Kensington Gardens—a house in which Maud can display her new wealth, her Victorian ormolu and brass.

This wider realm is a marketplace of commerce and newspapers, of boulevards and public parks. The corresponding private realm is one of ostentatious dinner parties, of combat and striving, in which everyone wears a costume and plays a part. At dinners, tea parties, social calls, encounters in Aunt Maud's parlor, each player strives to charm while concealing and protecting her own personal world, her secrets, the core of selfhood. When Kate and Merton Densher first meet at an evening party, they fall in love and open their secrets to each other:

> It wasn't, in a word, simply that their eyes had met; other conscious organs, faculties, feelers had met as well, and when Kate afterwards imaged to herself the sharp, deep fact she saw it, in the oddest way, as a particular performance. She had observed a ladder against a garden wall, and had trusted herself so to climb it as to be able to see over into the probable garden on the other side. On reaching the top she had found herself face to face with a gentleman engaged in a like calculation at the same moment, and the two inquirers remained confronted on their ladders. The great point was that for the rest of that evening they had been perched—they had not climbed down.

Onward the camera sweeps, across the West End and into the countryside, to an estate where the wealthy and powerful gather, the cosmopolitan world glimpsed in a similar setting in Paris, in *The Ambassadors*, where personality and life may have their fullest expression, where great art is found.

James is delicate in his treatment of intimacy, of shared secrets, of passionate relations, of what he calls the "occult" (in the old sense of "hidden") and "sacred." He speaks often of the "sacred" inner life, as opposed to the "profane" or public one, but he is reluctant to intrude too much into the realm of the sacred. His respect for his characters and their reality is such that we never see them undressed, never see their secrets except through a veil. We do not quite see Kate's embraces and are not told precisely what is her father's crime. Yet we feel the palpable reality of the strong forces that are at work in the darkness, and we understand them as it were directly, immediately. We feel without being told of Kate's almost ungovernable passion for the blond, smiling Densher. She is an artist, attempting to manage divergent forces within, and she successfully conceals this passion from her aunt and from Milly. She inspires love in men and women alike and binds them to her; she all but seduces Milly Theale. A critic will remark on James's

> remarkably scrupulous efforts . . . to write about sex and gender without bowing to the pressure of explanation, without figuring a cause or supplying a name to the necessarily tantalizing phenomena of human passion and human preference . . . most scrupulously unexplained, most astonishing, and most enchanted.

But after these opening chapters were written, James had set the novel aside, two years earlier. When he picked up the abandoned novel again, in the spring of 1901, he was moved not so much by reawakened interest as by the fact that he had already made a beginning and hoped now to finish quickly.

He had evidently dropped the tale after the fourth of what were to be ten installments or acts. From that point on, the story now unbuttoned and expanded. As he was no longer writing for the illustrated magazines, his treatment of sexuality became more frank. Kate Croy and Merton Densher are in an agony of frustrated passion; Densher's is such as to make him ill. He will soon insist that Kate spend a night with him.

But the center of consciousness shifts to Milly, and what had begun as Kate's story, almost an homage to Thackeray and Becky Sharp, became Milly's and then Densher's. Although the reader has just been told (in a passage written perhaps two years earlier) that Milly will be seen only from a distance, through the eyes of others, we are now plunged into her own young awareness. Through her, James relives the unique, "the first and only prime" of life, the time of first encounters with embodied, material life in full. A new character, the benevolent physician Sir Luke Strett, steps forward. He replaces Milly's duenna as her mentor and gently confers upon Milly the knowledge that her illness is fatal. He urges her to live, in the time that remains.

Milly's experience of her own mortality, her common humanity, is rendered precisely and movingly; it is an epiphany. From this other side of the coin, she learns the life-altering lesson that life is spirit embodied. From the awareness that she may die, under her physician's gentle guidance, she gains the courage to live.

To experience all that Europe has for her, Milly rents a palace in Venice, recognizably the beloved Barbaro. Merton Densher follows Milly to Venice and at Kate's urging courts her. Milly falls in love with him, and the promise of a happy fulfillment gives her energy and life. But when she discovers that her friends are betraying her, she turns her face to the wall.

Milly, the dove, who is dying, leaves a letter in which she confers a gift of wealth and freedom upon the lovers who together have betrayed her. Densher receives her word on Christmas Eve. He has insisted that Kate sleep with him, but he has fallen in love with Milly, with her beauty and clarity of spirit. When she dies, he remains in love with her memory, and, ennobled by his love and disenchanted with Kate, he refuses to profit from their crime. He offers to sign over to Kate the inheritance that Milly offers, but he tells Kate that, if she accepts the money, he cannot marry her.

"She died for you then that you might understand her," Kate replies, and in a chilling gesture she flings the "sacred script" of Milly's letter into the fire.

Hendrik Andersen wrote from Rome with distressing news while James was still hard at work completing *The Wings of the Dove*. After a difficult winter in Rome, Hendrik had learned of the death from tuberculosis of his brother Andreas in Paris. James answered warmly, for once abandoning discretion:

My dear, dear, dearest Hendrik.
   Your news fills me with horror & pity, & how can I express the tender yearning with wh. it makes me think of you & the aching wish to be near you & put my arms around you? My heart fairly bleeds & breaks at the vision of you *alone*, in your wicked & indifferent old far-off Rome. . . . The sense that I can't *help* you, see you, talk to you, touch you, hold you close & long, or do anything to make you rest on me, & feel my deep participation—this torments me, dearest boy, makes me ache for you, & for myself. . . . I wish I could go to Rome & put my hands on you (oh, how lovingly should I lay them!) But that, alas, is odiously impossible. . . . I find myself thrown back on . . . [the] possibility of your coming to England, of the current of your trouble inevitably carrying you here—so that I might take consoling, soothing, infinitely close & tender & affectionately-healing possession of you . . . sooner or later to have you *there* [in Lamb House] & do for you, to put my arm around you & *make* you lean on me as on a brother & a lover, & keep you on & on, slowly comforted or at least relieved of the first bitterness of pain. . . . I embrace you with almost a passion of pity.

In Lamb House again, after Andersen replied at length, James wrote once more, comfortingly, to his "dearest, dearest Boy":

Now, at last, my weak arms can fold you close. Infinitely, deeply, as deeply as you will have felt, for yourself, was I touched by your 2d letter. I respond to every throb of it, I participate in every pang. I've gone through Death, & deaths, enough in my long life, to know how all that we *are*, all that we *have*, all that is best of us within, our genius, our imagination, our passion, our whole personal being, become then but aids & channels & open gates to *suffering*, to being flooded. But, it is better so. Let yourself go & *live*, even as a lacerated, mutilated lover, with your grief, with your loss, your sore, unforgettable consciousness. *Possess* them & let them possess you, & life, so, will still hold you in her arms, & press you to her breast, & keep you, like the great merciless but still *most* enfolding & never disowning mighty Mother, on & on for things to come. . . .
     [Andreas] is *all* yours now; he lives in you & out of all pain. Wait, & you will see.

Within days, another exchange of letters. James has just completed his novel and is still in character:

Beloved Boy! . . . I can't have your beautiful last letter without the necessity of putting my hand out & laying it upon you, touched as I am to the heart, with the tenderest, softest, most healing & soothing benediction. Let it rest on your shoulder, perch there, lightly, like a dove whose wing you may stroke with your cheek.

James renewed his invitation to be cared for and comforted at Lamb House, but Hendrik was obliged to return from Paris to Rome with his mother, widowed sister-in-law, and surviving brother, without a detour to Rye. James promised to visit him in Rome. He sent Andersen a copy of *The Wings of the Dove* when it appeared but urged him not to trouble himself to read it: "Put it on your table, if you like, that the world may see I've sent it to you; but don't think it necessary to plough *through* it."
     The death altered Hendrik's life in unforseen ways. Andreas's wife of only one month, Olivia, fled to Rome. She was the former Olivia Cushing, a daughter of a wealthy Boston family, artists and patrons of the arts. Olivia would be Hendrik's patron, as she had briefly been Andreas's. She established a new household in Rome, providing both living quarters and

a studio for Hendrik. With her help, Hendrik was able to make a home for his mother, Helene. They were soon joined by a lovely young woman, Lucia, who was at first Olivia's housekeeper and Hendrik's model, and then his adopted sister. The four would remain a close-knit family until the ends of their lives. Freed from financial pressures and able to have his work rendered in marble and bronze, encouraged and supported by Olivia, Andersen devoted himself henceforth to monumental visions.

Olivia and Henry James had many mutual friends in Boston, and curiously, they were related by marriage. Olivia's sister, Louisa, had married James's troubled nephew, Ned, Bob and Mary's son. When the Andersen and Cushing household was thoroughly settled, James was invited to visit as almost a member of the family.

The Wings of the Dove appeared in August 1902, in Great Britain and America. Arnold Constable brought it out in a single, six-shilling volume for direct sale to the public, circumventing the gatekeepers of illustrated magazines and lending libraries. Scribner's published it in two comparatively expensive volumes and promoted the book in the United States as a melodrama, a return to James's earlier and more popular style. It did reasonably well on both sides of the Atlantic, more popular with readers than with reviewers, who complained about the difficulty of the style. The new style, and the mixture of moral fable and frank realism in the tale, confused even some of James's warmest admirers. Arthur Benson confided to his diary that while the conception of the characters was fine, he could not make head or tail of the plot.

The Ambassadors had not yet appeared; *Wings* was the first published novel to display James's fully mature style. His brother William's reaction was typical of many readers over the following century and of the reaction that many people would have to modernist styles in literature and painting:

> I have read the Wings of the Dove (for which thanks!) But what shall I say. . . . You've reversed every traditional canon of story-telling (especially the fundamental one of *telling* the story) and have created a new *genre littéraire* which I can't help thinking perverse, but in which you *succeed*, for I read with interest to the end (many pages, and innumerable sentences twice over to see what the dickens they could possibly mean) and all with unflagging curiosity to know what the upshot might become. . . . "In its way" the book is most *beautiful*—the queer

thing is the way—I went fizzling about concerning it, and expressing my wonder all the while I was reading it.

There still had been no word from Harper about *The Ambassadors;* the editors were evidently worried about the adulterous love affair revealed in the closing chapters. Harper's paid the balance of the advance for the serial to James, but apparently the novel would not appear in its monthly magazine. Howells, who was an adviser and regular contributor to the monthly, intervened on James's behalf, however, and the novel was serialized in *The North American Review*, the old Cambridge-based journal of ideas that had given James his first cash payments as an author, almost forty years earlier. The *Review* was now owned by Harper, and *The Ambassadors* began its run there in January 1903, when sales of *The Wings of the Dove* had pretty much finished.

A few weeks later, Methuen and Scribner's brought out a volume of James's short stories, *The Better Sort*. In it were seven stories that he had written on his return from Italy and had placed in magazines, plus three more that he had somehow found time to write to fill out the volume, that had not previously appeared and would be among his best known and longest-lived: "The Beast in the Jungle," "The Birthplace," and "The Papers." Then in September, in time for another year's Christmas sales, *The Ambassadors* was published in an inexpensive single volume, bound in paper boards.

James was producing at high speed but at the top of his form, and reviewers wondered how such a "voluminous" writer managed to write with such care. William wrote, "Apparently you have been working very hard, and your last books have started you on a new career of popularity or at least of praise."

With three major works published on both sides of the Atlantic in the space of twelve months, James had indeed reestablished himself as a literary force and had managed also to keep his income at a high level— about $4,000 that year from writing, about $7,000 total. By circumventing the illustrated magazines and lending libraries and going directly to mass-market book publication, he was able to write more frankly and to experiment more freely. He found his old audience still waiting for him, refreshed and enlarged by a growing number of educated women. He promised himself never to trouble about serializing a novel again. He was writing once more for the young and in Great Britain was classed with the experimental new writers. A. T. Quiller-Couch, writing in the trade

publication *The Bookman* and consciously speaking for an older generation, remarked bemusedly:

> Of men writing fiction just now many are wonderful to me; but the
> two most wonderful, being almost admirable, are Mr. Henry James and
> Mr. Joseph Conrad. . . . Mr. James and Mr. Conrad move in an atmos-
> phere in which I feel myself inexpert, and follow as an amateur, fairly
> active on another level, stumbles after a Swiss guide. I know that here
> is good literature; I guess that it is literature touched with genius; I am
> pleased to find and even proud to find myself enjoying it wholeheart-
> edly.

Many writers whom *The Bookman* reviewed and reported upon in
those first years of the century were friends, admirers, or followers of
James: Mary Ward, Gertrude Atherton, Edith Wharton, Gosse, Benson,
Sturgis, Broughton, Elizabeth Robins (whose novel of Klondike adventures was well received), Max Beerbohm. The future Bloomsbury set
studied and imitated James's new style. Lytton Strachey wrote a short
story in the Jamesian manner, which he copied as well in letters and conversation. The young Rupert Brooke began "writing Henry James" before
he had read the master's work, picking up his style from the air, as an earlier generation had absorbed Robert Browning. Strachey and Duncan
Grant arranged for James to be invited to lunch with the Apostles at
Cambridge, and Strachey found it difficult to reconcile the actual *haut
bourgeois* James exterior with the marvelous aesthetic experiments of his
work, very much as the young James had wondered at Robert Browning's
smoothly social public face.

Rye, with James its presiding spirit, was becoming a center for a generation of writers and artists. Joseph Conrad, with his new family, was living cheaply nearby, and James (with Gosse's help) tried to obtain
financial assistance for him. George Gissing and H. G. Wells visited Rye
and stayed at Lamb House, and when they were there James invited
Conrad to join them for tea. Gissing and Wells, it was true, were pursuing a very different course from James's. They had taken up the new materialist sciences and quasi-sciences. Wells was making a success with his
science fiction novels, in which he explored the future evolution of the
human race and imagined its encounters with superior beings. He had recently turned to nonfiction to promote notions of a "New Republic," a
race of superior men. Wells sought James's advice and help, which the

older man happily gave. Arnold Bennett, pursuing yet another and different course, nevertheless recorded in his diary that "There is scarcely an author—unless it be Henry James—whom I find flawless, and whom, therefore, I can read in perfect comfort." Single volumes by some of these authors sold better than James's own, and he complained constantly of the meager sales of his titles, but few authors of literary fiction had sales and income that in the aggregate were greater than his.

Living on stimulants in a long spell of elevated mood, he visualized new projects while still at work on old ones; the day after completing a book he began another, dictating every morning, including Sundays, from notes prepared the night before. A dedicated workman, he had extracted a living from literature, periodically reinventing himself, for almost forty years.

After *The Ambassadors, The Wings of the Dove,* and *The Better Sort* had all appeared, after the labor of correcting and revising proofs was done and the books had been sent to friends and the reviews had appeared, James at last was able to complete his biography of William Wetmore Story. He had pursued his idea of describing the Roman setting of Story's expatriate life, and applying his now-settled method he wrote from a point of view within the scene, his own. The massive two-volume work was principally an evocation of their shared Rome, of James's experience of the background of Story's life. His new, evocative style was curiously well adapted to nonfiction, his own passions enriching and enlarging what might otherwise have been a pedestrian tale and evoking with rare power the life of an artist in the lost papal Rome.

James's health was better, now that the pressure was lifted and he had accomplished much of what he had set for himself in the past three years. He made regular visits to his small circle of young friends, when they were not able to visit him. And James was "Fletcherizing," to which he attributed an equal share of the improvement in his health. He ate slowly and mindfully, and the result was gratifying, and reinforced the comparative serenity he had reached. Fletcher's prescription was to eat simply and frugally, to chew slowly and throughly, tasting and enjoying each bite of food until it was liquefied. The results he promised were those of a spiritual awakening, but he also emphasized the beneficial effects of his regime upon the bowels—in his scheme, the stools were the index of mental and physical health—and promised his devoted followers that

like Indian holy men their "excreta" would be "no more offensive than
moist clay, and have no more odor than a hot biscuit."

James had taken to the regime cautiously at first, but, finding that his
health did improve and that he lost weight, he adopted it enthusiastically
and proselytized like the convert he was. Even his lifelong back trouble
eased. He sent copies of Fletcher's books to his neighbors and recommended them to his friends. To Hendrik Andersen he wrote after a long
experience of the method, "Try it, dearest boy—try it! *It has renewed my
elderly life!*"

His head crowded with visions, he began to plan new projects. For
Macmillan, returning to his old publishing house, he contracted to write
a book about his beloved London. To Methuen he promised to deliver
two new short novels, to be written solely for book publication in the following year. Just past his sixtieth birthday, he began writing the first of
these new novels, which was to be called *The Golden Bowl*.

Like other recent volumes, it was drenched in palpable sexuality,
evoked more vividly for never being made explicit. To play the part of
the good heroine, Maggie Verver, James cast his dear old friend Lizzie
Boott, her charming slim Bostonian person, dark hair pulled smoothly
down over her temples. Her mentor was her doting father. Maggie, like
Lizzie Boott, is devoted to her wealthy, indulgent, widowed father. They
racket about Europe in pursuit of artistic interests, sufficient unto themselves. They communicate without speaking, and no other woman incon-
veniently intrudes. The love of father and daughter is delicately and
richly portrayed; it is virtuous, yet no dimension is lacking.

The Ververs are richer than the Bootts, however. They are the new
American royalty: immensely, impossibly wealthy. Maggie is not a great
beauty, but she is sufficiently beautiful, and when she falls in love with an
impecunious Roman prince her wealth makes it possible for them to
marry and for her to marry for love. Verver is happy to make this possible; he wishes happiness for his daughter and in a manner of speaking
purchases a husband for her. The Roman prince, Amerigo, to whom
Verver marries his daughter, is modeled upon Count Joseph Primoli. Like
a Bonaparte heir, Amerigo is the prince of a vanished principality, although he is descended not from Napoleon but from a "wicked Pope."

We begin, accordingly, with a happy family. The prince joins the
Ververs, travels with them, and is careful not to interfere between father
and daughter. At the center of Maggie's life is a happy marriage, and more
than that, for she is able to keep her father, who perhaps means more to
her than her husband, with her. Adam Verver, by making his daughter's

marriage possible yet keeping her near, has sought a strange fusion of parental and husbandly love. He is able to hold his daughter close, while allowing her the passionate fulfillment of a marriage for love. The result is beautiful but obscurely troubling:

> The situation had been occupying, for months and months, the very centre of the garden of her life, but it had reared itself there like some strange, tall tower of ivory, or perhaps rather some wonderful, beautiful, but outlandish pagoda, a structure plated with hard, bright porcelain, coloured and figured and adorned, at the overhanging eves, with silver bells that tinkled, ever so charmingly, when stirred by chance airs. She walked round and round it . . . looking up, all the while, at the fair structure that spread itself so amply. . . .
>
> The pagoda in her blooming garden figured the arrangement—how otherwise was it to be named?—by which, so strikingly, she had been able to marry without breaking, as she liked to put it, with her past. She had surrendered herself to her husband without the shadow of a reserve or a condition, and yet she had not, all the while, given up her father by the least little inch.

James takes pleasure in playing the part of Maggie's father, whom he has magnified into a billionaire retired early from business affairs. Verver has taken up a second career as an art collector and has discovered within himself a talent for connoisseurship. He is an artist in this new medium, and the museum he plans for his American city is to be "civilization condensed, concrete, consummate, set down by his hands as a house on a rock." It is to be more than simply a house, it is be what seems impossible and a contradiction, a house that is civilized but whose doors and windows nevertheless would be open "to grateful, to thirsty millions" and from which "the higher, the highest knowledge would shine out to bless the land."

As James portrays Verver, it is difficult to believe in his business acumen. The character of Adam Verver indeed only calls to mind James himself, disguised in the costume of a western railroad man. He is beset by a sense of duty to those most closely him, he is "fatally stamped" with the desire to help and to please. His one indulgence in freedom is his insistence on sometimes being left alone; but the people around him constantly intrude. He is terribly beset by women seeking favors and assistance, offering themselves in marriage. Their pestering shows him, however, that he has succeeded, that he has "come out"

quite at the top of the hill of difficulty, the tall sharp spiral round which
he had begun to wind his ascent at the age of twenty, and the apex of
which was a platform looking down, if one would, on the kingdoms of
the earth with standing-room for but half-a-dozen others.

He is a man of strong passions kept carefully under control and is not
sentimental. In this second career, his love for the beautiful burns within
him, but "with a cold, still flame." There is something monstrous in his
collecting. His deepest aesthetic pleasures are derived from beautiful
people, and the works of art he treasures most highly are the "real," those
that like his daughter are not merely attractive but embody an idea, a fusion of noble character and personal beauty. Love was not less sensual for
having this added dimension:

> Adam Verver had in other words learnt the lesson of the senses, to
> the end of his book, without having, for a day, raised the smallest scan-
> dal . . . being in this particular not unlike those fortunate bachelors, or
> other gentlemen of pleasure, who so manage their entertainment of
> compromising company that even the austerest housekeeper, occupied
> and competent downstairs, never feels obliged to give warning.

James surely smiled here, dictating to Miss Weld, as he did a little later
when describing the manner in which those around Adam Verver kow-
tow to him. They behave like courtiers in a way that would be familiar to
"a Pope, a President, a Peer, a General, or just a beautiful Author."

The young couple have a son, and husband and wife grow a little less
intimate; but father and daughter draw still closer. Adam Verver's fierce
love for his grandson makes another bond between them. He continues
to spend long afternoons alone with his daughter, walking and talking
with her about their mutual loves.

Adam Verver, too, has married, however. He has made a marriage of
reason with his daughter's intimate friend Charlotte Stant, who is a great
beauty. He marries as much for his daughter's sake as for his own, to ensure her the company of a female companion and friend, but he is not
aware that Charlotte and the prince are old friends and that they have
concealed their intimate friendship from him and from Maggie.

The entranced reader sees Charlotte's and the prince's shared secret
deepen into love and their love blossom into betrayal. We are with Maggie as she slowly comes to understand what is happening and realizes she
must pretend that nothing is wrong, if she is not to make an irretrievable

breach in both marriages. Maggie must take command of the situation. Under the benevolent gaze of her father, Maggie ceases to be a victim and becomes an actor. She binds the prince to her with the force of her own well-governed passion and her clarity of spirit. He falls in love with his own wife and rests his head on her breast in a gesture of submission.

And Adam Verver, having conferred freedom upon his daughter, abandons his unreasonable hope of preserving their garden of intimacy. He takes his own wife, leading her with a golden leash, to the purgatory of America, leaving his daughter and her husband with all the world before them.

The novel is a play, with repeated references to Shakespeare; characters step out on balconies and staircases and speak silent monologues. Verver is a fanciful duke who succumbs to personal feeling and then restores his realm to harmony. The moral order is ancient, enduring; its next capital will be in America. Scene by scene, the drama proceeds to its climax.

Within this frame, however, which is simple and plain, lies the heart of the novel: the intricate sexual relations among the four central characters. Powerful ties bind the American businessman and the Roman prince, the wealthy heiress and her intimate friend the beautiful adventuress, father and daughter, husband and wife. The bonds of friendship and passion, of love in all its manifestations, of selfishness and greed, hold the group together in a deep harmony.

The form of the novel, its plot and setting, perfectly reflect its inner heart. The characters are on a grand scale that ennobles their passions and failures; the book is flawlessly dramatic, a perfection of Aristotelian form. Maggie's path to knowledge and freedom opens an invitation to the reader to follow and experience, in her own way, the intensity of the moment in which she embraces the prince.

There is no better exposition of the exercise of power in intimate relations in James's work, perhaps anywhere.

In five years he had written a massive biography, a volume of short stories, and three of the greatest novels in the English language, all the while maintaining a busy social life, managing his own business affairs and a complex household. To have created all this in such a short time seems scarcely credible. Even when compared with James's earlier periods of intense productivity, this one was remarkable.

Part of the explanation lies in his now complete mastery of technique, and of the mechanics of production. For forty years he had been training himself to write with little or no revision. And then, too, he was happy in his home and in his loves.

Each of the later works grew from a single germ—an anecdote or a glimpse of a relationship—and was hardly more than a tableau or a figure in a dance. He was always interested in the development of individual character, but in the great later works, each character is thoroughly and realistically embedded in intimate relationships.

In each of the novels of his major phase, which perhaps may be thought of as beginning with *The Spoils of Poynton* and *What Maisie Knew*, James finds his way into the heart of a shared situation and explores it in detail, using the consciousness of a participant alternately with his own. Each of the late works is essentially modest, a story or play that must be told rather than seen; an extended moment. To the reader, James seems to be observing rather than inventing.

The plots of these late works accordingly are simple, elemental as medieval morality plays, Bible stories. They seem complex and ambiguous on first reading, like elaborate mysteries, but this impression owes more to the complexity of style and description, the realistic intricacy of character and relation, than to any complications of the plot itself. It is a testimony to the accuracy of his observation and the fundamental realism of his method that after more than a century and after profound changes in language, culture, and sensibility in the English-speaking world, even in the America whose future he saw and feared, we can enter into and share the lives of his characters, who seem as real as on the day that he first imagined them. The greatness, let us say the sublimity, of these last completed works lies in their organic unity, the manner in which fact and idea, fable and incident, fuse.

The modern reader, it is true, does not always enter easily into James's moral universe. His belief in moral absolutes and spiritual realities is by no means forgotten, but the language for expressing such beliefs has been lost, at least in educated circles. We are obliged to speak in the language of materialism and science, and to modern criticism and many modern readers, desire for moral certainty is only a desire for the ideal, never to be fulfilled. We cannot help wishing for truth, but we cannot find it outside ourselves.

Where James saw an intricate harmony of opposites, a permanent and ever-changing pattern, moreover, we of his future often see ambiguity and fundamental uncertainty. Yet we recognize the self-same, mysteriously real intimacies, loyalties, and betrayals that James set before us. He somehow transformed his own unique experience, that of an elderly, conservative Victorian gentleman, into truths that if we cannot say with certainty are universal, at least can be shared by readers as diverse as a young modern American, an elderly Frenchman, a Korean critic, and an elderly translator who has grown up under Russian communism and yearns to go once to Paris, to see the setting of the novel she is struggling to render into Russian.

Each of the late novels and stories is unique, growing as it does out of its particular donnée. The form of expression of each grows from the initial premise, like a plant. The given situation expands in its own way, and, as James said of Turgenev, we expect the author to be able to produce photographs and documents. A lifetime of intense experience is brought to bear in these performances, all but the last written in haste against publisher's deadlines. Yet each is universal and permanent; James has accomplished in each the magical fusion of the abstract and the immediate, the individual and the type, the material and the ideal. This fusion is carried through from the largest to the smallest feature of his work. The anecdote from which he begins, seemingly trivial and particular, becomes part of a mystery play. Each character is intensely individual and unique, yet is a type, the exemplar of a pattern; each detail of description is painted by laying on minute touches of generic descriptors, adverbs, adjectives, and adjectival nouns and phrases that surround a simile or metaphor and expand it into a vivid representation of how a moment is seen and felt.

But the essential secret of James's late work rests finally on the mysterious genius of which he spoke so often, his ability to enter wholly into each of his diverse characters, to imagine and to render their experiences from inside their relationships, in compelling imagery, in a manner that allows the reader to feel she is both participating in and watching the scene herself. This is a kind of inspired performance: James's image for the artist is a dancer on the tightrope; his beau ideal is the actor Coquelin, the contemporary whom James calls a modern Balzac.

Modern literary critics sometimes refer to James's works of fiction as "performative," a term of art that is used with a double meaning. It conveys a sense that the work is somehow a performance; but it is also a technical term coined by the philosopher J. L. Austin to describe sentences that are not logical propositions but are meant to accomplish some result. The modern use (perhaps misuse) of this technical term

conveys the puzzling character of James's style. His sentences taken separately are often clumsy and sometimes violate the rules of grammar or
syntax. When James, writing in his journal, reminds himself of a personal
memory that he cannot express explicitly in a published work, he says it
is "for fatal, for impossible expansion." This is clear, but it is not a logical
proposition and not quite an idiomatic English sentence. In ordinary
written language one might say, "I dare not make an explicit account of
this remembered experience, as it could not be published without unac-
ceptable consequences and it is not safe even to write it here." The compact image, "for fatal, for impossible expansion," prompts us to feel all
this; we vaguely imagine a published text and its consequences and understand that James cannot write out what he has in mind. We are even
made to understand that the memory can be hinted at and will lend some
color to what he eventually writes, without being said directly. This is
imagery but of an unusual kind: words that prompt us to imitate the
author's internal motions.

In these late works, the growing complexity of James's sentences reflects not the ease of dictation and revision but the increasing realism and
detail of his imagery. His sentences are difficult to parse, not because of
their length but because imagery has replaced logic.

The change in his style, this development of a new sort of imagery, is
clearly evident in *What Maisie Knew*, the first consistent and unitary
novel to emerge from his playwriting and short-story experiments. The
purpose of the imagery there was plain: to re-create the naive experience
of a child and to allow the reader simultaneously to share her sensations
and to witness her growing awareness.

Narratives of the little girl's experience alternate with more objective
descriptions, so that the reader can see more than Maisie sees, but even
then the description is made in metaphor and simile, and through a pil-
ing up of simple adjectives and adverbs. In *What Maisie Knew* and the
works that follow, James alternates such allusive descriptions with scenes
that consist almost entirely of dialogue. The theatrical form is preserved:
each scene is set and then comes to life in speech. Images and the dialogue each somehow induce in the reader an imitative reflex, putting her
into Maisie's role even while observing it.

The new style is still more evident in the concluding chapters of *The
Wings of the Dove*. The opening chapters are narrated objectively, as in
James's early work, and we seem to be reading an updating of Dickens or
Thackeray. But after the interval in which he set the novel aside, the au-
thor entered into Milly's consciousness, and the complex imagery of his

later style. Quotations are difficult to extract; but the effect of the simple, homely language is cumulative and deeply moving. When Milly Theale learns from her doctor that she has a fatal illness (whose precise nature is never vulgarly specified), he urges her to live, because she is going to die. Over the course of seven pages James describes her thoughts as she wanders, a young, unprotected woman on the streets of London, absorbing the news of her common humanity:

> The beauty of the bloom had gone from the small old sense of safety— that was distinct: she had left it behind there forever. But the beauty of the idea of a great adventure, a big dim experiment or struggle in which she might, more responsibly than ever before, take a hand, had been offered her instead. It was as if she had had to pluck off her breast, to throw away, some friendly ornament, a familiar flower, a little old jewel, that was part of her daily dress; and to take up and shoulder as a substitute some queer defensive weapon, a musket, a spear, a battle-axe—conducive possibly in a higher degree to a striking appearance, but demanding all the effort of the military posture.
>
> Here [in Regent's Park] were benches and smutty sheep; here were idle lads at games of ball, with their cries mild in the thick air; here were wanderers anxious and tired like herself; here doubtless were hundreds of others just in the same box. Their box, their great common anxiety, what was it, in this grim breathing-space, but the practical question of life? They could live if they would; that is, like herself, they had been told so; she saw them all about her, on seats, digesting the information.

This is a flurry of mixed metaphors and colloquialisms, seemingly artless, the vocabulary of a young American woman. Yet each word is carefully chosen, each detail is precise: the white sheep dirtied by London's pervasive coal smuts, the air thick with summer heat. There is a profusion of adjectives; an odd simile expands under their pressure into a complex image. The feeling of safety is like a homely ornament; the ornament is friendly, familiar, little, old, part of her daily dress. We feel ourselves discarding it, imagine shouldering a battle-axe instead, and feel the change in posture and consciousness.

The shift to a broad view of the park, like a change in focus, is effortless, and the image of scattered solitary figures seated on benches is as powerful in its way as that of "Dover Beach."

Yet, while these effects are achieved with remarkable economy, there

is no striking phrase or metaphor that one can extract; the cumulative effect is not exactly visual, it is the picture of a living mind feeling its way
into simplest and greatest truths, which the reader is lead to discover or
recall for herself. A book of essays, a personal religion, lives in these few
pages.

In each of these last great novels there is a good deal of exposition, and
comic characters like the unkindly named Fanny Assingham of *The
Golden Bowl*, a living avatar of George du Maurier's Mrs. Ponsonby de
Tompkyns—the little London lady who is determined to be a greater
one—exist simply to explain events that have occurred offstage. But the
power and greatness of the novels are in the magnetic imagery of the
principal characters' naive experience.

Through lifelong study, like the painters who delved into the mechanism of seeing, the representation of perspective and the anatomy of
color, James had found a perhaps fundamental mechanism of representa-
tional art, even of civilized community. The scattered adverbs and adjectives compose themselves into a solid figure by touching the keys of
response in the reader, the general forms and qualities into which our
nervous system analyzes perceptions, and reflexively imagines itself into
the moment. His words are like the line drawings in perspective that we
see as rounded, three-dimensional objects. His medium was the solitary
imagination, but his subject was his passionate understanding, "love's
knowledge" in Martha Nussbaum's precise phrase, of the strong forces
that draw people together, despite all jealousies and violence. James
prompts us to use a sense that combines intelligence and emotion, that
allows us to imagine each other's experience and to enact in imagination
the bare descriptions that we read, as if they were stage directions; he is
the artist of empathy.

A painter's self-portrait is at the edge of the frame, he is seated with
his back toward us at an easel; a model lounges on her couch, on a little
platform, facing us, and we see that the painter has sketched the outlines
of her figure on the canvas before him. We imagine ourselves sitting
where the painter sits, the remarkable beauty of the model's nude flesh
mysteriously illuminating the experience.

20

❦

RETURN OF THE NATIVE

While still in the first stages of *The Golden Bowl*, James had begun definitely to plan a return visit to his family and a tour of the United States. He wrote to Frederick Macmillan in June 1903, saying that his proposed book on London might be delayed not only by the novel he had in hand but by his planned trip to the United States. He wrote more querulously to William, however, expressing his anxieties about the trip, his worries about his age and the expense of living in hotels for six months, but he had long ago formed the habit of expressing his anxieties and uncertainties to William, and despite his worries his plan was quite definite. His household expenses were under control, and he had begun to think that the journey to America might be paid for and even made profitable by magazine articles and a book of travel impressions.

He did wish to see his family; but, cosmopolite though he was, he also felt strongly the importance of maintaining his particular national identity, his intimate relation to his country. Then, too, there was the opportunity to restock his store of materials with American experiences. As he went along with *The Golden Bowl*, he was aware of the lack of grounding for the American characters. America was evidently going to be a great force in the world, one sensed that the capital of the world was moving westward; the encounters of Americans with Europe were of a different quality and on a larger scale than they had been forty years before, when he had first begun to write of them. The subject of the great American republic and its rise to imperial stature lay before him, and he was eager to experience America again, the tastes and smells and sounds of daily life in the wealthiest nation in the world.

Two intertwined questions presented themselves for examination, and he began to prepare himself for their study: whether America had been able to use its enormous wealth to create a civilization and whether it was able to create and preserve a distinct national character despite a wave of immigrants, in truth a tidal wave, arriving from eastern and southern Europe.

As to the first question, he was aware of promising developments. Isabella Stewart Gardner, having inherited $3 million in her own right, was planning to build in Boston an approximate replica of the Barbaro Palace, in which she would house the wealth of art that she had collected in Europe. Theodate Pope, a young architect, had designed a similar project to house her wealthy parents' collection of European art and antiquities in a hilltop town in Connecticut. Andrew Carnegie, J. P. Morgan, John D. Rockefeller, and lesser figures were turning to the creation of libraries and museums throughout the country. Gertrude Abbey was prominent among the philanthropists; her generosity allowed Sargent and Abbey to complete their enormous didactic murals for the Boston Public Library. Perhaps a uniquely American civilization was under construction, a new Venetian Republic to which the riches of Europe would contribute and into which, somehow, the immigrants from other cultures would be assimilated. This at least was the ideal to which Adam Verver aspired.

In a complementary movement, of which perhaps Maggie Verver and Milly Theale were both exemplary, American women were coming to Europe and spending the riches of the new world to preserve the treasures of the old. At the conclusion of James's play *Mrs. Gracedew*—the one-act curtain-raiser for Ellen Terry that James had recently recycled into a short story, "Covering End"—the American heroine uses her wealth to rescue an old English family estate (and marry its attaching owner). He had written it in 1895, the year in which Consuelo Vanderbilt had married the Duke of Marlborough and devoted her vast dowry to restoring Blenheim Palace. In the play and the story, James's Mrs. Gracedew bravely shows her English husband's old house to visitors, immigrant Jews.

> One of the invaders . . . a broad-faced gentleman with long hair tucked behind his ears and a ring on each forefinger—had lost no time in showing he knew where to begin. He began at the top—the proper place, and took in the dark pictures ranged above the tapestry. "Olt vamily bortraits?" . . . The question affected the lovely lady over by the fireplace [Mrs. Gracedew] as the trumpet of battle affects a generous steed. She flashed on the instant into the middle of the hall. . . . They met her with low salutations, a sweep of ugly shawls and a brush of

queer German hats. . . . [A] matron of a rich Jewish type, with small nippers on a huge nose and a face out of proportion to her little Frei-schütz hat, [broke] the spell by an uneasy turn and a stray glance at one of the other pictures. "Who's *dat?*"

Mrs. Gracedew's welcome to the visitors, if comic, was also admirable and in its way heroic.

The Boer War ground to its hideous conclusion: more than 26,000 civilians—men, women, and children—died in concentration camps, and casualties in the armed forces on both sides were still greater. Despite systematic repression, guerrilla warfare conducted by the "bitter enders" of the Boer regime continued to take its toll on the occupying forces, and at last Balfour's government agreed to a peace that would give substantial control to the Boers. The majority of the population, native black Africans, would be disenfranchised, as the Boers demanded, and Afrikaans would be taught in the schools. The British declared victory and withdrew, knowing that public opinion would not support continued protracted warfare, leaving behind a Boer republic that would soon become an autonomous and hostile white republic, the Union of South Africa. Balfour's government was wounded equally by the war and the peace, and it was plain that in the next election the Liberals and the new Labour Party would take a clear majority. To James as to many others, it seemed that the British Empire had received a mortal wound.

Holmes was in London for the Season once again, in much better spirits than he had been the year before. He was not troubled by the Boer War or by the American conquest of the Spanish island colonies. On the contrary, he shared the widespread view that America was more or less permanently at war, or threatened by war, with rival empires. The new president, Theodore Roosevelt, was a vigorous champion of this view and had appointed him to a vacant seat on the Supreme Court largely for this reason. He was enjoying Washington and his success, and now, on a first visit to England as a Supreme Court justice and a national figure, Holmes spent a weekend with James at Lamb House. They had a great deal to talk about.

Roosevelt had appointed Holmes to the Supreme Court believing that he would support military rule over the Philippines and Puerto Rico. This was the great issue of the day, and from Holmes's arrival in Washington,

Roosevelt had embraced him with personal friendship. He spoke to Holmes as a fellow soldier, and the newspapers dutifully reported their intimacy. Early in 1903, Holmes was able to vindicate Roosevelt's trust and cast his deciding vote in favor of the imperialist faction, in a Supreme Court decision upholding military rule in America's new island colonies.

Holmes had now come to Great Britain on a diplomatic errand. Roosevelt was eager to proceed with construction of a canal across the Isthmus of Panama, in pursuit of his dream of a world-straddling navy, but a long-standing treaty with Great Britain required the United States to proceed jointly, if at all. Great Britain, embroiled in its costly war, was not eager to share the expense of a canal. Roosevelt was inclined to abrogate the treaty and proceed with the canal, with or without British consent. He was similarly impatient with a long-standing dispute with Britain over a strip of coast, running southward from the Alaskan peninsula, that held the only deepwater ports giving access to the Klondike goldfields. Roosevelt was disposed to ignore British claims and draw the boundary with Canada himself.

To emphasize his impatience, the president put American armed forces on alert. Under John Hay's strenuous urging, however, he agreed to submit both issues to arbitration; but in that summer of 1903, he gave Holmes a strongly worded letter that the justice was "indiscreetly" to show to Arthur Balfour or the colonial secretary, Joseph Chamberlain. The letter said quite simply that if the arbitration of the Alaska boundary dispute did not produce the result demanded by the United States, Roosevelt would ignore it.

Readiness for "righteous" war was central to the president's foreign policy, and this was its first expression. When later describing his settled attitude, Roosevelt expressed his deep regret that no European nation had intervened to halt the mass murders of Christian Armenians in Turkey and he praised the interventions of the British in Africa. He was at work building a modern fleet of steel-clad, turbine-driven battleships— a Great White Fleet—that could project American force anywhere on the globe.

> Hitherto peace has often come only because some strong and on the whole just power has by armed force, or the threat of armed force, put a stop to disorder. . . . the Mediterranean was freed from pirates only by the "pax Britannica." . . . If England had disarmed to the point of being unable to conquer the Soudan and protect Egypt, so that the Mahdists

had established their supremacy in northeastern Africa, the result would have been a horrible and bloody calamity to mankind. . . . Unjust war is dreadful; a just war may be the highest duty.

Holmes spoke to Chamberlain and tried to soften the language of Roosevelt's letter, believing that a bald threat would not be helpful, but when he and James met, the two countries seemed to be on the verge of war. As Hay had expected, however, within a few weeks the arbitration commission delivered a decision in favor of the United States' boundary claim, with only minor concessions to Canada; Great Britain happily agreed that the United States might proceed with a canal across Panama at its own expense, so long as Great Britain was guaranteed unrestricted passage through the canal, and the whole affair dissipated.

John Hay continued to labor on behalf of closer relations with England, but he confided to his friends that formal alliance with England was not possible, as Democrats in the Senate were able to block any treaty. With their base in the Irish Catholic communities of northern cities and their pursuit of recent Irish and German immigrants, the Democrats were hostile to Great Britain. Their candidate for president, William Jennings Bryan, had already accused the Republicans of making secret alliances with England. Even limited agreements were difficult to ratify, and Hay had begun to rely ever more heavily on the personal diplomacy of which Bryan was so suspicious.

James too soon found himself enmeshed in Hay's efforts, of which he heartily approved, to strengthen the ties between their two countries. This was the sort of task in which he had long been engaged and in which he could help. He and Holmes in that summer were in the quiet storm center of events. Holmes was visibly enjoying his new role, and his new mood was welcome. James felt he was greeting once more the young Holmes he had known forty years before: "exactly his old self." Holmes was white-headed but vibrant as ever, and James listened happily to his talk.

The biography of Story—oddly titled *William Wetmore Story and His Friends*—was making a surprising stir, and friends in America who remembered Story wrote to James; they liked the book, but there were delicate inquiries as to how the Story family had received it. Henry Adams wrote a rare friendly letter; it brought back the early days of Bostonian ventures into Europe for him:

Henry James, about 1890. He had decided to abandon the novel and devote himself to short stories and plays. (Dartmouth College Library, Rauner Special Collections)

Alice James, before her illness and years of dependence upon her brother Henry. (Courtesy Houghton Library, Harvard University)

Edmund Gosse, 1886. James was a friend and mentor to Gosse, who eagerly supplied him with gossip. Portrait by their mutual friend John Singer Sargent. (Courtesy National Portrait Gallery, London)

Arthur Christopher Benson (*center*), with his brothers, about 1883, when he and James formed their lifelong, intimate friendship. (Courtesy Tilling Society)

Mary Ward, who wrote as "Mrs. Humphry Ward," in an 1889 publicity photograph. She was a follower whose books far outsold the Master's. (From Janet Penrose Trevelyan, *The Life of Mrs. Humphry Ward*, courtesy of the Mary Ward Web Site)

Louisa Wolseley, Viscountess Wolseley, about 1884. She was James's companion of shopping expeditions, and gave him a window on imperial politics. (Courtesy National Portrait Gallery, London)

Robert Louis Stevenson, 1884, portrait in oils by John Singer Sargent,
in the summer of Stevenson's first friendship with James.
(Courtesy Taft Museum, Cincinnati, Ohio)

THE BROADWAY ARTISTS

*Artists who gathered in the summers at the village of Broadway, in the Cotswolds,
where the roles of artist, mentor, patron, and lover happily mingled.*

Edwin Austin "Ned" Abbey,
1870s, principal model for Nick
Dormer in *The Tragic Muse*.
(Photograph collection, Archives of
American Art, Smithsonian Institution)

Alfred Parsons, who designed
Henry's garden at Lamb House,
in the 1880s. (From Henry James,
Picture and Text)

George Boughton, a celebrated
illustrator and Parsons's
intimate friend, in the 1880s.
(From Henry James, *Picture and Text*)

John Singer Sargent, self-
portrait, 1886. Sargent and
Ned Abbey shared studio space
under the joint patronage of
Gertrude Mead. (Aberdeen Art
Gallery and Museums, Scotland)

Wolcott Balestier, who Alice thought would be a life partner for James. (From Henry James, "Wolcott Balestier," *Cosmopolitan Magazine*, May 1892)

Elizabeth Robins, 1891, in a publicity photo as Madame de Cintré in Henry James's *The American*. (Fales Library, New York University)

The walk down Mermaid Street to Lamb House, 1899. The Mermaid
Inn is on the right; Lamb House is to the viewer's left, just out of
sight. (From Henry James, "Winchelsea, Rye, and *Denis Duval*," illustrated by
E. C. Peixotto, *Scribner's Magazine*, January 1901)

Oliver Wendell Holmes on a visit to the United Kingdom,
about 1900. After their early friendship, there was always a
certain tension between Holmes and James.
(Courtesy Harvard Law Art Collection)

Henry James and friend, probably Max, in the garden of Lamb House, about 1904. (Courtesy Dartmouth College Library, Rauner Special Collections)

Henry James and his intimate friend Hendrik Christian
Andersen in Andersen's studio in Rome, 1907. Photograph
by Andersen's adoptive sister; the decision to pose in
front of monumental nudes is curious.
(Courtesy Museo Hendrik Christian Andersen)

Andersen among the monumental nudes. James counseled him to do portrait busts instead. (Museo Hendrik Christian Andersen)

Olivia Cushing, who was related by marriage to both James and Andersen, became Andersen's mentor and encouraged his work on monumental figures, and on their World City project. (Courtesy Museo Hendrik Christian Andersen)

Giuseppe Primoli, holding a portrait of his mother, Carlotta Bonaparte, about 1890. Primoli was the model for the Prince in *The Golden Bowl*, and probably was in James's thoughts during his final hours. (Courtesy Fondazione Primoli)

Henry James on the steps of the Borghese Gallery in Rome, photographed by Giuseppe Primoli, 1899. (Courtesy Fondazione Primoli)

Henry James and Howard Sturgis, with whom he had hoped to live, on the terrace of Edith Wharton's house, The Mount, photographed by Wharton, about 1904. (From Miranda Seymour, *A Ring of Conspirators*)

Edith Wharton Christmas card portrait, 1905, at the time of James's visit to America and their first friendship. (Original in Beinecke Library, Yale University)

Mrs. William (Alice Howe), daughter Margaret Mary (Peggy),
and William and Henry James on Henry's visit to Cambridge,
Massachusetts, 1905. (Courtesy Professor Frank Pajare's William James
Web page [Emory University])

William and Henry James, at the James family summer house in
Chocurua, New Hampshire, 1904. (Courtesy Dartmouth College
Library, Rauner Special Collections)

Horace Walpole, to whom James wrote some of his least
discreet love letters. Drawing by their mutual friend Jane
Emmet von Glehn (later "de Glehn"), about 1909, the
time of his intimate friendship with James.
(From the collection of the late Sir Rupert Hart-Davis, reproduced
in David Newsome, *On the Edge of Paradise: A. C. Benson, Diarist*)

Henry James, portrait by Jacques-Émile Blanche, 1908.
(Courtesy National Portrait Gallery, Washington, D.C., Smithsonian Institution)

More than ever, after devouring your William Story, I feel how difficult a job was imposed on you. . . . The painful truth is that all of my New England generation . . . knew nothing—no! but really nothing! of the world. One cannot exaggerate the profundity of ignorance of Story in becoming a sculptor, or Sumner in becoming a statesman. . . . What you say of Story is at bottom exactly what you would say of Lowell, Motley, Sumner. . . . You cannot help smiling at them, but you smile at us all equally. . . . You strip us, gently and kindly, like a surgeon, and I feel your knife in my ribs.

No one else will ever know it. You have been extremely tactful. The essential superficiality of Story and all the rest, is painfully clear to us, but not, I think, to the family or the public.

James replied hastily. He was happy to hear from Adams and sorry that the book had affected him as it had. James's own motive was nostalgic, and his method was simply to use his own subjective awareness to make a story of the book. A few years later, James would adopt the same method—and be obliged to make some of the same apologies and explanations—for a memoir of his brother and father. For now, he merely continued his efforts to finish the novel that he had promised to have ready in the fall but that he was carefully revising and would not have ready until the spring of 1904. He was determined to finish it before leaving for America. Miss Weld came to Lamb House every morning, and when he was briefly too ill to work, he asked her to check in every hour or two in case he should be ready to resume.

Lamb House again opened its arms to Hendrik Andersen, who came for a visit after many delays and postponements. With Olivia Cushing Andersen's aid he was the head of his family now; his mother, his sister, and his brother's widow lived with him in Rome. His younger brother, Arthur, was living alone in Paris, and after paying a visit to him, Hendrik ran up to Rye for five days alone with James. Afterward, the older man included in his letters a reminiscence of their embraces: "Beloved Hendrik . . . I draw you close, I hold you long, & I am, ever so tenderly, dearest Hendrik, your Henry James."

Owing to an attack of gout, James remained in Lamb House further into the winter than usual. He went up to London only for brief visits, once to call upon an American writer—Edith Wharton—and her husband, who were on their way to the south of France. Wharton was a friend of Howard Sturgis's, who had recommended her first novel, *The Valley of Decision*, just published, to James. Another mutual friend, Mary Cadwalader Jones (Wharton's sister-in-law) was also lobbying him and had sent James copies of Wharton's short-story collections. In response to these recommendations, he had read her book and dutifully wrote Wharton a friendly letter of praise. *The Valley of Decision* was set in eighteenth-century Italy; it was a novel of ideas on the order of Mary Ward's early bestsellers. (Wharton had tried but failed to meet her: "Mrs. Ward . . . [was] of course in Italy.") James wrote vague and general praise but tactfully suggested that in future Wharton address American subjects.

Wharton, when they met, was a little, lantern-jawed, self-composed woman of forty with fine, red-brown hair piled unbecomingly but fashionably on top of her head. She had what the age called a masculine intelligence. Largely self-educated, like James, and like him a cosmopolitan New Yorker, a mistress of European languages, she had the confident manner of a woman of inherited wealth. They likely spoke of New York and of their mutual friend Howard Sturgis, whose novel *Belchamber* was soon to be published. Neither seemed to think the visit likely to lead to a friendship, although Wharton was glad to have James's encouragement and advice. She had admired James's early work, especially *The Portrait of a Lady*, but did not care for his recent fiction: "He . . . talks, thank heaven, more lucidly than he writes."

Sturgis also sent James the first set of galley proofs of his novel, *Belchamber*, covering the opening chapters, and asked James for his comments. It was too late to make any but trivial changes; James accordingly replied with friendly and general praise and eschewed making any detailed critique. "The thing goes on very solidly & smoothly, interesting & amusing." But Sturgis had undertaken to be a novelist, and he wanted to engage James's critical faculties. He continued to send proofs in batches as they came from the printer and insisted on James's responding. Pressed for criticism, James again generally praised the book but pointed to the protagonist's hollow interior. Sainty had no imaginative life of his own, evidently because he lacked any strong feeling. The "poor worm" Sainty allowed himself to be mercilessly abused and, on his wedding night, to be spurned by his bride. Cuckolded by his best friend, he dies without apparently having felt any strong emotion. Sainty is effeminate and seems to form warmer friendships with men than with women, but that side of his character is also left blank, and he is given no reason for his lack of feeling for his wife. James thought the inner, personal realm should not have been left empty:

> one feels, in general, that Sainty's physiology, as it were, ought to be definitely & authoritatively established & focused: one wants in it a *positive* side,—all his own—so that he shall not be *all* passivity & nullity.

The third and fourth batches of proofs came with further demands for criticism, and James replied to each with further praise in general, but with reiterations of his earlier complaint: Sainty lacked an inner life. When his wife tries to inveigle him into sex, to provide a cover for her pregnancy, Sainty declines. James found this incident emblematic.

> I wish [Sainty's] failure to conjoin with [his wife] about 2 a.m. that night on the drawing room sofa, could for his sake have been a stand-off *determined* by some particular interposing, disconcerting, adequate positive fact . . . something not so merely *negative* for him. He couldn't afford there (for interest,) to fail without a reason. . . .

Sturgis did not accept James's view, but evidently out of deference to the older man, for whom he felt the greatest admiration, he wrote to say that he was going to withdraw the novel from publication. James replied in alarm:

> If you think of anything so insane you will break my heart & bring my grey hairs, the few left me, in sorrow & shame to the grave. Why should you have an inspiration so perverse & so criminal? If it springs from anything I have said to you I must have expressed myself with strange & deplorable clumsiness. Your book will give joy to thousands of people. . . . My esoteric reflections over the subject will occur to nobody else at all . . . if you love me let your adventure take care of itself to the end.

Sturgis did indeed allow the book to proceed to publication, and it was widely reviewed—in part through Wharton's efforts—and moderately well received. He and James agreed to talk over their differences when they next met. Their calendars could not be brought together until spring, however, when James was able to pay a leisurely visit to Queen's

Acre. When they were at last together, James enlarged upon his view that the inner life of the protagonist, through whose eyes the characters and events were seen, would have made the principal interest of the story. He could not accept a purely passive and effeminate Sainty. But Sturgis, expressing distress at their disagreement and while still offering homage to James, explained his own view that Sainty was not an agent but a resultant of external forces. Sturgis maintained that his tale of quiet acceptance was beneficent and moral.

Sturgis made an anecdote of this encounter with James and repeated it to his friends, wickedly imitating James's distinctive manner, and even wrote a short story (not published in his lifetime but evidently shown to friends) in which a Sainty-like author is crushed by criticisms from an admired mentor. In later years, this incident would become a celebrated literary quarrel. Sturgis would not write another novel, and some of their mutual friends blamed James, but Sturgis himself said, "I would write [another] book if I could, I really would, in spite of all the trouble it is, & the fact that people hate it when it's done, but I'm obstinately barren."

Late in January, recovered from his attack of gout, James went up to London for the remainder of the winter and settled in his bed-sitting room at the Reform Club. London was very quiet, and he was able to work steadily. Mary Weld joined him in town and arrived at his door promptly every weekday morning for dictation. (She came up in the lift from a side entrance, rather than through the members' entrance.) He suffered only occasional distractions. Humphry and Mary Ward's daughter Janet was married at Oxford, and James went up in a special train with the other guests, an Oxonian and cultured group of matrons "in grey silk and grey hair," as the young Lytton Strachey recorded with amusement. He made a note of James's comment on the vows the young couple had written for themselves: "The ordinary service binds, and makes an impression—it's like a seal; this was nothing more than a wafer."

At a literary luncheon at the Kensington house of the writer and editor Sidney Lee, James encountered once more the admiring American novelist Gertrude Atherton, who listened breathlessly to his conversation. ("Nobody wanted to listen to anyone else," she said afterward, "and if a pause threatened he was gently prodded.") Atherton screwed up her courage and asked James if she might dedicate her next book of stories to him, to which he courteously agreed.

. . .

James's old friends Frederic Myers and Henry Sidgwick, the founders of the Society for Psychical Research at Cambridge, to whom he had introduced William so many years ago, had both died. Myers's widow had written to Henry and William to say she was collecting his letters for a projected life, and would they lend her the letters that they had? James was immersed in preparations for his journey and replied somewhat hastily from the Reform Club that he doubted he had anything much; he had burned a great many letters when he moved to Rye.

Neither had he received posthumous communications from the departed men, but he kept an open mind as to the possibility of telepathic messages. Sidgwick's widow, Eleanor, Arthur Balfour's sister, who had succeeded Sidgwick as president of the Society for Psychical Research, was conducting a large-scale experiment to determine whether the two departed spirits had communicated, as they had promised, the contents of sealed letters left behind when they died. William was participating in séances to assist the effort, so far without result.

The arrangements for James's return to America were falling into place. He had hoped to let his house in Rye for the fall and winter that he planned to be away, to reduce expenses and keep his servants busy and under supervision. At almost the last moment, three young Americans, two sisters and a brother, turned up. James lunched in London with the elder sister, Louise Horstmann, and was pleased to find that she was engaged to John Boit, a son of Bostonian friends. The three young people would live in and maintain the house and garden and would pay a modest rental of five pounds per week, which would cover the servants' salaries. James was charmed by Louise and provided her with a long letter of instructions for dealing with house and servants. Mrs. Paddington was a gem; she would present the household accounts each week; George Gammon was an excellent carpenter as well as gardener and would repair anything that needed repair; little Noakes would brush the young man's clothes and call him in the mornings.

> Lastly, I take the liberty of confiding to your charity & humanity the precious little person of my dachshund Max, who is the best & gentlest & most reasonable & well mannered as well as beautiful small animal of his kind to be easily come across—so that I think you will speedily find yourselves loving him for his own sweet sake. . . . Of course what

he most intensely dreams of is being taken out on walks, & the more
you are able to indulge him the more he will adore you.

Provision would have to be made for Mary Weld, who would be unemployed during his absence. After some discussion, she agreed to accept
the little studio he had purchased at the far end of the garden. She would
share it with a friend and, like Hyacinth Robinson, learn the craft of
bookbinding.

James continued to fret over the practicalities of the journey. How
would he pay for six months of travel and hotels? The profits from a book
of impressions would come only afterward, and James did not like to dip
into his modest savings. There were logistical questions as well, travel
arrangements and hotel reservations in what were to him foreign cities.
Howard Sturgis could simply take off on a whim, but he never counted
the expense, and he had his majordomo the Babe to make advance
arrangements.

James's worries were summarily resolved by the energetic Colonel
George Harvey. When Harper and Brothers had fallen into difficulties in
the panic of 1893, the book and magazine publisher had been taken over
by creditors, principally J. P. Morgan and Company. Young Harvey, who
had acquired the troubled *North American Review*, was brought in as
chief executive, and in 1899 he took the company through bankruptcy.
Harvey hired new editors, including Elizabeth Jordan, a promising journalist who had covered the Lizzie Borden trial and who had famously
spent a night in a haunted house. She was making a tremendous hit with
Harper's Bazar.

The new management was very twentieth century, eager to succeed
with the best writing and black-and-white illustrations. Harvey himself
had published James's controversial *The Ambassadors* and was now glad
of an opportunity to cultivate the author. They met in London, and Harvey proposed to arrange a lecture tour, which would likely pay for the
trip and might even be profitable. The lecture tour would publicize
James's newly published novels, as well as the proposed sketches of
American life for Harper magazines. Harper would book the lectures and
make James's travel arrangements.

The remedy would bring its own complications, however. At the age
of sixty-one, James would face for the first time the task of public speaking, which he had avoided all his life. He would have to learn to perform
this new skill and to deal with the other duties of a public man, even a
celebrity.

Du Maurier had struggled with this problem of celebrity and when he undertook a lecture tour to make some money had talked about *Punch* and his distinguished predecessors there, rather than talking about himself or his work. James had attended du Maurier's maiden lecture in London and had approved of it. The approach he now decided to take was the one du Maurier had chosen: to talk about his own work only indirectly, by discussing his great predecessors, the lessons he had learned from them, the tradition in which he was working. This would allow him to avoid, as it had allowed du Maurier to avoid, tasteless self-praise; nor would he have to address the awkward question of his impressions of America before he had had a chance to formulate them.

As to the inevitable newspaper interviews, he would prepare some anecdotes of life in England; but for the most part he thought he would avoid giving interviews as much as possible. He would need new clothes; publicity photographs; there was a myriad of details to attend to. Elizabeth Jordan, who hoped to secure James for her newly literary *Bazar,* helped with all this. Harvey had delegated to her the task of making arrangements, and she explained the economics of the lecture tour, and promised that it would be profitable. She wrote to Howells and others with whom James expected to stay, made hotel arrangements in cities where he needed them, and generally reassured James about the wisdom of the trip. Harper and Brothers began to publicize the forthcoming journey, and newspaper paragraphs of a familiar kind began to appear: "Henry James is on the point of returning to the United States for a number of months, in order to renew his impressions of this country."

He put his final travel arrangements into place. He would sail in August, spend the autumn with William and his family, making side trips around New England, and then work his way southward to Florida as the weather grew colder. He hoped also to travel west as far as California, where he had never been, and to return to England in the spring. It was to be the completion of the journey he had planned twenty-three years earlier, interrupted then by the deaths of his parents.

Arthur Andersen, Hendrik's younger brother, who was trying to make his way as a painter in Paris, came to Lamb House for a visit, and James was touched and pleased by the attention. It was possible that Hendrik too would be traveling to America, perhaps to teach, Arthur told him. Hendrik sent photos of his newest, monumental works:

> I find them, dear Hendrik, difficult to speak of to you—they terrify me
> so with their evidence as of *madness* (almost) in the scale on which you

are working! It is magnificent—it is sublime, it is heroic; & the idea &
composition of your group-circled fountain, evidently a very big thing.
Only I feel as if it were let loose into space like a blazing comet—with
you, personally, dangling after like the tail, & I ask myself where my
poor dear confident reckless Hendrik is being whirled, through the
dark future, & where he is going to be dropped. I want to be there,
wherever it is, to catch you in my arms.

Howard Sturgis was planning a trip to America as well, and they tried
to coordinate their schedules so as to travel together; but Sturgis delayed
until the last minute, and James (choosing the cheaper route) took a
berth in a German ship, the *Kaiser Wilhelm der Grosse*, from Southampton to New York, while Sturgis went more directly to Boston. They
agreed to meet, perhaps at the Wharton place in Massachusetts, where
Sturgis would be staying. On August 18, James left Lamb House for London and Southampton. His parting from Lamb House and its comfortable hospitality was painful, as he told Miss Horstmann:

> I left L.H. yesterday looking so dreadfully sorry to part with me & so
> easy & pleasant to stay in withal, that I took refuge in burying my nose
> in Max's little gold-coloured back & wetting it (the back) with my
> tears.

James's ship docked at Hoboken, where all was confusion. His nephew
Harry had come to meet him, as had a minion of Harper and Brothers,
who pressed James to come first to Colonel Harvey's summer house on
the New Jersey shore for a day or two, to relax after his trip and discuss
the lecture arrangements. Harry wired his parents that Uncle Henry
would be delayed and forwarded his trunks to Boston while James went
off to Colonel Harvey's grand new house in Deal Beach, on the New Jersey shore, luxurious but oddly lacking in privacy. Mark Twain was there,
on a similar errand, and after dinner regaled them with stories.

Harvey explained that the Pond Lecture Bureau had booked James's
engagements, one appearance in each city that he visited, working his
way down the East Coast to Florida, thence to New Orleans, with perhaps a detour to newly American Cuba. From New Orleans, he would go
up the Mississippi River Valley to Chicago and then westward to California on the transcontinental railroad. His tour would begin after the first
of the year and take about six months. Until January, James would be free

to visit with his family in New England and to make little excursions on his own to gather impressions there, but when the cold weather arrived he would journey south; by the time it turned warm again, he would be on his way north once more.

He woke to a still, cool, sunny New England morning, a beneficent change from the heat and noise of New York. William and Alice had been among the first summer people from Boston to settle in Chocorua, New Hampshire, at the foot of the White Mountains, beside a pleasant cold lake. More recent newcomers in the village were painting the old wooden houses white and planting flowers in the long-neglected dooryards. The James house remained unpainted, however: a rambling, weathered clapboard-and-shingle farmhouse on what had been a ninety-acre farm. It was a house for summer vacations with small children, for lake swimming and mountain hikes, pleasant and disorderly. Billy was away in Geneva, where William hoped he might begin medical studies, and Harry was living in Boston, about to begin law practice there, but the younger children, Peggy and Alexander, were at home.

Peggy was seventeen and entering her last year of secondary school. Her plan was to attend college, but at her mother's suggestion this was to be put off while she performed the customary rituals of "coming out" in Boston society, an experiment about which she was somewhat dubious.

Alexander, the youngest at fourteen, was the subject of familiar Jamesian vacillations. His parents had been indecisive about his name, and had at first called him Francis Tweedy James, honoring one of William's colleagues and some cousins. William had called the boy "Tweedy" and his mother had called him "Francis." This would not do, and for a while they tried to compromise by calling him "John." Uncle Henry then suggested naming him after their maternal grandfather, Alexander Robertson, and after some hesitation William and Alice accepted the suggestion. When the child was about seven, therefore, his father began calling him "Aleck," but his mother was slower to change and still sometimes called him "Francis." Aleck was struggling with eyeglasses and was not doing well at school; there were the usual disagreements about his education.

Uncle Henry, as he was in these surroundings, settled in for a leisurely and happy stay. His friendship with the older children gave him a good deal of pleasure, and he began to know Aleck, whom he had heretofore seen only as an infant. The house was noisy with children and friends, busy with work and social activities. Uncle Henry took long walks with them in turn. He went birding with Aleck, who was an expert bird-watcher and had already compiled an imposing list of birds, including a rarely seen woodcock. Aleck's precocity in these matters seemed to balance his struggles with reading and arithmetic: seemed "quite to give feathers & wings & elated song to one's hope for him."

William's Gifford Lectures, published the year before, had been successful critically and commercially. The tolerance he expressed, his acceptance of the diversity of religious experience, had been especially welcomed. William said that he planned to give up teaching and devote himself entirely to what he had always felt to be his true calling, the pursuit of philosophy. He wished to erect a system of thought on purely empirical grounds, one that would explode all the old myths and superstitions of metaphysics. Now that he had achieved a substantial success of his own, he was easier with his brother and spoke kindly for the first time of his respect for Henry's courage in having chosen from the first to devote himself to the calling of letters.

William and Alice also were busy with the spiritual phenomena seemingly demonstrated in séances being conducted in Boston by a remarkable woman, Leonora Piper. Both the British and American branches of the Society for Psychical Research had investigated, had sent observers to her "sittings," had hired private detectives to investigate and follow her. One by one, all other mediums had been exposed as charlatans, but Leonora Piper alone defied explanation. Alice was persuaded that she had received communications from their dead son, Herman. William tried to remain skeptical but continued to attend Piper's séances. It seemed possible that Piper had in highly developed form a sensibility that allowed her to detect the traces of a personality that had passed through the material world, perhaps even to receive telepathic communications from such a spirit.

Physical manifestations of spirits were not in question; these were consistently debunked. Spirits, if such there were, did not have material form. But the transfer of thoughts from one mind to another seemed a distinct possibility, and if a personality could survive bodily death, perhaps it could make telepathic communications from the spiritual realm. Mrs. Piper had recently begun speaking in the voice of a young philosophy student who had attended her séances years before and who had since died of tuberculosis. She repeated details of his life and his personal acquaintance that it seemed impossible she should know. Henry James, like many others, was impressed by the seeming rigor of the experiments and was willing to believe in the almost limitless power of a superior imagination to perceive things unseen.

The third of the surviving James brothers, Robertson, was in Concord, where his wife and daughter had settled, although he continued to live apart from them. William and Alice now invited Bob to join the family gathering in Chocorua, and Henry seconded their invitation:

> [It would] minister greatly to the richness of family life, & the sense of reunion offered to my long-starved spirit, to have you here. The Dead we cannot have, but I feel as if they would be, will be, a little less dead if we three living can only for a week or two close in together here.

Bob answered at length but without accepting the invitation. James then wrote again to say that he would go to Bob in Concord.

New Hampshire was not picturesque, as the English countryside was; it lacked the institutions built up over feudal centuries, of church and squire, that had shaped the landscape. There was no guiding spirit to manage its appearance, and some villages were all but abandoned now that farming had moved westward with the railroads. But New Hampshire had its own history, recorded in the touching landscape, the abandoned farms, the granite skeleton breaking through the thin soil in the gentle, still, feminine September air.

James would confess, when writing of this visit, that his impressions were colored by his own memories, as they must inevitably be. New Hampshire evoked for him not only its own history but also that time of his own youth so recently celebrated in his novels, "the sense of some bedimmed summer of the distant prime, flushing back into life," when he had first experienced the cardinal facts of material life, of cash, love, and death. An excursion to North Conway especially recalled for him the long-vanished summers when he and Wendell Holmes together had visited the Temple sisters.

In October, James went with his brother's family to their house in Cambridge. Harry came from Boston, and they spent a precious day together.

Harry showed him the changes at Harvard and the new law school building, and Uncle Henry made notes, something that he rarely did.

The house that William and Alice had built at 95 Irving Street, a big,
commodious, vaguely Dutch Colonial clapboard house with a classical
portico, was—like the farmhouse in Chocorua—a noisy, busy place,
where William had carved out for himself a corner, a book-lined study on
the ground floor, where despite interruptions he could work. With only
two children now still at home, there was ample space for a guest, and
James was given what amounted to a private apartment on the second
story, with its own sitting room and bath. The pleasant, golden autumn
continued; he ran up to Concord for a long, pleasant visit with Robertson, Mary, and their daughter, Mary (called Mamie). Their son, Edward
(called Ned), had settled on the West Coast, and James hoped to see him
later in his journey.

Cambridge and Boston did not seem to him greatly changed. James
was sentimental about the old parts of the towns and again felt that there
lay over the whole scene an evening light of reminiscence of his young
manhood, his "prime initiation" to love and success, "full of both public
and of intimate vibrations." He visited the Boston Public Library, the vast
new cathedral of democracy, and admired the first panels of Sargent's
portrayal of the development of religion, from its presumably primitive
origins to the advanced Unitarianism of Boston, and Ned Abbey's nostalgic re-creation of a vanished age of Romance, all of which he had
watched in preparation at Morgan Hall. He tried to see Belle Gardner's
house and museum but found it closed on the day he had set aside for a
visit. Boston's efforts to create a new civilization intrigued him, but the
verdict on their success would evidently lie with the future.

Edith and Edward Wharton—Puss and Teddy to their oldest friends—
invited him to spend a few days with them at their new country house in
the Berkshire hills, holding out as an inducement the presence of their
mutual friend Howard Sturgis—and James happily accepted.

The Whartons' house was a square white structure of multiple floors
and chimneys, planted on a low hill. The dining room opened onto a wide
terrace, below which Edith had laid out a formal garden in the Italian
style. Sweeping away beyond the garden were meadows, making a vista,
with a pond in the middle distance and woods beyond. The house was

new, built to Edith's order and completed just the year before; the furnishings and decorations were new; everything was tasteful, comfortable, and new.

After dinner, the little company moved out to the cool terrace for coffee, cigarettes, and conversation: James, Edith and Edward Wharton, Howard Sturgis, and Walter Van Rensselaer Berry, an intimate friend of both Howard and Edith. He was tall, gray-haired and aquiline-featured, a bachelor of middle age, a lawyer with an international practice. They were all cosmopolite New Yorkers, the two little Whartons and the three large men, with mutual friends in Europe and shared memories of old Manhattan. Their talk was anecdotal, personal, gossipy. James was the guest of honor, and the others all prompted him to talk, which he obligingly did.

Over the years there would be other meetings of this little circle, from which the silent Teddy would gradually escape. They would gather in later years at Queen's Acre, where a young admirer, Percy Lubbock, would describe their long, happy gossips. Edith Wharton would sit between Sturgis and James, upright and straight-backed, intelligently alive. Over the years, James remained at the center of their circle, and it was always for him to begin. Wharton watched and waited as he began from far back,

> while he hesitated and cast around over the vast field of possible utterances . . . while his eyes grew rounder and larger with their rolling twinkle as he foresaw his discovery and relished his approaching success; wait, wait! he seemed to say—you shall enjoy this with me in a moment—give me time! She waited, still precariously on the edge, all alert to receive it. Out it came, the period achieved, with a gathering momentum, and she snatched it away with her peal of mirth and carried it off on a further, wilder, airier flight. There was no hesitation in *her*; everything she possessed was at her finger's end, as quick as she needed it.

This repartee, their shared and often malicious humor, would be the basis of a long and warm rivalry and friendship between James and Wharton. The peculiarities of his talk required a reciprocal understanding and appreciation, which he rarely found in other settings. James was not often so at ease as he was with Wharton and in Sturgis's circle. The graceful, handsome Walter Berry, too, would become an intimate friend. He and James would travel to London together and would meet and correspond frequently in the years to come, and Berry would be a regular overnight visitor at Lamb House, one of those to whom James would write letters drenched in sexuality.

The other great asset of the Whartons in Lenox was their motorcar. The newly purchased American car had frequent halts and breakdowns, obliging the chauffeur regularly to turn mechanic; but when it was running it was magical. James immediately fell in love with the sensation of riding fast in an open car, and Edith took him, often with Sturgis and Berry, on long excursions into the Berkshire countryside. Setting off was always something of a trial for the efficient Edith, waiting impatiently for the cautious and dilatory James. But once they were under way, it was all frolic. As she later recalled:

> On one of our happy motor-trips among the hills of Western Massachusetts . . . allusions to Roman ruins and Gothic cathedrals furnished a great part of the jests . . . and one day, when his eye caught the fine peak rising alone in the vale between Deerfield and Springfield, with a wooden barrack of a "summer hotel" on its highest ledge, I told [James] that the hill was Mount Tom, and the building "the famous Carthusian monastery." "Yes, where the monks make Moxie," he flashed back.

James reveled in the freedom, the liberation from practical constraints that the motorcar bestowed. Miraculously transported from valley to mountain pass and down into the next valley, they whisked from the grim Shaker village near Lebanon to Hudson, New Hampshire, on the Massachusetts border, where the car broke down. They were obliged to have dinner in an inn there while the car was repaired, but it was all adventure. "The Whartons' commodious new motor . . . had fairly converted me to the sense of all the thing may do for one & one may get from it," he reported; and Wharton added, "This mode of locomotion seemed to him, as it had to me, an immense enlargement of life." The automobile allowed James to tour New England and to visit Theodate Pope's hilltop country house–cum–museum in Farmington, Connecticut. He lingered at The Mount for ten days before returning to Cambridge and gladly accepted an invitation to visit the Whartons in their house in Manhattan on the next leg of his journey.

For the months of November and December, James remained in Cambridge with William and his family, making frequent excursions into the countryside to visit old friends and relations. Making notes of his impressions, he ranged from Newport to Connecticut, with frequent dips into Boston and occasional forays as far as New York. With William, he went out to Concord again and spent two days with Bob and Mary. While they were there, Ellen Emerson, the elderly daughter of the sage, gave a supper party in honor of James's return to America. Miss Emerson had become distinctly odd in her old age, and on this occasion she reminded her guests that as children they had often performed for her a song called "Rumpty-Ho!" She asked them to sing it for her after dinner. Henry demurred, but William and Bob did their best.

James went to Cape Cod to visit Howard Sturgis in Cotuit; ran down to New York for a celebratory dinner that George Harvey had arranged. *The Golden Bowl* had just been published in the United States, and while it was not a Harper book, the dinner served to launch publicity for his tour, for the Harper magazine series and books that were to follow, and for *The Ambassadors*, which Harper had published within the year. *The Golden Bowl* added to the general air of triumphant return to America and to the novel.

James visited Newport, the island community in which his family had settled for a time, and the profound changes there deeply impressed him. The old Newport that he remembered was a cosmopolitan community of old Quaker, Beacon Hill, and southern plantation families, of Julia Ward Howe's outdoor teas, Holman Hunt's painting classes, and sketching expeditions with John La Farge; of French-speaking southerners and Dutch Calvinist New Yorkers, summering together in the cool north. That old cosmopolitan Newport had lasted for centuries and then utterly vanished. The only place in America where such cosmopolites could have existed, it seemed to James, was now gone. In its place he found the gigantic new "cottages" of the railroad and steel barons, large and senseless. The cottages were "white elephants," "all house and no garden," "witless," reminders that there were "prohibited degrees of witlessness." They bragged loudly to him of their owners' wealth and showed that in America the newly wealthy were as yet unable to create either a civilized nationality or a cosmopolitan community.

Exhausted by constant travel, he was yet enjoying himself thoroughly and had what amounted to a vacation among friends and relatives. For the first time in many years, he was not writing, had hardly put pen to paper except to make notes and answer letters. He was absorbing impressions, it was true, but he found little opportunity to set them down in systematic form, and when he wrote to Gosse he said that he might have to wait until his return to England to wring himself out.

Toward the end of his stay in Cambridge he did make a beginning on his first magazine article, dictating to William's stenographer, and began to struggle with problems of exposition. He was surprised by the pleasure he took in the New England countryside and by the golden haze with which memory suffused Cambridge and Boston. The constant problems of his art began to present themselves for solution. How to convey external phenomena through the medium of his own impressions?

The house in Cambridge helped him frame some of his themes. William was playing host that fall to a succession of European visitors, scientists and philosophers, primarily German, who were visiting the United States for the centennial celebration of the Louisiana Purchase, a sort of world's fair being held in Saint Louis, and who were stopping at Harvard on their way home. Partly through William's efforts Harvard was providing a home for the new German philosophy, an empirical, scientific idealism: experimental epistemology. William had persuaded Hugo Münsterberg to leave Germany and serve as head of a new laboratory of experimental psychology in Cambridge, for instance. James was struck by the contrast to English universities, which seemed to him enclaves of national culture and national identity. Harvard was growing, was becoming a great institution and marking its boundaries, setting itself off as an institution, like Oxford and Cambridge, but it was at the same time losing its national character. He searched for an image that would give a sense of Harvard's future, but that would also convey

> the "sinister," the "Münsterberg" possibility—the sort of class of future phenomena repres'ted by the "foreigner" coming in & taking possession; the union of the large purchasing power with the absence of prejudices; the easy submission to the foreign imposition . . . the very sovereign little truth that no branch, no phase, no face, nor facet is perhaps more "interesting" (than this) of the question that hangs so forever before one here . . . what the effect of the great Infusion (call it that) is going to be.

As autumn gave way to a cold and sunny winter, he walked out to Mount Auburn Cemetery, where so many of the great figures of Boston's past were buried, and then to the municipal cemetery in Cambridge where his parents and Alice's ashes lay. That moment certainly was an image of past love and the realities of loss: "Do that (the picture) with pink winter sunset & the ghosts," he told himself.

> To present these accidents is what it is to be a *master:* that & that only. Isn't the highest deepest note of the whole thing the never-to-be-lost memory of that hour . . . when I took my way alone . . . to that unspeakable group of graves. It was late, in November; the trees were all bare, the dusk to fall early, the air all still more turning to that terrible, deadly, pure polar pink that shows behind American winter woods. But I can't go over this—I can only, oh, so gently, so tenderly, brush it & breathe upon it. . . . I seemed then to know why I had done this; I seemed then to know why I had come . . . it made everything priceless.

William had designed the urn for Alice's grave, on which was carved a couplet from Dante that James noted in his journal when he returned to the house:

> *Dopo lungo exilio e martiro*
> *Viene a questa pace—*
>
> [Roughly: "After long exile and martyrdom
> He has come to this peace—"]

> This had taken him by the throat, and when he recorded it in his notebook, after a brief beginning he was able to say only, "But why do I write of the all unutterable & the all abysmal . . . the cold Medusa-face of life, of all the life *lived*, on every side. *Basta, basta!*"

He walked across the familiar bridge from Cambridge to Boston and up to the low crest of Beacon Hill, where on Ashburton Place the modest house the James family had briefly rented still stood. There, on the third floor, were the green-shuttered windows of his old bedroom. He traced again the familiar walk across Beacon Hill and down the sharp slope to Charles Street, which in those vanished years had marked the margins of the bay. On the water side of Charles Street he found Dr. Holmes's narrow redbrick row house, the "door of importances, in fact of immensities." The visit to Boston, to Ashburton Street and to Dr. Holmes's house, called up memories of the young Wendell Holmes.

In the spring of 1865, Holmes was back from the war and studying law. Holmes and James had exchanged visits, had become intimate friends. How could James, at sixty-one, write of Boston and Cambridge, except through the glow of that remembered intimacy of forty years before? How could he render for readers the quality that his memories had bestowed on the silent houses on Ashburton Place and Charles Street? He could not write frankly about the past.

> The point for me (for fatal, for impossible expansion) is that I knew there, *had* there, in the ghostly old C[ambridge]. . . *l'initiation première* (the divine, the unique), there & in Ashburton Place. . . . Ah, the epoch-making weeks of the spring of 1865! . . . Something—some fine, su-perfine, supersubtle mystic breath of that may come in perhaps. . . . Ah, that pathetic, heroic little *personal* prime of my own . . . of unforget-table gropings & findings & sufferings & strivings & play of sensibility & of inward passion there. The hours, the moments, the days, come back to me . . . particular little thrills & throbs & daydreams there.

These memories led swiftly to another, a memory of the following summer when he had called at Doctor Holmes's house to inquire after Wendell:

> I can't help, either, just touching with my pen-point (here, here, only here) the recollection of that (probably August) day when I went up to Boston from Swampscott & called in Charles St. for news of O.W.H., then on his 1st flushed & charming visit to England . . . & *vibrated* so with the wonder & romance & curiosity & dim weak tender (oh, ten-der!) envy of it. . . . Oh, strange little intensities of history, of efface-ability; oh, delicate little odd links in the long chain, kept unbroken for the fingers of one's tenderest touch! Sanctities, pieties, treasures, abysses!

James lingered in Cambridge well into December, somewhat to the dis-appointment of Elizabeth Jordan, who was eager to introduce him in New York as a *Bazar* contributor. Newspapers and literary journals had been gossiping and speculating about his arrival: What would this chron-icler of manners, this author whose books were read by the elite of two continents, say about his native country? "The Return of Henry James," promised *The Literary Digest;* "The Return of the Native," said *Outlook,* inevitably. *The New York Times Saturday Review of Books* editorialized that James would do well to visit the originals of his fictional New England mill town, "Woollett," that he had portrayed so meagerly in *The Ambassadors* and the following week again editorialized grumpily that he was more a "literary topic" than at any time since the publication of "Daisy Miller." The weeklies agreed, as *Harper's Weekly* put it, that James's visit was of considerable interest to the public, since people wondered what his impressions would be. *Life* wrote humorously, twice, just before and just after his arrival, about the discomfiture that Americans would suffer under his critical gaze. *The Golden Bowl* was reviewed, and James was universally conceded to be the leading American novelist, perhaps the greatest writer in English now that Hardy and Meredith were no longer publishing, although his eminence was often grudgingly conceded and nearly every reviewer complained of the obscurity of his late style.

Dozens of newspapers along his expected route across the continent reviewed his recent work, and *The Independent* said that he was to the literary world what William Astor was to the social order, an arbiter at the summit. The *New-York Tribune* published an interview, the sort of personal account of his living arrangements in London and Rye, with a photograph of the author himself, that had so upset du Maurier.

Despite Elizabeth Jordan's eagerness to display her lion, James returned briefly to Boston. His teeth were hurting, a Boston dentist had ordered a major renovation of his mouth, and this would be a trial. Safe and effective anesthetics for dentistry were not yet known. As he told Bob:

> At the last my Dentist-Dr. man couldn't *touch* me without torture, & yet I had to be drilled by him for hours together. . . . I am . . . still in terror of possible inflammations, & *re*-openings of the ordeal.

Even aside from dental problems, he had ceased to Fletcherize while dining at others' tables. He was eating richer foods and was gaining weight, and his digestion suffered its old disorders. As he again set off southward, he took with him a supply of cascara, an herbal laxative. Later in the winter, when he ran out of cascara while traveling and found that it could not be obtained locally, he was obliged to wire William for a supply.

While still in Boston, James called on Olivia Cushing Andersen, Hendrik's widowed sister-in-law and patron who was visiting her own family, and they had a pleasant visit and a long talk. Hendrik had suffered from headaches and attacks of vertigo that past summer and had been obliged to leave Rome for Turin, where he had consulted a specialist. His planned trip to America would be delayed. Olivia reported that Hendrik was now recovered, however, although he would probably not arrive in America while James was there. Before leaving Boston for New York, James wrote to Hendrik at length:

> [F]or God's sake, dear, dear, boy, work gently & *sanely*, watch yourself well, put on the brake, twiddle your thumbs . . . & think of your poor helpless far-off but all-devoted H.J., who seems condemned almost never to be near you. . . .
>
> You must come to me at dear little Lamb House next summer. Think of me there with an easy mind & let me only yearn for your enabling me to think in somewhat the same way of you. I hold you, dear boy, in my innermost love & count on your feeling me—in every throb of your soul & sense—to do it. Keep up your heart & swing your hammer wide, & we will have good days together again yet.

As he made his way to New York and southward that winter, he sent behind him a steady stream of letters to Hendrik Andersen, to Howard Sturgis, to other friends in England, to William and Alice in Cambridge, to Bob, Mary, and Mamie in Concord.

21

AMERICANISM

America had emerged from its long depression and was prosperous again, but the industrial organization of the country had changed. The United States Steel trust now held roughly 90 percent of the iron- and steelmaking capacity of the nation; the railroads had been reorganized into a handful of regional monopolies; the petroleum, beef, sugar, and tobacco industries had each been organized as monopolies. A new class of unimaginably wealthy men, industrialists and financiers, organized and controlled these consolidations. The du Ponts, Carnegies, Morgans, Rockefellers, and a few other American families rivaled the royalty of Europe and Asia in wealth and ostentation.

Much of this personal wealth was held in real estate, and the magnates competed to build houses in New York that were on the scale of the great palaces of Europe. The Census Bureau estimated that the land and buildings on Manhattan Island represented more than 5 percent of the entire national wealth. But real estate in Manhattan was not like the great estates of Europe, entailed, bracketed, and walled, permanent as human ingenuity could make it. There were no entailed estates in America, land was a commodity bought and sold daily, and the great houses that fronted on the new avenues passed from hand to hand. "The whole costly up-town demonstration" struck James with its air of pathos: "Massive private ease attended with no force of assertion beyond the hour."

He could describe this new society only by contrasting it to the older civilizations of England, France, and Italy. There was a great flattening of social distinctions, which was admirable in its way. But forms were lost, shopkeepers were rude, and workmen came to the front door without ceremony. Liberty and wealth manifested themselves not merely as a flattening but also more distressingly as a loosening of social bonds. The

European extended family was a permanent institution, rooted in place and extending over generations, encompassing wide circles of relationship and dependency. The New York family was a temporary arrangement between husband and wife, readily severable. Democracy had extended its reach into the home, and children seemed as independent as their parents. In Europe, established churches and aristocratic, landowning families, tied to the graves and altars of their ancestors, had shaped their communities and the landscape. A family in Europe was rooted in the soil. Elite schools and universities, far from being engines of absorption of foreign influence, were enclaves in which a national culture was nurtured and transmitted. In America, there were no feudal institutions, there never had been any, no primogeniture or entailed estates, which was all to the good so far as justice was served; but the newly rich did not seem to feel the need to create a civilized equivalent. The churches, European institutions transplanted to America, were literally overshadowed by commerce: office buildings with their open, provisional air now dominated the skyline. Trinity Church, whose slim spire had dominated the foot of Manhattan as James remembered it, now stood in the shade of the office towers that loomed over it like Alpine cliffs. The men's clubs were filled with businessmen talking shop; there was nothing like the Reform or the Athenaeum. The featureless grid of Manhattan, the destruction of the surrounding landscape by sprawling development: these too were expressions of democracy and the free sale of land, unhindered by any aesthetic or historic sense.

Instead of finding the self-contained assurance of older aristocracies, James encountered newly wealthy Americans eager to please him and insistently curious about his appraisal of America. He was constantly asked by his hosts what he thought of them and of the world they were constructing, questions that struck him as touching and almost pathetic.

When he came to write of the intrusions of the marketplace into every corner of life, of the loosening of social bonds and the loss of civility, he was constrained from writing about his hosts. Yet he was obliged by his sensibility and his art to recount his impressions as they arose from a personal relationship, in a uniquely embodied moment. Instead of wealthy New Yorkers, therefore, when he began to write out his impressions he spoke of houses, clubs, and office buildings that spoke to him, opened their windows and doors to the public generally, made of themselves a single vast public market, where there were no enclosures in which privacy and civilization could flourish. The mansions on upper Fifth Avenue reached out to him for approval, but they spoke to him of nothing but temporary business success, placing themselves between an absent future and an absent past. "No," James lectured the houses, "you overdo it for what you are—you overdo it still more for what you may be." James met the superrich, visited their houses, looked with a cold eye on the civilization they were building. There was nothing visible here except money getting, a new culture of wealth without history or future.

He was uneasy on another score. In the year of his return, 1904, about one million new immigrants were admitted to the United States, a nation of 90 million. Perhaps a fourth of the immigrants were Jews from eastern Europe, and many spoke little or no English. The great question of the day was how they were all to be assimilated. Jane Addams in Chicago had begun the great venture of her Settlement House, patterned in part after Mary Ward's, where immigrants from abroad and migrants from the South were to be housed and taught, educated and acculturated. Settlement houses also sprang up in the East, along with athletic leagues, basketball leagues, workmen's circles. But the greatest engine of acculturation was the public school. All children were required to attend, and there the children of immigrants learned English through abrupt immersion and acquired the rudiments of cultural literacy. Internal migrants from the South and the inhabitants of Indian reservations were also subjected to compulsory public education. For the Indians, this often meant removing children from their homes and families.

Theodore Roosevelt spoke and wrote about the importance of "Americanism." His view of the question, ironically, was essentially European: the white, Protestant, English-speaking people who governed the United States were both a race and a nation. They faced dangers abroad and at home, dangers of being swamped by unassimilated immigrants, corrupted by foreign ideologies, outbred by the colored races. As police commissioner of New York, he had waged war against opium, prostitution, and other foreign evils and had championed a manly patriotism that he called "True Americanism."

> One may fall very far short of treason and yet be an undesirable citizen in the community. The man who becomes Europeanized, who loses the power of doing good work on this side of the water, and who loses his love for his native land, is not a traitor; but he is a silly and undesirable citizen. He is as emphatically a noxious element in our body politic as is the man who comes here from abroad and remains a for-

eigner. . . . It is not only necessary to Americanize the immigrants of foreign birth who settle among us, but it is even more necessary for those among us who are by birth and descent already Americans not to throw away our birthright. . . . We believe in waging relentless war on rank-growing evils of all kinds. . . .

With reference to the Americanizing of the newcomers to our shores[:] We must Americanize them in every way, in speech, in political ideas and principles, and in their way of looking at the relations between Church and State. We welcome the German or the Irishman who becomes an American. We have no use for the German or Irishman who remains such. We do not want German-Americans or Irish-Americans to figure as such in our social and political life; we want only Americans.

Roosevelt's Americanism was vigorous and manly, a warrior's and sportsman's creed. He was at pains to distinguish it from the simple bigotry of the Know-Nothings and he emphasized the American tradition of tolerance for belief. But he was uncompromising: the cosmopolite and the immigrant must accept American nationalism whole.

Foreign immigration and the failure to absorb large dependent populations of African Americans and Indians were being met with violence. Lynchings of blacks in the South and of immigrants of Asian ancestry in the West were increasing; the Ku Klux Klan was expanding its ranks, and its racialism would be celebrated in the first feature-length motion picture, *Birth of a Nation*. In popular fiction, a sentimental image of the "cowboy" and the western gunfighter, the vigilante, became the embodied image of Americanism. Owen Wister's racially charged *The Virginian* was a bestselling novel and the model for countless imitators. The remaining Indian lands were being overrun, broken up, and sold. The newly powerful trade unions demanded and got national bans on the importation of contract labor from abroad; immigration from China was banned outright, in violation of a long-standing treaty.

The recent assassination of President McKinley by a foreign-born anarchist had fed the fires of bigotry. Federal law now barred the admission to the United States of foreign "anarchists," and political radicals were being rounded up and deported. New York, the portal of immigration, adopted a virulent "antisedition" law aimed at foreign ideologies.

Just as James was embarking on his journey southward, John Hay was privately consulting Wendell Holmes about the constitutionality of the

Chinese Exclusion Act, which Senate Democrats had put up for renewal. Holmes thought it a reasonable measure, well within the power of the Congress to protect the national identity. Japan, eager for American support in the Pacific and wishing to avoid the stigma of such a legislative ban, had grudgingly agreed to a "gentleman's agreement" to prohibit working-class emigration to the United States.

Despite such measures to limit migrant and contract labor, the tide of immigration continued to rise, swelled by the millions fleeing pogroms in eastern Europe—the failing regime of the czar had turned to war against the supposed alien within—and Turkey, fleeing grinding destitution in the south of the new Italian kingdom, fleeing war and poverty in the collapsing Austro-Hungarian Empire. New legislation was accordingly being planned. Congress would shortly reaffirm a doctrine that dated from the founding of the republic, that only "free, white" persons were eligible to become naturalized citizens of the United States, a rule modified only by Civil War amendments that admitted persons of African descent. The courts began to puzzle over the question of whether Syrians and high-caste Indians were "white."

From his first days in New England, James noted the universal presence of immigrants, even in the New Hampshire woods. He thought that little could be done to Americanize these new arrivals, who brought other languages and cultures with them. Their children were another matter, however. Public schools and the other machinery of Americanization would have its chance with them:

> The machinery is colossal—nothing is more characteristic of the country than the development of this machinery, in the form of the political and social habit, the common school and the newspaper; so that there are always millions of little transformed strangers growing up in regard to whom the idea of intimacy of relation may be as freely cherished as you like. They are the stuff of whom brothers and sisters are made.

In the note with which he prefaced his published observations, however, he warned readers that they would not find this machinery described in his book. He would not rely on the "prodigious reports," the numberless "newspapers, reports, surveys and blue-books" that addressed such questions. He would rely solely on his own impressions. He had found that personal impressions had unique value and a truth that could

not be found in statistics and documents. James was an artist, not a journalist, and was determined to employ the methods he had so painstak-
ingly developed. He would observe America through the lens of his own
sensibility, with all the artistry, self-awareness, and vivid recall of which
he was capable.

His own remembered New York was a little world, a stretch of Fifth Avenue and a long block to the east and west, along the half mile from Washington Square to Union Square. It was a world that he, the Whartons,
Walter Berry, and Howard Sturgis knew and had shared, an old Dutch
and Scots Calvinist New York, a village of moderate wealth, of solid
brownstone row houses with walled gardens behind them. He was glad
to accept Mary Cadwalader's invitation to stay in her brownstone house
in this tiny world, on Eleventh Street just off Fifth Avenue, for the holiday season. In the new year, he migrated only a short way, to the Whartons' house on Fourth Avenue. There he was close to Elizabeth Jordan, to
his cousins in Gramercy Park Square, to the photographer to whom he
went for publicity portraits, and to Bay Emmet, who had established a
studio in Manhattan and was painting portraits.

Elizabeth Jordan held a dinner for him on his arrival in her house in
Gramercy Park, to which she invited writers of his own generation, old
friends for the most part, as well as the younger authors whom he did not
know.

Although there were new faces, this insular world had changed little
since the years of his childhood, and he was able to recapture his vivid
memories of that time. As with New England impressions, when he came
to write of his return to Manhattan he would lay down a wash of memories over his impressions of the present scene. The old New York that he
found still intact, with its long history and settled sense of itself, was in
danger of being overshadowed and crushed by the mansions of the newly
wealthy closing in upon it from the north, the skyscrapers from the
south, and the crowds that beat upon its walls from east and west, where
the streets and avenues were filling with immigrants.

Early in January, he began his journey southward through the former
Confederacy, hoping to reach Florida quickly. His family had ties to
Florida from Reconstruction times. Mary and Mamie James had gone

ahead of him, planning to winter in Florida, and he expected to meet them there. He still hoped to dip down to Cuba, to catch a glimpse of this new American outpost, and to return via New Orleans, Saint Louis, and Chicago, lecturing in each city, and thence westward on the fabled transcontinental railroad, reaching California by the spring.

His first address was given to a friendly audience in Philadelphia. The hall was packed to suffocation with five or six hundred people and was a fashionable crowd for a literary address. He delivered the speech he had prepared in advance, "The Lesson of Balzac."

Later critics would note Balzac's influence on James's novels, especially the social commentaries of *The Bostonians* and *The Princess Casamassima* period. But the importance to him of Balzac went far beyond social commentary. James's career as an author had begun, in a manner of speaking, with his reading of *Eugénie Grandet*, in the summer of his seventeenth year. In the long-ago Newport days John La Farge and James had gone on sketching expeditions together, La Farge had painted James's portrait, and they had formed a lifelong friendship. James had learned to observe, and acquired something of the religion of experience, from John Ruskin's manual of drawing and Hunt's exercises in capturing the light. But La Farge had given him a decisive turn by lending him a magnificent leather-bound edition of Balzac. Unlike the writers in English whom James knew, Balzac's fiction was intensified realism, a sort of history. His novels and tales were infused with the strong forces of greed and sexuality, and the lesson that Balzac taught was the art of living consciously, imaginatively, engaged with one's world; of fashioning art from that life and life from art.

> [Balzac's] plan was to handle, primarily, not a world of ideas, animated by figures representing those ideas; but the packed and constituted, the palpable, provable world before him. . . . His happy fate is accordingly to *partake* of life, actively, assertively, not passively, narrowly, in mere sensibility and sufferance.

At every moment, Balzac engaged his experience imaginatively, seeking to penetrate and understand; this active engagement enabled him to paint his immense portrait of the France of his day, an image of life. After gathering experience within himself, for "no other economy explains his achievement," he would retreat to his study and in perfect solitude, "positively that of a Benedictine monk leading his life within the four walls of his convent," write his great work. James called Balzac the greatest master of the novel, the man who was really the father of them all.

> I can only speak of him, and can only speak, as a man of his own craft, an emulous fellow-worker, who has learned from him more of the lessons of the engaging mystery of fiction than from anyone else. . . .
> He was always living in the particular necessary, the particular intended connection—was always astride of his imagination, always charging, with his heavy lance at rest, at every object that sprang up in his path.
> What it comes back to, in other words, is the intensity with which we live . . . and his intensity is recorded on every page of his work.

These were only preconditions; what counted in the end was the work itself. Balzac's life and work had to be taken together to be properly understood, and the work, taken as a whole, taught a still more fundamental lesson:

> the lesson that there is no convincing art that is not ruinously expensive. . . . Nothing counts but the excellent; nothing exists . . . but the superlative.

The lecture was a great success with audiences, and bookings multiplied. As he was speaking from a prepared and memorized text, James's stammer subsided. He was revealed to himself as a public speaker. He was an old man, it was too late, perhaps; but he would see. Before the end of his tour he would regret that he had prepared only a single address for general audiences; he would have liked to accept more of the invitations that began to stream in. He was almost immediately asked to make a second talk, at Bryn Mawr. But before he could deliver this address, he was obliged to make a detour to Washington, to meet the president.

The invitation from John and Clara Hay had reached him in Cambridge, in November, soon after the national election in which Roosevelt was returned to the White House in his own right. Now, in January, there was to be a private dinner at Hay's house on Lafayette Square, opposite the White House. The president and Mrs. Roosevelt would attend this dinner. On the following day, James was to attend the annual diplomatic reception at the White House and remain for a second dinner there with the president, with whom he would be seated.

The two dinners were evidently meant, among other things, to effect a reconciliation. Ten years earlier, the energetic Roosevelt, who had just begun his rhetorical crusade for manly "Americanism," had publicly denounced James as an exemplar of Europeanized, un-American effeminacy. James, in reply, had called Roosevelt a dangerous jingo. Now James's old mentor John Hay was the senior member of the president's cabinet and was attempting to reconcile Roosevelt to a more cosmopolitan circle. The dinners early in the new year to which James was invited were part of an elaborate launching of the new social season and the newly ratified administration. The diplomatic corps and the leaders of society were being introduced to the idea of Washington as an equal partner of London, a world capital with a newly won empire to govern. Early in the new year, Hay and his intimate friend and next-door neighbor Henry Adams were instrumental in organizing a series of meetings and festivities, and Hay had invited Henry James, John La Farge, and Augustus Saint-Gaudens—all old friends—to Washington. Adams added his own invitation to stay with him when they came. They remained for a week with Adams, and had a fond reunion among themselves.

The private dinner at Hay's house was therefore a remarkable occasion. In addition to the president and Edith Roosevelt, and the Hays, the guests included Adams, La Farge, Saint-Gaudens, and Henry James, nearly all the newly elected members of the American Academy of Arts and Letters. Except for the president, they were old men. Henry James, at sixty-one, was the youngest of the guests, and both Hay and Saint-Gaudens were close to death; there would not be another such gathering. But no record of the conversation was kept, Roosevelt did not bring his secretary, and Hay noted in his journal only that the dinner had been a success.

On the following day, James attended the annual diplomatic reception at the White House and remained afterward for supper, seated at a table of eight with the president himself. As James recounted the occasion, he was seated "next to the lady (wife of a cabinet member) who was next to [the president], so that I had a great deal of his extraordinary talk and indescribable overwhelming, but really very attaching personality."

A reconciliation with Roosevelt was accomplished; the president ceased to inveigh against James and spoke of him, at least in public, in friendly terms. In his letters and published account of his travels in America, James responded with a warm appreciation of the cultural atmosphere in Washington, for which he gave the president credit—which in itself was a modest propaganda victory for Hay. Aside from personal considerations, the rapprochement was planned as one small element in

Hay's efforts to bring the United States and Great Britain together. James had been the intimate friend of successive American ministers to the Court of St. James's, beginning with James Russell Lowell and Hay himself; he was well acquainted in both Liberal and Conservative circles in London and was a friend of the present prime minister. Hay evidently saw that, aside from the importance of putting American culture on suitable display, James's personal stature and diplomatic usefulness would be enhanced if the diplomatic corps saw him dining with the president. Responding to Hay's suggestion, James expressed in a jocular and self-deprecating tone his happy willingness to assist in personal diplomacy:

> I think indeed I ought to become the special ward, pupil, pensioner (moral,) object of pathetic yet hopeful interest, in short, of the Department of State, & that under some such fostering care & cultivation I might be made, somehow, internationally, to "pay."

After the diplomatic reception and dinner, James lingered in Washington for a week, longer than planned, camping at Henry Adams's house, where he received invitations and some calls; he lunched with the Hays and the Henry Cabot Lodges and dined with the new French ambassador, Jules Jusserand, an old friend from Jusserand's posting as consul in London.

James wrote to Holmes immediately on his arrival in Washington, hoping to see him, and Holmes answered promptly, but their schedules could not be made to coincide. James promised to write again when he returned to Washington on his lecture tour.

His extensive American friendships and his new celebrity combined to deluge James with invitations that he could not easily refuse. His hostess in New York, Mary Cadwalader, began calling him "Célimare," the eponymous hero of a French play who was well loved by women, and James with a smile now signed himself "Célimare" when he wrote to her, explaining his complex movements and the reasons for declining another of her generous invitations. He hastened back from Washington to Philadelphia, to deliver his address at Bryn Mawr, and then spent an unforeseen four days at Butler Place, Fanny Kemble's well-remembered country house, with her daughter Sarah Wister and her grandson the novelist Owen Wister. His temporarily repaired right front tooth came out, and he was afraid he would have to return to Boston, but William located a dentist for him in Philadelphia, and he remained for three days at the Rittenhouse Club until the tooth and his appearance could be repaired. He then resumed his much-delayed journey south.

Railroads themselves were one of the principal features of his journey: "the great straddling, bellowing railway, the high, heavy, dominant American train that so reverses the relation of the parties concerned, suggesting somehow that the country exists for the 'cars,' which overhang it like a conquering army." The railroads were the embodiment of the heedless power of commerce. The ugly stations and the unfenced level crossings, the "localization of death and destruction," contributed to his sense of the railroads' dominance, their general air of bossing things. The proliferation of rail lines, and of the still newer automobiles and paved roads, had facilitated a great sprawl of characterless houses, unconnected to one another or to any village or town, blighting the landscape. Yet he adored the long-haul passenger trains, their comfort and speed, as much as he had enjoyed Edith Wharton's automobile.

The journey south continued in dreary fashion. The weather was bad, snow was falling in Richmond, Virginia, and the earth was covered with snow all the way to South Carolina. He was in a hurry to reach Florida and to experience at least briefly a tropical climate. He paused, however, at Biltmore, in North Carolina, to visit George Vanderbilt at his Biltmore House estate, where the weather was still vile and James was kept in his room by an attack of gout. He felt obliged to cut down his visit to Charleston, where he was to lecture, to an overnight stay. He was running far behind his optimistic schedule and now wrote to Mamie James about the delays. To save time, he would drop his plan to visit Daytona Beach and would travel instead to Palm Beach and meet her and her mother in Saint Augustine.

This Southland that he had not visited before was strange to him, and he to it. Outside the Charleston Hotel, waiting for his bags to be loaded onto the ancient yellow horse-drawn bus that would carry him to the railroad station, a gentleman standing beside him and, likewise waiting, said for some reason, "I guess we manage our traveling here better than in your country!"—to which James could find no reply.

He lectured as he went and gained the impression from his hosts and his audiences, and from glimpses of the towns through which he passed, that the South had not yet after forty years recovered from slavery or the war that had been fought to end it. The marks of physical devastation had healed, but the community of whites seemed impoverished and meager, and if the blacks were still poorer they seemed to have more sense of themselves and of their dignity. James remarked that W. E. B. Du Bois, a black man, had written the best book to have come from the South since the war. (This was a little inaccurate, as Du Bois was a New Englander, then teaching in Atlanta; but it served to strike a comparison.) The white men who were James's hosts and whom he met in passing in railroad cars or hotels were often charming, but he sensed a capacity for violence behind their excellent manners. He was not collecting data about lynchings, however, only gathering direct impressions.

Palm Beach was a blur of brilliant sky, lush vegetation, resort hotels, and well-dressed women: "this (almost) coral strand, where the sea today is sapphire, [and] the women (there are five thousand of them) are in fluttering white." Hastily he continued on to Saint Augustine, a brief visit with Mary and Mamie there, and glimpses of the four-hundred-year-old Spanish conquest. He was distinctly disappointed with the ordinary Protestant Americanness of Florida, having vaguely expected to find it exotically and historically Spanish, Creek, and Seminole, the Florida of the Seminole Wars of which he had read as a child. A journey to the South should have taken him at least to Naples, as it were, but "a south without church-fronts and church interiors [was] superficially as strange, in its way, as a Methodism of the sub-tropic night." These were only glimpses; he was obliged to hasten northward again, back to Boston and his dentist. Infection had evidently set in, James was again in pain, and renewed surgery was required.

In Boston, after an exhausting journey, James was obliged to spend ten days of agony under the drill, presumably replacing temporary prostheses and completing the plan for renovation of his teeth. Toward the end of his ordeal James gave an account of it to Howells, who had just returned from abroad:

My whole time has been ravaged by the Dentist—through the circumstance of my having fallen, early in the winter, a victim to the fiendish ambition of a very perfect performer, in that line, in Boston, who conceived a vast and comprehensive plan of campaign at my expense, which he is still (whenever I can scramble back to him) ruthlessly carrying out. That whole business has made, truthfully speaking, such a deep dark hole in my time, my nerves, my strength, my ability to do anything else, that I literally came near going to pieces under it.

Much of the planned tour of the United States, derailed by deaths on his first attempt, would again have to be abandoned, blocked once more by the intractability of material life. He would set off straight from Boston to Chicago, making a detour to Saint Louis, where he was committed to give a lecture although it was no longer on his route; to Indianapolis to lecture; back to Chicago for the scheduled lecture there; and then to California.

Three days in Saint Louis, giving two lectures; three days in Chicago, again lecturing twice. Although he and Pond's Lecture Bureau had agreed to keep the number of lectures low by demanding high fees, from $250 to $500, he had an audience of seven hundred in Chicago and was booked for a second evening for the overflow. If he had prepared a second lecture, he reflected, he might have earned as much more again. But Chicago itself did not attract him. On the day of his lecture he was accompanied into the city by a young professor, Robert Herrick, from the new university founded by John D. Rockefeller, which he had been invited to visit. Herrick recalled the occasion later:

> I accompanied him from a luncheon engagement [at the university] on the far South Side via the suburban train along the wintry shore of the Lake—it was then bleak March—through the smudged purlieus of the untidy city into the black gloom of the Loop. I have still in memory a quite vivid picture of the distinguished expatriate sitting huddled on the dingy bench of the suburban car, draped in the loose folds of a nondescript British mackintosh, hands clasped about a baggy British umbrella, his face haggard under the shuttling blows of the Chicago panorama. "What monstrous ugliness!" he murmured once, in a tone of pure physical anguish.

He went from Chicago to Notre Dame and Indianapolis to lecture and then on to Milwaukee for a day's visit with Wilky's widow, Caroline, and her son Cary. They had kept a slight distance from the Jameses, but Henry was glad to be able to see them and refresh the relation. Cary saw him onto the train to Chicago; from Chicago he set off across the country via the Southern Pacific Railroad, across the great American desert to Los Angeles.

> I reached this racketing spot at 10 o'clock last night many hours late, & after an ordeal, of alkali deserts & sleep-defying "sleepers" drawn out almost to madness. The *noise* that surrounds me is Bedlamitical . . . but I have been walking about for a couple of hours & detect (mainly in the flower-shops,) symptoms of a climate. Also, this hotel [the Van Nuys] seems excellent . . . [but] I want to get off to woods & waters.

And so he did, leaving Los Angeles promptly after giving his lecture for Monterey and San Francisco, where he settled for a few pleasant days. Lending a particular happy quality to his memories of San Francisco was his meeting with Bruce Porter, a young architect. They met at the Bohemian Club, a gathering of artists, musicians, writers, and performers. It was a men's club to which some prominent businessmen also belonged but more to his taste than the businessmen's clubs in New York. The Bohemian Club reminded him of his circle of cosmopolitan London bachelors, and he found Porter in particular a most congenial companion. A few days later, Porter described his encounter with James to a friend:

> We hit it off from the very first instant that he came in—the good round man in clothes that had a hint of shabbiness—with the fine head & the kind, sad eyes. . . . O! I'm set up! The police man on the corner knows there is something wrong with me. It's perceptible . . . that I've had a romantic adventure. . . . It *is* a case—*my* case—but then it's evidently his. He did not for a moment let me doubt that; & when his trunk was packed, & we stood face to face in the gaudy little hotel parlor to say good bye, we fell into each other's arms (literally). Well, the tears were in *his* eyes—& I'd forgotten hours back that he was Henry James—he was just the dearest friend of my earliest recollection.

Porter accompanied him to the railroad station and later confessed that for a moment he had been tempted to follow James to Seattle. James, for his part, kept up this new friendship as well as he could at long range. Porter visited him in London, and when James returned to America years later he made efforts to see him. The lapses were filled by affectionate letters, which, as so often with other lifelong friends, began with elaborate apologies and explanations for long silences and concluded with

James's declaration, far beyond the conventional expressions of affection between men,

> simply believe me & trust me & "like" me still, simply take the inevitability of the whole thing from me as part of the penalty of having so calculably incalculable & so irregularly regular a *lover.*

James stopped for a day in Portland, Oregon, to give a lecture and then went on immediately to Seattle for a visit with Bob's son, Edward, who had married and settled there. From Seattle, he was to go back across the continent to New York City, and he sent a message ahead to George Higginson, who had been his host in Chicago. James would stop in Chicago only long enough to change trains. He asked Higginson to reserve a stateroom for him on the

> next & swiftest night express to New York. . . . The best of everything please & damn the expense: I am so travel-sore that I am reckless. . . . I got here only this a.m. from San Francisco—sorry, very sorry, to have seen the last of the really very handsome California & to have had to see it all too briefly & meagerly. . . . Still it remains *the* impression (it *will* do so), of all my months in the U.S.

On his return from California, James hastened down to Washington again to deliver yet another lecture. These engagements were very profitable, and he did not like to miss any opportunity. He wrote ahead to tell Holmes of his brief visit.

"Henry James is here," wrote Justice Holmes from Washington to a mutual friend on the last day of April 1905. "He discoursed," Holmes reported from Washington, "mainly to ladies, yesterday afternoon, on the lesson of Balzac & said some good things."

This "mainly to ladies" was a dig. There was a certain edginess in their relation. James, gossiping after his lecture, remarked that Holmes had "chosen success," which also was not complimentary. But James was glad to be in Washington again and to see his old friend. On this second passage through the city, the aspect of Washington had utterly changed. The midwinter city that he had visited, the city of boulevards and public monuments, was now engulfed by the blossoms of a luxurious southern summer. The streets had become leafy refuges, and the whole city had a rural air. Congress had adjourned, and the president was in Portsmouth, New Hampshire, presiding over negotiations that would bring an end to the war between Russia and Japan. Holmes was obliged to remain in Washington until the end of the term of his Court, however, before removing himself to the Massachusetts shore for the summer, and they dined on the first of May, a few days past James's sixty-second birthday and Holmes's sixty-fourth.

Holmes was not as well known to the public as he would later be. He was still a newcomer in Washington, moreover, and there was a hint of defensive arrogance in the wide wings of his mustache, now turning white, and the rattle of his monologues. His initial intimacy with Roosevelt, who had appointed him to the Court, was over. Roosevelt was ostentatiously displeased by a dissenting opinion Holmes had written gratuitously, as it seemed, in an important antitrust case, and he was no longer a social lion nor sought out by the diplomatic corps. James, by contrast, had been making a royal progress through the country, dining with the president, his movements widely reported in the newspapers. So there was a little edge to their relations. But Holmes came to hear his old friend lecture, and James went to his house on I Street for dinner.

The house was a narrow brownstone not unlike Dr. Holmes's house in Boston, and Fanny had brought their furniture with them, so that the house was a Boston enclave amid the tropical greenery of Washington in summer. Fanny and their adopted niece, Dorothy, had already departed for New England, so the two men dined alone and lingered at the table to smoke. They might indeed have been in Boston, these two old men with their ghostly memories standing beside them. In the dark, paneled dining room were Copley's portraits of James Fenimore Cooper and Holmes's great-grandfather Jonathan Jackson. Holmes smoked his carefully rationed cigar, James a cigarette. Perhaps they shared a bottle of port, in the English fashion, although both men were careful of their health and had grown abstemious.

22

❧

WORK AND LIFE AS A WHOLE

Manhattan from the Battery to Gramercy Park was his childhood home: the crooked streets and parks like village squares, where James was born, where his father and uncles had had offices, where his father had lectured. This was still the locus of his mother's large family. Particularly in the narrow streets between Washington Square and Union Square, James felt that continuity from generation to generation that was for him the sense of family and of place. In Manhattan and in the still-rural region along the Hudson north of the city, where the James family built its country houses, even the quality of the light evoked his past. In his young manhood James had tried to settle in Manhattan, before fleeing finally to Europe, and he had returned in his old age with a sense of anticipation. On his last visit, twenty-two years earlier, he had spoken of returning to New York—"when I am sixty years old!"—to enjoy his success. He would call the definitive edition of his collected fiction the New York Edition.

Over the course of its first three centuries New York had crept northward up Manhattan Island only as far as Gramercy Park. Its tall, gray-eyed young men and women were the models for James's fictional Americans, and New York was at the core of his sense of himself. The ideal American was one who had traveled, who had acquired confidence and cosmopolitan culture, but, like Lambert Strether and Chad Newsome, like Adam Verver and James himself, kept his ties to place and family. He thought of himself as a cosmopolitan American; to be only cosmopolitan would have been to lose something precious.

Returning now to New York, James's perceptions were touched with personal apprehensions. He revisited the places of his childhood and found a guide to show him the neighborhoods in which immigrants had settled. He went to Ellis Island for an afternoon; he ranged on foot throughout Manhattan and was frightened and horrified. In his tale of Mrs. Gracedew, he had shown her cheerfully preserving an old estate by opening it to a handful of vulgar Jews, who paid for the privilege. Like Trollope, he had observed and written of the growing influence of German-speaking Jews in the worlds of finance and commerce in London. He had written a graceful, fictional tribute to his friend William Heinemann. But the phenomena he now observed were entirely outside his previous experience: the movements of whole peoples, settlements that were cities in themselves where languages were spoken that he did not even recognize. He felt at home in London, Paris, and Rome and had written comfortably and knowledgeably of "Europe," but Warsaw, Vienna, and Budapest were hardly more than names to him. In the New Hampshire woods he had encountered a young man whose language and nationality of origin he could not even guess (Armenian?) but who had proudly declared himself an American. Now in the New York of his best memories James found whole communities whose origins he did not know, that were alien to him in a new way.

The representative image of the new immigrant was an eastern European Jew, and James arranged to have himself conducted through the Jewish quarter in the Lower East Side of Manhattan by a "high public functionary" who lived in the ghetto and who spoke knowledgeably of it as they drove downtown on a warm summer night. Writing of this experience afterward, James fell back on the imagery of scientific investigation, as he had when writing of London's underclass. Children were out in the crowded streets, escaping the heat of the tenements; to James they did not play but "swarmed."

> There is no swarming like that of Israel when once Israel has got a start, and the scene bristled at every step, with the signs and sounds, immitigable, unmistakable, of a Jewry that has burst all bounds. That it has burst all bounds in New York, almost any combination of figures or of objects taken at hazard sufficiently proclaims; but I remember how the rising waters, on this summer night, rose, to the imagination, even above the housetops and seemed to sound their murmurs to the pale distant stars. It was as if we had been thus, in the crowded, hustled roadway, where the multiplication, the multiplication of everything, was the dominant note, at the bottom of some vast aquarium in which innumerable fish, of over-developed proboscis, were to bump together, for ever, amid heaped spoils of the sea.

The impression the crowded streets made upon him was one of "race," of the overwhelming presence of an alien people, of "the Hebrew conquest of New York." He did not mask his revulsion, yet he was conscious of a great advance in social justice, and that this teeming ghetto was a refuge from the horrors of Europe. The fire escapes that disfigured the fronts of the tenements, and on which the children swarmed, were, for all their ugliness, like the hideous festoons of wire that carried telephone service and electric light everywhere even in these impoverished regions, modern improvements. The blaze of electric lights in the shop fronts, where visitors from uptown were invited to leave their money, the sanitary staircases and community gardens,

what did it all really come to but that one had seen with one's eyes the New Jerusalem on earth? What less than that could it all have been, in its far-spreading light and its celestial serenity of multiplication? There it was, there it is, and when I think of the dark, foul, stifling Ghettos of other remembered cities, I shall think by the same stroke of the city of redemption.

James was conducted to cafés that might have been reminiscent of Vienna, if he had had such a point of reference, and where to his surprise no alcoholic beverages were served. He wondered whether the proprietors were Slavs? Hungarians? He went to a beer cellar where German was spoken and pictures of prizefighters adorned the walls. It was the fashion to visit the ghetto, as it would be a fashion a few years later to visit clubs in Harlem, and he returned to the Lower East Side with friends to a performance, or part of one, of a Yiddish play in a crowded little theater. Hearing their performances praised, he then attended an uptown performance in English, on Broadway, by newly celebrated Yiddish actors. He was puzzled by all this and troubled by what it meant for him and for his New York. The dominant tone of the city was now set by the immigrant:

The alien himself fairly makes the singleness of impression. Is not the universal sense his sense and do we not feel ourselves feeding, half the time, from the ladle, as greasy as he chooses to leave it for us, that he holds out?

Stopping in Philadelphia on his way from Washington to New York, it struck him that Philadelphia, at least the region around Rittenhouse

Square, had more of what one might call a national feeling than the other cities he had visited. Philadelphia had avoided the fashion for skyscrapers. What he saw of it was an organic community, with its native history and English language, living for the most part privately and socially. The highly selective country clubs struck him as admirable. Clubs to which both men and women could belong were a novelty, and he thought them an advance over the businessmen's clubs of New York. Country clubs treated "families" as their members, and this too was a uniquely American idea, to consider the family a horizontal structure, without past or future, and take it as the basic unit of society. The contrast between Philadelphia's settled neighborhoods and clubs and the chaotic immigration overwhelming Manhattan was striking.

James was not troubled by the racial exclusions of the country clubs. It was an old story that civilization rested on injustice. Privacy and democracy were often in conflict, and the question for America, for the future, was whether the two could be reconciled. He saw glimpses, even in New York, of possibilities. A country club on the Hudson, open to families without much discrimination except with regard to wealth, open apparently even to the newly arrived wealthy, gave him a glimpse of aristocratic values that might be maintained even in a democracy:

> the ample, spreading, galleried house, hanging over the great river, with its beautiful largeness of provision . . . all one could say face to face with it, treading its great verandahs and conversation rooms, its halls of refreshment, repose and exercise, its kitchens and its courts and its baths and its gardens . . . was that it positively revealed new forms of felicity. It was thus a new and original thing—and actually an "important" one; for what did it represent (all discriminations made and recognized) but the active Family, as a final social fact, or in other words the sovereign People, as a pervasive and penetrative mass, "doing" themselves on unprecedented lines.

Perhaps America was inventing new cultural institutions that might replace family estates and the ancient Church. New public libraries in Boston and New York impressed him with their beauty and their presence. Andrew Carnegie and other wealthy men and women were endowing libraries in the way that the aristocrats of Europe had endowed churches. He had admired the Boston Public Library. The public library in Manhattan, on Fifth Avenue and Forty-second Street, was still incomplete but was already both dignified and beautiful, and when it was finished the following year it would be the largest marble structure in the United States. The new Library of Congress building in Washington was even more magnificent. These libraries were evidently the cathedrals of a new humanist faith. In the upper reaches of Manhattan, on Riverside Heights, there was a collection of grand, even grandiose, new buildings to house Columbia University and the Presbyterian Hospital. These too were churches of democracy. Despite the busy individuality and featureless sprawl of so much of the landscape, there were even hopes for a new democratic architecture. James was struck by the loveliness of Grant's Tomb on a bluff overlooking the Hudson, the simple classical lines of a temple that stood symbolically open.

> The tabernacle of Grant's ashes stands there by the pleasure-drive, unguarded and unenclosed, the feature of the prospect and the property of the people, as open as an hotel or a railway-station to any coming or going . . . without mystery or ceremony to "back" it, without Church or State to intervene on its behalf. . . . And yet one doesn't conclude, strange to say, that the Riverside pavilion fails of its expression a whit more than the Paris dome [of the Invalides]; one perhaps even feels it triumph.

These were glimmers of the possibility that the old sensibilities of Europe were not being entirely lost but were embodied in new forms. But these glimmers were infrequent. The dominant notes were struck by the immigrants, on the one hand, and by a roaring new commercial Americanism, on the other.

"Americanism" was not only a political slogan but a movement. It seemed to James that a culture was literally being manufactured, that whole industries, newspapers and magazines, photographs and illustrations, even fine arts, were devoted to "faking"—creating an imaginary or romanticized history, idealized ancestors, an illusory nationality represented by heroic but anonymous figures.

This manufactured American culture was hotel culture, from Boston to Palm Beach. Making the long pilgrimage to Florida, one found the hotel spirit in sole articulate possession. The hotel was the epitome of the national character: "The jealous cultivation of the common mean, the common mean only, the reduction of everything to an average of decent suitability." In Boston and New York, so in the Breakers and the Royal Poinciana, society—said to be drawn from all over the United States— was a uniform, characterless bourgeois respectability and business success, even in the oldest European settlement in America, Saint Augustine, "proving primarily, and of course quite legitimately, but an hotel." The young women in the lobbies struck him as actors abandoned on a stage or like fish in a bowl.

The country was all a vast marketplace, founded on the new dogma of "free trade" and its corollary, free immigration. New housing developments in the cities and across the landscape were being laid out in unlovely geometric lines, leading not to a vista but only to a mathematical vanishing point. The precious cultivated landscape was being squandered. There was no principle except that of exchange, no restraint on the rudeness or vulgarity of the traders, no sense of incommensurable values. Everything and everyone was a potential commodity.

The vast machinery of Americanization, in short—the public schools and libraries and newspapers and magazines, even the settlement houses and hospitals—was turning the new immigrants into Americans whose only culture was that of the market. The immigrants enthusiastically participated, to James's puzzled surprise; each of the "aliens" whom he met declared himself an American; in the new coffeehouses and cafés, the lively conversation was all in heavily accented English. The Yiddish-speaking actors performing on Broadway spoke an English that was hardly intelligible to him. The speech of Americans had been bad enough, and a man of letters had sufficient difficulty finding a milieu and an audience in America. But at least the works of Shakespeare and the English tradition provided a value and a standard. What would come of the mechanical assimilation of so many millions of alien adults? What language, what culture, would result?

The image that embodied for him the terrors of this experiment was that of the great hall of Ellis Island on a winter morning. It had been one of the first sights he asked to see, and the commissioner of immigration, to whom Colonel Harvey had introduced him, was glad to show him through the enormous facility. They left early from the Battery; seen from the harbor, the geologic scale of the office towers, emerging sublimely from the morning fog, seemed to justify itself for the first time. Their boat banged against ice floes in the foggy bay, and the terrible morning seemed to set the tone of the whole experience:

> Anything blander, as a medium, would have seemed a mockery of the facts of the terrible little Ellis Island, the first harbour of refuge and stage of patience for the million or so of immigrants annually knocking at our official door. Before this door which opens to them there only

with a hundred forms and ceremonies, grindings and grumblings of the key, they stand appealing and waiting, marshaled, herded, divided, subdivided, sorted, sifted, searched, fumigated, for longer or shorter periods . . . an intendedly "scientific" feeding of the mill. . . . It is a drama that goes on, without a pause, day by day and year by year, the visible act of ingurgitation. . . . The wonder that one couldn't keep down was the thought that these two or three hours of one's own chance vision of the business were but as a tick or two of the mighty clock that never, never stops. . . . I think indeed that the simplest account of the action of Ellis Island on the spirit of any sensitive citizen who may have happened to "look in" is that he comes back from his visit not at all the same person that he went. He has eaten of the tree of knowledge, and the taste will be forever in his mouth.

The aliens in their inconceivable numbers, entering the vast factory of Americanization, affected him intimately. James was not speaking of statistics or norms; he was facing a phenomenon that intruded into his innermost being.

He had thought he knew before, thought he had the sense of the degree in which it is his American fate to share the sanctity of his American consciousness, the intimacy of his American patriotism, with the inconceivable alien; but the truth had never come home to him with any such force. In the lurid light projected upon it by these courts of dismay it shakes him . . . to the depths of his being.

This was an experience early in his journey, but it remained with him and seemed to grow in significance as he traveled and studied. When he came to make a book of his impressions, he would add some later reflections:

[T]his affirmed claim of the alien, however immeasurably alien, to share in one's supreme relation was everywhere the fixed element, the reminder not to be dodged. One's supreme relation, as one had always put it, was one's relation to one's country—a conception made up so largely of one's countrymen and one's countrywomen. Thus it was as if . . . the idea of the country itself underwent something of that profane overhauling through which it appears to suffer the indignity of change. Is not our instinct in this matter, in general, essentially the safe one—that of keeping the idea simple and strong and continuous, so that it shall be perfectly sound? To touch it overmuch, to pull it about, is to put it in peril of weakening; yet on this free assault upon it, this readjustment of it in *their* monstrous, presumptuous interest, the aliens, in New York, seem perpetually to insist. This sense of dispossession, to be brief about it, haunted me so, I was to feel . . . the fond alternative vision . . . of the luxury of some such close and sweet and *whole* national consciousness as that of the Switzer or the Scot.

This Anglicized man, who from his youth had been criticized in the American press as lacking in American nationality and manliness, had nevertheless clung to his identity as an American and a New Yorker. He imagined himself living in Manhattan and felt like a man who has seen a ghost in his own supposedly safe old house.

In New York he had business to address. The Academy of Arts and Letters met in New York City while he was there, to take advantage of his presence, and he had the pleasure of joining in the election of William James, whose candidacy had been postponed until his brother could be present. William for his part was abroad, but he was reducing his career obligations and declining invitations of all kinds, and he sent a jocular letter refusing this invitation from friends, alleging as one of his reasons the prior election of his "younger and vainer" brother.

James had not written much of his American impressions as yet. While still in Boston he had dictated an account of his travels in the New England countryside, and this, under the pressure of his realistic methods of portrayal, had grown to excessive length. He had held it for a while, hoping to revise it, but at last sent it off to Colonel Harvey with the suggestion that this and subsequent articles be published in *The North American Review,* as they were too long and literary for *Harper's New Monthly.* He now set to work on subsequent articles, for which he had begun to make some notes while in California. His descriptions of New England would eventually require three long articles and could have made a small volume in themselves. New York and the South would also take a good deal of space; he began to think that the western states would have to wait for a second volume.

A question of moment was the proposal by Scribner's to bring out a collected edition of his fiction. *The Golden Bowl* was selling well, propelled by numerous reviews, by the publicity generated by his tour, and by the momentum created by his well-received books of the past two years. It went into a second printing in the United States shortly after its first issue, just as the British edition was appearing, and would sell better than any of his books since *The Portrait of a Lady*. Critics began to look back over his work as a whole. Joseph Conrad called him "the historian of fine consciences," and a new book published just as he returned to New York from California was devoted entirely to an admiring assessment of his novels:

> [James's] cumulative statement of his impressions has the dignity of mature, considered, highly developed art. . . . His method is closely akin to that of the painter. . . . He reaches depths and crannies of character and temperament, to which none of his predecessors could have penetrated, . . . by means of *a passion for truth*.

The author of this praise, Elisabeth Luther Cary, arranged for James to address a women's club in Brooklyn, where he evidently was all but worshiped. She introduced him, in all likelihood, with the words with which she had begun her book:

> It is time to think of him not as the author of independent works . . . but as the creator through his accumulated accomplishments of an impression both definite and general.

Scribner's Sons had proposed a collected edition several years earlier, when James was engaged with his last series of big novels, and he had put them off until he should have more time. In the spring of 1905, with James's star ascendant in America, Edward Bellingame of Scribner's again proposed bringing out a collected edition of James's work.

Such collections, a staple of the publishing business on both sides of the Atlantic, were referred to as "library" editions in America and were aimed at the upper end of the book market, people who had the interest and means to own fine books and bindings, as well as at the newly proliferating municipal and university libraries. Library editions had an economic logic of their own, which Scribner's had perfected. With their own modern rotogravure printing plant and a sales and advertising force, Scribner's had specialized in these editions, sold directly to purchasers by subscription. Authors were not given advances for the works, and the volumes were printed and sold by the publisher to people and institutions who had ordered them in advance, eliminating margins that otherwise would be allowed for wholesalers and bookstores. Without much risk, Scribner's could count on a steady stream of income from a library edition over a period of years or decades. The author, although paid little or nothing at the outset (and, as it transpired in James's case, forced to pay other publishers for the rights to reprint his scattered works), might hope for a steady stream of royalties running long into the future, for his own retirement and for his heirs.

This was not a decision to be made lightly. Selecting among and preparing the early works for publication would be a substantial task. A complete edition that would include all his voluminous works was never a realistic prospect: James had published seventeen volumes in the past ten years alone. Even restricting the edition to novels and short stories, the work of selecting and arranging would consume months when he was not producing anything new, and James was by no means at the end of his productive career. He had already fallen into arrears on his promised book about London and on his articles and book of American impressions, all of which should produce more immediate income than a library edition. His tour of America was meant to generate material for new stories and novels, ideas for which were already bubbling; all this might have to be set aside for a time if he were to devote himself to a collected edition. Aside from creative considerations, the felt need to pursue his new ideas and his domestic economy both required the publication of a more or less popular book each year; but royalties from a library edition would be a modest and long-term affair.

He talked the matter over with Howells, his longtime friend and adviser. Howells had been in Europe for most of the time James was in America, but he returned shortly before James's departure, and the two men revived their old comradery. On one miserably hot and humid summer afternoon they sat outdoors and talked of the proposal for a collected edition, and Howells was encouraging. He thought it would allow the public to see James's works of fiction as a single whole, in which he had carried out his conscious intentions better than any of his contemporaries. Howells's remark evidently chimed with James's own sense. He had been lecturing repeatedly on "The Lesson of Balzac," the writer whose numerous linked novels and stories had been collected into a single, gigantic portrait of France. His own "definitive edition" would be more complex, a kind of artistic autobiography, his work seen in retrospect through his own eyes, as well as a history of the transatlantic world portrayed in his fiction. Encouraged by Howells, James was sufficiently interested in this notion to suggest that Pinker open practical discussions with Scribner's. The complexities were considerable—his work had been published by so many different houses over the years, all of whom might claim some rights—but Pinker came to New York and began the discussions.

Toward the end of his visit in America, obligations and distractions again began to accumulate. James was by no means finished with lecturing; invitations continued to arrive, and he agreed to give a talk at Smith College in May. Howard Sturgis was in Newport, and James was determined to make a detour both to see him and to collect more impressions of the famous "cottages," which now seemed a paradigm of American wealth, and which he would choose as the setting for his long-planned but never-finished American novel, *The Ivory Tower.* James was invited to attend a celebration in Cornish, New Hampshire, that was planned to honor his friend and fellow Academy member Augustus Saint-Gaudens, who was gravely ill, and then he was invited to give the commencement address at Bryn Mawr College. Hendrik Andersen wrote to say that he would be visiting his family in Boston that summer after all; perhaps they could meet? James was also determined to spend a little more time in Cambridge with his brother and sister-in-law. And the Whartons invited him to return to their estate for a few days' rest before setting off across the Atlantic again. Edith had published the first installments of her new American novel, *The House of Mirth,* and James had promised to sit down and talk with her about it and about his own American impressions. She now repeated her invitation somewhat insistently, promising to invite William Dean Howells as well and to carry James in her automobile to the other New England locations that he wanted to visit. She was "like [the archangel] Michael driving Satan," James said, and he acquiesced to her invitation as well. But she needn't bring Howells to him; he would visit Howells separately.

To make all these movements possible, James delayed his departure slightly and arranged to sail directly from Boston on the Fourth of July. He tried once again to coordinate his movements with Howard Sturgis's, but was defeated.

A last dip into Philadelphia, to make his farewells and to deliver the commencement address at Bryn Mawr College. He could hardly give his talk on Balzac again, however, and so he wrote a new speech. In the talk he prepared now, he began to develop a topic that he would only touch on in his travel notes but that was to be the basis of a second series of essays promised to *Bazar*. This was what he called the "abdication of the American male," the disappearance of American men from the social realm.

In *The Ambassadors*, James had described the curious division of labor between a New England husband and wife visiting Paris. Only the wife had any real interest in the city as a capital of civilization and culture, as a place at all different from Woollett, Massachusetts. Her husband was interested only in more primitive amusements. Now, after his tour of America, James was prepared to state as a general principle that in America the whole task of civilization—art, religion, culture, the domestic arts, and the education of children—had been turned over to women. Men concerned themselves solely with business, politics, blood sports, and primitive amusements and left women to manage as best they could. The sole exception that he found in the East was in Washington, D.C., that democratic replacement for the royal courts of Europe. In Washington men joined in conversation, and the talk was never of business. He kept for his planned later volume his reflections on San Francisco and the Bohemian Club.

Bryn Mawr was a comparatively new college founded only twenty years before to provide higher education for Quaker women, although it was open to women of all faiths. The curriculum was classical, modeled upon that of men's universities, and the faculty included both men and women. The management of the college provided a good deal of freedom and independence for the students, and it posed for James the same dilemma that he had observed in Boston and New York, the conflict between liberty and civilization. Adults had abandoned the young people to their own devices in every respect except the formal curriculum; James thought that even these elite young women were being denied a proper education, a serious matter in a country where women were the bearers of civilization. Democracy and the abdication of the American male, his liberty unhampered by duty, combined to leave young women stranded and vulnerable.

James had no intention of shirking what he saw as his own share of responsibility. Bryn Mawr was not only a women's college, it was the college that his favorite niece, Peggy, was planning to attend when her coming-out year was completed, and he perhaps felt a special obligation. He himself had only with pain and effort acquired the education that was being denied to these young women, the education that the schools and families of America were failing to provide, and he set out in his brief talk, quixotically, to explain in simple and clear terms the character of civilized life, of life as an art.

The image he chose to illustrate his lecture was the pronunciation of English in America. This was not a new topic for him: his niece and his young female cousins had amused their family with tales of his persistent lectures on pronunciation. He was often horrified at the manner in which even educated Americans spoke: the nasal tones that he had so often described in his fiction, the slovenly enunciation, the elision of consonants, the insertion of extraneous sounds, so that even educated Americans said "Mommer" and "Popper" instead of Mama and Papa, and said "leastways" and "anyways." James was not alone in his concern. The new American Academy of Arts and Letters to which he had been elected was taking as one of its principal tasks (in imitation of its French model) to set standards for American English. A Yale professor and leader in the new movement to teach English literature in the colleges, Thomas R. Lounsbury, had addressed the Academy at one of its first meetings on this subject and had only a few weeks before published his book on the need for standards for American speech.

For James, the question had a special significance. Spoken language, far more than the written texts that were taught in colleges, was the medium of social relations and hence of civilized life.

> All life therefore comes back to the question of our speech, the medium through which we communicate with each other; for all life comes back to the question of our relations with each other. These relations are made possible, are registered, are verily constituted by our speech, and are successful (to repeat my word) in proportion as our speech is worthy of its great human and social function: is developed, delicate, flexible, rich—an adequate accomplished fact. The more it suggests and expresses the more we live by it—the more it promotes and enhances life.

To speak well and charmingly was to to perform one's part in relationships with conscious care. The secret of this art was conscious self-mastery, and the result, constrained by history and circumstances, would be a conscious national *tone*. The tone of educated speech necessarily reflected centuries of history, imposed by teachers and guardians, by

Church and State, by the conservative impulse that imposed itself upon the freedom of the young. Freedom, by all means; but the conservative spirit must be dominant.

He spoke for more than an hour, inveighing against the public schools and the newspapers for their failure to set any sort of standard; he launched a half-humorous attack on immigrants, the "Dutchmen" (Germans) and "dagos" who were making free with the language of America, turning it into a simple commercial instrument. The machinery of Americanization and the freedom granted to the immigrant, precious in its own way, was creating a debased and ugly national language.

The young people were not to blame, of course, and he commiserated with them on the lack of guidance, the absence of models, for them to follow. He obliquely blamed the system of education of which Bryn Mawr College was a part; the abdication by the male, as he would say at more length in his essays, as he had said in his fiction, left the female without any help or guidance. It would take fifty years to make an adequate spoken American language, distinct from the English, he told the young women. They, unaided, would have to make a beginning themselves.

He went to Cambridge to visit with William and Alice, Peggy and Aleck, in June and then made a dash from there to Cornish, New Hampshire, for the celebration to honor Saint-Gaudens. John La Farge and other newly elected members of the Academy were there, as well as the painters, sculptors, and actors who came to the art colony in Cornish in the summers. It was a rural enclave with inexpensive lodgings, not far from the railroad station in Windsor, Vermont, and in many ways resembled the Broadway colony of which James had fond memories. Saint-Gaudens was the founder and leader of this community. He had purchased an abandoned inn on a little hilltop, with sweeping meadows below and a magnificent view of Mount Ascutney. The colonists planned to perform an original play in his meadow, with music written by Arthur Whiting and performed by members of the Boston Symphony Orchestra. The play was an affectionate parody of the Greek mythology of which Saint-Gaudens was fond, called *The Masque of 'Ours,'* and the sets had been designed by Maxfield Parrish, who was to appear as a centaur in a ludicrous costume of his own invention. The climax of the play was to be the presentation to Saint-Gaudens of an ornamental sundial. When the organizers of the performance learned of James's expected presence, however, they hastily rewrote the ending and added a subtitle to the play: *The Gods and the Golden Bowl* (*with no apologies to H.J.*) At the close of the performance, the gods and goddesses chose a new ruler, Saint-Gaudens, and presented to him not the sundial they had planned but a hastily purchased, antique golden bowl.

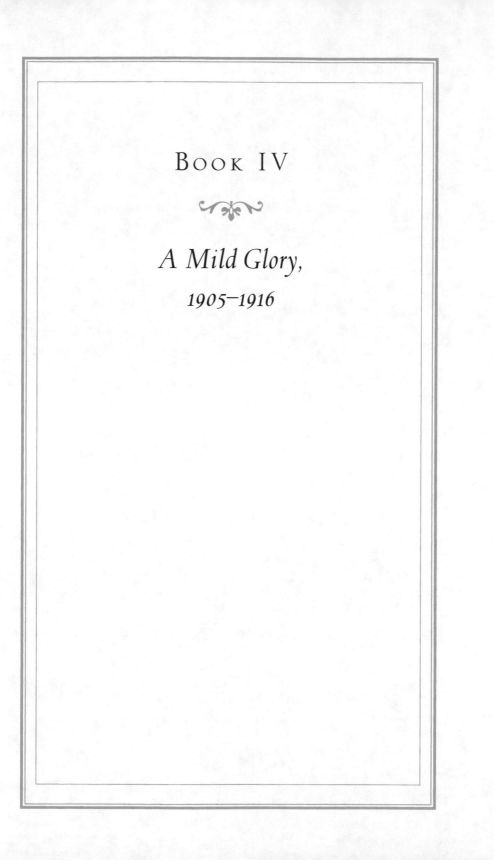

BOOK IV

A Mild Glory,

1905–1916

23

❦

SOME FAREWELLS

Before he sailed from Boston, James made last-minute efforts to see Hendrik Andersen, who planned to be in Boston only briefly and then to sail directly for Italy, foreclosing a visit to Rye.

> I shall be back at Lamb House by July 15th (heaven send!) But what good will that do either of us if you are streaking off to 3000 miles away? However, we will talk of these things, dear boy, when I really can lay my hands on you, & how I *shall* lay them!

They did manage to meet briefly in Boston and then again for three days in Newport, where Sturgis also was visiting family. James appears carefully to have managed matters so that Andersen and Sturgis, to each of whom he spoke as a lover, did not meet. Andersen evidently changed his plan and promised to arrange a passage to England, and to visit Rye, before continuing on to Italy. On the eve of his own departure, James sent a hasty note from Cambridge:

> I sail to-morrow a.m. . . . without seeing you. This is a hasty, tired scrawl of the final fagged hour of preparation, to make up, a little, for that. . . . Write me a word to Lamb House, I beseech you, & let me know that I may expect you & when. . . . I embrace you & am your affectionate old friend, very tenderly expectant of you.

This was only one of many farewell letters written late into the night. To Mary James: "it is late . . . & I am weary & spent. . . . But I must thank you for your good & sweet last word of farewell. . . . Yes, I long for the peace of home."

His departure was the closing of a chapter: it did not seem likely that he would make such a tour of his scattered family again, and his contemporaries were passing from the scene. On July 1, John Hay died at his home in New Hampshire, of heart failure.

Walter Berry was traveling to Europe on business: he and James shared the week's journey on the *Ivernia*. James's old friend of theater days, Elizabeth Robins, was returning from her own tour of North America and wrote to ask him to reserve a stateroom for her; she would be on the ship as well.

At home and at peace in Lamb House in mid-July, after almost a year abroad, two or three years of steady work lay ahead. He owed travel impressions to *The North American Review*, to be collected into at least one volume, probably two. There was to be a third volume on the speech and manners of American women. And he had begun to turn over in his mind the idea of a novel that would grow out of the separation of the sexes and the abdication of duty by American men, their curious resignation of civilization to the unaided care of women. As he told Elizabeth Robins on the voyage home, he "marveled that up to now [the subject] had so blessedly been let alone . . . the complete separation of the sexes in modern America . . . a state of segregation beyond anything existing out of the Orient." James had decided as well to proceed with Scribner's selective New York Edition.

Nor had he forgotten his promise to write a book about London. He thought of making it the sort of portrait that he was painting of the whole of America. He described this last plan with great enthusiasm to Edmund Gosse shortly after returning to England. Indeed, on visits to London that fall he began his research for this study, even though he had so many other projects under way. Gosse was now the librarian of the House of Lords, and he escorted a gleeful James into the garrets of the Palace of Westminster, from which strangers were ordinarily barred.

James's interlinked projects would make a portrait of his English-speaking world, from San Francisco to the West End, from the House of Lords to the New York ghetto, as seen through his own eyes and imagination: a vast extended moment in history that he had been privileged to observe from its heights. Balzac had described the first coming of democracy to France; James was portraying on an even more grandiose scale the final rise of democracy and its conquest of the last remnants of the Old Regime.

George Harvey had been nagging him to choose an overall title for his American travel articles, and he had put the question off. The perfect title, he thought, would have been "The Return of the Native," which would have emphasized his loyalty to his own nation; but, Thomas Hardy having used that title, he would have to find another. After a long delay, he chose *The American Scene*. This was an allusion to Balzac's *Human Comedy:* the stage was always for him *la scène*, "the scenic art."

During his absence, his tenant Miss Horstmann had married young Mr. Boit; they had spent their honeymoon in Lamb House and had moved to Washington. The house was in reasonably good order; a few pieces of the Robertson china had been broken and replaced with plates that looked well enough. Mrs. Paddington had kept good order, and there had been no collapse during his absence, as there had been under the reign of the Smiths. James reinstituted his regime of Fletcherized fish-and-barley-water lunches and abstemious dinners.

There were changes in his household, however. During his absence Mary Weld had met and married a local young man and had given up both bookbinding and typing. Miss Petherbridge's, the employment agency that had served him well in the past, sent a typist whose name has not been preserved, to whom he began to dictate the magazine articles that would become *The American Scene*.

Arthur Benson, to James's surprise, left his post at Eton in order to allow himself time for some large writing projects. He was just completing a biography of Walter Pater; he planned to write his father's biography; and the royal household had asked him to edit an edition of Queen Victoria's letters and to write her life—all tasks that required undivided attention. Freedom from the calendar of the school year allowed him more control of his schedule, as James happily noted, however, and perhaps there would be more opportunities for them to meet now that he was no longer tied to Windsor.

Hendrik Andersen was obliged to sail directly from Boston to Genoa, after all, to save time and money; but they promised each other to meet soon, somehow, and James resolved to travel to Italy as soon as his accumulated writing obligations would allow. With the proceeds of his lecture tour in hand, he could think of traveling to the Continent once more.

Sturgis too had returned from America, and there was a congenial circle around him at Queen's Acre in Windsor: Arthur Benson, Edmund Gosse, Edith Wharton on her regular visits to Europe with her husband, Gaillard Lapsley, Percy Lubbock, and other young writers—James's friend from from his Paris days Morton Fullerton—Walter Berry on his way from Paris to New York and back again. While visiting Sturgis in Windsor, James took advantage of his proximity to call upon his long-term friend, the now-aged Hamilton Aïdé, who had settled nearby at Ascot. He would particularly recall a two-day visit to Aïdé that fall, driving through Windsor Forest on an exquisite summer day, a visit that would be their last.

William was in California, preparing to give a course at Stanford University, near San Francisco. In a public lecture, "The Moral Equivalent of War," he would propose his own peaceful answer to Roosevelt's militarist Americanism: a national corps of young men who would carry out public service projects, works of engineering and conservation.

On April 18, 1906, an earthquake struck San Francisco. The earth ruptured at a point beneath the ocean just outside the Golden Gate. Much of the city was built of wood on marshy, filled land, and hundreds of buildings collapsed during the brief earthquake. Water and gas mains were broken, electrical lines fell, and dozens of fires were ignited in the rubble of the collapsed houses. For three days, fires swept through the city unchecked, and except for an area of brick buildings on the hills and along shorelines where water was available, the city was destroyed. It was not known at first how many had died, but almost the whole surviving population was homeless.

The news came quickly to London. James was just completing the first serial installments of *The American Scene* and beginning to think of the second series, which was to deal with the western states and to dwell on San Francisco, when he heard the news. He received no message from William, however, which alarmed him, and he cabled to the family in Cambridge. A reply from Harry soon assured him that William was not hurt.

Young Billy James was at that moment en route from Boston on his way to Paris to study painting, however, and fearing that he would hear the news of the earthquake and fire without knowing whether his father had survived, James hurried to Liverpool to meet his nephew's steamer when it docked. He went aboard before Billy and his companion, Sam

Crothers, were able to disembark, and gave them his report. As Crothers remembered it:

> He stood upon the deck and poured out, not the news, but the impressions which the catastrophe made upon his sensitive mind. We were made to see it all as he saw it in his imagination. The fear, the uncertainty, the vastness, all were reproduced. It was like hearing of the destruction of Babylon the Great from a contemporary.

Years later, Harry James would recall that the San Francisco earthquake and fire interrupted his uncle's account of his journey to America and in the end would oblige him to leave it unfinished. "He felt it [the earthquake and fire] as an event so stupendous and sensational that it must throw what he had to say into the shade." He abandoned his plan for a second volume of American travel notes and turned instead to his essays for *Bazar* on the speech and manners of American women, which were to make a third volume.

He continued to work at the New York Edition as well. The prospectus he gave Scribner's was for a reasonably compact set, considering the actual bulk of his work, to be published in sixteen volumes, arranged chronologically. Much of his early fiction and all of his nonfiction would be omitted, and he took to calling it a "severely selected" edition.

The set would be divided into halves; the first culminating with the final novel of his first period, *The Tragic Muse*, and the second half to cover his later work in the dramatic, realistic style that had emerged from the experiments within a small frame. To emphasize the character of the edition as a new work in itself, a comprehensive view of his fiction as he wished it to be understood, he decided early on to revise those of his early works that were included to bring them up to his present standards.

As he set to work, he perhaps had in mind the illustrated library edition of Sir Walter Scott's novels, admired by him as a child, to each of which Scott had added a preface in the first person, describing his working methods, and footnotes explaining the historic models for characters and settings. That "Magnum Opus" edition—a single vast work—had rescued Scott from bankruptcy and had given his early novels, reissued when he was a celebrity, a new life.

Whether or not James recalled Scott's edition, he began to form similar visions for the success of his own, prompted by his sense of the fame he had now achieved in America. He began with *Roderick Hudson*, which he misrepresented as his first novel—this was evidently not to be a scrupulously accurate self-portrait. He sketched out a preface in which he explained the project as a whole. In prefaces to subsequent volumes, he said, he would describe the process by which each novel had developed from the germ of an idea (which in fact was his consistent method only in his later works), the manner in which he had made use of his own memories of places and people, and the manner in which the writing had been influenced by his circumstances of the moment. He told Gosse, with some excitement, that the prefaces to the volumes in this definitive edition would be full and confidential; they were to throw to the winds all restraints of conventional reticence and would take the reader into the inmost sanctum of his soul.

Charles Scribner was pleased with the prospectus, and Pinker set to work to obtain rights to reprint James's works from his several publishers, but there the project languished for many months. Houghton, Mifflin, Heinemann, and Macmillan all demanded a chance to recoup what they considered to be their losses on the earliest editions of James's works. Houghton, Mifflin even insisted that they and not Scribner's print the volumes of the new edition to which they still claimed rights.

This question of "losses" going back thirty years was vexing. Publishers considered advances to authors as personal loans, and they were carried on the publisher's books until royalties from book sales had canceled them out. Any unrecovered portion of the advance remained on the publisher's books as a loss, whatever the overall balance sheet for a volume or an author might show.

James's early publishers, hearing from Pinker that a new edition of his early work was planned, accordingly demanded to have his old, unearned advances repaid. The stubbornness of their demands was all the greater, in the cases of Houghton, Mifflin and Heinemann, because they objected to dealing with a literary agent. The old paternalistic relation of publisher and author was being destroyed by the pressures of the marketplace, but James in this particular instance seemed to have no regrets at the destruction of the old order. He insisted on the publishers' dealing with Pinker, and for a while it seemed the project would collapse entirely, but after some months of impasse the publishers made an agreement among themselves. Scribner's made modest payments to all three publishers of James's early work. James supplemented these payments from his own funds and agreed to accept a lower royalty rate for the early volumes first published by Houghton, Mifflin. As part of the overall settlement, James also agreed to give Heinemann, with whom he had parted company years before, the right to collect and republish (as *English Hours*) some of his early travel writings, which he brought up to date with a hastily written essay on Rye and the Cinque Ports.

In the fall of 1905, Balfour's government resigned, and in the election that followed, Liberals, led by Sir Henry Campbell-Bannerman, gained an overwhelming majority, the largest in parliamentary history, and the new Labour Party won two dozen seats. Early in the new year, when James made his usual migration to London, the streets were noisy with motor-cars, and the Reform Club, usually quiet before the sitting of Parliament, was swamped by a new "Liberal flood." Liberal candidates had been re-turned even from what were thought to be safe Tory districts. James Bryce, a mutual friend of James and Holmes, was to be ambassador to the United States. Another old friend, Herbert Asquith, who had clashed with Balfour, was in the cabinet. Asquith had married Margot Tennant, still another friend from ancient days. The young people who had been known as "the Souls" were now middle-aged and in positions of power.

Hard at work at his American notes, and selecting works for inclusion in the New York Edition, James lightened his concentrated efforts by regular attendance at the theater, often with his old friends Elizabeth Robins, Lucy Clifford, or Rhoda Broughton. A new theater companion was Jocelyn Persse, the handsome young nephew of Augusta Gregory. James went with him to see the new plays by G. B. Shaw and Somerset Maugham and met some of Persse's friends, among whom was a young writer named Evelyn Waugh.

Persse was a cheerful, attractive youth with whom James was glad to be seen, but when he proposed Persse for membership in the Athenaeum Club he was obliged to instruct him, "*Athenaeum* (not 'Ethenaeum'— horror of horrors!)" and to explain the origin of the name.

Hendrik Andersen wrote regularly but kept putting off his hoped-for trip to England. He sent photographs of his proliferating, monumental statues: great nude figures, the forms tending toward the abstract and geometrical. It was a new style, and James fretted over it and complained (as he had long ago complained of French Impressionist paintings) of a lack of finish. He worried that Andersen was overworking himself and that there would be no market in America for these monumental figures. But the dominant note was one of longing and affection:

Of course I have had punctually all your beautiful & blessed missives, & of course I've tenderly loved you, & yearningly embraced you, & passionately thanked you for them.

Your little postcard is a weight off my spirit & this is a bare word to tell you so & to embrace you in this faint & far & ineffectual way. . . . I wish to goodness I could be with you a little—such a breath of the colour & charm [of Italy] do your few words give me. . . . I throb responsive—*so* responsive—to your hint that a few days here may be possible to you. . . . I long for you alone & when you do come—*if* you only do—

James thought of sending Andersen a round-trip ticket, to facilitate his visit to Lamb House, but the moment passed, and he turned to planning his own journey to Italy.

I am laying out plans for our coming together somehow—somehow that will permit of my laying the firmest & kindest & closest of all arms about you & talking to you, "for your own good," for three uninterrupted days & nights.

In the interim, he showered Andersen with motherly advice, recommended Fletcherizing for his health, urged him not to work quite so hard and to take some time away from his monumental nudes to do portrait busts; he offered himself as a model and promised to pay for the portrait. If the young sculptor would find subjects for portrait busts, his work would prosper. Aside from the money itself, dear Hendrik would gain a benefit from that "*friction with the market* which is so true a one for solitary artists too much steeped in their mere personal dreams."

Dear, dear Hendrik, have patience with my words. . . . With what formidable & ferocious advice you will feel me drenching you! However, I'm not really afraid that you won't see in it, my dear dear Hendrik, all the tenderest tenderness of your insufferable old friend.

Prosperous for the moment, James was able at last to install at Lamb House hot-water pipes, for which he had long yearned, and to double-glaze the windows, which together would make it easier for him to remain there in winter. The improvements were a great aid to work and health, both of which prospered in the congenial environment he had built for himself in Rye and which suffered when he was in London or abroad.

In September, Billy James came again for a week; Bay Emmet came for a time, as did old friends from London. Joining the stream of visitors to Lamb House was Walter Berry, who came for a long visit. He fell ill while still at Lamb House, however. James nursed him and urged him to rest, to remain until he had recovered, but Berry persisted in what seemed to James a reckless plan of visiting Italy. Edith and Edward Wharton stopped on their way to France, bringing their automobile and their chauffeur with them. James met them in Dover and rode back to Rye with them, managing to pilot them into a confused wandering along the dikes of Romney Marsh. He was happy to be able to return their hospitality and to enjoy with them a tour of his own countryside in their open-topped car.

Hamilton Aïdé died that winter, and James went up to London for the funeral, a sad gathering of old friends, with many gaps in their ranks. He scanned the considerable crowd and thought of how many were absent because they had gone before.

> His death makes me feel how much I was attached to him, & how far back our happy relation went & of what ever-charming intimate human things it was mainly compounded.

Another old comrade of James's youth, Tom Perry, was in Paris, and James invited him to come over for a visit: "I totter toward the grave. I distinctly desire your visit before I go." Perry did as he was bid, and they went up to London together. James had the pleasure of putting him up as his guest at the Athenaeum. He introduced Perry to Sidney Colvin at the British Library and arranged for him to have access to its collections.

Bob and Mary's daughter, Mamie, was engaged to be married to George Vaux, a Philadelphian whom James had met, briefly, on his lecture tour. He wrote to Mamie with real pleasure, inviting her to bring her husband to Lamb House, and in due course they would name their first child for him.

He had planned to depart for Paris shortly after the first of the year and then return to London for the rest of the winter, but work kept him at his desk in Rye: he was heavily revising the first novels of the New York Edition and arranging for a young photographer, Alvin Coburn, to make a frontispiece, the sole illustration, for each volume. He was completing his essays on American manners, had agreed to contribute to a collective novel that Elizabeth Jordan was running in *Bazar,* and was writing his usual quota of potboiler reviews and prefaces. He remained in Lamb House, with its newly heated water and sealed windows, and made only brief journeys to London after the first of the year; he dictated in the mornings, revised in the afternoons, and wrote long letters laboriously by hand in the evenings.

With the first volumes of the New York Edition in Scribner's hands and a volume of his American notes completed, he was free for the moment and flush with cash. *The American Scene* was published early in 1907, while his notes on American manners were still running in *Bazar.* The book was well received in both England and America. Gosse wrote a puff for the *Daily Mail* that touched James's heart with its generosity. The American reviews were respectful and often admiring. Although he was critical of his native land, James's nostalgic descriptions of New England and his childhood memories of Manhattan, and his account of distress at the disturbing new waves of commerce and immigration, all struck responsive chords. *The New York World* particularly praised James's description of the "shock" given to his sense of nationality by the flood of immigrants. The *Boston Evening Transcript* thought James had penetrated to "the heart of the American scene." Reviewers and readers both seemed pleased, one almost might say flattered, that James wrote as an American, not as a visiting foreigner, and the book was selling reasonably well.

He set off on the long rail journey to Italy on March 5, accordingly, with a light heart and with no deadlines to meet. As usual, he planned to stop en route in Paris for a leisurely visit. Tom and Lilla Perry invited him to share their rented house in Paris, but Edith Wharton had written more insistently, and James agreed to stay in the Whartons' apartment at 58 rue de Varenne, an eighteenth-century *hôtel,* in the Faubourg Saint-Germain of which he had so many romantic memories. The Whartons had given up their house in New York City, professedly because the climate of Manhattan did not agree with Teddy, and had rented George Vanderbilt's apartment in the milder and supposedly more salubrious winter air of Paris. They were spending their first season in Paris, and

Edith was expanding in the rich atmosphere, but they were evidently glad to have James, who knew Paris to his fingertips, with them.

Visits to the Bourgets, who had a flat nearby, were necessary but difficult. Paul was growing ever more extreme in his nationalist views. The socialist government of Georges Clemenceau was implementing a rigorous separation of Church and State, with all the bitterness remaining from the Dreyfus Affair, and Bourget was among those who had moved still further to the right in reaction. Although not himself a believer, James regretted the brutal measures being taken to disestablish the Catholic Church at every level of society. The effort to purge the influence of religion from government had extended from Paris to every rural village clerk and schoolteacher. This seemed to him excessive and brutally done. The French "have nothing but hate in their hearts," he said bemusedly of this effort, but he was equally distressed by the reaction, "the almost *insane*, bad manners snobbishness & folly of Bourget."

Edith Wharton's new novel, *The House of Mirth*, was having a great success in America. Wharton had taken James's advice and set her novel in New York, and had embraced what appeared to reviewers to be a Jamesian style and Jamesian themes. The repeated comparisons to James annoyed Wharton but did not discourage her from taking command of him during his visit and proudly introducing him to her new neighbors in the quarter. "Our friend," James confided to Sturgis, "is a great graceful lioness, & I have come in for many odd bones & leavings. . . . In fact I have an indigestion of chères Madames."

Edward Wharton did not share Edith's enthusiasm for literary and aristocratic circles, but he liked to please his Puss, and he kept himself occupied in tinkering with the new French motorcar he had purchased, for whose open top he was constructing an enclosure. After ten days, Teddy, Puss, and their Yankee chauffeur, Charles Cook, carried James off on a motor tour of the south of France. The weather was mild, the newly constructed top of the car was left behind, Teddy sat beside the driver, and Edith and James shared the open rear seat of the Panhard, where the sensation was of weightless albeit noisy soaring, an untethered flight. The freedom of the horse-drawn carriage had been infinitely multiplied by the power of the machine, and the experience was continually interesting and exhilarating. James allowed himself to be carried along as the week's outing stretched into two, into three weeks. Rural France was a revelation: "This is a wondrous, exquisite, sympathetic country, which I can't rejoice enough to have become possessed of—as the marvelous motor masters and absorbs it." As he told Sturgis, "My three weeks of really seeing this large incomparable France in our friend's chariot of fire has been almost the time of my life."

He celebrated his sixty-fourth birthday in Paris, and early in May he went by rail to Rome. From rue de Varenne, he wrote ahead to Hendrik Andersen announcing his departure but declining Hendrik's invitation to stay with him at the house he had taken in Rome for himself and his mother, sister, and widowed sister-in-law. This seeming coolness may have been connected to the likelihood that James would visit other old friends in Rome, where indeed he expected also to meet Howard Sturgis.

James broke his journey again for a few days' rest in Turin and to do some work correcting proofs of the New York Edition that had been sent there to meet him.

Scribner's seemed willing to do the thing handsomely. There were to be eighteen "books," roughly the structure he had first proposed, filling a total of twenty-three volumes. (Some of the novels would require two volumes each.) James involved himself in the details of typography and design, as he always did when he could. He was making books, and their physical expression, their dress and speech, was an essential aspect of the art. He was infuriated by the cheap, one-volume English edition of *The Golden Bowl*, which he thought too ugly to give to his friends, and equally by Harper's cheap edition of *The American Scene*, from which the "indispensable" page headings had been omitted. Now he negotiated with a willing Scribner's every detail of the definitive edition, from the design of the covers and title pages to the length of the line and the width of the margin. The books were to be easy to hold and to read, their graphic elements dignified and beautiful, in harmony with the author's overall design.

Illustrations were to be limited to a single frontispiece photograph for each of the twenty-three volumes. James had always disliked illustrations for his fiction, especially drawings that substituted another artist's vision of the characters for his own, and the photographs that he commissioned were to portray only the settings that he had had in mind for critical scenes.

Each of the individual novels and collections of stories would have a long preface, explaining the circumstances of their production and giving James's own retrospective, critical view. The prefaces and the works of fiction, taken together, would be both an artistic autobiography and a comprehensive exposition of his views with regard to the making of fiction. These prefaces, and the revisions he felt were needed in the early novels and stories, now deeply engaged him in Turin, and he continued to set aside his mornings for them when he went on to Rome in May.

He took a suite of rooms at the fondly remembered old Hotel de Russie. James was paying his promised visit to Andersen, but he had other calls to make as well. This was likely to be his last visit to Rome. The old artistic and expatriate community of his fond memories had all but vanished beneath a tide of English- and German-speaking tourists, and the city itself was disappearing beneath its renovations and monuments and highways and the imperious demands of the automobile. But he had a new circle of friends in the new capital.

Among his first visits was a call on Joseph Primoli, who had undertaken to alter and enlarge his family's palace, closing off the old facade facing the Tiber, blighted now by the completed highway on the embankment, and had opened a new entrance to the palace on the quiet little street behind it. These were preparations, in part, for Primoli's planned museum devoted to the history of the Bonapartes. Primoli had inherited his cousin the Princess Mathilde's trove of Bonaparte archives, which he added to his mother's collection of memorabilia. This remarkable library was to be housed in his palace; he again gave James an exhibition of his photographs and memorabilia and spoke of his ambition to write a history of the Bonapartes, whose family records he now had in his keeping.

Howard Sturgis, too, was in Rome. He and James had exchanged letters over the course of the previous weeks, trying to make their itineraries coincide. As James approached Rome from the north, Sturgis came from the south, from Sicily, traveling with a dependent entourage—to which recently had been added his niece Mildred Seymour, who was in grave straits both spiritually and physically, difficulties that were a great distress to the sympathetic Sturgis. James counseled him not to engage himself so deeply in her difficulties and was relieved to learn that William Haynes Smith, "the Babe," was on his way to Rome to assist him.

James discouraged Sturgis from meeting him at the railroad station, where he was to be met by Andersen, and invited him instead to call at his hotel after a delay, presumably to compose himself after the long train journey. In his affectionate and gossipy letters before and after his visit to each, James did not mention one to the other, nor did he introduce either man to Primoli.

There were other farewells to say in Rome, but despite all the rivals for his attention James spent many hours with Hendrik Andersen. He sat to Andersen for his portrait as he had promised. They often shared their midday meal with Hendrik's sister Lucia, sister-in-law Olivia, and Mrs. Andersen and then spent a quiet afternoon together in the sculptor's studio. Andersen was modeling a life-size bust, with bared neck and shoulders. The completed portrait was severe and noble, rather like a portrait of a Roman senator but modern, polished, and geometrical. It would look well cast in metal.

On his last night in Rome, James and Andersen dined alone on Hendrik's terrace, in the high cool Roman night. They dined by candlelight on the roof of an old loggia above the Piazza del Popolo, overlooking the ancient gate to the walled city, and, as it seemed to James,

> the whole backward past, the mild confused romance of the Rome one had loved and of which one was exactly taking leave under the protection of the friendly lanterned and garlanded feast and the commanding, all-embracing roof-garden. It was indeed a reconciling, it was an altogether penetrating last hour.

As the weather grew uncomfortably hot, he went north to Florence, followed there shortly by Howard Sturgis and his entourage. James had few friends still living in Florence, but he wanted to see the city a last time, in company with Sturgis. Onward again to Venice and a farewell visit to the Curtises at the Palazzo Barbaro; then home to Lamb House.

24

CELEBRITY

While still in Italy, James wrote to Miss Petherbridge that he wanted a new typist as soon as he returned, and she accordingly had a candidate for him to interview when he came up to London in August: Theodora Bosanquet, fresh from University College London. She had volunteered for the job and had resigned a civil service position to take it, out of admiration for his work, and had spent the previous month practicing typing from a copy of *The Ambassadors*. James interviewed her in Petherbridge's London office. At sixty-four and at the peak of his fame, he was evidently an alarming presence:

> We sat in armchairs on either side of a fireless grate. . . . I suppose he found me harmless and I know that I found him amazing. He was much more massive than I had expected, much broader and stouter and stronger. . . . After the interview I wondered what kind of impression one might have gained from a chance encounter. . . . He might perhaps have been an eminent cardinal in mufti, or even a Roman senator amusing himself by playing the part of a Sussex squire. . . . His features were all cast in the classical mold of greatness. He might very well have been a merciful Caesar or a benevolent Napoleon.

James asked few questions, relying on the recommendation of the agency, but spoke at length of the conditions and terms of employment. Miss Bosanquet would be obliged to take lodgings in Rye near his house; he knew of rooms in Mermaid Street that were "very simple, rustic and antique" but conveniently near. The work would be dull, and she would likely find Rye dull. Bosanquet had no objections to any of this and was engaged to begin work in October.

• • •

He ordered new stationery from Mr. Adams, big folio sheets on which he could write without cramping, and his handwritten letters continued to fly in all directions. There was a joyous tone in them. James seemed in some ways relieved to have cut his ties with the Continent. Perhaps he had begun to outlive both duty and passion. With regard to Bourget, who was not aging well, for example:

> It is thus at any rate a positive joy to me (or almost,) that Bourget has now for long become of a *poncif* so abandoned that I find in him neither life nor style nor interest. . . . It relieves & simplifies that he has ceased to be an obsession—to constitute a demand on one's attention.

His letters to Andersen grew less frequent and less intense; he spoke of their respective obligations and discussed the question of showing his portrait bust in London, where it might be seen. Hendrik suggested the Royal Academy exhibition. The bust was finished in clay and was to be cast in bronze. James suggested a dark patina for the bronze but was discouraging about the Royal Academy. He continued to speak of his love for Andersen and signed himself still very affectionately, but as an old friend.

There was a little more distance in his letters to Howard Sturgis, as well. Sturgis was allowing himself in Sainty-like fashion, or so it appeared to James, to be overwhelmed by Mildred Seymour and her daughters, and "5 or 6 other waifs," and despite the assistance of the Babe was "literally in pieces." James rarely found him alone, and Sturgis no longer came to Lamb House.

Arthur Benson was very much absorbed in his new and successful projects, from which he was becoming prosperous. Benson had purchased a motorcar, and James was dimly annoyed and envious:

> We can't *all* be Arthur Christophers—we can't *all* be ideally constituted & masters of our fate—a mastery for which, & the example of which & the emoluments of which, & the motor-cars of which, I envy & revere & love A.C.!

Gosse, too, was newly prosperous. In addition to his happy sinecure as librarian of the House of Lords, his wife, Nellie, had come into a considerable inheritance, and they were abandoning their charming and mildly

Bohemian middle-class neighborhood in Little Venice, preparing to move into a grand new house north of Regent's Park, the world of Maud Lowder.

But if his male friends were growing older, less engaging, and a little more distant, younger men continued to join the circle. There was a new intimacy in his letters to Persse, who began to make visits to Lamb House, and James had a new companion on his long afternoon walks, twenty-eight-year-old Sydney Waterlow, who had settled nearby. Waterlow had been invalided out of the diplomatic service and had come to the mild climate of Rye to recover his health. He was lightly occupied in making translations from the Greek and was readily available for walks and long conversations, many of which he recorded in a diary:

> We fell to discussing the problem of tramps, who come out of the casual ward & ask for bread & cheese. Sh'd one give it them . . . incidentally defeating the purpose of the Poor Law? He said that . . . there was no problem for *him*: the supply *must* be arranged, in spite of the disagreeableness of having your maids spending their time distributing sustenance to possibly truculent tramps. As for the economic bugbear which was constantly poking its nose into these questions, he would like to kick its bottom.
>
> H.J. began talking about politics. . . . He said that the older he grew the more acutely & passionately did he feel the huge absurdity & grotesqueness of things, the monstrous perversity of evil. . . . He felt tempted to call himself a rabid Socialist, so often does a great wind carry him off his feet & set him down somewhere far beyond & ahead of the present world.

At Waterlow's house he met other young people, and early in 1908 he was introduced to a promising novelist then still in his twenties who signed his books "E. M. Forster." Forster was spending a week with Waterlow and was invited to tea at Lamb House, served in the Garden Room. Bay Emmet ("American and beautiful," Waterlow thought) was visiting; she poured out, and James was genial in this circle of youth.

Max Beerbohm was among the young Cambridge men whom he befriended in these years. Beerbohm's memorable caricatures and parodies of James's style date from this time. In 1907, Beerbohm published a book of caricatures, with two drawings of James. One showed him in London, in a fog, gazing with interest at his own hand; the second showed him in America, surrounded by racial types—Indians, Negroes, Bostonians, cowboys. For this latter drawing Beerbohm wrote a long caption, "Extract from His Unspoken Thoughts": "I might, in regarding . . . these dear good people, find hard to swallow, or even take by subconscious injection, the great idea that I am—oh, ever so indigenously!—one of them."

Privately with Gosse, Beerbohm composed a sonnet to accompany another of his caricatures of James, an unpublished drawing of an old man, a little stooped, with enormous lamp eyes:

> Say, indefatigable alchemist,
> Melts not the very moral of your scene,
> Curls it not off in vapour from between
> Those lips that labour with conspicuous twist?
> Your fine eyes, blurred like arc-lamps in a mist,
> Immensely glare; yet glimmerings intervene,
> So that your May-Be and your Might-Have Been
> Leave us still plunging for your genuine gist.
>
> How different from Sir Arthur Conan Doyle
> As clear as water, and as smooth as oil,
> And no jot knowing of what Maisie knew.
> Flushed with the sunset air of roseate Rye,
> You stand, marmoreal darling of the few,
> Lord of the troubled Speech and Single Eye.

William wrote from Cambridge that he was reading *The American Scene* and "fairly melting with delight. . . . Evidently that book will last and bear reading over and over again."

> After the fitful fever of your spring and summer you must be settling rather pleasantly into your winter's stretch of work. . . . I have the pleasantest picture of your writing away in your garden house. Long may it last.

While James was waiting for Bosanquet to arrive so that he might resume his routine of dictation, he opened a new notebook and began to make handwritten notes of his walks in London, like those he had made in America. He was walking with a purpose, peeping into corners that he had not seen before, familiarizing himself with the architectural residue of vanished ages, giving particular attention to old churches in little squares that lent their character to the city and whose absence in America he had so deeply felt. As he went, he seemed to see with a camera's eye, and photographic terms like "focus" crept into his language. His notes were not solely for his own use, but also to record opportunities for drawings. Joseph Pennell was to illustrate the book, and his publishers were anxious for him to begin.

The first two volumes of the New York Edition of his selected works in fiction appeared in America in time for Christmas sales. The first volume of this magnum opus was the strangely prophetic *Roderick Hudson*, a story of a sculptor and the patron who loved him, set in Rome; but there were no personal revelations to add spice to the preface. The frontispiece for the volume was a portrait of the author in left profile, a soft-focus photograph made to James's direction by the young Alvin Coburn. The response was muted, and there were few sales beyond the subscriptions ordered in advance.

Johnston Forbes-Robertson was a gaunt, graceful actor who had made his name as a Shakespearean, who, now in his fifties had married an American actress, Gertrude Elliott, twenty years younger than himself, with whom he had formed a touring company. They were a striking couple. He was tall and blond, with the high forehead and strong features that typecast him as an aristocrat. She too was tall but dark, slight, and delicately beautiful. Shortly after making her his leading lady, Forbes-Robertson asked James for rights to the short story "Covering End," which had begun its career as *Mrs. Gracedew*, a curtain-raiser for Ellen Terry. It evidently attracted him partly for the reason it had attracted Terry: the title role was written for a beautiful and charming American woman. A further attraction was evidently that her leading man was an English aristocrat, a role for which Forbes-Robinson himself seemed perfectly cast:

> Erect and slender, but as strong as he was straight, he was set up, as the phrase is, like a soldier, and yet finished, in certain details—matters of expression and suggestion only indeed—like a man in whom sensibility had been recklessly cultivated.

Forbes-Robertson had seen dramatic and comic possibilities in the novella into which James had recycled the one-act, but when he first asked for it James was busy with big novels. In the late summer of 1907, however, when he asked again, James agreed to turn the story back into a play. It had begun as a one-act comedy, but James thought the expanded narrative would require treatment as a full-length play. Forbes-Robertson agreed to this, agreed to everything, promised to take the play on tour and—if it proved successful—to bring it to London. James was tempted, and while he still had the New York Edition on his hands and Macmillan was asking for news of progress on the London book, he agreed to redramatize his tale.

With less at stake than in his first venture onto the stage, and with more experience behind him, the work of dramatization went easily and well. If the one-act had somewhat expanded in its translation to a novella, the story now required only compression to become a play again, renamed once more. Although the estate that was its subject remained Covering End, the play was to be called *The High Bid*.

In this latest version, Mrs. Gracedew is still the powerful, joyous, spontaneous, and immensely wealthy heroine. Visiting Europe, she buys up whole households of beautiful old things to bring back with her to America. She has come to see Covering End, an ancient family seat, and falls in love with it and its reluctant and impoverished heir, Captain Yule.

Captain Yule has taken to working in a settlement house in the East End of London and has become something of a socialist. He must give up his ancestral home to the vulgar Podmore, who has bought up the captain's obligations in order to squeeze him. Yule can keep his house only by giving Podmore what he wants. If the captain agrees to marry Podmore's daughter, conferring respectability on his family, and stand for Parliament as a Tory, his debts will all be discharged.

The elegant captain is willing to consider the daughter but not to give up his political convictions. His stubbornness prompts Mrs. Gracedew to make a passionate speech, in which her affection for the man and his house are mingled. She expresses James's opinions with a fluency that none of his characters have yet achieved. She asks how Yule can allow party rivalries to destroy the precious inheritance of Covering End.

In *The Tragic Muse*, party politics had been portrayed as a shabby rivalry. To Sydney Waterlow, James had recently confided his feeling that Parliament was "an immense waste of talk and energy and solemnity." In contrast to the frivolity of politics (and his moderate enthusiasm for the captain's views), James sets before his audience the permanence of Covering End and the family that has nurtured it over six centuries. We see the estate through the eyes of the old family servant and then with Mrs. Gracedew's fresh gaze. She gathers up some intruders, village folk, and gives them a spontaneous tour of the house, explaining that it is one

> for which the ages have been tender and the generations *wise:* letting it change so slowly that there's always more left than *taken;* living their lives in it, but (with charming persuasive unction) letting it *shape* their lives.

She dotes upon the hangings, the carved oak wainscot, the very flags with which the floor is paved. She twirls about with arms extended and sweeps everyone up with her enthusiasm. Yule confesses to her that he would keep the lovely old house if he could. But there are thousands who are homeless, and he will share their fate rather than abandon them for the sake of an old house. He will give up his own history and uniqueness and merge himself into the mass of humanity.

Mrs. Gracedew is incredulous. How can he give himself up in this way? She speaks of the house as if it were a person, as if it were Yule himself. The house is not simply another old place, it is the best of its type, it is a patiently constructed work of art, which is to say that it is *unique.* The villagers, like a chorus, echo, "Unique, unique, unique."

She treats his gesture of sacrifice with contempt. One cannot share a Tintoretto by cutting it into pieces. Surely Captain Yule will do more for humanity by preserving and carrying forward his family, the house they built, and the centuries of slow history embodied by it. Found his family anew but allow the house to be shown, share it democratically in a way that preserves more than it changes:

> MRS. GRACEDEW: What on earth is more precious than what the Ages have slowly *wrought?* . . . It's such a virtue, in anything, to have lasted; it's such an honour, for anything, to have been spared. . . . To all stragglers from the Wreck of Time hold out a pitying hand!

The climax of the play is altered from those of the earlier versions. All still ends happily, and Mrs. Gracedew gets both house and husband. A group of visitors still intrudes at the close, and Mrs. Gracedew shows them around. But instead of the vulgar Jews of his story, they are vulgar, ill-spoken American tourists.

There was only one set, and Forbes-Robertson was pleased with the parts written for him and for his wife; the play would open in Edinburgh in March.

Aside from the pleasure James had in seeing his work performed and in the chance of a success, the relation with Forbes-Robertson was one that he had long hoped to find. James was eager to write more parts for him and hastily set to work to dramatize another short story, "Owen Wingrave," whose hero was just such a graceful heir of an old family. This play would be *The Saloon*.

It is easy to overlook the ancient butler at Covering End, Chivers, who opens *The High Bid* and is present in the opening scenes and subsequent crises. Chivers is a type, a familiar character in fiction and drama, the Old Family Retainer. The genius of the theater allows James with great economy and the collaboration of a talented actor to present him as a flesh-and-blood person, an embodiment of the family and traditions of Covering End. When Captain Yule first begins to understand the importance of Covering End, it is to Chivers he turns and pledges loyalty.

The estate is part of the essential, material order of civilization; it embodies an older tradition of family than the new unit of American society, the unstable atom of temporarily linked parents and child. The feudal family extends over time and place, and, like James's own, it ramifies over generations and includes widening circles of relations and dependents. To found or maintain a family was the privilege of the aristocrat, whose place in feudal society was to head such a realm and to fight for it. A "family" encompassed a whole little nation and made a home for generations of husbands and wives, friends and lovers, bachelors in pairs, spinsters in pairs, brothers and sisters, nephews and nieces, cousins and servants. Often it was perhaps a tyranny founded upon injustices, but a "family" was just such a little world with its own traditions and household gods as James had founded at Lamb House, one that could and should be governed with benevolence and civility.

Although in form *The High Bid* was a light comedy, meant as a crowd-pleaser, James could not be false to his own vision. In this repeatedly reworked and slowly elaborated little play, the central image is an old house that is passing into the hands of the latest heir. The house was successively called "Summersoft," the title under which it was first published as a play, a name that conveyed some of the qualities of James's favorite image, late-afternoon tea in a walled garden, and then "Covering End," the name it was given in the story and final play versions, which carry more of the sense of a refuge. The house and family at Covering End were metaphors, embodiments of James's central ideas, his personal religion. The new title, *The High Bid*, signals the danger to this enclave of civilization, unrestrained buying and selling of the unique repositories of art and civilization.

His message was not entirely clear to his audiences, but the quality of his workmanship and his joyous tone made this the most popular of his plays, at least with critics. It would be warmly reviewed when it played in London, and a lifetime later Kenneth Tynan would include *Guy Domville* and *The High Bid* among those to be considered for the repertory of the new National Theatre.

Lamb House was crowded with proofs in process of correction, typescripts in process of revision, handwritten sheets waiting to be typed, anacondas of paper. The New York Edition was appearing in the United States two volumes at a time, stepping on the heels of *The American Scene*. Travel essays excluded from the magnum opus were collected in Heinemann's edition of *English Hours*, to be swiftly followed by *Italian Hours*. In the spring of 1908, a Boston publisher brought out a volume of James's literary criticism, *Views and Reviews*, and a bibliography of his published work. He was writing short stories again, some to be included in later volumes of the New York Edition, while others would be published in two separate books outside the edition. Some of his finest short stories would thus be omitted from the magnum opus.

From 1907 through 1909, therefore, rival publishers in the United States and Great Britain, seeking to capitalize on James's celebrity, issued—in addition to twenty-three volumes of the New York Edition—another half-dozen books of Jamesiana, many of them reprints of earlier work, all revised and supplemented to bring them up to date.

The sales of individual titles were disappointing, inevitably, given the number of James's books that were appearing and the finite size of his audience. The first printing of the early volumes of the New York Edition was 1,500 sets; but these early novels, heavily revised and laden with the detailed imagery of his later style that they could not easily carry, evidently were disappointing to his readers. New subscriptions for subsequent volumes did not materialize, and the print order was reduced to 1,000 for the second half of the series. Royalties in the first year were minuscule, after James's expenses were deducted. Macmillan issued a "de luxe" edition in Great Britain, but this sold poorly.

Contributing to the poor sales was one of the periodic collapses of the securities markets in the United States, a panic that swept back across the Atlantic to Great Britain and made the middle class cautious. But there were also difficulties in the fundamental conception of the project. James had a characteristically complex idea, hoping to show not only that his works of fiction made a coherent whole, like Balzac's, but also to show this vast work from a present point of view, making of it a single vast work as seen in retrospect by its author. As in his fiction and nonfiction works alike he had chosen an observer from whose point of view to narrate, so in the New York Edition the reader would be asked to see the work from the author's point of view; in itself a complex and divided one, for the author of today was recalling with fond memories the experiences of the young man who had first written the books. The prefaces that James wrote, and the revisions that he made, were from this complex point of view.

James wrote his prefaces and made his revisions in his new style, one that was infused with energy and life but was hardly crystalline. A reader quickly discovered that the preface held no enriching or elucidating commentary on the novel that followed but was part of a vast metawork, James's artistic autobiography, from which personalities and anything of a "private" character were omitted. The reader was asked to embark on a purely intellectual project, an inquiry into the art of representation, in which the only voice we hear is James's and the only sight we see is James with his back turned, at his desk before a window. These prefaces have been immensely valuable to critics and biographers, as James probably intended; but the New York Edition never succeeded with general readers.

In important ways, furthermore, the prefaces were misleading: self-absorbed and self-regarding but affixed, as they were, to novels and stories drenched with sexuality—sexuality that was emphasized and made vivid by the revisions that he made for this definitive edition. In his revised *Portrait of a Lady*, for instance, the climax of the book is Isabel Archer's decision to turn away from the embrace of a young man, Caspar Goodwood, who loves her. The impact of his passion was left to be imagined in the first edition; now James described it with extraordinary vividness:

> He said nothing at first; she only felt him close to her. . . . It almost seemed to her that no one had ever been so close to her as that. . . .
>
> "Turn to me," Goodwood repeated . . . [and] she felt . . . that she had never been loved before. She had believed it, but this was different; this

was the hot wind of the desert, at the approach of which the others dropped dead, like mere sweet airs of the garden. It wrapped her about; it lifted her off her feet, while the very taste of it, as of something potent, acrid and strange, forced open her set teeth. . . .

His kiss was like white lightning, a flash that spread, and spread again, and stayed; and it was extraordinarily as if, while she took it, she felt each thing in his hard manhood that had least pleased her, each aggressive fact of his face, his figure, his presence, justified of its intense identity and made one with this act of possession.

A reader understands that the temptation Goodwood poses must be portrayed vividly, Isabel must be tempted to surrender herself, before duty and self-mastery intervene and she turns away. But the prefaces give no hint that the sensations James describes of being loved by a young man, evoking tastes and odors, the sensation of an embrace, are reconstructed from memory. James speaks only of the solitary act of composition and not of the memories with which he clothes his work. His descriptions of ecstasies are given an uneasy onanistic quality. The reader who pursues the prefaces and reads the revised novels may easily believe—however improbable such a feat would be—that all the vivid sensory experience James describes, agonies of love and betrayal, upheavals of emotion, are only magically persuasive fantasies spun out of air.

In the midst of all his frenetic activity, his concentrated agonies over the New York Edition, James wrote a potboiler for Elizabeth Jordan—a chapter for her serialized "collective novel" *The Whole Family*—and when Forbes-Robertson turned down his dramatization of "Owen Wingrave" as a curtain-raiser early in the year—evidently hesitating to open in two plays by the same author in which he performed two essentially similar parts—James enlarged *The Saloon* to a full three acts and sent it to another producer. Meanwhile, he oversaw rehearsals, set design, and costuming for the production of *The High Bid* for a March opening in Edinburgh.

His book on London, for which Macmillan was now clamoring—Pennell had already produced a number of illustrations of James's suggested subjects—his American novel, and a still older unfinished project, *The Sense of the Past*, the companion to *The Golden Bowl* that had been promised to Methuen three years earlier, were all set aside for the time being while he met these more pressing demands. Despite the poor sales of the New York Edition, he was in excellent spirits and producing at a prodigious pace.

The High Bid required a week of rehearsals in London in February, and then another week of rehearsals while the company was on the road, in Manchester, and final dress rehearsals on the stage in Edinburgh, through all of which James was in attendance, gently encouraging and directing. Forbes-Robertson was an excellent Captain Yule, but James had doubts about Gertrude Elliott's ability to be as powerful as Mrs. Gracedew was required to be—"she is a scrap (personally, physically) where she should be a presence." She had doubts of her own and at one point asked James to rewrite the climax so that less was required of her—which James declined to do—but by opening night he was satisfied that she was sufficiently intelligent and talented to carry off her part.

Rehearsals at the theater in Manchester, where the company rehearsed in the afternoons and performed another play in the evenings, and then the special train with actors, sets, and baggage to Edinburgh, all brought back to him the pleasant Bohemian days on tour with Wolcott Balestier and the Compton Comedy Company. When James spoke of *The High Bid*, it was as the impresario of the affair:

> the journey from Manchester to [Edinburgh was] achieved an hour or two ago by special train for my whole troupe & its impedimenta—I traveling with the animals like the lion-tamer or serpent-charmer in person & quite enjoying the caravan-quality, the bariolée Bohemian or *picaresque* note of the affair.

For the opening, Jocelyn Persse came up to Edinburgh as James's guest and stayed at the Roxburghe Hotel, where James had taken a suite, as had Pinker. Lucy Clifford came up from London as well, and James, nervous as ever on an opening night, was grateful for their presence.

The play opened at the Royal Lyceum, a large theater satisfactorily filled with an expectant crowd. James, to spare himself, had arranged beforehand with Forbes-Robertson that he would not take the author's curtain call; he joined his friends in their box for a time but could not bear to watch his play and slipped away backstage. The audience's laughter and applause told him that the play was a success; Forbes-Robertson and Elliott assured him that it had been; and James happily played host to his friends and the cheerful cast that night at the Roxburghe.

James, Persse, and Pinker stayed over to see the second night's performance, which confirmed the success of the first. The little group of principals discussed the future of the play. The Forbes-Robertsons would take it on tour during the winter and would look for a London theater to lease; they would bring the play to London at the height of the Season, in May or June.

The following week, the play went to Glasgow, where it was again a success, and James returned to London. The opening in Scotland was "a real and unmistakable victory," but only London could provide financial success. Forbes-Robertson looked for a theater, but none was immediately available on short notice.

James's hopes for a second life for his early novels were disappointed, although sales of the New York Edition as a cumulative affair might eventually justify the labor involved ("I am building a little on the Edition," he told Howells). Nor did the royalties for *The American Scene* get much beyond the advances already paid, and his series on "The Speech and Manners of American Women" for *Harper's Bazar* was not very popular and did not appear separately as a book. *English Hours* was not earning very much, and although he was publishing a great deal he was earning very little at the moment from past work—"My books absolutely decline to do anything," he complained. For the short term, his hopes were invested in the theater again, although success there depended upon many factors converging, as he well knew.

> [*The High Bid*] has been done solely for sordid coin—in the hope of the same—& I am therefore praying that arrangements may take effect for its production in town early in May. But there is a terrific *treacherous* side—or possibility—to any theatric matter—& I tremble even while I yearn.

Returning to the comparative quiet of Lamb House, James resumed work on the New York Edition, held in abeyance during the month of rehearsals and the opening of *The High Bid*. Rye was suffering the effects of the motorcar, and the town was growing noisy and crowded with fashionable people down from London for a brief holiday. He complained of these intrusions on his quiet realm and of the pressure of work—printers were demanding corrected proofs for the New York Edition. But his late novels and stories did not require extensive revision, and in less than a month he was ahead of his schedule once again and thinking of going abroad, despite all previous resolutions to the contrary. Edith and Edward Wharton were in Normandy, just across the Channel, tempting him with the idea of an auto tour in the north of France.

Adding to the temptation was the possibility of seeing Hendrik Andersen, Henry Adams, and William Dean Howells, all of whom had plans to be in Paris that spring. Tom and Lilla Perry added their voice to the chorus summoning him to Paris, as they lingered there. With his work up to date and nothing definite decided yet about a venue for *The High Bid* in London, James gave himself a sixty-fifth birthday present of two weeks in France with old friends. Instead of joining the Whartons in Amiens and returning to Paris with them by motor, as they proposed, however, he went to Paris first for a few days to see friends and await their arrival.

At the Whartons' apartment on the rue de Varenne, earlier in the year, Teddy had suffered from vague illness and depression. He did not have Edith's enthusiasm for Paris, and her deepening friendship with Walter Berry, who shared her artistic and intellectual life in a way that he could not, excluded him further from her interests. Teddy was an American husband; he was not comfortable in Edith's circle of cosmopolitan men and women, he spoke little French and could not join her at the theater, nor did he have friends of his own in Paris. Early in April, he fled to America.

When James arrived, accordingly, he found the tour of Normandy abandoned and Edith living alone in a rented *hôtel* on the Right Bank, among Americans in the Place des États-Unis, that James called her "Palazzino." After a brief stay in Paris and some visits to friends, she and James set off to Beauvais in a truncated version of the planned automobile tour. They were accompanied by James's old friend and Ronald Gower's lover, Morton Fullerton. James was certainly aware that Edith and the polymorphous Fullerton were carrying on an affair. Wharton was grateful for James's friendly presence, which made the situation easier. This was her first extramarital affair, and she confided to her journal that she often felt shy and awkward when left alone with Fullerton, but "with our dear H.J. I felt at my ease."

Invitations for James streamed into the Palazzino, and Wharton loyally tried to fend them off. Jacques-Émile Blanche asked permission to paint

James's portrait, to which he agreed, and Wharton's chauffeur carried him out to Blanche's studio in the suburb of Passy for several sittings. Blanche began by sketching James full face, despite his subject's protestations. James insisted, as he had all his life, that his face was too round to be shown frontally and asked to be painted in left profile, a pose that would hide the scar in his upper lip. Blanche made no reply and continued to sketch him from the front, but as there were to be so few sittings he had photographs made from which to complete the portrait, and to James's astonishment when it was finished it showed him in left profile.

James had a round of pleasant farewell dinners in Paris, saying goodbye to Tom Perry, Henry Adams, and Howells, American friends whom he was not certain of seeing again. Perry, whose health was better, was planning a journey to Saint Petersburg and Moscow, and James asked him to look for signs, while he was in Saint Petersburg, whether "an old & very amiable Russian friend of mine . . . Paul Joukovsky, be alive or dead???"

William, Alice, and Peggy came to Lamb House for another extended visit. William had been invited to give the Hibbert Lectures at Manchester College, Oxford, and used the opportunity to begin his work in speculative philosophy, attempting, as he had long promised himself to do, a system of thought built upon empirical considerations. William and Alice went to Oxford just as Henry was returning from Paris, but when William's lectures had been delivered in June they came to Lamb House for a long visit, and Peggy came over to join them.

Host to his family again, James nevertheless continued to work intensely at the New York Edition, which was nearing completion. Late in June, Alice and Peggy set off for Switzerland, leaving William at Lamb House with his brother.

With William quietly ensconced in the garden, through unusually pleasant sunny days, James finished the last preface for the last volume of his magnum opus. In this final essay on *The Golden Bowl* he spoke of his consistent method throughout the novels and short stories he had chosen for the edition. In each case, the situation at the center of the tale was described by an observer, a sensitive consciousness that seemed to James to add a necessary dimension.

The choice of observer was important, for the more perceptive an observer, the richer would be the final portrait. James's careful elaborations of style, his efforts to render perception vividly and precisely, were therefore—as it seemed to him—a necessary development of the artist's task. As he read over the whole body of his work for this edition, he was struck by the constancy with which he had adhered to this duty. There remained only a single important point for him to make, more urgent than any so far addressed: the question of revision.

Reading over his work of the past twelve years, the time during which he had developed his new realistic style, he found that as a reader he was in harmony with the author. There were only minor corrections to make in this work. But when he read over the fiction of his first period, he had felt obliged to discard a great deal, and what he kept he found that he could no longer read as he had written. The extensive revisions he had made of these simpler early works, although readers had objected, had seemed to him a duty, one that evidently trumped his wish for commercial success.

His duty was not precisely to the works themselves but to the truths that they portrayed. Reading his early work had given him a renewed sense of their reality. Turning his imagination upon his earliest work and its underlying truth was like "a sudden large apprehension of the Absolute." He had hesitated for months over the question of revising his first novels and tales, but after this experience of rereading, he had no longer felt any hesitation. The form in which he had left his early work was not adequate fully to express its essential truths or their sensual human embodiment. His characters had an objective reality, the fusion of the ideal and the particular in a single unique work of art; they were not so much invented as discovered, and revisions were needed to keep the work faithful to them in their best expression.

He spoke of himself now as a poet, and of the poet's calling, in language one ordinarily reserved for religious experience. A poet passionately cultivates the image of life, and the art of transmitting his vision, in an ecstacy of inspiration: to present this image in less than perfect expression would be a sin.

> The seer and speaker under the descent of the god is the "poet," whatever his form, and he ceases to be one only when his form . . . is unworthy of the god.

Early in 1908, James began to feel the first symptoms of ischemic heart disease, what later generations would call "heart failure," the illness from which William and Robertson also suffered and from which their mother and perhaps Alice had died. The cause, a gradual weakening of the heart muscles, was not yet known, but the sensation of a great weight upon the chest and the painful, suffocating sensation called "angina" had recently been identified as the early stages of an illness whose most common conclusion was death.

In James's case, as in the classic progression of the disease, early symptoms of panting and breathlessness were soon followed in January by an episode of angina accompanied by severe pain, a frightening incident of the kind that had not yet been named a "heart attack."

When James had his attack, he consulted William Osler, the newly appointed Regius Professor of Medicine at Oxford, who had written the first systematic description of the disease. Osler—who had treated William while still in the United States—assured James that the disease was manageable, and referred him to a specialist in London, a Dr. Mackenzie, whom he might see regularly. Mackenzie prescribed exercise, which James had largely given up in the past year, and a weight-loss diet. He now Fletcherized with a vengeance.

Henry and William corresponded about their mutual "thoracic" symptoms. William had been taking digitalis for several years, but his heart condition was worsening, and he now reported that he was experimenting with "a semi-quack homeopathist" in Boston, who had been strongly recommended by friends but whose treatments so far had left him worse than before. William found that the illness depressed him and made it difficult for him to work.

Henry's local physician in Rye, a Dr. Skinner, gave him strychnine and digitalis tonics, which greatly relieved his symptoms and allowed him to exercise. With the aid of Skinner's tonics and Mackenzie's prompting, he renewed his routine of daily walks, although he went more slowly than before, and his heart seemed to strengthen. Although the symptoms of angina did not entirely disappear, James adapted himself to them, resting frequently when he walked, and pausing as he went up stairs. He was soon able to give up the various tonics entirely. Despite continued symptoms of a heart ailment, Mackenzie's regime was having a beneficent effect:

> I am definitely better & working out my salvation (my temporal salvation) . . . to go in for more movement & locomotion . . . above all to reduce my weight. So I've walked & walked more, & eaten less & less, & felt my clothes grow looser & looser—& all to my distinct benefit.

As spring came on, his depression also lightened. He was able, despite the distress and depression that accompanied his heart disease, to read the last proofs of the New York Edition. But he knew that he had been at a dangerous threshold. He confided to Edith Wharton in the spring of 1909, when he was feeling more fully recovered:

> I *have* had—to be frank—a bad & worried & depressed & inconvenient winter—with the serpent-tail of what seemed at the time . . . a tolerably ominous cardiac crisis. . . . I am definitely better . . . only that particular brush of the dark wing leaves one never quite the same.

Writing was always in part making love to his reader, and with the New York Edition he felt that he had bared himself for an ultimate intimacy, a complete intellectual and spiritual union of writer and reader. He was aware that he had few readers who would rise to such an invitation, and in his last preface he spoke indeed of how few they were. Subscriptions were meager, and few volumes beyond the subscribed number were being sold. But he was happy with the work he had done, and if fully responsive readers were few, they were precious and welcome. Young men gathered around him, and if they did not always understand his work, they accepted his invitation to intimacy and returned his affection.

Several friends left records of the impression he made at this time, of the long-remembered impact of a personality who fully inhabited his body and was wholly present in the moment. He looked out of his eyes and bared his face, scarred lip and all. The young Lytton Strachey, staying at the Mermaid Inn for the Christmas season, carefully recorded having seen James twice: once at the inn and once glimpsed through the window of Lamb House. "Both times exceedingly remarkable, but almost impossible to describe. . . . He has a colossal physiognomy . . . I long to know him."

Not long after he was observed and described by Strachey, James was in Cambridge, having been invited by some young men for May week, and took the opportunity to visit Arthur Benson, who was now a Fellow of Magdalen College. Benson's edition of Queen Victoria's letters had been well received, and James was among the admirers of the work (famously remarking that the queen was "more of a man" than he had imagined). Benson had purchased a motorcar and a country house in Sussex for himself and his mother. James rarely saw him alone now, except when Benson motored to Rye, but they continued to correspond regularly. Benson had his own circle of collegiate admirers, among whom James's work was a regular topic of admiring discussion.

On this visit to Cambridge, James lunched with the young men who had invited him: Charles Sayle, Geoffrey Keynes, and Rupert Brooke, who had walked over from Grantchester "in a fever of awed anticipation." After this meeting, Brooke's letters took on a distinctly Jamesian caste. A friend gently gibed him about his encounter with the great man:

"Of course you were frank and boyish?"

"Oh yes, of course I did the fresh, boyish stunt and it was a great success."

James also met John Maynard Keynes, Geoffrey's brother, and had breakfast with him, but of all the young men his sharpest memory was of Rupert Brooke, a golden youth, a poet whose personal beauty was already part of his legend.

Margaret Brooke (who was not related to Rupert) was spending more time in London, seeing to her sons' interest in the succession to the throne of Sarawak. She became a frequent visitor to Lamb House as well. The otherwise imperious ranee treated James with great deference and at about this time began to call him "chèr Maître," an honorific that had no equivalent in English. ("Master" sounded submissive; "guru" or "teacher" was closer.) Some other of his more cosmopolitan friends also adopted the practice. Joseph Conrad addressed his letters so; even some of James's neighbors in Rye picked up the mildly feudal form of address. If he had been a British subject, he would have been a candidate for a title; in France he might have been an Academician, but for an American there was no suitable term of respect.

Forbes-Robertson had leased Ellen Terry's theater, but despite his promises he had not yet produced James's play. Instead, he opened in September with Jerome K. Jerome's *The Passing of the Third Floor Back*. The reason may have been Ellen Terry's objections. She had purchased the one-act version of *The High Bid* outright and when the three-act version opened in Edinburgh had cabled Forbes-Robertson, "You have my play." Perhaps James had forgotten that she owned the theatrical rights to the original story or felt that her claim did not extend to the newly written play.

Forbes-Robertson later claimed that the matter had been amicably arranged, and perhaps it had been from his point of view. He told James that *The High Bid* could not be staged in Terry's theater, however, and offered instead to put it on as a matinee in Beerbohm Tree's new venue, His Majesty's Theatre, with a promise that it would move to evening performances in due course. James agreed.

The High Bid ran for its appointed week in February 1909, to full houses and adulatory reviews. James's winter theater companions— Margaret Brooke, Lucy Clifford, Jocelyn Persse—joined him for the opening. Max Beerbohm wrote a love letter of a notice. True, young Beerbohm thought the plot of the play trite and improbable. "Of all that I love in Mr. James's mind so very little can be translated into the sphere of the drama." But the bulk of his long notice was an admiring tour of James's whole body of work, of which the play gave some hints, and he pointed out exactly what had tempted James into the theater so often:

> [Forbes-Robertson] showed that for the interpretation of Mr. James's sort of thing he was admirably equipped. "What are you exactly?" asks Captain Yule of the aged and shabby butler who is in charge of the house; "I mean, to whom do you beautifully *belong?*" There, in the last six words, is quintessence of Mr. James; and the sound of them sent innumerable little vibrations through the heart of every good Jacobite in the audience. . . . The words could not have been more perfectly uttered than they were by Mr. Forbes-Robertson. . . . How crude a medium print is . . . for expression of what such a face and voice as Mr. Forbes-Robertson can express! In his eyes, as he surveyed the old butler, and in his smile, and in the groping hesitancy before the adverb was formed, and in the sinking tone of the verb, there was a whole world of good feeling, good manners, and humor.

Hugh Walpole was one of Arthur Benson's protégés. He was twenty-five years old and just beginning his climb to success and world celebrity. Having completed his first novel, he was at the moment waiting to learn its fate and trying to help it along as well as he could. Walpole had adopted the useful practice of writing admiring letters to successful authors, and after first securing an introduction from Benson, he wrote a charming letter to James, who replied with more than usual courtesy. They entered into a correspondence. Walpole had lodgings in Chelsea, and when James was briefly in London they had dinner together. There was forty years' difference in their ages. Walpole was tall, stout, and handsome, a clean-shaven rugby player with a big square jaw and a frank manner. His wavy brown hair was plastered down in the fashion of the day, and he wore gold-rimmed eyeglasses. A lion hunter and practiced charmer, Walpole was eager to make his way in London. He had written very warmly of James's work, his warmth was not feigned, and he had a genuine affection for the older man that was highly attractive. Afterward he made a brief entry in his diary:

> Dined with Henry James alone at the Reform Club. He was perfectly wonderful. By far the greatest man I have ever met—and yet amazingly humble and affectionate—absolutely delightful. He talked about himself and his books a good deal and said some very interesting things. It was a wonderful evening.

Walpole told Benson all about it, and Benson noted ruefully in his own diary, "He makes friends with everyone—his latest captive is Henry James, who writes to him often. All this is very delightful . . . though it makes me feel horribly old and cold."

James was indeed captive. He was particularly eager for affection in that winter of his first brush with death, and in April he invited Walpole to spend a weekend at Lamb House. Walpole carefully recorded afterward, "a wonderful weekend with Henry James. Much more wonderful than I had expected. . . . He is beyond words. I cannot speak about him."

James's account of the visit, when he wrote to Benson afterward to thank him for making them acquainted, was almost equally warm. Their friendship grew through the summer. With the New York Edition behind him at last, James came up to London more often than before and made valuable introductions for the young man. Walpole wrote to him when they were parted, to ensure that he was in the older man's thoughts. "Think of you?" James replied gallantly, "I think of you constantly." The affection of this powerful older man was particularly welcome to Walpole:

> [T]hat is a quite perfect affair in its own way and one begins to feel that the one thing that one really demands of the friend is perfect comprehension. Of course that is perhaps "a counsel of perfection" but H.J. has got it.

In August, Benson confided to his diary that "H.J. has formed a romantic friendship with Hugh Walpole, very good & happy for both, I expect. But I feel envious, alas."

Walpole, and other very much younger men, did make James feel his age. Hugh was as healthy and vital "as a merry-go-round at a fair," an "almost unbearably enviable youth." When he wrote to Hendrik Andersen, James (saying nothing about Walpole, however) confessed that he felt ancient, said that he was ninety-nine years old. Percy Lubbock and other young men around Benson and Sturgis affected him the way Walpole sometimes did. James told Benson:

> I am spending a dark, cold, dripping Sunday here [at Queen's Acre]— with two or three other amis de la maison; but above all with the ghosts, somehow, of a promiscuous past brushing me as with troubled wings, and the echoes of the ancient years seeming to murmur to me: "Don't you wish you were still young—or young again . . . as they so wonderfully are?" I don't know that I particularly do wish it.

Hugh Walpole asked how he should address his new mentor, and James replied genially that he might address him, not indeed by his first name nor as "chèr Maître," the way other acolytes did, but as " 'Très-chèr Maître,' or 'my very dear master.' " He spoke of them as master and pupil, or as Robinson Crusoe and his man Friday, and in those letters that have survived, Walpole addresses him as "My Dearest Master." The gap of forty years between them was too deep entirely to be bridged, but the friendship was a very warm one on both sides, as long years afterward Walpole recalled it:

> I loved him, was frightened of him, was bored by him, was staggered by his wisdom and stupefied by his intricacies, altogether enslaved by his kindness, generosity, child-like purity of his affections, his unswerving loyalties, his sly and Puck-like sense of humour.

One Friday in October, Walpole came down for a weekend and stayed for a full week. The visit evidently marked a watershed in their relations. James wrote to him beforehand, "Just a fond word to speed you on your way . . . & as a hint of how wide I open my arms—to say nothing of how tight I shall thereafter close them." Walpole recorded the visit in his diary briefly: "Most blissful time with H.J. Every day with him is better than the last." Promptly on his return to London, he wrote to James, who answered fondly, in a letter filled with heavily erotic puns. Walpole, he knows, has had to struggle through a "jungle" of waiting correspondence, but James is glad that he has cut through the jungle to come upon *this* elephant, who winds about him his "well-meaning old trunk."

> I abominably miss you—having so extravagantly enjoyed you; but it's a great enrichment of consciousness, all the while, that we are in such beautiful, such exquisite, relation. . . . I dream of the golden sands— with you there, along with me, for my man Friday. *Such* a run, now, on *the* Friday here! The elephant paws you oh so benevolently—which his name is your all devoted old H.J.

He carries the joke along in later letters, the clumsy old elephant careers in circles about the youth, he addresses Hugh as "dear" and "dearest" and lapses into a kind of baby talk. The old man was making himself a little ridiculous, and Gaillard Lapsley remarked to Arthur Benson that James had a craving for affection—indeed, that it was the only simple thing left in him.

Holmes came to England that summer, although he had long ago said his farewell to the Season, to receive an honorary degree from Oxford. James did not attend the ceremony and did not see him; which became an element in a later grievance.

Edith Wharton paid James a visit at Lamb House. They were good friends now; their relations, very much like James's with his sister, Alice, were enriched by their silent understandings and their shared sense of humor: teasing, ironical, often edged with cheerful malice. Wharton had been depressed and discouraged after her return to the United States. Walter Berry had accepted a position as a judge in an arbitration tribunal that sat in Cairo and did not expect to be in Europe or America, except for brief visits, for several years. Morton Fullerton had ceased to answer her letters, and in the winter that followed their affair it appeared that he had long been enmeshed with another woman and that he had perhaps become engaged to marry a third. Wharton was alone at the Mount with her husband, who required her care and attention, but Teddy was ill and self-absorbed, and even at his best shared none of her interests. When she came upon a passage in a book that she was moved to share with him, he only remarked, "Does that sort of thing really amuse you?" She felt imprisoned, and her restlessness verged upon desperation. She hauled

Teddy with her to Paris; she carried him about in the automobile and they made another tour in the south; but nothing availed to improve his spirits or her situation. James gave the only advice he could offer:

> I am deeply distressed at the situation you describe & as to which my power to suggest or enlighten now quite miserably fails me. I move in darkness; I rack my brains; I gnash my teeth; I don't pretend to understand or to imagine. And yet incredibly to you doubtless—I am still moved to say "Don't Conclude!" . . . Only sit tight & *go through the movements of life* . . . behind which, all the while, the deeper & darker & the unapparent, in which things *really* happen to us, learns, under that hygiene, to stay in its place.

James learned from Fullerton that he was in fact being blackmailed by a former mistress, Henrietta Mirecourt, who was still sharing his house and who had come upon and stolen letters he had received from Lord Ronald Gower, Margaret Brooke, Wharton, and James himself. Fullerton had the habit of letting letters accumulate, rarely answering but never discarding them.

Wharton learned of the situation, presumably through James, and wrote stiffly and formally to Fullerton, asking for the return of her letters. That winter she met with him in Paris, where he evidently confessed to her the whole depth of his embroilments with men and women. Teddy Wharton remained in America, and Edith took an apartment on the rue de Varenne, opposite the Vanderbilt apartment in which she had been so happy, and then came over to England to discuss her situation with James.

Gradually a plan emerged: Fullerton must accede to the blackmail and buy back all the letters that Mirecourt had taken. In order to convey the needed funds to Fullerton discreetly, they agreed to have him invited to write a book about Paris for Macmillan, in the series for which James was to write his London book. Wharton wrote to Fullerton, saying (untruly) that the assignment would come with a large advance, and James wrote to Frederick Macmillan that Fullerton was in need of money and that he would provide the cash anonymously if Macmillan would commission a book on Paris and characterize the payment as an advance against royalties, making no mention of his involvement. Wharton apparently provided one thousand pounds to be conveyed to Fullerton in this way.

The ruse was successful; Fullerton managed to propitiate Mirecourt, gave her the cash supplied by Wharton via James and Macmillan, and recovered his letters.

In July, when all these transactions were complete, James invited both Wharton and Fullerton to visit him in Lamb House. Wharton had reconciled herself to Fullerton's profligacy and was glad to be reunited with him. "It is just a month today since I came down to dinner at Rye," Wharton wrote to Fullerton in August, "and found you standing by the hearth in the drawing room talking to Henry. . . . During that month I have had everything in life I ever longed for, & more than I ever imagined!"

After their brief stay at Lamb House, Fullerton returned to Paris and his work as correspondent for *The Times;* nothing was ever heard again of his book on Paris. James accompanied Wharton to Queen's Acre, where he left her, and she prepared to return to Paris. Walter Berry was to have a brief vacation that summer, and after Wharton's happy month with Fullerton, Berry came to see her in Paris. At first they planned to accept James's invitation to Lamb House, but Berry's time was short. Wharton then invited James to join them in Paris, but he answered that he was too busy. He settled into his green study with a sigh of relief after six weeks of immersion in Wharton's complex affairs.

While these matters were being untangled, James one evening read Otto Weininger's *Sex and Character,* which had swept across Europe after its publication in Vienna. Its author was only twenty-two when it was composed, and after its remarkable success he had committed suicide.

The book was a work of would-be idealist science, an analysis of sexual character into ideal types. Male and female, heterosexual and homosexual were intelligently characterized and subdivided; but the masculine spirit was praised and the feminine condemned, equally in homosexual and heterosexual characters. The Jewish author's suicide seemed to lend drama to his agonized portrayal of imagined polarities—Aryan and Semitic, Male and Female. When he read the book, James remarked with gallows humor, "I thought [it] so portentous on the part of the mere boy who produced it that nothing indeed could be left him but to blow his brains out."

He spent a weekend with the Byron papers, investigating old accusations that had so bestirred his father's generation, that the poet had abused his wife and committed incest with his half sister. James's neighbor Lady Lovelace, now widowed, had inherited the Byron papers from the late earl, and the countess asked James and her nephew novelist John Buchan to look through the papers and prepare a report on the poet's relations with his wife and sister, a document to be deposited in the British Museum. James always had a lively appetite for gossip and took up the task with alacrity. Buchan, who was a comparatively young man, recalled that "the thing nearly made me sick" but that James never turned a hair. Byron had abused his wife by forcing upon her knowledge of his incestuous relations with his sister. Coming upon some special vileness in the letters, James would calmly remark, " 'singular,'—'most curious'—'nauseating, perhaps, but how inexpressibly significant.' "

With the New York Edition completed—the "Nightmare Edition" as James took to calling it—he looked for ways to repair his income. "The Edition has played for me . . . a terrible Dog-in-the-Manger part," as he told Frederick Macmillan. He was eager to recycle already published work and leaped at the chance when Nelsons, a publisher of cheap reprints, offered £135 for *The American*. James stipulated only that the newly revised version rather than the original text be reprinted.

As he had done in his earlier playwriting period, James was energetically writing short stories. Pinker sent them around to magazines in the United States and Great Britain. These stories were popular, and James was able to fill two volumes with previously published magazine pieces. (Some were rather long. Harper serialized and then brought out as a slim book the story "Julia Bride," with a substantial first printing of four thousand copies.) James also agreed to contribute an essay to *Bazar*, which was running a series of reflections on the afterlife by various prominent figures. In July, James sent his contribution, "Is There a Life After Death?" to Elizabeth Jordan, who made it the concluding piece in the series and in the book edition, *In After Days*.

He expressed in this essay his tentative belief, at least his willingness to believe, that his personality might survive his death. He viewed this possibility as William did, as a natural phenomenon. There was no evidence at all for ghosts, that is to say for physical manifestations of the departed spirit, James wrote; but seeming telepathic communications reported by the Society for Psychical Research were difficult to explain on any other basis than the survival of the personality. Perhaps not every personality would survive the dissolution of the body—"immense numbers" of people didn't wake up enough to live in either this world or the next—but if a personality had been carefully built and maintained, had been nurtured and strengthened throughout a lifetime, had *lived* in each moment, perhaps it would not simply evaporate when the body died.

When in London, James attended the theater faithfully. Elizabeth Robins had retired from the stage, settled in the country, and was now rarely found in London. With women friends close to his own age—Lucy Clifford, Rhoda Broughton, Florence Bell—and with ever-younger men—Jocelyn Persse, Hugh Walpole—James attended opening nights of the new plays. Florence Bell had a new play, *Where the Money Goes*, that he happily attended with Walpole. He also saw Guy du Maurier's play *An Englishman's Home*, which was produced and published by his brother, Gerald, who took one of the parts. In the play, an English home was shown besieged by an invading foreign army, against which civilians fought bravely but futilely. It was a plea for a standing British army, to protect the nation from German invasion. The lord chamberlain would not allow the invading nation to be named, but the invaders wore highly recognizable spiked helmets. The production was so popular and created so much excitement that the army opened a recruiting station in the theater lobby.

In the summer of 1909, the stage was again offering James more dangerous temptations. An Irish poet, Herbert Trench, with the backing of a wealthy young friend, Thomas Evelyn Ellis, was starting a resident repertory company at the Haymarket Theatre and sought James's aid and support. James happily offered a play of his own for this effort, his melodrama *The Other House*, which had had success as a novel but had never been produced as a play. Trench accepted and purchased the theatrical rights for a period of five years. Staging would have to await the end of the run of Maurice Maeterlinck's new play, *The Blue Bird*, however, with which Trench had opened his season.

A group of well-known playwrights was making yet another effort to establish a national theater, in which to perform both classics and the best new plays. James agreed to lend his celebrated name and his talents to this renewed effort, as well. The organizers were distinguished and highly successful playwrights: Somerset Maugham, the most popular playwright of the day, James M. Barrie, George Bernard Shaw, John Masefield, John Galsworthy, and Harley Granville-Barker. Young Allan Wade, who was directing the Abbey Theatre's successful repertory season in London and who would later edit a book of James's theatrical criticism, was secretary for the group. Granville-Barker was the artistic director. Their effort was to be financed by Charles Frohman, an American producer.

The playwrights working to establish a repertory theater were anxious to end the censorship of plays. Protests against censorship were an old story, but times were changing. King Edward VII, whatever his personal failings may have seemed, continued to be a generous patron of the arts, and he was less interested than his late mother had been in maintaining the royal prerogative to censor plays. Herbert Asquith was prime minister, and his Liberal administration, responding to the appeals of the playwrights, established a select joint committee of Parliament to look into the question, without objection from the royal household. James, who had earlier written a letter of protest against censorship, attended the proceedings and submitted a forceful written statement to the committee.

Anticipating a new atmosphere, the playwrights had set to work. For the Frohman–Granville-Barker group Shaw wrote *Misalliance*, John Galsworthy wrote *Justice*, J. M. Barrie contributed two one-act plays, and James set to work on a new full-length play, *The Outcry*.

He worked at it while in London, writing the first draft out by hand. Miss Bosanquet had remained behind in Lamb House, and James sent handwritten drafts down to Rye, receiving typed copy by return mail. Frohman, meanwhile, leased the Duke of York's Theatre. James's new play was to be performed in that first season. He struggled to have it finished and set in type for the players before the first of the year.

The Outcry was James's first and only partisan political effort. He had become radicalized, as it were, by recent events. Earlier that year, the duke of Norfolk had announced his intention to sell Holbein's magnificent portrait of Queen Christina of Denmark, which had been on loan to the National Gallery for forty years. The painting was considered a national treasure, and James knew it well. The proposed buyer was Henry Frick, the American steel magnate, who was assembling one of the world's great private art collections in New York City.

Norfolk was a leader of the Tory opposition in the House of Lords, and the proposed sale was meant to dramatize his objections to the Liberal administration's budget for 1909, prepared by the radical David Lloyd George. The budget included a 20 percent inheritance tax to be imposed on the great landed estates, and Norfolk claimed that he was obliged to sell the painting in order to pay his taxes.

A proviso in the duke of Norfolk's agreement with Frick, however, would allow the Holbein portrait to remain at the National Gallery if the museum could match the American's offer of £72,000. The proposed sale to Frick was announced on May 1, and a campaign to match Frick's offer was quickly launched by the new National Arts Collection Fund. The fund issued an appeal that appeared in newspapers on May 7, and the press took up the cause. There was a great outcry and within a month the needed funds were obtained.

James was an early member and supporter of the National Arts Collection Fund, whose patron was Edward VII. James knew well the founding members of the fund and its moving spirit, the young art critic Roger Fry. The struggle over the Holbein seemed to James an important one both in itself and as a symbol of the greedy decline of the aristocracy, who were willing to sell away the embodied history and culture of England.

The Outcry was a recognizable dramatization of those events. The play was set at the height of the Season, and the initial stage direction said that the action was "highly contemporaneous." Norfolk became the belligerent widower "Lord Theign," who in the play was determined to sell his youngest daughter as well as a treasured painting, in order to pay family debts. Henry Frick was impersonated by the dignified "Breckenridge Bender," a new sort of American aristocrat who was more interested in preserving European culture than was Theign.

Roger Fry appears as the art critic "Hugh Crimble," the hero of the tale. Crimble conspires with Theign's young, beautiful daughter to keep the painting in England. He reports to Theign and to the audience that an immense patriotic outcry has broken out in the press over the sale of the precious painting. Embarrassed by the outcry, Theign acquiesces and donates his picture to the National Gallery. He instead recoups his fortunes by marrying a wealthy woman. His daughter, Grace, is then free to marry Crimble, and all ends happily. James has contrived a harmonious joinder of democracy and the old order. Newspapers (for a wonder) and young lovers ally themselves in the great cause of simultaneously preserving the heritage of the past and opening it to the public. The play ends with a courteous appearance by a British royal, who cannot be directly named.

The producer of the planned repertory season and its artistic director were pleased to have such a lively and topical play from James and scheduled *The Outcry* to make its first appearance in a West End theater at the height of the Season. This was precisely what James had earlier wished for *The High Bid*. He was at last on the verge of popular success in the theater. When he went down to Lamb House for Christmas, he took with him the text of *The Outcry* to make cuts and revisions for which Granville-Barker had asked. Rehearsals were to begin in the new year.

At this time he still expected that *The High Bid* would be performed in His Majesty's Theatre after the Jerome play's run. James also expected the *The Other House* to follow Maeterlinck's *Blue Bird* at the Haymarket. He would have two or even three plays being performed in the West End in the Season, and the script for *The Saloon* was still making the rounds. The plays were fables, rather than realist fictions; they depended greatly upon the actors to bring them down to earth. But they were well made and in their way beautiful. James seemed on the threshold of his long-sought popular and commercial success, with works in which he could believe he was assisting the theater and even, however modestly, the advance of civilization.

25

EVENING SOLITUDE

As Christmas approached, James's health and spirits declined. The demands of art and friendship had drained him, and when he retreated to Lamb House for the holidays he learned that Jonathan Sturges, his companion at Christmas in recent years, had died. His hosts during his early years in London—Houghton, Kemble, du Maurier, Smalley—were all dead. James had hoped to visit Howard Sturgis, but Sturgis was fully absorbed by the family he had assembled in Queen's Acre. Arthur Benson, too, was absorbed in family and work. James was lonely and fretted about his health and his finances.

Lamb House was filled with papers—typescripts, proofs, revised texts—after the extraordinary efforts of the past two years, and James had Gammon make a bonfire to dispose of them and added some of his accumulated correspondence to the blaze. As he told Annie Fields, who too had asked for any letters he might have had from Sarah Orne Jewett, who had died, "I have made tolerably absolute these last years . . . as I myself grow older and think more of my latter end: the law of not leaving personal and private documents at the mercy of any accidents, or even of my executors!" He feared the indiscretion of others more than his own, however, and made no effort to retrieve or destroy his own artful letters.

If he was lonely, he was not alone. In addition to Miss Bosanquet, with whom he worked and took his meals, and her companion Ellen Bradley—Nelly—who joined them at tea, Joan Paddington, Burgess Noakes, George Gammon, and Minnie Kidd waited upon, cared for, and indeed doted upon James. Neighbors called regularly, and family members visited. Bob's son, Ned, ran over from Paris and spent a day with him and brought James up to date on the Concord branch of the family. James was a great-uncle again, and, as he assured Robertson when he wrote to report his son's visit, he himself was not solitary—indeed he was rarely alone—but Lamb House in the winter darkness and wind was "solitudinous."

He had suffered another prolonged siege of gout and was bedridden for a while with another ailment that he feared was a return of the "jaundice" from which he had suffered in Venice. James continued to have regular bouts of angina, he was tired, and his spirits were very low after the long strain of recent years, the stresses both good and bad of the past few months. He felt that his reduced vitality and his continuing illnesses were the aftereffects of his "heart crisis," and although he rarely spoke of them, he confessed to William that the attacks of angina had continued to trouble him ever since the crisis of the previous winter. Darkness and unrelenting wind and rain also had their effect; as winter came on, he felt himself imprisoned in Lamb House. Three days before Christmas, he felt a definite downturn in mood.

> I have now spent some ten or eleven winters mainly in the country and find myself reacting violently at last in favour of pavements or street lamps and lighted shop fronts—places where one can go out at 4 or at 5 or at 6. . . . Here at 5 or 6 the plunge is only into black darkness and the abysmal *crotte* [mire].

Christmas dinner was a modest affair. Theodora Bosanquet and her "lady-pal," her "second self," Nelly Bradley, were now settled members of his Lamb House family, and on Christmas Eve an old friend, Bailey Saunders, turned up without notice, very glum; his wife had left him alone while she journeyed on the Continent.

James's end-of-year letters were subdued. He dwelt upon the difficulties and illnesses of the past year. To Margaret Brooke he wrote, "How beautiful & faithful you are to the poor old obscured & absent & so very muddling 'Master.' " It had been a detestable year, he said, and the dark Christmastide, "with only a lone & lorn & sad & rather stranded melancholy friend to keep him company" had been a fit climax to it.

> Dearest Hendrik.
>   Your tender little letter awakens in me the most tender response,— & I greet you all affectionately & faithfully, I put out my arms & hold you fast across Channel & Alps & Apennines. . . . I sit again in your high cool studio with all your brilliant creations about. . . . Above all, how-

ever, I rejoice in your telling me of your plan of coming to Paris this spring & of the happy chance of your coming to *me* by the same stroke.

He finished revising the last act of *The Outcry*, sent it to Granville-Barker in London, and sat down to make some needed cuts in the first act. Shortly after the first of the year, he learned that the opening was to be somewhat delayed, apparently because of difficulty in securing John Hare for the role of Lord Theign.

The High Bid would also be delayed. *The Third Floor Back* was playing to full houses, and Forbes-Robertson confessed that he would keep it on for some months. *The Blue Bird*, too, was doing well and would hold the stage at the Haymarket for several weeks more.

None of this meant defeat, but it was difficult for James to put off his hopes for a renewed income. He turned to his notebooks and began to work with redoubled energy at a new potboiler, a serialized novel for Harper.

The new light novel was to be based on the "K.B. case" recorded in his notebooks. "K.B." was the late Katherine Bronson, his first hostess in Venice in years gone by. Mrs. Bronson in her early Venetian days was a young widow, freedom abruptly conferred upon her by the unregretted death of her husband, to whom she had been unhappily married. The situation began to open up to him with the ramifications of a novel.

But he was not able to continue. On January 10, 1910, he suffered a thorough collapse and ceased writing. He felt apprehensive and weak, agitated and depressed. He found that he could not eat, indeed had developed a loathing for food, and was seized with vague anxieties. James grew frightened and sent for Dr. Skinner, who comforted him and relieved his loneliness and anxiety to a degree. When he felt the worst of the episode was over, James described it to his brother:

> I struggled in the wilderness, with occasional & delusive flickers of improvement (of a few hours) for many days—& with Skinner cooperating most kindly—and then 18 days ago [about January 21] I collapsed & went to bed & he instantly sent an excellent Nurse (who is still with me for a few days more;) whereby the worst of the burden was lifted & the worry & anxiety soothed & the fairly dismal loneliness assuaged.

Despite the temporary improvement, Miss Bosanquet thought that his family should be notified, and she cabled to Cambridge. Harry set off for England, and shortly his uncle wrote, in pencil and bedridden, to report that he had taken a turn for the worse.

> Dearest Ones,
>
>   It is an unspeakable relief & blessing to have Harry with me, & I cling to him with almost frenetic intensity. But I am sorry to say I haven't been able to do justice to his advent by any continuous or valid improvement. My flares & flickers up are followed so damnably by relapses, & the drops seem so deep & disheartening that I am afraid I am rather demoralized & abject. . . . It seems in fact all difficult & endlessly uphill—& I have a kind of terror of finding myself alone here again with my misery.

James yearned for his family but feared the journey to America and isolation there. Henry pleaded with William, Alice, and Peggy to follow Harry and join him in Rye—he would make over Lamb House to them, if only they would come and *take care* of him until he was on his feet again.

> I am writing this on a bad day, I know—& I shall still again have better; but I can't help it, & the form of my appeal (how the mighty are fallen!) drives me & makes me rush it . . . it seems so long—& as if it would outlast *me* rather than I *it*.

James blamed his plunge into depression and anxiety upon his severe diet and his Fletcherizing, which had ended by making him loathe food, but he suspected the heart condition behind all and tried to arrange a consultation with William Osler. Harry went up to Oxford to see the great man, who was attentive and kind and who agreed to see James in London.

The most distressing aspect of the whole affair, James complained, was that it kept him from his work.

> My sense of the matter is that I *can* get better & that I am worth saving for such magnificent work as I want still to do,—& oh so *can*!—& was never more full of the ardent dream of.

Indeed, despite all, he managed to work at further revisions to *The Outcry* that Granville-Barker had requested. He still expected his play to open at the height of the Season that spring. But his anxieties, which now centered upon the play, were acute. William wrote to say that he and Alice were coming to care for him.

William, too, was suffering from his heart ailment. He was now taking nitroglycerin three times a day, to suppress the otherwise constant angina, and had given up trying to walk. He would go on to Paris to consult a heart specialist and perhaps go on to Bad Nauheim but would come first to Rye.

In March, while awaiting William's arrival, Henry succeeded in having a consultation with Osler in London. The doctor's famous bedside manner was greatly reassuring to James. Osler had his patient undress and made a complete examination, which was modern and scientific and therefore comforting in itself. He assured James that if he would return to a normal manner of eating and abandon Fletcherizing, his appetite and health would return. James's anginal symptoms had subsided, presumably because of his considerable loss of weight. The physician invited James and his nephew to come down to him in Oxford for a weekend, and James was greatly cheered and comforted.

On James's return to Rye, the cheering effects of the consultation dissipated, and he had another downturn. Skinner put him to bed and sent another nurse. James thought now that his illness was primarily "*nervous distress & agitation*"; William was soon calling it "nervous melancholia"; but while it was reassuring to know that he was not dying of his heart ailment, the struggle with depression was still "a hard battle to fight alone." Harry had been a comfort but by the end of March was obliged to return to Boston and his law practice.

A week later, on April 8, William and Alice arrived at Lamb House. The week between Harry's departure and their arrival was difficult for James, and he greeted William and Alice with pathetic joy. William was now completely sedentary, as any but the mildest activity would bring on the distressing symptoms of heart disease, but he had gamely answered his brother's cry for help. Alice was head of the family now, managing the servants and the care of two invalids. Each morning, Minnie Kidd brought an early breakfast to her room, and she then saw to the brothers' breakfasts and sat with Henry as he had his morning coffee and roll in bed. Alice gave Paddington her instructions for the day and presided over the two brothers' sometimes lively luncheon. She walked slowly and with frequent pauses with Henry in the afternoons, leaving William to read or work at a paper he was writing, under the mulberry tree in the blooming spring garden.

Edith Wharton, learning from Bosanquet of James's illness, sent her automobile and chauffeur across the Channel to Lamb House. This handsome gesture was very welcome. Alice thereafter took the two brothers for long afternoon rides along the coast, a great pleasure for all three.

The brothers evidently were happy in each other's company. Henry continued to have his ups and downs of mood, a nearly regular cycle, and in his brighter moments continued to work at revisions for *The Outcry*. Casting was complete, and he was glad to know that Gerald du Maurier would be the principal young man. He sent the last revisions to Granville-Barker early in May.

William set off for Paris to see a specialist in coronary artery disease, a Dr. Moutier, traveling with Charles Strong, an American friend of independent means. William was fêted in Paris and made a foreign member of the Académie-Française. But Moutier concluded (reasonably, it appears) that he had no treatment to offer, and William decided to go on alone to Bad Nauheim to try the efficacy of the baths once more. Afraid to remain alone, he begged Alice and Henry to join him. At first, Alice felt divided in her duties. Henry felt unable to leave England while *The Outcry* was preparing and his other plays were hanging fire, but he too greatly feared being left. Yet Alice did not like to send William to Germany alone.

In the evening of May 6, 1910, King Edward died, and the next morning Great Britain was again plunged into official mourning. Theaters and other places of public amusement closed, not to reopen during the usual Season. The second son and heir of Edward and Alexandra took the throne as King George V. The Edwardian Age had come to an early conclusion, just short of Edward's seventieth birthday, and one of the minor unforeseen consequences of the king's death was to simplify the Jameses' situation. As the theaters would remain closed for the balance of the Season, James was no longer tied to England. The meaningless chance of death had again diverted the course of his life; all of his theatrical projects were suspended, perhaps permanently. Hopes for the end of royal censorship were dashed, and the heavy hand of the lord chamberlain's office would not be lifted for decades. Frohman's repertory season was canceled in the face of enormous losses. Herbert Trench's repertory season evaporated as well, and there was no further point, for the moment, in looking for a producer for *The Saloon*.

Henry—who accepted the end of the theatrical season with mingled relief and regret—thereupon agreed to join William in Bad Nauheim, and

William reserved rooms for them all to live *en famille* for an extended stay. Henry also agreed to Alice's insistent suggestion that he return to America with them after William had exhausted the benefits of the baths. She wrote to her children in America that Henry would come to live with them in Cambridge, give up his room at the Reform Club, and let Lamb House to tenants, greatly reducing his expenses. James told his friends in England of the news. Arthur Benson recorded the fact with regret:

> A very distressing letter from Henry James [Benson wrote in his diary] who is suffering much as I did, only worse, under black melancholy & poisonous "trepidation" one is so utterly helpless. He speaks of great & urgent worries, I fear of money. Where does the theory of punishment come in here, in the case of this loving, peaceable, high-minded man.

The visit to Bad Nauheim had its pleasant side. While Henry did not submit to a course of baths, the climate was beneficent and he was able to walk in the afternoons. He had just completed a synthesis of his life work, the sort of project on which his elder brother was just beginning, and they had time for leisurely conversations. William's "radical empiricism" pointed toward a new metaphysics of experience, a phenomenology.

But, in the past three years, William had set the larger project aside and had published three important books on the subject of "pragmatism." He had made himself the spokesman of a movement. The first volume, *Pragmatism*—the title was like a banner—had struck a chord with the general public, and was then in its tenth printing. He had felt obliged to follow it with a sequel, *The Meaning of Truth*, in which he answered his critics, and with *A Pluralistic Universe*, in which he collected lectures he had been asked to give at Manchester College on the new ways of thinking. Like his earlier study of religious experience, in *Pragmatism*, William sought what was evidently an important personal goal, to vindicate scientific idealism, the faith, if one may put it so, in which he had been raised. Although he had hoped to go beyond the disputes of his youth, it seemed to him necessary to rescue idealism from the rigidity of his colleagues at Harvard, believers in an Absolute revealed only through logic. He attacked these mild Bostonians as if they were the bishops of a universal church, and declared that pragmatism "will be an alteration in 'the seat of authority' that reminds one almost of the protestant reformation."

It seemed equally necessary to rescue empirical science from the merely mechanical systems of certain natural scientists. Even materialists must be obliged to accept the truth of spiritual phenomena. "To any one who has looked on the face of a dead child or parent the mere fact that matter *could* have taken for a time that precious form, ought to make matter sacred ever after." The mystery of life and thought remained, whether one spoke of material substances or of God; a merely mechanical system was not adequate to capture experience.

Fifty years earlier, before the Civil War scattered them, Henry and William James and Wendell Holmes had debated idealism and materialism late at night in smoky, gaslit bedrooms. William had fought then to defeat Holmes's materialsim; as he grew older he struggled to reconcile his father's and his brother's "tender-minded" spirituality with Wendell's "tough-minded" science. His method of reconciliation was simply to reject rigid and comprehensive a priori systems, as such; no system could do justice to the richness of experience. As he had said years before, in his *The Will to Believe*, "After all that reason can do has been done, there still remains the opacity of the finite facts." The warring systems of idealism and materialism, like the seemingly inconsistent religious systems of his earlier studies, were only expressions of different characters and different perspectives, the world seen from different windows.

What we experience as "truth" is not a system of logical deductions; it is something that we come to feel about a thought or idea, through the experience of having it validated by experience, and by seeing it find its place among other beliefs and ideas felt to be true. Tested by experience, a thought proves its worth and hence its truth.

William's thought and Henry's (and indeed even Holmes's), in that time so dominated by Kant, had a shared premise. Reading William's essay, Henry was moved to declare that he felt like the man in the play, who discovered he had been speaking prose all his life. The combative Wendell, who had attended the Lowell Lectures in Boston on which *Pragmatism* was based, refused to accept William's formulation, and sneered that pragmatism was only a method for turning down the lights, to allow a chance for miracles. But his own formula was not far off. He called himself a "mystical materialist," and with his fondness for paradox insisted that what he meant by truth was only the system of his limitations, what he could not help believing.

William's exposition captured the public's imagination, and his name thenceforth would always be associated with it; but the originality of his own contribution, and the coherence of his thought, would always be debated. As a sympathetic philosopher would later put it,

Paradoxically, it is Henry [James] who writes with the careful qualifications and minute attention to detail that one might expect of a psychologist or philosopher, and William who carries the reader away with his humor and zest and the vividness of his imagery. If his meaning is not always clear, the reason partly is that he so strongly felt the importance of his message and was so eager to make converts. . . . He thought along broad lines which left room for some uncertainty, perhaps in his own mind as in the minds of his critics, as to the precise implications of the theories that he held.

Despite his depression, Henry too continued to work, writing letters, preparing his income tax return, and making a substantial contribution to a fund for support of George Smalley's widow. Alice remarked that his depression was evidently constitutional and resembled her Aunt Nannie Webb's "visceral melancholy." Henry James now suffered under the same fear of solitude and anxiety about the future, but Henry, she thought, had "the habit of self-control, of a trained will, and the interests of a great brain to steady him."

The three Jameses abandoned Bad Nauheim in June and began to work their way slowly back to Lamb House. While in Switzerland, en route, Henry began feeling better. The bright sunshine, moderate exercise, and the moderate diet that he and Alice were following evidently helped both his health and spirits. William's health grew worse, however, his lungs beginning to fail under the accumulation of fluid that was a consequence of his disease. As they went up into the Alps, he began to have trouble breathing.

A telegram from Harry, forwarded from Lamb House, reached them in Geneva. Robertson James, the youngest of the brothers, had died on July 3 of heart failure. A letter from Peggy followed:

He just passed out, smiling, in his sleep, & the poor storm-tossed spirit is at rest. It was the most beautiful way to go. We must draw the circle closer while we are here together, and do all we can for one another while it is still time.

The news was at first kept from William, as both Alice and Henry feared the effects of such a shock to his heart. The task of writing condolence letters fell largely to Henry. "My dear Mary. How shall I tell you how my heart turns to you . . ." The family treated Bob's death as a release, not to be regretted on his behalf, but it was nevertheless frightening. Peggy's account was romanticized: Bob had died alone in his house in Concord, and two days had passed before his body was found.

Theodora Bosanquet was given notice and returned to London, where she and Nelly Bradley found a flat to share. James carefully noted her address, however. He was not yet ready to give up his room at the Reform Club, which he had waited years to obtain, nor did he give up Lamb House. His staff remained there to maintain the house in his absence; only Burgess Noakes accompanied him to America. Henry did not feel able to face the coming winter without his American family but was not yet ready to cut his ties to his own home in England, after all.

Passing through London, they briefly saw William Dean Howells, who had just lost his wife, Elinor, and the three old friends commiserated briefly. William was overcome by a severe attack of angina, however, and was obliged to take morphine for the pain. He was plainly growing worse, and when they repaired to Lamb House, Henry began to take up part of the burden of caring for him. Henry himself was somewhat better, and Alice was able to confide to a friend that his attack of "neurasthenia" was evidently an acute, rather than a chronic, state.

The three Jameses sailed from London for Quebec on August 12, on a new Canadian vessel, *The Empress of Britain*, and made the crossing in only six days. The crossing was smooth, but William was now in constant distress. Harry met them in Quebec and accompanied them on the rail trip into New Hampshire. At North Conway, Alice cabled to Aleck and Billy to come home. A local physician, Dr. Shedd, came to stay with them at the farmhouse, and Alice hired a nurse. Henry telephoned to Boston to summon a specialist to the bedside.

The end was very difficult. William's legs and feet were swollen, and his lungs were filling with fluid. He was in constant pain and gasping for breath, evidently in the last stages of congestive heart failure. The muscles of the heart had been weakened and no longer provided enough pressure to draw fluid from his lungs. Henry and Alice sat with William through the days of his last struggles, when William was in constant pain, slowly suffocating, and wishing only for death.

On August 24, William was given morphine and slipped into unconsciousness. He died in the afternoon of August 26, 1910, at the age of sixty-eight, with his head cradled in Alice's arms. Henry, who had been writing a letter to his niece Mary James Vaux, opened it to add a post-script: "I open my letter of 3 hours ago to say that your Uncle William died an hour since—unconsciously, without apparent pain or struggle. Think of us, dear Mary, all tenderly."

William had asked for a traditional Christian service, which was held in Harvard's Appleton Chapel. Six old men carried his coffin to the hearse that took his body to be cremated. Fanny and Wendell Holmes were among the mourners, and Wendell was a pallbearer. Henry, William, and Wendell had been closest friends in the time of their young manhood and had kept up their friendship, with whatever intermissions, for a lifetime. But Henry was ill and preoccupied. After the funeral, Holmes wrote to their mutual friend Alice Green in an oddly bitter mood:

> H. James at William's funeral looked distinguished but far from well. I wrote a line afterward to him but I don't know whether he would care for it—he also has seemed remote the last few years—I don't know why, except the vicissitudes of the Irish temperament & the difference of emphasis in our respective interests.

But Henry was glad to get his note.

> My dear Wendell.
>   I thank you kindly for your note of sympathy of the other day. I sit here infinitely stricken & in deep darkness—but imperfectly recovered, myself, from a long & dismal & dreadful illness of many months. My beloved brother & my sister came out angelically, to minister to me—he himself already much menaced—& she & I returned with him, later on, but to see him horribly suffer & die. My privation is unutterable—he filled such a place in my personal & intellectual world. And he was in the plenitude of his admirable genius & his unique magnanimity. It has all been a black nightmare to
>
> > Yours ever
> > Henry James

Henry and Alice managed the complex aftermath of death together, and Henry remained at Irving Street for almost a year. He helped with the enormous task of answering the condolence letters that poured in and helped Alice and Harry arrange the estate. He made a new will of his own, designating Alice instead of William his principal heir.

William had not been able to accumulate much by way of savings. The royalties from the sale of his works would be an important source of support for Alice, who had no means of her own, and Harry began to prepare editions of William's unpublished writings. The meaningless accident of death had broken off William's work on his great philosophical treatise, the reshaping of metaphysics he had envisioned, but he had left behind a scattering of published and unpublished essays on radical empiricism that could be collected into a volume. Harry told his uncle that he also wished to prepare an edition of his father's letters, and Henry offered to write a preface.

James could not cut his ties to Lamb House, which still seemed to him the home of his extended family, far more than the white frame house on Irving Street. Lamb House and the staff it required were expensive, however, and beyond his means unless he continued to write. As the new year dawned and his family responsibilities diminished, he returned to writing to pay his bills. But he vowed to cut his ties to the stage and its stresses, which had so nearly killed him. He wrote to Theodora Bosanquet in London to ask for a copy of *The Outcry*, not to pursue it as a play but so that he could turn it into a short novel.

In January 1911, the symptoms of his heart ailment worsened again, however, and James went to New York "for a few days" to consult a specialist there and to pursue discussions with publishers. The days stretched into a month. James's health somewhat improved with renewed treatment of his angina and with the lightening of spirit that accompanied his escape from Cambridge. He luxuriated in Mary Cadwalader's hospitality once again, in her comfortable house on Eleventh Street that was in such easy walking distance of Washington Square and Gramercy Park, where he lunched regularly at the Players' Club. Manhattan was his home in the United States, and he sank into its winter activities gratefully.

Late in February, having placed his novelized *Outcry* with Scribner's Sons, James returned to Cambridge, where he found that he had been elected to the Saturday Club, the once-a-month dining club at the Parker House of which his father, Dr. Holmes, Emerson, and Hawthorne had been founders. He attended politely but did not find the company or the conversation stimulating. To Rhoda Broughton: "I beguile the tedium of vast wastes of homesickness here—where, frankly, the sense of aching exile attends me the livelong day."

He soon fled to New York again, and another round of baths, walks, and visits to friends and physicians, that greatly cheered him and revived his sense that he was recovering from illness.

One of the great topics of the day was the new Rockefeller Institute for Medical Research (now Rockefeller University) in Manhattan, where a research hospital—the first in the United States—opened in October. In the era before modern scientific medical schools, the Rockefeller family had endowed a laboratory and hospital patterned after the Pasteur and Koch institutes, purchasing for the purpose the old Schermerhorn Farm on the East River. The laboratory had had a spectacular success in 1907, finding a vaccine to halt an epidemic of meningitis in the city. More recently it had grown controversial, however, embroiled in accusations of cruel experiments upon animals.

James asked Lawrence Godkin, the son of his old friend and editor of *The Nation*, to obtain an invitation for him, and in February he and Godkin spent a day at the institute. Jerome Greene, the general manager, met them in his office and introduced them to Simon Flexner, the scientific director. As Greene later recalled the visit, "Mr. James was full of interest and curiosity and lingered so long in each laboratory as to exhaust Mr. Godkin's patience."

Greene took James and Godkin into a laboratory where Peyton Rous (later a Nobel Prize winner) was studying the development of cancerous tumors that he induced to grow in mice. Rous was introduced to the visitors and explained the experiment that was being conducted. Greene and Godkin went out, but James lingered, hesitated, and then asked, with a wave of his hand at the cages of mice, "Has the individuality—I might say, the personality—of these little creatures impressed itself upon you?"

Rous was taken aback, but after a moment, he told James a story. He had recently had to kill a mouse with a newborn litter and to save her young had given them to another mouse. The foster mother mouse had raised them with her own, and the experiment had turned out so well that Rous had given her another litter of newborn young, to see what would happen. These too she raised, and again she was given a litter. All went well until they were more than an inch long—attractive, bright-eyed, and furred—and then, one night, she ate them all.

James listened with attention, and to Rous he seemed lost to time. But Godkin was at the door, saying, "Mr. James, will you please come?" and with reluctance he hurried off.

With summer came the humid, dusty heat of Cambridge that James so disliked, and he began to plan his return to England. His depression had lifted, and a few days free of angina sufficed to persuade him that he was on the road to recovery from his heart ailment. The return of symptoms would repeatedly surprise and discourage him, but optimism now again prevailed. He planned to finish the novelization of *The Outcry* by August and began to prepare for a return to Lamb House.

Having abandoned Fletcherizing and any restrictions upon his diet, James returned to the meat and potatoes that he loved and that were in any case difficult to avoid when traveling. He again grew stout and gave up his lifelong efforts to keep his weight under control and to dress fashionably. Comfort was now to be the rule, especially in the summer heat that was now so unpleasant to him. An open automobile was accordingly now doubly delicious, and when he wrote a letter on black-bordered Cambridge notepaper, he confessed:

> I am really not where my paper-head indicates, but deep in the heart of the country, amid admirable mountains, vales & streams, embordered in prodigious elms & maples, & taking long & most fortifying & reviving motor-runs every day of my life.

He freely accepted the hospitality of everyone he knew who had a motorcar, but the most constant and generous was Edith Wharton, who had returned to The Mount for the summer months and whose Panhard and chauffeur were always at James's disposal.

He was invited to receive an honorary degree at the Harvard College commencement exercises that summer. Harvard was sparing with its honorary degrees, and James had never attended the college (or any other); he had been enrolled in the law school for only a single semester. But the new president of Harvard, Abbott Lowell, considered him a member of the community to which he was so closely tied, and James came down for the exercise from Nahant to receive the honor. He was obliged to rise at the crack of dawn to attend the Saturday-morning exercises in Sanders Hall, and by the time they were concluded and he had lunched with the dignitaries, he was exhausted and suffering from a bout of angina. An old friend, John T. Morse, took him to Irving Street to lie down, and when he was a little recovered, Henry Cabot Lodge carried him back to Nahant in his motorcar.

James's indisposition was doubly unfortunate, because that year marked the fiftieth anniversary of the graduation of the Civil War class of 1861, and Holmes had been asked to speak on the occasion. Holmes took a good deal of trouble over his short address and ended it with an image that echoed one of James's. Regretting, as James did, the manner in which tradition and idealism both were being overwhelmed by commerce, he spoke of the way that in Manhattan skyscrapers overshadowed the slender tower of Trinity Church: "Commerce has outsoared the steeples." Holmes's address was delivered in the afternoon of that long day, however, by which time James had fled, and there was a pointedly empty chair beside Holmes on the podium.

Holmes wrote to James immediately afterward, sending him a copy of the printed address, remarking bitterly on the manner in which James seemed to be avoiding him, recalling their old friendship, and making observations, even more pointed than those he had expressed to Alice Green, of what he imagined were the reasons for James's neglect, blaming what a later generation would call their differences of sexual orientation. James replied at length, explaining his indisposition and recalling all the long years through which he had praised Holmes's addresses and yearned to hear them delivered.

> It was with a pang at any rate that I renounced, under such stress, the other day, the chance of listening to you . . . for I felt even then how it would have rekindled for me the *general* light of other days . . . so much so that I ask myself frankly today, dear Wendell—or rather, still more frankly, ask *you*—why you should "feel a doubt" as to whether I should care to see you again & what ground I ever gave you for the supposition that the "difference in the sphere of our dominant interests" might have made "a gulf that we cannot cross." As I look back at any moment of our contact—which began so long ago—I find myself crossing & crossing with a devotedness that took no smallest account of gulfs, or, more truly, hovering & circling & sitting on your side of the chasm altogether (if chasm there were!)—with a complete suspension, as far as

you were concerned, of any other side. Such was my pleasure & my affection & my homage—& when & where in the world did you ever see any symptom of anything else?

Edith Wharton had returned to The Mount alone. Teddy had broken out in bizarre behavior in Boston the year before, while she was in Paris. Instead of pursuing cures for his ailments, he had dipped into her trust fund and with the stolen money kept a mistress in a Boston apartment. When the defalcation was discovered, Edith had had a series of painful conversations with the remorseful Wharton and tried to negotiate a modus vivendi, but for the moment they had separated.

She was not unhappy, having largely freed herself from an uncongenial marriage, and was surrounded by older accomplished men and young courtiers. Walter Berry had his own guest apartment in her new flat in Paris, and her relations with Morton Fullerton were happy, so long as she did not insist on his being faithful. On her return to The Mount after three years' absence that summer, James came up for a week, and her young acolytes John Hughes Smith and Gaillard Lapsley joined them.

Edith would later recall the days at The Mount as a particularly happy moment. The Mount was her creation, and its raw newness had passed away. The plantings she had designed six years earlier had matured. In her pleasure at the sight, "so much leafier and *fondu*" than she had last seen it, she told Fullerton that "Decidedly, I'm a better landscape gardener than a novelist, and this place, every line of which is my own work, far surpasses the House of Mirth."

James and Wharton were easy with each other, enjoying their mutual badinage, the motherly old man and the restless, sharply intelligent younger woman. Wharton was impatient with James's age and disabilities, but she suppressed her impatience and made him welcome and as comfortable as he could be in the heat.

A drought had blighted much of the countryside, and outside the oasis of The Mount the landscape was bleak and brown. The days were miserably hot, and the oppressive weather exacerbated James's discomfort and apprehensions about his health. He was overweight, and the conventions of the day required a great deal of clothing. An electric fan, iced drinks, and constant motoring relieved him somewhat. In the pleasant evenings, after dinner, the heat abated and the little party gathered on the terrace. They talked easily and idly, and for this little company, who had looked into each other's gardens, there were no chasms to bridge. They read to each other from books in Wharton's library, to pass the hours. Someone spoke of Walt Whitman, *Leaves of Grass* was fetched, and James read while the others sat rapt.

When he read Whitman, James seemed to be speaking directly from his innermost self. His stammer vanished, and he read with unaffected emotion, chanting to emphasize the rhythms of the songs. When he came to the elegy for Lincoln, his voice deepened with emotion, and at the passage that begins "Come lovely and soothing death," his voice "filled the hushed room like an organ adagio":

When lilacs last in the dooryard bloom'd,
And the great star early droop'd in the western sky in the night,
I mourn'd, and yet shall mourn with ever-returning spring.

Ever-returning spring, trinity sure to me you bring,
Lilac blooming perennial and drooping star in the west,
And thought of him I love. . . .

Come lovely and soothing death,
Undulate round the world, serenely arriving, arriving,
In the day, in the night, to all, to each. . . .

Dark mother always gliding near with soft feet,
have none chanted for thee a chant of fullest welcome?
Then I chant it for thee, I glorify thee above all,
I bring thee a song that when thou must indeed come, come unfalteringly.

After a few days, Teddy arrived, filled with energy and determined to reestablish himself as a husband. He insisted that he should again take charge of his dear Puss's affairs. He could not accept that The Mount was utterly Edith's and insisted that he be given management of the estate. When Edith refused, he picked a quarrel with her, then collapsed into tears and pleading. Lapsley and Smith fled, but James lingered for another day and in the afternoon accompanied Edith for a long walk in the shady wood and listened to her account of all her struggles to arrive at some mode of life with Teddy, to whom she had been married for twenty-five years. James gently suggested that perhaps the time had come for them to separate permanently.

• • •

The heat at last broke, and Edith sent James off in her automobile, in a cold rain, to join Alice at Chocorua. He had decided to make the summer crossing to his home in England, had booked passage, and now began to pack. New England was a desert for him, the climate was intolerable, family affairs no longer required his presence, and his health was sufficiently recovered for him to return to his own home.

On the first of August, as James was preparing for his return to Lamb House, word came that Ned Abbey had died after a return of the hepatic cancer with which he had long been troubled. He was only fifty-nine years old. James wrote to Gertrude:

> One can but stretch out one's hand. . . . I can only wonder at the cruelty and perversity of his extinction—to say nothing of his suffering. The tenderness of my affection abides with me, however, thank Heaven, and the vividness of his presence and genius . . . and, above all, the happiness of his life—the rich felicity, every way of his career. He had *had* it, he hadn't missed it: he had sat at the full feast and had manfully, splendidly, lived.

During his illness, James had lacked the energy needed to maintain his numerous intimacies. He had not answered his friends' letters. Hendrik Andersen had been in America briefly, to attend to family matters, while James was there, but the older man had made no real effort to see him and noticeably had failed to invite him to Chocorua, Irving Street, or The Mount. After James's return to Lamb House, Andersen, Edmund Gosse, Arthur Benson, and Howard Sturgis all complained of his silence and neglect.

Once at home, accordingly, James began to restore the tattered fabric. He and Benson exchanged letters, struggling to find a meeting ground. He hastened to invite the long-neglected Edmund Gosse down to Rye for a visit and a good gossip. As soon as he could, he paid a visit to Queen's Acre, where Howard Sturgis was generous and understanding and was readily reassured. Walter Berry had at last escaped from his Egyptian bondage and was now often in London, on his way to and fro from Paris to New York. When he was in London, he was a frequent visitor at Queen's Acre and would sometimes come from Windsor to Lamb House for a weekend alone with James.

· · ·

Sturgis kept his friendly door open to James, Edith Wharton, Benson, Walter Berry, and a constantly refreshed circle of young former Etonians, ambitious for literary careers, who became admirers and friends of both James and Wharton. The conversation around Sturgis's fireside was relaxed and happily filled with gossip. The once-modern white-paneled sitting room, with its chintz curtains and upholstery, the coal fire always burning low in the grate, had grown comfortably shabby. Sturgis was a relaxed and complacent host on his lounge beside the fireplace, keeping his fingers busy with knitting or embroidery, and James was often in the place of honor opposite him in a deep armchair. The young people, then still early in their careers, would later remember and celebrate James in this firelit circle, an old man close to the end of his life with his work behind him: "the Master" who had outlived the world in which he had formed his life and art.

Edith Wharton and Teddy were separated in law, as James had advised, and The Mount was sold with all its contents. Paris would henceforth be Edith's home. She invited James confidently, a little imperiously, to join her and Walter Berry in Paris and to go on a five-week motor tour with them, an invitation he could not accept. His hunger for affection had not abated, however. To Walpole he wrote—"Dearest, dearest Hugh" and then again "Darling, darling little Hugh!"—to apologize for and explain his long silence. He came up to London in September, and they spent a quiet morning together at the Reform Club. James began again to attend the theater with Jocelyn Persse.

He had been away for a year, but his loyal staff remained at Lamb House. House and garden had been well maintained in his absence, and he hoped to burrow in for a rest from his travels. His neighbors in Rye were welcoming; only Sydney Waterlow had vanished, having moved his quarters to Cambridge. Theodora Bosanquet was living in London with Nelly Bradley in Chelsea, but promptly replied that she would be glad to return to work for James.

The Outcry was published shortly after his return to England, and was very rapidly successful. James had not published a novel since *The Golden Bowl*, six years earlier, and had published little of any kind since the New York Edition had been completed two years before. In Great Britain, Methuen had its long-promised novel, and in the United States,

Scribner's was glad to cash in at last on James's carefully cultivated celebrity. His patient audience had only this one book offered to them by James that year, and it was a still topical story, brief and clearly written, published in an inexpensive, single volume. For once, James caught the moment. Printings were quickly exhausted, one after another, and the book ran through six editions in the year following publication. He had a modest bestseller, and his income was restored.

With the problem of maintaining Lamb House settled for the moment, he began to prepare a memoir of his elder brother, the preface he had promised Harry. He had kept William's letters to himself, and he now wrote to ask Mary and Carrie James for those William had written to Bob and Wilky. He wanted also to have William's letters to Alice and his children, all of which set up a little tiff with Harry, who was trying to prepare the edition of William's letters for which James was writing the preface and did not wish Uncle Henry to keep them long or include very much of them in his own work.

But James was not done with his heart ailment, as he had allowed himself to believe, and his gain in weight, return to work, social nights and days, dependence on stimulants and laxatives took their toll. His angina returned, and the weather in Rye turned bleak. When the days grew shorter and darker, the winter wind and rains began and he was immobilized indoors. He realized that he could not remain in Lamb House that winter. He confided to Sturgis that the house and staff were "rather an incubus & a millstone" if he could not live there, but he was not prepared to give them up. His "little old house" was as dear to him as ever, and he wanted to spend long summers there, even if in the winter months he would be obliged to retreat to London, where it was possible to walk and to see his intimate friends, where "miles of pavement & lamplight & shopfronts are good for me."

His bed-sitting room at the Reform Club was too confining to serve day and night as office and bedroom. James asked the faithful Theodora Bosanquet to find a furnished room where his typewriter could be kept on its stand, one that was furnished with tables and chairs and a fireplace and where he would have room to pace. This was easily accomplished. She and Nelly had taken a flat for themselves in an old house in Chelsea, near the river, which included a large room that she thought would serve: "A quiet room, running back into a silent yard."

Beginning in October he took the Underground or a taxi every workday from Pall Mall to Bosanquet's flat in Chelsea, where he resumed his morning routine, reading over the dictation of the previous day, composing his mind, and then dictating until it was time for lunch, often resuming after lunch until tea.

A number of his friends had settled in Chelsea, in easy visiting distance. Abbey was gone, but Sargent still had his studio there, and Rhoda Broughton had settled nearby, as had Augusta Gregory. The Albert Bridge and the park to which it led on the opposite bank of the Thames were admirable for strolls when the weather allowed them, although his former brisk twenty-mile walks were now reduced to two or three miles, stretched out over an afternoon by frequent pauses. Bosanquet often accompanied him on these walks.

He was a Londoner again and would be so for the few years remaining to him. He became a familiar fixture in the Reform Club, where he lunched with evident relish upon veal or lamb chops and where he was often joined by friends.

He was a massive figure, impressive to the young writers who saw him at a little distance, and who would later recall their encounters with the great man. H. G. Wells brought Upton Sinclair to lunch and pointed out to him the "Grand Khan of Anglo-American letters." The young expatriate American Ezra Pound remembered James's conversation, intimate and frankly confiding,

> the massive head, the slow uplift of the hand ... the long sentences piling themselves up in elaborate phrase after phrase, the lightening incision, the pauses, the slightly shaking admonitory gesture with its "wu-w-wait a little, wait a little, something will come," blague and benignity and the weight of so many years' careful, incessant labor, of minute observation.

His memoir of his older brother had far outgrown any possible bounds for a preface and would be published as a separate volume; it continued to expand beyond even those limits and plainly would require at least two volumes. For the first volume, when it was completed, he chose the title *A Small Boy and Others*. The small boy was himself. As in his other nonfiction works, he used his own memories as the medium in which to portray his subject. Throughout their shared childhood, William was "in isolated eldest superiority." James's characteristic memory was of William glimpsed through an open door, sitting at a desk with his back turned. As in the biography of Story, James portrayed the shared surroundings in which William had grown to maturity, a little family world that only Henry had survived to describe. Imagery flourished and all but concealed the narrative, such as it was; James's self-awareness, the consciousness of his process of recollection, became the subject. Each recollection set off a chain of associations: "Gertrude Pendleton's mere name, for instance, becomes . . . the frame of another and a better picture." A page-long sentence follows, studded with semicolons and dashes; not so much a sentence as a firm grasp on the reader's attention, while James fires off similes in rapid succession, until the image of a moment on the rue Saint Honoré forms itself in the air, mysteriously detailed, arriving even with odors and tastes.

Freed from commercial considerations, without limits of space or time, James luxuriated in the task. Each evening he summoned his earliest recollections, the bright images that his remarkable memory was able to provide, and put them into an orderly, temporal sequence: the houses in Albany and Manhattan, summers on Staten Island and Long Island, the father who had so dominated William's childhood and youth; the remarkable months spent in Paris under the Second Empire. Here was little Florence Bell, one of the daughters of a famous physician; and the father himself ("whose emphasized type much impressed itself"). With relish he awoke again the memories of his first taste of glory, of the Napoleonic Louvre, of the empress on her Avenue and the infant prince carried in state in his own carriage with his nurse, surrounded by the imperial guard. In the spare room in Chelsea offered to him by Miss Bosanquet and Miss Bradley, he traveled in time and dictated triumphantly and confidently, dispensing ever more with the mechanics of sentence structure, of ordinary syntax, creating vivid images one after another as it were directly in the medium of memory, infused with sensuous power, crowded with sexual imagery.

> But the Avenue of the Empress, now, so much more thinly, but of the Wood itself, had already been traced, as the Empress herself, young, more than young, attestedly and agreeably *new*, and fair and shining, was, up and down the vista, constantly on exhibition; with the thrill of that surpassed for us, however, by the incomparable passage, as we judged it, of the Prince Imperial borne forth for his airing or his progress to Saint-Cloud in the splendid coach that gave a glimpse of appointed nursing breasts and laps, and beside which the *cent-gardes*,

all light-blue and silver and intensely erect quick-jolt, rattled with pistols raised and cocked.

In the early days of this effort, James learned from Alice that his nephew and namesake Harry had been offered a post at the Rockefeller Institute, the position of manager that had been held by James's guide on his tour, Jerome Greene. James may have suggested his nephew for the post and now strongly urged him to take the offer when it came. He was overjoyed when Harry accepted.

Roger Fry invited James one afternoon to an informal private view of Postimpressionist paintings at the Grafton Gallery, with Virginia Stephen, Vanessa and Clive Bell, Sydney Waterlow, and other mutual friends. As Virginia Stephen (not yet Virginia Woolf) recalled the occasion, Fry took them down to the basement of the gallery, where, among the packing cases and brown paper, tea was offered. Seated on a hard chair, James tried to express "in convoluted sentences the disturbed hesitations which Matisse and Picasso aroused in him."

Hendrik Andersen was thoroughly immersed in the atmosphere of twentieth-century Rome and wrote to James a long and excited letter about a new project that was wholly absorbing him, the design of a new "World City." With Olivia's support, he had hired draftsmen to work through his ideas in detail and was laboring to rough out models for the many monuments the city would require. James had no hesitation in framing his reaction:

> Your mania for the colossal, the swelling & the huge, the monotonously
> & repeatedly huge, breaks the heart of me for you. . . . What am I to say
> to you, gentle & dearest Hendrik . . . when you write to me . . . that you
> are extemporizing a World-City from top to toe, & employing 40 architects to see you through with it? . . . As *if*, beloved boy, any use on all
> the mad earth can be found for a ready-made city. . . . Cities are *living*
> organisms, that grow from within & by experience & piece by piece;
> they are not bought, all hanging together, in *any* inspired studio anywhere whatsoever.

Andersen defended his project, and James wrote again, more mildly. The project was charming and interesting to him simply as Andersen's, as a sort of dream that a prince in a fairy tale might make for himself if imprisoned by a wizard and shut off from the world and its possibilities and complications. But how was dear Hendrik to convert these dream images into the material reality that was required to give it sense?

> You see, dearest Hendrik, I live myself in the very intensity of reality and can only conceive of any art-work as producing itself piece by piece and touch by touch, in close relation to some immediate form of life.

He had similar advice and criticism for H. G. Wells, whom he met that winter again, after an interval of several years. As Waterlow put it, observing them at a dinner party, it was their first encounter "since Wells became disreputable, and they circled around one another suspiciously, like cat and dog." Wells had been quarreling with the people around him, nursing old literary grudges, attacking Bernard Shaw, labor socialists, and the gathering feminist movement in violent, contemptuous terms. He was for a new order, indeed a new world order, of superior men, a new warrior class; his books were propaganda for this grandiose vision, oddly similar in its way to Hendrik's, each foreshadowing in its way the dark abysses of the century to come.

Hoping to reconcile Wells with his fellows, to restore him to healing personal relations, James invited him to join the Academic Committee of the Royal Society of Literature, of which he and Bernard Shaw were members. But Wells declared himself an anarchist with regard to such societies, refused the invitation, and sent James his new novel, *Marriage*, an antifeminist tract and celebration of martial, masculine virtues.

James wrote to Wells much as he had to Andersen. He enjoyed Wells, enjoyed the book because it was Wells's, but the younger man had not devoted the care and attention that were needed to make his characters real and for them to behave in realistic fashion. Nor had he taken the trouble to give his tale meaningful shape. Wells answered like a schoolboy, "I will seek earnestly to make my pen lead a decent life, pull myself together, and think of Form." And as James was ill, he added, "I hope very earnestly for your recovery. The *Reform Club* is a poor place without you."

When *Marriage* came out, the Wellses held a fancy-dress ball at their house in Hampstead; although they were middle-aged they counted themselves among the party of the future and invited young people as well as dignitaries of the older generation. They asked Henry James, who adored fancy dress and happily accepted. He came as a contemporary of Lord Byron. For the most part, he sat out the evening and watched the dancing. Sydney Waterlow was there, in a rented rajah's costume, and sat beside him. Duncan Grant was beautiful in a purple turban and Virginia Stephen's Turkish robe; Virginia's brother Adrian was in cardinal's robes. The most striking costume was James Strachey's—Waterlow said he was "ravishing"—as Nijinsky, in a low-necked blouse, bangles, billowing pantaloons.

Waterlow confided in James as he had in past years, but Wells's wife, Amy, did not like him monopolizing her lion. She interrupted their conversation to introduce James to other guests and finally drew him away: "Oh, Mr. James, will you dance Sir Roger de Coverly with me?" "With reserves, dear lady, with reserves!" he answered, rising.

Oxford University conferred an honorary doctorate of letters upon James that summer, and he spent a few days as the guest of the president of Oxford's Magdalen College. This was a most satisfactory experience. In July, he retired to Lamb House, where he welcomed his usual stream of visitors and caught up on his correspondence. Edith Wharton came that summer, accompanied as always by her Alsatian maid, her chauffeur, and her glorious automobile. Playing host to Wharton was always a trial and an expense for James, but he was glad to see her, to return her hospitality, and grateful for the automobile. After a week's visit at Lamb House with almost daily outings, they motored together to Queen's Acre for a leisurely stay, saving James the wearisome journey by rail. The openhanded generosity of the Sturgis establishment was a pleasant change for both of them from the frugality of Mrs. Paddington's regime at Lamb House.

The French doors of Sturgis's white sitting room opened on an ill-maintained rose garden, where James and Sturgis took their afternoon walk. Wharton accompanied them, eager for movement and activity, and years later could still recall her impatience. Sturgis walked slowly and potteringly, and James who was obliged by his heart ailment to halt frequently, covered his pauses with observations or conversation; they spent more time standing still in the damp than walking, and Wharton complained that "I have known few more chilly forms of exercise, on a cold damp day than a 'constitutional' with [Sturgis] and James."

. . .

Bosanquet obligingly came down to Rye for the summer to take dictation, and despite visitors and distractions James once again was at work in the Garden Room each morning. His working summer at Lamb House had begun late, however, and after a few weeks was further interrupted by a new illness that Skinner diagnosed as shingles, an intensely painful ailment that came on in mid-September, gradually worsened, and kept James bedridden into October. There was no treatment; one simply had to live through the disease, which prolonged itself week after week. Bosanquet continued to come to him each morning, and when he was well enough he would dictate. When he remained in bed, she brought her notebook and took his dictation in shorthand, but James preferred to dictate to the familiar rhythm of the typewriter, and after a while he had it brought into his bedroom.

As his illness dragged on, James realized that he would not be able to return to the Reform Club for the winter, dependent as he was when ill upon Burgess and Paddington as well as on Bosanquet. He began to discuss with her his need for a flat in London to which he could bring his staff, and when Bosanquet returned to Chelsea for two weeks she told him of a flat on the top floor of a new building, Carlyle Mansion, that looked out over the treetops on the new Chelsea Embankment. James went up to see it as soon as he could. The recently constructed building had an elevator, essential for him now, and electric lights. The flat had two good rooms at the front, facing the river, and smaller and dimmer but quiet rooms to the rear, where he thought he would put his bedroom. There was a bedroom for Noakes beside his and additional rooms for servants under the eaves. The flat was available unfurnished for little more than he was paying for his bedroom at the Reform Club, and the outgoing tenant, a young woman, showed him around.

Recognizing the famous name, she expressed interest.

"Are you any relation of the writer, Mr. James?"

"Writer, what writer?"

"Oh, I mean the novelist Henry James—the novelist. Are you perhaps, by any chance, his son?"

"Well, no," James replied, enjoying himself. "The novelist hasn't got a son. But I feel somehow that if he *had* a son, I should be!"

The flat was not available for a long-term lease, the proprietor warned, but James told her that he wanted it only for a foot on the ground in London for his few remaining years and took it on a three-year lease, beginning in the new year; which turned out to be precisely the time for which it would be needed.

In December, a new spell of depression descended upon him, in addition to his other ills. His chest pain was worsening, and he was obliged to bring himself up to London and check into a hotel, as the Chelsea flat was not yet ready. Bedridden again, he scribbled a note in pencil to Rhoda Broughton to explain why he could not honor an engagement:

> I came to town by my doctors' urgency on Friday last, expecting happier things from the change. But they have not come to pass yet, & matters have within the last 24 hours in particular gone so wrong with me that I lie here again helpless . . . [in] extreme present dreariness—a dark back bedroom at an expensive hotel.

Early in the new year, however, he was able to move into his flat in Chelsea, with Burgess Noakes beside him, Joan Paddington and Minnie Kidd comfortably housed in servants' quarters, and Theodora Bosanquet a short walk away. He brought over his furniture from the Reform Club, supplemented by a few pieces that Bosanquet and Bradley had lent him for his office.

The shingles had abated, but his chest pain was now severe and constant, and he must have recognized the progression of the disease as he had seen it in William. He was now a thorough invalid,

> having to reckon with so much chronic pectoral pain, now so seated & settled—moreover it is astonishing with how much pain one can with long practice learn constantly & not too defeatedly to live.

Paul Zhukowsky, who had been ill, went to Baden-Baden early in the year, as was his recent custom, but, growing still more gravely ill, went on to Weimar to join his sister. He died on August 26, 1912. He and James had long been out of touch, and it was some time before James learned of his death.

Margaret Brooke was in England, struggling once again with her husband over the succession to the throne of Sarawak, which would be decided by the new Liberal administration. She was again troubled by deaths, by the loss of a grandson upon whom her hopes had depended, and James wrote to her in sympathy:

> But life will still be there for [your son] after a while—his youth has all to *do* yet—How one doesn't, no, absolutely doesn't, envy him that; but in a manner pities him only the more. Oh, how I feel with you about the soft-bosomed death—it's like the lap of my dear Mother opening out for me again after all the torments of years for me to bury my head in it & cry. How we shall glide on the great strange stream!

26

WITHIN THE RIM

The first volume of James's memoir of his brother had reached only his own fifteenth year, and he and Harry had agreed that it would appear as a separate book, with a second and final volume that would take James to his twenty-fifth year, his departure for Europe, and the end of their shared family life. But what would the second volume be called? If the first was *A Small Boy and Others*, surely the second would have to be *A Big Boy and Others*? The first volume appeared in March 1913, with a note on the title page that it was to be followed quickly by a second, *Notes of a Son and Brother*, whose title promised that the ostensible subject of the work would move to the foreground and that William would be joined there by their father.

Recovering sufficiently from shingles to resume his regime of daily walks, James set off down the Chelsea Embankment every afternoon, weather permitting. One Sunday in February, as dusk was falling on a cold wet gray day, Sydney Waterlow met him on his doorstep. James was determined to have his walk, so Waterlow turned about and walked with him. They walked along the embankment eastward to Westminster, a distance of a little more than two miles, James leaning heavily on Waterlow's arm and talking steadily. They walked slowly, with frequent pauses. Although they set off at 4:30 from Cheyne Walk, they did not reach Westminster, wet and tired, until seven. Waterlow then suggested stopping at the Cheshire Cheese, and James happily agreed. He insisted he would eat nothing, but when they were comfortably seated in the warm interior he ate a heavy dinner of fried sole and a chop. They continued their conversation well into the evening—this was what London was for—and James spoke of his pleasure at Max Beerbohm's affectionate parody, "A Mote in the Middle Distance," in the just-published *Xmas Garland*. It had affected him in a curious way: whatever he wrote now, he felt that he was parodying himself.

Throughout that difficult winter he continued to call on his friends, continued to plead for their visits and expressions of affection. He had a telephone installed—it was a novelty to him, as he had none in Lamb House—and immediately took to it. Telephoning replaced note writing and even, to some degree, paying calls. It was difficult but possible even to have a chat and a gossip on the telephone.

For friends who were out of range of the telephone, however, letters were still necessary. To Walter Berry he sent particularly pointed, funny, and lascivious invitations, urging him to make an overnight stay and speaking in metaphor but with startling vividness of their overnight encounters:

> I am crawling but a bit slowly out of my hole, and my chin, I think, would have been by no means even yet quite above ground, had not your letter this morning, produced within me a thrill of satisfaction that jerked it a good inch higher. . . . I insatiably long to see you.
>
> I hunger and thirst for your discourse. . . . I somehow kind of feel that you have wondrous newses for me; that you can't *not* have. I shall have nothing for you but a great gaping mouth at them—think of me therefore as just a waiting, panting abyss and yours all devotedly.

After an overnight visit, Berry—who had recently come into a substantial inheritance—sent to him a luxurious traveling case, bound in soft leather and lined with red silk. This expensive gift was so noticeably grand, so much out of character with James's other belongings, that it would have been indiscreet for him to appear in public with it; nor could he afford to reciprocate. He thereupon wrote to Berry a mock-angry acknowledgment:

> What is a poor man to do, mon prince, mon bon prince, mon grand prince, when so prodigiously practiced upon? There is nothing, you see: for the proceeding itself swallows at a gulp with its open crimson jaws (such a rosy mouth!) like Carlyle's Mirabeau, "all formulas." . . .
>
> Ah, Walter, Walter, why do you do these things? they are magnificent, but they're not—well, discussable or permissible or forgiveable. At least not all at once. It will take a long, long, time, only little by lit-

tle and buckle-hole by buckle-hole shall I be able to look, with you, even one strap in the face . . . you are victor, winner, master, Oh Irresistible One—you've done it, you've brought it off and got me down forever and I must just feel your weight and bear your might.

Bosanquet was so thoroughly a member of his family that James dictated these letters to her; but to this invitation he added a handwritten postscript that was later torn off and destroyed.

February brought a new attack of angina, and James was in bed again, attended by two physicians—the local doctor, de Voeux, and his London heart specialist, Mackenzie—and a nurse. The accumulation of fluids in his body had begun to affect his lungs. Bed rest and digitalis helped him through this attack, but from then on he was aware that he would have to manage his day-to-day activities with his heart disease always in mind, "to reckon with this pectoral menace in every act of life."

At the end of February, nurse and doctors withdrew, and the local Chelsea physician called only occasionally to see how he was doing. Long walks were not possible, but during his recovery from the attack James rented a bath chair, and Burgess Noakes wheeled him along the Chelsea Embankment or across the Albert Bridge into Battersea Park.

Correspondence that had once been filled with gossip about love affairs now dwelt upon illnesses. Sturgis was ill; Howells was ill; Miss Allen had a grave heart ailment; Grace Norton was ill; Tom Perry was recovering. Hendrik Andersen wrote to ask why he had been silent for so long: Was James offended with him?

Yes, I have been silent—because I have been endlessly *ill* & the writing of letters a burden & effort beyond my power . . . the dreadful illness that broke upon me at the New Year of 1910 is a thing I have never but very imperfectly recovered from, & never *shall*, completely; & let that plead with you for my sorry old shortcomings. . . . I am yours, dearest Hendrik, all as faithfully & tenderly as ever.

Hendrik promptly invited James to join him in the warmth of Italy, but this was out of the question.

Alas, . . . my travel-power of every sort is dead & buried & I don't even weep on its tomb. You will come in your young might to England &

then we will meet (still embracingly) over the abyss of our difference
in years & conditions. I do so greatly rejoice in yours.

He worried constantly now about money, his brother's illness and
death and his own illness having kept him from much remunerative work
for three years and the royalties from *The Outcry* now faltering. Alice, the
"white-haired angel," again invited him to live with her in Cambridge and
to give up once and for all the burden of supporting his staff and two
households, but fond as he was of her and the children he could not think
of becoming so completely dependent on them or of living in what still
seemed to him the desert of Cambridge. "Dearest Alice, I could come
back to America (could be carried back on a stretcher) to die—but never,
never to live." How happy he would be, though, if Alice could come and
live with him in London for part of the year; then he could visit her in
Cambridge for the other part.

> You see my capital—yielding all my income, intellectual, social, associ-
> ational, on the old investment of so many years—my capital is *here*, and
> to let it all slide would be simply to become bankrupt. Oh if you only,
> on the other hand, you and Peg and Aleck, could walk beside my bath-
> chair down this brave Thames-side I would . . . half live there for the
> sake of your company.

He was anxious, almost desperate, to get back to work, and as he began
to see the end of his long memoir, he concluded negotiations with Scribner's for his long-postponed American novel. James Pinker had told
Scribner's of his plan for such a novel, but at first they had not responded. In September 1912, however, Charles Scribner had made an
unusual proposal directly to him: he would like to have a new American
novel as a complement to *The Golden Bowl*, to conclude the New York
Edition. If James were willing to begin work immediately, setting aside
other projects, Scribner's was prepared to offer the unusually large advance of $8,000, half to be delivered on signing a contract, half when the
book was finished.

The proposal was a curious echo of Edith Wharton's urging to him
that he set aside potboilers and write the big American novel he had had
in his mind for years. If the similarity struck him, he undoubtedly set it
down to Wharton's perspicacity; he was not aware that she had spoken to
Scribner's on his behalf and that the money would be hers.

James did not respond immediately but consulted Pinker. He did not want to set aside the concluding volume of the memoir on which he was engaged, and he was a little frightened by the size of the advance and the commitment it would represent. Pinker opened discussions with Charles Scribner, however, and Scribner was accommodating. Early in 1913 a contract was signed that would allow James to complete his memorial to father and brother before beginning work on the American novel. Early in March, he received a check for the first half of the advance, less Pinker's commission, as well as a nearly comparable amount from royalties and advances on the two volumes of memoirs, plus modest royalties from sales of the New York Edition and of Nelsons's cheap edition of *The American*. His income from writing for the year would be more than $7,000. His immediate worry was relieved, although the long-term problem remained. He was impatient for his health to improve so that he could get to work.

As his seventieth year drew toward its close, James was given the honors that a democratic society had to offer. In Great Britain, *The Bookman* devoted a special supplement to an illustrated account of his life and work. This was an honor given to the leaders of the world of letters: Emerson, Meredith, Hardy, and Mary Ward had all preceded him. He gave the editors a signed photograph of himself, as requested, but that was as far as he would go, and he declined to admit a photographer to his study. The March issue of the journal was adorned with a tipped-in "presentation plate portrait" of James, suitable for framing, and a long biographical article by Dixon Scott of the laudatory, uncomprehending school of criticism. But there were no pictures or descriptions of his domestic or working habits.

The editors of a new London weekly, *The Times Literary Supplement*, had a graceful acknowledgment to offer: they asked James to write an essay on the new fiction of the twentieth century. Despite his illness he happily agreed. The young English fiction writers were his friends, nearly all addressed him as "chèr Maître," and in his essay he spoke to them directly, in the tone of Matthew Arnold, urging on them counsels of perfection.

The burgeoning new fiction, he said, was one of the symptoms of spreading democracy and had democracy's virtues and defects. The new writers—some, like Wells and Arnold Bennett, no longer young but still to be classed with the new—had broken decisively with the sentimentality and romanticism of the past. This was a tremendous event, a revolution, and admirable as far as it went. The new writers painted on a broad canvas, took for their subject ordinary people living ordinary lives, and were frank about intimacies. Even the great Jane Austen had stopped where "the pressure of appetite" began; the Victorian Age had "bristled" with such retreats from actuality. Not so the new fiction writers, to whom no doors were closed. So much was all to the good; the new fiction was "saturated" with material fact—*War and Peace* was their great model—the new authors squeezed their orange dry; they gave us good bread, a "slice of life." A reader was glad to have this great new feast of material fact—"Yes, yes—but is this *all?*"

All art was an amusement; but it was a noble amusement, the most noble of all. Bread was not merely material fact, it was also manna from Heaven. One could not cut a slice from the loaf without selecting, shaping, giving form. And the new writers were sadly neglectful of craftsmanship and form and the meaning they conveyed. Embodied fact was dead, without an idea to vivify it. Continuing his conversation with Wells, James urged the new generation to devote themselves to the painstaking methods by which senseless material fact was given shape and meaning.

He wrote with affection of his young friends; found words of praise for the young Compton Mackenzie, in whose birthday book he had inscribed his name when Mackenzie was eight and James was writing for his father's Compton Comedy Company. He was frankly affectionate to Wells and Walpole, but the only writers of the new generation whom he placed in the first rank were Joseph Conrad and Edith Wharton, and it was only for Conrad that he had unqualified praise.

In the United States, numerous books and articles were assessing the state of American literature; critics and professors in the newly established field of study were attempting to establish a curriculum and standards. James and Howells were being named the heads of a distinctively American school of realist fiction, and James was widely acknowledged to be the leading novelist of his generation. *The New York Times* reported that James's "influence on the younger school of English novelists is perhaps greater than any other living writer." When *A Small Boy and Others* was published, his evocation of childhood in New York City before the Civil War was praised and contributed to a general feeling that he was one of their own, an American who had risen to the pinnacle of Anglo-Saxon letters.

On both sides of the ocean, efforts were under way to celebrate his seventieth birthday in traditional fashion. In England, Edmund Gosse invited a small circle of James's friends—Percy Lubbock, Howard Sturgis, and one or two others—to discuss what should be done, in light of James's poor health. They decided to enlist James's friends in purchasing a gift of some kind; a suggestion was made that a portrait be commissioned—perhaps Sargent would paint it, although he had given up portrait painting? It was a somewhat confused effort, and Sargent himself was enlisted as one of the subscribers to the gift. Percy Lubbock managed the logistics of organizing a committee of leaders in the theater, painting, and literature—Barrie, Sargent, Gosse, W. E. Norris, Walpole, Lucy Clifford, and Lubbock himself—drafting a letter for them to sign, which was then printed and sent to a long list of names that Gosse and the others compiled.

When he learned of this effort, William Dean Howells—James had contributed to *his* seventy-fifth birthday celebrations—thought that James's American friends should organize their own efforts and enlisted Edith Wharton to join him in a letter to James's cisatlantic circle. But time was now growing short, and Wharton suggested that perhaps they should simply make a gift of money to James, so that he could purchase something suitable for his new apartment.

When Harry learned of this second project, he wrote to his uncle to inform him that a sum of money was being raised, and James telegraphed immediately asking Harry to put a stop to the effort by whatever means necessary; plainly it was too much like the funds for broken-down writers to which James had contributed over the years. He did not want his financial difficulties made a matter of public concern, no matter how often he had complained to his friends about money problems. Harry accordingly wrote peremptory letters to Edith Wharton and Howells, as well as to some of the people to whom they had appealed, deeply offending Wharton; but the effort was halted and the money returned.

James was aware of all this scurrying in the shadows, but on the morning of April 15 he was surprised by the scale and warmth of the celebration. Burgess Noakes, with a smile, brought him the morning newspapers. *The Times'* leader was a birthday greeting, and there was a news item (a paragraph written by Percy Lubbock): "Mr. Henry James has been asked by a large number of his friends on this side of the Atlantic to sit for and accept his portrait by J. S. Sargent, R.A." *The Pall Mall Gazette* had a long editorial entitled "Henry James." The doorbell began to ring early, and Minnie brought in armloads of flowers that soon covered his worktable in the front parlor. Letters and telegrams filled the chimneypiece and overflowed onto the furniture.

The most treasured of these was the letter of birthday greetings organized by Gosse and signed by more than 250 of his London friends, congratulating James and asking whether he would consent to sit for a portrait by Sargent. The letter was delivered by young Lubbock, who brought with it a golden bowl—gilt silver—a careful reproduction of a handsome piece from the reign of Charles II. The signers were a remarkable collection of disparate personalities, leaders of his several worlds in London. Whole families had appended their names, with two and even three generations represented. His oldest surviving friends were there—Gosse, Florence Bell, Margaret Brooke, Arthur Balfour, Ariana Curtis, Lawrence Alma-Tadema, Arthur Benson, Paul Bourget, Lucy Clifford, William Heinemann, Frederick Macmillan, Alfred Parsons, John Sargent, Mary Ward. Friends who had died were represented by their children: Fanny Kemble's daughters, the du Maurier children, Virginia Woolf, the young Lord Houghton. Other, younger friends were there in their own right: Bernard Shaw, Arthur Pinero, Rudyard Kipling, Joseph Pennell, Max Beerbohm, H. G. Wells, and the still younger men, Jocelyn Persse, Hugh Walpole, Rupert Brooke, and Sydney Waterlow, among them a catalogue of future luminaries.

Lubbock reported afterward to Gosse, "I had to the last a slight fear that he might be over-whelmed & oppressed, even though gratified. But not a bit of it—he seemed to thrive & grow vigorous on our homage!"

Howard Sturgis, who was himself ill, had not been able to add his name to the list of signers in time for the presentation of the birthday gift, but he sent a penciled note that arrived along with the more elaborate messages, and James replied to him first of all, before sleeping that night: "Darling, darling Howard!" But none of James's friends knew to include Hendrik Andersen in the celebration, and he was for the moment forgotten.

Bosanquet was with James all the next day, as he began the long task of answering and thanking. To the signers of the gift he wrote, in a letter that would be printed and sent to each:

Dear Friends All,

Let me acknowledge with boundless pleasure the singularly generous and beautiful letter, signed by your great and dazzling array. . . . I was drawn to London long years ago as by the sense, felt from still earlier, of all the interest and association I should find here, and I now see how my faith was to sink deeper foundations than I could presume ever to measure . . . it is so wonderful indeed to me as I count up your numerous and various, your dear and distinguished friendly names, taking in all they recall and represent, that I permit myself to feel at once highly successful and extremely proud. . . . I remain all faithfully and gratefully yours,

Henry James

P.S. And let me say over your names.

James appended his enlarged list of those to whom thanks were due, adding Howard's name and those he knew had subscribed to the abortive American gift, 270 in all.

A few more days were required to sort out the confusion about the money that had been raised from the British group. A large sum had been raised for a gift, and with a portion of it the golden bowl had been purchased, but the bulk of the money was for a portrait. Sargent refused to take any fee, however, and James, while he agreed to sit for a portrait, refused to take ownership of it (hoping thereby to mollify his American friends, whose gift he had refused). After some discussion, James agreed to accept the portrait on the understanding that he would offer it to the National Portrait Gallery, and, at Sargent's request, the fee was redirected to a young sculptor, Francis Derwent Wood, who was in London assisting with the memorial to Queen Victoria and to whom James would sit for a portrait in bronze. And so the matter was composed.

Sittings for two portraits kept James in London well into the summer. The painting was completed late in June—"Sargent at his very best & poor old H.J. not at his worst"—and in July James began to sit in the mornings for Derwent Wood. But he was anxious to escape from London, and the sculptor had some photographs taken to help him complete the portrait bust.

When the Sargent portrait was finished, a great many people wished to see it. Sargent had long ago given up portrait painting, and his having agreed to do this last portrait was in itself news and had been widely reported both in the United States and Great Britain. Interest in the result was great, especially as the picture was said to be a masterpiece. James began to receive requests from America for photographs of the painting and from London for a glimpse of the original. Sargent obligingly held his studio open to visitors for several days. Printed invitations were sent out for this extended private view; James brought callers around from his flat to the studio on Tite Street and played host in the studio, standing beside the portrait and demonstrating for visitors the remarkable likeness that Sargent had achieved.

It was the portrait of an old man in ill health, his fragile skin stretched like parchment over the knuckles of his clenched left hand. The technique was impressionist, but, viewed at a little distance the strokes of color merged into a solid, massive figure posed against a dark background. James was painted full face, to show his remarkable eyes, now somewhat dimmed, his sensitive mouth—teeth parted, lips faintly pursed, as if he were listening and framing a responsive thought into words. The vast expanse of rumpled waistcoat, the round face, puffy from illness, the slight twist in the upper lip, the inscrutable expression of the bottomless eyes were rendered plainly, unsentimentally.

> Dear Charles de Kay.
>
> It was touching of you to write me so kind & much-remembering—much appreciating a letter. . . . I am touched by your stirring of old chords. . . . I hope life is using you not too unkindly. . . . For myself, I won't say blatantly that I've had what I want; but I haven't had, to excess, what I didn't want & that's a kind of mild glory. . . . Good night, & believe me yours very truly,
>
> Henry James

At the end of July, the James household prepared to remove itself to Rye. Mrs. Paddington and Minnie Kidd went ahead to open the house and air the rooms, while Burgess helped James pack. On the eve of his departure, however, James suffered the most severe chest pain that he had yet experienced and fell to the floor. As he lost consciousness, he thought—was certain—that he was dying.

Noakes went immediately to bring Dr. de Voeux from around the corner. Together they put James to bed and telephoned for the heart specialist Mackenzie, who sent a nurse and followed as quickly as he could. Noakes wired to Lamb House, and the maid Minnie Kidd was back with them by evening. When James recovered consciousness, he was well attended, and with the aid of nitroglycerin and bed rest he was able to resume his journey to Rye after three or four days.

Peggy James came over from Cambridge to spend the summer with him at Lamb House, and he was utterly grateful for her presence and her care. Harry, too, came over but stayed only briefly. Peggy fussed over her uncle's diet—de Voeux told him to eat lightly, and as many green vegetables as he could manage, for the sake of his heart, but Mackenzie (perhaps because he had a clearer sense of the irresistible progress of the disease) told James to follow his own instinct and to eat what he liked. To Peggy's horror, he insisted on eating heavy meals of fried fish and potatoes, with a meat course thrown in at dinner—to keep up his spirits, as he told her. He had a revulsion now for the stimulants, even coffee and cocoa, on which he had for so many years depended and that had carried him through his birthday celebrations, fearing the downturn and attacks that followed upon their use. ("He swears that a cup of cocoa is at the bottom of his troubles this time," Peggy reported to her mother. "Oh, it is too pathetic for words.")

Before he left London, James saw the Wolseleys, who were settled now in an apartment at Hampton Court for the winter. Wolseley was again agitating for a large standing army and the universal military service that was the rule on the Continent. The argument for a large army was the same as in past years—to defend the homeland—except that Germany rather than France was now the source of feared invasion.

Alice Green, to whom Holmes had complained of James, held a dinner for Holmes to which she invited James. At seventy-two, Holmes was on yet another visit to England and Ireland, his ailing wife having sent him off for his own health, and Green brought the two men together for a brief reconciliation. James, although he had given up dining out, accepted the invitation and brought nitroglycerin tablets with him in case of a heart attack. Neither of the men left any record of the occasion, and they did not meet again.

The news from America was disquieting. In the presidential election of 1912, Roosevelt and Taft factions had divided the Republican Party, and the first Democratic administration in a generation had resulted. Woodrow Wilson owed his election in part to the populist, isolationist core of his party, and he promptly appointed the Bible Belt candidate William Jennings Bryan secretary of state, senior member of his cabinet, and dispenser of ambassadorships. James Bryce came home from Washington; the arbitration treaty he had negotiated with Hay had been rejected by the Senate and now lay in ruins. Disturbing rumors circulated in London about the prospective American ambassador. The era of Anglo-Saxon alliance, in which James could play a role in personal diplomacy, seemed to have ended for a time.

He had ceased in his illness to issue invitations to handsome young men for overnight visits to Lamb House. Peggy provided some companionship and helped to drive away the demon of loneliness, walking with him as he crept along in the afternoons, lunching and dining with him, and her conversation and her presence was enough and all that he could bear.

Howard Sturgis, who had recovered his health, in the fall invited James to join him at Queen's Acre. James declined and regretfully wrote to say that he could not even invite Sturgis to spend a night in Lamb House: "cohabitation is under the stress of chronic angina a sad producer of attacks."

When he wrote to Walpole now, he repeated advice that his own parents had given their sons in their young manhood—"drink in health of body and mind in following out your own safe and innocent attractions"—but offered no attractions of his own. Hugh Walpole had written guiltily about indulging in "high jinks," and James responded in paternal fashion that when they met again, Hugh must expect only the lowest of "jinks" from him, evidently meaning that his own time for sexual adventures was past. But Hugh was not to take that as jealousy or disapproval:

> Don't say to me . . . à propos of jinks—the "high" kind that you speak of . . .—that I ever challenge you as to *why* you wallow, or splash or plunge, or dizzily & sublimely soar (into the jinks element,) or whatever you may call it: as if I ever remarked on anything but the absolute inevitability of it for you at your age & with your natural curiosities, as it were, & passions. It's good healthy exercise, when it comes but in bouts & brief convulsions, & it's always a kind of thing that's good, & considerably final, to *have* done. We must know, as much as possible, in our beautiful art, yours & mine, what we are talking about—& the only way to know it is to have lived & loved & cursed & floundered & enjoyed & suffered—I don't think I regret a single "excess" of my responsive youth—I only regret, in my chilled age, certain occasions & possibilities I didn't *embrace*. Bad doctrine to impart to a young idiot or a duffer; but in place for a young friend (pressed to my heart,) with a fund of noble passion, the preserving, the defying, the dedicating, & which always has the last word.

. . .

November in Chelsea: gray overcast sky, lamps in early afternoon, black barges moving on the broad yellow river. James had finished the second volume of his memoir. Alice had obtained and sent him letters that Minny Temple had written to their mutual friend John Gray, whom she had loved, and these allowed him to give a living portrait of this brave young woman with whom William had been in love and who had served as the model for the best of James's heroines.

James had taken the story of shared family life up to the moment of his own departure for Europe, and he began to think of writing an autobiography that would take up his own story from that point. But first there was the American novel to write—with ample time and space and no worries for the moment about money. He began dictating to Bosanquet a long memorandum to himself, thinking through out loud the background of the story and the structure of the novel.

It was to be a complement to *The Golden Bowl*, whose flawed, gilded crystal was an image of passionate friendship and betrayal between women. The new book was to be called *The Ivory Tower*, and an emblematic carved ivory pagoda, pierced with drawers and hidden recesses, was an image of friendship and betrayal between men.

The setting was to be Newport, with its hideous new "cottages," and New York City; a world of money getting and boastful spending, the arid world of the American male. Perhaps, he thought, he would set some scenes in Lenox; perhaps also California? Simply to show that he knew there was more to America than Manhattan and Newport. The young men would be rivals for a woman and for an inheritance. The amount of the inheritance was important; the money should be substantial, enough to be worth fighting over, but should not be a great fortune, not great enough for its owner to be able to carry out philanthropies and make atonement for the means by which it had been gathered.

In April, when Peggy returned to England to keep him company, James, with Peggy, Paddington, and the other servants, moved to Lamb House for the summer. He began to catch up his arrears of correspondence. *Notes of a Son and Brother* had appeared, and there were friendly messages from old friends to answer. Lilla Perry sent him a photograph of Mary Temple as she had been in the brief months of her prime, a photograph that he now gave pride of place on his desk.

. . .

The presumptive heir to the Hapsburg throne, Archduke Franz Ferdinand, and his bride, Sophie, were murdered on June 28, while visiting Sarajevo. The archduke was in Bosnia-Herzegovina to review the empire's troops in this newly acquired province and had brought his wife with him to make a holiday of the trip. They were assassinated by the Black Hand, a gang of criminals that included serving Serbian army officers that had carried out other terrorist acts, the now hideously familiar "propaganda of the deed," on behalf of a Greater Serbia. The old emperor of Austria-Hungary, Franz Josef, issued an ultimatum to Serbia. Finding that it was not promptly obeyed, on July 28 he declared war and ordered a mobilization of his armies.

In Great Britain, the crisis that began in Sarajevo seemed only another upheaval in the chronically troubled Balkans, at the shifting boundaries of three rival empires. Less than two years had passed since Serbia, Greece, and Bulgaria had united to drive the Ottoman Turks from the Balkans; less than a year since Austria-Hungary had annexed the former Turkish provinces of Bosnia and Herzegovina, seizing—over Serbian protests—one of the prizes of its victory. The empires of central Europe were preparing for a new war in the Balkans; Londoners prepared for a holiday weekend at the seashore.

At the highest levels of government, it was true, frantic diplomatic efforts were under way to forestall a general war. If Russia acted to defend Serbia from invasion, Germany would be drawn in to assist its ally Austria, and France would be drawn in on the side of Russia. Great Britain would be hard pressed to remain aloof from such a war.

On July 29, the day after Austria's declaration of war, Czar Nicholas II—he who had convened a peace congress and championed a court of arbitration—ordered the mobilization of the Russian armies in support of his fellow Slavs in Serbia. A wider war was now inevitable. Kaiser Wilhelm ordered the mobilization of the German armies and declared war on Russia. France mobilized in support of Russia.

Much as Herbert Asquith's administration was inclined to support France, even then it still seemed possible that the dispute could be contained in the east. He waited, but on August 3, Germany invaded neutral Belgium, sending its armies rapidly by rail and motor toward France's lightly defended northeastern border. Under a seventy-year-old treaty, Great Britain was committed to respecting Belgian neutrality, and the following day Herbert Asquith appeared on the floor of the House of Commons to announce that Germany was at war with France and had invaded Belgium. He asked permission to assist in Belgium's defense. With full support from the Unionist opposition and only wavering dissent in his own party, Asquith issued an ultimatum to Germany to withdraw its troops by midnight. The ultimatum was refused, and on the morning of August 5, Great Britain was at war.

James was at Lamb House, writing long-delayed replies to letters received in London. At midnight, August 4, when the British ultimatum to Germany expired, he was in the act of writing to Howard Sturgis, who had complained more bitterly than in the past of having been neglected. James began a long, somewhat impatient reply:

> [W]hy *should* I treat you at this time of day—or to speak literally, of night—as if you had begun suddenly not to be able to understand without a vulgar demonstration on the blackboard . . . that I tenderly & unabatedly love you . . . ?

He had not been able to maintain a stern tone, however, and had ended with a cordial greeting:

> I think the great public blackness most of all makes me send out this signal to you—as if I were lighting the twinkle of a taper to set over against you in my window.

In the morning, with the newspaper before him, he reopened the letter.

> Aug. 5. The taper went out last night, & I am afraid I now kindle it again to a feeble ray—for it's vain to try to talk as if one weren't living in a nightmare of the deepest dye. How can what is going on not be to one as a huge horror of blackness? Of course that is what it is to you, dearest Howard, even as it is to your infinitely sickened inditer of these lines. The plunge of civilization into this abyss of blood & darkness by the wanton feat of those 2 infamous aristocrats is a thing that so gives away the whole long age during which we had supposed the world to be with whatever abatements, gradually bettering, that to have to take it all now for what the treacherous years were all the while really making for & *meaning* is too tragic for words.

For a century afterward, the causes of and reasons for the war would be argued, but James never wavered from his view that regardless of plans and preparations that had been made beforehand, alliances formed, weapons prepared, interests engaged, regardless of all that had come before, two men, the German and Austrian emperors, had had the power to decide between civilization or war—and had chosen war.

> Black & hideous to me is the tragedy that gathers, & I'm sick beyond care to have lived to see it. . . [We] should have been spared this wreck of our belief that through the long years we had seen civilization grow & the worst become impossible. The tide that bore us along was then all the while moving to *this* as its grand Niagara—yet what a blessing we didn't know it. It seems to me to undo everything, everything that was ours, in the most horrible retroactive way.

In "the most beautiful English summer conceivable," his garden was blooming. From his green parlor window and from the ramparts of the old castle grounds just below him, the Channel lay on the horizon, beyond peaceful diked fields, like the blue rim of a world. Beyond that rim, almost as it seemed within hearing, German and French armies were maneuvering.

Doubly glad now to have Peggy's company and that of the faithful Bosanquet, he continued to dictate in the mornings and to take slow afternoon walks, keeping to the high street and the paved roads. The American novel was set aside; he could not think of writing about the present world. But he wanted work to occupy him and thought of taking up his old, long-abandoned potboiler, *The Sense of the Past*, about a modern American historian who is mysteriously transported to the age of Byron.

Those few first weeks of August and September were eerily reminiscent of the opening days of the American Civil War. The British Expeditionary Force was moving southward in silence, and in Rye they waited for news, as once he had waited for news of the Union Army's advance. The atmosphere of his village was suddenly altered; in the streets he was conscious of new expressions, hushes, clustered groups, detached figures pacing meditatively. It was all as he remembered, and he remembered too that those first early days of waiting, the calls for volunteers, were the prelude to a long and bitter struggle.

The first news, as in that earlier time, was bad. The Germans' advance through Belgium was barely slowed by the small Belgian Army and a British force hastily sent to its aid. The wounded and refugees began to stream across the Channel. French forces raced eastward, hoping to flank the German Army advancing in the north and encircle it, while the German forces raced southward toward Paris, hoping to cut off and encircle the French. No one on either side thought the war in the west would be prolonged. As Austria and Russia mobilized vast, slow-moving forces in the east, the rapidly moving and destructive armies of the west raced to outmaneuver and destroy each other.

On September 5, the German advance reached the Marne on the outskirts of Paris and was met by a hastily assembled rear guard brought out from Paris in taxis and private automobiles. There the German advance was halted, and the invading army retreated, in good order, to consolidate its forces.

A new race northward to the Channel began, as each side hastened to outflank the other, leaving behind them a long front. German forces assaulted Antwerp, whose ancient fortifications could not withstand the new high-explosive artillery shells. Hasty British reinforcements helped the Belgians to hold out briefly, but by mid-October Antwerp had been taken and the Channel ports were threatened. Only a thin defensive line stood between the enormous German armies and the crossing to England.

James could not recall the precise moment when his sense of the situation changed, from that of a Northerner in a remote seaport, waiting for news in a long war but expecting eventual victory, to the sense that he was now a Southerner, with an invading army poised on his doorstep. He had slowly gained an intense awareness that German armies were converging on the Channel ports in France, just out of sight beyond the blue rim of his home.

In September, Peggy returned to America, and James took his little household back to Chelsea and lent his house in Rye to the town council to be used to house refugees.

He found London transformed. Within days after the declaration of war, Parliament had enacted without discussion the administration's Defense of the Realm Act, effectively suspending civil liberties and allowing arrest and detention without charge. War news was censored, and wild rumors circulated of fantastic victories, terrible defeats. Resident aliens were required to register and report their movements; James had duly registered in Rye and had reported his departure for London. Persons of German origin or with Germanic names were heavily under suspicion, and many left the country. The prime minister and the clergy of the established Church speaking from their pulpits denounced the German emperor, Victoria's grandson by marriage, as an earthly personification of evil and proclaimed the war a moral crusade. There was as yet no conscription, but enormous public pressure was put on young men to volunteer. Lord Kitchener, the hero of the slaughter at Omdurman and architect of the South African concentration camps, was appointed secretary of state for war. Recruiting posters with Kitchener's stern visage were everywhere, seemingly on every blank surface, and the newspapers proclaimed that service was a moral duty.

Belgian refugees brought home the reality of the war. To James, the mark of barbarism of the German emperor was the disdainful manner in which he had taken and used a whole nation simply as a means, a roadway to conquest, destroying numberless precious lives and whole communities. The scale and violence of modern warfare threatened whole nations. Acutely engaged as his sympathies were on behalf of Belgium, the image that presented itself to him most vividly was that of the spiked helmet clapped down on the priceless genius of France, as the beauty, spontaneity, and individuality of the nations of Europe fell victim to the German Reich:

> a world squeezed together in the huge Prussian fist and with the variety and spontaneity of its parts oozing in a steady trickle, like the blood of sacrifice, between those hideous knuckly fingers.

James recorded his outrage in letters to friends and in articles and essays on behalf of the war effort. He told Pinker that he could not write anything except what was connected to the war effort: "I am unable really to care for anything but what happens to, and above all by, our armies." More angry now than he had ever been, this man of strong feelings began to look about for what more he could do. He who had disliked men's dinners and formal functions joined one committee after another: a committee to raise money for the Fund for the Relief of the Invaded Departments; the Committee for National Patriotic Organizations; the committee to support the work of the American Volunteer Ambulance Corps, of which he was made honorary chairman. He assiduously wrote fund-raising appeals, wrote articles for inclusion in pamphlets, even gave an interview to a *New York Times* correspondent in London, Preston Lockwood, carefully concluding with a New York address to which contributions should be sent. When the interviewer asked him to speak about his literary work in progress, James held up a hand and spoke with impatience: that was irrelevant now. "All I want is to invite the [American] public, as unblushingly as possible, to take all the interest in us it can."

Crosby Hall, at the foot of Cheyne Walk on the Chelsea Embankment, most recently a residence hall for the University of London, was converted to an emergency shelter for Belgian refugees. James made frequent visits to the gray stone medieval hall, with its arched and traceried windows, and the high vaulted ceiling of what had once been the duke of Gloucester's banqueting hall. Its bedrooms were now filled with refugees. James joined the Chelsea committee for aid to the refugees, helped in writing letters, making arrangements, giving information, and giving money. He brought refugees to see his doctor and his dentist.

Edith Wharton was in Paris, making similar efforts, and she sent him small sums to distribute to the refugees. Once a week, the Chelsea committee arranged a tea party in the great banqueting hall for refugees who were housed in the neighborhood. Those of the refugees who spoke French the committee members could engage in conversation, but the Flemish speakers were quiet and did not converse much even among themselves. Many had lost contact with their families and were helplessly trying to find husbands, wives, children, parents.

Wounded Belgian soldiers also came to London, and James began to visit hospital wards that recalled for him memories of visits to the hospital tents of the Civil War. The first casualties to arrive were the "lacerated Belgians," whose silent expressiveness was eloquent to James. These first casualties were Flemish-speaking, and James could not converse with them as he could with the British enlisted men. But at St. Bartholomew's there were some French-speaking Belgian soldiers, and James was able to establish a helpful relation with them, which gave him a sense of doing something useful.

Wounded survivors of the British Expeditionary Force soon also came home, and James was deeply touched by the rows of enlisted men in their beds at St. Bartholomew's, strangely quiet. The long wards stretched away, as it seemed, to an infinite vanishing point, the infinite patience and capacity for sacrifice of ordinary men in all their personal diversity.

By November 1914, Allied and German forces were stretched along a vast front, from the Swiss border to the North Sea. The war would not be a short one; the boys would not be home for Christmas, despite promises made to the volunteers. Both sides dug in along the extended front, a complex line of trenches and barbed wire across France, for the winter. The encounters of the rapidly moving armies had been short and limited, the casualties modest when compared in memory with those of the Civil War, of Antietam and Gettysburg. But the war had just begun, and planning for a protracted land war, the first for Britain in a century, began. "We were so unthinkably *unprepared* . . . and now the whole country is a huge workshop of war," James said.

On behalf of the Rockefeller philanthropies, Harry returned to Europe to make a tour in Belgium, France, and Serbia, to assess the need for assistance. James's young friends were volunteering for service; Hugh Walpole went to the eastern front as war correspondent for the *Daily Mail:* "Dearest Master. This is a hurried little letter of farewell. I'm just off to Russia . . . AMLTY [all my love to you]!" Within weeks, Walpole was serving with the Red Cross on the Russian front. Burgess Noakes enlisted in the Royal Sussex Regiment and was soon at the front in France; James hired another young man but was prepared to give him up soon to the army. Jocelyn Persse obtained a commission in Guy du Maurier's Royal Welsh Fusiliers, and although James was not able to see him off, he sent fond letters after him: "How can anyone imagine anything more 'right' than to do what you have done? . . . I intensely envy you the sense, & the fact, of *doing.*" When du Maurier took his regiment to France, James was greatly moved by reports of the warm reception they received on disembarking at Marseille. Rupert Brooke enlisted and went to the Royal Naval Division.

Young American men were volunteering, with their automobiles, for the ambulance corps—the British Army had no motorized ambulances of its own—and James began to frequent the headquarters that had been established for the volunteers in London. He raised money for the corps from friends in America, and the *New York Times* reporter who had interviewed him early in the new year remarked that this headquarters was the only social setting in which James was now likely to be found.

Asquith had organized a committee of the cabinet, a "War Council," to direct the war effort, with Kitchener and the young Winston Churchill, to which he invited Arthur Balfour, the leader of the opposition. James took to dropping in at 10 Downing Street for tea with Margot Asquith and any news. "I lunched yesterday with the Prime Minister," James confided to the Perrys, "on the chance of catching some gleam between the chinks—which was idiotic of me, because it's mostly in those circles that the chinks are well puttied over." But Margot Asquith in fact was willing to be indiscreet, partly out of friendship and partly because of James's value as a link to America. She lent him the latest volume of her diary, in which she characterized some of the inner workings of the War Council, and James learned how critically important they thought American munitions and war materiel would be in what Kitchener told them would be a protracted war.

Rupert Brooke was briefly home on sick leave early in the year. As he was a good friend of their daughter Violet Bonham Carter, the Asquiths put him up at 10 Downing Street, and Violet asked James to visit. He sat by the young poet's bedside and read aloud, and they agreed that James would write a preface for a little book of Brooke's, the collected newspaper reports of his journey to America. This would be an iota of propaganda urging the United States to join in the war effort. Brooke had also just published a book of war sonnets, and in a passion James read it and, thinking of Brooke, wrote that the sick and wounded British officers, with their beauty and modesty, affected him as the very flower of the human race.

Young men who had known him only in the years of age and illness were struck by the passionate engagement of the old man. The pondering hesitation of his speech left him when he was speaking of the war; Percy Lubbock recalled afterward that "the challenge of the war with Germany roused him to a height of passion he had never touched before, and if the strain of it exhausted his strength, as well it might, it gave him one last year of the fullest and deepest experience." But older friends were worried about him. W. E. Norris wrote to Gosse that he didn't quite like Henry James's account of himself in a recent letter:

> He tells me that he is only just recovering from a complete breakdown, and he seems to suffer at more frequent intervals from angina, which he says the slightest perturbation (and he is so easily perturbed!) brings on. Apparently these attacks are only warded off by or cured by a persistent regimen of explosives.

James was now in constant pain and was taking nitroglycerin tablets twice or thrice daily, as William had in the last months of his life, and to emphasize his martial character he liked to tell his friends that he was subsisting on a diet of dynamite. He rarely went out now in the mornings, which were his worst time, but was generally ready by teatime for meetings, visits, telephone calls, and letters. He began to dictate the opening chapters of *The Sense of the Past* again, taking comfort and distraction from his ability to work. He also dictated a reminiscence of his early friendship with Annie Fields, who had died early in the year. The Fields and Holmes houses had been close to each other on Charles Street in Boston, when he had known them in the Civil War years, and perhaps with a touch of malice he allowed his recollection to drift to Wendell Holmes and their intimate friendship, with references that only Holmes could be expected to understand.

James lunched with Arthur Benson, for what would be the last time, at the Athenaeum, consuming with his accustomed relish veal chops and a pudding. Benson confided to his diary that James "looked worn & small but sturdy." They gossiped about mutual friends, as of old, and James threw up his hands over Gosse, who was making himself somewhat ridiculous over a young sculptor. Mrs. Gosse cried out, "Again!—Again!" at this new outbreak, James said, of his friend's "frivolity."

A little later in the spring, James collected mail that had accumulated at the Reform Club and found among the circulars that the porter gave him H. G. Wells's new book, *Boon*. This was a hastily compiled pastiche of ruminations, purportedly the literary remains of a once-popular writer, who greatly resembled H. G. Wells. The eponymous Boon supposedly had been killed by the outbreak of the war and would be seen no more. The third chapter was titled "Of Art, of Literature, of Mr. Henry James" and was simply a long insult illustrated with Wells's stick-figure caricatures. Wells portrayed James as a practitioner of Art for Art's Sake, an effete character whose finicky work he contrasted with his own vigorous, no-nonsense books. The diatribe was a continuation of Wells's conversation with James about *Marriage* and was heavy with the spirit of the staircase. Why should a novel have unity, or artistry at all? Boon demands. James is a "leviathan retrieving pebbles," he is the culmination of the "Superficial type." His people are bloodless, passionless, his tales artificial. His novels put Wells in mind of "a magnificent but painful hippopotamus resolved at any cost, even at the cost of its dignity, upon picking up a pea which has got into a corner of its den."

James read this with considerable surprise and sent off a letter to Wells, remarking on their long friendship and asking for an explanation.

My dear James,

You write me so kind and frank a letter after my offenses that I find it an immense embarrassment to reply to you . . . my sparring and punching at you is very much due to the feeling that you were "coming over" me. . . . I would rather be called a journalist than an artist, that is the essence of it, and there was no other antagonist possible than yourself. . . .

Yours most gratefully and affectionately,
H. G. Wells

James began his reply calmly: "I am bound to tell you that I don't think your letter makes out any sort of case for the bad manners of *Boon*" and then went on, dictating to Bosanquet with slowly gathering anger. He treated with contempt Wells's characterization of James's work and the supposed opposition between Wells's journalism and James's art. All art was for use, in the same kind and degree. "It is art that makes life, makes interest, makes importance . . . and I know of no substitute whatever for the force and beauty of its process."

Wells replied, "I don't clearly understand your concluding phrases," and they did not speak again.

Rupert Brooke died on the way to Gallipoli; Guy du Maurier died on the western front. Burgess Noakes was struck by shrapnel and invalided home. James began to be occupied with writing condolence letters to friends who had lost their sons or their husbands. ("Dear Mrs. Harrison. . . . The sense of your signal bereavement has cut the knot of all my awkwardness." "My dear, dear Clare [Sheridan], I languish with you . . . and I press the mighty little Margaret to my aged breast.")

A new kind of warfare was being conducted along the western front, "trench warfare." The name seemed innocuous, but it concealed gigantic brutality. The deep trenches of the opposing sides, protected by barbed wire and machine guns, were separated by barren ground. Unlike fortifications, the trenches could not be destroyed by artillery fire, and the "no-man's-land" between them could not be crossed by infantry without enormous casualties. Even when a line of trenches was successfully attacked, after heavy shelling, the success was not the capture of a garrison but simply the gain of a few yards, with the enemy retreating to new entrenchments. Neither side made use of armored vehicles; infantry were ordered to advance on foot against barbed wire and machine guns. The casualties were immense, stupefying. Newspapers were censored, but at the headquarters of the volunteer ambulance corps James heard reports of five thousand casualties in twenty minutes.

Early in the year, he paid a weekend visit to the prime minister and his daughters at Walmer Castle in Kent. The occasion likely gave James an opportunity to explore once again the possibilities of joining in personal diplomacy. Italy was loosely allied with the German-speaking empires but had as yet taken no part in the war. After his weekend, James wrote to Hendrik Andersen and other friends in Italy, apologizing for his recent neglect of them and urging upon them the importance of Italian neutrality. Joseph Primoli came to England; he met with James and others, and they talked of the need for Italy to remain neutral.

But the principal object of his efforts was the United States. James's anger toward the American administration grew as the horrors gathered. Henry Adams had come over to London, and they met and talked over the situation. It appeared that the United States would be neutral in this war. The two men shared a deep contempt for Woodrow Wilson,

> who seems to be *aware* of nothing but the various ingenious ways in which it is open to him to make difficulties for us. . . . Most of my correspondents at home . . . minister to my dread of him and the meanness of his note as it breaks into all this heroic air.

Was this how his story would end—with a new Germanic empire in Europe, with Great Britain invaded, and the United States too busy with moneymaking and elections to help? German ships had shelled northeastern British coastal towns, and zeppelins had begun bombarding London, killing civilians at random. On May 7, a German submarine sank the British passenger ship *Lusitania* as it approached the Irish coast, killing more than a thousand civilians, including many Americans, friends and acquaintances of James among them. Theodate Pope was aboard but survived; Alfred Vanderbilt and Charles Frohman, who was to have produced *The Outcry*, went down with the ship. But Woodrow Wilson continued to assure the kaiser of the United States' friendship and neutrality. James could barely contain his outrage. He haunted the American embassy, calling regularly on the new ambassador, Walter Hines Page, to urge upon him the need for aid to Britain.

He evidently discussed with Asquith, perhaps on their weekend in the country, the possibility of becoming a British subject. An American friend, Logan Pearsall Smith, had adopted British citizenship in order to volunteer for service and urged the step upon James as a way of enlisting in the Allied cause. Aside from his own wish to enlist to the extent possible for him, James was galled by the label of "foreigner" that was affixed to him by Defense of the Realm Act procedures. In June, he telephoned Pearsall Smith to ask how naturalization was done. "You go to a solicitor," Pearsall Smith replied, and James went the same afternoon to see Nelson Ward, in Gray's Inn. Four sponsors were needed, Ward told him, adult male householders who could testify to his respectability and his ability to speak and write English. James wrote to Gosse, asking him to be one of the sponsors of his application.

> The force of the public situation now at last determines me to testify to my attachment to this country, my fond domicile for nearly forty years . . . by applying for naturalization here: the throwing of my imponderable moral weight into the scale of her fortune is *the geste* that will best express my devotion—absolutely nothing else *will*.

Gosse replied with considerable tact and understanding, "It is splendid of you and beautifully like yourself, to make this sacrifice for us. You give us the most intimate thing you possess." James then spoke with Asquith, asking him to be his leading sponsor, to which Asquith agreed. In a formal letter to the prime minister, James then recited the facts that were required for his application, but he dwelt upon the heart of his reasons:

> I find my wish to testify at this crisis to the force of my attachment and devotion to England, and to the cause for which she is fighting, finally and completely irresistible. It brooks at least no inward denial whatever. I can only testify by laying at her feet my explicit, my material and spiritual allegiance, and throwing into the scale of her fortune my all but imponderable moral weight.

It was of the essence of the act that it should be known in the United States, and James supplied Pinker with a summary statement of his reasons, for distribution to newspapers. On July 28, when he surrendered his passport and took his oath of allegiance to the king, the statement was published in *The New York Times*.

. . .

James believed that by taking an oath of allegiance to the king he had at the same time renounced his American citizenship. In letters to Edmund Gosse he referred to the act as his "Gran Rifiuto" and said that henceforth he would be no longer a "child of the West"—hence Gosse's remark that he had given up something intimate and precious. Explaining to Sargent that he was waiting for America to abandon its neutrality, James complained that "It would really have been *so* easy for the U.S. to have 'kept' [me] (if they had cared to!)." To Lilla Perry he said that Woodrow Wilson could have saved James the need to make such a sacrifice "with one wiggle of his little finger." Observers in the United States, even those who supported him, took the act as a renunciation. Ezra Pound fumed:

> The "Americans" . . . have understood nothing about it. They do not even know what they have lost. They have not stopped for eight minutes to consider the meaning of his last public act. After a year of ceaseless labor, of letter writing, of argument, of striving in every way to bring America on the side of civilization—civilization against barbarism, civilization not Utopia . . . ! After a lifetime spent in trying to make two continents understand each other . . . America has not yet realized that never in history has one of her great men abandoned his citizenship out of shame. It was his last act—the last thing left.

This was too violent—James's renunciation was an act of loyalty to Britain, not primarily rejection of America—but Pound's understanding was the common one, and James's act became a source of bitter recriminations.

In August he grew more severely ill and at first mistook the symptoms for a new gastric disorder. He once again lost his appetite for food, and, as in Alice's case twenty years earlier, a dentist extracted decayed teeth, but this did not improve matters. He suffered a steep decline in spirits, and, feeling that it was time to do so, went back to his solicitor to make some final changes in his will. He made the solicitor, Nelson Ward, his executor jointly with Harry. With his usual meticulous care he amended this public document, which, as he knew, would be reported in the press. He made the customary bequests of one hundred pounds to each of his servants. Sargent's portrait was to be given to the National Portrait Gallery, as agreed, if it would accept it. A bequest to Ned James, his brother Robertson's unhappy son, he was obliged to revoke, as Ned had just published an antiwar tract that contained what were in Great Britain criminal libels against the king, which in the circumstances he could not ignore. There were modest gifts to his constant companions in the theater, which could be made without indiscretion: Lucy Clifford, Jocelyn Persse, Hugh Walpole. He made no mention of his intimate friends Arthur Benson, Howard Sturgis, and Hendrik Andersen. To his niece Peggy he left the proceeds of his life insurance, which he hoped would confer upon her a measure of freedom. The principal provisions made at the time of William's death, leaving his interest in the Syracuse properties and his copyrights to Alice, he left as they were. Lamb House, which would only have been a burden to Alice, was to go to Harry. He appointed no literary executor, trusting that Harry would perform that function for Alice's financial benefit—James viewed his copyrights as property, like the Syracuse real estate, whose principal importance was monetary. There were final instructions to consider. He could not live in America, but he would not renounce his deep ties to his first home:

> I direct that my body shall be cremated at Golders Green (if I shall die in England) and my ashes afterward laid near those of my parents my elder brother and my sister in the Cemetery of Cambridge Massachusetts

He went briefly to Lamb House, but the old mulberry tree under which he was accustomed to sit in the summers had fallen in a gale, and he took no pleasure in the denuded garden. Depressed and finding himself too ill to remain at Lamb House, he soon returned to his flat in Carlyle Gardens. Turning over Lamb House to refugees once more, he cleared out his drawers of personal papers, burning most of his remaining letters from friends.

In London, the nature of his physical discomfort revealed itself clearly as a new and grave heart crisis, and this discovery at least allowed proper treatment with digitalis. His depression lifted somewhat, and the return to London improved both his spirits and his energy. He became more optimistic about an eventual Allied victory, although he was well informed and knew that the Allies' best hopes lay in a protracted war and eventual American support. The Americans surely would soon enter the war, in response to the continued torpedoing of passenger ships carrying Americans. There was a certain excitement in seeing, from his privileged height, the great forces of history at their brutal work. As he imagined the future, he foresaw a Western triumph, and he began to recover a degree of optimism. The horrors of the war surely would ensure that such a fall into barbarism would never be allowed to happen again.

There were to be no more walks along the embankment, but a bath chair was again rented and James was happy to be wheeled along beside the river, watching the life there. John Sargent came by often from his studio on Tite Street. On December 4, 1915, he wrote to Gosse:

> I write in case you have not already learnt that Henry James has had two slight strokes within the last forty-eight hours. He is paralysed on the left side—his brain is clear, and his speech. A nephew has been called for from America, and he is well looked after by his friends and neighbors.

Bosanquet had summoned Harry. She was friend, secretary, and neighbor, a constant presence in the apartment. As James was too ill to do so himself, she wrote to his close friends to tell them of the crisis. Fanny Prothero came and continued to visit every day, as did Margaret Brooke. James could not walk but was carried out from his bedroom to the front parlor in the afternoons to look out the window at the life on the river. Bosanquet spent her days at the flat. Nelson Ward supplied her with cash for household expenses and to pay servants and nurses. She telegraphed to Cambridge to alert Alice to a further downturn in James's health and wrote to Edith Wharton, Edmund Gosse, and other of James's friends.

The heart specialist Mackenzie came and ordered day and night nurses. About a week after the first stroke, Bosanquet thought James had improved. "He wanted to dictate some sentences describing his psychological condition," she noted in her diary. The two strokes had left him physically disabled, with his left side paralyzed, but his mind evidently was not greatly affected, except that he seemed uncertain of where he was. The strokes may have caused some loss of recent memory; he knew the people around him and spoke lucidly to Bosanquet but did not recognize the flat.

He began to dictate to Bosanquet again and asked her to bring the Remington into his bedroom, as she had done on other occasions when he was too ill to leave his bed. He spoke half to her responsive machine and half to himself, as he had long been accustomed to do, chronicling his own dissolution. The process of dying was in its way a drama, with its ups and downs: "I find the business of coming round about as important and glorious as any circumstance I have had occasion to record, by which I mean that I find them as damnable and as boring." But he wasn't up to the effort, and after dictating three sentences he agreed he ought to stop and rest.

With James immobilized and with fluid accumulating in his lungs, pneumonia set in. James's temperature spiked sharply on December 10, but on the following morning the night nurse reported to Bosanquet that James had had an easier night and that his temperature had dropped back almost to normal. Lucy Clifford came in and saw that James was sleeping peacefully.

Later in the day, he asked for Bosanquet and she went into the bedroom. The night nurse had reported that he was delirious, but when Bosanquet entered James seemed to recognize her. He spoke to her clearly and made some remarks about the Bonaparte family, about whom he apparently had been thinking. Later, in the evening, he sent for her again because he wanted to dictate, and Bosanquet brought the typewriter.

He appeared to be dictating one of his preparatory memoranda for a book, perhaps a historical novel, about the Bonapartes. The scene he imagined was a royal procession. Napoleon had suffered his first reverses, "during these days of cold grey Switzerland weather, on the huddled and haggard campaigns of the first omens of defeat," and had returned to Paris. Bonaparte brothers and sisters watched the procession; they were behaving badly in this crisis, having had no preparation for their sudden elevation to power or their equally sudden fall.

> They pluck in their terror handfuls of plumes from the imperial eagle, and with no greater credit in consequence that they face, keeping their equipoise, the awful bloody beak that he turns round upon them.

Among them is a girl, the future heir. The point of view will shift to her—"We simply shift the sweet nursling of genius from one maternal breast to the other and the trick is played, the false note averted." She is evidently to be one of James's heroines, an "astounding little stepchild of gods, astounding young stepmother!"

On Sunday morning, the night nurse again reported that James had called for Bosanquet, apparently wishing to dictate again. The nurse reported that James was delirious, as he had been trying to dictate to the nurse during the night. He seemed to think he was writing a book. Although James was still confused about where he was, Bosanquet thought him otherwise clear of mind. He resumed his dictation, continuing his ruminations about the Napoleonic work:

> The Bonapartes have a kind of bronze distinction that extends to their finger-tips and is a great source of charm in the women. Therefore they don't have to swagger after the fact; fortune has placed them too high. . . . You can believe anything of the Queen of Naples or of the Princess Caroline Murat. There have been great families of tricksters and conjurors, so why not this one, and so pleasant withal?

As he went on, he shifted his point of view into the character he was describing, a young woman in the second generation, watching the procession as it reached the palace of the Louvre. "Our admirable father keeps up the pitch. . . . He is the dearest of men," she says of Napoleon, and James slides into the manner of one writing a letter, reporting the scene, and concludes the dictation, "I am, devotedly yours."

James sleeps and in the evening awakes and resumes. He has stepped onto the stage of his drama now and is Napoleon himself, in the midst of his renovations of the Louvre, writing letters to his brother and sister in America. The first he signs, "Napoleone," giving the name Primoli's Italian pronunciation. But in the second letter, in which he speaks of provisions he is making for his family in America, he signs himself, "your faithful brother and brother-in-law, Henry James." For the next two days, the night nurse reported each morning that James appeared to think he was dictating to her, and Bosanquet assumed that he was trying to continue his Napoleonic work, but no notes were made of what he said. During the day his fever would return, and he would sleep or would be too disoriented to work.

Alice arrived in London on the evening of December 13 and came to the flat the next morning. Shortly afterward, she discharged Bosanquet and took over the management of the household herself. This was understandable, but Bosanquet was deeply hurt.

Alice found James feverish and increasingly confused about his surroundings. He recognized her and greeted her joyfully but did not know where he was and began to guess that he was in Ireland, or perhaps in California or at home in Lamb House. He grew more agitated, and the doctor recommended complete quiet and rest. He began to administer morphine.

Bosanquet had carried messages to and from his friends, but Alice barred the door to all visitors, intercepted telephone calls, and took over the task of writing to James's worried friends herself. Bosanquet's frank reports were replaced by Alice's more conventional reassurances:

> Dear Mr. Gosse. This is a belated answer to your kind note . . . [Henry] does not suffer and the mental confusion which distressed him at first no longer weighs on him. He thinks he is in foreign cities, among old friends, and that his brother William, the only one he asks for, will be coming ere long. Such serenity of spirit shines through the wrecked brain that his presence is still a comfort to us.

The prime minister proposed Henry James for the Order of Merit, and his name was included on the honors list for the new year. James Bryce, briefly ambassador to America and now Viscount Bryce, an old friend, came to deliver the red-and-blue medal to James in his darkened bedroom.

Burgess Noakes, injured and deafened by an artillery shell, remained with James until the end. Peggy arrived in January and tried to make notes of her uncle's continued efforts at dictation, but he was now feverish and heavily sedated, and the fragments of speech were disconnected. The nurses continued to say that he was delirious, but Peggy thought that often they simply were unable to understand his elaborate speech. At times, James moved his hand as if he were writing. His lungs were filling with fluid, and he had to struggle harder to breathe. In mid-January, he suffered a new heart attack.

Yet James still had lucid moments. At one point, he asked Peggy to see that some competent person be chosen to bring order to his dictations for the Napoleonic work, unaware of how little had been recorded. He complained that there were only women around him. "In one of his vivid and conscious moments," Alice told Gosse, "he said to me, 'tell the boys to *follow*, to be *faithful*, to *take me seriously*.' "

Pneumonia and morphine spared him the agonies that William had suffered. On February 28, 1916, Henry James died in his flat in Chelsea. A memorial service was held in the Chelsea Old Church, and shortly afterward Alice carried James's ashes home to America for burial.

HENRY JAMES IN MEMORY

Almost a century after his death, James's readers remain faithful and novelists continue to admire his success and rebel against his example. His works are nearly all still in print in Great Britain and North America, and much of his fiction is in print in French translation. There are some German and Italian editions, and the late Soviet Academy of Sciences had in hand a project to translate his novels into Russian, which I believe collapsed for lack of funds but got at least as far as a Russian translation of *Portrait of a Lady*. James has also, through film and television, reached a mass audience. Although his plays have not been performed since the First World War, his novels and stories have been regularly adapted for stage and screen, in both French and English. Versions of *The Turn of the Screw* and *Washington Square* have been particularly popular in America, and it was charming to see Helena Bonham Carter, a great-granddaughter of James's friends the Asquiths, starring as Kate Croy in a fine film adaptation of *The Wings of the Dove*. Even *The Golden Bowl* has been adapted for television and film.

James's critical reputation has suffered a more complex history. Shortly after the First World War, Percy Lubbock published two volumes of Henry James's letters, a traditional "life and letters." James's correspondence with Robert Louis Stevenson was published separately, and writers who had known him published memoirs in which he figured. These were for the most part admiring, and James was fondly remembered as a great figure of the Victorian Age by the young people who had known him only as an old man.

His critical standing quickly began to falter. In the United States, there was a strong reaction after the war to America's involvement with Europe. "Americanism" returned to the fore, and in the academy, James was now condemned in Rooseveltian terms as effete and effeminate. His adoption of British citizenship, and his frequent and pointed criticisms of America, were certainly held against him, but there was a deeper, almost racial hostility to the figure of the cosmopolite.

The centerpiece of this school of criticism was Van Wyck Brooks's *The Pilgrimage of Henry James*, published in 1925, in which Brooks, drawing heavily on *A Small Boy and Others*, portrayed James as a child who had a pathetic yearning for the fairyland of Europe, known only from picture books, a child who never grew up. Edmund Wilson adopted Brooks's account, giving it a Freudian spin, and subjected James's (and his characters') supposed repression of feeling to scholarly analysis. This portrait was soon given support by H. G. Wells's venomous *Experiment in Autobiography*, in which Wells, now an embittered old man, renewed his attack on James, portraying him as effeminate and cowardly.

For various reasons, perhaps his insistence on the barrenness of the American desert and its need for transplanted European gardens, university professors who were constructing the new field of "American literature" disliked James. Vernon Parrington spoke of James's final expatriation: cut off from the "blood and soil" of America, James's work was inferior to such authentic American products as Sherwood Anderson's *Winesburg, Ohio*.

Praise in those years from the expatriate writers Ezra Pound and T. S. Eliot did not really help matters greatly, especially in the universities, where a purely American literature was being taught. James became a cult figure but was not thought to be suitable reading for undergraduates. One senses in the critical disapproval of these years an undercurrent of uneasiness about James's late novels, drenched in erotic feeling, and the widely circulated rumors of his liaisons with men.

The Second World War and a renewed alliance with Great Britain prompted a change of heart in the United States. Bennett Cerf at Random House led the recanonization. On the centennial of James's birth in 1943, collections of James's stories were issued in inexpensive editions, his novels appeared in the Modern Library and the Book-of-the-Month Club. In the academy, Alfred Kazin, in *On American Ground*, recalled that James was one of the leaders of a distinctively American school of realism. W. H. Auden's poem on the centenary of James's birth, his preface to *The American Scene*, and F. O. Matthiessen's *Henry James: The Major Phase*, published in 1943 and 1944, sounded a note of critical approval that has continued to the present day. Jacques Barzun defended James from the charge that he lacked feeling; F. R. Leavis and Richard Poirier, among other leading figures, treated him seriously and rescued his works from the imputation that they were merely formal exercises.

Academic professionals in the United States were also uneasy about

James's conservative views, his racial prejudices and seeming anti-Semitism, his sometimes severe moral judgments, reminders of the Victorian Age. But these perceived failings were set aside—as they were for T. S. Eliot—for the sake of his art and were attributed to the neurotic fears of a pre-Freudian age or simply ignored. James was one of only a handful of American writers who had attained European stature, who could be ranked with the masters of French and English literature, and we were proud of him again.

His star has continued to rise. Theoretical criticism has happily plumbed James's complexities. James's own theory of fiction is out of fashion, and the author's own views have been dethroned from the seat of authority, but modern theoretical criticism has happily embraced James's complexities in its own way.

In Great Britain, there have not been such wild swings of reputation, perhaps because James was accepted into the canon of English literature during his lifetime but never had or could have the sort of prominence there that he achieved in the United States. The Bloomsbury group turned against him after the war, classing him with the despised eminent Victorians. Some authors, such as E. M. Forster and Somerset Maugham, reacted against him very strongly. But his place in the canon has never seemed in doubt. James died a British subject and was given a tablet in the Poets' Corner of Westminster Abbey. In the land of Shakespeare and Milton, he was never as prominent nor as controversial as in the United States.

Biographies of James followed the ups and downs of his critical fortunes in the United States. Percy Lubbock's life and letters was reasonably frank and wholly admiring. Theodora Bosanquet's intimately knowledgeable *Henry James at Work* (published by Hogarth Press in 1924) was a graceful introduction to James's worldview and his later work. Rebecca West's critical biography, *Henry James*, spoke especially to female readers and writers who admired James both for his art and for his portrayals of women (and perhaps further infuriated her lover, H. G. Wells). Leon Edel's early work on James's plays and the influence of playwriting on his later novels was respectful and brought attention to an otherwise forgotten side of his career.

But Van Wyck Brooks's imaginative study seemed to capture the man's inner life in a way that formal biography could not. James, Brooks argued persuasively, must have been afraid of the realities of life, afraid of passion and engagement, to have retreated to Europe and into his obscurities. The realism of his late style, its internal complexity, paradoxically gave many readers a sense of willful obscurity, as if he were concealing rather than revealing himself.

This was far from his intention. Although James systematically destroyed most of the letters he received, he never tried to recapture his own letters, nor did he ask his correspondents to destroy them (as, for instance, Holmes did). James, like George Sand, evidently was content to allow his own letters to speak for him. In requests to his nephew, James asked Harry to protect his reputation and his papers but never asked him to destroy the mass of James's letters that he knew had been kept by his friends. Harry took it as within his uncle's mandate to publish an edition of James's own letters, at least those written in the years after the period described in his memoirs. Shortly after James's death, therefore, and after taking Edmund Gosse's advice, he authorized Percy Lubbock to compile *The Letters of Henry James*, which remains an invaluable resource. Representative examples even of James's very frank and affectionate letters to Howard Sturgis, Hugh Walpole, and Walter Berry were included, albeit stripped of their passionate salutations—"Dearest dearest," "Darling Boy," etc. (Correspondence in the Gosse Papers shows that Gosse prompted this modest bowdlerization.) The Lubbock edition gave a clear if sketchy account of James's life and work, although his letters, like his fiction, sometimes required energetic efforts and a knowledge of context from the reader to be understood.

After Henry James's death, his nephew Harry steadfastly refused all requests for further publication of James's letters, as well as all requests for access to his papers for the purpose of writing a new biography. Interestingly, Leon Edel was among those whose requests were refused when he asked to publish both a biography and an additional volume of James's letters.

Harry did give the Harvard literature professor F. O. Matthiessen access to the papers and permission to publish James's notebooks. Matthiessen's invaluable edition appeared in 1947, and Harry did authorize Leon Edel, by then also an English professor, to publish James's plays, but he steadfastly hewed to James's request, of which he perhaps approved, to bar any other outside biographer and to allow James alone to speak for himself.

Aside from the Lubbock letters, therefore, and a few privately printed volumes, access to James's letters and other papers was difficult to obtain until recently. The imaginative efforts of Van Wyck Brooks and others held the field for a generation. Except for those who had heard the anecdotes or read the privately printed letters, James was thought or at least said to be a kind of monk, in Auchincloss's word a "churchman," a celibate aesthete, occupying himself with a literary version of Howard Sturgis's embroidery.

Despite Harry's effort to discourage them, biographies began to accumulate, based largely on secondary materials that seemed to flesh out what was becoming the established portrait of James. F. W. Dupee wrote several well-regarded volumes on the James family, taking as a premise once again James's memoirs of his brother and father. Dupee used them to create what now seems clearly a myth, that Henry James had been in love with Mary Temple, a romantic love for a dead girl, in which he supposedly sheltered himself from actual involvement with women. In his one-volume *Henry James*, Dupee used an episode from *A Small Boy and Others*, "the dream of the Louvre," to exemplify James's supposed lifelong romanticism about Europe, a fantasy to which he would flee, marking the "Napoleonic theme" that Edel and other scholars would pursue. Dupee also seems to have originated the theory that "James's invalidism . . . was itself the symptom of some fear of or scruple against, sexual love on his part." This was very much in accord with the popular American Freudianism of the day. A picture of Henry James as a repressed and neurotic Bostonian accordingly was well established by the best authorities when Harry died in 1947.

When Harry had planned his own estate, in which so many family records were held, he had evidently faced a dilemma. Henry's works were precious but no longer remunerative. Like Lamb House, they were, financially speaking, a burden rather than an asset. Harry—who had spent his career in the nonprofit organizations for which his uncle had such high hopes—resolved the difficulty by leaving Lamb House to the National Trust of Great Britain and the family archives to Harvard University. Instead of merely donating the papers themselves, he left Henry's copyrights in the donated materials, including the right of first publication of the donated letters, to the university—in effect making the Fellows of Harvard College his uncle's literary executors.

It was at this point that the remarkable figure of Leon Edel again entered the picture, and a separate word needs to be said about his contribution to James biography.

Having long had in mind the ambition to write a comprehensive biography of James, after Harry's death Edel made energetic efforts to obtain access to the papers at Harvard. Edel's own papers, which are now at McGill, show that he sought Theodora Bosanquet's aid early in this effort. He had long before described to her his wish to write a full-length biography in which the "Napoleonic theme" would be prominent. Evidently impressed by Dupee's use of the dream of the Louvre, he had also learned of James's final dictation, in which a Napoleonic theme returned. Harry James had denied him access to this material, but Bosanquet now entered into the project, introduced Edel to some of James's friends in Europe who were still living, and prepared for him an excerpt from her own diary notes of the deathbed dictation.

Edel then obtained permission to make use of materials that were still in the family's hands. William's grandson, Alexander Robertson James, represented the James family in such matters, under an informal arrangement among cousins that was carried forward into the next generation. Alexander James agreed that Edel would have exclusive access to the Henry James copyrights for the purpose of preparing a full biography. There seem to have been some differences in the family at this time, other heirs having retained a literary agent to protect their interests, but eventually those disputes were resolved without hindering Edel's project. Harvard for its part readily agreed to Edel's proposal, supported by the other copyright owners, that he be given exclusive access to Henry James's letters for the purpose of preparing both a biography and an enlarged edition of the letters.

Edel worked hard to maintain what he called his "priority" in access to the papers, and some folders of letters at the Houghton Library are still marked "reserved for Leon Edel." The late Henry James Vaux, Robertson's grandson, told me that he had gained the impression Edel himself had acquired the copyrights to Henry James's unpublished works. Professor Edel's papers at McGill hold copies of numerous letters to libraries, asking them (not always successfully) to close their James archives to other scholars until his own work was finished.

The efforts to maintain his priority reached a sort of climax with a lawsuit brought at Edel's behest in a London court by attorneys for Rupert Hart-Davis, Edel's British publisher, to enjoin publication of Henry Montgomery Hyde's study, frequently cited in this volume, *Henry James at Home*. Edel was by then preparing the last of the five volumes of his biography and was evidently suffering a good deal of stress. He expressed alarm that Montgomery Hyde had gained access not only to James's letters but also to Sydney Waterlow's diary, which Edel himself had not yet seen, and to materials Bosanquet had prepared on the Napoleonic theme. Edel wrote to Harvard and to Bosanquet's heir, insisting that Montgomery Hyde be barred from further access to the Bosanquet papers. He traced the provenance of Waterlow's diary, which had found its way to a rare-book dealer and then to the research division of the New York Public Library, and obtained the assistance of Waterlow's children in claiming that it had been stolen from them. He then brought his suit to prevent the imminent publication of Montgomery Hyde's book, which was then in proof. The lawsuit rested on the theory that Edel represented the copyright owners of both the James and Waterlow materials and that Hyde's work would violate their common-law right to make first publication.

Edel's suit eventually had to be abandoned when he could not document his claims, but publication of Montgomery Hyde's book was considerably delayed, and in the interval Edel published in the weekly *Times Literary Supplement* excerpts from Bosanquet's materials and from Waterlow's diaries.

Edel's *Henry James* appeared in five volumes from 1953 to 1972. When the biography was complete, Edel launched a new edition of James's letters, and while this was a highly selected collection of materials, primarily those on which he had relied for his biography, the title— *Henry James: Letters*—and the seeming bulk of the work conveyed the impression that it was an essentially complete record. Many scholars evidently believed that these letters were the entire surviving correspondence, although more than ten thousand more are known to have survived.

The last volume of Edel's last edition of James letters was published in 1984, and he then largely abandoned his efforts to control the James papers. But Edel had effectively controlled access to the James papers and hence biographical work on James for more than thirty years. Because of the system of peer review, Edel, as the acknowledged expert on James's life and work, also had considerable influence on what appeared in print.

Edel's biography was compellingly written and seemed to be strongly validated by his editions of James's letters. It achieved canonical status as an authoritative work of scholarship, difficult to challenge except in details. The image of James that it conveyed was essentially that already well established in the critical literature, an image drawn from James's memoir *A Small Boy and Others*, of a little boy with his nose pressed against the glass of a shop window or breathlessly racing after his big brother. The psychoanalytic framework in which Edel worked and that was widely accepted when he began to publish made it seem natural that these childhood experiences should determine the whole course of James's life and that he would remain a frightened observer of adults.

Those of James's stories that were narrated from the point of view of a passive observer, or portraying irresponsible aesthetes, were taken to be autobiographical.

The psychoanalytic image remained unchallenged until recently. Fred Kaplan's biography accepted Edel's account of James as a passive and isolated observer, although Kaplan added some details about James's friendships with young men and substituted his own explanation for James's supposed neurotic fearfulness and celibacy. According to Kaplan, James was afraid not of women, as Edel had claimed, but of his own homosexual feelings, which he never admitted to himself. R. W. B. Lewis's massive *The Jameses* repeated the now-orthodox account of James as a son and brother who never escaped from his childhood, more or less accepting the older Freudian explanation.

For all Edel's remarkable talents, however, and his unrivaled access to materials, he had labored under severe difficulties. James's 10,500 unpublished letters were scattered across Europe and North America. The invaluable apparatus of scholarly work that has appeared in recent years did not yet exist, there was no "calendar" of James's letters, no bibliography of James's work, no encyclopedia of Jamesiana; details of James's financial affairs had not yet been investigated; the hundreds of contemporary reviews of his work had not yet been excavated from their published sources. Edel did not have transcripts or published editions of any but a relative handful of James's thousands of letters, many of them written in an all but indecipherable scrawl, and many collections of letters and many diaries kept by James's contemporaries had not yet come to light. Finally, Edel was hindered by the surviving contemporaries of Henry James. Friends of his old age such as Hugh Walpole, Morton Fullerton, and Edith Wharton proved to be unreliable sources or, like H. G. Wells, had axes to grind but could not be ignored or safely disputed.

It is not surprising in view of all this that Edel accepted the received image of James as a querulous old maid, afraid of sexual contact or any real engagement with his surroundings, a solitary figure retreating into childish fantasies of omnipotence—the "Napoleonic theme"—who seemed to pass directly from adolescence to a querulous old age. Although he cited copiously from James's fiction and treated many of his stories and characters as autobiographical, the general outline of Edel's work was the conventional wisdom of his day, to which he stubbornly assimilated everything new that he found.

The particular American Freudianism of Edel's generation has waned, but the portrait of James as a disembodied observer continues to have some interest for academic writers, and in the newer reader-response theoretical work one finds portraits of the imputed author of James's works that are oddly similar to that first painted by Van Wyck Brooks eighty years ago, of an adolescent frightened by women. So powerful has this image proven to be, especially among teachers of the young, that all of James's ailments are said to be neurotic in origin—not only his periodic plunges into depression but even the family back trouble and the heart disease that killed him.

James's surviving letters are now open to all scholars, however, and many contemporaneous accounts have been identified and published. A new generation of scholars has been at work in these fertile fields and has portrayed James as the active, passionate, engaged man his contemporaries knew. The picture that is emerging is essentially that which James himself seems to have tried to convey and is quite different from the canonical account to which we all had grown accustomed. In the preceding pages I have tried to summarize his own self-portrayal, enriched by these later investigations of the man and the world in which he wrote.

Notes

Sources

I have worked from original documents or photocopies where possible but have included parallel citations to published versions where they are available. Unpublished documents are so indicated. My transcriptions of James's notebook entries have been compared with the Matthiessen edition, which is accurate save for alterations of punctuation and substitution of "and" for James's habitual ampersands; I have cited corresponding pages in that admirable edition, as well as page references in Leon Edel's later edition for material found only there. A published edition of all of Henry James's letters is in progress at the University of Nebraska Press; the first volume has just been announced as I write. A digital database is also planned but is evidently still some years in the future. I have therefore included citations to published versions of letters to which I have compared my own transcripts, for the convenience of scholars. Some of James's more famous letters have been republished several times, and new editions have continued to appear while this volume was in progress; I have cited only the edition with which I worked. I note here with regret that Zorzi's edition of James's letters to Hendrik Andersen appeared too late for me to have made use of it; letters to Andersen marked "unpub." in my notes are included in that edition. Many originals of the letters included in Lubbock's edition have been lost, and I have necessarily quoted and cited his version. References to living persons were deleted by Lubbock, and the affectionate salutations to young men were bowdlerized at Edmund Gosse's insistence (see the Epilogue), but the published versions otherwise seem faithfully to follow the typescripts prepared for Lubbock, in the James Family Archive in the Houghton Library. In other cases, where I have cited only a published edition, I have not found it necessary to compare it with the original.

James's publishing income, unless otherwise indicated, is based on Anesko.

Victorian pounds are given their modern equivalents based on the ratio of fifty to one used by Roy Jenkins in *Gladstone: A Biography* (New York: Random House, 1997), although inflation affected the value of the pound toward the end of the period described here. Dollars were fixed at approximately five to the pound throughout James's life.

An American writing about Victorian Britons is certain to go wrong with regard to names and titles. Although James was relentlessly proper and in his letters always addressed Louisa Wolseley as "Lady Wolseley," such formalities have a misleading tone today. I have generally followed modern American conventions and have given women their own names, rather than those of husbands or fathers. I have given men their titles, undoubtedly making errors in the process, but have not noted subsequent changes in rank and have used the more familiar name, for instance, Disraeli rather than Beaconsfield.

ABBREVIATIONS

James Family

AHJ: Alice Howe (Gibbens) James (Mrs. William James)
AJ: Alice James (sister)
CW: Catherine Walsh (Aunt Kate)
GWJ: Garth Wilkinson James (Wilky, brother)
HJ: Henry James
HJ Sr.: Henry James (father)
MHJ: Mary Holton James (Mrs. Robertson James)
MRJ: Mary Robertson (Walsh) James (mother)
RJ: Robertson James (Bob, brother)
WJ: William James (brother)

Others

OWH: Oliver Wendell Holmes
WDH: William Dean Howells

Manuscript Collections

American Academy: American Academy of Arts and Letters, New York City.
Austin: Harry Ransom Humanities Research Center, University of Texas at Austin.
Barrett: C. Waller Barrett Collection, University of Virginia, Charlottesville, Virginia.
Benson Diary: A. C. Benson Diaries, Pepys Library, Magdalene College, Cambridge.
Berg: Berg Collection, Research Division, New York Public Library.
BL: The Manuscript Collections, British Library, London.
Bodleian: Bodleian Library, Oxford University.
BPL: Boston Public Library.
Brooke Papers: Lady Margaret Brooke Papers, Columbia University, New York City.
Brown: John Hay Collection, Brown University, Providence, Rhode Island.
Bruce Porter Papers: Bancroft Library, University of California, Berkeley.
Chester: Cheshire Libraries, Arts and Archives, Chester.
Colby: Papers of T. S. and Lilla Perry, Special Collections, Colby College, Waterville, Maine.
Dartmouth: Special Collections, Dartmouth College Library, Hanover, New Hampshire.
Edel: Leon Edel papers, Rare Books and Special Collections Division, McGill University Libraries, Montreal.
Fales: Fales Library, New York University.
Fields: Annie Adams Fields Papers, Massachusetts Historical Society, Boston.

Fitzwilliam Museum: Department of Manuscripts and Printed Books, The Fitz-william Museum, Cambridge University.

Frewen: Frewen Papers, East Sussex Records Office, Lewes.

Gardner: The Elizabeth Stewart Gardner Museum Archive, Boston.

HLS: Manuscript Collections, Harvard Law School Library, Cambridge, Massachu-setts.

Houghton: James Family Papers, Houghton Library, Harvard University, Cambridge, Massachusetts.

Hove: Viscount and Lady Wolseley Papers, Hove Central Library, Hove, East Sus-sex.

Huxley: Thomas Huxley Papers, College Archives, Imperial College of Science, Technology and Medicine, London.

Jordan: Elizabeth Jordan Papers, Research Division, New York Public Library.

Leeds: Brotherton Collection, Leeds University Library, Leeds.

LoC: Manuscript Division, Library of Congress, Washington, D.C.

Magdalene: Pepys Library, Magdalene College, Cambridge.

Marlboro: Marlboro College Kipling Collection, Marlboro, Vermont.

Morgan Library: Pierpont Morgan Library, New York.

Myers: F. W. H. Myers Papers, Trinity College, Cambridge University.

Notebooks: Henry James's notebooks and pocket diaries, James Family Papers, Houghton Library, Harvard University, Cambridge, Massachusetts.

Novickova Papers: Papers of Alexeyevna Novickova, Pushkin House, St. Petersburg.

NYPL: Research Division, New York Public Library.

Pepys: Pepys Library, Magdalene College, Cambridge.

Vaux: Robertson James Archive, the estate of the late Henry James Vaux, Berkeley, California.

Waterlow Diary: Diary of Sir Sydney Waterlow, Berg Collection, Research Division, New York Public Library.

Weld Diary: Diary of Mary Weld, private collection.

Yale: Beinecke Rare Book and Manuscript Library, Yale University, New Haven, Connecticut.

Zhoukovsky Papers: Papers of V. A. and Pavel V. Zhoukovsky, Pushkin House, St. Pe-tersburg.

Published James Family Letters and Journals

AJ Diary: Leon Edel, ed. *The Diary of Alice James.* New York: Penguin Books, 1964.

Burr: Anna Robeson Burr, ed. *Alice James—Her Brothers, Her Journal.* New York: Dodd, Mead & Company, 1934.

Dearly Beloved Friends: Susan E. Gunter and Steven H. Jobe, eds. *Dearly Beloved Friends: Henry James's Letters to Younger Men.* Ann Arbor: University of Michi-gan Press, 2001.

Dear Munificent Friends: Susan E. Gunter, ed. *Dear Munificent Friends: Henry James's Letters to Four Women.* Ann Arbor: University of Michigan Press, 1999.

Harlow: Virginia Harlow. *Thomas Sergeant Perry: A Biography and Letters to Perry from William, Henry, and Garth Wilkinson James.* Durham: Duke University Press, 1950.

HJ-Adams Letters: George Monteiro, *The Correspondence of Henry James and Henry Adams, 1877–1914*. Baton Rouge: Louisiana State University Press, 1992.

HJ-Allen Letters: Rosella Mamoli Zorzi, ed. *Henry James: Lettere a Miss Allen—Letters to Miss Allen, 1899–1915*. Milan: Rosellina Archinto, 1993.

HJ-Barbaro Letters: Rosella Mamoli Zorzi, ed. *Letters from the Palazzo Barbaro*. London: Pushkin Press, 1998.

HJ-Benson Letters: E. F. Benson, ed. *Henry James: Letters to A. C. Benson and Auguste Monod*. New York: Charles Scribner's Sons, 1930.

HJ-Berry Letters: Walter Berry, ed. *Letters of Henry James to Walter Berry*. Paris: Black Sun Press, 1928.

HJ-Gosse Letters: Rayburn S. Moore, ed. *Selected Letters of Henry James to Edmund Gosse, 1882–1915*. Baton Rouge: Louisiana State University Press, 1988.

HJ-Hay Letters: George Monteiro, ed. *Henry James and John Hay: The Record of a Friendship*. Providence: Brown University Press, 1965.

HJ-Howells Corresp.: Michael Anesko. *Letters, Fictions, Lives: Henry James and William Dean Howells Correspondence*. New York: Oxford, 1997

HJL: Leon Edel, ed. *Henry James Letters*. 4 vols. Cambridge: Harvard University Press, 1974–1984.

HJ-Macmillan Corresp.: Rayburn S. Moore, ed. *The Correspondence of Henry James and the House of Macmillan, 1877–1914*. Baton Rouge: Louisiana State University Press, 1993.

HJ-OWH Letters: Mark DeWolfe Howe, ed. "The Letters of Henry James to Mr. Justice Holmes." 38 *Yale Review* (1948–1949), p. 410.

HJ-RLS Letters: Janet Adams Smith, ed. *Henry James and Robert Louis Stevenson: A Record of Friendship and Criticism*. London: Rupert Hart-Davis, 1948.

HJ-Robins Letters: Elizabeth Robins. *Theatre and Friendship: Some Henry James Letters*. New York: G. P. Putnam's Sons, 1932.

HJ-Wells Letters: Leon Edel and Gordon N. Ray, eds. *Henry James and H. G. Wells: A Record of Their Friendship, Their Debate on the Art of Fiction, and Their Quarrel*. Westport, Conn.: Greenwood Press, 1958.

HJ-Wharton Letters: Lyall H. Powers, ed. *Henry James and Edith Wharton: Letters, 1900–1915*. New York: Charles Scribner's Sons, 1990.

Horne: Philip Horne, ed. *Henry James: A Life in Letters*. London: Allen Lane, 1999.

Lubbock: Percy Lubbock, ed. *The Letters of Henry James*. 2 vols. New York: Charles Scribner's Sons, 1920.

Notebooks (Edel ed.): Leon Edel and Lyall H. Powers, eds. *The Complete Notebooks of Henry James*. New York: Oxford University Press, 1987.

Notebooks (Matthiessen ed.): F. O. Matthiessen and Kenneth Murdock, eds. *The Notebooks of Henry James*. New York: Oxford University Press, 1947.

Selected Letters (1955): Leon Edel, ed. *The Selected Letters of Henry James*. New York: Farrar, Straus and Cudahy, 1955.

———— (1987): Leon Edel, ed. *Henry James: Selected Letters*. Cambridge, Mass.: Harvard University Press, 1987.

WJ Corresp.: Ignas Skrupskelis and Elizabeth Berkeley, eds. *The Correspondence of William James*, vols. 1–3, *William and Henry, 1861–1910*. Charlottesville: University of Virginia Press, 1992–1997.

WJ Letters: Henry James, ed. *The Letters of William James.* Boston: Little, Brown and Company, 1926.

Yeazell: Ruth Bernard Yeazell, ed. *The Death and Letters of Alice James: Selected Correspondence Edited, with a Biographical Essay.* Berkeley: University of California Press, 1981.

Zorzi: Henry James, *Beloved Boy: Letters to Hendrik C. Andersen, 1899–1915* (Rosella Mamoli Zorzi, ed.). Charlottesville, Virginia: University of Virginia Press, 2004.

Prologue: Henry James at Home, 1904

xviii **"It would give me":** HJ to Gertrude Atherton, April 25, 1904; Atherton, *Adventures,* p. 374.

xix **"a kind of mild glory":** HJ to Charles de Kay, June 12, 1913, Austin; unpub.

xix **"the effort":** *The Tragic Muse* (Penguin ed.), p. 17.

xix **"I can work":** HJ to J. B. Pinker, May 20, 1904, Yale; 2 Lubbock, p. 15.

xix **"with such perfection":** HJ to WJ, April 13, 1904, Houghton; 3 WJ Corresp., p. 268.

Chapter 1: London in Winter

4 **"You know that":** HJ to RJ, Jan. 11, 1880, Vaux; Burr, pp. 66–67.

4 **"a society":** "London," p. 28.

5 **"A dapper little gentleman":** Robins, *Both Sides,* p. 9.

5 **"An aesthetic bachelor":** HJ to AJ, "New Year's Eve," [1878?,] Houghton; 2 HJ Letters, p. 198.

5 **"he gave the impression":** Charles Millar (George du Maurier's son-in-law), quoted in Ormond, *George du Maurier,* p. 465.

7 **"We are far":** "London," p. 19.

7 **"Christmas week":** "London," pp. 20–21.

7 **"The uglinesses":** "London," pp. 18–19.

8 *The Bitter Cry of Outcast London:* See Himmelfarb, *Poverty and Compassion,* pp. 55–65, and sources cited there.

10 **"The condition":** HJ to C. E. Norton, Dec. 6, 1886, Houghton; 1 HJ Letters, p. 124.

10 **"I think it is":** "London," p. 16.

11 **"It was a very hot day":** Ward, 2 *Recollections,* p. 17.

12 **James seemed to her:** Quoted in Sutherland, *Mrs. Humphrey Ward,* p. 100.

12 **"Nothing *lives*":** HJ to T. S. Perry, Sept. 26, 1884, in Harlow, *Thomas Sargeant Perry,* pp. 317–318.

13 **Edmund Gosse:** Gosse, *Aspects and Impressions,* pp. 35, 42.

Chapter 2: The Past Intrudes

16 "I care for the newspapers": HJ to Henry Adams, Dec. 27, 1881, HJ-Adams Letters, p. 51.

17 "The implements": HJ, *The Portrait of a Lady* (1881 ed.), p. 7.

18 "James's sympathy": Lesser, *His Other Half*, p. 99 (quoting Elizabeth Hardwicke's remark that James was America's "greatest female novelist").

21 Alice too: See Jamison, *Touched with Fire*, which devotes a chapter to the James family disorder.

21 pelvic massage: See Maines on the pelvic massage to orgasm typically prescribed for hysteria. For Henry's own massages, see Novick, *Henry James: The Young Master*, p. 156. In "The Middle Years," a young doctor is also a lover; compare the clever male doctor with female patients in *Washington Square* and the benevolent physician in *The Wings of the Dove*.

21 When Robertson became engaged: The correspondence concerning consanguinity is in the Vaux archive and is summarized in Maher, *Biography of Broken Fortunes*, pp. 110–111.

22 "[God] has no anger": HJ Sr. to RJ, April 28, 1865, Vaux; unpub.

24 "a good fellow": HJ to Isabella Stewart Gardner, Jan. 23, 1882, Gardner; 2 *HJL*, p. 373.

24 Newspapers: Marian Adams, *The Letters of Mrs. Henry Adams*, p. 329, n.

24 "I have learned": HJ to RJ, Jan. 7, 1882, Vaux; unpub.

25 "I should only": Ibid.

25 "We have lost": Quoted in Gernsheim, *Victorian and Edwardian Fashion*, p. 73.

26 "Reelly": Hyde, *Oscar Wilde*, p. 60.

26 Wilde was a "cad": Marian Adams to Robert Hooper, Jan. 22, 1882, *The Letters of Mrs. Henry Adams*, Marian Adams, p. 333.

27 "We have all": RJ to MHJ, "Saturday," [February 4?, 1882,] Vaux, pub. in part in Burr, pp. 55–56.

Chapter 3: Head of His Family

29 "He is a good . . . man": GWJ to MRJ, Aug. 7, 1872, Houghton; unpub.

30 "Harry James is spending": Howells, 1 *Life in Letters*, pp. 310, 311.

30 "The self-absorbed Holmes": HJ to WJ, Jan. 1, 1883, Houghton; 1 WJ Corresp., p. 342.

32 "a simple, serious, wholesome, time": Notebooks, [Winter 1882–1883,] entry following Nov. 11, 1882, p. 44.

33 "I soon perceived": HJ to E. L. Godkin, June 5, [1882,] Houghton; Horne, 139.

33 "My dear Mary": HJ to MHJ, May 25, 1882, Vaux; unpub.

34 Alone in his room: Novick, *Henry James: The Young Master*, p. 42.

34 "This lady is a real creation": "George du Maurier," in HJ, *Partial Portraits*, pp. 366–367. Louisa Wolseley also bore some resemblance to Mrs. Ponsonby de Tomkyns and her avatar Fanny Assingham, but Wolseley himself, unlike the cartoon husband, was entirely her equal.

36 "Alice sends much love": KPL to MHJ, Dec. 11, [1882,] Vaux; unpub.

37 "Darling father's": AJ to HJ, "Wednesday," [Dec. 20, 1882,] Houghton; Strouse, *Alice James*, p. 209.

38 William was still in London: WJ to HJ Sr., Dec. 14, 1882, Houghton; Matthiessen, *The James Family*, pp. 132–133.

38 "Harry makes one miserable": AHJ to WJ, Jan. 1, 1883, Houghton; quoted in *Dear Munificent Friends*, p. 18.

38 "How beautiful": HJ to WJ, Jan. 2, 1885; 2 WJ Corresp., p. 1.

39 "It comes over me": HJ to WJ, Jan. 2, 1885; 2 WJ Corresp., p. 1.

39 "My dear Bob": HJ to RJ, Dec. 30, [1882,] Vaux; quoted in Maher, *Biography of Broken Fortunes*, pp. 147–148.

41 He wrote and telegraphed: HJ to WJ, Jan. 11, [1883,] Houghton; 2 WJ Corresp., p. 348.

41 "The worst of the West": HJ to Fanny Kemble, Lubbock typescript, Houghton; unpub.

41 Wilky was sadly changed: HJ to WJ, Jan. 23, [1883,] Houghton; 1 WJ Corresp., pp. 356, 358.

42 "Your visit here": GWJ to HJ, Feb. 6, 1883, Maher, *Biography of Broken Fortunes*, p. 156.

42 the "handsomest" of American streets: HJ to WJ, Jan. 23, [1883,] Houghton; 1 WJ Corresp., pp. 356, 358.

43 "What you say": HJ to WJ Feb. 5, [1883,] Houghton; 1 WJ Corresp., pp. 359, 360.

43 "the 'rich bachelor uncle' ": WJ to HJ, Feb. 26–28, [1883,] Houghton; 1 WJ Letters, p. 367.

44 "but she has shrewdly declined": HJ to Fanny Kemble, Feb. 1, 1883, Lubbock typescript, Houghton; unpub.

44 "If I can only *concentrate*": Notebooks, [Winter 1882–1883,] entry following Nov. 11, 1882, p. 44.

44 He wrote each article: See, e.g., the manuscript of "The Impressions of a Cousin," written at this time, in the Morgan Library, MA 203, showing his method of composition.

45 "I expect the success": HJ to Clover Adams, Feb. 28, [1883,] Houghton; 2 HJL, pp. 407, 408. James was not aware that Henry Adams was the author of *Democracy*.

45 "She . . . has thrown herself": Notebooks, Apr. 8, 1883, p. 46. The proposal for the novel is contained in a letter to J. R. Osgood, April 8, 1883, [LoC,] which James copied into his notebook.

46 "She passed her nights": Notebooks, Feb. 9, 1882, p. 41.

46 "this morning I went out": HJ to WJ, Jan. 11, [1883,] 1 WJ Corresp., pp. 349–350.

46 "In a story, someone says": Notebooks, [1879?,] p. 14. This much-quoted passage was incorporated with minor changes into James's biography of Hawthorne.

47 "out of harmony": HJ, "Ivan Turgenev," p. 975.

47 "visibly killed": George Santayana, quoted in E. Wilson, *The Shock of Recognition*, p. 743.

48 **"The world is moving"**: Renan, *Recollections,* pp. xiii, xix.

49 **"She was our life"**: Notebooks, Feb. 9, 1882; p. 40.

50 **"I never return"**: HJ to George du Maurier, Apr. 17, 1883, Houghton; Matthiessen, *American Novels,* p. xii.

CHAPTER 4: THE CONTINUAL RENEWAL OF DAILY LIFE

52 **Alice wrote to Bob:** Letter signed "Alice," no date, among Robertson James papers, Vaux archive. This appears to be a letter from AHJ, but the date and context are conjectural.

53 **"I know too many people"**: Notebooks, Aug. 3, 1882, p. 42.

54 **Mrs. Thomas Huxley:** The correspondence is in Huxley, May 1879– November 1880.

54 **Matthew Arnold confided:** Matthew Arnold to William Dean Howells, Dec. 3, 1883, Houghton; unpub.

54 **regularly took guarana:** AJ to CW, Nov. 21–25, [1885?,] Houghton; Yeazell, *The Death and Letters of Alice James,* p.105. Guarana is a Brazilian herb, still fashionable, that resembles coffee in its effects.

55 **the germ of *The Tragic Muse*:** Notebooks, June 19, 1884, pp. 63–64.

55 **essay by "Mme Bentzon":** Pen name of Marie-Thérèse Solms, who published unauthorized translations of two of James's stories during his brief siege of Paris in 1875–1876.

55 **Macmillan, like other genteel houses:** Retail price-fixing in the book trade, under the Net Book Agreement, as it came to be called, continued until 1995.

56 **"We have the [suburban] villa"**: George Moore, *Confessions of a Young Man* (1888), quoted in Whyte, *William Heinemann,* p. 19.

57 **"the delicious ring"**: HJ to WJ, June 15, 1879, Houghton; 1 WJ Corresp., p. 315.

58 **"The Macmillans"**: HJ to WJ, June 15, 1879, Houghton; 1 WJ Corresp., p. 315.

60 **a story by Alphonse Daudet:** "L'Évangéliste," Notebooks, Apr. 8, 1883, p. 47.

60 **an anecdote . . . about Lady Byron:** Kemble, p. 129; see Novick, *Henry James: The Young Master,* pp. 357–358.

61 **"Daudet is a dear little man"**: HJ to Grace Norton, Feb. 23, 1884, Houghton; 3 *HJL,* p. 33.

61 **"There is nothing more interesting"**: HJ to WD Howells, Feb. 21, 1884, 1 Lubbock, p. 104.

62 **"the society of artists"**: HJ, *The Reverberator,* p. 44. See also James's essay "Alphonse Daudet," in which he speaks in the same terms of French writers, calling Daudet a writer with a brush and a painter with a pen.

63 **"half-stripped and covered with paint"**: HJ to Elizabeth Boott, [June 2,] 1884, Houghton; 3 *HJL,* p. 43.

63 **I find life *possible*:** HJ to T. E. Child, March 8, 1884, Barrett; 3 *HJL,* p. 36.

64 **"my young man"**: HJ to Edmund Gosse, June 5, 1884, Leeds; HJ-Gosse Letters, 31. Gosse made a fuss, however, about seconding a man he had not met.

64 **she "loved entertaining":** E. F. Benson, *Mother*, pp. 26–27. For James's frequent visits, see AJ to CW, April 23, [1886,] Houghton (where it is misdated 1885); Yeazell, *Death and Letters*, p. 113. The Bensons had six children, but the eldest boy, Martin, died in 1878.

66 **"The young lady living in a village":** HJ, "The Art of Fiction," p. 44.

67 **"The Art of Fiction" . . . extended its influence:** One scholar calls it "perhaps the most popular and surely the most influential brief statement of fictional theory ever made"; Miller, ed., *Theory of Fiction*, p. 29.

67 **The successful application of any art:** Quoted passages from HJ: "The Art of Fiction," in Miller, ed., *Theory of Fiction*, pp. 29–35.

68 **The patterned web . . . Kant's transcendental idealism:** For the reconstruction of Kant's philosophy, especially of the faculty of imagination, as James's generation understood it, I was greatly aided by Gibbons, *Kant's Theory of Imagination*. See also Martin, "The Portrait Without a Subject," discussing James's "Art of Fiction" in Kantian terms. Fogel views James's idealism as Romantic and Hegelian rather than Kantian.

69 **"when it happens to be":** HJ, "The Art of Fiction," in Miller, ed., *Theory of Fiction*, p. 35.

69 **"If one must indulge":** Ibid., p. 44.

69 **"my pages, in *Longman's*":** HJ to RLS, Dec. 5, [1884,] HJ-RLS Letters, p. 101.

70 **"My dear Robert Louis Stevenson":** HJ to RLS, Dec. 5, [1884,] HJ-RLS Letters, p. 101.

70 **"As you know":** RLS to HJ, Dec. 8, 1884, Houghton; 5 Stevenson Letters, pp. 42, 43.

Chapter 5: Bournemouth and Broadway

72 **Alice cabled:** HJ to Louisa Wolseley, Nov. 6, 1884, Hove; unpub.

73 **"It requires the strength":** AJ to WJ, Jan. 3–4, 1886, Houghton; Yeazell, *The Death and Letters of Alice James*, p. 105.

73 **The diagnosis:** Literary convention long attributed Alice's pain and weakness to a neurosis rooted in sexual frustration. A physician today would be more likely to diagnose an organic disorder, perhaps polymyositis (a chronic inflammatory disease of the muscles), fibromyalgia, or lupus.

73 **"To have a tornado":** AJ to CW, Nov. 21–24, [1885?,] Houghton; Yeazell, *Death and Letters*, p. 104.

74 **"His kindness & devotion":** AJ to WJ, Dec. 23, 1884, Houghton; Yeazell, *Death and Letters*, p. 100.

74 **We must accept it:** HJ to CW, May 12, [1885,] Houghton; Strouse, *Alice James*, pp. 240–241.

75 **James had attended:** HJ to Mary Anderson, Feb. 3, 1885; Edel, *Les Années Dramatiques*, p. 16.

76 **"He is a gentle":** May 1885, 5 Stevenson Letters, p. 104.

76 **"You sat enthroned":** Quoted in HJ-RLS Letters, p. 13.

76 **"But he, attended":** The poem was published as "Henry James" in *Under-*

wood's (1887) with slight changes in the opening lines. The women are characters in "Madame des Mauves," "Georgina's Reasons," "Daisy Miller," "Lady Barberina," and *The Bostonians*, respectively.

77 **"a cruel, a barbaric, fortune":** HJ to Grace Norton, Jan. 24, 1885, 1 Lubbock, p. 114.

77 **"I give you my blessing":** HJ to J. R. Lowell, May 29, [1885,] Lubbock typescript, Houghton; 3 *HJL*, p. 90.

77 **a "semi-detached villa":** Charlotte Clark to John Hay, Nov. 1, [1883]; HJ-Hay Letters, p. 25.

79 **" 'The Bostonians' ":** Frederick Macmillan to HJ, May 6, 1885, HJ-Macmillan Corresp., pp. 100–101.

79 **as Alice wrote:** AJ to CW, Apr. 23, [1885?,] Houghton; Yeazell, *Death and Letters*, p. 113 (dated "1886?").

80 **"Leaving aside":** R. W. Gilder to HJ, May 18, 1885; typescript copy, NYPL Miscellaneous Papers, Cent. L.B.E. 9.

80 **"I am sickened":** HJ to WDH, Apr. 23, [1885,] HJ-Howells Letters, pp. 248–249.

81 **"amid such a tumult":** Quoted in Hayes, *Henry James*, p. 157.

81 **The staid Springfield *Republican:*** Ibid., p. 165.

83 **Alfred Parsons, Edwin Abbey:** See HJ, "Our Artists in Europe," *Harper's New Monthly Magazine*, June 1889, reprinted as "Black and White" in *Picture and Text*, p. 19.

83 **James felt a kinship:** HJ, *Picture and Text*, p. 28.

83 **"If there be anything happier":** Ibid. The book was George H. Boughton, *Sketching Rambles in Holland* (New York: Harper and Sons, 1885).

83 **"We all treated him":** Edmund Gosse, "Reminiscences of Broadway," holograph, Berg. Gosse placed these events in 1886 but perhaps conflated several visits.

84 **Alice had not been doing well:** AJ to AHJ and WJ, Nov. 20, [1887?,] Houghton; Yeazell, *Death and Letters*, pp. 134, 138–139 (recalling summer of 1885).

84 **"He was a broad generous patient":** WJ to HJ, July 11, 1885, Houghton; 1 WJ Corresp., p. 21.

84 **"You have my full sympathy":** HJ to WJ, July 24, [1885,] Houghton; 2 WJ Corresp., p. 23.

84 **Alice would remember:** AJ Diary, June 17, 1891, pp. 212–213.

85 **"I adore the darkness":** AJ to WJ, Jan. 3–7, [1886?,] Houghton; Yeazell, *Death and Letters*, pp. 105, 109.

85 **"You seem very comfortable":** AJ to WJ, Sept. 10, [1886,] Houghton; Yeazell, *Death and Letters*, pp. 116, 117.

CHAPTER 6: *THE PRINCESS CASAMASSIMA*

86 **"who hesitate at nothing":** *The Times*, March 16, 1883, pp. 5, 9; quoted in Tilley, *The Background of* The Princess Casamassima, p. 19.

87 **"The country is gloomy":** HJ to Grace Norton, Jan. 24, 1885, 1 *HJL*, pp. 113–114.

87 "The revolutionary": Joll, *The Anarchists*, pp. 78–79.

87 anarchist plots: For an account of the press coverage with which James was likely familiar, see Tilley, *Background*.

88 "Tall, thin, and haggard": For the *Times'* coverage of the trial, see Tilley, *Background*, pp. 37–42. Tilley argues that Reinsdorf was the model for Hoffendahl in *The Princess Casamassima*.

89 Edmund Gosse and J. A. Symonds: Hyde, *The Cleveland Street Scandal*, pp. 16–19; Thwaite, *Edmund Gosse*, pp. 264–265.

89 "I can imagine": HJ to Grace Norton, Jan. 24, [1885,] Houghton; 1 Lubbock, pp. 113, 114.

90 Paul Zhukovsky had introduced James: Novick, *Henry James, The Young Master*, p. 411.

91 In the shops and pubs: Notebooks, Aug. 22, [1885,] p. 69.

92 "I gave poor old Lord Houghton": HJ to Grace Norton, Aug. 23, [1885,] Houghton; 3 *HJL*, pp. 96, 97.

93 William H. Huntington . . . Madame Childe: Novick, *Young Master*, pp. 322–345.

93 "Ah, to whom do you say it": HJ to Fanny Stevenson, Sept. 18, 1885, Horne, p. 180.

93 "He was bright and charming": HJ to Sidney Colvin, Nov. 17, [1885,] Fitzwilliam Museum; unpub.

94 James wrote congratulating her: HJ to Elizabeth Boott, Feb. 22, [1886,] Houghton; 3 *HJL*, p. 111.

94 What was now a mob: A Tory demonstration was followed by Hyndeman's socialist counterdemonstration; the destruction that followed was probably carried out by nonpolitical toughs. See Himmelfarb, *Poverty and Compassion*, pp. 330–331.

94 His flat: James first headed his notepaper "13 De Vere Mansions West." Shortly after he moved, however, he changed his notepaper to "34 De Vere Gardens," which is now Hale House, opposite, but presumably was once the principal address of the Mansions.

95 "flooded with light": HJ to WJ, March 9, [1886,] Houghton; 2 HJ-WJ Corresp., pp. 33, 34.

95 Alice arranged: AJ Diary, June 3, 1889, p. 27.

95 In the afternoons: HJ to Lady Wolseley, Dec. 8, 1887, Hove; unpub. From his letters one gathers that he also accompanied her and a friend on her own shopping expeditions.

95 "The place is excellent": HJ to WJ, March 9, [1886,] Houghton; 2 WJ Corresp., pp. 33, 34.

95 To ensure his ability: C. Mackenzie, *My Life and Times*, pp. 213–214.

96 as Benson later recalled: Benson, *Memories and Friends.*

96 "Dear Miss Townley": HJ to "Miss Townley," June 10, [1886,] Berg; unpub.

97 "We drove about": Quoted in Lucas, *Edwin Austin Abbey*, p. 158.

97 "Compte Joseph Primoli": Henri de Régnier, *De mon temps*, quoted in Richardson, *Portrait of a Bonaparte*, p. 209.

98 James invited Maupassant and Primoli: HJ to Edmund Gosse, Aug. 12, 1886, and Jan. 21, 1914, Leeds; HJ-Gosse Letters, pp. 40, 295.

 98   **Despite these adventures:** HJ to Lady Wolseley, Dec. 6, [1886,] Hove; unpub.

 98   **The American reviews of *The Princess:*** Summarized in Foley, *Criticism; Harper's New Monthly Magazine,* April 1887, p. 829, quoted in Foley, p. 41.

 99   **"Hyacinth Robinson":** *Punch,* Nov. 20, 1886, p. 245.

 99   ***The Scottish Review . . . The Times:*** Reprinted in Hayes, *Henry James,* pp. 163–182.

 99   **James's new effort:** New York *Sun,* April 4, 1886, quoted in Hayes, *Henry James,* p. 163.

100   **"Mr. Henry James":** *The Saturday Review,* Nov. 27, 1886, p. 728; quoted in Hayes, *Henry James,* p. 182.

CHAPTER 7: INTERVAL IN ITALY

101   **Constance Fenimore Woolson:** In Edel's widely followed interpretation, Woolson was in love with James; when he failed to respond adequately, she killed herself; Edel, *The Life of Henry James,* vol. 3. There is no direct evidence for this account, and Woolson scholars generally have taken the friendship of the two writers at face value. See Torsney, *Constance Fenimore Woolson,* pp. 11–21 ("Edel's text . . . a convention-laden male fantasy").

102   **"At the Chateau of Corinne":** Woolson, *Women, Artists, Women Exiles,* p. 211.

102   **"Flooded as we have been":** "Miss Woolson," in *Partial Portraits,* p. 177.

102   **Her mastery of character:** Ibid., p. 187.

103   **Vernon Lee and had published her first book:** *Les Aventures d'une pièce de monnaie,* published serially in the Lausanne journal *La Famille* in 1870, a first-person account of history by a Roman coin; see Colby, *Vernon Lee,* p. 11. Violet Paget used her birth name in personal letters and reserved the more masculine nom de plume Vernon Lee for her published writings and business correspondence. In the text I refer only to "Violet Paget," which is how James addressed his letters.

103   **Anatole France described her:** *The Red Lily,* p. 7, quoted in Colby, *Vernon Lee,* p. 132.

103   **Paget's first novel:** The dedication reads: "TO HENRY JAMES, I DEDICATE, FOR GOOD LUCK, MY FIRST ATTEMPT AT A NOVEL."

103   **"an awful want of taste & tact":** HJ to Grace Norton, Jan. 25, [1885,] Houghton; 3 *HJL,* p. 66.

103   **"You are really too savage":** HJ to Violet Paget, May 10, [1885,] Colby; Gardner, "An Apology," p. 691.

103   **Paget replied:** Paget's letter has not been found, but this much of it can be reconstructed from James's reply of June 8; Gardner, "An Apology," p. 692.

104   **"The Aspern Papers":** Notebooks, Jan. 12, 1887, p. 71.

104   **Years later, in a preface:** HJ, Preface, "The Aspern Papers," p. 1179.

104   **"All those years of work":** Vernon Lee, "Lady Tal," in Showalter (ed.), *Daughters of Decadence,* p. 194. The story was first published in 1892, in her collection of tales *Vanitas.*

107 **"As you live in it":** HJ, "The Grand Canal" (published 1892), in *Italian Hours*, p. 39.

108 **the "sympathetic Bourget":** HJ to Lady Wolseley, Aug. ?, [1885,] Hove; unpub.

108 **His sister, Alice, wrote to him:** Notebooks, Jan. 12, 1887, p. 70; see also Edel edition, p. 32, n. Alice's letter appears not to have survived. "The Marriages" would first be published in *The Atlantic Monthly*, August 1891, but was noted in the journal as the premise for a story at this time. Sir John Rose had been married to James's late cousin Charlotte Temple, and their country house provided the setting for *The Portrait of a Lady.*

108 **Plot followed plot:** See Notebooks, Jan. 12, 1887, p. 73, noting the germ of "Louisa Pallant," published in *Harper's New Monthly Magazine*, February 1888; Notebooks, Nov. 17, 1887, p. 82, in HJ, *The Reverberator* (James notes that he heard the anecdote "Last winter, in Florence").

109 **Howells had advised:** Notebooks, Nov. 17, 1887, p. 85.

109 **"More than any girl":** HJ, "Louisa Pallant," p. 199.

CHAPTER 8: EMINENT VICTORIANS

111 **"I can't tell you":** HJ to Daniel Curtis, Sept. 7 [1887,] Berg; unpub.

112 **His uncle Graham Balfour:** G. Balfour, *The Life of Robert Louis Stevenson*, vol. 2, p. 30.

112 **"It is a fine James":** RLS to HJ, Aug. 22, [1887,] HJ-RLS Letters, p. 120.

112 **"May you find":** HJ to RLS, Oct. 30, 1887, HJ-RLS Letters, p. 64.

113 **"My dear Louis":** HJ to RLS, July 31, [1888,] HJ-RLS Letters, p. 173.

114 **"a palace of week-ending":** W. R. Lethaby, quoted in Abdy and Gere, *The Souls*, p. 86.

114 **"I am sorry for Dillon":** See Balfour, *The Letters of Arthur Balfour and Lady Elcho, 1885–1917*, pp. 42–43; Lambert, *Unquiet Souls*, p. 62.

115 **Blunt angrily told newspaper reporters:** *The Times*, quoted in 2 WJ Corresp., p. 83, n. 3; *Letters of Arthur Balfour and Lady Elcho*, pp. 47–48; HJ to WJ, Feb. 20, 1888, Houghton; 2 WJ Corresp., p. 82.

115 **"Balfour I should":** HJ to WJ, Feb. 20, 1888, Houghton; 2 WJ Corresp., p. 82.

117 **He spoke of British losses:** "The Reassembling of Parliament," *The Nation*, March 20, 1879, pp. 197–199, in *Henry James on Culture*, p. 31.

117 **In November . . . a terrier bitch . . . Tosca:** Or so I understand his note of Nov. 17, [1887,] Hove, unpub., with its ponderous, jocular references to the "little friend." One of those details: Kaplan says firmly a Scottie, a breed not yet known in England; Montgomery Hyde says dachshund, but that was Max, who came later. Annie Field, who knew dogs, mentions in her diary James's "black-and-tan terrier." Despite the tradition that the dog was named for an opera heroine, the opera by Puccini did not premiere until 1900.

118 **"Since Kath. has again":** AJ to AHJ & WJ, Nov. 20, [1887?,] Houghton; Yeazell, *The Death and Letters of Alice James*, p. 139.

118 **"At the risk of stirring":** Ibid.

118 **"Nearly all my friends":** AJ to WJ, April 24, 1887, Houghton; Yeazell, *Death and Letters,* p. 127.

119 **For his own part:** HJ to Daniel Curtis, Feb. 24, [1888,] Berg; unpub.

119 **"I look forward":** HJ to Grace Norton, July 23, 1887, Lubbock, *Portrait of Edith Wharton,* p. 128.

119 **"[N]ow that autumn is closing in":** HJ to WJ, Oct. 1, 1887, Houghton; 2 HJ-WJ Corresp., p. 72.

119 **"It is really too beastly dear":** Quoted in HJ to Rhoda Broughton, Mar. 18, [1888,] Chester; unpub.

120 **"Coquelin was remarkable":** See HJ, "Coquelin," *The Century,* January 1887, reprinted in Wade, *The Scenic Art,* p. 198.

120 **Coquelin was "enchanted":** AJ to AHJ and WJ, Nov. 20, 1887, Houghton; Yeazell, *Death and Letters,* p. 137.

120 **At the end of the year:** HJ to Edmund Gosse, Dec. 18, 1887, Leeds; unpub.

121 **James and Gosse were both members:** Hyde, *Oscar Wilde,* p. 112.

121 **"I miss you":** HJ to RLS, Dec. 5, 1887; HJ-RLS Letters, pp. 168–169.

122 **After reading:** HJ to Mrs. Ward, n.d., Barrett; Horne, p. 202.

122 **"[Mrs. Ward] is incorrig[i]bly wise":** HJ to Edmund Gosse, Aug. 22, 1895, Duke; HJ-Gosse Letters, p. 131.

122 **Despite the absence of early notices:** For this account I am indebted to Sutherland. In *Mrs. Humphry Ward,* p. 125, Sutherland describes family and Oxford efforts to ensure attention for the book; first-year sales are given on pp. 130–131.

123 **he attributed Mary Ward's success:** HJ to Edmund Gosse, Dec. 24, [1888?,] Leeds; HJ-Gosse Letters, p. 50 (misdated "1887"; see HJ to Howells, Jan. 2, 1888, Houghton; HJ-Howells Letters p. 265).

123 **"I feel as if I had whined":** HJ to Edmund Gosse, Dec. 24, [1888?,] Leeds.

CHAPTER 9: A PRIVATE SEASON

124 **"I succumb to your arguments":** HJ to T. B. Aldrich, March 3, 1888, Houghton; 3 *HJL,* p. 223.

124 **"I must tell you":** HJ to Frederick Macmillan, May 24, 1888, BL, HJ-Macmillan Corresp., p. 140.

125 **He agreed to write four reviews:** Notebooks, Feb. 2, 1889, M. ed. p. 92; The four probably were "The Journal of the Brothers de Goncourt," *The Fort-nightly Review,* Oct. 1888, p. 501. HJ, "An Animated Conversation," *Scribners' Magazine,* March, 1889, p. 371. HJ, "After the Play," *The New Review,* June 1889, p. 30. HJ, "Our Artists in Europe," *Harper's New Monthly Magazine,* June 1889, p. 50. James's "London" appeared in Dec. 1888 in *Longman's Magazine* but was accompanied by thirteen illustrations and therefore had been composed months earlier.

125 **"It was very curious . . . the cruelty of men!":** AJ to CW, Dec. 29, 1888, Houghton; Yeazell, *The Death and Letters of Alice James,* p. 156.

125 **"The little waxen":** Ibid.; pp. 156–157.

125 **Balestier was very much:** Compare the description of Christopher Newman in the opening pages of *The American*.

126 **Legislation was pending:** The statute was not adopted until 1891, but its eventual passage seems not to have been in serious question in 1889. It did not change the situation appreciably for James, as works by Americans were protected only if manufactured in the United States; simultaneous publication in both countries was still required.

126 **Balestier seemed:** Henry James, "Wolcott Balestier," *The Cosmopolitan*, May 1892, pp. 43, 45.

127 ***The American* had been reissued:** Compton's wife told Leon Edel she had seen a magazine notice of the novel, presumably prompted by the republication. *Complete Plays*, p. 47.

127 **"I had practically given up . . . but on a new . . . basis":** Notebooks, May 12, 1889, p. 99.

128 **"two or three":** HJ to RLS, April 29, 1889, HJ-RLS Letters, p. 181.

129 **"I . . . think, just now":** HJ to AHJ, March 1, [1889]; *Dear Munificent Friends*, p. 25.

131 **"Last evening":** Notebooks, March 25, 1889, p. 97.

133 **"I am sorry to say":** WJ to AHJ, July 29, 1889, 6 WJ Corresp., p. 519.

CHAPTER 10: AN END TO NOVEL WRITING

134 **This proposal was accepted:** Anesko, *"Friction with the Market,"* pp. 124–125.

134 **Unless I can put:** HJ to Frederick Macmillan, March 28, 1890; HJ-Macmillan Corresp., pp. 160–161.

134 **James left it:** HJ-Macmillan Corresp., p. 161, n. 2.

137 **" 'To be what one *may* be' ":** HJ, *The Tragic Muse* (Penguin, reproducing 1890 ed.), p. 975.

138 **"From being outside":** HJ, *The Tragic Muse* (LoA), p. 1235.

138 ***The Picture of Dorian Gray:*** In "James Amongst the Aesthetes," Richard Ellmann noted that *The Picture of Dorian Gray* likely was a play on James's fable; but in his biography of Wilde, Ellmann played down the influence of James's tale, I think without sufficient ground.

138 **Scudder thought readers:** Unsigned review [by Horace E. Scudder], "The Tragic Muse," *The Atlantic*, Sept. 1890, p. 419, in Gard, ed., *Henry James*, p. 213.

138 **"I have been able":** HJ to H. E. Scudder, Aug. 30, 1890, Houghton; quoted in HJ-Hay Letters, p. 77.

138 **"At last you've done it":** WJ to HJ, June 26, 1890, Houghton; 2 WJ Corresp., p. 143.

139 **English reviewers:** For the contemporary reviews, see Gard, ed., *Henry James*, pp. 195–219.

142 **"I want to leave":** HJ to RLS, July 31, 1888, HJ-RLS Letters, p. 175.

142 **"*The Tragic Muse* is to be my last long novel":** HJ to WJ, May 16, 1890, Houghton; 2 WJ Corresp., p. 136.

142 "Since the immortal Docker's Strike": AJ to WJ, Nov. 25, 1889, Houghton; Yeazell, *The Death and Letters of Alice James*, p. 175.

143 James was well aware: See AJ Diary, March 7, 1890, p. 98 (HJ reports on the collapse of Labouchère's motion).

144 "I have just been reading": HJ to WJ, May 16, 1890, Houghton; 2 HJ-WJ Corresp., p. 136.

144 "the intensest throb": HJ to RLS, March 21, 1890, HJ-RLS Letters, p. 185.

Chapter 11: Collaboration

150 "I must extract": Notebooks, May 12, 1899, pp. 99–100.

150 "Then he [Newman] does . . . *but* get his wife": Ibid., p. 100. The story is a study in national character, and "characteristic" evidently means characteristically American.

150 On the stage, dialogue: Notebooks, Feb. 6, 1890, p. 102.

151 "I have an exquisite": AJ Diary, March 30, 1890, p. 105.

151 "Henry the patient": Ibid., March 25, p. 78.

151 "On May 5, Compton": C. Mackenzie, *My Life and Times*, pp. 213–214.

152 He confided to Alice: AJ Diary, May 13, 1890, p. 114.

152 Alice . . . "placid and cheerful": HJ to Carrie and Alice [James], May 20, 1890, Vaux; unpub.

152 released from duty: See, e.g., HJ to Rhoda Broughton, May 15, 1890, Chester; unpub.; HJ to Carrie and Alice [James,] May 20, 1890, Vaux; unpub.

152 one or two more plays: James may have begun *The Album* the clumsiest of his plays, at this time; but he may also have worked on another comedy, *The Reprobate.*

152 "The peace and leisure": HJ to Lady Gregory, June 13, 1890, Berg; unpub.

152 The Curtises: HJ to AJ, June 6, 1890, Houghton; 3 *HJL*, p. 287.

153 "I am ravished": HJ to AJ, June 6, 1890, Houghton; 3 *HJL*, p. 285.

153 "Her weakness": HJ to WJ, Feb. 6, [1891,] Houghton; 2 WJ Corresp., p. 168.

154 "I must tell you plainly . . . I was never fond": RLS to HJ, "August" 1890, HJ-RLS Letters, p. 190 (italics in original).

154 "I couldn't—I didn't—protest": HJ to RLS, Jan. 12, [1891,] HJ-RLS Letters, p. 196.

154 Now he confided in Florence Bell: HJ to Florence Bell, Aug. 13, 1890, Austin; unpub.

154 A few days later, he wrote: HJ to Florence Bell, Oct. 19, 1890, Austin; unpub.

155 "Many thanks": HJ to Florence Bell, Oct. 20, 1890, Austin; unpub.

155 He took plot and characters: The story was identified by Leon Edel as Henri Rivière, "Flavien: scènes de la vie contemporaine," *Revue des Deux Mondes*, Nov. 1, 1874. See *Complete Plays*, p. 257.

155 "The reading yesterday": HJ to Florence Bell, Dec. 7, 1890, Austin, unpub.; John Hare was actor-manager of the new Garrick Theatre, one of the principal venues of the West End.

156 **Wendell wrote:** OWH to WJ, Nov. 10, 1890, HLS; unpub.

156 **He was glad to help:** See HJ to F. W. H. Myers, Oct. 7, 1890; 3 *HJL*, p. 332; and Nov. 18, 1890, Myers; unpub.

156 **"No one need be told":** W. James, 1 *The Principles of Psychology*, 22–23.

157 **"I am much obliged":** HJ to William Archer, Dec. 27, 1890, BL Add'l 45292 ff. 267–271; 3 *HJL*, p. 309.

157 **"the curtain may never rise":** HJ to Florence Bell, Dec. 29, 1890, Austin; 3 *HJL*, p. 310.

158 **"Going?—Rather":** HJ to Florence Bell, Jan. 8, 1891, Austin; 1 Lubbock, p. 173. Lubbock omits the salutation to Hugh Bell.

158 **They talked of their plans:** Ibid.; AJ Diary, Jan. 7, 1891, pp. 161–163.

158 **James and Balestier went with them:** "Wolcott Balestier," *The Cosmopolitan*, pp. 43, 47.

159 ***Mrs. Vibert:*** See HJ to WJ, Feb. 6, [1891,] Houghton; 2 WJ Corresp., pp. 167, 168; HJ to Florence Bell, April 13, 1891, Austin; unpub.

160 **Reviewing . . . *Hedda Gabler:*** "Henrik Ibsen," in Wade, *The Scenic Art*, p. 243.

160 **"lamps burning":** "London Notes," in *Essays on Literature: English and American Writers*, LoA, p. 1388.

161 **The working title was "The Servant":** Published as "Brooksmith," p. 775. The story appeared with illustrations in *Black and White* in London and in *Harper's Weekly* in New York, May 2, 1891.

161 **A couple of Cockney models:** Notebooks, Feb. 22, 1891, p. 104; HJ, "The Real Thing," p. 32.

162 **These stories were . . . "little gems":** Notebooks, Feb. 22, 1891, p. 104.

163 **Sargent was to do:** The initial plan was for a third room to be done by James's old friend John La Farge, but this was not carried out, perhaps because there was no subsidy for La Farge's contribution.

163 **She and Henry agreed:** AJ Diary, Nov. 7, 1890, p. 150.

164 **"We are so absurdly happy":** AJ Diary, April 26, 1891, p. 200.

164 **All that could be done:** AJ Diary, May 31, 1891, p. 207.

164 **"To any one":** Ibid.

165 **Oxford was quiet:** HJ to Edmund Gosse, July 24, 1891, Leeds; unpub.

165 **"I must hammer away":** Notebooks, July 13, 1891, pp. 105–106.

167 **"In art there are no countries":** HJ, "Collaboration," p. 250.

167 **"There are still other details":** HJ, "Collaboration," pp. 253–254.

168 **"It was given all to a long drive":** HJ, "Wolcott Balestier," *The Cosmopolitan*, May 1892, p. 47.

168 **Alice wrote in her diary:** AJ Diary, Dec. 11, 1891, p. 223.

169 **The actors made notes:** Robins's copy of the script, showing her revisions, is now at the Fales Library, NYU.

169 ***Mrs. Vibert:*** See Alice's reflections, AJ Diary, April 23, 1891, p. 198.

170 **That fall he was at work:** See Gates, *Elizabeth Robins*, p. 45. HJ to Elizabeth Robins, June 1, 1891, BPL; Horne, *Henry James: A Life in Letters*, p. 238.

170 **"I am doing what I can":** HJ to RLS, Feb. 18, 1891, HJ-RLS Letters, p. 204.

171 **"she is slowly dying":** HJ to RJ, Sept. 8, 1891, Vaux; unpub.

171 **"A first night in London":** Constance Woolson to Katherine Livingstone

Maher, Oct. 20, 1891, quoted in Benedict, *Constance Fenimore Woolson*, pp. 371–372.

172 **"When the performance was ended"**: Ibid., p. 372.

172 **"I have had all the air"**: HJ to Edmund Gosse, "Sunday," [Sept. 27, 1891,] Leeds; HJ-Gosse Letters p. 82.

CHAPTER 12: THE LANDSCAPE IS ALTERED BY DEATH

173 **Frederick Pollock . . . wrote**: Frederick Pollock to OWH, Nov. 11, 1891, HLS; 1 Holmes-Pollock Letters, p. 42. The published text has "Rehan" instead of Robins.

173 **"Whatever may happen"**: HJ to WJ, Nov. 15, [1891,] Houghton; 2 WJ Corresp., p.193.

174 **"It is all one quest"**: Notebooks, Feb. 2, 1892, p. 113.

174 **"I am busy with the *short*"**: HJ to RLS, March 19, 1892, HJ-RLS Letters, p. 213.

174 **Alice recorded**: AJ Diary, Dec. 4, [1891,] pp. 222–223.

175 **He read the early chapters**: Carrington, *Rudyard Kipling*, p. 181.

175 **Balestier and Heinemann**: The details of these arrangements became evident when, after Balestier's death, Ouida tried to extricate herself from the agreement she had made with him. St. John, *William Heinemann*, pp. 23–24.

176 **"poor little concentrated, passionate Carrie"**: HJ to Edmund Gosse, "Thursday," [Dec. 10, 1891]; HJ-Gosse Letters, p. 84.

176 **"She is a worthy sister"**: HJ to Edmund Gosse, "Thursday," [Dec. 10, 1891]; HJ-Gosse Letters, pp. 84–85. James told Gosse that Carrie was up to meeting "any trouble but one," apparently something concerning Kipling. James said Carrie would have to face this difficulty unless spared by the "complexity of [Kipling's] 'genius.' " What this unique tribulation was or would be, he did not care to write. One naturally thinks of something that would be an obstacle to the marriage. Martin Seymour-Smith, in *Rudyard Kipling*, speculated that Kipling and Wolcott Balestier were lovers, but there is no real evidence one way or the other. If James thought Kipling to be homosexual, that would be sufficient to account for his remarks.

177 **"I have had success"**: HJ to WJ, Dec. 13, 1891, Houghton; 2 HJ-WJ Corresp., p. 197.

177 **a new comedy**: The two comedies James wrote for Compton were most likely *The Album* and *The Reprobate*. It is not possible to say which came first.

177 **"the undertakers had run out"**: Kipling, *Something of Myself*, p. 96.

177 **"I *ain't* doing a comedy"**: HJ to Florence Bell, Feb. 10, 1892, Austin; unpub. This letter was not mentioned in previous accounts, and the failure of the theater has been blamed on James's play.

178 **It was a "dreary little wedding"**: HJ to WJ, Feb. 6, 1892, Houghton; 2 WJ Corresp., p. 200.

178 **"The Long Trail"**: Quoted in Carrington, *Rudyard Kipling*, p. 193. Carring-

ton notes that the poem was an appeal to Wolcott Balestier and then altered for Carrie but is puzzled by "Tents of Shem." The latter seems a reference to Heinemann's Semitic origins.

179   **"Tenderest love to all"**: Telegram, AJ to WJ, Mar. 5, 1892, Houghton; 7 WJ Corresp., p. 246.

179   **"For about seven hours"**: HJ to WJ, March 8, 1892, Houghton; 2 WJ Corresp., p. 208.

180   **"Strange & rare"**: HJ to WJ, March 19, 1892, Houghton; 2 WJ Corresp., p. 212.

180   **"It is the last"**: HJ to WJ, March 9, 1892, Houghton; 2 WJ Corresp., p. 211.

180   **"You will need"**: WJ to HJ, March 22, 1892, Houghton; 2 WJ Corresp., p. 213.

181   **"to the young"**: HJ to Edmund Gosse, March 17, [1892,] Leeds; HJ-Gosse Letters, p. 86.

181   **"I hope you are not"**: HJ to RJ, March 8, 1892, Vaux; unpub.

181   **"I carry everywhere"**: HJ to George du Maurier, March 2, [1887,] Houghton; 3 *HJL*, p. 174.

181   **He had begun a second novel**: George du Maurier to HJ, Feb. 6, 1892, Houghton; unpub.

182   **"I confess"**: AHJ to HJ, Mar. 22, 1892, Houghton; unpub., quoted in Gunter, *A Vocation for Jameses*.

182   **Wendell Holmes sent**: O. W. Holmes, *Speeches*. See Novick, 3 *Holmes's Collected Works*, p. 461.

182   **"Nothing for a long time"**: HJ to OWH, Nov. 13, 1891, HLS; HJ-OWH Letters, p. 417.

183   **he had made a brief note**: Notebooks, March 26, 1892, p. 118.

183   **While he sat**: *Prefaces*, p. 1262. The notebook entry prompted by this experience is dated May 8, 1892, on the eve of James's departure for Italy. The story apparently was written while he was in Venice and published with illustrations on Nov. 28, 1892.

184   **He would return three more times**: In "The Jolly Corner," with which "Owen Wingrave" is paired in the New York Edition, the martial ghost is a doppelgänger. In the unfinished novel *The Sense of the Past*, the modern young man and his military ancestor change places, and James follows out his original idea of setting the story "at the beginning of the present century—at the time of the Napoleonic wars," Notebook, May 8, 1892, p. 120. The theme will reappear in James's deathbed dictations; see p. 581. The play based on "Owen Wingrave" was *The Saloon*.

184   **"a constant and painfully"**: Paul Zhukowsky to HJ, Mar. 13 [n.s., Mar. 31], 1898, Houghton; unpub.

185   **With these arrangements**: WJ to HJ, July 20, 1892, Houghton; 2 WJ Corresp., p. 224.

186   **James responded warmly**: HJ to Ada Rehan, Jan. 6, 1892; 3 *HJL*, p. 368. James's letter refers to John Hare's earlier praise of the play, which would seem to identify it as *Mrs. Vibert*. (Rehan, although still playing romantic leads and giving her age as thirty, was thirty-five and could have played the

middle-aged seductress.) Edel speculates that James had in mind *Mrs. Jasper* (published as *Disengaged*) which he did later send to Daly.

186 **James had no illusions:** HJ to Augustin Daly, Sept. 1, 1892, Houghton; 3 *HJL*, p. 395.

186 **Daly spoke of producing:** HJ to WJ, Nov. 15, 1892, Houghton; 2 WJ Corresp., p. 242.

187 **Gosse and James:** HJ to Gosse, Dec. 25, [1892,] Leeds; unpub.

187 **"those marvelous outpourings":** HJ to Gosse, Jan. 7, [1893,] Leeds; quoted in part in Hyde, *Henry James at Home*, pp. 49–50. The book came and went from the Board of Trade presumably because Gosse (like Symonds) was married.

187 **"I know all you speak of":** Grosskurth, *The Woeful Victorian*, pp. 280–281.

187 **"I don't wonder":** HJ to Gosse, Jan. 7, [1893,] Leeds; quoted in Hyde, *Henry James at Home*, p. 50; see also HJ-Gosse Letters, p. 90.

188 **"She had been on her":** HJ to Rhoda Broughton, Jan. 18, 1893, Chester; unpub.

188 **"The Middle Years":** Notebooks, May 12, 1892, pp. 121–122.

189 **"It *is* glory—to have been tested":** "The Middle Years," p. 354.

CHAPTER 13: RENEWED EXPERIMENTS

191 **an excited little group:** John, *Elizabeth Robins*, pp. 49–70. The translation was published as the joint work of Gosse and Archer; accounts published before John's had neglected Robins's role.

191 **"It is like an uncanny trick":** HJ to Florence Bell, Nov. 16, [1892,] Austin; Robins, *Theatre and Friendship*, p. 82.

192 **they read the play aloud:** The now-celebrated reading was held Dec. 7, 1892; see St. John, *William Heinemann*, p. 120; the playbill is reproduced in Thwaite, *Edmund Gosse*, p. 344. See also Gosse to G. B. Foote, Dec. 8, 1892; Charteris, *The Life and Letters of Sir Edmund Gosse*, pp. 226–227.

192 **"I am Hilda Wangel":** John, *Elizabeth Robins*, p. 66.

192 **Her collaborator Marion Lea:** Lea married the American playwright Langdon Mitchell, in whose play she had appeared, and retired from the stage. James, churning out short stories, at this time wrote "Nona Vincent," the tale of a playwright who marries his leading actress, who thereupon retires from the stage. Although he equips the young novice playwright with some of his own experiences on the stage, the story is not otherwise autobiographical, as has been suggested.

192 **He reassured his readers:** "Ibsen's New Play," *The Pall Mall Gazette*, Feb. 17, 1893, in Robins, *Theatre and Friendship*, p. 56. Wade, ed., *The Scenic Art*, pp. 256, 259, has a later version revised for book publication.

192 **"The freshness, the brilliancy":** HJ to Elizabeth Robins, Feb. 21, [1893]; Robins, *Theatre and Friendship*, p. 101.

193 **" 'The most beautiful word' ":** Notebooks, undated entry preceding first entry dated from Paris, April 8, 1893, p. 133.

194 **The young Alexander Woollcott:** Dawick, *Pinero: A Theatrical Life*, pp. 193–194.

195 **Alice told him:** HJ to AHJ, June 26, [1893,] Houghton; quoted in Gunter, *A Vocation for Jameses.*

195 **He left William and Alice:** HJ to MHJ, July 4, 1893, Vaux; unpub.

196 **"Dear Mrs. Bell":** HJ to Florence Bell, June 5, [1893?,] Austin; unpub.

196 *Salomé* **in its French edition:** HJ to Florence Bell, "Tuesday," [April 1893?,] Austin; unpub.

197 **"this frequent, fruitful, intimate battle":** Notebooks, Jan. 23, 1894, p. 145.

197 **"that literature sits patient":** Notebooks, May 7, 1893, p. 134.

197 **"Hew out a style":** E. F. Benson, *Final Edition*, p. 2.

197 **"All my previous work":** E. F. Benson, "Introduction," HJ-Benson Letters, p. vii. Benson is quoting, apparently from a letter now lost, to Mary Benson late in 1892 or early in 1893. Benson gives the date as "round about" the dates of the first letters he includes in his collection, of which the first is Sept. 3, 1892, and the second Sept. 8, 1894. The "hew out a style" quote dates from fall 1892, when Mary Benson asked James to look at the draft of *Dodo.* Arthur Benson and Edmund Gosse later made similar remarks about James's transformation during this period.

197 **he filled his notebook:** Notebooks, Nov. 12, 1892–Mar. 16, 1894, pp. 126–151. By November 1894 he had added the outline of what would become *The Wings of the Dove*, pp. 169–174, so that all the novels of his "major phase" except *The Ambassadors* were first conceived as short subjects, either plays or short stories, during this second playwriting year, 1893–1894.

198 **One Sunday afternoon:** HJ, "The Lesson of the Master," *Prefaces*, p. 1225. James remembered this call being paid in the spring of 1894, but on Jan. 9, 1894, he refers to a definite engagement having already been made.

199 **"This young man":** HJ, *Prefaces*, p. 1226.

199 **As it was a cooperative venture:** The plan to make it a cooperative venture proved impractical, and after trying unsuccessfully to sell stock, Harland and Beardsley accepted financing from Lane, who became the sole proprietor and, after 1895, coeditor.

199 **"I was invited":** HJ, *Prefaces*, p. 1227.

199 **The nominal business offices:** John Lane and Elkin Matthews were nominally partners at the outset, but Lane kept the magazine for his own project and soon pushed Matthews out of the Bodley Head entirely.

200 **"I withdraw it":** HJ to Augustin Daly, Dec. 7, 1893, Houghton; 3 *HJL*, pp. 444–445.

200 **Daly responded:** See 3 *HJL*, p. 445, n.1.

200 **("Oof!—it's a relief"):** HJ to Florence Bell, Dec. 14, 1893, Austin; unpub.

201 **"I have been sitting here":** Notebooks, Dec. 26, 1893, p. 138.

201 **Early in January 1894, he held:** HJ to [William] Squire, Jan. 14, 1894, Fitzwilliam Museum; unpub.

203 **"A close & valued friend":** HJ to Margaret Brooke, Jan. 28, 1894, Columbia; quoted in Edel, 3 *The Life of Henry James*, p. 360.

203 **"Miss Woolson was so valued":** HJ to John Hay, Jan. 28, 1894, Brown; HJ-Hay Letters, p. 110.

204 **"I have been terribly overwhelmed":** HJ to Rhoda Broughton, Jan. 28 and Jan. 29, 1894, Chester; unpub.

204   **He wrote to Gosse:** HJ to Edmund Gosse, Jan. 30, 1894, Leeds; HJ-Gosse Letters, p. 97.

204   **"a day of despair":** A. C. Benson to Edmund Gosse, Jan. 31, 1894, Leeds; unpub.

204   **He wanted to treat:** Notebooks, January 23, 1894, pp. 145–146.

204   **"Could not something":** Notebooks, February 3, 1894, pp. 147–148.

205   **"intensely a vision of youth":** "George du Maurier," *Harper's Weekly*, April 14, 1894, in *Collected Essays*, p. 873.

206   **Trilby is a picture:** Ibid., p. 875.

206   **"I am making love":** HJ to Rhoda Broughton, Mar. 27, 1894, Chester; unpub.

207   **"My dear Ralph":** HJ to Ralph Curtis, Jan. 14, 1895, Austin; unpub.

207   **John Briggs Potter:** HJ to Henrietta Reubell, Nov. 5, 1894, Houghton; quoted in Horne, p. 272, n. 3.

207   **"He made a frightfully":** Alida Cagidemetrio, "Recollections of Henry James in His Later Years," BBC broadcast, June 14, 1956, transcript in Houghton; published in part in Perosa, *Henry James e Venezia*, pp. 54–55. Gordon, *A Private Life*, pp. 1–6, has a highly colored version. I have not found confirmation of this improbable story, but as it has become canonical I include it here.

207   **"Dear Lady Carnavon":** HJ to Lady Carnavon, May 16, 1894, BL; unpub.

207   **In his illustrations:** The anti-Semitism is explicit. James and his contemporaries thought of Jews in racial terms, and du Maurier praises racial mixtures in which there is some Jewish ancestry and praises Western or Sephardic Jews, but he paints a repellant stereotypic portrait of Svengali, an Eastern, "oriental" Jew. James, untroubled, describes him as "pagan."

208   **"Only see":** HJ to George du Maurier, "Thursday," [May 1894,] 1 Lubbock, pp. 212–13.

208   **In that first issue:** Max Beerbohm, " A Defence of Cosmetics," *The Yellow Book*, April 1894; reprinted in *The Yellow Book: A Selection*, p. 137.

209   **"I hear your sister's":** HJ to WJ, May 28, 1894, Houghton; 2 WJ Corresp., p. 310.

209   **"I have been immensely":** HJ to WJ, May 28, 1894, Houghton; 2 WJ Corresp., p. 311.

210   **The Palazzo Primoli:** Contemporary references are confusing. In 1894, the modest palace fronted on what was then Piazza dell'Orso, now Piazza Ponte Umberto I. In 1901, Primoli enlarged the house, closed off the entrance on the embankment, and added a new entrance facade on Via Zanardelli. The building now houses the Museo Napoleonico.

211   **On his return to England:** HJ to Arthur Benson, Sept. 8, 1894, HJ-Benson Letters, p. 3.

211   **"The arrival of the eggs":** HJ to Gertrude Abbey, summer 1894, Lucas, 2 *Edwin Austin Abbey*, p. 276.

212   **"We are very unhappy":** HJ to Gertrude Abbey, Nov. 1, 1894, quoted in Lucas, 2 *Edwin Austin Abbey*, pp. 276–277.

212   **"I particularly envy":** HJ to T. H. Huxley, Nov. 2, 1894, Huxley Papers; unpub.

212   **Aside from wanting:** HJ to T. H. Huxley, Oct. 27, 1894, Huxley Papers; unpub.

212 **He felt that a new:** HJ to W. D. Howells, Jan. 22, 1895, Houghton; HJ-Howells Corresp., p. 297.

213 **"This was a mood":** HJ to Sidney Colvin, Aug. 23, [1894,] Fitzwilliam Museum; unpub.

213 **"Situation of that":** Notebooks, [fall 1892?,] p. 126.

214 **James thought he could solve:** HJ to John Hay, Feb. 9, 1895, Brown; HJ-Hay Letters, p. 113.

215 **"Since I wrote this":** HJ to Florence Bell, Dec. 17, [1894,] Austin; unpub.

215 **"with a shock":** Gosse, *Aspects and Impressions*, p. 29.

215 **"I meant to write":** HJ to Edmund Gosse, Dec. 17, 1894, BL; HJ-Gosse Letters, p. 121, with small changes.

216 **"You must know":** W. D. Howells to HJ, Dec. 13, 1894, Houghton; HJ-Howells Letters, p. 296.

CHAPTER 14: CLOSING THE CHAPTER

217 **"My dear Gosse":** HJ to Edmund Gosse, Dec. 27, 1894, Leeds; HJ-Gosse Letters, p. 123.

217 **"Forgive the uncontrollable":** HJ to Florence Bell, Jan. 1, 1895, Austin; unpub. HJ to Hugh Bell, Jan. 4, 1895, Austin; unpub.

218 **He was not a man of business:** HJ to Sidney Colvin, Dec. 20, 1894, 1 Lubbock, pp. 224–225.

218 **"The ghost of poor R.L.S.":** HJ to Edmund Gosse, Dec. 27, 1894, Leeds; HJ-Gosse Letters, p. 123.

218 **Sidney Colvin pleaded:** Benson Diary, Mar. 6, 1895; quoted in part in Newsome, *On the Edge of Paradise*, pp. 88–89.

219 **At the interval:** HJ to Louisa Wolseley, Oct. 4, 1895, Leeds; unpub.

219 **"There followed":** HJ to WJ, Jan. 9, 1895, Houghton; 2 WJ Corresp., p. 337.

219 **James "stood before":** See Thwaite, *Waiting for the Party*, pp. 154–155.

219 **"the opinion of the public . . . a charming scene":** HJ to WJ, Jan. 9, 1895, Houghton; 2 WJ Corresp., p. 337.

219 **"No one after":** Margaret Brooke to E. Gosse, May 15, 1920, Leeds; unpub. (quoting HJ's letter).

220 **"I swore to myself an oath":** HJ to Virginia Compton, Mar. 15, 1895, C. Mackenzie, *My Life and Times*, pp. 113–114.

220 **"I was astonished":** Gosse, *Aspects*, pp. 33–34. There are similar accounts in Benson's diary, other contemporary sources, and James's correspondence. His behavior after the opening, described below, continued to be energetic and optimistic. In Edel's psychoanalytic account, however, James's cheerfulness was superficial and masked a deep and prolonged depression. Edel's account has been widely followed, but the weight of evidence seems to be the other way.

220 **"All *private* opinion":** HJ to WJ, Jan. 9, 1895, Houghton; 2 WJ Corresp., p. 337.

220 **"to gossip a bit":** HJ to Hugh Bell, Jan. 6, 1895, Austin; unpub.

221   " 'Guy Domville' is a story": George Bernard Shaw, "The Drama's Laws," *The Saturday Review*, Jan. 12, 1895, reprinted, *Guy Domville*, p. 205.

221   *The Times'* anonymous reviewer: *The Times*, Jan. 7, 1895, quoted in 2 WJ Corresp., 339 n. 2.

221   "My dear Norris": HJ to W. E. Norris, Jan. 10, 1895; *Selected Letters*, p. 285. HJ to Ralph [Curtis,] Jan. 14, 1895, Austin; unpub. HJ to Henschel, Jan. 15, 1895; Edel Archive. Edel, *Henry James: Les Années Dramatiques*, appendix 3. HJ to [W. Barclay] Squire, Jan. 8, 1895, Fitzwilliam Museum; unpub. HJ to Henrietta Reubell, Jan. 10, 1895, Houghton; *Selected Letters*, p. 153. WJ to HJ, Jan. 19, 1895, Houghton; 2 WJ Corresp., p. 340. HJ to [Eugenia] Phillips, Jan. 15, 1895, Austin; unpub. HJ to Rhoda Broughton, Jan. 14, 1895, Chester; unpub.

222   As he told Gertrude: Lucas, *Edwin Austin Abbey*, p. 278.

222   He wrote to Louisa: HJ to Lady Wolseley, Jan. 17, 1895, Hove; unpub.

222   "the story of [two] young children": Notebooks, Jan. 12, 1895, p. 178.

223   " 'What sort of a play' ": *St. James's Gazette*, January 18, 1895, quoted in Hyde, *Oscar Wilde*, p. 176.

224   "the withdrawal": HJ to John Hay, Feb. 9, 1895, Brown; HJ-Hay Letters, p. 113.

224   James renewed his relations: HJ to WJ, Feb. 26, 1895, Houghton; 2 WJ Corresp., p. 350 ("I am full of engagements to produce [2 one-volume novels, this year, for Heinemann].") James's letter of Jan. 22 to Howells seems already to refer to these short novels.

225   "I shall never again": HJ to W. D. Howells, Jan. 22, 1895, Houghton; HJ-Howells Letters, p. 298.

225   "I take up my own": Notebooks, Jan. 23, 1895, p. 179.

225   "But all that": These entries follow that for January 23 but are not dated separately.

225   James expressed his willingness: Notebooks, Feb. 6, 1895, p. 184.

227   "there are depths in London": HJ to WJ, April 26, 1895, Houghton; 2 WJ Corresp., p. 359.

227   In later trials for "homosexualism": Hoare, *Oscar Wilde's Last Stand*, pp. 8–10, 28.

227   "Yes . . . it has been": HJ to Edmund Gosse, [April 8, 1895,] Leeds; HJ-Gosse Letters, p. 126.

228   "What a pity": Ibid. ("Quel dommage—mais quel bonheur—que J.A.S. ne soit plus de ce monde!")

228   "fond outpourings of poor J.A.S.": HJ to Edmund Gosse, [April 28, 1895,] Leeds; HJ-Gosse Letters, p. 127.

228   "I have my head": Notebooks, Feb. 14, 1895, p. 187.

CHAPTER 15: THE LESSON OF THE THEATER

229   "I am singularly accessible": HJ to A. C. Benson, Feb. 26, 1895, HJ-ACB Letters, p. 6.

229   "Ah, if you knew": HJ to A. C. Benson, May 11, [1895,] 1 Lubbock, p. 240.

230 **Atherton stared:** Atherton, *Adventures of a Novelist*, pp. 110–111, 248–249.

230 **"Yes, I will finish":** HJ to Ellen Terry, May 23, [1895?,] Berg; unpub.

231 **The success of the stage:** "Trilby" is still the name given to a style of hat worn in the West End staging.

231 **"The whole phenomenon":** "George du Maurier," *Harper's New Monthly Magazine*, September 1897; *Collected Essays*, p. 903.

231 **"the most affectionate":** Du Maurier, *The Martian*, pp. 1–2.

232 **This female genius:** Ibid., p. 288.

232 **"There is no longer":** Ibid., p. 374.

232 **The Wolseleys:** HJ to Edmund Gosse, July 4, [1895,] Leeds; unpub.

233 **His guests:** Benson Diary, June 6, 1895; unpub. "H James tho' ill came frm town to dine. V.P., H. Sturgis, Ainger, Luxmore." "Ainger" is A. C. Ainger (1841–1919). From other entries it is clear that "V.P." refers to the vice provost, Warre-Cornish.

233 **would soon write a fanciful story:** HJ, "The Great Good Place," first published in *Scribner's Magazine*, January 1900.

234 **The dinner was ample:** HJ to A. C. Benson, Aug. 5 and Sept. 14, 1895, HJ-Benson Letters, pp. 14–15, 19.

234 **"Henry James":** Benson Diary, July 17, 1895; unpub.

234 **Shortly afterward:** HJ to A. C. Benson, Aug. 5, 1895, HJ-Benson Letters, pp. 14–15.

235 **"I have got over":** OWH to Nina Gray, Sept. 2, 1895, HLS; Novick, *Honorable Justice*, p. 207. His letter to James, now lost, presumably was similar.

235 **James spoke of the experience:** HJ to Gertrude Mead, [September? 1895,] Lucas, *Edwin Austin Abbey*, p. 278.

236 **"[I]n the midst":** 3 *Collected Works*, p. 486; see Novick, *Honorable Justice*, p. 205.

236 **"I've told you before":** HJ to OWH, Oct. 13, 1895, HLS; HJ-OWH Letters, p. 418.

236 *Mrs. Gracedew:* Notebooks, Feb. 6, 1895, pp. 185–187. The play was published as *Summersoft*, recycled as a short story, "Covering End," and then re-dramatized as *The High Bid*, see pp. 574 and 575.

237 **In notes he made:** Notebooks, March 4, 1895, p. 196. James notes the return to the themes of *The Bostonians*.

237 **"insane frenzy":** Notebooks, July 14, 1895, p. 207.

238 **The anger . . . disappeared:** Notebooks, June 4, 1895, pp. 200–205. The story appeared in *The Yellow Book* in July.

238 **"May I not instantly":** Notebooks, Feb. 14, 1895, p. 188 (italics in original).

239 **Instead of a branching:** The now-famous passage describing James's discovery of the principle of the "scenario" has sometimes been misinterpreted. In James's day, "scenario" was not yet a general term for plan or outline but was still only a technical term describing the structure of a play or opera libretto, a succession of scenes. See "Scenario" in *Oxford English Dictionary.* Today's equivalent might be the storyboard.

239 **"the situation of the mother":** Notebooks, Dec. 24, 1893, pp. 136–137.

240 **"What then is it . . . When I ask myself":** Notebooks, Aug. 11, 1895, p. 208.

241　"I've been too proud": Notebooks, Sept. 8, 1895, p. 212.

242　He spoke in the first person: HJ, "Glasses," *The Atlantic*, February 1896, pp. 169–172.

243　Sturges was one: HJ to Jonathan Sturges, Oct. 19, 1893; 3 *HJL*, p. 435 (Lubbock typescript in Houghton) ("keep also for life, if you can, yours ever, my dear Sturges").

243　"Oh the old full": Notebooks (Edel ed.), July 1914, "Thursday"–Aug. 3, 1914, "Monday," p. 407, recalling Sturges's visit.

243　James made a note: Notebooks, Oct. 31, 1895, p. 225 ("a *sujet de nouvelle*").

243　" 'Oh, you are young' ": Notebooks, Oct. 31, 1895, p. 226. HJ added: "I amplify & improve a little—but that was the tone."

244　The committee had found: Hyde, *Oscar Wilde*, p. 296.

244　Wilde's state of collapse: HJ to Alphonse Daudet, Nov. 10, 1895; Horne, *Henry James: A Life in Letters*, p. 287. James describes his visitor only as "un homme politique," but, as Horne notes, the visitor was almost certainly R. B. Haldane, who as a member of the committee on prison reform had the authority to visit Wilde and who had intervened on his behalf. See Hyde, *Oscar Wilde*, p. 300.

244　Haldane may also: Harris, *Oscar Wilde*, p. 204.

245　A petition would not: Jonathan Sturges to Stuart Merrill, quoting James, in Ellman, *Oscar Wilde*, p. 493.

245　Surely there would: James did sign at least four public letters, including one assuredly futile protest against the lord chamberlain's censorship of plays; see Edel and Laurance, *A Bibliography of Henry James*, p. 352.

245　"The House Beautiful": The title had been used not only by Wilde but also on a recent American book, which put it off limits for *The Atlantic*.

245　Arthur Benson's new book: Arthur Christopher Benson, *Essays* (1896).

246　"my dear Arthur": HJ to A. C. Benson, Nov. 25, 1895, HJ-Benson Letters, p. 22–23. HJ to A. C. Benson, Dec. 17, 1895, HJ-Benson Letters, pp. 25–26.

247　*The Other House:* First noted Dec. 26, 1893; Notebooks, pp. 138–147; thought of as a novel, *The Promise*, entry following Dec. 21, 1895; Notebooks, p. 233.

247　he wrote to George Brett: HJ to George Brett, April 14, 1896, HJ-Macmillan Letters, p. 178.

248　"The admirers of James": Harris, 2 *My Life and Loves*, pp. 159–160.

248　The twenty-four-year-old Crane's: "Comment on New Books," *The Atlantic Monthly*, March 1896, p. 422.

248　"Henry James is an effeminate": Quoted in Beer, pp. 151–152.

249　he was "panting": HJ to A. C. Benson, Jan. 16, 1896, HJ-Benson Letters, p. 28.

249　"if I can pick your bones": HJ to A. C. Benson, April 5, 1896, HJ-Benson Letters, pp. 29–31.

250　"He just said": Lady Gregory's Diaries, pp. 100–104; Augusta Gregory, *SeventyYears*, p. 182.

250　"Think? *Think?*": Ellman, "James Among the Aesthetes," in Bradley, *Henry James and Homoerotic Desire*, p. 41.

252　"a laughing azure": Gosse, *Aspects and Impressions*, p. 36.

252 "My dear Arthur": HJ to A. C. Benson, June 29, 1896, HJ-Benson Letters, pp. 34–35; Sept. 2, 1896, HJ-Benson Letters, p. 37.

252 "my little hovel": HJ to OWH, April 11, 1896, HLS; HJ-OWH Letters p. 419. "Tuesday," [June 30, 1896,] HLS; HJ-OWH Letters, pp. 419–420.

253 Wendell was "in admirable youth": HJ to WJ, July 24, 1896, Houghton; 2 WJ Corresp., p. 405. OWH calendar, July 23, 1896, HLS.

253 "My dear Wendell": HJ to OWH, n.d., HLS; quoted in part in Novick, *Honorable Justice*, p. 210.

253 I began to pay: HJ to Edmund Gosse, Aug. 28, [1896,] Houghton; HJ-Gosse Letters, p. 145.

254 "Forgive me . . . I launch this note . . . I jump at the chance": HJ to OWH, Aug. 7, [1896,] HLS; unpub. HJ to OWH, "Monday," [August 10, 1896,] HLS; unpub. "Friday," [August 14, 1896,] HLS; unpub.

254 "Standing before me": HJ to OWH, Oct. 17, 1901, HLS; HJ-OWH Letters, p. 427.

255 "There can be for him": HJ, "The Spoils of Poynton," *Prefaces*, p. 1141.

255 "wonderful book": Ford, *Henry James*, p. 31; HJ, *Portraits from Life*, p. 8.

256 sales of the book: HJ to WJ, Oct. 30, 1896, Houghton; 2 WJ Corresp., pp. 415, 416.

256 he recalled a dream: HJ, *A Small Boy and Others*, p. 196; Novick, *Henry James: The Young Master*, p. 53. James does not give a date for this dream, except to say that it occurred in summer. As he emphasizes his sense of triumph, I have placed it here. It is susceptible of other interpretations; see the Epilogue.

256 "I never had more": HJ to A. C. Benson, Dec. 28, 1896, 1 Lubbock, pp. 250, 252.

CHAPTER 16: RYE

260 his Robertson grandmother's house: I was able to visit the house, 10 Washington Square North, the setting of James's *Washington Square*, before the building was razed to make way for rental apartments. For James's investigations of Lamb House and his "sheep's eyes," see HJ to AHJ, Dec. 1, 1897, 1 Lubbock, p. 265.

260 "I have been living . . . I must always cling": HJ to Daniel Curtis, Oct. 14, 1896, Berg; unpub.

261 "I doubt if you": HJ to MRJ, "Wednesday," [Sept. 2, 1896?,] Vaux; unpub. As for "Jews, etc.": James was revolted by Continental anti-Semitism and was a Dreyfusard, but he freely applied racial labels and shared the common conviction that these were scientific designations, and that Jews were a racially distinct group. We should note that race, nationality, and ethnicity were not clearly distinguished at this time; the French and English were also considered racially distinct.

261 Sultan Abd al-Hamid II: In James's day usually rendered as "Abdul Hamid II."

262 "During the past few years": "Mr. James Bryce, 'The Armenian Question,' "

The Dial, Feb. 16, 1897, p. 113. Bryce, author of *The American Common-wealth* (1889) and later ambassador to the United States, was a mutual friend of James and Holmes and twenty years later would deliver to James the Order of Merit.

262 **"This has been":** HJ to WJ, Sept. 17, 1896, Houghton; 2 WJ Corresp., pp. 411–412.

263 **a peaceful globalization . . . "from far back":** *Prefaces*, pp. 1209–1218.

263 **"This is tremendous":** HJ to John Hay, Feb. 22, 1897, Brown; HJ-Hay Letters, pp. 115–116.

264 **Adams would later say:** Henry Adams, *The Education of Henry Adams*, p. 1180.

264 **"Her performance":** HJ, "Mr. Henry Irving's Production of 'Cymbeline,' " *Harper's Weekly*, Nov. 21, 1896; Wade, ed., *The Scenic Art*, p. 283.

265 **" 'Burn' it, quotha!":** HJ to A. C. Benson, Dec. 28, 1896, 1 Lubbock, p. 252.

265 **"the march of an action":** Notebooks, Dec. 21, 1897, p. 263.

266 **"The author who":** HJ, "London," *Harper's Weekly*, Feb. 6, 1897 (with date-line "January 15"); Wade, ed., *The Scenic Art*, pp. 292–293.

267 **"Ruminating over it":** Notebooks, Nov. 12, 1892, pp. 126–127.

267 **"the torch of rapture":** HJ, *Prefaces*, pp. 1156–1157.

267 **portraying fully what she *saw*:** HJ, *Prefaces*, p. 1160. See Greg W. Zacharias's interesting notes to the preface, in the Modern Library edition of *What Maisie Knew* (2002), on James's use of "consciousness" and "seeing," giving also citations to the principal recent works on James's lifelong study of the perceptive functions of the mind.

267 **"It was to be":** "What Maisie Knew," *The Chap-Book*, Jan. 15, 1897, p. 215. For the book edition James removed several commas, which I have allowed to stand as likely to be closer to the first draft, later extensively revised, and corrected a typographical error ("stare" instead of "stars").

268 **"In that lively sense . . . Some of these gentlemen":** *The Chap-Book*, pp. 215–217.

269 **The Boulogne that Maisie:** See Novick, *Henry James, The Young Master*, p. 58.

270 **As Rebecca West:** West, *Henry James*, p. 95.

270 **"portrait of the artist as a young girl":** See the much-cited article by Juliet Mitchell, "*What Maisie Knew*."

270 **More than a century:** See Mackenzie, *Communities of Honor and Love*, which describes HJ's late novels as a series in which love is a fundamental ground of identity and the medium of participation in community.

271 **When a neighbor's door:** Hyde, *Henry James at Home*, p. 119.

271 **"I remember in particular":** Wharton, *A Backward Glance*, pp. 177–194.

272 **"the whole thing":** HJ to Louisa Wolseley, Mar. 8, 1897, Hove; *Dear Munificent Friends*, p. 263.

272 **He refused Augusta Gregory's:** HJ to Lady Gregory, Feb. 26, 1897, Berg; unpub.

272 **James spoke of his fondness:** HJ to Edward Warren, Sept. 15, 1897, 1 Lubbock, p. 261.

273 **The next morning:** HJ to WJ, Sept. 1, 1897, Houghton; 3 WJ Corresp., pp. 20–21.

274   **He thought them:** HJ to WJ, Sept. 1, 1897, Houghton; 3 WJ Corresp., p. 19. Jane Emmet to Lydia Emmet, Aug. 6, 1897, quoted in part in Edel (one-vol. ed.), p. 459. WJ to AHJ, Aug. 7, 1897, 3 WJ Corresp., p 13. The three sisters and their cousin Ellen all had careers as painters; the family papers are now in the Smithsonian's art archives.

274   **"The reader unexpectedly":** "Mr. James' Latest Novel," *The Saturday Review*, Oct. 31, 1896, pp. 474–75; Hayes, *Henry James*, pp. 249, 251.

275   **"If you debar":** *The Athenaeum*, Mar. 6, 1897, pp. 308–309; Hayes, *Henry James*, p. 272.

275   **"Considering their nature":** *The Athenaeum*, Nov. 6, 1897, p. 629; Hayes, *Henry James*, p. 287; Foley, *Criticism in American Periodicals*, p. 69.

275   **"The vulgar, selfish":** Nov. 24, quoted in Gard, *Henry James: The Critical Heritage*, pp. 537–538; Hayes, *Henry James*, p. 289. HJ, "High Water," *The Pall Mall Gazette*, Oct. 11, 1897; Hayes, *Henry James*, pp. 283–284.

276   **At this time . . . Athenaeum:** Notes by Isaac H. Lionberger of James's talk at a University Club (Saint Louis) dinner, [1905?,] Berg; unpub.

276   **"Even to the end":** HJ, "A Tribute from Mr. Henry James," *The Illustrated London News*, April 2, 1898, p. 3, col. 1. This is a fragment of the complete essay, published the following week as "The Late James Payn." (Both were omitted from the generally complete Library of America edition of James's essays on writers.)

277   **"At any rate":** HJ to A. C. Benson, Oct. 1, 1897, HJ-Benson Letters, p. 46; Benson Diary, vol. 2, p. 104, unpub.

277   **The publication of her letters:** HJ, "She and He: Recent Documents," *The Yellow Book*, January 1897, p. 15; HJ, *European Writers*, pp. 738–753.

279   **"John Delavoy":** *Cosmopolis*, January and February 1898, pp. 1–21, 317–332; HJ, *Complete Stories 1898–1910*, p. 1.

279   **"Paste":** HJ, "Paste" (1899), *Complete Stories 1898–1910*, p. 135.

280   **The Turn of the Screw:** See HJ, "The Aspern Papers, Etc." *Prefaces*, pp. 1181–1182.

280   **When the book edition:** Macmillan Co. Records, Berg, quoting Elisabeth Cady in *Scribner's Magazine*.

281   **"I am just drawing":** HJ to A. C. Benson, Sept. 25, 1897, 2 Lubbock, p. 262.

CHAPTER 17: LAMB HOUSE

282   **"Parsons, best of men":** HJ to AHJ, Dec. 1, 1897, 1 Lubbock, pp. 263, 266.

282   **"We are here":** HJ to Daniel Curtis, Dec. 26, 1897, Berg; unpub.

283   **"impressions of his condition":** HJ to MHJ, Feb. 25, 1899, Vaux; unpub.

283   **"My very dear friend!":** Paul Zhukowsky to HJ, "Mar. 13/31" [1898], Houghton; unpub. ("Y viendrez vous, cher ami? Pensez y un peu sérieusement. . . . Maintenant laissez-mois vous embrasser bien affecteusement et vous prier de m'écrire, ne fut-ce que deux lignes pour me dire comment vous vous portez. A vous de coeur, P. Joukovsky.")

284   **"Vera had oriented":** Atherton, *Adventures of a Novelist*, p. 285.

285 **"feels burningly":** F. H. Bradley, *Appearance and Reality* (1893), p. 229, quoted in A. N. Wilson, *The Victorians*, p. 569.

287 **"Rye society":** Hyde, *Henry James at Home*, p. 115.

287 **"the special note of Rye":** HJ to AHJ, Dec. 19, 1898, 1 Lubbock, p. 303.

288 **A dinner with Rosebery:** HJ, "The Real Right Thing," see Notebooks, May 7, 1898, p. 265.

288 **"He was waiting":** Annie Fields Diary, Sept. 13, 1898, BPL.

289 **But Holmes was engaged:** This was a romantic encounter, as James knew; see HJ to OWH, Sept. 23, 1898, HLS; HJ-OWH Letters, p. 421; Novick, *Honorable Justice*, pp. 211 ff.

289 **His working space . . . "Garden Room":** This room and the view from the window were made famous by E. F. Benson, who with his brother Arthur rented Lamb House after James's death. He set his Mapp and Lucia novels there and called it "Mallards."

289 **He wrote a short novel:** *The Awkward Age*, quoted passages from chapters xxiv, xxv, pp. 196–197, 204. In the New York Edition the frontispiece for the volume is a photograph of the front door of Lamb House.

291 **He wrote to Pinker:** HJ to James Pinker, Oct. 23, 1898; 4 *HJL*, p. 85.

292 **James ran over from Rye:** HJ to John Hay, April 3, 1900, Brown; HJ-Hay Letters, p. 123. See also the opening scene of Gore Vidal, *Empire* (1987).

292 **"the wail of the elements":** HJ to WJ, Jan. 26, 1899, Houghton; 3 WJ Corresp., p. 48.

292 **"I greatly applaud":** HJ to Howard Sturgis, May 19, 1899, Houghton; *Dearly Beloved Friends*, p. 122.

293 **"George Alexander":** Notebooks, Jan. 22, 1899, p. 268. The "obstacles" presumably included Ellen Terry's ownership of stage rights to the story, which had begun as the play *Mrs. Gracedew*.

293 **"How, through all":** Notebooks, Jan. 27, 1899, p. 269.

294 **The two men:** HJ to A. F. de Navarro, Monday–Tuesday night, [Feb. 27–28, 1899,] 1 Lubbock, pp. 312–313.

294 **"We rushed":** HJ to Edward Warren, February 27, 1899; Hyde, *Henry James at Home*, pp. 95–96.

295 **"My dear Tony":** HJ to A. F. de Navarro, Monday–Tuesday night, [Feb. 27–28, 1899,] 1 Lubbock, pp. 312–314.

295 **William remarked . . . Henry agreed:** WJ to HJ, Mar. 19, 1899, Houghton; 3 WJ Corresp., p. 56. HJ to WJ, Apr. 2, 1899, Houghton; 3 WJ Corresp., p. 59.

295 **"We have ceased":** HJ to WJ, June 3, 1899, Houghton; 3 WJ Corresp., p. 63.

296 **"my old circle here". . . clasped the hands:** HJ to Ariana and Daniel Curtis, Mar. 16, 1899, HJ-Barbaro Letters, p. 155.

296 **He thought it "exquisite":** HJ to Edmund Gosse, Nov. 9, 1894, 1 Lubbock, p. 221.

296 **"France . . . will":** HJ to Ariana Curtis, Oct. 30, 1898, Dartmouth; HJ Barbaro Letters, p. 132.

296 **James thought the place:** HJ to WJ, April 22, 1899, Houghton; 3 WJ Corresp., p. 58.

297 **"Think, my dear":** Mary Temple to HJ, Aug. 15–22, 1869, Houghton; Le

Clair, "Henry James and Minny Temple," pp. 46–47; Novick, *Henry James: The Young Master,* p. 203.

297 **At work in Venice:** Despite later scholarly speculation to the contrary, James was at work on the novel by October 1899, shortly after his return from Italy; see Vincec, " '*Poor Flopping Wings,*' " p. 65. We know from the preface to the New York Edition that he began with the image of Milly Theale, who resembles Minny Temple; the central scene and climax of the novel are set in the Palazzo Barbaro.

298 **Julia Ward:** Notebooks, May 16, 1899, p. 290. This was the germ of "The Beldonald Holbein," 1901.

299 **"I crawl, depleted":** HJ to Howard Sturgis, [July? 1899,] Houghton; unpub.

300 **"I've never in all":** HJ, *Prefaces,* p. 1129.

300 **"Mr. Henry James Exasperates":** May 8, 1899, p. 4; Hayes, *Henry James,* p. 318.

300 **"enigma, the very":** May 2, 1899, p. 4; Hayes, *Henry James,* p. 317.

300 **"A charm, sometimes":** *The Athenaeum,* May 27, 1899, p. 651; Hayes, *Henry James,* pp. 324, 326.

300 **"You must take time":** June 1899, p. 81; Hayes, *Henry James,* p. 330.

301 **"The book has done":** HJ, *Prefaces,* p. 1129.

301 **"Nothing I've ever done":** HJ to WDH, Nov. 25, 1899, Houghton; WJ-Howells Letters, p. 352.

301 **James angrily called:** HJ to Henrietta Reubell, Nov. 12, 1899, Houghton; 1 Lubbock, p. 333.

301 **Arthur Bellingham had died:** Bellingham died in South Africa, not in the Yukon.

302 **"It fixes me":** HJ to WJ, July 31, 1899, Houghton; 3 WJ Corresp., p. 67.

302 **Then Alice wrote:** The three-cornered correspondence is AHJ to HJ, Aug. 3, 1899, Houghton; 3 WJ Corresp., p. 71. HJ to WJ, Aug. 4, 1899, Houghton; 3 WJ Corresp., pp. 71–72, 75.

303 **The bust had arrived:** HJ to Hendrik Andersen, July 21, 1899, Virginia; unpub.

304 **"I will spend":** Hendrik Andersen to his parents, Aug. 16, 1899; *Dearly Beloved Friends,* p. 25, n.

304 **James walked alone:** HJ to Hendrik Andersen, Oct. 23, 1899, Virginia; *Dearly Beloved Friends,* p. 27.

304 **"My dearest little Hans":** HJ to Hendrik Andersen, Sept. 7, 1899, Virginia; *Dearly Beloved Friends,* p. 26.

CHAPTER 18: CENTURY'S END

306 **"Lamb House":** HJ to Louisa Wolseley, Nov. 5, 1899, Hove; *Dear Munificent Friends,* p. 266.

306 **First were potboilers:** "Two Old Houses and Three Young Women" (Venetian scenes), *The Independent,* September 1899, and "The Present Literary Situation in France," *North American Review,* October 1899; *The Soft Side,*

1900. "Paste," "The Great Good Place," and "The Real Right Thing" appeared in December and January. Three other stories were included in the volume that did not appear first in magazines ("The Tree of Knowledge," "The Abasement of the Northmores," and "The Third Person"), which also were likely written at this time.

307 **The first of these:** The novel had not yet been given a title, and James destroyed the prospectus. Edel and others have argued on psychological grounds that the 1899 proposal was for *The Ambassadors* and that *The Wings of the Dove* was conceived later. Vincec shows persuasively, however, that the scenario written in the fall of 1899 was for *The Wings of the Dove*, when its opening chapters were written, and that *The Ambassadors* was a distinct project first proposed the following year. The proposal for *The Ambassadors* has survived and is dated Sept. 1, 1900.

307 **"It has bothered me":** Notebooks, Nov. 3, 1894, p. 170.

307 **She will learn:** The gradual elaboration of the plot is described in James's preface in the New York Edition, see *Prefaces*, pp. 1287 ff.

308 **But the tale:** HJ to WD Howells, Aug. 9, 1900, HJ-Howells Corresp., p. 358.

308 **"The writer of these":** Notebooks, May 16, 1899, p. 291.

308 **He began to sketch:** Notebooks, Nov. 11, 1899, p. 295. The play, presumably for George Alexander, centering on a "celibate bachelor," was never written. The stories became "Fordham Castle" and "The Abasement of the Northmores."

308 **Stopford Brooke:** Son of the Unitarian minister of the same name; no relation to either Rupert Brooke or Margaret Brooke, the ranee of Sarawak. Notebooks, Feb. 17, 1894, p. 151; Feb. 19, 1899, p. 275.

310 **it was only a joke:** The vampire theme struck so strongly resonant a chord with Freudian critics that this became one of James's most celebrated and controversial tales. If one takes the vampire theory as an expression of the neurotic fears of the author, the tale becomes self-satire—which it is, a little—a performance in drag. It was popular at the time simply as a satire of country-house licentiousness.

311 **"When . . . I broke up":** HJ to Mrs. F. W. H. Myers, April 8, 1904; Myers 22/74, unpub. This letter contradicts the well-established myth that James made a huge bonfire of letters at the close of his life.

311 **Jonathan Sturges:** HJ to Henrietta Reubell, Nov. 12, 1899, 1 Lubbock, p. 334.

311 **conversations . . . with other friends:** W. E. Norris to Edmund Gosse, Dec. 19, 1898, Leeds; unpub.

312 **William, Alice, and Peggy:** WJ to HJ, Oct. 9, 1899, Houghton; 3 WJ Corresp., p. 89. HJ to WJ, Nov. 13, 1899, Houghton; 3 WJ Corresp., p. 93.

312 **"It is all sad work":** HJ to MHJ, Nov. 29, 1899, Vaux; unpub.

312 **"I sit in the garden":** HJ to Mary Ward, Sept. 22, 1898, Virginia; Horne, *Henry James: A Life in Letters*, p. 308. HJ to WJ, Aug. 9, [1899,] Houghton; 3 WJ Corresp., p. 78. WJ to HJ, Aug. 20, 1899, Houghton; 3 WJ Corresp., p. 82. HJ to WJ, Sept. 6, 1899, Houghton; 3 WJ Corresp., p. 85.

313 **"I confess I live":** HJ to Edmund Gosse, Aug. 19, 1899, Duke; HJ-Gosse Letters, p. 167. HJ to AHJ, Aug. 19, 1899, Houghton; *Dear Munificent Friends*, p. 36.

313 **"This miserable murderous war"**: HJ to Louisa Wolseley, Nov. 5, 1899, Hove; *Dear Munificent Friends*, p. 266.

314 **"There is something sinister"**: HJ to WJ, Nov. 1, 1899, Houghton; 3 WJ Corresp., p. 92.

314 **"The war drags"**: HJ to WJ, Feb. 10, 1900, Houghton; 3 WJ Corresp., p. 101.

314 **Ellen Terry called:** Benson Diary, Dec. 7, 1899.

314 **Alice still remembered:** I am indebted to Gunter, *A Vocation for Jameses*, for these details.

315 **"May these words"**: HJ to Hendrik Andersen, Dec. 22, 1899, Virginia; *Dearly Beloved Friends*, pp. 28–29.

315 **"This house is sadly shrunken"**: HJ to WJ, Jan. 15, 1900, Houghton; 3 WJ Corresp., p. 97.

316 **The hundredth year:** HJ to W. E. Norton, Nov. 24, 1899–Jan. 13, 1900, 1 Lubbock, p. 343. HJ to A. F. de Navarro, Dec. 29, 1900, 1 Lubbock, p. 369.

316 **"This dreadful gruesome New Year"**: HJ to Rhoda Broughton, Jan. 1, 1900, Chester; unpub.

316 **"I have met Mr. Yeats"**: HJ to Lady Gregory, Jan. 24, 1900, Berg; unpub. Almost certainly W. B. and not John Yeats. Lady Gregory Diaries, Jan. 24, 1900, p. 229.

317 **"[T]here is nothing cheerful"**: HJ to Mrs. Everard Cotes [Sara Jeannette Duncan], Jan. 26, 1900, 1 Lubbock, p. 348.

317 **"How I wish, dear"**: HJ to Margaret Brooke, n.d., from extract in Brooke Papers; unpub. Although undated, internal references suggest this letter was written in the winter of 1899–1900.

317 **James feared falling more gravely ill:** HJ to Sidney Colvin, Nov. 6, 1903, Fitzwilliam Museum; unpub.

318 **"H.J. works hard. . . . He seemed to know"**: Benson Diary, p. 40, Jan. 17, 1900; Hyde, *Henry James at Home*, pp. 110–111, Newsome, *On the Edge of Paradise*, pp. 91–92.

319 **Howard Sturgis would be:** HJ to Howard Sturgis, Mar. 4, 1900, Houghton; *Dearly Beloved Friends*, p. 126 (happily recalling Benson's suggestion).

319 **"You will stay over"**: HJ to Howard Sturgis, Feb. 9, [1900,] Houghton; unpub.

320 **"Your good letter"**: HJ to Howard Sturgis, Feb. 25, [1900,] Houghton; *Dearly Beloved Friends*, p. 124.

320 **"our so-happy little congress"**: HJ to Howard Sturgis, Mar. 4, 1900, Houghton; *Dearly Beloved Friends*, p. 125. The editors remind us that one of the commonly accepted meanings of "congress" is "coitus," ibid., p. 125, n.

320 **Sturgis would not:** Aside from practical considerations, Sturgis remained close to his old tutor A. C. Ainger in Windsor for the rest of their joint lives.

321 **He set aside:** HJ to WDH, Aug. 9, 1900, HJ-Howells Letters, p. 509.

321 **In one story . . . In another:** "The Tone of Time" and "Hugh Merrow," an unfinished, unpublished story Leon Edel found among James's papers, probably from September 1900. See Notebooks, Sept. 11, 1900, p. 304. James apparently planned "The Tone of Time" for *The Soft Side*, was put off briefly by Paul Bourget telling him that another author had such a story, and then set to work on it again when he learned in September that the topic was in fact free

for him to use; the other stories were "Maud-Evelyn," "Europe," and "The Third Person."

322　**"The wind . . . was often high":** HJ, "The Third Person," p. 258.

323　**he shaved his beard:** HJ to WJ, May 12, 1900, Houghton; 3 WJ Corresp., p. 119.

324　**Their presence in Lamb House:** HJ to Louisa Wolseley, June 6, 1900, Hove; unpub.

325　**Her mother and sisters:** HJ to Mary James [Vaux], Nov. 14, 1900, Vaux; unpub.

325　**He happily commissioned Bay:** HJ to WJ, July 18, 1900, Houghton; 3 WJ Corresp., p. 123.

325　**William soon had a new plan:** HJ to W. E. Norris, Sept. 26, 1900, 1 Lubbock, p. 361.

326　**James privately decided:** HJ to WJ, Nov. 17, 1900, Dec. 9, 1900; 3 WJ Corresp., pp. 145, 148–149.

326　**"This is brave news":** HJ to Hendrik Andersen, Nov. 3, 1900, Barrett; unpub.

326　**the unhappy time, thirty years earlier:** See Novick, *Henry James: The Young Master,* p. 238 ff.

326　**when James wrote to Louisa:** HJ to Louisa Wolseley, Dec. 30, 1900, Hove; unpub.

327　**His niece Mary:** HJ to Mary James [Vaux], Nov. 14, 1900, Vaux; unpub.

327　**The room faced south:** HJ to W. E. Norris, Dec. 23, 1900, 1 Lubbock, p. 367.

327　**In the quiet time:** Ibid., p. 366.

327　**"Here by the Xmas fireside":** HJ to Anthony de Navarro, Dec. 19, 1900, 1 Lubbock, p. 369.

Chapter 19: The Major Phase

328　**"It's a very dusky":** HJ to Hendrik Andersen, January 12, 1901, Barrett; unpub.

329　*Speriamo:* HJ to WJ, Jan. 24, 1901, Houghton; 3 WJ Corresp., p. 159.

330　**"This rather fatigued":** HJ, "Project of a Novel," Sept. 1, 1900, typescript, Morgan Library.

331　**"little artist man":** Du Maurier was very much in James's mind. In the English edition of *Trilby*, which James read, du Maurier portrayed his youthful friendship with James McNeill Whistler, illustrated it with a very recognizable caricature of Whistler, and named the character "Gloriano" after a shrewd, unscrupulous artist in James's early novel *Roderick Hudson*. Setting a scene in what had become Whistler's garden in Paris, James borrowed back the name and called the garden's owner "Gloriani."

331　**"generous and open-handed":** Du Maurier, *The Martian,* p. 2.

331　**mill town belongings:** The Boott family wealth was founded on woolen mills in Lowell, Massachusetts; George Smalley was the son of a Calvinist minister and grew up in Worcester, the model for the novel's "Woollett."

331　**"Chad raised his face":** Book Fourth, chapter 1, p. 170 (New York Edition).

332 "How could he wish": Book Seventh, chapter 1, p. 176.

332 "He felt, strangely": Book Eleventh, chapter 1, p. 282.

333 she was "a gem": HJ to WJ, May 27, 1901; 3 WJ Corresp., p. 172.

333 Years later, composing . . . "like a monotony": HJ, Prefaces, p. 1306.

336 "Not God, but life": W. James, The Varieties of Religious Experience, p. 497.

336 "Everywhere they ask": Josiah Royce to WJ, Feb. 7, 1900; Allen, William James, p. 412.

336 " 'Oh! oh! oh!' ": Quoted in Gunter, A Vocation for Jameses.

337 There was a sudden uproar: These events were reported to Montgomery Hyde by Noakes, long after the fact. A more nearly contemporary but characteristically garbled version is given by Ford, Portraits, pp. 2–3.

338 Noakes still remembered: Godden, A House with Four Rooms, p. 267. Godden, who had the story from Noakes, is unsure of the name of the dog and guesses that it was "Max," the name of the dog who followed Nick.

338 "I've had the rest": E. F. Benson, Final Edition, p. 5. This is James's account; Montgomery Hyde has Joan Paddington's version of the same story.

338 "What a sad": HJ to Hendrik Andersen, July 1, 1901, Barrett; Dearly Beloved Friends, p. 34.

338 "Now that you're": HJ to Hendrik Andersen, Oct. 5, 1901, Barrett; Dearly Beloved Friends, p. 37.

343 "It wasn't, in a word": HJ, The Wings of the Dove, p. 46.

343 She is an artist: Compare Mrs. Medwin (1901, reprinted in The Better Sort). Mamie Cutter sells her disreputable brother's affections to Lady Wantridge in exchange for an introduction to society for a wealthy client, Mrs. Medwin. This is a brilliant stroke, and Cutter congratulates herself, "I'm something of an artist"; p. 375.

344 "remarkably scrupulous efforts": Dimick, "Gender," p. 26, speaking of James's method generally, not of Wings in particular.

344 "the first and only prime": The Wings of the Dove, p. 173.

345 "My dear, dear, dearest": HJ to Hendrik Andersen, Feb. 9, 1902, Barrett; Dearly Beloved Friends, p. 37.

346 "Now, at last": HJ to Hendrik Andersen, Feb. 28, 1902, Barrett; Dearly Beloved Friends, pp. 39–40.

346 "Beloved Boy!": HJ to Hendrik Andersen, Mar. 19, 1902, Barrett; Dearly Beloved Friends, p. 40.

346 "Put it on your table": HJ to Hendrik Andersen, Nov. 15, 1902, Barrett; Dearly Beloved Friends, p. 42.

347 Arthur Benson confided: Benson Diary, vol. 19, p. 53; unpub.

347 "I have read the Wings": WJ to HJ, Oct. 25, 1902, Houghton; 3 WJ Corresp., 220.

348 "Apparently you have": WJ to HJ, Apr. 7, 1903, Houghton; 3 WJ Corresp., p. 229.

349 "Of men writing": A. T. Quiller-Couch, "Four Tales by Mr. Conrad," The Bookman, vol. xxiv (June 1903), p. 108.

349 The young Rupert Brooke: Hassall, Rupert Brooke, p. 71.

350 "There is scarcely an author": Bennett, The Journal of Arnold Bennett, Dec. 21, 1897, p. 70.

350 **Fletcher's prescription:** See Fletcher, *The A.B.–Z of Our Own Nutrition*, pp. 5, 11.

351 **"Try it, dearest":** HJ to Hendrik Andersen, Nov. 25, 1904, Barrett; *Dearly Beloved Friends*, p. 62.

352 **"The situation":** HJ, *The Golden Bowl* (first U.S. ed., 1904), pp. 413–415.

352 **"to grateful, to thirsty":** Ibid., p. 47.

353 **"quite at the top":** Ibid., p. 132.

353 **"Adam Verver had":** Ibid., pp. 200–201.

353 **"a Pope, a President":** Ibid., p. 209.

358 **"The beauty of the bloom":** HJ, *The Wings of the Dove* (first English edition, 1902), pp. 206–207.

CHAPTER 20: RETURN OF THE NATIVE

360 **He wrote more querulously:** HJ to WJ, May 24, 1903, Houghton; 3 WJ Corresp., p. 236.

361 **"One of the invaders":** HJ, "Covering End," *Complete Stories, 1892–1898*, p. 833.

363 **Early in 1903, Holmes:** Novick, *Honorable Justice*, p. 263. Holmes's pocket diary, HLS, shows that he called on Chamberlain, but it does not appear that he spoke with the prime minister.

363 **The letter said:** Thayer, *Theodore Roosevelt*, p. 176.

363 **"Hitherto peace has":** Theodore Roosevelt to Carl Schurz, Sept. 8, 1905, in Roosevelt, *Autobiography*, p. 560, under the heading "The Peace of Righteousness." Roosevelt is answering Schurz's call for reductions of armaments, but he quotes his own letter as expressing his more general view.

364 **Holmes was visibly:** OWH to Ellen Curtis, Mar. 21, 1903, HLS; Novick, *Honorable Justice*, p. 262. HJ to Frances R. Morse, Aug. 12, 1903, HLS; Novick, *Honorable Justice*, p. 263.

364 **"More than ever":** Henry Adams to HJ, Nov. 18, 1903, HJ-Adams Letters, pp. 59–60. Later commentary notwithstanding, American reviews of the book were excellent, and the Story family accepted the judgment of the reviewers. See HJ-Adams Letters, p. 63, n. 2; Taylor, *Henry James*, pp. 330–345.

365 **James replied hastily:** HJ to Henry Adams, Nov. 19, 1903, HJ-Adams Letters, p. 62.

365 **"Beloved Hendrik":** HJ to Hendrik Andersen, Dec. 3, 1903, Barrett; *Dearly Beloved Friends*, p. 45.

366 **Mary Cadwalader Jones:** With what was for him unusual informality, James addressed her as "Mary Cadwal."

366 **Wharton had tried:** Edith Wharton to Sara Norton, May 5, [1904,] Wharton, *The Letters of Edith Wharton*, p. 88.

366 **"He . . . talks, thank heaven":** Edith Wharton to William Cary Brownell, Jan. 7, 1904; Wharton, *The Letters of Edith Wharton*, p. 87.

366 **"The thing goes on":** HJ to Howard Sturgis, Nov. 8, 1903, Houghton; *Dearly Beloved Friends* p. 131. Sturgis explained the need to make the otherwise pathetic protagonist a good catch for his unscrupulous bride.

367 **"one feels, in general"**: HJ to Howard Sturgis, Nov. 18, Nov. 23, Dec. 2, 1903, Houghton; *Dearly Beloved Friends*, pp. 133–136.

368 **Sturgis maintained**: Benson Diary, vol. 51, openings 58–59, unpub., repeating Sturgis's account of the conversation, undated but apparently spring 1904.

368 **"I would write [another]"**: Sturgis to Edith Wharton, Dec. 5, 1905, in Goodman, *Edith Wharton's Inner Circle*, p. 81. For support of the trauma theory, see Borkland and Goodman.

368 **"The ordinary service"**: Holroyd, *Lytton Strachey*, pp. 218–219.

369 **he had burned**: HJ to Mrs. F. W. H. Myers, April 8, 1904, Myers; unpub.

369 **"Lastly, I take"**: HJ to Louise Horstmann, Aug. 12, 1904, *The Atlantic Monthly*, August 1946.

370 **Harper would book**: Arrangements for the lecture tour apparently were agreed upon at a dinner on April 10, 1904; HJ to George Harvey, April 9, 1904, LoC; unpub.

371 **"Henry James is on"**: Herbert Croly, "Henry James and His Countrymen," *The Lamp*, Feb. 1904; Dupee, ed., *The Question of Henry James*, p. 28.

371 **It was possible that Hendrik**: HJ to Hendrik Andersen, June 4, Aug. 10, 1904, Barrett; *Dearly Beloved Friends*, pp. 46–49.

372 **"I left L.H. yesterday"**: HJ to Louise Horstmann, August 19, 1904, *The Atlantic Monthly*, August 1946.

373 **Aleck's precocity**: HJ to Billy James, July 8, [1903,] (typescript copy), Edel Papers; unpub.

375 **"[It would] minister"**: HJ to RJ, Sept. 4, 1904, Vaux; 4 *HJL*, p. 320. HJ to RJ, Sept. 14, 1904, Vaux; unpub.

375 **New Hampshire evoked**: HJ, *The American Scene*, p. 13; Novick, *Henry James: The Young Master*, pp. 108–111, 120–123.

376 **his "prime initiation"**: HJ, *The American Scene*, pp. 227–229. HJ is speaking of his awakening to his own sexuality as well as to his first public successes; see Novick, *Young Master*, pp. 108–111.

377 **Their talk was anecdotal**: Wharton, *A Backward Glance*, p. 178.

377 **"while he hesitated"**: Lubbock, *Portrait of Edith Wharton*, p. 4.

378 **"On one of our happy"** . . . **"This mode of locomotion"**: Wharton, *A Backward Glance*, pp. 180, 177. "Moxie" is a soft drink still popular in northern New England.

378 **Miss Emerson**: Burr, *Alice James*, pp. 21–22.

379 **The only place**: HJ, *The American Scene*, pp. 222–225. The opening scenes of *The Ivory Tower* would be set in such "cottages."

379 **He was absorbing**: HJ to Edmund Gosse, Oct. 27, 1904, LoC; HJ-Gosse Letters, p. 210.

380 **"the 'sinister' "**: Notebooks, Dec. 11, 1904, p. 317.

380 **"To present these"**: Notebooks, March 29, 1905, pp. 320–321.

381 **a couplet from Dante**: James misremembered the inscription, which reads "ed essa da martiro e da essilio venne a questa pace," *Paradiso* 10:128. See WJ to HJ, Mar. 10, 1893, 2 WJ Corresp., p. 259.

381 **"But why do I write"**: Notebooks, March 29, 1905, p. 321.

381 **"door of importances"**: Notebooks, March 29, 1905, p. 319; the quoted pas-

sage is at *Notes of a Son and Brother*, p. 414; see Novick, *Young Master*, pp. 94 and 468, n.14.

381 **"The point for me"**: Notebooks, Mar. 29, 1905, pp. 319–320. As there has been some discussion of this passage since I first called attention to it in *Young Master*, p. 109, it is worth remarking here that in the novels written at this time, James uses the word "prime" to refer to a first young love, and the nature of the "initiation" recalled here can hardly be mistaken. The linking of these memories to Wendell Holmes is striking, and James will link them again and more explicitly later. *Young Master*, p. 472, n. 48.

382 **Newspapers**: See Taylor, *Henry James*, pp. 350–365, listing and summarizing dozens of notices.

383 **"At the last my Dentist-Dr."**: HJ to RJ, Dec. 22, 1904, Vaux; unpub.

383 **Later in the winter**: HJ to WJ, Feb. 9, 1905, Houghton; 3 WJ Corresp., p. 286. This is presumably *cascara sagrada*, the "sacred bark," still in wide use.

383 **"[F]or God's sake"**: HJ to Hendrik Andersen, Dec. 9, 1904, Barrett; *Dearly Beloved Friends*, p. 49.

Chapter 21: Americanism

387 **"No," James lectured**: HJ, *The American Scene*, pp. 159–161.

387 **"One may fall"**: Theodore Roosevelt, "True Americanism," *The Forum*, April 1894.

389 **"The machinery is colossal"**: HJ, *The American Scene*, p. 120

389 **personal impressions had unique value**: HJ, *The American Scene*, p. xxvi.

391 **In the long-ago**: See Novick, *Henry James: The Young Master*, pp. 68–71.

391 **[Balzac's] plan**: HJ, *The Question of our Speech, and the Lesson of Balzac*, pp. 86–87.

391 **"I can only speak of him"**: Ibid., pp. 67, 76–77, 84–85, 101–102.

392 **He was revealed**: James wrote to his brother in characteristically dramatic and lugubrious terms: "I really quite feel as if *je m'étais révélé conférencier* (to myself;) so sadly & strangely, in my old age, after having lived too long in a hole—& too late, too late! Such is the perversity of life! But I must see, yet." HJ to WJ, Jan. 14, 1905; 3 WJ Letters, pp. 279, 280.

392 **reception at the White House**: See HJ to Clara Stone Hay, Dec. 17, 1905, Brown; HJ-Hay Letters, p. 134. The dinner at the Hays' on January 10, 1905, has been overlooked by the numerous biographers of Hay, James, and Roosevelt.

393 **Hay had invited Henry James**: Henry Adams to Louise Hooper, Jan. 8, 1905; *The Letters of Henry Adams*, vol. 5, p. 625.

393 **Hay noted in his journal**: HJ-Hay Letters, p. 186, note to letter 49.

393 **As James recounted**: HJ to Jessie Allen, Jan. 16, 1905, Houghton; 4 *HJL*, p. 339.

393 **A reconciliation with Roosevelt**: The president's private opinion of James did not change, however. In later years, he said that Hay had been injured by the company of such men as Henry James and Henry Adams, "charming

men . . . of refined and cultivated tastes . . . [but] wholly lacking in robustness of fiber." TR to Henry Cabot Lodge, quoted in HJ-Hay Letters, pp. 4–5.

394 **"I think indeed":** HJ to John Hay, Sept. 13, 1904, Hay LoC; HJ-Hay Letters, p.133. "Moral" is inserted in parentheses after "pensioner," presumably to dispel any implication that James expected to be paid for his services.

394 **James wrote to Holmes:** HJ to OWH, Jan. 14, 1905, HLS; unpub.

394 **"Célimare":** Eugène Labiche, "Célimare le bien aimé" (1863).

394 **Railroads themselves:** HJ, *The American Scene*, pp. 27, 9, 44.

395 **To save time:** HJ to "Mary jr." and "Mamie" James, Feb. 1, 4, and 10, 1905, Vaux; unpub.

395 **"I guess we manage":** HJ, *The American Scene*, p. 423.

396 **"this (almost) coral strand":** HJ to Elizabeth Jordan, Feb. 17, 1905, NYPL; HJ-Jordan Letters.

396 **"a south without church-fronts":** HJ, *The American Scene*, p. 313.

396 **"My whole time":** HJ to WDH, Mar. 1, 1905, Houghton; HJ-Howells Letters, p. 410.

397 **"I accompanied him":** Herrick, "A Visit to Henry James," p. 723.

397 **"I reached this racketing":** HJ to George Higginson, Mar. 24, 1905, Berg; unpub.

398 **"We hit it off":** Bruce Porter to Katherine Hooker, April 16, 1905; Gunter, "Henry James," p. 8.

398 **"simply believe me":** HJ to Bruce Porter, May 15, 1911; Gunter, "Henry James," pp. 8–9.

399 **"next & swiftest":** HJ to George Higginson, April 17, 1905, Berg; unpub.

399 **"Henry James is here":** OWH to Nina Gray, April 30, 1905, OWH papers HLS 35–14; unpub.

399 **James was glad to be in Washington:** HJ to Louise Boit, Nov. 2, 1905; Louise Boit, "Henry James as Landlord," *The Atlantic Monthly*, August 1946.

399 **they dined on the first of May:** This second visit to Washington and the meeting of old friends, like the dinner with Hay, has been overlooked by scholars.

CHAPTER 22: WORK AND LIFE AS A WHOLE

401 **On his last visit:** HJ to Hamilton Aïdé, April 24, [1883,] Berg; unpub.

402 **"There is no swarming":** HJ, *The American Scene*, pp. 131, 133.

403 **"The alien himself":** Ibid., pp. 117–118, 325.

404 **Privacy and democracy:** See W. H. Auden, "Introduction," *The American Scene* (1946 ed.).

404 **A country club on the Hudson:** HJ, *The American Scene*, p. 327.

405 **Grant's Tomb:** Ibid., pp. 145–146.

406 **"Saint Augustine":** Ibid., pp. 457–459.

406 **The young women:** Ibid., pp. 451–456.

406 **a vast marketplace:** Ibid., pp. 234–238.

406 **Ellis Island:** Ibid., pp. 84–86.

408. **He imagined himself:** Ibid., p. 85. In "The Jolly Corner" James imagines himself into the place of the intruder: a Europeanized expatriate returning to his own old house in New York, where he encounters a violent, manly apparition—the ghost of the American owner.

408   **his "younger and vainer" brother:** William was writing to people he knew well, and everyone concerned at the time seems to have understood this as a characteristic joke, as it was probably intended, but some later biographers have taken it for a sign of buried sibling rivalry. The correspondence and later commentary, and the sparse records of these early meetings, are in the files of the Academy in New York.

409   **an admiring assessment:** Cary, *The Novels of Henry James*, p. 13 (emphasis in original), p. 1.

410   **James's works of fiction as a single whole:** Howells to HJ, Aug. 2, 1908, Houghton; HJ-Howells Corresp., p. 423.

410   **"The Lesson of Balzac":** Leon Edel emphasized that Balzac's edition and James's both appeared in a set of twenty-three volumes, but, as Michael Anesko later demonstrated, the size and division of James's edition into volumes was chosen by the publisher, not by James. See Anesko, "Friction with the Market," pp. 141–162. Edel's error should not obscure the correctness of his perception that Balzac was likely an influence.

411   **"like [the archangel] Michael":** HJ to Edith Wharton, June 7, 1905, HJ-Wharton Corresp., p. 50.

412   **he wrote a new speech:** "The Question of Our Speech." The talk was published in *Appleton's Booklovers Magazine* in August. The frugal James gave "The Lesson of Balzac" to *The Atlantic Monthly*, and the two speeches were published in a slim volume that fall by Houghton, Mifflin. The longer essay that developed from the germ of the Bryn Mawr address appeared in *Harper's Bazar* from November 1906 to February 1907 but was not collected in book form until 1973 as *The Speech and Manners of American Women* (E. S. Rigs, ed.). Both versions are now long out of print. Quotations given in the text are from the 1905 Houghton, Mifflin text, p. 10.

414   ***The Gods and the Golden Bowl:*** Saint-Gaudens' estate, Aspet, is now a national park, and in the summer of 2005, the play was revived on its centenary. Dr. Henry Duffy, curator, traced the references to Henry James and found a local newspaper story reporting his presence at the performance. The text of the play, showing the late emendations, is in the archive of the museum there.

CHAPTER 23: SOME FAREWELLS

419   **"I shall be back":** HJ to Hendrik Andersen, May 11, 1905, Barrett; *Dearly Beloved Friends*, p. 51.

419   **"I sail to-morrow":** HJ to Hendrik Andersen, [July 3, 1905,] Barrett; unpub.

419   **To Mary James:** HJ to Mary James, July 3, 1905, Vaux; unpub.

420   **He owed his travel:** HJ to Arthur Benson, [May ?,] 1906; extract, June 1, 1906, Benson Diary, vol. 86, n.p.

420   **As he told Elizabeth Robins:** Robins, *Theatre and Friendship*, pp. 256–257.

420   **He described this last:** Gosse, *Aspects*, p. 46. Gosse places this conversation in November 1905 and calls the book a "novel," but the Macmillan series were nonfiction.

422   **He would particularly recall:** HJ to Rhoda Broughton, Dec. 21, 1906, Chester; unpub.

423   **"He stood upon the deck":** Crothers, "Henry James," in *The Later Years of the Saturday Club*, (E. Emerson, ed.) p. 385.

423   **"He felt it":** Harry James to Percy Lubbock, May 20, 1919, Gosse papers, Leeds; unpub. See also HJ to Bruce Porter, Feb. 19, 1907; 2 Lubbock, p. 65.

423   **To emphasize the character:** HJ to Charles Scribner's Sons, May 12, 1906; Horne, p. 432. HJ to Robert Herrick, Aug. 7, 1905, 4 *HJL*, p. 370. Martha Banta has discussed the New York Edition as a self-portrait; see "The Excluded Seven," in McWhirter, ed., *Henry James's New York Edition*, p. 240. See also Nussbaum's discussion in *Love's Knowledge*.

423   **He began:** *Watch and Ward* had in truth been the first.

424   **He told Gosse:** Gosse, *Aspects and Impressions*, pp. 17–18.

425   **"Athenaeum (not 'Ethenaeum')":** HJ to Jocelyn Persse, n.d.; *Dearly Beloved Friends*, p. 85.

425   **"Of course I have had":** HJ to Hendrik Andersen, May 31, Aug. 22, 1906, Barrett; unpub.; Nov. 25, 1906, Barrett; *Dearly Beloved Friends*, p. 60.

426   **"I am laying":** Ibid.

426   **"Dear, dear Hendrik":** Ibid.

427   **Hamilton Aïdè died:** HJ to Rhoda Broughton, Dec. 21, 1906, Chester; unpub.

427   **"I totter toward":** HJ to T. S. Perry, Oct. 22, 1906, HJ-Perry Letters, p. 321.

427   **He wrote to Mamie:** HJ to Mary Walsh James, Dec. 13, 1906, Vaux; unpub.

429   **The French "have nothing":** HJ to WJ, April 30, 1907, Houghton; 3 WJ Corresp., pp. 335–336.

429   **"Our friend":** HJ to Howard Sturgis, March 20, 1907, Houghton; *Dearly Beloved Friends*, p. 146.

429   **"This is a wondrous" . . . "My three weeks":** HJ to Willy James, "Easter Day," 1907, Berg; unpub. HJ to Howard Sturgis, April 13, 1907, 2 Lubbock, p. 80.

429   **From rue de Varenne:** HJ to Hendrik Andersen, April 3, 1907, Barrett; unpub.

430   **He was infuriated:** See, e.g., HJ to WJ, May 31, 1907, Houghton; 3 WJ Corresp., p. 341. In 1946, Scribner's reissued the British edition of *The American Scene* with the invaluable page headings and an introduction by W. H. Auden.

431   **The completed portrait:** The portrait is now at Lamb House, on a pedestal said to bring the head to James's height. Lucia took photographs of James and Andersen during and after the sittings; HJ to Hendrik Andersen, July 18, 1907, Barrett; unpub.; the photos are in the Museo Hendrik Christian Andersen in Rome.

431   **On his last night in Rome:** HJ to Hendrik Andersen, July 18, 1907, Barrett; *Dearly Beloved Friends*, p. 63. The quoted passage is from HJ, *Italian Hours*, p. 227.

CHAPTER 24: CELEBRITY

433 **"We sat in armchairs":** Bosanquet, *Henry James at Work*, p. 4.

434 **"It is thus":** HJ to Edmund Gosse, Aug. 7, 1907, Berg; HJ-Gosse Letters, p. 127 (with slight inaccuracies). "Poncif" is a hackneyed or stereotyped work.

434 **James suggested a dark patina:** HJ to Hendrik Andersen, Jan. 24, 1908, Barrett; *Dearly Beloved Friends*, p. 64.

434 **"literally in pieces":** HJ to Edith Wharton, Aug. 11 [and 12], 1907, HJ-Wharton Letters, p. 72.

434 **"We can't *all* be":** HJ to Edmund Gosse, Aug. 7, 1907, Berg; HJ-Gosse Letters, p. 127 (from inaccurate Lubbock typescript).

435 **"We fell to discussing":** Sir Sydney Waterlow Diary, Nov. 3 and 9, 1907, Jan. 31, 1908, Berg; quoted in part in Hyde, *Henry James at Home*, pp. 122, 125–126.

435 **"E. M. Forster":** Waterlow Diary, Jan. 16, 1908, Berg; Forster's diary, Jan. 24, 1908, from extract in Edel Papers.

436 **For this latter drawing:** Behrman, *Portrait of Max*, p. 245.

436 **"Say, indefatigable alchemist":** Gosse Papers, Leeds, unpub. The "twisted" right upper lip, visible in some portraits, may be the result of early dental work and probably accounts for James's insistence on being photographed and painted in left profile.

436 **William wrote:** WJ to HJ, Dec. 6, 1907, Houghton; 3 WJ Corresp., pp. 346, 344.

437 **"Erect and slender":** HJ, "Covering End," p. 755.

438 **To Sydney Waterlow:** Sir Sydney Waterlow Diary, Jan. 31, 1908; quoted in part in Hyde, *Henry James at Home*, p. 125.

439 **"for which the ages":** HJ, "The High Bid," pp. 573, 574, 581.

444 **"she is a scrap":** HJ to Edith Wharton, March [22,] 1908; HJ-Wharton Letters, p. 95; *Complete Plays*, pp. 551–552.

444 **"the journey from Manchester":** HJ to Edith Wharton, March [22,] 1908, HJ-Wharton Letters, p. 95.

445 **"a real and unmistakable":** HJ to Harry James, April 3, 1908, 2 Lubbock, pp. 96–97.

445 **"I am building a little":** HJ to W. D. Howells, March 10, 1908, Houghton; HJ-Howells Letters, p. 422.

445 **"My books absolutely decline":** HJ to W. D. Howells, March 10, 1908, Houghton; HJ-Howells Letters, p. 422.

445 **[*The High Bid*]:** HJ to Edmund Gosse, April 6, 1908, HJ-Gosse Letters, p. 236.

446 **"with our dear H.J.":** Quoted in Lewis, *Wharton*, p. 219. The late R. W. B. Lewis and Millicent Bell had dueling accounts of this period. Bell is probably right to identify Walter Berry as the subject of some journal entries in which Wharton spoke of both love and intellectual companionship, but Lewis was correct, having the benefit of Wharton's letters to Fullerton, in saying that she and Fullerton had an affair at this time. Neither of them mentioned that Berry was thought to have been homosexual and was dividing his time between Wharton and James.

447 **Blanche made no reply:** Now in the (U.S.) National Portrait Gallery. Wharton called it the best likeness of James.

447 **"an old & very amiable":** HJ to Lilla Perry, April 29, 1908; Colby, unpub. HJ to T. S. Perry, May 20, 1908, Colby; Gardner, "An Apology," p. 326.

447 **In this final essay:** Preface, *The Novels and Tales of Henry James* (New York Edition), vol. 23, *The Golden Bowl*, pp. v–vi.

448 **"a sudden large apprehension":** 23 New York Edition, p. xiv.

448 **"The seer and speaker":** Ibid., p. xviii.

449 **an episode of angina:** Bosanquet's diary records the "heart trouble" on January 17; on January 19 James is "better" but still not working in the mornings.

449 **William had been taking:** WJ to HJ, Dec. 8, 1908, Houghton; 3 WJ Corresp., p. 372.

449 **With the aid of Dr. Skinner's:** HJ to WJ, Feb. 5, 1909, Houghton; 3 WJ Corresp., p. 379–380.

449 **"I am definitely better":** HJ to RJ, Oct. 14, 1909, Vaux; unpub.

450 **"I *have* had":** HJ to Edith Wharton, April 19, 1909, 2 Lubbock, pp. 123–124. See also HJ-Wharton Letters, p. 110. Both Lubbock and Lewis have "serpent-trail" instead of "serpent-tail" for the heart attack that climaxed James's thoracic symptoms.

450 **"Both times exceedingly":** Holroyd, *Lytton Strachey*, p. 397.

451 **A friend gently gibed:** Hassall, *Rupert Brooke*, 277.

451 **Forbes-Robertson later claimed:** The plan to produce only a matinee version of *The High Bid* was announced in June, long before the Jerome play was performed. See "Drama," *The Nation*, June 18, 1908.

452 **"Of all that I love":** HJ, "The High Bid," *The Saturday Review*, Feb. 27, 1909.

453 **"Dined with Henry James":** Hart-Davis, *Hugh Walpole*, p. 68

453 **"He makes friends":** Newsome, *On the Edge of Paradise*, p. 231.

453 **"a wonderful weekend":** Hart-Davis, *Hugh Walpole*, p. 68; HJ to A. C. Benson, June 5, 1909, 2 Lubbock, pp. 125–126.

453 **"[T]hat is a quite perfect":** Sir Sydney Walpole Diary, July 6, 1909; *Dearly Beloved Friends*, p. 179.

453 **Benson confided:** Aug. 27, 1909, Benson Diary, vol. 106, opening 84, unpub.

454 **"I am spending a dark":** HJ to A. C. Benson, June 5, 1909, 2 Lubbock, p. 127.

454 **" 'Très-chèr Maître' ":** HJ to Hugh Walpole, April 27, 1909, Austin; *Dearly Beloved Friends*, p. 186.

454 **Robinson Crusoe and his man:** HJ to Hugh Walpole, Oct. 23, 1909, Austin; *Dearly Beloved Friends*, p. 193.

454 **"I loved him":** Hugh Walpole, *The Apple Trees*, pp. 52–53; *Dearly Beloved Friends*, p. 176.

454 **"Just a fond word":** HJ to Hugh Walpole, Oct. 14, 1909, Austin; *Dearly Beloved Friends*, p. 192.

454 **"Most blissful time":** Walpole Diary, Oct. 23, 1909, Austin; *Dearly Beloved Friends*, p. 193.

455 **"I abominably miss you":** HJ to Hugh Walpole, Oct. 23, 1909, Austin; *Dearly Beloved Friends*, p. 193.

455 **Gaillard Lapsley remarked:** Benson Diary, Dec. 27, 1909, vol. 108, opening 55.

455 "Does that sort": Bell, *Edith Wharton and Henry James*, p. 152.

456 "I am deeply distressed": HJ to Edith Wharton, Oct. 13, 1908, HJ-Wharton Letters, p. 101.

456 Wharton apparently provided: Edith Wharton to Morton Fullerton, [July 1909?]; Wharton, *Letters of Edith Wharton*, p. 184. Wharton says the advance will be a thousand pounds, which has been taken as an error but is more likely her supplement to what Macmillan (and James) could offer.

457 "It is just a month": Edith Wharton to Morton Fullerton, August 12, 1909; Wharton, *Letters of Edith Wharton*, p. 189.

457 Wharton's complex affairs: The complex relations among Wharton, Berry, Fullerton, and others of Wharton's followers have been the subject of much gleeful conjecture. See Bell, pp. 150–162; Lewis, *Edith Wharton*, pp. 248–262; Wharton, *Letters of Edith Wharton*, pp. 160–189; HJ-Edith Wharton Letters, pp. 104–116.

457 "I thought [it] so portentous": HJ to Herbert Gilchrist, Sept. 7, 1913, Berg; unpub. Otto Weininger's *Geschlecht und Charakter* (Vienna: Braumüller Verlag, 1903) was published by Heinemann as *Sex and Character* (1906), the edition that James presumably read.

458 Buchan . . . recalled: John Buchan, *Memory Hold-the-Door*, quoted in Notebooks (Matthiessen ed.), p. 181, n. The material James must have seen, in which Byron appears to be abusing his wife with open display of his incestuous adultery, is quoted and reproduced in Mayne, *The Life and Letters of Anna Isabella, Lady Byron*.

458 "The Edition has played": HJ to Frederick Macmillan, Mar. 17, 1909, HJ-Macmillan Corresp., p. 217.

459 An Irish poet: Edward Garnett, "Drama," *The Nation*, Aug. 5, 1909.

460 a forceful written statement: HJ, "Statement to the Commission, August 12, 1909," *Collected Plays*, p. 762.

461 a British royal: The character of the "Prince" is presumably meant as a compliment to Edward VII, who could not be named directly.

Chapter 25: Evening Solitude

463 "I have made": HJ to Annie Fields, Jan. 2, 1910; 4 *HJL*, p. 541.

464 "solitudinous": HJ to RJ, Oct. 14, 1909, Vaux; unpub.

464 "heart crisis": HJ to RJ, Oct. 14, 1909, Vaux; unpub. HJ to WJ, Oct. 31, 1909, Houghton; 3 WJ Corresp., p. 403.

464 "I have now spent": HJ to Laura Wagnière, Dec. 22, 1909, 2 Lubbock, pp. 144, 145–146.

464 her "lady-pal": HJ to Edith Wharton, Dec. 13, 1909, HJ-Wharton Letters, p. 130.

464 To Margaret Brooke: HJ to Margaret Brooke, Dec. 27, 1909, Brooke Papers; unpub.

464 "Dearest Hendrik": HJ to Hendrik Andersen, "New Year's Night," 1910, Barrett; *Dearly Beloved Friends*, p. 68.

465　He turned to his notebooks: Notebooks, Jan. 4, 1910, p. 347. The putative novel had the working title "Mrs. Max," but James never got past making notes for it. When he had finally abandoned it, he used the names he had given some of the characters for his long-delayed American novel, *The Ivory Tower*. The recycled names have led some commentators to say that James began *The Ivory Tower* at this time, but there is no other similarity between the two.

465　"I struggled": HJ to WJ, Feb. 8, 1910, Houghton; 3 WJ Corresp., p. 410.

466　"Dearest Ones": HJ to WJ and AHJ, Mar. 4, 1910, Houghton; 3 WJ Corresp., pp. 413–414.

467　The physician invited: HJ to WJ, Mar. 15, [1910,] Houghton; 3 WJ Corresp., p. 416.

467　"a hard battle": HJ to WJ and AHJ, Apr. 4, 1910, Houghton; 3 WJ Corresp., p. 419.

467　Edith Wharton: Gunter, *A Vocation for Jameses*, [pp. 511–512].

468　At first, Alice felt: AHJ's unpublished letters to her children are summarized in Gunter, *A Vocation for Jameses*.

469　"A very distressing": Benson Diary, [May?] 1910.

469　"will be an alteration": William James, *Pragmatism*, p. 123.

469　"To any one": Ibid., p. 95.

471　"Paradoxically, it is Henry": A. J. Ayer, "Introduction," in William James, *Pragmatism and the Meaning of Truth*, p. ix.

471　Despite his depression: Notebooks (Edel ed.), June 1910, p. 603.

471　Henry, she thought: AHJ to Eliza Gibbens, June 14, 1910, private collection; unpub., quoted in Gunter, *A Vocation for Jameses*.

471　"He just passed": Margaret Mary James to AHJ, July 9, 1910, Bancroft; Gunter, *A Vocation for Jameses*.

472　"My dear Mary": HJ to MHJ, July 9, 1910, Vaux; unpub.

473　"I open my letter": HJ to Mary James Vaux, August 26, 1910, Vaux; unpub.

473　"H. James at William's": OWH to Alice S. Green, Sept. 4, 1910, HLS; unpub. When he was quarreling with William or Henry, Holmes liked to refer to their supposed Irish race, prejudice against the Irish in Boston still being fashionable, as anti-Semitism would soon be. The "difference of emphasis" likely refers to sexual orientation.

473　"My dear Wendell": HJ to OWH, Sept. 14, 1910, HLS; HJ-OWH Letters, p. 429.

474　James went to New York: HJ to Mrs. La Rose, Jan. 12, 1911, Colby; unpub.

475　He luxuriated: See, e.g., HJ to Clayton Hamilton, Jan. 29, 1911, Berg; unpub.

475　To Rhoda Broughton: HJ to Rhoda Broughton, Feb. 25, 1911, Chester; 2 Lubbock, pp. 178–179, with slight changes.

475　"Mr. James was full": Jerome D. Greene to Herbert S. Gasser, Feb. 20, 1948, Rockefeller University Archive, unpub. Greene dates the visit in 1912, but James was in New York only once, in 1911, after the hospital was built.

475　Greene took James and Godkin: Peyton Rous to Herbert S. Gasser, Apr. 1, 1948, Rockefeller University Archive, unpub.

476 "I am really not where": HJ to Margaret [Clifford,] May 27, 1911, Berg; unpub.

477 "Commerce has outsoared": Holmes likely read *The American Scene*, with its references to their early friendship, but it was Fanny who suggested using this image. Novick, *Honorable Justice*, p. 304.

477 "It was with a pang": HJ to OWH, July 16, 1911, HLS; HJ-Holmes Letters, pp. 430–431.

478 "Decidedly, I'm a better": Edith Wharton to W. Morton Fullerton, July 3, [1911,] Wharton Letters, p. 242.

479 When he read Whitman: Wharton, *A Backward Glance*, pp. 184–186.

480 "One can but stretch": HJ to Gertrude Abbey, August 1911; Lucas, *Edwin Austin Abbey*, p. 491.

480 Hendrik Andersen had been: HJ to Hendrik Andersen, Sept. 4, 1911, Barrett; *Dearly Beloved Friends*, p. 70; Jan. 2, 1912, Barrett; unpub.

481 She invited James: HJ to Edith Wharton, Sept. 27, 1911, HJ-Wharton Letters, p. 192.

482 His "little old house": HJ to Miss Betham-Edwards, Jan. 5, 1912, BL; unpub.

483 "A quiet room": Bosanquet, "Henry James: Notes for a Talk at St. Anne's House, May 31, 1954," Houghton; unpub.

483 The Albert Bridge: See Bosanquet, *Henry James at Work*, pp. 11, 23.

483 "the massive head": Ezra Pound, "A Brief Note," in McWhirter, *Henry James's New York Edition*, p. 27.

484 "in isolated eldest superiority": HJ to RJ, Oct. 14, 1909, Vaux; unpub.

485 "But the Avenue": Ibid., p. 332.

485 He was overjoyed: HJ to Harry James, [February?] 1912, transcript of excerpt, Rockefeller University Archive; unpub.

485 Seated on a hard chair: Woolf, *Roger Fry*, p. 180. See also Waterlow Diary, Jan. 16, 1912. There were two Postimpressionist shows at the gallery that year, the first in January and the second, which sent many paintings to the famous Armory Show in New York, in October–December, but James was ill and in bed in Rye during the second show.

486 "Your mania": HJ to Hendrik Andersen, April 14, 1912, Barrett; *Dearly Beloved Friends*, pp. 71–72.

486 "You see, dearest": HJ to Hendrik Andersen, Nov. 28, 1912, Barrett; *Dearly Beloved Friends*, p. 73.

486 As Waterlow put it: Waterlow Diary, Nov. 29, 1911, Berg; Hyde, *Henry James at Home*, p. 128.

487 James wrote to Wells: HJ to HG Wells, Oct. 18, 1912, HJ-Wells Letters, p. 165.

487 "Oh, Mr. James": Waterlow Diary, Mar. 8, 1912, Berg; unpub.

488 "I have known": Wharton, *A Backward Glance*, p. 236.

489 "Are you any relation": Hyde, *Henry James at Home*, p. 230.

489 "I came to town": HJ to Rhoda Broughton, Dec. 12, 1912, Chester; unpub.

490 "But life will": HJ to Margaret Brooke, Nov. 11, [1912?,] Brooke Papers; unpub.

CHAPTER 26: WITHIN THE RIM

491 *A Big Boy:* HJ to Harry James, Sept. 23–24, 1912, 4 *HJL*, p. 795.

491 **They continued:** "February 1913," Waterlow Diary, Berg; unpub.

492 **"I am crawling":** HJ to Walter Berry (dictated), Oct. 7, 1912, HJ-Berry Letters, letter 11.

492 **"What is a poor man":** HJ to Walter Berry (dictated), Feb. 8, 1912, HJ-Berry Letters, letter 10.

493 **Bed rest and digitalis:** HJ to Ethel Harrison, June 4, 1915, Austin; unpub.

493 **"Yes, I have been silent":** HJ to Hendrik Andersen, March 5, 1913, Barrett; *Dearly Beloved Friends,* p. 74.

493 **"Alas, . . . my travel-power":** Ibid., March 15, 1913, Barrett; *Dearly Beloved Friends,* p. 75.

494 **"You see my capital":** HJ to AHJ, April 1, 1913, 2 Lubbock, p. 306.

494 **negotiations with Scribner's:** James and Wharton apparently talked about his plans for work during his visit in 1912, and while Wharton urged him to begin work on his American novel, he continued to speak of potboilers like *The Outcry* and the projected Venetian serial for Harper. This conversation apparently led to Wharton's intervention at Scribner's, their joint publisher. Lewis, *Edith Wharton,* p. 342 (but with a garbled account of James's work in progress).

494 **If James were willing:** Charles Scribner to HJ, Sept. 27, 1912; 4 *HJL*, p. 789. Edith Wharton supplied the funds, as in the maneuver devised for Fullerton. Lewis, *Edith Wharton,* p. 342.

495 **He gave the editors:** HJ to the editor of *The Bookman,* Jan. 9, 1913, Berg; unpub.

495 **The burgeoning new fiction:** "The Younger Generation," *The Times Literary Supplement,* Mar. 19 and Apr. 2, 1914. A revised version was published as "The New Novel" in HJ, *Notes on Novelists* (1914).

496 **James's "influence":** *The New York Times,* March 22, 1914; Taylor, *Henry James,* p. 460.

497 **Percy Lubbock managed:** The preparations are described in letters from Lubbock to Gosse, April 11–16, 1913, Gosse Papers, Leeds; unpub.

497 **Harry accordingly wrote:** The often-quoted letters and telegrams for this period are in 4 *HJL.*

497 **written by Percy Lubbock:** Percy Lubbock to Edmund Gosse, April 11, 1913, Gosse Papers, Leeds; unpub.

498 **Lubbock reported afterward:** Percy Lubbock to Edmund Gosse, April 16, 1913, Gosse Papers, Leeds; unpub.

498 **"Darling, darling Howard!":** HJ to Howard Sturgis, April 15, 1913, Houghton; *Dearly Beloved Friends,* p. 168.

498 **Dear Friends All:** "To the Friends of Henry James," printed, Houghton; 2 Lubbock, p. 311; 4 *HJL*, p. 664.

499 **"Sargent at his":** HJ to Rhoda Broughton, June 26, 1913, Chester; unpub.

500 **"Dear Charles de Kay":** HJ to Charles de Kay, June 12, 1913 (typescript copy), Austin; unpub.

500 **As he lost consciousness:** HJ to Edmund Gosse, Aug. 11, 1913, Leeds; HJ-Gosse Letters, p. 287.

501 **"He swears that":** Margaret Mary James to AHJ, Aug. 1, 1913, Bruce Porter Papers, Bancroft (courtesy of Susan Gunter); unpub.

502 **"cohabitation is under":** HJ to Howard Sturgis, Sept. 7, 1913, Houghton; unpub.

502 **"Don't say to me":** HJ to Hugh Walpole, Aug. 21, 1913, Austin; *Dearly Beloved Friends*, p. 220.

505 **"[W]hy *should* I":** HJ to Howard Sturgis, Aug. 4–5, 1914, Houghton; 2 Lubbock, p. 382. The printed version has slight alterations from the original. I have corrected the spelling of "bear."

506 **"Black & hideous":** HJ to Rhoda Broughton, Aug. 10, 1914, Chester; 4 *HJL*, 713.

506 **In "the most beautiful":** HJ "Within the Rim," *Henry James on Culture*, p. 179.

508 **"a world squeezed":** Ibid., p. 183.

509 **"All I want":** HJ, "Henry James's First Interview," *Henry James on Culture*, p. 138. (James had in fact given interviews during his tour of America.)

510 **"We were so unthinkably":** HJ to Tom Perry, Jan. 15, 1915, Colby; Harlow, *Thomas Sargeant Perry*, p. 347.

510 **"Dearest Master":** Hugh Walpole to HJ, Sept. 9, 1914, Austin; unpub.

510 **"How can anyone":** HJ to Jocelyn Persse, Nov. 4, [1914,] Houghton; *Dearly Beloved Friends*, p. 111.

510 **"I lunched yesterday":** HJ to Tom Perry, Mar. 26, 1915, Colby; 2 Lubbock, p. 459.

511 **She lent him:** HJ to Margot Asquith, Apr. 9, 1915; 4 *HJL*, p. 748.

511 **Brooke had also just:** HJ, "The Long Wards," in Walker, *Henry James on Culture*, p. 173.

511 **Percy Lubbock recalled:** 2 Lubbock, p. xxxi.

511 **"He tells me":** W. E. Norris to Edmund Gosse, Jan. 1, 1915, Leeds; unpub.

512 **Wendell Holmes:** See Novick, *Henry James: The Young Master*, p. 472, n. 48.

512 **James "looked worn":** Benson Diary, Apr. 12, 1915, vol. 152; Lubbock, p. 280.

512 **Mrs. Gosse cried out:** Benson Diary, Apr. 21, 1915, vol. 152; unpub.

512 **Wells portrayed James:** Wells, *Boon*, pp. 99–101.

512 **"My dear James":** H. G. Wells to HJ, July 8, 1915, Bodleian; HJ-Wells Letters, p. 263.

513 **James began his reply:** HJ to HG Wells, July 10, 1915, Bodleian; HJ-Wells Letters, p. 267.

513 **"I don't clearly understand":** 2 Lubbock, p. 488.

513 **condolence letters:** HJ to Mrs. Harrison, June 4, 1915, Austin; unpub. HJ to Clare Sheridan, 4 *HJL*, p. 755.

513 **James heard reports:** HJ, "James's First Interview," *Henry James on Culture*, p. 144.

514 **"who seems to be":** HJ to Elizabeth Norton, Jan. 25, 1915, 2 Lubbock, p. 441.

514 **James could barely:** See, e.g., HJ to Lilla Perry, June 17, 1915, Colby; 4 *HJL*, p. 758.

515 **"The force of the public":** HJ to Edmund Gosse, June 25, 1915, Leeds; HJ-Gosse Letters, pp. 307–308; Charteris, *The Life and Times of Sir Gosse*, p. 382.

515 **"I find my wish":** HJ to Herbert Asquith, June 28, 1915, Bodleian; Mont-

gomery, *Henry James at Home*, p. 265. James speaks throughout this process of "England" rather than Great Britain, but it was not unusual to speak this way at the time.

515   **On July 28:** See, e.g., *The New York Times*, July 28, 1915; see also Horne, p. 556.

515   **In letters:** HJ to Edmund Gosse, July 9, 1915, Leeds; HJ-Gosse Letters, p. 310. HJ to J. S. Sargent, July 30, 1915; Horne, *Henry James: A Life in Letters*, p. 550; HJ to Lilla Perry, Sept. 17, 1915, Colby; unpub.

516   **"The 'Americans' ":** Ezra Pound, "A Brief Note," in McWhirter, ed., *Henry James's New York Edition*, pp. 27–30.

517   **trusting that Harry would:** See the correspondence between them in 4 *HJL*, Appendix IV.

517   **In London . . . heart crisis:** HJ to Rhoda Broughton, Nov. 3, 1915, Chester; unpub.

518   **"I write in case":** J. S. Sargent to Edmund Gosse, Dec. 4, 1915, Leeds; unpub.

518   **"I find the business":** "Bosanquet Diary Notes" (see the Epilogue), Dec. 8, 1915, Houghton; 4 *HJL*, Appendix V.

519   **He spoke to her clearly:** Theodora Bosanquet to Eric S. Pinker, July 6, 1925, Houghton; unpub.

519   **"They pluck in their terror":** Bosanquet, transcript of "Final Dictation," Dec. 11, 1915, Houghton; 4 *HJL*, p. 810.

519   **"astounding little stepchild":** Ibid. Bosanquet first typed "Astounding little stepchild of God's astounding young stepmother," which does not make sense. In her transcript of the dictation she notes " 'gods' more probable." The published text in *HJL* does not include the suggested correction.

520   **"The Bonapartes":** Bosanquet, transcript of "Final Dictation," December 12, 1915, Houghton; unpub.

520   **The first he signs:** It is not clear whether the spelling "Napoleone" is James's or Bosanquet's. James may have been influenced by Primoli's pronunciation. ("Napoleone" was one of his names.) Confusingly, in the published version, Edel added an accent to the spelling of "Napoléone" and remarked that this was the original Corsican spelling, but the accent is not present in the surviving Bosanquet typescripts.

521   **Dear Mr. Gosse:** AHJ to Edmund Gosse, February 11, 1916, Leeds; unpub.

521   **"In one of his vivid":** AHJ to Edmund Gosse, Mar. 4, 1916, Leeds; unpub.

BIBLIOGRAPHY

WORKS BY HENRY JAMES

Henry James's letters and notebooks are cited in abbreviated form; full citations are given at the head of the endnotes. As to James's published work, the Library of America is very slowly republishing all or most of it, and where these volumes are available I have cited to them, with exceptions noted below. Library of America volumes are published by Literary Classics of the United States, 14 East 60th Street, New York, and distributed in the United States by Penguin. The Library of America volumes are far from complete at this writing, however. The late novels, those published after 1899, have not yet appeared, and many of James's essays, and his biography of Story, are still missing.

James's novels and stories appeared in more than one version during his lifetime, and many remain in print in more than one edition. Where James's work in progress is described, I have cited the text closest to the one on which James was working at the time. *The American Scene* is cited to the first British edition, which has been reproduced by the Library of America, and by Charles Scribner's Sons in a 1946 edition with a valuable preface by W. H. Auden. Other editions of James's works cited are as follows (citations to magazine articles given in full in the notes are not repeated here):

The Ambassadors. London: Penguin Books, 1987 (first pub. Methuen, 1903).

Complete Plays: Leon Edel, ed., *The Complete Plays of Henry James.* New York: Oxford University Press, 1990.

Complete Stories 1864–1910. New York: Library of America, 1996–1999 (six volumes).

The Golden Bowl. New York: Charles Scribner's Sons, 1904 (Book of the Month Club facsimile ed. 2000).

Guy Domville: Henry James, *Guy Domville: A Play in Three Acts.* (Leon Edel, ed.) London: Rupert Hart-Davis, 1961.

Henry James on Culture: Pierre A. Walker, ed., *Henry James on Culture: Collected Essays on Politics and the American Social Scene.* Lincoln: University of Nebraska Press, 1999.

Ivory Tower: The Ivory Tower, in F. O. Matthiessen, ed., *The American Novels and Stories of Henry James.* New York: Alfred A. Knopf, 1947.

Lesson of Balzac: Henry James, *The Question of Our Speech, The Lesson of Balzac: Two Lectures.* Boston: Houghton, Mifflin and Company, 1905.

LoA: Library of America.

"London," in Henry James, *English Hours* (illustrations by Joseph Pennell). Boston: Houghton, Mifflin and Company, 1905.

"The Married Son," in Henry James, et al., *The Whole Family: A Novel by Twelve Authors*. New York: Ungar Publishing Company, 1986 (first published Harper and Brothers, 1908).

The Novels and Tales of Henry James (New York Edition). New York: Scribner's Sons, 1907–1909 (24 volumes).

Outcry: Henry James, *The Outcry*. New York: Charles Scribner's Sons, 1911.

Painter's Eye: John L. Sweeney, ed., *The Painter's Eye: Notes and Essays on the Pictorial Arts*. London: Rupert Hart-Davis, 1956.

Picture and Text: Henry James, *Picture and Text*. New York: Harper and Brothers, 1893.

Question of Our Speech: Henry James, *The Question of Our Speech, The Lesson of Balzac: Two Lectures*. Boston: Houghton, Mifflin and Company, 1905.

Reverberator: Henry James, *The Reverberator*. New York: Grove Press, 1957 (reprint of 1888 Macmillan ed.).

"Rupert Brooke," preface: Rupert Brooke, *Letters from America*. New York: Beaufort Books, 1988 (first pub. Scribner's, 1916).

Sense of the Past: Henry James, *The Sense of the Past*. Fairfield, Conn.: Augustus M. Kelley, 1976 (reissue of vol. 26 of New York Edition, first pub. 1917).

Story: Henry James, *William Wetmore Story and his Friends: From Letters, Diaries and Recollections*. New York: DaCapo Press, 1969 (one vol.) (first published, in 2 vols., 1903).

Theatricals. London: Osgood, McIlvaine & Co., 1894.

Theatricals: Second Series. New York: Harper & Brothers, 1895.

Wade: Allan Wade, ed., *Henry James: The Scenic Art: Notes on Acting and the Drama, 1872–1901*. New Brunswick: Rutgers University Press, 1948.

Wings: Henry James, *The Wings of the Dove*. New York: The Modern Library, 1937 (first pub. 1902).

OTHER WORKS CITED

Abdy, Jane, and Charlotte Gere. *The Souls*. London: Sidgwick & Jackson, 1984.

Ackerman, Gretchen P. *Ibsen and the English Stage, 1889–1903*. New York: Garland Publishing, 1987.

Adams, Henry. *The Education of Henry Adams*, in *Henry Adams: Novels, etc*. New York: Library of America, 1983.

———. *The Letters of Henry Adams*, vol. 5: *1899–1905* (J. C. Levenson et al., eds.). Cambridge: Harvard University Press, 1988.

Adams, Marian. *The Letters of Mrs. Henry Adams, 1865–1883* (W. Thoron, ed.). Boston: Little, Brown, and Company, 1936.

Allen, Gay Wilson. *William James: A Biography*. New York: Viking Press, 1967.

Anesko, Michael. *"Friction with the Market": Henry James and the Profession of Authorship*. New York: Oxford University Press, 1986.

Appiah, Kwame Anthony. *The Ethics of Identity*. Princeton, N.J.: Princeton University Press, 2005.

Appignanesi, Lisa. *Femininity and the Creative Imagination: A Study of Henry James, Robert Musil and Marcel Proust*. London: Vision, 1973

Arnold, Matthew. *Complete Prose Works* (11 vols.) (R. H. Super, ed.). London: Macmillan, 1903–1904.

Atherton, Gertrude. *Adventures of a Novelist*. New York: Liveright, 1932.

Balfour, Arthur. *The Letters of Arthur Balfour and Lady Elcho, 1885–1917* (Jane Ridley and Clayre Percy, eds.). London: Hamish Hamilton, 1992.

Balfour, Graham. *The Life of Robert Louis Stevenson*. London: Methuen and Co., 1901.

Behrman, S. N. *Portrait of Max: An Intimate Memoir of Sir Max Beerbohm*. New York: Random House, 1960.

Bell, Millicent. *Edith Wharton and Henry James: The Story of their Friendship*. New York: George Braziller, 1965.

Benedict, Clare. *Constance Fenimore Woolson*. London: Ellis, 1945.

Bennett, Arnold. *The Journal of Arnold Bennett, 1896–1928*. New York: Viking Press, 1933.

Benson, A. C. *The Diary of Arthur Christopher Benson* (Percy Lubbock, ed.). London: Hutchinson & Co., 1926.

———. *Edwardian Excursions: From the Diaries of A. C. Benson*. (David Newsome, ed.). London: John Murray, 1981.

———. *Essays*. New York: Macmillan, 1896.

———. *The House of Quiet: An Autobiography*. London: John Murray, 1906.

———. *Memories and Friends*. London: John Murray, 1924.

Benson, E. F. *Final Edition: Informal Autobiography*. London: Longmans Green and Co., 1940.

———. *Mother*. London: Hodder and Stoughton, 1925.

Besant, Sir Walter. *Autobiography of Sir Walter Besant*. New York: Dodd, Mead and Company, 1902.

Borkland, Elmer. "Howard Sturgis, Henry James, and *Belchamber*," 58 *Modern Philology* (May 1966), p. 268.

Bosanquet, Theodora. *Henry James at Work*. London: Hogarth Press, 1927.

Boughton, George H. *Sketching Rambles in Holland*. New York: Harper and Sons, 1885.

Bourget, Paul. *Cruelle Enigme*. Paris: Librairie Plon, n.d. (1st ed.1885).

Bradley, John R. *Henry James and Homoerotic Desire*. London: Macmillan, 1999.

———. *Henry James on Stage and Screen*. New York: Palgrave, 2000.

———. *Henry James's Permanent Adolescence*. New York: Palgrave, 2000.

Burr, Anna Robeson. *Alice James: Her Brothers—Her Journal*. New York: Dodd, Mead & Company, 1934.

Carrington, Charles. *Rudyard Kipling: His Life and Work*. London: Macmillan & Co., 1955.

Cary, Elizabeth Luther. *The Novels of Henry James: A Study*. New York: G. P. Putnam's Sons, 1905.

Charteris, Evan. *John Sargent*. New York: Charles Scribner's Sons, 1927.

———. *The Life and Letters of Sir Edmund Gosse*. New York: Harper, 1931.

Colby, Vineta. *Vernon Lee: A Literary Biography*. Charlottesville: University of Virginia Press, 2003.

Dawick, John. *Pinero: A Theatrical Life.* Niwot: University of Colorado Press, 1993.

Denny, Norman, ed. *The Yellow Book: A Selection.* London: Bodley Head, 1949.

di Majo, Elena. "Hendrik Christian Andersen and Olivia Cushing, Birth of a Utopia in Rome, at the Dawn of a New Century," in *Spellbound by Rome: Anglo-American Community in Rome (1890–1914).* Catalogue of an exhibition February 16– April 16, 2005. Rome: Palombi & Partner, 2005.

Dimick, Wai Chee. "Gender, the Market, and the Non-trivial in James." *Henry James Review,* vol. 15 (1994), p. 26.

du Maurier, George. *The Martian: A Novel.* New York: Harper & Brothers, 1897.

———. *Trilby: A Novel.* London: Osgood, McIlvaine & Co., 1895.

Dupee, F. W., ed. *The Question of Henry James: A Collection of Critical Essays.* New York: Henry Holt and Company, 1945.

Edel, Leon. *The Complete Plays of Henry James.* New York: Oxford University Press, 1990.

———. *Henry James: A Life.* New York: Harper & Row, 1985.

———. *Henry James: Les Années Dramatiques.* Paris: Jouve & Cie., 1931.

———. *The Life of Henry James* (5 vols.). Philadelphia: J. P. Lippincott Company, 1953–1972.

———, ed. *Guy Domville, by Henry James; with comments by Bernard Shaw, etc.* Philadelphia: J. P. Lippincott, 1960.

———, and Dan H. Laurance, *A Bibliography of Henry James,* 3rd edition (James Rambeau). Winchester: St. Paul's Bibliographies, 1982.

Egan, Michael. *Henry James: The Ibsen Years.* London: Vision Press, 1972.

Ellmann, Richard. "James Amongst the Aesthetes," in John R. Bradley, ed., *Henry James and Homoerotic Desire.* London: Macmillan Press, 1999.

———. *Oscar Wilde.* New York: Alfred A. Knopf, 1988.

Fletcher, Horace, A.M. *The A.B.–Z. of Our Own Nutrition.* New York: Frederick A. Stokes, 1903.

Fogel, Daniel Mark. *Henry James and the Structure of the Romantic Imagination.* Baton Rouge: Lousiana State University Press, 1981.

Foley, Richard Nicholas. *Criticism in American Periodicals of the Works of Henry James from 1866 to 1916.* Washington, D.C.: Catholic University of America Press, 1944.

Ford, Ford Madox [Hueffer]. *Henry James: A Critical Study.* New York: Octagon Books, 1972.

———. *Memories and Impressions: A Study in Atmospheres.* New York: Harper & Brothers, 1911.

———. *Portraits from Life.* New York, Houghton, Mifflin and Company, 1937.

Gard, Roger (ed.). *Henry James: The Critical Heritage.* London: Routledge & Kegan Paul, 1987.

Gardner, Burdett. "An Apology for Henry James's 'Tiger Cat,' " *Proceedings of the Modern Language Association,* vol. 68 (1953), p. 688.

Gates, Joanne E. *Elizabeth Robins, 1862–1952: Actress, Novelist, Feminist.* Tuscaloosa: University of Alabama Press, 1994.

Gernsheim, Alison. *Victorian and Edwardian Fashion: A Photographic Survey.* New York: Dover, 1963.

Gibbons, Sarah. *Kant's Theory of Imagination: Bridging Gaps in Judgement and Experience.* New York: Oxford University Press, 1994.

Godden, Rumer. *A House with Four Rooms.* New York: William Morrow and Co., 1989.

Goode, John, ed. *The Air of Reality: New Essays on Henry James.* London: Methuen & Co., 1972.

Goodman, Susan. *Edith Wharton's Inner Circle.* Austin: University of Texas Press, 1994.

Gordon, Lyndall. *A Private Life of Henry James: Two Women and His Art.* New York: W. W. Norton & Co., 1999.

Gosse, Edmund C. B. *Aspects and Impressions.* London: Cassell and Company, 1922.

Green, John Richard. *A Short History of the English People* (rev. ed.). New York: Harper & Brothers, 1888.

Gregory, Isabella Augusta [Lady Gregory]. *Lady Gregory's Diaries, 1892–1902* (James Pethica, ed.). New York: Oxford University Press, 1996.

———. *Seventy Years: Being the Autobiography of Lady Gregory* (Colin Smythe, ed.). Gerrards Cross, Bucks.: Smythe, 1974.

Grosskurth, Phyllis. *The Woeful Victorian: A Biography of John Addington Symonds.* New York: Holt, Rinehart and Winston, 1964.

Gunter, Susan E. "Henry James, Peggy James, and Bruce Porter." Paper delivered at the Conference of the Henry James Society, Venice International University, July 12–15, 2005 (typescript).

———. *A Vocation for Jameses: The Story of Alice Howe Gibbens James.* Lincoln: University of Nebraska Press, forthcoming 2007.

Harlow, Virginia. *Thomas Sergeant Perry: A Biography (and Letters to Perry from William, Henry, and Garth Wilkinson James).* Durham, N.C.: Duke University Press, 1950.

Harris, Frank. *My Life and Loves* (3 vols.). Paris: privately printed, 1922–1926.

———. *Oscar Wilde.* New York: Dorset Press, 1989.

Hart-Davis, Rupert. *Hugh Walpole: A Biography.* New York: The Macmillan Company, 1952.

Hassall, Christopher. *Rupert Brooke: A Biography.* London: Faber & Faber, 1964.

Hayes, Kevin J., ed. *Henry James: The Contemporary Reviews.* Cambridge, England: Cambridge University Press, 1996.

Herrick, Robert. "A Visit to Henry James," *Yale Review* 1923, p. 728.

Himmelfarb, Gertrude. *Poverty and Compassion: The Moral Imagination of the Late Victorians.* New York: Alfred A. Knopf, 1991.

Hoare, Philip. *Oscar Wilde's Last Stand: Decadence, Conspiracy, and the Most Outrageous Trial of the Century.* New York: Arcade Publishing, 1998.

Hobsbawm, E. J. *The Age of Empire, 1875–1914.* New York: Pantheon Books, 1987.

Hocks, Richard A. *Henry James and Pragmatistic Thought.* Chapel Hill: University of North Carolina Press, 1974.

Holmes, Oliver Wendell. *Holmes-Pollock Letters: The Correspondence of Mr. Justice Holmes and Sir Frederick Pollock, 1874–1932* (2 vols.) (Mark DeWolfe Howe, ed.). Cambridge, Mass.: Harvard University Press, 1941.

Holroyd, Michael. *Lytton Strachey: A Biography.* London: William Heinemann, 1973.

Horne, Philip. *Henry James: A Life in Letters*. London: Penguin Books, 1999.

Howells, Mildred, ed. *Life in Letters of William Dean Howells* (2 vols.). Garden City, N.Y.: Doubleday, Doran, 1928.

Hyde, H. Montgomery. *The Cleveland Street Scandal*. London: W. H. Allen, 1976.

———. *Henry James at Home*. London: Methuen & Co., 1969.

———. *Oscar Wilde: A Biography*. London: Eyre Methuen, 1976.

Jacobson, Marcia. *Henry James and the Mass Market*. University of Alabama Press, 1983.

James, William. *A Pluralistic Universe*. New York: Longmans, Green and Co., 1909.

———. *Pragmatism: A New Name for Some Old Ways of Thinking*. New York: Longman's, Green and Co., 1907.

———. *Pragmatism and the Meaning of Truth*. Cambridge, Mass.: Harvard University Press, 1978.

———. *The Principles of Psychology* (2 vols.). New York: Henry Holt and Company, 1890.

———. *The Varieties of Religious Experience*. New York: Modern Library, 1936.

Jamison, Dr. Kay Redfield. *Touched with Fire: Manic-Depressive Illness and the Artistic Temperament*. New York: Free Press, 1993.

John, Angela V. *Elizabeth Robins: Staging a Life—1862–1952*. London: Routledge, 1995.

Joll, James. *The Anarchists*. Cambridge, Mass.: Harvard University Press, 1980.

Jordan, Elizabeth. *Three Rousing Cheers*. New York: D. Appleton-Century Company, 1938.

Kelly, Richard. *The Art of George du Maurier*. Aldershot: Scolar Press, 1996.

Kemble, Frances Anne. *Records of a Girlhood*. New York: Henry Holt & Co., 1879.

Keynes, Geoffrey. "Henry James in Cambridge." *The London Magazine*, March 1959.

Kipling, Rudyard. *Something of Myself: For My Friends Known and Unknown*. London: Penguin Books, 1977 (1st ed. 1936).

Kropotkin, P[eter]. *Memoirs of a Revolutionist*. Boston: Houghton, Mifflin and Company, 1899.

———. *Mutual Aid: A Factor of Evolution*. New York: Alfred A. Knopf, 1925 (1st ed. 1902).

Lambert, Angela. *Unquiet Souls: A Social History of the Illustrious, Irreverent, Intimate Group of British Aristocrats Known as "the Souls."* New York: Harper & Row, 1984.

Le Clair, Robert C. "Henry James and Minny Temple," *American Literature*, vol. 21 (March 1949), p. 35.

Lee, Vernon [Violet Paget]. *Miss Brown: A Novel* (3 vols.). Edinburgh: Blackwood and Sons, 1894.

———. *Vanitas*. London: Lovell, Coryell, 1892.

Lesser, Wendy. *His Other Half: Men Looking at Women Through Art*. Cambridge, Mass.: Harvard University Press, 1991.

Lewis, R. W. B. *Edith Wharton: A Biography*. New York: Harper & Row, 1975.

———. *The Jameses: A Family Narrative*. New York: Farrar, Straus and Giroux, 1991.

Lubbock, Percy. *Portrait of Edith Wharton*. New York: D. Appleton-Century Company, 1947.

Lucas, E. V. *Edwin Austin Abbey, Royal Academician: The Record of His Life and Work* (2 vols.). London: Methuen and Company, 1921.

Mackenzie, Compton. *My Life and Times, Octave One: 1883–1891*. London: Chatto & Windus, 1963.

Mackenzie, Manfred. *Communities of Honor and Love in Henry James*. Cambridge: Harvard University Press, 1976.

Maher, Jane. *Biography of Broken Fortunes: Wilkie and Bob, Brothers of William, Henry and Alice*. Hamden, Conn.: Archon Books, 1986.

Maines, Rachel P. *The Technology of Orgasm: "Hysteria," the Vibrator, and Women's Sexual Satisfaction*. Baltimore: Johns Hopkins University Press, 1999.

Martin, Michael S. "The Portrait Without a Subject: German Re-visioning, the Self, Nature, and the Jamesian Novel," no. 5, The Henry James E-Journal (July 29, 2002), available at the Henry James Scholars Page, www2.newpaltz.edu/~hathaway/ejourn5.html.

Matthiesen, F. O. *Henry James: The Major Phase*. New York: Oxford University Press, 1944.

———. *The James Family: Including Selections from the Writings of Henry James, Senior, William, Henry, and Alice James*. New York: Alfred A. Knopf, 1947.

———. *Sarah Orne Jewett*. Boston: Houghton, Mifflin and Co., 1929.

———, ed. *The American Novels and Stories of Henry James*. New York: Alfred A. Knopf, 1947.

Mayne, Ethel Coburn. *The Life and Letters of Anna Isabella, Lady Noel Byron*. New York: Charles Scribner's Sons, 1929.

McWhirter, David, ed. *Henry James's New York Edition: The Construction of Authorship*. Stanford, Calif.: Stanford University Press, 1995.

Miller, James E., Jr., ed. *Theory of Fiction: Henry James*. Lincoln: University of Nebraska Press, 1972.

Mitchell, Juliet. "*What Maisie Knew*: Portrait of the Artist as a Young Girl," in John Goode, ed., *The Air of Reality: New Essays on Henry James*. London: Methuen & Co., 1972.

Newsome, David. *On the Edge of Paradise, A. C. Benson: the Diarist*. London: John Murray, 1980.

Novick, Sheldon M. *Henry James: The Young Master*. New York: Random House, 1996.

———. *Honorable Justice: The Life of Oliver Wendell Holmes*. Boston: Little, Brown and Co., 1989.

———, ed. *The Collected Works of Justice Holmes* (3 vols.). Chicago: University of Chicago Press, 1995.

Nuland, Sherwin B. *How We Die: Reflections on Life's Final Chapter*. New York: Alfred A. Knopf, 1994.

Nussbaum, Martha C. *Love's Knowledge: Essays on Philosophy and Literature*. New York: Oxford University Press, 1990.

———. *Poetic Justice: The Literary Imagination and Public Life*. Boston: Beacon Press, 1995.

Ormond, Leonée. *George du Maurier.* Pittsburgh: University of Pittsburgh Press, 1969.

Page, Norman, ed. *Henry James: Interviews and Recollections.* New York: St. Martin's Press, 1984.

Perosa, Sergio. *Henry James e Venezia.* Firenze: Leo S. Olschke Editore, 1987.

Perrot, Jean. *Henry James: Une écriture énigmaticque.* Paris: Aubier-Montaigne, 1982.

Pope Hennessy, James. *Monckton Milnes* (2 vols.). London: Constable, 1949–1951.

———. *Robert Louis Stevenson.* London: Jonathan Cape, 1974.

Powers, Lyall H. *The Portrait of a Lady: Maiden, Woman, and Heroine.* Boston: Twayne Publishers, 1991.

Renan, Ernest. *Recollections of my Youth* (C. B. Pitman, trans.). New York: G. P. Putnam's Sons, 1883.

Richardson, Joanna. *Portrait of a Bonaparte: The Life and Times of Joseph-Napoleon Primoli, 1851–1927.* London: Quartet Books, 1987.

Robins, Elizabeth. *Both Sides of the Curtain.* London: William Heinemann, 1940.

———. *Ibsen and the Actress.* London: Hogarth Press, 1928.

———. *Theatre and Friendship.* London: Jonathan Cape, 1932.

Roosevelt, Theodore. *Theodore Roosevelt: An Autobiography.* New York: Charles Scribner's Sons, 1913 (Da Capo Press ed. 1985).

St. John, John. *William Heinemann: A Century of Publishing, 1890–1990.* London: Heinemann, 1990.

Santayana, George. *The Works of George Santayana,* vol. 1, *Persons and Places: Fragments of Autobiography* (W. G. Holzberger & H. J. Saatkemp, Jr., eds.). Cambridge, Mass.: MIT Press, 1986.

Seymour-Smith, Martin. *Rudyard Kipling.* London: Queen Anne Press, 1989.

Stetz, Margaret D., and Mark S. Lassner. *The Yellow Book: A Centenary Exhibition.* Cambridge, Mass.: Houghton Library, 1994.

Stevenson, Robert Louis. *The Letters of Robert Louis Stevenson* (Bradford A. Booth and Ernest Mayhew, eds.). New Haven: Yale University Press, 1995.

———. *Prince Otto: A Romance.* London: Chatto & Windus, 1885.

———. *Underwoods.* London: Chatto & Windus, 1902.

——— and Fanny Van de Grift Stevenson. *The Dynamiter: More New Arabian Nights.* London: Longmans, Green, 1885.

Strouse, Jean. *Alice James: A Biography.* Boston: Houghton, Mifflin and Co., 1980.

Sturgis, Howard O. *Belchamber.* London: Oxford University Press, 1935 (1st ed. 1904).

Sutherland, John. *Mrs. Humphry Ward: Eminent Victorian, Pre-eminent Edwardian.* Oxford: Clarendon Press, 1990

Symonds, John Addington. *The Memoirs of John Addington Symonds* (Phyllis Grosskurth, ed.). New York: Random House, 1984.

———. *A Problem in Modern Ethics: Being an Inquiry into the Phenomenon of Sexual Inversion, Addressed Especially to Medical Psychologists and Jurists.* London: privately printed, 1896.

Taylor, Linda J. *Henry James, 1866–1916: A Reference Guide.* Boston: G. K. Hall, 1982.

Thayer, William Roscoe. *The Life and Letters of John Hay* (2 vols.). Boston: Houghton, Mifflin and Company, 1915.

———. *Theodore Roosevelt: An Intimate Portrait.* New York: Grosset & Dunlap, 1919.

Thwaite, Ann. *Edmund Gosse: A Literary Landscape, 1849–1928.* London: Secker & Warburg, 1984.

———. *Waiting for the Party: The Life of Frances Hodgson Burnett, 1849–1924.* London: Secker & Warburg, 1974.

Tilley, W. H. *The Background of* The Princess Casamassima. Gainesville: University of Florida Monographs no. 5, "Fall 1960" [1961].

Tintner, Adeline R. *Henry James and the Lust of the Eyes: Thirteen Artists in His Work.* Baton Rouge: Louisiana State University Press, 1993.

Todorov, Tzvetan. *On Human Diversity: Nationalism, Racism, and Exoticism in French Thought.* (Catherine Porter, trans.). Cambridge, Mass.: Harvard University Press, 1993.

———. *The Poetics of Prose* (Richard Howard, trans.). Ithaca, N.Y.: Cornell University Press, 1977.

Torsney, Cheryl B. *Constance Fenimore Woolson: The Grief of Artistry.* Athens: University of Georgia Press, 1989.

Van de Water, Frederic. *Rudyard Kipling's Vermont Feud.* Rutland, Vt.: Academy Books, 1981.

Vincec, Sister Stephanie. " 'Poor Flopping Wings': The Making of Henry James's *The Wings of the Dove,*" Harvard Library Bulletin, vol. 24 (1976), p. 60.

Walker, Pierre A., ed. *Henry James on Culture: Collected Essays on Politics and the American Social Scene.* Lincoln, Nebraska: University of Nebraska Press, 1999.

Walpole, Hugh. *The Apple Trees: Four Reminiscences.* Waltham, Mass.: Golden Cockeral Press, 1932.

Ward, Mrs. Humphry [Mary Augusta]. *A Writer's Recollections.* New York: Harper & Brothers, 1918.

Weber, Carl J. "Henry James and His Tiger-Cat," PMLA, vol. 68 (1953), p. 672.

Wells, H. G. *Boon, The Mind of the Race, the Wild Asses of the Devil, and The Last Trump.* London: Fisher Unwin, 1915.

West, Rebecca. *Henry James.* New York: H. Holt & Co., 1916.

Wharton, Edith. *A Backward Glance.* New York: Charles Scribner's Sons, 1934.

———. *The Letters of Edith Wharton* (R. W. B. Lewis and Nancy Lewis, eds.). New York: Scribner, 1988.

Whyte, Frederic. *William Heinemann: A Memoir.* London: Jonathan Cape, 1928.

Wilson, A. N. *The Victorians.* New York: W. W. Norton & Company, 2003.

Wilson, Edmund, ed. *The Shock of Recognition: The Development of Literature in the United States Recorded by the Men Who Made It.* New York: Farrar, Straus and Cudahy, 1955.

Wolseley, Garnet [Lord Wolseley]. *The Letters of Lord and Lady Wolseley* (Sir George Arthur, ed.). London: William Heinemann, 1923.

Woodcock, George, and Ivan Avakumovic. *The Anarchist Prince: A Biographical Study of Peter Kropotkin.* New York: T. V. Boardman, 1950.

Woolson, Constance Fenimore. *Anne: A Novel.* New York: Harper & Brothers, 1882.

———. *Women Artists, Women Exiles: "Miss Grief" and Other Stories.* (Joan Myers Weimer, ed.). New Brunswick, N.J.: Rutgers University Press, 1988.

Yeazell, Ruth Bernard. *The Death and Letters of Alice James.* Berkeley: University of California Press, 1981.

INDEX

About the Author

SHELDON M. NOVICK is the author of *Henry James: The Young Master* and *Honorable Justice: The Life of Oliver Wendell Holmes,* and editor of *The Collected Works of Justice Holmes.* He is Adjunct Professor of Law and History at Vermont Law School and lives in Norwich, Vermont.

ABOUT THE TYPE

This book was set in Berling. Designed in 1951 by Karl Erik
Forsberg for the Typefoundry Berlingska Stilgjuteri AB in Lund,
Sweden, it was released the same year in foundry type by
H. Berthold AG. A classic old-face design, its generous propor-
tions and inclined serifs make it highly legible.